Philosophic Classics, Fourth Edition
Volume II

MEDIEVAL PHILOSOPHY

FORREST E. BAIRD, EDITOR
Whitworth College

WALTER KAUFMANN
Late, of Princeton University

Prentice
Hall

Upper Saddle River, New Jersey 07458

Library of Congress Cataloging-in-Publication Data

Philosophic classics / Forrest E. Baird, editor.—4th ed.
    p.   cm.
    "Walter Kaufmann, late, of Princeton University."
    Includes bibliographical references.
    Contents: v. 1. Ancient philosophy—v. 2. Medieval philosophy—
v. 3. Modern philosophy—v. 4. Nineteenth-century philosophy. 3rd
ed.—v. 5. Twentiety-century philosophy. 3rd ed.
    ISBN 0–13–048556–x (v. 1).—ISBN 0–13–048557–8 (v. 2).—ISBN
0–13–048558–6 (v. 3).—ISBN 0–13–048550–0 (v. 4).—ISBN
0–13–048563–2 (v. 5).
    1. Philosophy.   I. Baird, Forrest E.   II. Kaufmann, Walter
Arnold.
B21.P39   2000
100—dc21   98–32332
                                                      CIP

VP, Editorial Director: *Charlyce Jones Owen*
Senior Acquisition Editor: *Ross Miller*
Assistant Editor: *Wendy Yurash*
Editorial Assistant: *Carla Worner*
Sr. Managing Editor: *Jan Stephan*
Production Liaison: *Fran Russello*
Project Manager: *Bruce Hobart, Pine Tree Composition, Inc.*
Prepress and Manufacturing Buyer: *Sherry Lewis*
Art Director: *Jayne Conte*
Cover Designer: *Bruce Kenselaar*
Cover Art: *Effects of Good Government in the City,* by Ambrogio Lorenzetti. Palazzo Pubblico,
    Siena, Italy. Scala/Art Resource, NY.
Line Art Coordinator: *Guy Ruggiero*
Director, Image Resource Center: *Melinda Lee Reo*
Manager, Rights & Permissions: *Zina Arabia*
Image Specialist: *Beth Boyd*
Marketing Manager: *Chris Ruel*

This book was set in 10/12 Times Roman by Pine Tree Composition, Inc.,
and was printed and bound by Courier Companies, Inc.
The cover was printed by Phoenix Color Corp.

 ©2003, 2000, 1997, 1994 by Pearson Education, Inc.
Upper Saddle River, New Jersey 07458

Printed in the United States of America

10 9 8 7 6 5 4 3 2 1

ISBN 0-13-048557-8

Pearson Education Ltd., *London*
Pearson Education Australia Pty, Limited, *Sydney*
Pearson Education Singapore, Pte. Ltd.
Pearson Education North Asia Ltd. *Hong Kong*
Pearson Education Canada, Ltd., *Toronto*
Pearson Educación de Mexico, S.A. de C.V.
Pearson Education—Japan, *Tokyo*
Pearson Education Malaysia, Pte. Ltd.
Pearson Education, *Upper Saddle River, New Jersey*

This volume is dedicated to my wife,

JOY LYNN FULTON BAIRD

> *A capable wife is far more precious than jewels.*
> *Strength and dignity are her clothing,*
> *and she laughs at the time to come.*
> *She opens her mouth with wisdom,*
> *and the teaching of kindness is on her tongue.*

(Proverbs 31:10 25–26)

Contents

ISLAMIC AND JEWISH PHILOSOPHY IN THE MIDDLE AGES   217

WILLIAM OF OCKHAM   468

MEISTER ECKHART   495

CATHERINE OF SIENA   502

NICHOLAS CUSANAS   515

EPILOGUE: GIOVANNI PICO DELLA MIRANDOLA   523

Preface

The Middle Ages have been depicted as a time of intellectual sterility obsessed with trivial and tiresome questions; as a valley between two great mountain ranges—Greek philosophy on one side, which medievalism distorted, and modern philosophy on the other, which happily rejected medieval precedents entirely. As late as the 1960s, medieval philosophers were described by many as being incapable of independent thought, saddled with a "sacramental" view of a God-pointing world. For example, W.T. Jones wrote in *The Medieval Mind* (New York: Harcourt, Brace & World, 1969),

> It can hardly be denied that this sacramental point of view was a block to progress
> . . . [and to] many it seems equally obvious, now that this viewpoint has disap-
> peared, that men have rid themselves of much that was a liability—ignorance, su-
> perstition, intolerance. (p. xix)

This attitude led many to skip almost two millennia of human thought—from the Hellenistic philosophers to Francis Bacon or René Descartes—with only a passing nod to Augustine and Thomas Aquinas.

Much has changed. Most scholars no longer see Bacon and Descartes as the saviors of philosophy from a long medieval night. Following the lead of Étienne Gilson and others, philosophers now recognize that modern philosophy cannot be understood apart from its roots in medieval thought, that medieval philosophy was much richer than previously believed, and that medieval philosophers were as intelligent and thoughtful as the philosophers of any age. Although it is true that most debates during the medieval period were framed in a "sacramental" way and that the medievals considered some answers unacceptable for religious reasons, Christian, Jewish, and

Muslim thinkers in this period did original philosophical work. Furthermore, whereas medieval topics may often appear only theological, they are, in fact, related to virtually every area of philosophy.

The readings included in this volume of the Philosophic Classics series represent the towering medieval thinkers—Augustine, Thomas Aquinas, and William of Ockham—discussing a variety of topics, along with representative texts of other medieval figures. The readings consider ethics and politics, but the focus is on metaphysics and epistemology—questions on the nature of universals, the nature and essence of God, the relationship of God to time and creation, and the ability of humans to know God and creation.

For this fourth edition, a number of small changes have been made, including the translations for Plotinus, Anselm, and Pico and additional material from Augustine's *City of God,* Boethius's *The Consolation of Philosophy,* Anselm's *Proslogion,* and Thomas Aquinas's *Summa Theologica.* In choosing texts for this volume, I have tried wherever possible to follow three principles: (1) to use complete works or, where more appropriate, complete sections of works (2) in clear translations (3) of texts central to the thinker's philosophy or widely accepted as part of the "canon." To make the works more accessible to students, most footnotes treating textual matters (variant readings, etc.) have been omitted and all Greek words have been transliterated and put within angle brackets. In addition, each thinker is introduced by a brief essay composed of three sections: (1) biographical (a glimpse of the life), (2) philosophical (a résumé of the philosopher's thought), and (3) bibliographical (suggestions for further reading).

Those who use this volume for a one-term course in medieval philosophy, philosophy of religion, or metaphysics will find more material here than can easily be read in a normal semester. But this embarrassment of riches offers teachers some choice and, for those who teach the same course year after year, an opportunity to change the menu.

*   *   *

I would like to thank the many people who assisted me in this volume, including the library staff of Whitworth College, especially Hans Bynagle, Gail Fielding, and Jeanette Langston; my colleagues, F. Dale Bruner, who made helpful suggestions on all the introductions and provided suggestions for material on the early Christian documents, Barbara Filo, who helped make selections for the artwork, Roger Mohrlang, who made suggestions on the early introductions, and Corliss Slack, who provided historical context; Timothy A. Robinson, The College of St. Benedict, who read some of the introductions and gave helpful advice; Suzanne Noffke, Sisters of St. Dominic, who gave advice on selections for the medieval mystics; Michelle Seefried; my production editor, Bruce Hobart; my acquisitions editor, Ross Miller of Prentice Hall; and my former acquisitions editors, Karita France, Angela Stone and Ted Bolen. I would also like to acknowledge the following reviewers: James W. Allard, Montana State University; Robert C. Bennett, El Centro College; Herbert L. Carson, Ferris State University; Mary T. Clark, Manhattanville College; Stephen T. Davis, Claremont McKenna College; David Griesedieck, University of Missouri, St. Louis; Sandra S. Edwards, University of Arkansas; Helen S. Lang, Trinity College; Scott MacDonald, University of

Iowa; Angel Medina, Georgia State University; Katherine Rogers, University of Delaware; Reginald Savage, North Carolina State; Stephen Scott, Eastern Washington University; Walter G. Scott, Oklahoma State University; and Donald Phillip Verene, Emory University. New as reviewers to this edition, I would also like to thank R. James Long, Fairfield University; and Nicholas More, Westminster College.

I am especially thankful to my wife, Joy Lynn Fulton Baird, and to our children, Whitney Jaye, Sydney Tev, and Soren David, who have supported me in this enterprise. To use Anselm's famous words, they have been to me a family "than-which-none-greater-can-be-thought."

Forrest E. Baird
Professor of Philosophy
Whitworth College
Spokane, WA 99251
email: fbaird@whitworth.edu

Philosophers In This Volume

Philo
of
Alexandria

Jesus
Paul

Justin Martyr
Clement of Alexandria
Tertullian
Origen
Plotinus

Augustine

Boethius
Pseudo-Dionysius
Areopagite

Other Important Figures

Lucretius

Epictetus

Marcus Aurelius
Ptolemy (astronomer)
Sextus Empiricus
Porphyry

Justinian

Mohammed

A Sampling of Major Events

Furthest extent of the Roman Empire
Council of Nicea
Roman Empire divided
Fall of Rome
School of Philosophy in Athens
closed by Justinian
Buddhism introduced in Japan
Muslim conquest of
North Africa and Spain

0   A.D. 200   A.D. 400   A.D. 600

John Scotus Eriugena
Avicenna

Anselm
al-Ghazālī
Peter Abelard
Hildegard of Bingen
John of Salisbury
Averroës
Maimonides
Robert Grosseteste
Roger Bacon
Bonaventure
Thomas Aquinas
Meister Eckhart
Duns Scotus
William of Ockham
Catherine of Siena
Nicholas Cusanas
Pico Dell Mirandola

Charlemagne

Thomas Becket
Zhu Xi (Chu Hsi)
Genghis Khan
Dominic
Francis of Assisi
Marco Polo
Dante Alighieri
John Wycliffe

Leonardo da Vinci

Peak of Mayan civilization in Central America
Construction of Romanesque cathedrals
First Crusade
Construction of Gothic cathedrals
Paris University founded
Magna Carta

Hundred Years War between
France and England
Bubonic Plague
Ming Dynasty in China
Gutenberg invents
moveable-type
printing

A.D. 800   A.D. 1000   A.D. 1200   A.D. 1400

PROLOGUE I: EARLY CHRISTIAN DOCUMENTS

◄○►

With only a few exceptions, European medieval thought was deeply imbued with the Christian faith. As a result, it is not possible to understand medieval philosophy without at least a rudimentary understanding of the Christian documents from which that philosophy is drawn. Whether or not today's readers accept the veracity of the claims put forth in these writings, most medievals did believe them, and that belief formed the foundation of their thought.

Beginning as a Jewish sect, Christianity continued to hold a number of beliefs in common with Judaism, including the following bedrock convictions: that the Hebrew Bible (called the "Old Testament" by Christians) is the revealed Word of God; that God is superior to and distinct from the created world; that the world was created by God at a specific point in time and that the world will come to an end; that God is personal and desires a special relationship with each member of the human race; that humans have sinned against God's Law and are in need of God's forgiveness; that God requires righteousness as a means of a right relationship with God and others; and that God would send the Anointed One ("Messiah" in Hebrew, "Christ" in Greek) to set the people of God free. The following readings from the Hebrew scriptures include these beliefs and greatly influenced medieval thinkers:

GENESIS 1–3: The Creation and the Fall
GENESIS 12:1–8: The Call of Abraham and the beginning of Israel
EXODUS 20:1–20: The Ten Commandments
ISAIAH 52:13–15; 53:1–13: The Suffering Servant Song, Hope of Israel
AMOS 5:18–24: The Social Justice of Yahweh

1

Even though Christians accepted the foundational beliefs of their Jewish ancestors, they differed on one key point: the identity of the Messiah. Whereas the Jews anticipated a spiritual-political figure to save them from the oppression of their enemies, Christians believed the Christ saved his people mainly from the spiritual oppressors of sin and death. Whereas the Jews believed the Messiah would scrupulously follow the Law, favoring and associating only with those who did likewise, the Christians' Christ seemed to enjoy a remarkable freedom in relation to several of Israel's most venerable institutions—for example, Sabbath observances, the Temple, and ritual purity—while associating with the "lowlifes" of society. In short, whereas the Jewish people were (and still are) awaiting the Messiah, Christians believe that Jesus of Nazareth *was* the Messiah.

Christians hold that after his death by crucifixion, Jesus rose from the dead (the Resurrection) and taught his followers for forty days before ascending into heaven. As a part of that teaching, Jesus promised that he would return again (the Second Coming ⟨*parousia*⟩) and that in the meantime his followers should spread the Christian faith to all the world.

The basic Christian belief was (and still is) that Jesus is the Son of God who became a human (the Incarnation) to atone for human sin (Redemption). The severed relationship between the Holy God and sinful humanity could only be restored through the sacrifice of one who was consummate righteousness. As the Word ⟨*logos*⟩ of God made flesh, Jesus was that righteousness, made that sacrifice, and offered that restoration. Through faith, Christians accept this work done on their behalf (Justification) and receive the power of God's spirit to overcome sin and to serve others (Sanctification).

As Christians spread this message throughout the Roman Empire, they encountered resistance and persecution from both Jewish and Roman authorities. The first Christian martyr, Stephen, was stoned to death by orthodox Jews for the blasphemy of claiming Jesus as God's Son (Acts 7). Among those who participated in the stoning was an eager Christian-hunter, Saul of Tarsus. This man subsequently underwent a dramatic conversion on the road to Damascus and became the Apostle Paul.

While many Jewish leaders objected to the Christian identification of Jesus with God, Roman authorities objected to the Christians' unwillingness to participate in emperor worship. Jews, too, had refused to participate in state religion and had often been persecuted. But Christians posed a unique threat to the Romans because, unlike the Jews, Christians proclaimed a supranational, supraracial, universal Lord—one very much in competition with Caesar. And Christians indefatigably sought converts to their universal Savior. Accordingly, they were persecuted on and off for three centuries.

Despite persecution, Christianity grew steadily in the centuries after Christ. Many explanations are offered for that growth. The eighteenth-century historian Edward Gibbon* listed five causes: (1) Christianity's inheritance of the zeal of the Jews; (2) its connection to the philosophical doctrine of the immortality of the soul; (3) its claim of miracles; (4) the virtue of the early Christians; and (5) the organization of the church. Recent historians have pointed to the moral

---

The Decline and Fall of the Roman Empire, Chapter XV.

exclusivity of Christians, who demanded deep commitment; the definite and absolute character of Christian belief in an age of uncertainty; and the social dimensions of Christianity, which made it attractive to women, the poor, and the oppressed.*

As Christianity grew, doctrinal disputes inevitably arose. What is true Christianity? The answers tended to reflect deep convictions about two essential issues: the nature of the person and work of Jesus Christ and the relationship between faith and reason. What was the relationship between Jesus and God? Did Jesus have two distinct natures: one divine and one human? Or were they merged into a single unique nature? Moreover, if there is only one God, how could God also be three (Father, Son, and Holy Spirit)? And how could reason resolve issues of faith?

The first issue, the nature of Christ, was resolved at the Council of Nicea, convened and presided over by the first Christian emperor, Constantine, in A.D. 325. The council determined that the Son was exactly the same substance, "consubstantial" ⟨homoousios⟩, and not just "of like substance" ⟨homoiousios⟩, with God the Father. (The single Greek letter "iota" meant a great deal more than "one iota of difference" to the early church.) By the middle of the first millenium, the "Nicene Creed" was confessed by virtually all Christendom as the orthodox answer to the nature-of-Christ question. The Nicene Creed is still authoritative in Orthodox, Catholic, and Protestant churches.

Even though the Christological question was answered at Nicea, the question of the right relation between faith and reason continued to be argued throughout the medieval period. The early Christians had a simple faith in Jesus as Messiah (if they were Jewish Christians) and as Lord (if they were Gentile Christians); and they believed Jesus had lived, taught, died, and risen for them and all others. But almost immediately that simple faith encountered sophisticated Hellenistic thought throughout the Roman Empire. How much should Christian faith concede to the competence of philosophic reason? What was the relation between sacred writings (i.e., the Bible) and secular writings (e.g., philosophy)? In Acts 17, reprinted here (pages 21–23), Paul used reason and quoted pagan poets to help him preach the gospel to Epicurean and Stoic philosophers in Athens. Yet later, in Colossians 2:8, he warned, "See to it that no one takes you captive through philosophy and empty deceit." Some early Church Fathers, such as Justin Martyr, Clement of Alexandria, and Origen, used philosophy to help interpret Christian faith. Other Church Fathers, such as Tertullian, argued that reason could be inimical to faith: "What has Jerusalem to do with Athens?" he asked.

Some in the early church even claimed to have special esoteric knowledge not available to the rabble either in sacred Scriptures or through secular reason. They were known as Gnostics, from the Greek word for knowledge ⟨gnosis⟩. These Gnostics emphasized the Platonic belief in the soul as good and the body as evil, and they sought to free the soul from the body by extreme ascetic practices. Some of the Gnostics taught that Jesus was not really a physical person (since the body is evil) and that the Old Testament God, Yahweh, who had created bodies and matter, was really the devil. Manicheaism, which rivaled Christianity in

---

*Of course, Christians have always claimed that none of these reasons is entirely adequate and that the most acceptable explanation for the rise of Christianity is a supernatural one.

the third and fourth centuries, and for a time claimed Augustine as a member, was based on Gnostic thought.*

As Christians sought wisdom in all these complex issues, they were sustained by a peculiar faith, inherited from Judaism and deepened by their founders. As Anne Fremantle put it,

> The Christian believes that not only does he search for wisdom, but wisdom also searches for him, and with more immediate success. God is not only that than which nothing greater can be imagined, but a person who, while declaring Himself to be wholly unimaginable, has yet revealed Himself and given Himself to man. . . . Christian philosophy is an intellectual inquiry into the nature of being, which accepts as a premise the possible existence of a Power outside man that is both the object and the instigator of man's search; or, as Christ put it, that He is Himself "the Way, the Truth and the Life."**

*   *   *

For extrabiblical source material on Christianity, see C.K. Barrett, *The New Testament Background: Selected Documents* (New York: Harper Torchbooks, 1961) and Howard Clark Kee, *The New Testament in Context: Sources and Documents* (Englewood Cliffs, NJ: Prentice Hall, 1984). For discussions of the interaction between Christianity and its surrounding culture, see A.H. Armstrong and R.A. Markus, *Christian Faith and Greek Philosophy* (New York: Sheed and Ward, 1960); E.R. Dodds, *Pagan and Christian in an Age of Anxiety* (Cambridge: Cambridge University Press, 1965); Jaroslav Pelikan, *The Christian Tradition: A History of the Development of Doctrine,* five volumes (Chicago: University of Chicago Press, 1971–1989); and R.A. Markus, *Christianity in the Roman World* (London: Thames & Hudson, 1974). Relevant histories of Christianity include Kenneth Scott Latourette, *A History of Christianity* (New York: Harper & Row, 1953); Martin E. Marty, *A Short History of Christianity* (New York: Meridian, 1959); Henry Chadwick, *The Early Church* (Harmondsworth, Middlesex: Penguin Books, 1967); W.H.C. Frend, *The Rise of Christianity* (Philadelphia: Fortress Press, 1984); and Williston Walker et al., *A History of the Christian Church,* 4th edition (New York: Scribner's, 1985). For a discussion of Christian beliefs in their historical context, see J.N.D. Kelly, *Early Christian Doctrines,* 5th edition (London: Black, 1978). For basic introductions to traditional Christian beliefs, see John R.W. Stott, *Basic Christianity* (Downers Grove, IL: Inter-Varsity Press, 1971), and Hans Küng, *On Being a Christian,* translated by Edward Quinn (Garden City, NY: Doubleday, 1976).

---

*Similar contests between faith, reason, and extrarational experience would play out later in Islam, when Muslims sought to reconcile their sacred writings (the *Qur'ān*) with philosophy. Some thinkers, such as Avicenna (Ibn-Sīnā), argued for a special interpretation of the *Qur'ān* available only to the philosophically enlightened; and other thinkers, such as al-Ghazālī, protested that Islam should avoid philosophy and that Mecca, too, should have nothing to do with Athens.

**Anne Fremantle, *The Age of Belief: The Medieval Philosophers* (New York: New American Library, 1954), pp. 15–16.

JESUS
ca. 6 B.C.—ca. A.D. 30

Jesus was born in Bethlehem in Judea sometime around 6 B.C. (the currently accepted date of Jesus' birth corrects the error of a sixth-century monk who established the Western calendar). Virtually all data about the life of Jesus come from the first four books of the New Testament, called the Gospels (*gospel* means "good news"). The accuracy of the gospel accounts is a matter of debate, but most medieval philosophers believed that the gospel records were not only essentially trustworthy but also actually inspired. Therefore, to understand medieval thought, it is especially necessary to understand something of the life of Jesus as presented in the Bible.

According to two of the Gospels (Matthew and Luke), Jesus was conceived by the Holy Spirit and born of the Virgin Mary—a young woman engaged to a carpenter by the name of Joseph. According to Matthew, Mary and Joseph took Jesus to Egypt while he was still a small child to avoid Jesus' death at the hands of King Herod of Judea. Following Herod's death, the family settled in the northern Palestinian town of Nazareth in the province of Galilee. Apart from one temple visit in Jerusalem when Jesus was twelve (recorded in Luke), nothing further is found in the New Testament about Jesus' life until he began his adult ministry.

When Jesus was about thirty years old, John the Baptist began preaching that the "kingdom of heaven" was near. John lived an ascetic life in the wilderness and called on Israel to repent from its evil ways, return to God in good faith, and be baptized in order to express and begin a new life of repentance. Jesus left Nazareth and was baptized by John in the Jordan River. As Jesus came out of the water, the Spirit of God descended upon him, and a voice from heaven said,

"This is my Son, the Beloved, with whom I am well pleased." Following a period of intense personal struggle with the Devil, Jesus began his public ministry in Galilee. For the next one to three years, Jesus healed the sick, cast out demons, and preached the kingdom of heaven. A number of people followed Jesus as he traveled, including twelve specially chosen by him to be his disciples.

Jesus' preaching focused on the reality of God and the importance of other people, summarized in the "two greatest commandments": to love God deeply and to love one's neighbor heartily. In loving God, Jesus advocated moving beyond mere formal or ritual observance and being open to a divinely given "rebirth" that would change the person completely. As Jesus told the Pharisee Nicodemus, this rebirth could be received by believing in Jesus. As for love of neighbor, in the Parable (or Story) of the Good Samaritan, Jesus urged expanding the concept of neighbor beyond race, nation, or religion to include anyone in need. Perhaps the most impressive collection of Jesus' teachings is found in the Sermon on the Mount in Matthew's Gospel.

After one to three years of teaching in Galilee, Jesus and his followers moved south to Jerusalem where he was soon arrested and put to death by crucifixion. The religious leaders in Jerusalem objected to Jesus' claims to a special relationship to God. With the help of one of Jesus' own disciples, Judas Iscariot, they arrested Jesus, charging him with blasphemy. Following conviction by a religious court, Jesus was handed over to the Roman governor, Pontius Pilate, who condemned him to death by crucifixion. Three days after his death, Christians believe, Jesus rose bodily from the grave and appeared first to Peter and to some of his women followers, then to his eleven remaining disciples, and finally to a large group of followers. After forty days of further teaching, Jesus ascended into heaven, from which he will one day come again to judge all human beings, determining their eternal destiny. This is a bare outline of essential Christian faith—the *Credo* (literally "I believe") or creed of the medieval Western and now worldwide church.

Our first reading, from the Gospel of John, identifies Jesus as the Word ⟨*logos*⟩ of God made flesh. This Greek philosophical term (⟨*logos*⟩ was a key concept in Heraclitus's thought and in Stoic writings) in a gospel book presaged the interaction that was to follow between Greek philosophy and the Christian church. The other readings should provide a rudimentary introduction to the fundamental deeds and teachings of Jesus of Nazareth. They are all taken from Christendom's main book, a collection of writings called the New Testament. Although many people today might take exception to at least the supernatural elements in New Testament texts, every one of the medieval philosophers represented in this volume, with the exception of the Jewish and Islamic thinkers, believed the Gospels to be, as we say, the "gospel truth."

*   *   *

There is no such thing as an objective account of the life of Jesus. Perhaps the best starting point for further reading, after the New Testament itself in a modern translation, is C.H. Dodd's short book, *The Founder of Christianity* (New York: Macmillan, 1970), or from a more liberal position, Adolf Harnack's still useful and classic *What Is Christianity?* (New York: Putnam's, 1901). Albert Schweitzer's *The Quest of the Historical Jesus: A Critical Study of Its Progress from Reimarus to Wrede,* translated by W. Montgomery (New York: Macmillan, 1910) is, after Harnack, the classic work on the historical Jesus, whereas Harvey

K. McArthur, ed., *In Search of the Historical Jesus* (New York: Scribner's, 1969), continues the quest. More recent works representing a variety of Christian interpretations of Jesus' life, death, and teachings include Oscar Cullmann, *The Christology of the New Testament,* translated by Shirley C. Guthrie and Charles A.M. Hall (Philadelphia: Westminster, 1963); Wolfhart Pannenberg, *Jesus, God and Man,* translated by Lewis L. Wilkins and Duane A. Priebe (Philadelphia: Westminster Press, 1968); A.M. Hunter, *The Work and Words of Jesus,* revised edition (London: SCM Press, 1973); Günther Bornkamm, *Jesus of Nazareth,* translated by I. McCluskey and F. McCluskey (New York: Harper & Row, 1975); Gerard S. Sloyan, *Jesus in Focus: A Life in Its Setting* (Mystic, CT: Twenty-Third, 1984); Graham N. Stanton, *The Gospel and Jesus* (Oxford: Oxford University Press, 1989); and Raymond Edward Brown, *The Death of the Messiah,* two volumes (New York: Doubleday, 1994).

NEW TESTAMENT: GOSPELS (in part)

PROLOGUE TO THE GOSPEL OF JOHN (JOHN 1:1–18)

1 [1]In the beginning was the Word ⟨*logos*⟩ and the Word was with God, and the Word was God. [2]He was in the beginning with God. [3]All things came into being through him, and without him not one thing came into being. What has come into being [4]in him was life and the life was the light of all people. [5]The light shines in the darkness, and the darkness did not overcome it.

[6]There was a man sent from God, whose name was John. [7]He came as a witness to testify to the light, so that all might believe through him. [8]He himself was not the light, but he came to testify to the light. [9]The true light, which enlightens everyone, was coming into the world.

[10]He was in the world, and the world came into being through him yet the world did not know him. [11]He came to what was his own, and his own people did not accept him. [12]But to all who received him, who believed in his name, he gave power to become children of God, [13]who were born, not of blood or of the will of the flesh or of the will of man, but of God.

[14]And the Word became flesh and lived among us, and we have seen his glory, the glory as of a father's only son full of grace and truth. [15]John testified to him and cried out, "This was he of whom I said, 'He who comes after me ranks ahead of me because he was before me.'" [16]From his fullness we have all received, grace upon grace. [17]The law indeed was given through Moses, grace and truth came through Jesus Christ. [18]No one has ever seen God. It is God the only Son, who is close to the Father's heart, who has made him known.

*   *   *

St. Matthew, from the Lindisfarne Gospels, before A.D. 698. *(The British Library/SuperStock, Inc.)*

THE BAPTISM OF JESUS (MATTHEW 3:13–17)

3 [13]Then Jesus came from Galilee to John at the Jordan, to be baptized by him. [14]John would have prevented him, saying, "I need to be baptized by you, and do you come to me?" [15]But Jesus answered him, "Let it be so now for it is proper for us in this way to fulfill all righteousness." Then he consented. [16]And when Jesus had been baptized, just as he came up from the water, suddenly the heavens were opened to him and he saw the Spirit of God descending like a dove and alighting on him. [17]And a voice from heaven said, "This is my Son, the Beloved, with whom I am well pleased."

*   *   *

THE TEMPTATION OF JESUS (MATTHEW 4:1–11)

4 [1]Then Jesus was led up by the Spirit into the wilderness to be tempted by the devil. [2]He fasted forty days and forty nights, and afterwards he was famished. [3]The tempter came and said to him, "If you are the Son of God, command these stones to become loaves of bread." [4]But he answered, "It is written 'One does not live by bread alone, but by every word that comes from the mouth of God.'" [5]Then the devil took him to the holy city and placed him on the pinnacle of the temple, [6]saying to him, "If you are the Son of God, throw yourself down; for it is written, 'He will command his angels concerning you,' and 'On their hands they will bear you up so that you will not dash your foot against a stone.'" [7]Jesus said to him, "Again it is written, 'Do not put the Lord your God to the test.'" [8]Again, the devil took him to a very high mountain and showed him all the kingdoms of the world and their splendor; [9]and he said to him, "All these I will give you, if you will fall down and worship me." [10]Jesus said to him "Away with you, Satan! for it is written 'Worship the Lord your God, and serve only him.'" [11]Then the devil left him, and suddenly angels came and waited on him.

*   *   *

THE SERMON ON THE MOUNT (MATTHEW 5–7)

5 [1]When Jesus saw the crowds, he went up the mountain; and after he sat down, his disciples came to him. [2]Then he began to speak, and taught them, saying:

[3]"Blessed are the poor in spirit, for theirs is the kingdom of heaven.

[4]"Blessed are those who mourn, for they will be comforted.

[5]"Blessed are the meek, for they will inherit the earth.

[6]"Blessed are those who hunger and thirst for righteousness, for they will be filled.

[7]"Blessed are the merciful, for they will receive mercy.

[8]"Blessed are the pure in heart, for they will see God.

[9]"Blessed are the peacemakers, for they will be called children of God.

[10]"Blessed are those who are persecuted for righteousness' sake, for theirs is the kingdom of heaven.

[11]"Blessed are you when people revile you and persecute you and utter all kinds of evil against you falsely on my account. [12]Rejoice and be glad, for your reward is great in heaven, for in the same way they persecuted the prophets who were before you.

[13]"You are the salt of the earth, but if salt has lost its taste, how can its saltiness be restored? It is no longer good for anything, but is thrown out and trampled under foot.

[14]"You are the light of the world. A city built on a hill cannot be hid. [15]No one after lighting a lamp puts it under the bushel basket, but on the lampstand, and it gives light to all in the house. [16]In the same way, let your light shine before others, so that they may see your good works and give glory to your Father in heaven.

[17]"Do not think that I have come to abolish the law or the prophets, I have come not to abolish but to fulfill. [18]For truly I tell you, until heaven and earth pass away, not one letter, not one stroke of a letter, will pass from the law until all is accomplished. [19]Therefore, whoever breaks one of the least of these commandments, and teaches others to do the same, will be called least in the kingdom of heaven, but whoever does them and teaches them will be called great in the kingdom of heaven. [20]For I tell you, unless your righteousness exceeds that of the scribes and Pharisees, you will never enter the kingdom of heaven.

[21]"You have heard that it was said to those of ancient times, 'You shall not murder'; and 'whoever murders shall be liable to judgment.' [22]But I say to you that if you are angry with a brother or sister you will be liable to judgment, and if you insult a brother or sister, you will be liable to the council, and if you say, 'You fool,' you will be liable to the hell of fire. [23]So when you are offering your gift at the altar, if you remember that your brother or sister has something against you [24]leave your gift there before the altar and go, first be reconciled to your brother or sister, and then come and offer your gift. [25]Come to terms quickly with your accuser while you are on the way to court with him, or your accuser may hand you over to the judge, and the judge to the guard, and you will be thrown into prison. [26]Truly I tell you, you will never get out until you have paid the last penny.

[27]"You have heard that it was said 'You shall not commit adultery.' [28]But I say to you that everyone who looks at a woman with lust has already committed adultery with her in his heart. [29]If your right eye causes you to sin tear it out and throw it away; it is better for you to lose one of your members than for your whole body to be thrown into hell. [30]And if your right hand causes you to sin, cut it off and throw it away, it is better for you to lose one of your members than for your whole body to go into hell.

[31]"It was also said, 'Whoever divorces his wife, let him give her a certificate of divorce.' [32]But I say to you that anyone who divorces his wife, except on the ground of unchastity, causes her to commit adultery; and whoever marries a divorced woman commits adultery.

[33]"Again, you have heard that it was said to those of ancient times, 'You shall not swear falsely, but carry out the vows you have made to the Lord.' [34]But I say to you, Do not swear at all, either by heaven, for it is the throne of God, [35]Or by the earth, for it is his footstool, or by Jerusalem, for it is the city of the great King. [36]And do not swear by your head, for you cannot make one hair white or black. [37]Let your word be 'Yes, Yes' or 'No, No'; anything more than this comes from the evil one.

[38]"You have heard that it was said 'An eye for an eye and a tooth for a tooth.' [39]But I say to you, Do not resist an evildoer. But if anyone strikes you on the right cheek, turn the other also; [40]and if anyone wants to sue you and take your coat, give your cloak as well; [41]and if anyone forces you to go one mile, go also the second mile. [42]Give to everyone who begs from you, and do not refuse anyone who wants to borrow from you.

[43]"You have heard that it was said, 'You shall love your neighbor and hate your enemy.' [44]But I say to you, Love your enemies and pray for those who persecute you, [45]so that you may be children of your Father in heaven, for he makes his sun rise on the evil and on the good, and sends rain on the righteous and on the unrighteous. [46]For if you love those who love you what reward do you have? Do not even the tax collectors do the same? [47]And if you greet only your brothers and sisters, what more are you doing than others? Do not even the Gentiles do the same? [48]Be perfect, therefore, as your heavenly Father is perfect.

6 [1]"Beware of practicing your piety before others in order to be seen by them, for then you have no reward from your Father in heaven.

[2]"So whenever you give alms, do not sound a trumpet before you, as the hypocrites do in the synagogues and in the streets, so that they may be praised by others. Truly I tell you, they have received their reward. [3]But when you give alms, do not let your left hand know what your right hand is doing, [4]so that your alms may be done in secret, and your Father who sees in secret will reward you.

[5]"And whenever you pray, do not be like the hypocrites; for they love to stand and pray in the synagogues and at the street corners, so that they may be seen by others. Truly I tell you, they have received their reward. [6]But whenever you pray, go into your room and shut the door and pray to your Father who is in secret; and your Father who sees in secret will reward you.

[7]"When you are praying, do not heap up empty phrases as the Gentiles do; for they think that they will be heard because of their many words. [8]Do not be like them, for your Father knows what you need before you ask him.

[9]"Pray then in this way:

Our Father in heaven,
hallowed be your name.
[10]Your kingdom come.
Your will be done,
on earth as it is in heaven.
[11]Give us this day our daily bread.
[12]And forgive us our debts,
as we also have forgiven our debtors.
[13]And do not bring us to the time of trial,
but rescue us from the evil one.

[14]For if you forgive others their trespasses, your heavenly Father will also forgive you; [15]but if you do not forgive others, neither will your Father forgive your trespasses.

[16]"And whenever you fast, do not look dismal, like the hypocrites, for they disfigure their faces so as to show others that they are fasting. Truly I tell you, they have received their reward. [17]But when you fast, put oil on your head and wash your face, [18]so that your fasting may be seen not by others but by your Father who is in secret and your Father who sees in secret will reward you. [19]"Do not store up for yourselves treasures on earth where moth and rust consume and where thieves break in and steal; [20]but store up for yourselves treasures in heaven, where neither moth nor rust consumes and where thieves do not break in and steal. [21]For where your treasure is there your heart will be also.

[22]"The eye is the lamp of the body. So, if your eye is healthy, your whole body will be full of light; [23]but if your eye is unhealthy, your whole body will be full of darkness. If then the light in you is darkness, how great is the darkness!

[24]"No one can serve two masters for a slave will either hate the one and love the other, or be devoted to the one and despise the other. You cannot serve God and wealth.

[25]"Therefore I tell you, do not worry about your life, what you will eat or what you will drink, nor about your body, what you will wear. Is not life more than food, and the body more than clothing? [26]Look at the birds of the air; they neither sow nor reap nor gather into barns, and yet your heavenly Father feeds them. Are you not of

more value than they? [27]And can any of you by worrying add a single hour to your span of life? [28]And why do you worry about clothing? Consider the lilies of the field, how they grow they neither toil nor spin, [29]yet I tell you, even Solomon in all his glory was not clothed like one of these. [30]But if God so clothes the grass of the field which is alive today and tomorrow is thrown into the oven, will he not much more clothe youyou of little faith? [31]Therefore do not worry, saying, 'What will we eat?' or 'What will we drink?' or 'What will we wear?' [32]For it is the Gentiles who strive for all these things; and indeed your heavenly Father knows that you need all these things. [33]But strive first for the kingdom of God and his righteousness, and all these things will be given to you as well.

[34]"So do not worry about tomorrow, for tomorrow will bring worries of its own. Today's trouble is enough for today.

7 [1]"Do not judge, so that you may not be judged. [2]For with the judgment you make you will be judged, and the measure you give will be the measure you get. [3]Why do you see the speck in your neighbor's eye, but do not notice the log in your own eye? [4]Or how can you say to your neighbor, 'Let me take the speck out of your eye,' while the log is in your own eye? [5]You hypocrite, first take the log out of your own eye, and then you will see clearly to take the speck out of your neighbor's eye.

[6]"Do not give what is holy to dogs and do not throw your pearls before swine, or they will trample them under foot and turn and maul you.

[7]"Ask, and it will be given you; search, and you will find; knock, and the door will be opened for you. [8]For everyone who asks receives, and everyone who searches finds, and for everyone who knocks, the door will be opened. [9]Is there anyone among you who, if your child asks for bread, will give a stone? [10]Or if the child asks for a fish, will give a snake? [11]If you then who are evil, know how to give good gifts to your children, how much more will your Father in heaven give good things to those who ask him!

[12]"In everything do to others as you would have them do to you; for this is the law and the prophets.

[13]"Enter through the narrow gate; for the gate is wide and the road is easy that leads to destruction, and there are many who take it. [14]For the gate is narrow and the road is hard that leads to life, and there are few who find it.

[15]"Beware of false prophets, who come to you in sheep's clothing but inwardly are ravenous wolves. [16]You will know them by their fruits. Are grapes gathered from thorns, or figs from thistles? [17]In the same way, every good tree bears good fruit, but the bad tree bears bad fruit. [18]A good tree cannot bear bad fruit, nor can a bad tree bear good fruit. [19]Every tree that does not bear good fruit is cut down and thrown into the fire. [20]Thus you will know them by their fruits.

[21]"Not everyone who says to me 'Lord, Lord,' will enter the kingdom of heaven, but only the one who does the will of my Father in heaven. [22]On that day many will say to me, 'Lord, Lord did we not prophesy in your name, and cast out demons in your name, and do many deeds of power in your name?' [23]Then I will declare to them, 'I never knew you; go away from me, you evildoers.'

[24]"Everyone then who hears these words of mine and acts on them will be like a wise man who built his house on rock. [25]The rain fell, the floods came, and the winds blew and beat on that house, but it did not fall, because it had been founded on rock. [26]And everyone who hears these words of mine and does not act on them will be like a foolish man who built his house on sand. [27]The rain fell, and the floods came and the winds blew and beat against that house, and it fell—and great was its fall!"

²⁸Now when Jesus had finished saying these things, the crowds were astounded at his teaching ²⁹for he taught them as one having authority, and not as their scribes.

*   *   *

Nicodemus Visits (John 3:1–21)

3 ¹Now there was a Pharisee named Nicodemus, a leader of the Jews. ²He came to Jesus by night and said to him, "Rabbi, we know that you are a teacher who has come from God, for no one can do these signs that you do apart from the presence of God." ³Jesus answered him, "Very truly, I tell you, no one can see the kingdom of God without being born from above." ⁴Nicodemus said to him, "How can anyone be born after having grown old? Can one enter a second time into the mother's womb and be born?" ⁵Jesus answered, "Very truly, I tell you, no one can enter the kingdom of God without being born of water and Spirit. ⁶What is born of the flesh is flesh, and what is born of the Spirit is spirit. ⁷Do not be astonished that I said to you, 'You must be born from above.' ⁸The wind blows where it chooses, and you hear the sound of it, but you do not know where it comes from or where it goes. So it is with everyone who is born of the Spirit." ⁹Nicodemus said to him, "How can these things be?" ¹⁰Jesus answered him, "Are you a teacher of Israel, and yet you do not understand these things?

¹¹"Very truly, I tell you, we speak of what we know and testify to what we have seen; yet you do not receive our testimony. ¹²If I have told you about earthly things and you do not believe, how can you believe if I tell you about heavenly things? ¹³No one has ascended into heaven except the one who descended from heaven, the Son of Man. ¹⁴And just as Moses lifted up the serpent in the wilderness so must the Son of Man be lifted up ¹⁵that whoever believes in him may have eternal life.

¹⁶"For God so loved the world that he gave his only Son, so that everyone who believes in him may not perish but may have eternal life.

¹⁷"Indeed, God did not send the Son into the world to condemn the world, but in order that the world might be saved through him. ¹⁸Those who believe in him are not condemned, but those who do not believe are condemned already, because they have not believed in the name of the only Son of God. ¹⁹And this is the judgment, that the light has come into the world, and people loved darkness rather than light because their deeds were evil. ²⁰For all who do evil hate the light and do not come to the light, so that their deeds may not be exposed. ²¹But those who do what is true come to the light, so that it may be clearly seen that their deeds have been done in God."

*   *   *

The Crucifixion and Resurrection of Jesus (Matthew 27:27–28:20)

27 ²⁷Then the soldiers of the governor took Jesus into the governor's headquarters, and they gathered the whole cohort around him. ²⁸They stripped him and put a scarlet robe on him, ²⁹and after twisting some thorns into a crown, they put it on his head. They put a reed in his right hand and knelt before him and mocked him, saying, "Hail, King of the Jews!" [30]They spat on him, and took the reed and struck him on the head. [31]After mocking him, they stripped him of the robe and put his own clothes on him. Then they led him away to crucify him.

[32]As they went out, they came upon a man from Cyrene named Simon; they compelled this man to carry his cross. [33]And when they came to a place called Golgotha (which means Place of a Skull), [34]they offered him wine to drink, mixed with gall, but when he tasted it, he would not drink it. [35]And when they had crucified him, they divided his clothes among themselves by casting lots; [36]then they sat down there and kept watch over him. [37]Over his head they put the charge against him, which read, "This is Jesus, the King of the Jews."

[38]Then two bandits were crucified with him, one on his right and one on his left. [39]Those who passed by derided him, shaking their heads [40]and saying, "You who would destroy the temple and build it in three days, save yourself! If you are the Son of God, come down from the cross." [41]In the same way the chief priests also, along with the scribes and elders, were mocking him, saying, [42]"He saved others; he cannot save himself. He is the King of Israel, let him come down from the cross now, and we will believe in him. [43]He trusts in God; let God deliver him now, if he wants to; for he said, 'I am God's Son.'" [44]The bandits who were crucified with him also taunted him in the same way.

[45]From noon on, darkness came over the whole land until three in the afternoon. [46]And about three o'clock Jesus cried with a loud voice, "Eli, Eli, lema sabachthani?" that is, "My God, my God, why have you forsaken me?" [47]When some of the bystanders heard it, they said, "This man is calling for Elijah." [48]At once one of them ran and got a sponge, filled it with sour wine, put it on a stick, and gave it to him to drink. [49]But the others said "Wait, let us see whether Elijah will come to save him." [50]Then Jesus cried again with a loud voice and breathed his last. [51]At that moment the curtain of the temple was torn in two, from top to bottom. The earth shook, and the rocks were split. [52]The tombs also were opened, and many bodies of the saints who had fallen asleep were raised. [53]After his resurrection they came out of the tombs and entered the holy city and appeared to many. [54]Now when the centurion and those with him, who were keeping watch over Jesus saw the earthquake and what took place, they were terrified and said, "Truly this man was God's Son!"

[55]Many women were also there, looking on from a distance, they had followed Jesus from Galilee and had provided for him. [56]Among them were Mary Magdalene, and Mary the mother of James and Joseph, and the mother of the sons of Zebedee.

[57]When it was evening, there came a rich man from Arimathea, named Joseph, who was also a disciple of Jesus. [58]He went to Pilate and asked for the body of Jesus, then Pilate ordered it to be given to him. [59]So Joseph took the body and wrapped it in a clean linen cloth [60]and laid it in his own new tomb, which he had hewn in the rock. He then rolled a great stone to the door of the tomb and went away. [61]Mary Magdalene and the other Mary were there, sitting opposite the tomb.

[62]The next day, that is after the day of Preparation, the chief priests and the Pharisees gathered before Pilate [63]and said, "Sir, we remember what that impostor said while he was still alive, 'After three days I will rise again.' [64]Therefore command the tomb to be made secure until the third day; otherwise his disciples may go and steal him away, and tell the people, 'He has been raised from the dead,' and the last deception would be worse than the first." [65]Pilate said to them, "You have a guard of soldiers go, make it as secure as you can." [66]So they went with the guard and made the tomb secure by sealing the stone.

28 [1]After the sabbath, as the first day of the week was dawning Mary Magdalene and the other Mary went to see the tomb. [2]And suddenly there was a great earthquake; for an angel of the Lord, descending from heaven, came and rolled back the stone and sat on it. [3]His appearance was like lightning, and his clothing white as snow. [4]For fear of him the guards shook and became like dead men. [5]But the angel said to the women "Do not be afraid; I know that you are looking for Jesus who was crucified. [6]He is not here; for he has been raised, as he said. Come, see the place where he lay. [7]Then go quickly and tell his disciples, 'He has been raised from the dead, and indeed he is going ahead of you to Galilee; there you will see him.' This is my message for you." [8]So they left the tomb quickly with fear and great joy, and ran to tell his disciples. [9]Suddenly Jesus met them and said "Greetings!" And they came to him, took hold of his feet, and worshiped him. [10]Then Jesus said to them, "Do not be afraid; go and tell my brothers to go to Galilee; there they will see me."

[11]While they were going, some of the guard went into the city and told the chief priests everything that had happened. [12]After the priests had assembled with the elders, they devised a plan to give a large sum of money to the soldiers [13]telling them, "You must say, 'His disciples came by night and stole him away while we were asleep.' [14]If this comes to the governor's ears, we will satisfy him and keep you out of trouble." [15]So they took the money and did as they were directed. And this story is still told among the Jews to this day.

[16]Now the eleven disciples went to Galilee, to the mountain to which Jesus had directed them. [17]When they saw him, they worshiped him but some doubted. [18]And Jesus came and said to them, "All authority in heaven and on earth has been given to me. [19]Go therefore and make disciples of all nations, baptizing them in the name of the Father and of the Son and of the Holy Spirit, [20]and teaching them to obey everything that I have commanded you. And remember, I am with you always, to the end of the age."

Paul and the
Early Church
ca. A.D. 10–ca. 67

The Apostle Paul, originally named Saul, was raised in Tarsus, a small city in southeastern Asia Minor (near the south coast of present-day Turkey). He was both a Jew and a Roman citizen—a status that afforded him special privileges. He studied Hebrew Law under Rabbi Gamaliel and gave evidence in his writings of a respectable knowledge of Hellenistic thought. As a young man, Saul was a zealously observant Jew and a persecutor of Christians. According to the New Testament Book of Acts, he was present at the death of Stephen, the first Christian martyr. While on his way to Damascus to attack a group of Christians, Saul underwent a dramatic conversion. He went on to become the outstanding missionary and theologian of the early Church.

One of the questions facing the early Church was whether or not Christianity should remain a Jewish sect. Should converts to Christianity also undertake the ritual steps needed to become Jewish? Sometime around A.D. 48, a council met in Jerusalem to discuss the issue. This council determined that gentile converts did not have to undergo circumcision, but they should observe the dietary and sexual prescriptions of the Law. In so doing, the council effectively endorsed Paul's work among the gentiles.

By the time of the Jerusalem council, Paul had already completed one missionary journey. Over the next ten years, he traveled extensively throughout the Mediterranean world, preaching in Jewish synagogues and planting Christian communities. The Book of Acts chronicles many of these journeys. Despite his success in missionary work, Paul was not a skilled public speaker. He admitted his lack of rhetorical talents, and Acts records that on one occasion Paul talked so long into the night that an exhausted young man fell asleep and plunged three

16

stories from his perch in the gallery, almost killing himself (Acts 20:7–12). But what Paul lacked in oratorical skills, he more than made up for in his writings. He dictated powerful letters, many of which are still extant and form almost a third of the New Testament. Selections from three of these letters are reprinted here, along with the account from Acts of the foundation of the early Church, Paul's recounting of his conversion, his exchange with the philosophers in Athens, and the influential end-times description of the new heaven and new earth from the Revelation to St. John.

Sometime around A.D. 58, Paul was arrested and imprisoned in Jerusalem. Using the privilege of Roman citizenship, Paul requested that his case be tried by the highest Roman authority. After a long and eventful journey, Paul arrived in Rome about A.D. 60 and spent the next two years under house arrest. The outcome of his trial and the date of his death are not known, but according to tradition at some later point he was found guilty and beheaded. (Execution by beheading rather than crucifixion was another privilege of Roman citizenship.)

* * *

Despite his own Jewish ancestry, Paul taught a universal Christianity that went well beyond ethnic Judaism. The Jesus of which Paul preached was the God-Man, the Lord Christ whose death was an atonement for the sins of *all* humanity. Paul argued that human good works done in obedience to even the best and highest Law, the Law of Israel, were worthless in acquiring righteousness before God. While the Law could indeed point out the inadequacy of one's "flesh" (or human power) in the presence of God, the Law could not transform human nature into the consummate righteousness required for association with the holy God. Only through faith in Jesus as the Christ, a faith that was itself a gift of God, could one be restored to a right relationship with God and given the gift of God's Spirit. Such a restored relationship would be characterized by humbly accepting God's gift and by an answering love for others.

Besides his teachings on Justification and Sanctification, the passages reprinted here include such significant Pauline doctrines as the universal knowledge of God's nature and power (similar to the Stoic concept of Natural Law), the incontinent nature of the unconverted will, the divine ordination of governmental authority, the acknowledgment of the seeming "foolishness" of the Gospels to human reason, and the bodily resurrection of human beings before a judgment at the end of history. All of these tenets were accepted and developed by the Christians of the Middle Ages.

* * *

The classic work by Adolf Deissmann, *Paul: A Study in Social and Religious History,* 2nd edition, translated by W.E. Wilson (Garden City, NY: Doubleday, 1927), is a good beginning in the study of Paul. Günther Bornkamm, *Paul,* translated by D.M.G. Stalker (New York: Harper & Row, 1971); Michael Grant, *Saint Paul* (New York: Scribner's, 1976); John Ziesler, *Pauline Christianity* (Oxford: Oxford University Press, 1983); Joseph A. Fitzmyer, *Paul and His Theology: A Brief Sketch* (Englewood Cliffs, NJ: Prentice Hall, 1989); and E.P. Sanders, *Paul* (Oxford: Oxford University Press, 1991) are also helpful. E.P.

Sanders, *Paul and Palestinian Judaism* (London: SCM Press, 1977), and W.D. Davies, *Paul and Rabbinic Judaism: Some Rabbinic Elements in Pauline Theology,* 4th edition (Philadelphia: Fortress Press, 1980) stress Paul's roots in Jewish thought, whereas Abraham J. Malherbe's books, *Paul and the Theologians: The Philosophic Tradition of Pastoral Care* (Philadelphia: Fortress Press, 1987) and *Paul and the Popular Philosophers* (Philadelphia: Fortress Press, 1989), focus on the connections between Paul and Hellenistic philosophy. For discussions of Paul's social environment, see Wayne Meeks, *The First Urban Christians: The Social World of the Apostle Paul* (New Haven, CT: Yale University Press, 1983). For a general study on the relationship between Jesus and Paul, see F.F. Bruce, *Paul & Jesus* (Grand Rapids, MI: Baker Book House, 1974). For a study specifically comparing their ethics, see Roger Mohrlang, *Matthew and Paul: A Comparison of Ethical Perspectives* (Cambridge: Cambridge University Press, 1984).

NEW TESTAMENT: ACTS, PAULINE LETTERS, AND REVELATION (in part)

THE BIRTH OF THE CHRISTIAN CHURCH
(ACTS 2:1–21, 37–47)

2 [1]When the day of Pentecost had come, they were all together in one place. [2]And suddenly from heaven there came a sound like the rush of a violent wind, and it filled the entire house where they were sitting. [3]Divided tongues, as of fire, appeared among them, and a tongue rested on each of them. [4]All of them were filled with the Holy Spirit and began to speak in other languages, as the Spirit gave them ability.

[5]Now there were devout Jews from every nation under heaven living in Jerusalem. [6]And at this sound the crowd gathered and was bewildered, because each one heard them speaking in the native language of each. [7]Amazed and astonished, they asked, "Are not all these who are speaking Galileans? [8]And how is it that we hear, each of us, in our own native language? [9]Parthians, Medes, Elamites, and residents of Mesopotamia, Judea and Cappadocia, Pontus and Asia, [10]Phrygia and Pamphylia, Egypt and the parts of Libya belonging to Cyrene, and visitors from Rome, both Jews and proselytes, [11]Cretans and Arabs—in our own languages we hear them speaking about God's deeds of power." [12]All were amazed and perplexed, saying to one another, "What does this mean?" [13]But others sneered and said, "They are filled with new wine."

[14]But Peter, standing with the eleven, raised his voice and addressed them, "Men of Judea and all who live in Jerusalem, let this be known to you and listen to what I

say. [15]Indeed these are not drunk, as you suppose for it is only nine o'clock in the morning. [16]No, this is what was spoken through the prophet Joel:

[17]'In the last days it will be, God declares,
that I will pour out my Spirit upon all flesh,
and your sons and your daughters shall prophesy,
and your young men shall see visions,
and your old men shall dream dreams.
[18]Even upon my slaves, both men and women,
in those days I will pour out my Spirit;
and they shall prophesy.
[19]And I will show portents in the heaven above
and signs on the earth below,
blood, and fire, and smoky mist.
[20]The sun shall be turned to darkness
and the moon to blood,
before the coming of the Lord's great and glorious day.
[21]Then everyone who calls on the name of the Lord shall be saved.'

*   *   *

[37]Now when they heard this, they were cut to the heart and said to Peter and to the other apostles, "Brothers, what should we do?" [38]Peter said to them, "Repent, and be baptized every one of you in the name of Jesus Christ so that your sins may be forgiven and you will receive the gift of the Holy Spirit. [39]For the promise is for you, for your children, and for all who are far away, everyone whom the Lord our God calls to him." [40]And he testified with many other arguments and exhorted them, saying, "Save yourselves from this corrupt generation." [41]So those who welcomed his message were baptized, and that day about three thousand persons were added. [42]They devoted themselves to the apostles' teaching and fellowship, to the breaking of bread and the prayers.

[43]Awe came upon everyone, because many wonders and signs were being done by the apostles. [44]All who believed were together and had all things in common, [45]they would sell their possessions and goods and distribute the proceeds to all, as any had need. [46]Day by day, as they spent much time together in the temple, they broke bread at home and ate their food with glad and generous hearts [47]praising God and having the goodwill of all the people. And day by day the Lord added to their number those who were being saved.

*   *   *

THE CONVERSION OF SAUL (ACTS 9:1–22)

9 [1]Meanwhile Saul, still breathing threats and murder against the disciples of the Lord, went to the high priest [2]and asked him for letters to the synagogues at Damascus, so that if he found any who belonged to the Way, men or women, he might bring them bound to Jerusalem. [3]Now as he was going along and approaching Damascus, suddenly a light from heaven flashed around him. [4]He fell to the ground and heard a voice saying to him,

"Saul, Saul, why do you persecute me?" [5]He asked, "Who are you, Lord?" The reply came, "I am Jesus, whom you are persecuting. [6]But get up and enter the city, and you will be told what you are to do." [7]The men who were traveling with him stood speechless because they heard the voice but saw no one. [8]Saul got up from the ground, and though his eyes were open, he could see nothing; so they led him by the hand and brought him into Damascus. [9]For three days he was without sight, and neither ate nor drank.

[10]Now there was a disciple in Damascus named Ananias. The Lord said to him in a vision, "Ananias." He answered, "Here I am, Lord." [11]The Lord said to him, "Get up and go to the street called Straight, and at the house of Judas look for a man of Tarsus named Saul. At this moment he is praying, [12]and he has seen in a vision a man named Ananias come in and lay his hands on him so that he might regain his sight." [13]But Ananias answered, "Lord, I have heard from many about this man, how much evil he has done to your saints in Jerusalem; [14]and here he has authority from the chief priests to bind all who invoke your name." [15]But the Lord said to him, "Go, for he is an instrument whom I have chosen to bring my name before Gentiles and kings and before the people of Israel; [16]I myself will show him how much he must suffer for the sake of my name." [17]So Ananias went and entered the house. He laid his hands on Saul and said, "Brother Saul, the Lord Jesus, who appeared to you on your way here, has sent me so that you may regain your sight and be filled with the Holy Spirit." [18]And immediately something like scales fell from his eyes, and his sight was restored. Then he got up and was baptized [19]and after taking some food, he regained his strength.

For several days he was with the disciples in Damascus, [20]and immediately he began to proclaim Jesus in the synagogues, saying, "He is the Son of God." [21]All who heard him were amazed and said, "Is not this the man who made havoc in Jerusalem among those who invoked this name? And has he not come here for the purpose of bringing them bound before the chief priests?" [22]Saul became increasingly more powerful and confounded the Jews who lived in Damascus by proving that Jesus was the Messiah.

*   *   *

PAUL WITH THE PHILOSOPHERS IN ATHENS
(ACTS 17:16–34)

17 [16]While Paul was waiting for them in Athens, he was deeply distressed to see that the city was full of idols. [17]So he argued in the synagogue with the Jews and the devout persons, and also in the marketplace every day with those who happened to be there. [18]Also some Epicurean and Stoic philosophers debated with him. Some said, "What does this babbler want to say?" Others said, "He seems to be a proclaimer of foreign divinities." (This was because he was telling the good news about Jesus and the resurrection.) [19]So they took him and brought him to the Areopagus and asked him, "May we know what this new teaching is that you are presenting? [20]It sounds rather strange to us, so we would like to know what it means." [21]Now all the Athenians and the foreigners living there would spend their time in nothing but telling or hearing something new.

[22]Then Paul stood in front of the Areopagus and said, "Athenians, I see how extremely religious you are in every way. [23]For as I went through the city and looked carefully at the objects of your worship, I found among them an altar with the inscription, 'To an unknown god.' What therefore you worship as unknown, this I proclaim to you. [24]The God who made the world and everything in it, he who is Lord of heaven and earth, does not live in shrines made by human hands, [25]nor is he served by human hands, as though he needed anything, since he himself gives to all mortals life and breath and all things. [26]From one ancestor he made all nations to inhabit the whole earth, and he allotted the times of their existence and the boundaries of the places where they would live, [27]so that they would search for gods and perhaps grope for him and find him—though indeed he is not far from each one of us. [28]For

'In him we live and move and have our being,'

as even some of your own poets have said,

'For we too are his offspring.'

[29]Since we are God's offspring, we ought not to think that the deity is like gold, or silver, or stone, an image formed by the art and imagination of mortals. [30]While God has overlooked the times of human ignorance, now he commands all people everywhere to repent, [31]because he has fixed a day on which he will have the world judged in righteousness by a man whom he has appointed, and of this he has given assurance to all by raising him from the dead."

[32]When they heard of the resurrection of the dead, some scoffed; but others said, "We will hear you again about this." [33]At that point Paul left them. [34]But some of them joined him and became believers, including Dionysius the Areopagite and a woman named Damaris, and others with them.

*   *   *

PAUL'S NATURAL THEOLOGY (ROMANS 1:16–32)

1 [16]For I am not ashamed of the gospel, it is the power of God for salvation to everyone who has faith, to the Jew first and also to the Greek. [17]For in it the righteousness of God is revealed through faith for faith; as it is written, "The one who is righteous will live by faith."

[18]For the wrath of God is revealed from heaven against all ungodliness and wickedness of those who by their wickedness suppress the truth. [19]For what can be known about God is plain to them, because God has shown it to them. [20]Ever since the creation of the world his eternal power and divine nature, invisible though they are, have been understood and seen through the things he has made. So they are without excuse, [21]for though they knew God, they did not honor him as God or give thanks to him, but they became futile in their thinking, and their senseless minds were darkened. [22]Claiming to be wise,

they became fools, [23]and they exchanged the glory of the immortal God for images re-sembling a mortal human being or birds or four-footed animals or reptiles.

[24]Therefore God gave them up in the lusts of their hearts to impurity, to the de-grading of their bodies among themselves [25]because they exchanged the truth about God for a lie and worshiped and served the creature rather than the Creator, who is blessed forever! Amen.

[26]For this reason God gave them up to degrading passions. Their women ex-changed natural intercourse for unnatural [27]and in the same way also the men, giving up natural intercourse with women, were consumed with passion for one another. Men committed shameless acts with men and received in their own persons the due penalty for their error.

[28]And since they did not see fit to acknowledge God, God gave them up to a de-based mind and to things that should not be done. [29]They were filled with every kind of wickedness, evil covetousness, malice. Full of envy, murder, strife, deceit, craftiness, they are gossips, [30]slanderers, Godhaters, insolent, haughty, boastful, inventors of evil, rebellious toward parents, [31]foolish, faithless, heartless, ruthless. [32]They know God's decree that those who practice such things deserve to die—yet they not only do them but even applaud others who practice them.

*   *   *

RIGHTEOUSNESS THROUGH FAITH
(ROMANS 3:21–31)

3 [21]But now, apart from law, the righteousness of God has been disclosed, and is at-tested by the law and the prophets; [22]the righteousness of God through faith in Jesus Christ for all who believe. For there is no distinction, [23]since all have sinned and fall short of the glory of God, [24]they are now justified by his grace as a gift through the re-demption that is in Christ Jesus, [25]whom God put forward as a sacrifice of atonement by his blood, effective through faith. He did this to show his righteousness, because in his divine forbearance he had passed over the sins previously committed; [26]it was to prove at the present time that he himself is righteous and that he justifies the one who has faith in Jesus.

[27]Then what becomes of boasting? It is excluded. By what law? By that of works? No, but by the law of faith. [28]For we hold that a person is justified by faith apart from works prescribed by the law. [29]Or is God the God of Jews only? Is he not the God of Gentiles also? Yes, of Gentiles also, [30]since God is one, and he will justify the circumcised on the ground of faith and the uncircumcised through that same faith. [31]Do we then overthrow the law by this faith? By no means! On the contrary, we up-hold the law.

*   *   *

Results of Justification (Romans 5:1–11)

5 [1]Therefore, since we are justified by faith, we have peace with God through our Lord Jesus Christ, [2]through whom we have obtained access to this grace in which we stand; and we boast in our hope of sharing the glory of God. [3]And not only that but we also boast in our sufferings knowing that suffering produces endurance, [4]and endurance produces character, and character produces hope, and hope does not disappoint us, because God's love has been poured into our hearts through the Holy Spirit that has been given to us. [6]For while we were still weak, at the right time Christ died for the ungodly. [7]Indeed, rarely will anyone die for a righteous person—though perhaps for a good person someone might actually dare to die. [8]But God proves his love for us in that while we still were sinners Christ died for us. [9]Much more surely then, now that we have been justified by his blood, will we be saved through him from the wrath of God. [10]For if while we were enemies, we were reconciled to God through the death of his Son, much more surely having been reconciled, will we be saved by his life. [11]But more than that, we even boast in God through our Lord Jesus Christ, through whom we have now received reconciliation.

*   *   *

The Struggle Between the Flesh and the Spirit (Romans 7:14–8:39)

7 [14]For we know that the law is spiritual, but I am of the flesh, sold into slavery under sin. [15]I do not understand my own actions. For I do not do what I want, but I do the very thing I hate. [16]Now if I do what I do not want I agree that the law is good. [17]But in fact it is no longer I that do it, but sin that dwells within me. [18]For I know that nothing good dwells within me that is, in my flesh. I can will what is right, but I cannot do it. [19]For I do not do the good I want, but the evil I do not want is what I do. [20]Now if I do what I do not want, it is no longer I that do it, but sin that dwells within me.

[21]So I find it to be a law that when I want to do what is good, evil lies close at hand. [22]For I delight in the law of God in my inmost self [23]but I see in my members another law at war with the law of my mind, making me captive to the law of sin that dwells in my members. [24]Wretched man that I am! Who will rescue me from this body of death? [25]Thanks be to God through Jesus Christ our Lord!

So then, with my mind I am a slave to the law of God, but with my flesh I am a slave to the law of sin.

8 [1]There is therefore now no condemnation for those who are in Christ Jesus. [2]For the law of the Spirit of life in Christ Jesus has set you free from the law of sin and of death. [3]For God has done what the law, weakened by the flesh, could not do: by sending his own Son in the likeness of sinful flesh, and to deal with sin, he condemned sin in the flesh, [4]so that the just requirement of the law might be fulfilled in us, who walk not according to the flesh but according to the Spirit. [5]For those who live according to the flesh set their minds on the things of the flesh, but those who live according to the Spirit set their minds on the things of the Spirit. [6]To set the mind on the flesh is death, but to set the mind on the Spirit is life and peace. [7]For this reason the mind that is set on the flesh is hostile to God, it does not submit to God's law—indeed it cannot [8]and those who are in the flesh cannot please God.

[9]But you are not in the flesh; you are in the Spirit, since the Spirit of God dwells in you. Anyone who does not have the Spirit of Christ does not belong to him. [10]But if Christ is in you, though the body is dead because of sin, the Spirit is life because of righteousness. [11]If the Spirit of him who raised Jesus from the dead dwells in you, he who raised Christ from the dead will give life to your mortal bodies also through his Spirit that dwells in you. [12]So then, brothers and sisters, we are debtors, not to the flesh, to live according to the flesh—[13]for if you live according to the flesh, you will die; but if by the Spirit you put to death the deeds of the body, you will live. [14]For all who are led by the Spirit of God are children of God. [15]For you did not receive a spirit of slavery to fall back into fear, but you have received a spirit of adoption. When we cry, "Abba! Father!" [16]it is that very Spirit bearing witness with our spirit that we are children of God [17]and if children, then heirs, heirs of God and joint heirs with Christ— if, in fact, we suffer with him so that we may also be glorified with him.

[18]I consider that the sufferings of this present time are not worth comparing with the glory about to be revealed to us. [19]For the creation waits with eager longing for the revealing of the children of God [20]for the creation was subjected to futility, not of its own will but by the will of the one who subjected it, in hope [21]that the creation itself will be set free from its bondage to decay and will obtain the freedom of the glory of the children of God. [22]We know that the whole creation has been groaning in labor pains until now [23]and not only the creation, but we ourselves, who have the first fruits of the Spirit, groan inwardly while we wait for adoption, the redemption of our bodies. [24]For in hope we were saved. Now hope that is seen is not hope. For who hopes for what is seen? [25]But if we hope for what we do not see, we wait for it with patience.

[26]Likewise the Spirit helps us in our weakness; for we do not know how to pray as we ought, but that very Spirit intercedes with sighs too deep for words. [27]And God, who searches the heart, knows what is the mind of the Spirit, because the Spirit intercedes for the saints according to the will of God.

[28]We know that all things work together for good for those who love God, who are called according to his purpose. [29]For those whom he foreknew he also predestined to be conformed to the image of his Son, in order that he might be the firstborn within a large family. [30]And those whom he predestined he also called; and those whom he called he also justified, and those whom he justified he also glorified.

[31]What then are we to say about these things? If God is for us, who is against us? [32]He who did not withhold his own Son, but gave him up for all of us, will he not with him also give us everything else? [33]Who will bring any charge against God's elect? It is God who justifies. [34]Who is to condemn? It is Christ Jesus, who died, yes, who was raised, who is at the right hand of God, who indeed intercedes for us. [35]Who will separate us from the love of Christ? Will hardship, or distress, or persecution, or famine, or nakedness, or peril, or sword? [36]As it is written,

> "For your sake we are being killed all day long;
> we are accounted as sheep to be slaughtered."

[37]No, in all these things we are more than conquerors through him who loved us. [38]For I am convinced that neither death, nor life, nor angels, nor rulers, nor things

present, nor things to come, nor powers, [39]nor height, nor depth, nor anything else in all creation, will be able to separate us from the love of God in Christ Jesus our Lord.

*   *   *

The Christian Ethic of Paul (Romans 12–13)

12 [1]I appeal to you therefore, brothers and sisters, by the mercies of God, to present your bodies as a living sacrifice, holy and acceptable to God, which is your spiritual worship. [2]Do not be conformed to this world, but be transformed by the renewing of your minds, so that you may discern what is the will of God—what is good and acceptable and perfect.

[3]For by the grace given to me I say to everyone among you not to think of yourself more highly than you ought to think, but to think with sober judgment, each according to the measure of faith that God has assigned. [4]For as in one body we have many members and not all the members have the same function, [5]so we, who are many, are one body in Christ, and individually we are members one of another. [6]We have gifts that differ according to the grace given to us: prophecy, in proportion to faith; [7]ministry, in ministering; the teacher, in teaching; [8]the exhorter, in exhortation; the giver, in generosity; the leader, in diligence; the compassionate, in cheerfulness.

[9]Let love be genuine, hate what is evil, hold fast to what is good; [10]love one another with mutual affection; outdo one another in showing honor. [11]Do not lag in zeal, be ardent in spirit, serve the Lord. [12]Rejoice in hope, be patient in suffering, persevere in prayer. [13]Contribute to the needs of the saints; extend hospitality to strangers.

[14]Bless those who persecute you; bless and do not curse them. [15]Rejoice with those who rejoice, weep with those who weep. [16]Live in harmony with one another; do not be haughty but associate with the lowly; do not claim to be wiser than you are. [17]Do not repay anyone evil for evil, but take thought for what is noble in the sight of all. [18]If it is possible, so far as it depends on you, live peaceably with all. [19]Beloved, never avenge yourselves but leave room for the wrath of God; for it is written, "Vengeance is mine, I will repay, says the Lord." [20]No, "if your enemies are hungry, feed them; if they are thirsty, give them something to drink, for by doing this you will heap burning coals on their heads." [21]Do not be overcome by evil, but overcome evil with good.

13 [1]Let every person be subject to the governing authorities, for there is no authority except from God, and those authorities that exist have been instituted by God. [2]Therefore whoever resists authority resists what God has appointed, and those who resist will incur judgment. [3]For rulers are not a terror to good conduct, but to bad. Do you wish to have no fear of the authority? Then do what is good, and you will receive its approval; [4]for it is God's servant for your good. But if you do what is wrong, you should be afraid, for the authority does not bear the sword in vain! It is the servant of God to execute wrath on the wrongdoer. [5]Therefore one must be subject not only because of wrath but also because of conscience. [6]For the same reason you also pay taxes, for the authorities are God's servants, busy with this very thing. [7]Pay to all what is due them—taxes to whom taxes are due, revenue to whom revenue is due, respect to whom respect is due, honor to whom honor is due.

[8]Owe no one anything, except to love one another; for the one who loves another has fulfilled the law. [9]The commandments, "You shall not commit adultery, You shall not murder, You shall not steal, You shall not covet," and any other commandment are summed up in this word, "Love your neighbor as yourself." [10]Love does no wrong to a neighbor; therefore, love is the fulfilling of the law.

[11]Besides this, you know what time it is, how it is now the moment for you to wake from sleep. For salvation is nearer to us now than when we became believers; [12]the night is far gone the day is near. Let us then lay aside the works of darkness and put on the armor of light; [13]let us live honorably as in the day, not in reveling and drunkenness, not in debauchery and licentiousness, not in quarreling and jealousy. [14]Instead, put on the Lord Jesus Christ, and make no provision for the flesh, to gratify its desires.

*   *   *

THE FOOLISHNESS OF THE GOSPEL (I CORINTHIANS 1:18–31)

1 [18]For the message about the cross is foolishness to those who are perishing, but to us who are being saved it is the power of God. [19]For it is written,

> "I will destroy the wisdom of the wise,
> and the discernment of the discerning I will thwart."

[20]Where is the one who is wise? Where is the scribe? Where is the debater of this age? Has not God made foolish the wisdom of the world? [21]For since, in the wisdom of God, the world did not know God through wisdom, God decided, through the foolishness of our proclamation, to save those who believe. [22]For Jews demand signs and Greeks desire wisdom [23]but we proclaim Christ crucified, a stumbling block to Jews and foolishness to Gentiles, [24]but to those who are the called, both Jews and Greeks, Christ the power of God and the wisdom of God. [25]For God's foolishness is wiser than human wisdom, and God's weakness is stronger than human strength.

[26]Consider your own call, brothers and sisters: not many of you were wise by human standards, not many were powerful, not many were of noble birth. [27]But God chose what is foolish in the world to shame the wise, God chose what is weak in the world to shame the strong; [28]God chose what is low and despised in the world, things that are not, to reduce to nothing things that are [29]so that no one might boast in the presence of God. [30]He is the source of your life in Christ Jesus, who became for us wisdom from God, and righteousness and sanctification and redemption, [31]in order that, as it is written, "Let the one who boasts, boast in the Lord."

*   *   *

THE GIFT OF LOVE (I CORINTHIANS 13)

13 [1]If I speak in the tongues of mortals and of angels, but do not have love, I am a noisy gong or a clanging cymbal. [2]And if I have prophetic powers, and understand all mysteries and all knowledge, and if I have all faith, so as to remove mountains, but do not have love, I am nothing. [3]If I give away all my possessions, and if I hand over my body so that I may boast, but do not have love, I gain nothing.

[4]Love is patient, love is kind, love is not envious or boastful or arrogant [5]or rude. It does not insist on its own way; it is not irritable or resentful; [6]it does not rejoice in wrongdoing, but rejoices in the truth. [7]It bears all things, believes all things, hopes all things, endures all things.

[8]Love never ends. But as for prophecies, they will come to an end; as for tongues, they will cease; as for knowledge, it will come to an end. [9]For we know only in part, and we prophesy only in part; [10]but when the complete comes, the partial will come to an end. [11]When I was a child, I spoke like a child, I thought like a child, I reasoned like a child; when I became an adult, I put an end to childish ways. [12]For now we see in a mirror, dimly, but then we will see face to face. Now I know only in part; then I will know fully, even as I have been fully known. [13]And now faith, hope, and love abide, these three; and the greatest of these is love.

*   *   *

THE RESURRECTION OF THE BODY
(I CORINTHIANS 15:16–26; 51–58)

15 [16]For if the dead are not raised then Christ has not been raised. [17]If Christ has not been raised, your faith is futile and you are still in your sins. [18]Then those also who have died in Christ have perished. [19]If for this life only we have hoped in Christ, we are of all people most to be pitied.

[20]But in fact Christ has been raised from the dead, the first fruits of those who have died. [21]For since death came through a human being, the resurrection of the dead has also come through a human being, [22]for as all die in Adam, so all will be made alive in Christ. [23]But each in his own order: Christ the first fruits, then at his coming those who belong to Christ. [24]Then comes the end, when he hands over the kingdom to God the Father, after he has destroyed every ruler and every authority and power. [25]For he must reign until he has put all his enemies under his feet. [26]The last enemy to be destroyed is death.

*   *   *

[51]Listen I will tell you a mystery! We will not all die, but we will all be changed, [52]in a moment, in the twinkling of an eye, at the last trumpet. For the trumpet will sound, and the dead will be raised imperishable, and we will be changed. [53]For this perishable body must put on imperishability, and this mortal body must put on immortality.

[54]When this perishable body puts on imperishability, and this mortal body puts on immortality, then the saying that is written will be fulfilled:

> "Death has been swallowed up in victory."
> [55]"Where, O death, is your victory?
> Where, O death, is your sting?"

[56]The sting of death is sin, and the power of sin is the law. [57]But thanks be to God, who gives us the victory through our Lord Jesus Christ.

[58]Therefore, my beloved, be steadfast, immovable, always excelling in the work of the Lord, because you know that in the Lord your labor is not in vain.

*   *   *

WARNING AGAINST PHILOSOPHY (COLOSSIANS 2:8–10)

2 [8]See to it that no one takes you captive through philosophy and empty deceit, according to human tradition, according to the elemental spirits of the universe, and not according to Christ. [9]For in him the whole fullness of deity dwells bodily, [10]and you have come to fullness in him, who is the head of every ruler and authority.

*   *   *

THE NEW HEAVEN AND THE NEW EARTH (REVELATION 21:1–8; 22:1–5)

21 [1]Then I saw a new heaven and a new earth; for the first heaven and the first earth had passed away, and the sea was no more. [2]And I saw the holy city, the new Jerusalem, coming down out of heaven from God, prepared as a bride adorned for her husband. [3]And I heard a loud voice from the throne saying,

> "See, the home of God is among mortals.
> He will dwell with them as their God;
> they will be his peoples,
> and God himself will be with them;
> [4]he will wipe every tear from their eyes.
> Death will be no more;
> mourning and crying and pain will be no more,
> for the first things have passed away."

[5]And the one who was seated on the throne said, "See, I am making all things new." Also he said, "Write this for these words are trustworthy and true." [6]Then he said to me, "It is done! I am the Alpha and the Omega, the beginning and the end. To

Christ as Ruler of the Universe, Byzantine Mosaic, twelfth century. Byzantine domes often included an image or icon of Christ as ruler. Notice that the text on the left-hand page of the Bible is in Greek (the language of Byzantium), while the right-hand page is in Latin (the language of Western Europe). *(Art Resource)*

the thirsty I will give water as a gift from the spring of the water of life. [7]Those who conquer will inherit these things, and I will be their God and they will be my children. [8]But as for the cowardly, the faithless, the polluted, the murderers, the fornicators, the sorcerers, the idolaters, and all liars, their place will be in the lake that burns with fire and sulfur, which is the second death."

*   *   *

22 [1]Then the angel showed me the river of the water of life, bright as crystal, flowing from the throne of God and of the Lamb [2]through the middle of the street of the city. On either side of the river, is the tree of life with its twelve kinds of fruit, producing its fruit each month, and the leaves of the tree are for the healing of the nations. [3]Nothing accursed will be found there any more. But the throne of God and of the Lamb will be in it, and his servants will worship him; [4]they will see his face, and his name will be on their foreheads. [5]And there will be no more night, they need no light of lamp or sun, for the Lord God will be their light, and they will reign forever and ever.

THE CHURCH FATHERS

One of the earliest questions facing the growing church was the proper relationship between Christianity and Greek philosophy. On the one hand, some of the early Christian writers, known as the *Church Fathers,* pointed to Paul's use of pagan concepts in preaching (Acts 17) and to his appeal to universal knowledge of God's power and nature (for example, Romans 1:20). They took this as proof that Greek philosophy might *supplement* revelation. Yet others claimed that Paul's warnings against philosophy (in Colossians 2:8, for example) and his claim that the Gospels were "foolishness" to the Greeks (e.g., I Cor. 1:18–31) indicated that Greek thought had been *superseded* by divine revelation.* Justin Martyr, Clement of Alexandria, and Origen are among the Church Fathers who advocated a rapprochement between divine revelation and secular reason, whereas Tertullian is the most prominent Church Father to urge a strong distinction between the two.

Justin Martyr (ca. A.D. 110–ca. 165), the first of the major Church Fathers, claimed that Christianity represented the completion of all true philosophy. Following studies in philosophy at Ephesus, Justin Martyr was converted to Christianity in his thirties. As he explained in his *Dialogue with Trypho,* he tried various philosophies but found peace only when he encountered the Christian Scriptures. Rather than seeing all his previous learning as false, he claimed that each of the pagan philosophers had a "dim glimpse of the truth" because of "the engrafted seed of the Word which was implanted in them."

*I am indebted to James N. Jordan, *Western Philosophy: From Antiquity to the Middle Ages* (New York: Macmillan, 1987), p. 277, for this distinction.

Clement of Alexandria (ca. A.D. 150–ca. 215) went even further than Justin Martyr in his estimation of philosophy. As the head of a Christian school in Alexandria, Clement claimed in his *Stromateis* (or *Miscellanies*) that philosophy was "a preparation, paving the way for the man who is brought to perfection by Christ." Borrowing an idea from his Jewish predecessor, Philo of Alexandria (ca. 20 B.C.–ca. A.D. 50; see following section), Clement claimed that Plato was able to come so close to the truth because Plato had directly studied the writings of Moses and had personally met the prophet Isaiah. Clement believed that parts of God's truth could be found in all philosophies—even in such apparently secular philosophies as Epicurianism.

Clement also borrowed from Philo the allegorical interpretation of scripture. But it was Origen (ca. A.D. 185–ca. 254), Clement's successor at the school in Alexandria, who took this approach to the Bible to its limits. According to Origen, every story, every teaching in the Bible can be seen as an allegory containing some deeper spiritual meaning. Using this approach to scripture, Origen combined Neoplatonic teachings with Christianity. For example, Origen accepted the biblical position that God freely created the world at a certain point in time, yet he also agreed with the Neoplatonic doctrine that God eternally and necessarily emanated creative power. Origen reconciled these apparently incompatible teachings by claiming that all souls preexisted from eternity, that all but one soul fell and became united with bodies in "the world" (Jesus being the exception), and that the biblical story of creation refers only to this particular world, not to the many others that God has created and will create. Although Origen's teachings were later rejected by the church, the question of God's relation to creation continued to be a controversial topic and echoes of Origen can be heard in Augustine.

The fourth major Church Father, Tertullian (ca. A.D. 155–ca. 220), took a position very different from that of Justin Martyr, Clement, and Origen. A successful lawyer from the northern African city of Carthage, Tertullian argued passionately against the use of philosophy to support Christianity. According to Tertullian, philosophy had already discredited itself by its patent inability to come to any unanimity about truth. And whereas philosophers, such as Socrates, may have occasionally said something true, it was only by chance or by the influence of biblical writings that they managed to intuit even partial truth.

But even in the best cases, Tertullian claimed, whatever partial truth might have been found in philosophy has been more than superseded by God's revelation. Tertullian went so far as to write, "The Son of God died; it must be believed because it is absurd. He was buried and rose again; it is certain because it is impossible." Tertullian's eloquent denial of the power of reason was to have great influence on the church. When the Council of Nicea rejected human wisdom in declaring Jesus to be both fully God and yet fully human, it was following the instincts and teachings of Paul and Tertullian.

*   *   *

The brief selections given here are from the translations of Thomas B. Falls (Justin Martyr), Henry Scowcroft Bettenson (Clement of Alexandria), Peter Holmes (Tertullian), and Frederick Crombie (Origen).

For further readings from the Church Fathers, see J.B. Lightfoot and J.R. Harmer, eds., *The Apostolic Fathers* (Grand Rapids, MI: Baker Book House,

1956); Henry Scowcroft Bettenson, ed., *Documents of the Christian Church,* 2nd edition (Oxford: Oxford University Press, 1967); and Eberhard Arnold, *The Early Christians After the Death of the Apostles* translated and edited by the Society of Brothers at Rifton (Rifton, NY: Plough, 1970). For comparative studies of the Church Fathers, see Henry Chadwick, *Early Christian Thought and the Classical Tradition: Studies in Justin, Clement, and Origen* (Oxford: Oxford University Press, 1966), and Hamilton Baird Timothy, *The Early Christian Apologists and Greek Philosophy Exemplified by Irenaeus, Tertullian and Clement of Alexandria* (Assen, The Netherlands: Van Gorcum, 1973). For the relations between Christian doctrine and the surrounding culture, the best introduction is Jaroslav Pelikan, *The Emergence of the Catholic Tradition (100–600)* (Chicago: University of Chicago Press, 1971).

For specific Church Fathers see the following:

JUSTIN MARTYR: Leslie W. Barnard, *Justin Martyr: His Life and Thought* (Cambridge: Cambridge University Press, 1967).

CLEMENT OF ALEXANDRIA: R.B. Tollinton, *Clement of Alexandria: A Study in Christian Liberalism* (London: Williams and Norgate, 1914); Eric Francis Osborn, *The Philosophy of Clement of Alexandria* (Cambridge: Cambridge University Press, 1957).

TERTULLIAN: John B. Delaunay, *Tertullian and His Apologetics: A Study of Early Christian Thought* (Notre Dame, IN: Notre Dame University Press, 1914); Timothy David Barnes, *Tertullian: A Historical and Literary Study* (Oxford: Clarendon Press, 1971).

ORIGEN: Jean Danielou, *Origen,* translated by Walter Mitchell (New York: Sheed and Ward, 1955); Joseph Wilson Trigg, *Origen: The Bible and Philosophy in the Third-Century Church* (Atlanta, GA: John Knox, 1983); Henri Crouzel, *Origen,* translated by A.S. Worrall (San Francisco: Harper & Row, 1989).

JUSTIN MARTYR
ca. A.D. 110–ca. 165

DIALOGUE WITH TRYPHO (in part)

2. "I will explain to you,"* I replied, "my views on this subject. Philosophy is indeed one's greatest possession, and is most precious in the sight of God, to whom it alone leads us and to whom it unites us, and they in truth are holy men who have applied themselves to philosophy. But, many have failed to discover the nature of philosophy, and the reason why it was sent down to men; otherwise, there would not be Platonists, or Stoics, or Peripatetics [i.e., Aristotelians], or Theoretics,** or Pythagoreans, since this science of philosophy is always one and the same. Now, let me tell you why it has at length become so diversified. They who first turned to philosophy, and, as a result, were deemed illustrious men, were succeeded by men who gave no time to the investigation of truth, but, amazed at the courage and self-control of their teachers as well as with the novelty of their teachings, held that to be the truth which each had learned from his own teacher. And they in turn transmitted to their successors such opinions, and others like them, and so they became known by the name of him who was considered the father of the doctrine. When I first desired to contact one of these philoso-

*[Justin Martyr is speaking to Trypho, a Jewish exile from Corinth, Greece.]
**[Possibly the Skeptics, or the name may be used here to indicate a group of philosophers who devoted themselves primarily to speculation and meditation.]

Thomas B. Falls, *Saint Justin Martyr, The Fathers of the Church,* Vol. 6 (Washington, DC: Catholic University of America Press, 1948), Chapters 2, 7, and 8. Reprinted with permission.

phers, I placed myself under the tutelage of a certain Stoic. After spending some time with him and learning nothing new about God (for my instructor had no knowledge of God, nor did he consider such knowledge necessary), I left him and turned to a Peripatetic who considered himself an astute teacher. After a few days with him, he demanded that we settle the matter of my tuition fee in such a way that our association would not be unprofitable to him. Accordingly, I left him, because I did not consider him a real philosopher. Since my spirit still yearned to hear the specific and excellent meaning of philosophy, I approached a very famous Pythagorean, who took great pride in his own wisdom. In my interview with him, when I expressed a desire to become his pupil, he asked me, 'What? Do you know music, astronomy, and geometry? How do you expect to comprehend any of those things that are conducive to happiness, if you are not first well acquainted with those studies which draw your mind away from objects of the senses and render it fit for the intellectual, in order that it may contemplate what is good and beautiful?' He continued to speak at great length in praise of those sciences, and of the necessity of knowing them, until I admitted that I knew nothing about them; then he dismissed me. As was to be expected, I was downcast to see my hopes shattered, especially since I respected him as a man of considerable knowledge. But, when I reflected on the length of time that I would have to spend on those sciences, I could not make up my mind to wait such a long time. In this troubled state of mind the thought occurred to me to consult the Platonists, whose reputation was great. Thus it happened that I spent as much time as possible in the company of a wise man who was highly esteemed by the Platonists and who had but recently arrived in our city. Under him I forged ahead in philosophy and day by day I improved. The perception of incorporeal things quite overwhelmed me and the Platonic theory of ideas added wings to my mind, so that in a short time I imagined myself a wise man. So great was my folly that I fully expected immediately to gaze upon God, for this is the goal of Plato's philosophy."

[While still in this Platonic "folly," Justin Martyr recounts that he met an old man and engaged in conversation about the value of pagan philosophy. After discussing several philosophical issues, the old man concluded, "Those philosophers, then, know nothing . . . about such matters, for they can't even explain the nature of the soul." This led Justin Martyr to ask the following question.]

7. "'If these philosophers,' I asked, 'do not know the truth, what teacher or method shall one follow?'

"'A long time ago,' [the old man] replied, 'long before the time of those reputed philosophers, there lived blessed men who were just and loved by God, men who spoke through the inspiration of the Holy Spirit and predicted events that would take place in the future, which events are now taking place. We call these men the Prophets. They alone knew the truth and communicated it to men, whom they neither deferred to nor feared. With no desire for personal glory, they reiterated only what they heard and saw when inspired by the Holy Spirit. Their writings are still extant, and whoever reads them with the proper faith will profit greatly in his knowledge of the origin and end of things, and of any other matter that a philosopher should know. In their writings they gave no proof at that time of their statements, for, as reliable witnesses of the truth, they were beyond proof; but the happenings that have taken place and are now taking place force you to believe their words. They also are worthy of belief because of the miracles which they performed, for they exalted God, the Father and Creator of all things, and made known Christ, His Son, who was sent by Him. This the false prophets, who are filled with an erring and unclean spirit, have never done nor even do now, but they undertake to perform certain wonders to astound men and they glorify the demons and spirits of error. Above all, beseech God to open to you the gates of light, for no one can perceive or understand these truths unless he has been enlightened by God and His Christ.'"

8. "When he had said these and many other things which it is not now the fitting time to tell, he went his way, after admonishing me to meditate on what he had told me, and I never saw him again. But my spirit was immediately set on fire, and an affection for the prophets, and for those who are friends of Christ, took hold of me; while pondering on his words, I discovered that his was the only sure and useful philosophy. Thus it is that I am now a philosopher. Furthermore, it is my wish that everyone would be of the same sentiments as I, and never spurn the Savior's words; for they have in themselves such tremendous majesty that they can instil fear into those who have wandered from the path of righteousness, whereas they ever remain a great solace to those who heed them. Thus, if you have any regard for your own welfare and for the salvation of your soul, and if you believe in God, you may have the chance, since I know you are no stranger to this matter, of attaining a knowledge of the Christ of God, and, after becoming a Christian, of enjoying a happy life."

*   *   *

APOLOGY (in part)

PART II, CHAPTER 13: HOW THE WORD HAS BEEN IN ALL MEN

When I learned of the evil camouflage which the wicked demons had thrown around the divine doctrines of the Christians to deter others from following them, I had to laugh at the authors of these lies, at the camouflage itself, and at the popular reaction. I am proud to say that I strove with all my might to be known as a Christian, not because the teachings of Plato are different from those of Christ, but because they are not in every way similar; neither are those of other writers, the Stoics, the poets, and the historians. For each one of them, seeing, through his participation of the seminal Divine Word, what was related to it, spoke very well. But, they who contradict themselves in important matters evidently did not acquire the unseen [that is, heavenly] wisdom and the indisputable knowledge. The truths which men in all lands have rightly spoken belong to us Christians. For we worship and love, after God the Father, the Word who is from the Unbegotten and Ineffable God, since He even became Man for us, so that by sharing in our sufferings He also might heal us. Indeed, all writers, by means of the engrafted seed of the Word which was implanted in them, had a dim glimpse of the truth. For the seed of something and its imitation, given in proportion to one's capacity, is one thing, but the thing itself, which is shared and imitated according to His grace, is quite another.

CLEMENT OF ALEXANDRIA
ca. A.D. 150–ca. 215

STROMATEIS (in part)

BOOK 1, CHAPTER 1: PHILOSOPHY A PREPARATION
FOR CHRISTIANITY

Philosophy was necessary to the Greeks for righteousness, until the coming of the Lord: and even now it is useful for the development of true religion, as a kind of preparatory discipline for those who arrive at faith by way of demonstration. For "your foot will not stumble," [Proverbs 3:28] as the Scripture says, if you attribute to Providence all good things, whether belonging to the Greeks or to us. For God is the source of all good; either directly, as in the Old and New Testaments, or indirectly, as in the case of philosophy. But it may even be that philosophy was given to the Greeks directly; for it was "a schoolmaster," [Galatians 3:24] to bring Hellenism to Christ, as the Law was for the Hebrews. Thus philosophy was a preparation, paving the way for the man who is brought to perfection by Christ.

* * *

Henry Scowcroft Bettenson, ed., *The Early Christian Fathers* (Oxford: Oxford University Press, 1956). Reprinted by permission of Oxford University Press.

CHAPTER 20: PHILOSOPHY A "CONTRIBUTORY" CAUSE OF THE TRUTH

If our critics force us to make a distinction by calling philosophy a *contributory* cause towards the apprehension of truth, as being a search for truth, we shall admit it to be a preparatory discipline for the "gnostic," without making it a *necessary* as opposed to a *contributory* cause, or asserting philosophy to be a *sine qua non*. For almost all of us have received the word about God through faith, without having a secondary education or a training in Greek philosophy, some of us without elementary education. But we have been moved by the power of the divinely inspired, non-Greek philosophy, trained by a self-taught wisdom.... And yet philosophy by itself did once justify the Greeks, not indeed to the attainment of complete righteousness, to which it proved a contributory cause, as the first two steps are to one mounting to an upper story, or a primary teacher to the budding philosopher.

TERTULLIAN
ca. A.D. 155–ca. 220

A TREATISE ON THE SOUL (in part)

CHAPTER 1: IT IS NOT TO THE PHILOSOPHERS THAT WE RESORT FOR INFORMATION ABOUT THE SOUL BUT TO GOD.

... It is not surprising that Socrates in prison ... asserts the immortality of the soul ... All the wisdom of Socrates, at that moment, proceeded from the affectation of an assumed composure, rather than the firm conviction of ascertained truth. For by whom has truth ever been discovered without God? By whom has God ever been found without Christ? By whom has Christ ever been explored without the Holy Spirit? By whom has the Holy Spirit ever been attained without the mysterious gift of faith? Socrates, as none can doubt, was actuated by a different spirit ... The teachings of the power of Christ had not yet been given—(that power) which alone can confute this most pernicious influence of evil that has nothing good in it, but is rather the author of all error, and the seducer from all truth.

Now if Socrates was pronounced the wisest of men by the oracle ... of how much greater dignity and constancy is the assertion of the Christian wisdom! ... You can show us no more powerful expounder of the soul than the Author thereof. From God you may learn about that which you hold of God; but from no one else will you get this knowledge, if you get it not from God. For who is to reveal that which God has hidden? To that quarter must we resort in our inquiries whence we are most safe even in deriving our ignorance. For it is really better for us not to know a thing, because He has not revealed it to us, than to know it according to man's wisdom, because he has been bold enough to assume it.

PRESCRIPTIONS AGAINST THE HERETICS (in part)

CHAPTER 7: PAGAN PHILOSOPHY THE PARENT OF HERESIES. THE CONNECTION BETWEEN DEFECTIONS FROM CHRISTIAN FAITH AND THE OLD SYSTEM OF PAGAN PHILOSOPHY.

. . . Philosophy is the material of the world's wisdom, the rash interpreter of the nature and the dispensation of God. Indeed heresies are themselves instigated by philosophy. From this source came the Aeons, and I know not what infinite forms, and the trinity of man in the system of Valentinus, who was of Plato's school. From the same source came Marcion's better god, with all his tranquillity; he came of the Stoics. Then, again, the opinion that the soul dies is held by the Epicureans; while the denial of the restoration of the body is taken from the aggregate school of all the philosophers; also, when matter is made equal to God, then you have the teaching of Zeno; and when any doctrine is alleged touching a god of fire, then Heraclitus comes in. The same subject-matter is discussed over and over again by the heretics and the philosophers; the same arguments are involved. Whence comes evil? Why is it permitted? What is the origin of man? And in what way does he come? Besides the question which Valentinus has very lately proposed—Whence comes God? Which he settles with the answer: From enthymesis [conception] and *ectroma* [abortion]. Unhappy Aristotle! who invented for these men dialectics, the art of building up and pulling down; an art so evasive in its propositions, so farfetched in its conjectures, so harsh, in its arguments, so productive of contentions—embarrassing even to itself, retracting everything, and really treating of nothing! . . .

From all these the apostle would restrain us, when he expressly names *philosophy* as that against which he would have us be on our guard. Writing to the Colossians [2:8], he says, "See that no one beguile you through philosophy and vain deceit, after the tradition of men, and contrary to the wisdom of the Holy Ghost." He had been at Athens, and had in his interviews (with its philosophers) become acquainted with that human wisdom which pretends to know the truth, while it only corrupts it, and is itself divided into its own manifold heresies . . . What indeed has Athens to do with Jerusalem? What concord is there between the Academy and the Church? What between heretics and Christians? Our instruction comes from "the porch of Solomon," who had himself taught that "the Lord should be sought in simplicity of heart." Away with all attempts to produce a blended Christianity of Stoic, Platonic, and dialectic composition! After Christ Jesus we want no subtle theories, no inquisition after enjoying the gospel! With our faith, we desire no further belief. For this is our victorious faith, that there is nothing which we ought to believe besides.

ORIGEN
ca. A.D. 185–ca. 254

ON FIRST PRINCIPLES (in part)

BOOK III, CHAPTER 5: THAT THE WORLD TOOK ITS BEGINNING IN TIME

1. . . . Concerning, then, the creation of the world, what portion of Scripture can give us more information regarding it, than the account which Moses has transmitted respecting its origin? And although it comprehends matters of profounder significance than the mere historical narrative appears to indicate, and contains very many things that are to be spiritually understood, and employs the letter, as a kind of veil, in treating of profound and mystical subjects; nevertheless the language of the narrator shows that all visible things were created at a certain time. But with regard to the consummation of the world, Jacob is the first who gives any information, in addressing his children in the words: "Gather yourselves together unto me, ye sons of Jacob, that I may tell you what shall be in the last days," or "after the last days." If, then, there be "last days," or a period "succeeding the last days," the days which had a beginning must necessarily come to an end. David, too, declares: "The heavens shall perish, but Thou shalt endure; yea, all of them shall wax old as doth a garment: as a vesture shalt Thou change them, and they shall be changed: but Thou art the same, and Thy years shall have no end." Our Lord and Savior, indeed, in the words, "He who made them at the beginning, made them male and female," Himself bears witness that the world was created; and again, when He says, "Heaven and earth shall pass away, but My word shall not pass away," He points out that they are perishable, and must come to an end. The apostle, moreover, in declaring that "the creature was made subject to vanity, not willingly, but by reason of Him who hath subjected the same in hope, because the creature itself also shall be delivered from the bondage of corruption into the glorious liberty of the children of God," manifestly announces the end of the world; as he does also when he again says, "The fashion of this world passeth away." Now, by the expression which he employs, "that the creature was made subject to vanity," he shows that there was a beginning to this world: for if the creature were made subject to vanity on account of some hope, it was certainly made subject from a cause; and seeing it was from a cause, it must necessarily have had a beginning: for, without some beginning, the creature could not be subject to vanity, nor could that (creature) hope to be freed from the bondage of corruption, which had not begun to serve. But any one who chooses to search at his leisure, will find numerous other passages in holy Scripture in which the world is both said to have a beginning and to hope for an end.

2. Now, if there be any one who would here oppose either the authority or credibility of our Scriptures, we would ask of him whether he asserts that God can, or cannot, comprehend all things? To assert that He cannot, would manifestly be an act of impiety. If then he answer, as he must, that God comprehends all things, it follows from the very fact of their being capable of comprehension, that they are understood to have a beginning and an end, seeing that which is altogether without any beginning cannot be at all comprehended. For however far understanding may extend, so far is the faculty of comprehending illimitably withdrawn and removed when there is held to be no beginning.

3. But this is the objection which they generally raise: they say, "If the world had its beginning in time, what was God doing before the world began? For it is at once impious and absurd to say that the nature of God is inactive and immoveable, or to suppose that goodness at one time did not do good, and omnipotence at one time did not exercise its power." Such is the objection which they are accustomed to make to our statement that this world had its beginning at a certain time, and that, agreeably to our belief in Scripture, we can calculate the years of its past duration. To these propositions I consider that none of the heretics can easily return an answer that will be in conformity with the nature of their opinions. But we can give a logical answer in accordance with the standard of religion, when we say that not then for the first time did God begin to work when He made this visible world; but as, after its destruction, there will be another world, so also we believe that others existed before the present came into being. And both of these positions will be confirmed by the authority of holy Scripture. For that there will be another world after this, is taught by Isaiah, who says, "There will be new heavens, and a new earth, which I shall make to abide in my sight, saith the LORD"; and that before this world others also existed is shown by Ecclesiastes, in the words: "What is that which hath been? Even that which shall be. And what is that which has been created? Even this which is to be created: and there is nothing altogether new under the sun. Who shall speak and declare, 'Lo, this is new'? It hath already been in the ages which have been before us." By these testimonies it is established both that there were ages before our own, and that there will be others after it. It is not, however, to be supposed that several worlds existed at once, but that, after the end of this present world, others will take their beginning; respecting which it is unnecessary to repeat each particular statement, seeing we have already done so in the preceding pages.

4. This point, indeed, is not to be idly passed by, that the holy Scriptures have called the creation of the world by a new and peculiar name, terming it ⟨katabola⟩, which has been very improperly translated into Latin by "constitutio"; for in Greek ⟨katabola⟩ signifies rather "dejicere," i.e., to cast downwards,—a word which has been, as we have already remarked, improperly translated into Latin by the phrase "constitutio mundi," as in the Gospel according to John, where the Saviour says, "And there will be tribulation in those days, such as was not since the beginning of the world"; in which passage ⟨katabola⟩ is rendered by beginning (constitution), which is to be understood as above explained. The apostle also, in the Epistle to the Ephesians, has employed the same language, saying, "Who hath chosen us before the foundation of the world": and this foundation he calls ⟨katabola⟩, to be understood in the same sense as before. It seems worth while, then, to inquire what is meant by this new term;

and I am, indeed, of opinion that, as the end and consummation of the saints will be in those (ages) which are not seen, and are eternal, we must conclude (as frequently pointed out in the preceding pages), from a contemplation of that very end, that rational creatures had also a similar beginning. And if they had a beginning such as the end for which they hope, they existed undoubtedly from the very beginning in those (ages) which are not seen, and are eternal. And if this is so, then there has been a descent from a higher to a lower condition, on the part not only of those souls who have deserved the change by the variety of their movements, but also on that of those who, in order to serve the whole world, were brought down from those higher and invisible spheres to these lower and visible ones, although against their will—"Because the creature was subjected to vanity, not willingly, but because of Him who subjected the same in hope;" so that both sun, and moon, and stars, and angels might discharge their duty to the world, and to those souls which, on account of their excessive mental defects, stood in need of bodies of a grosser and more solid nature; and for the sake of those for whom this arrangement was necessary, this visible world was also called into being. From this it follows, that by the use of the word ⟨*katabola*⟩, a descent from a higher to a lower condition, shared by all in common, would seem to be pointed out. The hope indeed of freedom is entertained by the whole of creation—of being liberated from the corruption of slavery—when the sons of God, who either fell away or were scattered abroad, shall be gathered together into one, or when they shall have fulfilled their other duties in this world, which are known to God alone, the Disposer of all things. We are indeed, to suppose that the world was created of such quality and capacity as to contain not only all those souls which it was determined should be trained in this world, but also all those powers which were prepared to attend, and serve, and assist them. For it is established by many declarations that all rational creatures are of one nature: on which ground alone could the justice of God in all His dealings with them be defended, seeing every one has the reason in himself, why he has been placed in this or that rank in life.

PROLOGUE II: OTHER FOUNDATIONAL DOCUMENTS

––––––◄○►––––––

Although Christianity was clearly the dominant influence in the European Middle Ages, Neoplatonism also enjoyed a considerable vogue—especially in the early medieval period. Plato's successors in the Athenian Academy developed the skeptical side of their founder's thought, but in northern Egypt a different kind of Platonism emerged. A number of thinkers began to emphasize the mystical and religious Plato. The *Timaeus,* with its description of God as the "demiurge" who brings the physical world into being, was especially important. Among these "middle" Platonists, the most influential was Philo of Alexandria (ca. 20 B.C.–A.D. 50). Philo provided a way to integrate religous beliefs with the claims of Plato and other philosophers. For example, using an allegorical method to understand scripture, Philo attempted to reconcile the creation story of *Genesis* with that of the *Timaeus.*

Two centuries later another Egyptian, Plotinus (A.D. 204–270), developed Plato's thought even further. Plotinus took the religious doctrines of virtually every philosophy of his time and combined them with dualistic Platonic thought to produce a new philosophy, Neoplatonism. Plotinus emphasized the reality *beyond* the world of experience and the need for mystical experience in order to be united to that world.

Neoplatonism received a boost from a group of works supposedly written by Dionysius, St. Paul's convert at the Areopagus in Athens. Appearing about A.D. 500, these texts combined Plotinus' teachings with an unorthodox version of Christianity. Though the writings were later condemned by the Catholic church (and it was demonstrated that they could not have been written by the real Dionysius), they were influential for centuries.

*   *   *

Further introductions to these three thinkers and their works, as well as suggestions for further reading, can be found on the following pages. For general overviews of middle Platonism at this time, see John Dillon, *The Middle Platonists: 80 B.C. to A.D. 220* (Ithaca, NY: Cornell University Press, 1977) and Robert M. Berchman, *From Philo to Origen: Middle Platonism in Transition* (Chico, CA: Scholars Press, 1984).

PHILO OF ALEXANDRIA
ca. 20 B.C.–A.D. 50

Philo of Alexandria has been proclaimed the inventor of religious philosophy, the first to develop a way of thinking that attempts to harmonize the philosophies of Greece and Rome with the accepted truths of revelation. His voluminous writings were the dominant influence on Jewish philosophy for at least a thousand years and his impact on succeeding Christian philosophers of religion was so great that one writer claims, "the history of Christian philosophy begins not with a Christian but with a Jew, Philo of Alexandria, elder contemporary of St. Paul."*

Yet despite his extensive writings (twelve volumes in the Loeb Classics edition) and his philosophical importance, little is known about the life of Philo. The few facts available tell us that he came from a wealthy family in Alexandria. The historian Josephus records that Philo's immensely wealthy brother once loaned a large sum to Agrippa, the grandson of Herod the Great, and donated silver and gold for the gates of the temple in Jerusalem. Philo himself once visited the temple and also headed the Jewish delegation to the Emperor Caligula in 40 A.D. In his account of this visit, *Legacy of Gaius,* Philo calls himself an "old man"—the only clue we have about his age. Given that he wrote two lengthy treatises after this visit, it is assumed he lived another five to ten years.

While little is known about his life, much is known about the northern Egyptian city in which he lived and wrote. Alexandria was at the height of its glory during Philo's lifetime. It was a center for artistic achievement and intellectual ferment. Hellenistic thought, particularly the Neoplatonic version of Platonism,

*Henry Chadwick, "Philo," *The Cambridge History of Later Greek and Early Medieval Philosophy,* edited by A.H. Armstrong (London: Cambridge University Press, 1970), p. 137.

was dominant, but mystery religions and new cults were constantly developing as well. The famous library, one of the seven wonders of the ancient world, was still intact with the accumulated wisdom of centuries. For the thousands of Jews living there, it was difficult to maintain the purity of their religious beliefs in such a syncretistic culture.

Philo's approach to this intellectual environment was "to deliver his Jewish compatriots from an oppressive sense of inferiority that came from living in the shadow of a pervasive, powerful and alluring Hellenistic culture." Turning the tables, Philo sought to show that "Judaism was superior to Hellenism—that Plato took his great insights from Moses and that the Hebrew Scriptures were both compatible with and superior to Hellenism."* At the same time, Philo used philosophy to understand Moses. The truth of God could be found in both philosophical writings and scripture. Using allegorical interpretations of scripture, Philo wrote philosophical interpretations of revelation in order to harmonize the strands of reason and faith which informed his world.

In our selection from *On the Account of the World's Creation Given by Moses,* translated by F.H. Colson and G.H. Whitaker, we can see this allegorical method at work. While expositing the text of *Genesis,* Philo uses Pythagorean numerology and the Stoic conception of a "Divine breath" (*logos*) as the essence of a human soul which animates the body. But it is the writings of "the most holy Plato," particularly the creation account of the *Timaeus,* that is the underlying philosophical basis for much of this work. Philo agreed with Plato's claim that this material world was only a reflection of a higher, immaterial world. Plato held that this higher world was the place where the "Forms," the eternal, unchanging Ideas, existed. Holding the orthodox Jewish idea that God alone was eternal, Philo could not accept a separate existence for such Ideas. Instead he harmonized Plato and scripture by claiming that the Forms existed as God's thoughts until, prior to creating the material world, God made those thoughts into real beings, the "Divine image," in an intelligible world. This intelligible world in turn became the basis for the creation of the material world: "this entire world perceived by our senses . . . is a copy of the Divine image. . . ."

Philo also recognized that there were times when philosophy and scripture could not be harmonized—and he generally sided with revelation. But it was his attempt at a unified synthesis that was most influential. Some of Philo's specific beliefs, such as his conception of the Platonic Forms as God's Ideas and his disdain for the body, would later be echoed in the works of Plotinus and Augustine. Beyond the particular teachings, it is Philo's attempt to do philosophy as a believer and to believe as a philosopher that had the greatest impact.

*   *   *

For a collection of readings from Philo, see Nahum H. Glatzer, ed., *The Essential Philo* (New York: Schocken Books, 1971) and *Philo of Alexandria: The Contemplative Life, The Giants, and Selections,* trans. with introduction by David Winston (New York: Paulist Press, The Classics of Western Spirituality, 1981). The classic study of Philo's life and work remains H.A. Wolfson, *Philo:*

---

*Calvin J. Roetzel, *The World That Shaped the New Testament,* p. 81, as quoted in Colin Brown, *Christianity and Western Thought,* Volume I (Downers Grove, IL: Inter-Varsity Press, 1990), p. 64.

Foundations of Religious Philosophy in Judaism, Christianity and Islam, 2 vols. (Cambridge, MA: Harvard University Press, 1947). A more recent work is Samuel Sandmel, *Philo of Alexandria: An Introduction* (New York: Oxford University Press, 1979). For specialized studies in specific areas of Philo's thought, see Erwin R. Goodenough, *The Politics of Philo Judaeus, Practice and Theory* (New Haven, CO: Yale University Press, 1938); Thomas H. Billings, *The Platonism of Philo Judaeus* (New York: Garland, 1979); Thomas H. Tobin, *The Creation of Man: Philo and the History of Interpretation* (Washington, DC: Catholic Biblical Association of America, 1983); David Winston, *Logos and Mystical Theology in Philo of Alexandria* (Cincinnati, OH: Hebrew Union College Press, 1985); David T. Runia's pair of works, *Philo of Alexandria and the Timaeus of Plato* (Leiden, Netherlands: Brill, 1986) and *Philo in Early Christian Literature: A Survey* (Minneapolis, MN: Fortress Press, 1993); and the *Studia Philonica* series published by the Philo Institute (1972–).

ON THE ACCOUNT OF THE WORLD'S CREATION GIVEN BY MOSES

II. There are some people who, having the world in admiration rather than the Maker of the world, pronounce it to be without beginning and everlasting, while with impious falsehood they postulate in God a vast inactivity; whereas we ought on the contrary to be astonished at His powers as Maker and Father, and not to assign to the world a disproportionate majesty. Moses, both because he had attained the very summit of philosophy, and because he had been divinely instructed in the greater and most essential part of Nature's lore, could not fail to recognize that the universal must consist of two parts, one part active Cause and the other passive object; and that the active Cause is the perfectly pure and unsullied Mind of the universe, transcending virtue, transcending knowledge, transcending the good itself and the beautiful itself; while the passive part is in itself incapable of life and motion, but, when set in motion and shaped and quickened by Mind, changes into the most perfect masterpiece, namely this world. Those who assert that this world is unoriginate unconsciously eliminate that which of all incentives to piety is the most beneficial and the most indispensable, namely providence. For it stands to reason that what has been brought into existence should be cared for by its Father and Maker. For, as we know, it is a father's aim in regard of his offspring and an artificer's in regard of his handiwork to preserve them, and by every means to fend off from them aught that may entail loss or harm. He keenly desires to provide for them in every way all that is beneficial and to their advantage: but between that which has never been brought into being and one who is not its Maker no such tie is formed. It is a worthless and baleful doctrine, setting up anarchy in the well-ordered realm of the world, leaving it without protector, arbitrator, or judge, without anyone whose office it is to administer and direct all its affairs. Not so Moses. That great master, holding the unoriginate to be of a different order from that which is visible, since everything that is an object of sensible perception is subject to becoming and to constant change, never abiding in the same state, assigned to that which is invisible and an object of intellectual apprehension the infinite and undefinable as united with it by closest tie; but on that which is an object of the senses he bestowed "genesis," "becoming," as its appropriate name.

Seeing then that this world is both visible and perceived by the senses, it follows that it must also have had an origin. Whence it was entirely to the point that he put on record that origin, setting forth in its true grandeur the work of God.

III. He says that in six days the world was created, not that its Maker required a length of time for His work, for we must think of God as doing all things simultaneously, remembering that "all" includes with the commands which He issues the thought behind them. Six days are mentioned because for the things coming into existence there was need of order. Order involves number, and among numbers by the laws of nature the most suitable to productivity is 6, for if we start with 1 it is the first perfect number, being equal to the product of its factors (i.e. $1 \times 2 \times 3$), as well as made up of the sum of them (i.e. $1 + 2 + 3$), its half being 3, its third part 2, its sixth part 1. We may say that it is in its nature both male and female, and is a result of the distinctive power of either. For among things that are it is the odd that is male, and the even female. Now of odd numbers 3 is the starting-point, and of even numbers 2, and the product of these two is 6. For it was requisite that the world, being most perfect of all things that have come into existence, should be constituted in accordance with a perfect number, namely six; and, inasmuch as it was to have in itself beings that sprang from a coupling together, should receive the impress of a mixed number, namely the first in which odd and even were combined, one that should contain the essential principle both of the male that sows and of the female that receives the seed.

Now to each of the days He assigned some of the portions of the whole, not including, however, the first day, which He does not even call "first," lest it should be reckoned with the others, but naming it "one" He designates it by a name which precisely hits the mark, for He discerned in it and expressed by the title which He gives it the nature and appellation of the unit, or the "one."

IV. We must recount as many as we can of the elements embraced in it. To recount them all would be impossible. Its pre-eminent element is the intelligible world, as is shown in the treatise dealing with the "One." For God, being God, assumed that a beautiful copy would never be produced apart from a beautiful pattern, and that no object of perception would be faultless which was not made in the likeness of an original discerned only by the intellect. So when He willed to create this visible world He first fully formed the intelligible world, in order that He might have the use of a pattern wholly God-like and incorporeal in producing the material world, as a later creation, the very image of an earlier, to embrace in itself objects of perception of as many kinds as the other contained objects of intelligence.

To speak of or conceive that world which consists of ideas as being in some place is illegitimate; how it consists (of them) we shall know if we carefully attend to some image supplied by the things of our world. When a city is being founded to satisfy the soaring ambition of some king or governor, who lays claim to despotic power and being magnificent in his ideas would fain add a fresh lustre to his good fortune, there comes forward now and again some trained architect who, observing the favourable climate and convenient position of the site, first sketches in his own mind wellnigh all the parts of the city that is to be wrought out, temples, gymnasia, town-halls, market-places, harbours, docks, streets, walls to be built, dwelling houses as well as public buildings to be set up. Thus after having received in his own soul, as it were in wax, the figures of these objects severally, he carries about the image of a city which is the creation of his mind. Then by his innate power of memory, he recalls the images of the various parts of this city, and imprints their types yet more distinctly in it: and like a good craftsman he begins to build the city of stones and timber, keeping his eye upon his pattern and making the visible and tangible objects correspond in each case to the incorporeal ideas.

Just such must be our thoughts about God. We must suppose that, when He was minded to found the one great city, He conceived beforehand the models of its parts, and that out of these He constituted and brought to completion a world discernible only by the mind, and then, with that for a pattern, the world which our senses can perceive.

V. As, then, the city which was fashioned beforehand within the mind of the architect held no place in the outer world, but had been engraved in the soul of the artificer as by a seal; even so the universe that consisted of ideas would have no other location than the Divine Reason, which was the Author of this ordered frame. For what other place could there be for His powers sufficient to receive and contain, I say not all but, any one of them whatever uncompounded and untempered? Now just such a power is that by which the universe was made, one that has as its source nothing less than true goodness. For should one conceive a wish to search for the cause, for the sake of which this whole was created, it seems to me that he would not be wrong in saying, what indeed one of the men of old did say, that the Father and Maker of all is good; and because of this He grudged not a share in his own excellent nature to an existence which has of itself nothing fair and lovely, while it is capable of becoming all things. For of itself it was without order, without quality, without soul, (without likeness); it was full of inconsistency, ill-adjustment, disharmony: but it was capable of turning and undergoing a complete change to the best, the very contrary of all these, to order, quality, life, correspondence, identity, likeness, perfect adjustment, to harmony, to all that is characteristic of the more excellent model.

VI. Now God, with no counsellor to help Him (who was there beside Him?) determined that it was meet to confer rich and unrestricted benefits upon that nature which apart from Divine bounty could obtain of itself no good thing. But not in proportion to the greatest of His own bounties does He confer benefits—for these are without end or limit—but in proportion to the capacities of the recipients. For it is not the nature of creation to receive good treatment in like manner as it is the nature of God to bestow it, seeing that the powers of God are overwhelmingly vast, whereas creation, being too feeble to entertain their abundance, would have broken down under the effort to do so, had not God with appropriate adjustment dealt out to each his due portion. Should a man desire to use words in a more simple and direct way, he would say that the world discerned only by the intellect is nothing else than the Word of God when He was already engaged in the act of creation. For (to revert to our illustration) the city discernible by the intellect alone is nothing else than the reasoning faculty of the architect in the act of planning to found the city. It is Moses who lays down this, not I. Witness his express acknowledgement in the sequel, when setting on record the creation of man, that he was moulded after the image of God (Gen. i. 27). Now if the part is an image of an image, it is manifest that the whole is so too, and if the whole creation, this entire world perceived by our senses (seeing that it is greater than any human image) is a copy of the Divine image, it is manifest that the archetypal seal also, which we aver to be the world descried by the mind, would be the very Word of God.

*   *   *

XLIV. In his concluding summary of the story of creation he says: "This is the book of the genesis of heaven and earth, when they came into being, in the day in which God made the heaven and the earth and every herb of the field before it appeared upon the earth, and all grass of the field before it sprang up" (Gen. ii. 4, 5). Is he not manifestly describing the incorporeal ideas present only to the mind, by which, as by seals, the finished objects that meet our senses were moulded? For before the earth put forth its young green shoots, young verdure was present, he tells us, in the nature of things without material shape, and before grass sprang up in the field, there was in existence an invisible grass. We must suppose that in the case of all other objects also, on which the senses pronounce judgement, the original forms and measures, to which all things that come into being owe shape and size, subsisted before them; for even if he has not dealt with everything in detail but in the mass, aiming as he does at brevity in a high degree, nevertheless what he does say gives us a few indications of universal Nature, which brings forth no finished product in the world of sense without using an incorporeal pattern.

XLV. Keeping to the sequence of the creation and carefully observing the connexion between what follows and what has gone before, he next says: "and a spring went up out of the earth and watered all the face of the earth" (Gen. ii. 6). Other philosophers say that all water is one of the four elements out of which the world was made. But Moses, wont as he is with keener vision to observe and apprehend amazingly well even distant objects, does indeed regard the great sea as an element, a fourth part of the whole, which his successors, reckoning the seas we sail to be in size mere harbours compared to it, call Ocean; but he distinguished sweet drinkable water from the salt water, assigning the former to the land and looking on it as part of this, not of the sea. It is such a part, for the purpose already mentioned, that by the sweet quality of the water as by a uniting glue the earth may be bound and held together: for had it been left dry, with no moisture making its way in and spreading by many channels through the pores, it would have actually fallen to pieces. It is held together and lasts, partly by virtue of the life-breath that makes it one, partly because it is saved from drying up and breaking off in small or big bits by the moisture. This is one reason, and I must mention another which is a guess at the truth. It is of the nature of nothing earth-born to take form apart from wet substance. This is shown by the depositing of seeds, which either are moist, as those of animals, or do not grow without moisture: such are those of plants. From this it is clear that the wet substance we have mentioned must be a part of the earth which gives birth to all things, just as with women the running of the monthly cleansings; for these too are, so physical scientists tell us, the bodily substance of the *fetus*. And what I am about to say is in perfect agreement with what has been said already. Nature has bestowed on every mother as a most essential endowment teeming breasts, thus preparing in advance food for the child that is to be born. The earth also, as we all know, is a mother, for which reason the earliest men thought fit to call her "Demeter," combining the name of "mother" with that of "earth"; for, as Plato says, earth does not imitate woman, but woman earth. Poets quite rightly are in the habit of calling earth "All-mother," and "Fruit-bearer" and "Pandora" or "Give-all," inasmuch as she is the originating cause of existence and continuance in existence to all animals and plants alike. Fitly therefore on earth also, most ancient and most fertile of mothers, did Nature bestow, by way of breasts, streams of rivers and springs, to the end that both the plants might be watered and all animals might have abundance to drink.

XLVI. After this he says that "God formed man by taking clay from the earth, and breathed into his face the breath of life" (Gen. ii. 7). By this also he shows very clearly that there is a vast difference between the man thus formed and the man that came into existence earlier after the image of God: for the man so formed is an object of sense-perception, partaking already of such or such quality, consisting of body and soul, man or woman, by nature mortal; while he that was after the (Divine) image was an idea or type or seal, an object of thought (only), incorporeal, neither male nor female, by nature incorruptible. It says, however, that the formation of the individual man, the object of sense, is a composite one made up of earthly substance and of Divine breath: for it says that the body was made through the Artificer taking clay and moulding out of it a human form, but that the soul was originated from nothing created whatever, but from the Father and Ruler of all: for that which He breathed in was nothing else than a Divine breath that migrated hither from that blissful and happy existence for the benefit of our race, to the end that, even if it is mortal in respect of its visible part, it may in respect of the part that is invisible be rendered immortal. Hence it may with propriety be said that man is the borderland between mortal and immortal nature, partaking of each so far as is needful, and that he was created at once mortal and immortal, mortal in respect of the body, but in respect of the mind immortal.

PLOTINUS
A.D. 204–270

Plotinus was the most influential of the Neoplatonists. Born in Lykopolis, Egypt, in A.D. 204, he moved in his late twenties to Alexandria. There he studied with Ammonius Saccas, an unknown figure who was also the teacher of Origen. After eleven years with Ammonius, Plotinus joined an expedition to Persia to gain knowledge of Persian and Indian wisdom. The trek proved unsuccessful, and Plotinus moved on to Rome. There he established a school of philosophy and became friends with the emperor Gallenius. At one point, he sought permission to found a city based on Plato's *Republic,* but the plan came to naught. He stayed in Rome, teaching and writing, until the death of the emperor in A.D. 268. He then moved to the home of a friend where he died in A.D. 270, apparently from leprosy.

Developing Plato's dualistic understanding of reality, Plotinus taught that true reality lies "beyond" the physical world. This "reality beyond reality" has no limits and so cannot be described by words since words invariably have limits. Plotinus, again borrowing from Plato, calls it the "Good" or the "One." The One/Good has no limits and is so supremely rich that it overflows or "emanates" to produce "Intellectual-Principle" or "Divine Mind" ⟨*Nous*⟩. This Intellectual-Principle, in turn, overflows and "Divine-Soul" emanates from it. This process continues as Divine-Soul generates the material world. The lowest level of emanation, at the furthest extreme from the One/Good, is the utter formlessness and unreality of matter.

The goal of philosophy is to awaken individuals to recognize reality beyond the material world. But philosophy alone cannot take a person to the highest reality of the One/Good. Only in a mystical experience can an individual unite with the One/Good. Plotinus himself claimed to have achieved such a union, a "flight of the Alone to the Alone" to cite his famous words, four times during his life.

His experiences of nonmaterial reality were so powerful that he said he was ashamed to have a body.

Plotinus's writings were edited by one of his pupils, Porphyry, in the form of six groups of nine "Tractates" (treatises), published as the so-called *Enneads* (from the Greek word for "nine"). The selection given here, in the Stephen MacKenna translation, is Plotinus's "Treatise on Beauty." This tractate explains how the ascent of the soul to the One/Good depends on beauty of soul, a godlike disposition.

Neoplatonism, with its emphasis on the otherworldly and the need for escape from the physical world, was the perfect philosophy for the chaotic final days of the Roman Empire. St. Augustine, in particular, was strongly influenced by Neoplatonic thought. Indeed, if St. Thomas is considered an Aristotelian, St. Augustine may be called a Neoplatonist. Many later thinkers, such as Meister Eckhart, Nicholas Cusanas, John Comenius, Jacob Boehme, G.W.F. Hegel, and Friedrich Schelling, also had their philosophy molded by Neoplatonist doctrines.

*   *   *

Joseph Katz, *Plotinus' Search for the Good* (New York: King's Crown Press, 1950); Émile Bréhier, *The Philosophy of Plotinus,* translated by Joseph Thomas (Chicago: University of Chicago Press, 1958); and Lloyd P. Gerson, *Plotinus* (Oxford: Routledge, 1994) are good introductions to the study of Plotinus. For more advanced studies, see A.H. Armstrong, *The Architecture of the Intelligible Universe in the Philosophy of Plotinus* (Cambridge: Cambridge University Press, 1940); J.M. Rist, *Plotinus: The Road to Reality* (Cambridge: Cambridge University Press, 1967); Lloyd P. Gerson, ed., *The Cambridge Companion to Plotinus* (Cambridge: Cambridge University Press, 1996); and Margaret R. Miles, *Plotinus on Body and Beauty* (Oxford: Basil Blackwell, 1999). E.R. Dodds, *Select Passages Illustrating Neoplatonism,* translated by E.R. Dodds (New York: Macmillan, 1923), and Dominic J. O'Meara, *Plotinus: An Introduction to the Enneads* (Oxford: Oxford University Press, 1993), provide anthologies of the *Enneads* with discussions of important passages. For discussions of Neoplatonism as a school, see Thomas Whittaker, *The Neo-Platonists* (Cambridge: Cambridge University Press, 1918); Arthur O. Lovejoy's influential book, *The Great Chain of Being* (Cambridge, MA: Harvard University Press, 1936); R.T. Wallis, *Neoplatonism* (London: Duckworth, 1972); and the collection of essays, R. Baine Harris, ed., *The Structure of Being: A Neoplatonic Approach* (Norfolk, VA: International Society for Neoplatonic Studies, 1982).

ENNEADS (in part)

ENNEAD I, TRACTATE 6: BEAUTY

1. Beauty addresses itself chiefly to sight; but there is a beauty for the hearing too, as in certain combinations of words and in all kinds of music, for melodies and cadences are beautiful; and minds that lift themselves above the realm of sense to a higher order are aware of beauty in the conduct of life, in actions, in character, in the pursuits of the intellect; and there is the beauty of the virtues. What loftier beauty there may be, yet, our argument will bring to light.

What, then, is it that gives comeliness to material forms and draws the ear to the sweetness perceived in sounds, and what is the secret of the beauty there is in all that derives from Soul?

Is there some One Principle from which all take their grace, or is there a beauty peculiar to the embodied and another for the bodiless? Finally, one or many, what would such a Principle be?

Consider that some things, material shapes for instance, are gracious not by anything inherent but by something communicated, while others are lovely of themselves, as, for example, Virtue.

The same bodies appear sometimes beautiful, sometimes not; so that there is a good deal between being body and being beautiful.

What, then, is this something that shows itself in certain material forms? This is the natural beginning of our enquiry.

What is it that attracts the eyes of those to whom a beautiful object is presented, and calls them, lures them, towards it, and fills them with joy at the sight? If we possess ourselves of this, we have at once a standpoint for the wider survey.

Almost everyone declares that the symmetry of parts towards each other and towards a whole, with, besides, a certain charm of colour, constitutes the beauty recognized by the eye, that in visible things, as indeed in all else, universally, the beautiful thing is essentially symmetrical, patterned.

But think what this means.

Only a compound can be beautiful, never anything devoid of parts; and only a whole; the several parts will have beauty, not in themselves, but only as working together to give a comely total. Yet beauty in an aggregate demands beauty in details; it cannot be constructed out of ugliness; its law must run throughout.

All the loveliness of colour and even the light of the sun, being devoid of parts and so not beautiful by symmetry, must be ruled out of the realm of beauty. And how comes gold to be a beautiful thing? And lightning by night, and the stars, why are these so fair?

In sounds also the simple must be proscribed, though often in a whole noble composition each several tone is delicious in itself.

Again since the one face, constant in symmetry, appears sometimes fair and sometimes not, can we doubt that beauty is something more than symmetry, that symmetry itself owes its beauty to a remoter principle?

Turn to what is attractive in methods of life or in the expression of thought; are we to call in symmetry here? What symmetry is to be found in noble conduct, or excellent laws, in any form of mental pursuit?

What symmetry can there be in points of abstract thought?

The symmetry of being accordant with each other? But there may be accordance or entire identity where there is nothing but ugliness: the proposition that honesty is merely a generous artlessness chimes in the most perfect harmony with the proposition that morality means weakness of will; the accordance is complete.

Then again, all the virtues are a beauty of the soul, a beauty authentic beyond any of these others; but how does symmetry enter here? The soul, it is true, is not a simple unity, but still its virtue cannot have the symmetry of size or of number: what standard of measurement could preside over the compromise or the coalescence of the soul's faculties or purposes?

Finally, how by this theory would there be beauty in the Intellectual-Principle, essentially the solitary?

2. Let us, then, go back to the source, and indicate at once the Principle that bestows beauty on material things.

Undoubtedly this Principle exists; it is something that is perceived at the first glance, something which the soul names as from an ancient knowledge and, recognising, welcomes it, enters into unison with it.

But let the soul fall in with the Ugly and at once it shrinks within itself, denies the thing, turns away from it, not accordant, resenting it.

Our interpretation is that the soul—by the very truth of its nature, by its affiliation to the noblest Existents in the hierarchy of Being—when it sees anything of that kin, or any trace of that kinship, thrills with an immediate delight, takes its own to itself, and thus stirs anew to the sense of its nature and of all its affinity.

But, is there any such likeness between the loveliness of this world and the splendours in the Supreme? Such a likeness in the particulars would make the two orders alike: but what is there in common between beauty here and beauty There?

We hold that all the loveliness of this world comes by communion in Ideal-Form.

All shapelessness whose kind admits of pattern and form, as long as it remains outside of Reason and Idea, is ugly by that very isolation from the Divine-Thought. And this is the Absolute Ugly: an ugly thing is something that has not been entirely mastered by pattern, that is by Reason, the Matter not yielding at all points and in all respects to Ideal-Form.

But where the Ideal-Form has entered, it has grouped and coordinated what from a diversity of parts was to become a unity: it has rallied confusion into co-operation: it has made the sum one harmonious coherence: for the Idea is a unity and what it moulds must come to unity as far as multiplicity may.

And on what has thus been compacted to unity, Beauty enthrones itself, giving itself to the parts as to the sum: when it lights on some natural unity, a thing of like parts, then it gives itself to that whole. Thus, for an illustration, there is the beauty, conferred by craftsmanship, of all a house with all its parts, and the beauty which some natural quality may give to a single stone.

This, then, is how the material thing becomes beautiful—by communicating in the thought that flows from the Divine.

3. And the soul includes a faculty peculiarly addressed to Beauty—one incomparably sure in the appreciation of its own, never in doubt whenever any lovely thing presents itself for judgement.

Or perhaps the soul itself acts immediately, affirming the Beautiful where it finds something accordant with the Ideal-Form within itself, using this Idea as a canon of accuracy in its decision.

But what accordance is there between the material and that which antedates all Matter?

On what principle does the architect, when he finds the house standing before him correspondent with his inner ideal of a house, pronounce it beautiful? Is it not that the house before him, the stones apart, is the inner idea stamped upon the mass of exterior matter, the indivisible exhibited in diversity?

So with the perceptive faculty: discerning in certain objects the Ideal-Form which has bound and controlled shapeless matter, opposed in nature to Idea, seeing further stamped upon the common shapes some shape excellent above the common, it gathers into unity what still remains fragmentary, catches it up and carries it within, no longer a thing of parts, and presents it to the Ideal-Principle as something concordant and congenial, a natural friend: the joy here is like that of a good man who discerns in a youth the early signs of a virtue consonant with the achieved perfection within his own soul.

The beauty of colour is also the outcome of a unification: it derives from shape, from the conquest of the darkness inherent in Matter by the pouring-in of light, the unembodied, which is a Rational-Principle and an Ideal-Form.

Hence it is that Fire itself is splendid beyond all material bodies, holding the rank of Ideal-Principle to the other elements, making ever upwards, the subtlest and sprightliest of all bodies, as very near to the unembodied; itself alone admitting no other, all the others penetrated by it: for they take warmth but this is never cold; it has colour primally; they receive the Form of colour from it: hence the splendour of its light, the splendour that belongs to the Idea. And all that has resisted and is but uncertainly held by its light remains outside of beauty, as not having absorbed the plenitude of the Form of colour.

And harmonies unheard in sound create the harmonies we hear and wake the soul to the consciousness of beauty, showing it the one essence in another kind: for the measures of our sensible music are not arbitrary but are determined by the Principle whose labour is to dominate Matter and bring pattern into being.

Thus far of the beauties of the realm of sense, images and shadow-pictures, fugitives that have entered into Matter—to adorn, and to ravish, where they are seen.

4. But there are earlier and loftier beauties than these. In the sense-bound life we are no longer granted to know them, but the soul, taking no help from the organs, sees and proclaims them. To the vision of these we must mount, leaving sense to its own low place.

As it is not for those to speak of the graceful forms of the material world who have never seen them or known their grace—men born blind, let us suppose—in the same way those must be silent upon the beauty of noble conduct and of learning and all that order who have never cared for such things, nor may those tell of the splendour of virtue who have never known the face of Justice and of Moral-Wisdom beautiful beyond the beauty of Evening and of Dawn.

Such vision is for those only who see with the Soul's sight—and at the vision, they will rejoice, and awe will fall upon them and a trouble deeper than all the rest could ever stir, for now they are moving in the realm of Truth.

This is the spirit that Beauty must ever induce, wonderment and a delicious trouble, longing and love and a trembling that is all delight. For the unseen all this may be felt as for the seen; and this the Souls feel for it, every soul in some degree, but those the more deeply that are the more truly apt to this higher love—just as all take delight in the beauty of the body but all are not stung as sharply, and those only that feel the keener wound are known as Lovers.

5. These Lovers, then, lovers of the beauty outside of sense, must be made to declare themselves.

What do you feel in presence of the grace you discern in actions, in manners, in sound morality, in all the works and fruits of virtue, in the beauty of souls? When you see that you yourselves are beautiful within, what do you feel? What is this Dionysiac exultation that thrills through your being, this straining upwards of all your Soul, this longing to break away from the body and live sunken within the veritable self?

These are no other than the emotions of Souls under the spell of love.

But what is it that awakens all this passion? No shape, no colour, no grandeur of mass: all is for a Soul, something whose beauty rests upon no colour, for the moral wisdom the Soul enshrines and all the other hueless splendour of the virtues. It is that you find in yourself, or admire in another, loftiness of spirit; righteousness of life; disciplined purity; courage of the majestic face; gravity; modesty that goes fearless and tranquil and passionless; and, shining down upon all, the light of god-like Intellection.

All these noble qualities are to be reverenced and loved, no doubt, but what entitles them to be called beautiful?

They exist: they manifest themselves to us: anyone that sees them must admit that they have reality of Being; and is not Real-Being, really beautiful?

But we have not yet shown by what property in them they have wrought the Soul to loveliness: what is this grace, this splendour as of Light, resting upon all the virtues?

Let us take the contrary, the ugliness of the Soul, and set that against its beauty: to understand, at once, what this ugliness is and how it comes to appear in the Soul will certainly open our way before us.

Let us then suppose an ugly Soul, dissolute, unrighteous: teeming with all the lusts; torn by internal discord; beset by the fears of its cowardice and the envies of its pettiness; thinking, in the little thought it has, only of the perishable and the base; perverse in all its impulses; the friend of unclean pleasures; living the life of abandonment to bodily sensation and delighting in its deformity.

What must we think but that all this shame is something that has gathered about the Soul, some foreign bane outraging it, soiling it, so that, encumbered with all manner of turpitude, it has no longer a clean activity or a clean sensation, but commands only a life smouldering dully under the crust of evil; that, sunk in manifold death, it no longer sees what a Soul should see, may no longer rest in its own being, dragged ever as it is towards the outer, the lower, the dark?

An unclean thing, I dare to say; flickering hither and thither at the call of objects of sense, deeply infected with the taint of body, occupied always in Matter, and absorbing Matter into itself; in its commerce with the Ignoble it has trafficked away for an alien nature its own essential Idea.

If a man has been immersed in filth or daubed with mud his native comeliness disappears and all that is seen is the foul stuff besmearing him: his ugly condition is due to alien matter that has encrusted him, and if he is to win back his grace it must be his business to scour and purify himself and make himself what he was.

So, we may justly say, a Soul becomes ugly—by something foisted upon it, by sinking itself into the alien, by a fall, a descent into body, into Matter. The dishonour of the Soul is in its ceasing to be clean and apart. Gold is degraded when it is mixed with earthy particles; if these be worked out, the gold is left and is beautiful, isolated from all that is foreign, gold with gold alone. And so the Soul; let it be but cleared of the desires that come by its too intimate converse with the body, emancipated from all the passions, purged of all that embodiment has thrust upon it, withdrawn, a solitary, to itself again—in that moment the ugliness that came only from the alien is stripped away.

6. For, as the ancient teaching was, moral discipline and courage and every virtue, not even excepting Wisdom itself, all is purification.

Hence the Mysteries with good reason adumbrate the immersion of the unpurified in filth, even in the Nether-World, since the unclean loves filth for its very filthiness, and swine foul of body find their joy in foulness.

What else is *Sophrosyne,** rightly so-called, but to take no part in the pleasures of the body, to break away from them as unclean and unworthy of the clean? So too, Courage is but being fearless of the death which is but the parting of the Soul from the body, an event which no one can dread whose delight is to be his unmingled self. And Magnanimity is but disregard for the lure of things here. And Wisdom is but the Act of the Intellectual-Principle withdrawn from the lower places and leading the Soul to the Above.

The Soul thus cleansed is all Idea and Reason, wholly free of body, intellective, entirely of that divine order from which the wellspring of Beauty rises and all the race of Beauty.

Hence the Soul heightened to the Intellectual-Principle is beautiful to all its power. For Intellection and all that proceeds from Intellection are the Soul's beauty, a graciousness native to it and not foreign, for only with these is it truly Soul. And it is just to say that in the Soul's becoming a good and beautiful thing is its becoming like to God, for from the Divine comes all the Beauty and all the Good in beings.

We may even say that Beauty is the Authentic-Existents and Ugliness is the Principle contrary to Existence: and the Ugly is also the primal evil; therefore its contrary is at once good and beautiful, or is Good and Beauty: and hence the one method will discover to us the Beauty-Good and the Ugliness-Evil.

And Beauty, this Beauty which is also The Good, must be posed as The First: directly deriving from this First is the Intellectual-Principle which is pre-eminently the manifestation of Beauty; through the Intellectual-Principle Soul is beautiful. The beauty in things of a lower order—actions and pursuits for instance—comes by operation of the shaping Soul which is also the author of the beauty found in the world of sense. For the Soul, a divine thing, a fragment as it were of the Primal Beauty, makes beautiful to the fulness of their capacity all things whatsoever that it grasps and moulds.

7. Therefore we must ascend again towards the Good, the desired of every Soul. Anyone that has seen This, knows what I intend when I say that it is beautiful. Even the desire of it is to be desired as a Good. To attain it is for those that will take the upward path, who will set all their forces towards it, who will divest themselves of all that we have put on in our descent:—so, to those that approach the Holy Celebrations of the Mysteries, there are appointed purifications and the laying aside of the garments worn before, and the entry in nakedness—until, passing, on the upward way, all that is other than the God, each in the solitude of himself shall behold that solitary-dwelling Existence, the Apart, the Unmingled, the Pure, that from Which all things depend, for

*The principle of balance.

Which all look and live and act and know, the Source of Life and of Intellection and of Being.

And one that shall know this vision—with what passion of love shall he not be seized, with what pang of desire, what longing to be molten into one with This, what wondering delight! If he that has never seen this Being must hunger for It as for all his welfare, he that has known must love and reverence It as the very Beauty; he will be flooded with awe and gladness, stricken by a salutary terror; he loves with a veritable love, with sharp desire; all other loves than this he must despise, and disdain all that once seemed fair.

This, indeed, is the mood even of those who, having witnessed the manifestation of Gods or Supernals, can never again feel the old delight in the comeliness of material forms: what then are we to think of one that contemplates Absolute Beauty in Its es-

The School of Plato, Roman Mosaic, n.d. The Platonism of late antiquity (and the Middle Ages) was strongly influenced by Plotinus's development and modification of Plato's thought. (*Scala/Art Resource, N.Y.*)

sential integrity, no accumulation of flesh and matter, no dweller on earth or in the heavens—so perfect Its purity—far above all such things in that they are non-essential, composite, not primal but descending from This?

Beholding this Being—the Choragos of all Existence, the Self-Intent that ever gives forth and never takes—resting, rapt, in the vision and possession of so lofty a loveliness, growing to Its likeness, what Beauty can the soul yet lack? For This, the Beauty supreme, the absolute, and the primal, fashions Its lovers to Beauty and makes them also worthy of love.

And for This, the sternest and the uttermost combat is set before the Souls; all our labour is for This, lest we be left without part in this noblest vision, which to attain is to be blessed in the blissful sight, which to fall of is to fail utterly.

For not he that has failed of the joy that is in colour or in visible forms, not he that has failed of power or of honours or of kingdom has failed, but only he that has failed of only This, for Whose winning he should renounce kingdoms and command over earth and ocean and sky, if only, spurning the world of sense from beneath his feet, and straining to This, he may see.

8. But what must we do? How lies the path? How come to vision of the inaccessible Beauty, dwelling as if in consecrated precincts, apart from the common ways where all may see, even the profane?

He that has the strength, let him arise and withdraw into himself, foregoing all that is known by the eyes, turning away for ever from the material beauty that once made his joy. When he perceives those shapes of grace that show in body, let him not pursue: he must know them for copies, vestiges, shadows, and hasten away towards That they tell of. For if anyone follow what is like a beautiful shape playing over water-is there not a myth telling in symbol of such a dupe, how he sank into the depths of the current and was swept away to nothingness? So too, one that is held by material beauty and will not break free shall be precipitated, not in body but in Soul, down to the dark depths loathed of the Intellective-Being, where, blind even in the Lower-World, he shall have commerce only with shadows, there as here.

"Let us flee then to the beloved Fatherland": this is the soundest counsel. But what is this flight? How are we to gain the open sea? For Odysseus is surely a parable to us when he commands the flight from the sorceries of Circe or Calypso—not content to linger for all the pleasure offered to his eyes and all the delight of sense filling his days.

The Fatherland to us is There whence we have come, and There is The Father.

What then is our course, what the manner of our flight? This is not a journey for the feet; the feet bring us only from land to land; nor need you think of coach or ship to carry you away; all this order of things you must set aside and refuse to see: you must close the eyes and call instead upon another vision which is to be waked within you, a vision, the birth-right of all, which few turn to use.

9. And this inner vision, what is its operation?

Newly awakened it is all too feeble to bear the ultimate splendour. Therefore the Soul must be trained—to the habit of remarking, first, all noble pursuits, then the works of beauty produced not by the labour of the arts but by the virtue of men known for their goodness: lastly, you must search the souls of those that have shaped these beautiful forms.

But how are you to see into a virtuous soul and know its loveliness?

Withdraw into yourself and look. And if you do not find yourself beautiful yet, act as does the creator of a statue that is to be made beautiful: he cuts away here, he smooths there, he makes this line lighter, this other purer, until a lovely face has grown upon his work. So do you also: cut away all that is excessive, straighten all that is crooked, bring light to all that is overcast, labour to make all one glow of beauty and never cease chiselling your statue, until there shall shine out on you from it the godlike splendour of virtue, until you shall see the perfect goodness surely established in the stainless shrine.

When you know that you have become this perfect work, when you are self-gathered in the purity of your being, nothing now remaining that can shatter that inner unity, nothing from without clinging to the authentic man, when you find yourself wholly true to your essential nature, wholly that only veritable Light which is not measured by space, not narrowed to any circumscribed form nor again diffused as a thing void of term, but ever unmeasurable as something greater than all measure and more than all quantity—when you perceive that you have grown to this, you are now become very vision: now call up all your confidence, strike forward yet a step—you need a guide no longer—strain, and see.

This is the only eye that sees the mighty Beauty. If the eye that adventures the vision be dimmed by vice, impure, or weak, and unable in its cowardly blenching to see the uttermost brightness, then it sees nothing even though another point to what lies plain to sight before it. To any vision must be brought an eye adapted to what is to be seen, and having some likeness to it. Never did eye see the sun unless it had first become sunlike, and never can the soul have vision of the First Beauty unless itself be beautiful.

Therefore, first let each become godlike and each beautiful who cares to see God and Beauty. So, mounting, the Soul will come first to the Intellectual-Principle and survey all the beautiful Ideas in the Supreme and will avow that this is Beauty, that the Ideas are Beauty. For by their efficacy comes all Beauty else, but the offspring and essence of the Intellectual-Being. What is beyond the Intellectual-Principle we affirm to be the nature of Good radiating Beauty before it. So that, treating the Intellectual-Kosmos as one, the first is the Beautiful: if we make distinction there, the Realm of Ideas constitutes the Beauty of the Intellectual Sphere; and The Good, which lies beyond, is the Fountain at once and Principle of Beauty: the Primal Good and the Primal Beauty have the one dwelling place and, thus, always, Beauty's seat is There.

PSEUDO-DIONYSIUS AREOPAGITE
Late-fifth–early-sixth centuries(?)

Sometime around the beginning of the sixth century, a group of Neoplatonic writings appeared that attracted special attention. It was widely believed that the writings were the work of Dionysius the Areopagite, a man converted in the first century by the Apostle Paul's preaching in Athens (Acts 17:34). Because of his supposed connection with the Apostle, "Dionysius'" writings were held to be uniquely authoritative. However, scholars trace the writings of the Pseudo [or "false"]-Dionysius to about A.D. 500.*

These writings emphasize the Neoplatonic doctrines of the unity of God and the unity of the world. Every apparent diversity participates in the unity of the being "above" it, from which it emanates. God is at the top of this hierarchy. But emphasizing the unity of God posed problems for traditional explanations of the Christian doctrine of God's Tri-Unity (Trinity). Apparently the Pseudo-Dionysius considered the three realities of the Trinity to be eternal manifestations from within the oneness of God. This teaching was often held to be unorthodox, and orthodox Christians, who considered the Pseudo-Dionysius's writings authoritative, were in considerable consternation. The attempted synthesis of Christianity and Dionysian Neoplatonic notions of unity and emanation informed John Scotus Eriugena's thought and eventually led to his condemnation by the Catholic church.

But two other themes of the Pseudo-Dionysius had greater influence on medieval thought. The first was the Neoplatonic concept of evil as the absence of good. According to the Pseudo-Dionysius, what we experience as evil is, quite

---

*It was once wrongly supposed by others that the works were written by Denis (or Denys), the patron saint of France.

literally, nothing. Evil, as such, "is not be-ing nor in beings." This Neoplatonic idea was given a Christian interpretation by Augustine, but it was the Pseudo-Dionysius's formulation of it that influenced subsequent thinkers. The first selection given here from *The Divine Names,* translated by John D. Jones, summarizes the Pseudo-Dionysius's position.

The second important theme from the Pseudo-Dionysius was the knowledge of God. There are two ways of knowing God: the affirmative and the negative. The affirmative way predicates characteristics of God that are consistent with God's infinite being, such as goodness. The negative way denies predicating of God characteristics that apply to creatures, such as mutability. Our second selection from *The Divine Names* expresses these two ways of knowing God when the Pseudo-Dionysius says, "God is known through knowledge, and through unknowing." In presenting this negative way of knowing God through "unknowing," the Pseudo-Dionysius often used hymnlike poetry and mystical utterances. Both the content and style of his writings influenced medieval mystics.

* * *

Paul Rorem, *Pseudo-Dionysius* (Oxford: Oxford University Press, 1993) gives an excellent overview of our author as well as a discussion of the Pseudo-Dionysius's influence. The introductory essay found in the Pseudo-Dionysius Areopagite, *The Divine Names and Mystical Theology,* translated by John D. Jones (Milwaukee, WI: Marquette University Press, 1980), pp. 1–105 is also a good place to begin further study. A.H. Armstrong, ed., *The Cambridge History of Later Greek and Early Medieval Philosophy* (Cambridge: Cambridge University Press, 1959); Frederick Copleston, *A History of Philosophy, Volume II: Medieval Philosophy, Part I: Augustine to Bonaventure* (1950; reprinted Garden City, NY: Image Doubleday, 1962); E.R. Dodds, *The Greeks and the Irrational* (Oxford: Oxford University Press, 1968); and Andrew Louth, *The Origins of the Christian Mystical Tradition from Plato to Denys* (Oxford: Oxford University Press, 1981) also include discussions of the Pseudo-Dionysius.

THE DIVINE NAMES (in part)

CHAPTER 4: CONCERNING THE GOOD, LIGHT, BEAUTY, LOVE, ECSTASIS, AND ZEAL, THAT EVIL IS NEITHER BEING, NOR FROM BEING, NOR IN BEINGS

18. . . . In general, what is evil? From what source does it subsist? In which beings is it? How did the good will to produce it? How was such a will possible? If evil is from another cause than the good, what cause is there for beings beside the good? How

Pseudo-Dionysius Areopagite, *The Divine Names and Mystical Theology,* Chapter 4, Sections 18–21, 30; and Chapter 7, Section 3, translated by John D. Jones (Milwaukee, WI: Marquette University Press, 1980). Reprinted by permission of Marquette University Press.

is there evil if there is providence? How does evil come to be at all? Why is it not destroyed? Finally, how does any being desire it istead of the good?

19. Such questions as these will perhaps be raised in a perplexed discourse. But we demand that one look away from such a discourse into the truth of the matter. Thus we shall at first say this freely and boldly. Evil is not from the good; if something is from the good, it is not evil. As what is cold does not bring forth fire, what is not good does not bring forth what is good. Now it is the nature of the good to produce and to conserve while that of evil is to destroy and to ruin. Thus if all beings are from the good, no being is from evil. Indeed, evil itself will not be, for it would be evil to itself.

If this is not so, evil will not be wholly evil but will have some aspect of the good according to which it is able to be at all. Further, if all beings desire the good and beautiful, if all these produce whatever they produce through producing what appears good, and if the intention of beings has the good as its source and end—for no being focuses on the nature of evil to produce what it produces—how will evil be in beings or be produced from such a good desire? Now if all beings are from the good and the good is beyond all beings, then that which is not is in the good. Thus, evil is neither be-ing (if not, [evil is] not wholly evil) nor not being (for, nothing will be wholly non being unless it is said to be in the good according to what is beyond being). The good lies beyond and is much prior to what simply is and what is not. Evil is neither in what is nor in what is not. Rather, it has a greater absence and estrangement from the good than what is not; it is more greatly without being than what is not.

"But when, then, is evil?" someone will say. "For if there is no evil, both virtue and vice will be the same in whole and, by analogy, in part and what wars against virtue will not be evil." Nonetheless, temperance and intemperance are opposed and justice and injustice are opposed. I speak not only of just or unjust persons or temperate or intemperate persons. For even before the outward manifestation of their difference there is the much earlier opposition in the soul itself, in which the vices have already warred against the virtues, and the passions have already revolted against the logos. From these considerations some evil necessarily shows itself to be opposed to the good. For the good is not opposed to itself, but since it is from one source and has come to be from one cause, it rejoices in communion, unity and friendship. Further, the lesser good is not opposed to the greater good, just as lower heat or less cold are not opposed to greater heat or cold. Thus, evil is in beings and is be-ing; it is placed against and is opposed to the good. If evil is a destruction of beings this does not remove evil from *being* but it will itself be be-ing and generative of beings. For does not the destruction of one being frequently come to be the genesis of this other being? Thus evil contributes to the completion of all that is and provides through itself non-imperfection to the whole.

20. About these charges the true logos responds that evil as evil in no way produces being or genesis but only makes bad and destroys the subsistence of beings as far as it is able. But if someone says that evil is generative of beings and that by the destruction of one being genesis is given to another, one must respond truly that, as destructive, evil does not give genesis or being but that destruction and evil only destroys and makes bad. For genesis and being come to be through the good. Thus evil is destructive through itself but generative through the good. Evil as evil is neither be-ing nor productive of beings; through the good it is good, be-ing, and productive of what is good. Or, to put the matter another way, the same thing is not both good and evil in the same respect; the same power—whether itself a power or a destruction—will not be both productive and generative of the same thing in the same respect. Evil itself is neither be-ing, good, nor generative or productive of beings or what is good.

Now in those beings in which it comes to be complete, the good produces complete, unmixed, and whole goods. However, those which participate in less of it are non-complete and mixed goods through their lack of the good. Evil is neither good nor productive of good, but those which draw more or less near to the good will be analogically good. Further, the all-complete goodness wanders through all beings; it does not extend merely to the completely good beings about it but it stretches itself down to the last of beings. It is wholly present to some, present in a diminished fashion to others, and in the extreme it is present to others as each is able to partake of it. Thus some beings partake wholly of the good, some are more or less deprived of it, some have a share of the good in a more inferior manner, and to others, which are the last among beings, the good is present as an echo. For if the good were not analogically present to each, then the most divine and eldest beings would have the order of the least among beings. But how would it be possible for all to uniformly partake in the good since not all are enabled to partake in the whole of it in the same way?

Now this is the exceeding greatness of the power of the good: it empowers both those which are deprived of it and the privation of itself toward the whole participation of itself. And if it is necessary to speak the truth freely and clearly, those which war against it do and are able to do battle against it by its power. Hence to speak in a comprehensive fashion: all beings, in whatever way they are, are and are good and are from the good. Insofar as they are deprived of the good they are neither good nor be-ing. For with respect to other conditions such as heat or cold, there are those which are heated and those losing heat; further, many beings are without life and intellect. Even God is apart from being and "is" beyond every manner of being. And simply, with respect to everything else, there are many beings which are able to subsist, yet which have abandoned or have not achieved their own condition. But that which is deprived from the good in every respect was, is, will be, or is able to be in no manner whatsoever.

Thus the intemperate person who lacks the good by his irrational desires neither is nor desires what is; yet he shares the good according to the obscure echo of his unity and friendship. Even anger partakes of the good, for through its movement and desire it directs and returns what seems to be evil to what seems to be good. Moreover, even those who desire the worst life still desire life and what seems best to them; thus, they partake in the good by their very desire, their desire for life, and their search for [what seems to them to be] the best life.

If the good were wholly annihilated there would be neither being, life, desire, motion, or anything else. Hence the genesis which emerges from destruction is not a power of evil but is the presence of a lesser good. In this respect, disease is a lack of order, but not of every order. For if this were so the disease itself would not subsist; yet the disease is and it abides by having being with the least possible order. Nevertheless, it subsists along with the order.

That which is wholly apart from the good, is neither be-ing nor in beings. But that which is a mixed good is in beings on account of the good; thus it is be-ing and is in beings by partaking of the good. Hence all beings will be more or less insofar as they partake of the good. For even with respect to being itself, that which is in no manner whatever will not be. But that which somehow is, somehow is not. Insofar as it has fallen away from what always is, it is not. Insofar as it partakes in be-ing, it is and its whole being and non be-ing are protected and preserved.

Evil, that which has entirely fallen from the good, will not be in those which are more or less good. But that which is somehow good—thus, somehow not good—wars against some beings that are good but not against the whole good. It is protected by its participation in the good, for the good gives being to the privation of itself [with a view] towards the whole participation of itself. Given the complete absence of the good, nothing will be good, mixed or even evil itself. For if evil is non-complete good and the complete absence of the good would involve the absence of both mixed and complete goods, then evil will be and be seen only in respect to those to which it is opposed, and will be removed from others as good. For it is impossible for the same things in the same respect to war against one another in every respect.

21. Evil is not be-ing nor in beings. For if all beings are from the good and the good is in all beings and encompasses all, then evil will not be in beings; it will not be in the good; nor will it be destructive through the good. (For, clearly, evil will no more be in the good than cold is in fire.) Yet if this were so, how would evil be in the good? It is impossible and absurd that evil be from the good. For as the writings say, "a good tree does not bring forth evil fruit"; clearly, the opposite is not so. But if evil is not from the good, it is evident that it is from another source and cause. For either evil will be from the good or the good will be from evil. If this is not possible, then evil and the good will be from some other source and cause. However, no dyad is a source; for the source of every dyad is one. Nevertheless, it is absurd that before *being* "are" two which are completely opposed and that these are from one and the same; for this source would not be simple and one but opposed to itself, so that it would become other than itself.

Also it is clearly not possible for there to be two opposed sources of beings warring against one another and all beings. If this were so, God would be neither at rest nor separated from dispute, for something would be an adversary to him. Further, everything would be without order and always at war. Yet the good gives a share of friendship and peace itself to all beings; these gifts of peace are celebrated by the sacred writings. Wherefore, everything that is good is friendly, and harmonious, a descendant of one life, ordered together toward one life, and are like and gentle and agreeable with one another.

Evil is not in God nor is evil divine. Evil is not from God; for either God is not good or he is good-producing and productive of good things. Now God does not sometimes produce what is good and at other times not produce what is good, nor does God not produce all that is good. For this would bring change and otherness in God in regard to causality which is the most divine of all. But if the good constitution is in God then when he changes from the good he will sometimes be and at other times not be. Further if God participates in the good and derives this participation from another, he will sometimes have it and at other times not have it. Thus evil is not from God nor in God, neither simply nor temporally.

[Sections 22–29 argue that evil is not in angels, in irrational animals, in the whole of nature, in bodies, nor in matter as matter and that even demons are not evil by nature.]

*　　*　　*

30. To speak in a summary fashion: the good is from one whole cause; evil is from many partial defects. God knows evil as good and with God the causes of evils are good-producing powers. But if evil is everlasting, creates, has power, is, and acts, whence does it obtain these? For either they are from the good or the good is from evil or they are both from other causes.

All that is in conformity with nature comes to be from defined causes. But if nature is without cause and undefined, it is not by nature. For that contrary to nature [does not come to be] by nature any more than what is contrary to art [comes to be] by art. But is not the soul the cause of evils, just as fire is the cause of what is hot, so that whatever comes in contact with it is full of evils? Is the nature of the soul good but does it not sometimes act in one manner and sometimes in another? But if the being and nature of the soul are evil, whence does it obtain these except from the good creative cause of the totality of what is? But if the soul is from this how is it evil in being? For all that is good is descended from the good creative cause. But if it is evil in its activities, this is not unchangeable. For if not, from whence does it obtain its virtues unless it itself has come to be good formed? Thus it remains that evil is a weakness and lack of the good.

*   *   *

CHAPTER 7: CONCERNING WISDOM, INTELLECT, LOGOS, TRUTH, AND FAITH

*   *   *

3. According to our power,
>   we attain to that beyond all
>   by a path and order
>   in the denial and preeminence of all, and
>   in the cause of all.
God is known
>   in all, and
>   apart from all.
God is known
>   through knowledge, and
>   through unknowing.
Of God there is
>   intellect, reason, knowledge,
>   contact, sensation, opinion, imagination, name, and
>   everything else.
God is
>   not known, not spoken, not named,
>   not something among beings, and
>   not known in something among beings.
God is
>   all in all,
>   nothing in none,
>   known to all in reference to all,
>   known to no one in reference to nothing.
>   For we say all of this correctly about God
>   who is celebrated according
>   to the analogy of all,
>   of which it is the cause.
The most divine knowledge of God is
>   one which knows through unknowing
>   in the unity beyond intellect
>   when the intellect stands away from beings

       and then stands away from itself,
       it is united to the more than resplendent rays,
       and is then and there illumined
       by the inscrutable depths of wisdom.
Nevertheless, as we have said,
    it is known from all;
    (for according to the writings)
    it is
       productive of all,
       always harmonizing the all,
       cause of the indissoluable
          concordance and harmony of all,
       always joining together
          the end of those which are prior to
          the beginnings of secondaries, and
       beautifying the agreement and harmony of all.

AUGUSTINE

A.D. 354–430

◄○►

Aurelius Augustinus, Saint Augustine, was born of a Christian mother and a pagan father in Thagaste, a small town in what is now Algeria, North Africa. In many ways, his family's mixed religious background represented the crumbling Roman Empire. Even though the influence of Christianity had grown since Emperor Constantine's edict of religious toleration in A.D. 313, there were still many rivals to his mother's faith.

As a boy, Augustine showed intellectual promise, and at 17 he was sent to Carthage to study rhetoric. While there, Augustine found philosophy, rejected Christianity, took a mistress (who bore him a son), and began to investigate some of the religions of the time. He turned first to the followers of the prophet Mani—the Manichaeans. Mani was a third-century prophet who called himself "the apostle of God." He developed the ancient Persian teaching of Zoroaster (or Zarathustra), which said that there are two great forces in the world, one good and one evil, and that neither can overcome the other. Living a life of sensual indulgence, Augustine took comfort from the idea that God could no more overcome evil in the universe than Augustine could in his own life.

In 375, Augustine returned to Thagaste to begin teaching rhetoric. When his mother, Monica (later sainted for her perseverance in prayer for her son), discovered that he had become a Manichaean, she expelled him from her house. Finding Thagaste boring, and his mother difficult, Augustine returned to Carthage. Over the next seven years, he grew disenchanted with Manichaeism. In 384, he left Carthage for teaching positions in Rome and finally Milan. In Milan, Augustine encountered the writings of Plotinus and was converted to Neoplatonism. At the same time, he came into contact with a group of Christians led by the Bishop of Milan, Ambrose. Under the influence of this group, Augustine was forced to reconsider his earlier rejection of Christianity, yet he was still unwilling to give up his life of self-gratification. In 386, while sitting in a friend's garden, he heard what he thought was a child's voice saying, "Pick it up and read, pick it up and read." Augustine later recounted what happened:

> I returned to the place where Alypius was sitting, for on leaving it I had put down there the book of the apostle's letters. I snatched it up, opened it and read in silence the passsage on which my eyes first lighted: "Not in dissipation and drunkenness, nor in debauchery and lewdness, nor in arguing and jealousy; but put on the Lord Jesus Christ, and make no provision for the flesh or the gratification of your desires." [Rom. 13:13–14] I had no wish to read further, nor was there need. No sooner had I reached the end of the verse than the light of certainty flooded my heart and all dark shades of doubt fled away.*

The following year, Augustine was baptized and returned to Africa to found a monastic community. Within two years he left the cloister, answering the church's call to priesthood. He served as a priest, and later as bishop, in the African town of Hippo for the rest of his life.

*   *   *

While at Hippo, Augustine wrote voluminously on a variety of theological and philosophical topics. Many of his works sought to define exactly what was and was not "Christian." His doctrinal works, such as *The Trinity,* established Christian essentials; whereas his polemical works, directed against "heresies" (positions unacceptable to the church), outlined what was not admissible. Augustine fought two major heresies: the Pelagian and the Donatist. The Pelagians held that sin had affected only Adam, that the will is free from sin, and that God's grace is given on the basis of human merit. The Donatists maintained that the sacraments were effective only when administered by a priest in a state of grace. Augustine argued passionately that both heresies put too much emphasis on human ability and not enough on God's grace.

Augustine's most famous work, the *Confessions,* invented the genre of introspective autobiography. The *Confessions* are full of both psychological and spiritual insight and so can be read as either devotional tract or philosophical essay. Books I through IX are Augustine's life story from the perspective of Christian conversion (detailed in our selection from Book VIII). As Augustine reflects on his life, he sees both his sinfulness and his intellectual aimlessness apart from God's grace. He also gives early glimpses of his mature epistemological position that God must illumine the mind in order for an individual to gain wisdom. Following his conversion, Augustine continued to seek understanding—though now firmly founded on faith. Books X to XII illustrate this "faith seeking understanding," as Augustine examines the questions of memory, time, and creation. Our selection from Book XI explores the nature of time and God's relation to it. Augustine argues that God must be "outside" time in an eternal present. This view of God as timelessly eternal was developed by Boethius and is still influential today (see the suggested readings that follow). I am pleased to offer this selection in the outstanding new translation by Maria Boulding.

---

*Saint Augustine, *Confessions,* Book VIII. See reading on p. 104.

Among Augustine's early writings, *On the Free Choice of the Will* is one of the most interesting and provocative. Written against the Manichaeans, the book was later used by the Pelagians to support their view of radical free will. Augustine was forced to point out in his *Retractions* that even though he had argued that humans can fall into sin of their own free will, he had held that they cannot rise up to relationship with God on the same basis. Book II, given here complete in the Anna S. Benjamin and L.H. Hackstaff translation, includes Augustine's early theory of the will, his theory of knowledge, and his proof of God's existence on the basis of truth.

Of Augustine's many other works, *The City of God* is by far the most influential. During the fourth century, Christianity had become the state religion of the Roman Empire; in 410, Rome fell to the Visigoths, and the eternal city was sacked for the first time. Naturally, many considered the sack of Rome a punishment for the betrayal of the old Roman religion. Augustine wrote *The City of God* to answer this charge and in so doing he developed yet another first: the first Western philosophy of history. Rather than a cycle of repeated events, Augustine described history as being linear—from creation to consummation and final judgment. As history moves from beginning to end, we can observe two cities: the City of God, consisting of those who love God; and the City of Man, those who love self rather than God. The first selection, from Book VIII of this work, gives Augustine's history of philosophy and includes his favorable appraisal of Plato.

The brief second selection, from Book XI, presents Augustine's final argument against the skeptics. Augustine's insistence that he *knows* he exists anticipates Descartes's argument twelve centuries later. The third selection, from Book XII, explains the origin of evil and of the City of Man. Augustine begins by insisting, against the Manichaeans, that there is no being capable of opposing God: God is all-powerful. But, despite the presence of evil, God is also all-good and everything God created is good. Evil arises when a moral agent (angel or human) wills to love a lesser good (self) rather than the highest good (God). There is no evil "thing" to choose—there is only evil choosing. This leads to the question of what caused the will to choose evilly—a question Augustine says cannot be answered.

The final selection, from Book XIX, presents Augustine's treatise on peace: both earthly peace and the heavenly peace of the City of God. These four selections have been ably translated by Gerald G. Walsh, Daniel J. Honan, and Grace Monahan.

Augustine's impact has been enormous. Medieval Catholic philosophers, such as Anselm and Thomas Aquinas, as well as Protestant reformers, such as Martin Luther and John Calvin, wanted to be Augustine's heirs. Many contemporary Christian thinkers still appeal to Augustine's ideas, such as his defense of grace and his explanation of evil. But Augustine's influence has not been limited to theologians and philosophers of religion. Ludwig Wittgenstein began his *Philosophical Investigations* by examining Augustine's theory of language, and Bertrand Russell claimed Augustine's theory of time superior even to that of Kant. Echoes of Augustine's understanding of history as the unfolding of divine purpose can be heard in the writings of Hegel, whereas Augustine's idea that some kind of faith must precede fruitful understanding has been adapted by thinkers in such fields as the sociology of knowledge and philosophy of science.

*　*　*

The best general account of Augustine's philosophy remains Étienne Gilson, *The Christian Philosophy of Saint Augustine,* translated by L.E.M. Lynch (New York: Random House, 1960); Peter Brown, *Augustine of Hippo: A Biography* (Berkeley: University of California Press, 1967), provides an excellent biography. For brief introductions to Augustine's life and thought, see Henry Chadwick's pair of books, *Augustine* and *Augustine: A Very Short Introduction* (Oxford: Oxford University Press, 1986 and 2001). For more extensive discussions of Augustine's thought, see Robert E. Meagher, *An Introduction to Augustine* (New York: New York University Press, 1978); Christopher Kirwan, *Augustine* (London: Routledge, 1989); and Benedict J. Groeschel, *Augustine: Major Writings* (New York: Crossroads, 1995). J.N. Figgis, *The Political Aspects of St. Augustine's City of God* (London: Longmans, Green, 1921); Ronald H. Nash, *The Light of the Mind: St. Augustine's Theory of Knowledge* (Lexington: University Press of Kentucky, 1969); R.A. Markus, *Saeculum: History and Society in the Theology of St. Augustine* (Cambridge: Cambridge University Press, 1970); Robert J. O'Connell's pair of books, *St. Augustine's Confessions* and *Images of Conversion in St. Augustine's Confessions* (New York: Fordham University Press, 1989 and 1996); and Brian Stock, *Augustine the Reader* (Cambridge, MA; Harvard University Press, 1996) deal with the specialized topics indicated by their respective titles. John M. Rist, *Augustine: Ancient Thought Baptized* (Cambridge: Cambridge University Press, 1994) explores the connections between Augustine and Platonic thought. For collections of essays, see M.C. D'Arcy et al., *Saint Augustine* (New York: Meridian, 1957), and R.A. Markus, ed., *Augustine: A Collection of Critical Essays* (Garden City, NY: Anchor, Doubleday, 1972).

ON THE FREE CHOICE OF THE WILL
(in part)

BOOK II

1. Why did God give freedom of the will to men, since it is by this that men sin?

EVODIUS: Now, if possible, explain to me why God gave man free choice of the will, since if he had not received it he would not be able to sin.

AUGUSTINE: Are you perfectly sure that God gave to man what you think ought not to have been given?

EVODIUS: As far as I seem to understand the discussion in the first book, we have freedom of will, and could not sin if we were without it.

AUGUSTINE: I, too, remember that this was made clear to us. But I just asked you whether you know that it was God who gave us that which we possess, through which it is clear that we commit sin.

Saint Augustine, *On the Free Choice of the Will,* translated by Anna S. Benjamin and L.H. Hackstaff (New York: Macmillan/Liberal Arts Press, 1964), Book II.

EVODIUS: No one else. For we are from Him, and whether we sin or whether we do right, we earn reward or punishment from Him.

AUGUSTINE: I want to ask, as well: do you know this clearly, or do you believe it willingly without really knowing it, because you are prompted by authority?

EVODIUS: I admit that at first I trusted authority on this point. But what can be more true than that all good proceeds from God, that everything just is good, and that it is just to punish sinners and to reward those who do right? From this it follows that through God sinners are afflicted with unhappiness, and those who do right endowed with happiness.

AUGUSTINE: I do not object, but let me ask another question: how do you know that we are from God? You did not answer that; instead, you explained that we merit punishment and reward from God.

EVODIUS: The answer to *that* question, too, is clear, if for no other reason than the fact that, as we have already agreed, God punishes sins. All justice is from God, and it is not the role of justice to punish foreigners, although it is the role of goodness to bestow benefits on them. Thus it is clear that we belong to God, since He is not only most generous in bestowing benefits upon us, but also most just in punishing us. Also, we can understand that man is from God through the fact, which I proposed and you conceded, that every good is from God. For man himself, insofar as he is a man, is a good, because he can live rightly when he so wills.

AUGUSTINE: If this is so, the question that you proposed is clearly answered. If man is a good, and cannot act rightly unless he wills to do so, then he must have free will, without which he cannot act rightly. We must not believe that God gave us free will so that we might sin, just because sin is committed through free will. It is sufficient for our question, why free will should have been given to man, to know that without it man cannot live rightly. That it was given for this reason can be understood from the following: if anyone uses free will for sinning, he incurs divine punishment. This would be unjust if free will had been given not only that man might live rightly, but also that he might sin. For how could a man justly incur punishment who used free will to do the thing for which it was given? When God punishes a sinner, does He not seem to say, "Why have you not used free will for the purpose for which I gave it to you, to act rightly?" Then too, if man did not have free choice of will, how could there exist the good according to which it is just to condemn evildoers and reward those who act rightly? What was not done by will would be neither evildoing nor right action. Both punishment and reward would be unjust if man did not have free will. Moreover, there must needs be justice both in punishment and in reward, since justice is one of the goods that are from God. Therefore, God must needs have given free will to man.

2. If freedom is a good, given for good use, why can it be turned to evil uses?

EVODIUS: I concede now that God gave free will. But I beg you, don't you think that, if free will was given so that man might act rightly, it should not be possible to use it to sin? For example, justice itself was given so that man might live well. No one can live in evil through his own justice, can he? In the same way, no one could sin through his will, if the will is given for acting rightly.

AUGUSTINE: I hope that God will give me the power to answer you, or rather that He will give you power to find the answer yourself through that very thing which is the highest teacher of all—the truth within which teaches us. Please tell me briefly: if you acknowledge as certain what I questioned you about, namely that God gave us free will, tell me whether we ought to say that God should not have given what we concede

He did give. If it is uncertain whether He gave free will, we may properly ask whether it was a good gift, so that if we should discover that it is a good gift, we would discover also that it was given by Him who gave the soul all good gifts. If, on the other hand, we should discover that free will is not a good gift, we would know that He whom it is wicked to blame did not give it. Yet if it is certain that God Himself gave free will, however it was given, we must acknowledge that it neither ought not to have been given, nor has been given in any other way than it was given; for God gave free will and His deed can in no wise be justly condemned.

EVODIUS: Although I believe this with unshaken faith, nevertheless I do not understand it. Therefore, let us take up our investigation as though everything were uncertain. From the fact that it is uncertain whether free will was given so that man might live rightly, since we can sin through free will, it follows that it becomes uncertain whether free will ought to have been given. If we do not know that it was given so that man might live rightly, we also do not know that it ought to have been given. In consequence of this, it is uncertain whether God gave free will. For if it is uncertain that free will ought to have been given, it is also uncertain that free will was given by God, since it is wicked to believe that God gave anything that should not have been given.

AUGUSTINE: At least you are certain that God exists.

EVODIUS: I accept even this by faith, and not by reason.

AUGUSTINE: If any fool who has said in his heart, "There is no God," [Ps. 52:1] should say this to you and be unwilling to believe with you what you believe, but should want to know whether your belief was true—would you walk away from the man, or would you think that he should be persuaded of what you firmly believe, especially if he was eager to know, and not just to argue stubbornly?

EVODIUS: Your last question gives me a good hint as to how I should answer him. Surely, however unreasonable he might be, he would concede that I ought not to dispute with a sly and stubborn man about anything at all, let alone such an important thing. After he granted this, we should first hold a discussion so that I might believe that he raised the question in the right spirit, and that nothing which would affect the argument, like trickery or stubbornness, lay hidden in him. Then I would prove to him what I think is very easily proven: how much fairer it is, when he wants another who does not know to believe him concerning the secrets of his own spirit which he himself knows—how much fairer it is to believe that God exists by the authority of the books of those great men who left written testimony that they lived with the Son of God, since they wrote that they saw things which could not have happened if God did not exist. He would be foolish indeed if he, who wanted me to believe him, were to blame me for believing them. A man could find no reason why he should not be willing to imitate what he cannot justly blame.

AUGUSTINE: If you think that it is sufficient to judge that we have not been rash in believing such great men on the question of God's existence, why then, I beg you, don't you think that we can likewise believe these same men's authority in the other matters into whose investigation we entered assuming them to be uncertain and obscure? Then we would have to toil no further in investigating them.

EVODIUS: But we want to know and understand what we believe.

AUGUSTINE: You remember rightly; we cannot abandon the position we adopted at the beginning of the first discourse. Unless believing is different from understanding, and unless we first believe the great and divine thing that we desire to understand, the prophet has said in vain, "Unless you believe, you shall not understand" [Is. 7:9]. Our Lord Himself, by His words and deeds, first urged those whom He called to salvation to believe. Afterwards, when He spoke about the gift He was to give to those who believed, He did not say, "This is life eternal so that they may believe." Instead He said, "This is life eternal that they may know Thee, the one true God and Him whom Thou didst send, Jesus Christ" [John 17:3]. Then, to those who believed, He said, "Seek and you shall find" [Matt. 7:7]. For what is believed without being known cannot be said to have been found, and no one can become fit for finding God unless he believes first what he shall know afterwards. Therefore, in obedience to the teachings of our Lord, let us seek earnestly. That which we seek at God's bidding we shall find when He Himself shows us—as far as it can be found in this life and by such men as we are. We must believe that these things are seen and grasped more clearly and fully by better men even while they dwell in this world, and surely by all good and devout men after this life. So we must hope and, disdaining worldly and human things, must love and desire divine things.

3. To show that God exists, it is necessary to investigate man's consciousness of himself. The bodily senses and the inner sense.

AUGUSTINE: Let us take up our search in the following order, if you will. First, how is it proved [manifestum] that God exists? Second, are all things whatsoever, insofar as they are good, from God? Finally, is free will to be counted as a good? When we have answered these questions, it will be quite clear, I think, whether free will was rightly given. Therefore, to start at the beginning with the most obvious, I will ask you first whether you yourself exist. Are you, perhaps, afraid that you are being deceived by my questioning? But if you did not exist, it would be impossible for you to be deceived.

EVODIUS: Let us move on.

AUGUSTINE: Since it is clear that you exist, and since this would not be clear to you unless you lived, it is also clear that you are alive. So you understand that these two points are absolutely true?

EVODIUS: I fully understand.

AUGUSTINE: Then this third point is also clear: you understand.

EVODIUS: Yes.

AUGUSTINE: Which of these three things do you think is the best?

EVODIUS: Understanding.

AUGUSTINE: Why do you think so?

EVODIUS: Because, while there are these things—to be, to live, and to understand—the stone *is,* and the beast *lives,* yet I think that the stone does not live, nor the beast understand. Furthermore, it is very certain that he who understands both *is* and *lives.* For this reason, I do not hesitate to judge that in which all these three are present to be more perfect than that in which any one is lacking. For what lives, also is; but it does not follow that it also understands. Such, I think, is the life of a beast. Furthermore, what *is* does not necessarily live or understand. I can admit that a dead body *is,* yet no one would say that it lives. Likewise, what does not live surely does not understand.

AUGUSTINE: We maintain, then, that the dead body lacks two of these three; the beast, one; and man, none.

EVODIUS: Yes.

AUGUSTINE: We maintain this as well: of these three, what man has in addition to the two others—that is, understanding—is the most excellent. In having this, man consequently also is and lives.

EVODIUS: We also maintain this.

AUGUSTINE: Now tell me whether you know that you possess the ordinary bodily senses: sight, hearing, smell, taste, and touch.

EVODIUS: I know that I possess them.

AUGUSTINE: What do you think is the proper object of the sense of sight? That is, what do we perceive by sight?

EVODIUS: Anything corporeal.

AUGUSTINE: We don't perceive hardness and softness by sight, do we?

EVODIUS: We do not.

AUGUSTINE: What then is the proper object of the eyes; what do we perceive with them?

EVODIUS: Color.

AUGUSTINE: The ears?

EVODIUS: Sound.

AUGUSTINE: Smell?

EVODIUS: Odor.

AUGUSTINE: Taste?

EVODIUS: Flavor.

AUGUSTINE: Touch?

EVODIUS: Soft and hard, smooth and rough, and many other such things.

AUGUSTINE: What about the shapes of bodies: large, small, angular, rounded, and others of this kind? Don't we perceive them by touch and sight, so that they can properly be attributed, neither to sight nor to touch alone, but to both?

EVODIUS: I understand.

AUGUSTINE: Therefore, you understand both that each sense has certain objects of its own about which it reports, and that some senses have objects in common.

EVODIUS: I understand this also.

AUGUSTINE: We cannot, can we, discern by any one sense either what is the proper object of that individual sense, or what all or some senses possess in common among themselves?

EVODIUS: Of course not. This is discerned by something within.

AUGUSTINE: Can this be reason, which beasts lack? For it seems to me that by reason we grasp this and know it is so.

EVODIUS: No; I think, rather, that by reason we understand that there is a certain inner sense to which all things are referred by the five familiar senses. For the beast sees by one thing; by another, it avoids or seeks what it has perceived with its sight. For sight lies in its eyes, while the other sense lies within its soul. By this other sense, animals either seek and take (if pleased), or avoid and reject (if annoyed), what they see, hear, and grasp with the other senses. This sense cannot be called either sight, hearing, smell, taste or touch. It is something else which controls all the senses in common. While we grasp this with our reason, we cannot call it reason, since it is clearly to be found in beasts.

AUGUSTINE: I recognize this, whatever it is, and I do not hesitate to name it "the inner sense." But unless what we perceive by the bodily senses passes beyond the inner sense, we cannot arrive at knowledge *[scientia]*. Whatever we know, we grasp and hold to by reason. Moreover, we know that we cannot perceive colors with our hearing or voices with our eyes, to say nothing of the other senses. When we know this, we know it neither by the eyes, nor by the ears, nor by the inner sense which beasts do not lack. We must not believe that beasts know that light is not perceived by the ears nor a voice by the eyes, for we perceive this only by rational thought and reflection within the soul.

EVODIUS: I cannot say that I am clear about this. What if animals, too, discern that colors cannot be perceived by hearing and voices by sight, by means of that inner sense which you admit they do not lack?

AUGUSTINE: You don't think, do you, that animals can discern separately (1) the color which is perceived, or (2) the sense which is in the eyes, or (3) the inner sense in the soul, or (4) reason, by which these things are each distinguished and defined?

EVODIUS: Of course not.

AUGUSTINE: Could reason discern these four things separately and limit them by definition, unless color were referred to reason by the sense belonging to the eyes, and this in turn by the inner sense which controls it, and the inner sense in turn by itself, if nothing else were interposed?

EVODIUS: I do not see how else it could.

AUGUSTINE: Do you see that color is perceived by the sense belonging to the eyes, and that the sensation itself is not perceived by the same sense? You do not see that you see with one and the same sense by which you see color, do you?

EVODIUS: Absolutely not.

AUGUSTINE: Try also to distinguish these. I believe that you do not deny that (1) color is one thing, that (2) to see color is another, and that (3) when color is not present, it is still another thing to have the sense by which color could be seen if color were present.

EVODIUS: I do make such a distinction, and admit that they are quite different things.

AUGUSTINE: You don't perceive any of these three things, except color, by the eyes, do you?

EVODIUS: No.

AUGUSTINE: Tell me, therefore, how you see the two other things. For you could not distinguish them unless they were seen.

EVODIUS: I don't know how else. I do know that they exist, but know nothing more.

AUGUSTINE: You do not know, therefore, whether it is reason itself, or that life we call the inner sense that excels the bodily senses, or something else?

EVODIUS: I do not.

AUGUSTINE: Yet you do know this: that it is not possible to define these things except by reason, and that reason cannot do this except in the case of things which are brought to it to be examined.

EVODIUS: That is certain.

AUGUSTINE: Whatever that other thing is by which all that we know can be perceived, it is the servant of reason, to which it brings and reports whatever touches it, so that what is perceived can be distinguished by its own limits and grasped, not only by perception, but also by knowledge.

EVODIUS: Yes.

AUGUSTINE: That very reason which discerns its own servants and the objects that they bring to it, which likewise recognizes the differences between these things and itself, and affirms that it is more powerful than they—that very reason does not comprehend itself by anything other than itself, that is, reason, does it? Would you know that you possessed reason by any other means than perceiving it by reason?

EVODIUS: This is most true.

AUGUSTINE: Then, when we perceive color, we do not likewise perceive that we perceive it by the sense of sight itself; when we hear a sound, we do not hear our own hearing; when we smell a rose, something has fragrance for us, but not our sense of smell. When we taste something, the sense of taste itself does not taste in our mouth. We touch something, but we cannot touch the sense of touch itself. Since this is so, it is clear that these five senses cannot perceive themselves, although all corporeal objects may be perceived by them.

EVODIUS: Yes.

4. The inner sense perceives that it perceives; the bodily senses do not.

AUGUSTINE: It is also clear, I think, not only that the inner sense perceives what is presented by the five senses of the body, but also that it perceives the bodily senses themselves. Otherwise, a beast would not move either to seek or to avoid something, unless the beast were aware that it perceived—a thing not perceived by any of the five senses. It is not so that it may know (which is the function of reason) that a beast perceives that it perceives, but only so that it may move. If this is still obscure, it will become clearer if you turn your attention to one sense, like sight, which will furnish a quite sufficient example. A beast could not open its eye and move it to look at what it wanted to see unless when the eye was closed, or when it was not moved, the beast perceived that its eye did not see. Moreover, if a beast is aware that it does not see when it does not see, it is also aware that it sees when it sees; for when the beast sees, it does not move its eye because of the same impulse which causes it to move its eye when it does not see; and it notes that it perceives both of these conditions. Whether this life which is aware that it perceives corporeal objects also perceives itself is not so obvious, unless we consider the fact that everyone, when he seeks within himself, finds that every living thing avoids death. Since death is the opposite of life, necessarily life, which avoids its opposite, perceives itself. But if this is not yet clear, let us omit it, so that we may work toward what we want only by clear, proven evidence. This much is proven: corporeal objects are perceived by the senses of the body; a sense cannot perceive itself; moreover, by means of the inner sense, corporeal objects are perceived through the senses of the body, and the senses of the body themselves are also perceived by the inner sense; but by means of reason, all these things, and reason itself, become known and are included in knowledge. Do you not think so?

EVODIUS: I do indeed.

AUGUSTINE: Now tell me: how stands the question toward whose solution we have been struggling for so long upon this road?

5. The inner sense that controls and judges the bodily senses is more excellent than the bodily senses.

EVODIUS: As I remember, of the three questions that we proposed to form the order of this discourse a little while ago, we are now dealing with the first: how we can prove that God exists, even though we believe it firmly and steadfastly.

AUGUSTINE: Your memory is correct. I also want you to keep carefully in mind that when I asked whether you knew you existed, it became obvious that you knew not only this, but also two other things [that you live and that you understand].

EVODIUS: I remember this as well.

AUGUSTINE: Now see in which of these three belongs everything that the senses of the body perceive; that is, in which of these classes would you place whatever reaches our senses through the eyes (or, for that matter, any organ of the body whatsoever)? In that which merely exists, that which also lives, or that which understands?

EVODIUS: In that which merely exists.

AUGUSTINE: In which class would you place the sense itself?

EVODIUS: In that which lives.

AUGUSTINE: Which of these two do you judge to be the better, the sense or its object?

EVODIUS: The sense, of course.

AUGUSTINE: Why?

EVODIUS: Because what lives is better than what merely exists.

AUGUSTINE: What of the inner sense, which we investigated previously and found to be inferior to reason, yet common to man and beast? Will you hesitate to rank this higher than the senses of the body—which, in turn, are to be ranked higher than the body itself?

EVODIUS: No, I would not.

AUGUSTINE: I would like to hear why you would not. You cannot say that the inner sense should be placed in that one of the three classes which understands as well, but only in that which is or lives, since it lacks understanding; for the inner sense is present in beasts as well, and they do not have understanding. Since this is so, I ask you why you place the inner sense higher than the sense which perceives corporeal objects. Both belong to the class that lives. Moreover, you placed the sense that touches bodies over the bodies themselves, because bodies are in the class of things that merely exist, while this sense is in the class of things that live. Since the inner sense is also found in the class that lives, tell me why you think it better. If you say, "Because the inner sense perceives the bodily sense," I believe that you will not find a rule by which we can confidently assert that everything which perceives is better than what it perceives. For by this same rule, we would be forced to admit that everything which understands is better than what is understood. This is false; for man understands wisdom, yet he is not better than wisdom itself. Therefore, why do you think that the inner sense is to be placed above the sense by which we perceive bodies?

EVODIUS: Because I recognize that it controls and, as it were, judges the bodily senses. If something is missing in the performance of their function, the inner sense demands its debt, so to speak, from its servants, just as we proved a little while ago. For the sense of the eye does not see that it sees or does not see. Since it does not, it cannot judge what is missing or what is sufficient. The inner sense, however, advises the bodily sense, in the soul of a beast, to open the closed eyes and to complete what it perceives is lacking. No one can doubt that what judges is better than what is judged.

AUGUSTINE: You assert, then, that the bodily sense makes judgments in the same way about bodies? For pleasure and pain affect the bodily sense when it is touched gently or roughly by a body. Just as the inner sense judges what is lacking or what is sufficient in the sense of the eyes, so the sense of the eyes itself judges what is lacking or sufficient in color. Just as the inner sense judges whether or not our hearing is intent enough, so hearing itself judges voices, what flows in harmoniously or what makes a harsh noise. We need not continue with the rest of the senses. I think that you know what I mean: just as the inner sense makes judgments about the senses of the body, approving their completeness or demanding what is lacking, so the senses of the body make judgments about bodies, accepting from among them what is pleasing and rejecting what is not.

EVODIUS: I understand and agree.

6. Reason is the highest and most excellent faculty of man. God and that which is more excellent than reason.

AUGUSTINE: Now see if reason makes any judgment about the inner sense. I am not asking whether you doubt that reason is better than the inner sense, since I am sure you think it is. I think that now we do not need to question whether reason makes judgments about the inner sense. For, of the things that are under the reason—bodies, bodily senses, and the inner sense—how would one be better than another and reason more excellent than all, unless reason itself told us so? Certainly this is possible only if reason makes judgments concerning them.

EVODIUS: That is evident.

AUGUSTINE: Therefore, since the nature which merely exists and does not live or understand (for example, the inanimate body) is inferior to the nature that not only exists, but also lives, though it does not understand (for example, the soul of beasts); and since this in turn is inferior to that which at once exists, lives, and understands (for example, the rational mind in man)—you do not think then, do you, that anything can be found in us more excellent (that is, among those things by which our nature is perfected so that we are men) than this which we put in the third place? Clearly we have a body, and a kind of life that makes the body live and grow. We recognize these two conditions in beasts as well. We have also a third thing: a head or eye of our soul, as it were, or whatever term can be more aptly applied to our reason and understanding. This is what the nature of a beast does not have. Please see whether you can find anything in man's nature which is more noble than reason.

EVODIUS: I see absolutely nothing more noble.

AUGUSTINE: What if we should be able to find something which you would not doubt not only exists, but even is more excellent than our reason? Will you hesitate to say that, whatever it is, this is our God?

EVODIUS: If I could find something better than what is best in my nature, I would not immediately say that this is God. I am not inclined to call God that to which my reason is inferior, but rather that to whom no one is superior.

AUGUSTINE: Clearly. And God Himself has given your reason the power to think so devoutly and truly about Him. But, I ask you, if you find that there is nothing superior to our reason except what is eternal and immutable, will you hesitate to say that this is God? You know that bodies are mutable and that life itself, which animates the body in its varying conditions, is plainly subject to change. Reason itself is clearly proven to be mutable, now struggling to arrive at truth, now ceasing to struggle, sometimes reaching it and sometimes not. If, without the aid of any organ of the body or of any sense inferior to it, either touch, taste, smell, hearing, or sight, reason discerns that it is inferior and through its own power discerns something eternal and immutable, reason should at the same time admit that it is inferior and that this is its God.

EVODIUS: I shall admit that this is God to which nothing is granted to be superior.

AUGUSTINE: Good! It will be sufficient, then, for me to prove that there is something of this nature which you will admit to be God; or, if there is anything superior, you will grant that this superior being is God. Therefore, whether there is something superior or not, it will be proven that God exists when, as I promised, I show with God's aid that there is something superior to reason.

EVODIUS: Prove then what you promise.

7. How can the same object be known by many at the same time?

AUGUSTINE: I will. Let me ask first whether my bodily sense is the same as yours; or whether it is not really my sense, unless it be mine, and not really your sense, unless it be your own. Were it not so, I could not see through my eyes any object that you did not see.

EVODIUS: I admit this fully. Although senses are the same in kind, we each have our own senses of seeing, hearing, and so forth. Not only can one man see or hear what another cannot; but it is also possible for any person to perceive with any sense what someone else does not perceive. Thus it is proven that a sense is not yours unless it is yours, nor mine unless it is mine.

AUGUSTINE: Would you say the same thing about the inner sense, or something else?

EVODIUS: The same, surely. My inner sense perceives my senses, and yours perceives yours. For this reason, I am often asked by a man who sees something whether I see it too. For I perceive whether or not I see it; he who asks does not perceive whether or not I see it.

AUGUSTINE: Well, does not each one of us have his own reason? For it can happen that I understand something which you do not understand and which you cannot know whether or not I understand, while I, on the other hand, do know that I understand it.

EVODIUS: It is evident that each of us has his own rational mind.

AUGUSTINE: You could not say, could you, that each of us has his own sun, moon, stars, and so forth, which we see, although each perceives these with his own sense?

EVODIUS: Of course not!

AUGUSTINE: Many of us at the same time can see some one object. Yet each of us has his own senses, with which each perceives the one object that we all see simultaneously. Although my sense is different from yours, what we see is not necessarily mine or yours. One object is before both of us and is viewed by both of us at the same time.

EVODIUS: That is very evident.

AUGUSTINE: We can hear another voice at the same time; yet my hearing is distinct from yours, and the voice that we hear is neither mine nor yours. Whatever sound occurs is present in its entirety, to be heard by both of us.

EVODIUS: This is also evident.

AUGUSTINE: Now, please, turn your attention to what we say about the other senses of the body. They do not behave exactly as do the senses of the eyes or ears, because they have contact with the object; nor is their behavior entirely different. Both you and I can inhale the same air, and can perceive the character of this air from its odor. Likewise, we can both taste the same honey, or whatever food or drink you please, and we can perceive its character from its taste. Although the air or honey is the same, and although the odor or taste is the same when we both experience it, nevertheless you do not experience it with my sense, nor I with yours, nor do we experience it with some other sense which both of us possess in common. My sense is my own and yours is your own, even though the odor or taste experienced by both of us is the same. From the above reasoning, these senses are found to be something like the senses of sight and hearing. But for the purposes of our discussion, they differ from sight and hearing in the following way: both of us draw in the same air through our noses and taste the same food; nevertheless, I do not breathe that part of the air that you breathe and I do not take the same part of the food that you take. Each of us takes a different part. When I take a breath from the whole air, I take in the part which is sufficient for me, and you likewise breathe from the whole air the part which is sufficient for you. And although a certain food is completely consumed by both of us, nevertheless not all is consumed by you or by me, in the same way that we both at the same time hear a whole word or see the same sight. Different parts of the food or drink must enter each of us. Do you understand this?

EVODIUS: I agree that this is clear and true.

AUGUSTINE: You don't think, do you, that the sense of touch can be compared to the sense of the eyes and ears in the case we have just discussed? Not only can both of us perceive one body through the sense of touch, but even the same part of a body. This is not the case when we are both eating; we cannot both take all of the food placed before us, as, with the sense of touch, you could touch the same object that I touched, and all of it—so that both of us each touched, not just individual parts of the object, but the whole object.

EVODIUS: I admit that in this way the sense of touch is very like the sense of seeing and hearing. But I see a difference: both of us can see and hear one entire object at the same time. Both of us, however, cannot touch an entire object at one time, only a part at a time; and not the same part, except at different times. I cannot touch any part that you are touching unless you move away from it.

AUGUSTINE: A most acute answer! Yet attend to this: of all the objects that we perceive, there are some which both of us perceive at the same time and others which we each perceive separately. Yet each of us perceives his own sensations separately; I never feel yours and you never feel mine. What can each of us separately, not both together, perceive from among those things that are perceived by us through the bodily senses, that is, from among corporeal objects, except what becomes our own so completely that we change it into ourselves? For instance, food and drink. You cannot perceive any part of food or drink that I have perceived. Even though nurses give infants food that has already been chewed, the part that has already been tasted, chewed, and absorbed into the vitals of the one who chewed it cannot in any way be called back as food for the infant. When the palate has tasted something pleasant, however small that part may be, the palate claims it irrevocably as its own and forces it to conform to the nature of the body. Were this not so, there would remain no taste in the mouth after the food which was bitten off and tasted has been spit out. The same can also be said of the parts of the air that we inhale through the nose. Although you too can inhale all that I have exhaled, you cannot breathe in what has been used as nourishment because I cannot exhale that part. Doctors teach us that we take in nourishment through our nose. This nourishment I alone can perceive by inhaling, and I cannot restore it by exhaling for you to inhale and perceive through your nose. When we perceive other sorts of sensible objects we do not, in the act of perception, break them up and absorb them into our body. Both of us can perceive them either at one time or separately, so that either all or part of what I perceive may also be perceived by you. Examples of this are light, sound, or corporeal bodies, with which we come into contact but, in so doing, do not alter them.

EVODIUS: I understand.

AUGUSTINE: It is, therefore, clear that objects we do not change when we perceive them with our bodily senses do not become part of the nature of our senses and so are common to us, since they are not changed or turned into our own, as it were, personal property.

EVODIUS: I agree completely.

AUGUSTINE: By "our own" and "personal," I mean that which each one of us consumes for himself and what each alone perceives in himself as belonging properly to his own nature. By "common" and, as it were, "public," I mean what is perceived by everyone who perceives, without its being changed or destroyed.

EVODIUS: Yes.

8. The order of numbers, known as one and unchangeable, is not known by the bodily senses.

AUGUSTINE: Come! Listen and tell me whether we may find anything that all reasoning men see with their reason and mind in common with all others, while what is seen is present in all and, unlike food or drink, is not transformed into some use by those to whom it is present, instead remaining uncorrupted and complete whether or not men discern it. Perhaps you think that nothing like this exists?

EVODIUS: On the contrary, I see that many such things exist, one of which is quite enough to mention: the order and the truth of number *[ratio et veritas numeri]* are present to all who think. Everyone who calculates tries to understand the truth of number with his own reason and understanding. Some can do this rather easily; others have more difficulty. Yet the truth of number offers itself to all alike who are able to grasp it. When a man understands it, it is not changed into a kind of nourishment for him; when he fails to grasp it, the truth of number does not disappear; rather, it remains true and permanent, while man's failure to grasp it is commensurate with the extent of his error.

AUGUSTINE: Correct! I see that you are not inexperienced in this, and have quickly found your answer. If someone were to say to you that numbers were impressed upon our spirit not as a result of their own nature, but as a result of those objects which we experience with the bodily senses, what answer would you make? Or do you agree with this?

EVODIUS: No, I do not. Even if I did perceive numbers with the bodily senses, I would not be able to perceive with the bodily senses the meaning of division and addition. It is with the light of the mind that I would prove wrong the man who makes an error in addition or subtraction. Whatever I may experience with my bodily senses, such as this air and earth and whatever corporeal matter they contain, I cannot know how long it will endure. But seven and three are ten, not only now, but forever. There has never been a time when seven and three were not ten, nor will there ever be a time when they are not ten. Therefore, I have said that the truth of number is incorruptible and common to all who think.

AUGUSTINE: I do not disagree with your answer, for you spoke truly and clearly. But you will easily see that numbers themselves are not drawn from the bodily senses, if you realize how any number you please multiplied by one is that number. For example, two times one is two; three times one is three; ten times one is ten; any number times one is that number. Anyone who really thinks about the number one realizes that he cannot perceive it through the bodily senses, for whatever we experience through a sense is proven to be many, not one. This follows because it is a body and is therefore infinitely divisible. But I need not concentrate upon each small and indistinct part; however small such a bodily part may be, it has a right, left, upper, and lower side, or a farther and nearer side, or ends and a middle. These, we admit, must be in a body, however small it is; thus, we concede that no body is truly and purely one. Yet all these parts could not be counted, if they had not been distinguished by the concept of one. When, therefore, I look for one in a body, I do not doubt that I will not find it. I know what I am seeking there and what I shall not find there. I know that I cannot find one, or rather that it does not exist in a body at all. How do I know that a body is not one? If I did not know what one is, I could not count the many parts of the body. Moreover, however I may know one, I do not know it through the bodily senses, because through the bodily senses I know nothing except a body which, we have proven, is not really and simply one. Furthermore, if we have not perceived one through a sense of the body, we have not perceived by a sense any number of those numbers which we discern only through the understanding. There exists no number which does not get its name from the number of times it contains one. The perception of one does not occur through any bodily sense. The half of any body whatsoever, although the whole body consists of two halves, also has its own half; therefore, there are two parts of a body which are not simply two. Moreover, the number which is called two because it is twice what is irreducibly one, cannot be two parts of one, in other words, that which is simply one cannot again have a half or a third or whatever part you please, since it is simply and truly one. In observing the order of numbers, we see after one the number two, which is twice one. Twice two does not follow next in order; rather, three comes next, and then four, which is twice two. This order *[ratio]* continues throughout all the rest of the numbers by a fixed and unchangeable law. Thus after one, the first of all numbers, when one itself is excepted, the first number is the double of one, for two comes next. After this second number, that is, after two, when two is excepted, the second number is the double of two; for after two the first number is three, and the second number is four, the double of two. After the third, that is, after the number three, when it is itself excepted, the third number is the double of three; for after the third number, that is, after three, the first number is four, the second five, and the third six, which is the double of three. So after the fourth number, when it is itself excepted, the fourth number is the double of four; for after the fourth number, after four, the first number is five, the second is six, the third is seven, and the fourth number is eight, which is the double of four. Through all of the rest of the numbers you will find the same thing that is found in the first pair of numbers, one and two, namely, the double of any number is as many times after this number as such a number is from the beginning.

How do we discern that this fact which holds for the whole number series is unchangeable, fixed, and incorruptible? No one perceives all the numbers by any bodily sense, for they are innumerable. How do we know that this is true for all numbers? Through what fantasy or vision do we discern so confidently the firm truth of number throughout the whole innumerable series, unless by some inner light unknown to bodily sense?

Men to whom God has given ability in argument, and whom stubbornness does not lead into confusion, are forced to admit that the order and truth of numbers have nothing to do with the bodily senses, but are unchangeable and true and common to all rational beings. Therefore, although many other things could occur to us that are common and, as it were, public for rational beings, things that are seen by each individual with his mind and reason and still remain inviolate and unchanged, nevertheless, I am not unwilling to accept the fact that the order and truth of number are the best possible examples that you could have given when you wished to answer my question. Not without reason was number joined to wisdom in the Holy Scriptures where it is said, "I and my heart have gone round to know and to consider and to search out wisdom and number" [Eccles. 7:26].

9. Is wisdom, which is necessary for human happiness, one and the same in all men who are wise?

AUGUSTINE: Nevertheless, I beg you, what opinion should we have in the case of wisdom itself? Do you think that each man has his own individual wisdom? Or is there one wisdom that exists alike for all men, such that the more a man partakes of this wisdom, the wiser he is?

EVODIUS: I do not know what wisdom you mean. I see that men have various opinions as to what is said or done wisely. Men who serve as soldiers think that they are acting wisely, while men who despise military service, devoting their energy and effort to agriculture, praise agriculture and claim that this is wisdom. Men who are shrewd in devising ways of acquiring wealth think that they are wise. Men who disregard all this or put aside temporal things of this sort, devoting their whole effort to the search for truth so that they may know themselves and God—these men judge that this is the great gift of wisdom. Those who are not willing to devote themselves to the leisure of seeking and contemplating truth, but prefer toilsome business and official duties so that they may advise men and engage in the just government and management of human affairs—these men think that they are wise. Men who do both of these things and live some of the time in the contemplation of truth, and some of the time amid toilsome official duties which they think they owe to human society, think that they hold the prize of wisdom. I pass over innumerable sects, all of which rank their own followers over others and claim that they alone are wise. Therefore, since we are discussing the problem between us in such a way that we must assert, not our beliefs, but only what we clearly understand, I cannot answer your question unless I know by reflection and reasoning what wisdom itself is.

AUGUSTINE: You don't think, do you, that wisdom is anything other than the truth in which the highest good is discerned and held? All the different sects that you mentioned seek good and avoid evil. Their doctrines vary because different things appear to them to be good. Whoever, then, seeks what he should not seek, errs, even though he would not seek it if he did not think it good. The man who seeks nothing cannot err, nor can the man who seeks what he ought to seek. Insofar as all men seek the happy life, they do not err. Insofar as each man fails to follow the road of life that leads to happiness, although he may confess and profess that he is unwilling to arrive anywhere except at happiness, he is in error. His error is that he follows something that does not lead where he wishes to arrive. The greater his error on the road of life, the less his wisdom, and the farther he is from the truth in which the highest good is discerned and grasped. Moreover, when the highest good has been pursued and obtained, each man becomes happy—which beyond a doubt is what we all wish. Just as it is agreed that we all wish to be happy, so it is agreed that we all wish to be wise, since no one without wisdom is happy. No man is happy except through the highest good, which is to be found and included in that truth which we call wisdom. Just as the idea of happiness is impressed upon our minds before we are happy—through this idea we know confidently and say without hesitation that we wish to be happy—so, before we are wise, we have an idea of wisdom in our minds. Through this idea each one of us, if asked whether or not he wants to be wise, answers without any confusion or doubt that he does so wish.

If it is, therefore, agreed between us what wisdom is, although perhaps you could not explain wisdom in words—for if you did not discern wisdom at all with your spirit, you would not know either that you wish to be wise or that you ought to wish to be wise, which I do not think you will deny—I want you to tell me whether you think that wisdom offers itself alike to all who think, just as the order and truth of number do. Or since there are as many minds as there are men, so that I discern nothing in your mind and you discern nothing in mine, do you think that there can be as many wisdoms as there are wise men?

EVODIUS: If the highest good is one for all men, the truth in which it is discerned and grasped—that is, wisdom—must be one and common to all men.

AUGUSTINE: Do you doubt that the highest good, whatever it is, is one for all men?

EVODIUS: Yes, I do, because I see different men rejoicing in different things as their highest goods.

AUGUSTINE: Indeed, I wish that no one had any doubt about the highest good, just as no one has any doubt that a man cannot be happy without obtaining the highest good. Since the question is important, and may demand a long explanation, let us imagine that the highest goods are as many as the different things which are sought by various men as the highest good. It does not follow, does it, that wisdom itself is not common alike to all men, just because the goods which men discern in it and choose are many and varied? If you think this, you may also doubt that the light of the sun is one, because we see many different things in it. From these many things, each man chooses according to his will what he may enjoy through his sight. One man willingly looks at the height of a mountain and rejoices to see it; another at the level fields; another at the hollow of valleys; another at the greenness of the woods; another at the flickering surface of the sea; another compares all or some of these things at the same time, for the delight of seeing them. Just as the objects which men see in the sunlight and choose to enjoy are many and varied, yet the light in which the sight of each man watching sees and holds what he enjoys is one; so even if the goods are many and varied from which each man may choose what he wishes, determining to discern, grasp, and enjoy the highest good rightly and truly, nevertheless it is possible that the very light of wisdom, in which these goods can be discerned and grasped, is one wisdom common to all wise men.

EVODIUS: I grant that this can be so and that nothing is opposed to the existence of one wisdom common to all, even if there are many different highest goods. But I would like to know whether or not this is so; for when we grant that this may possibly be so, we do not necessarily grant that it *is* so.

AUGUSTINE: Meanwhile, we maintain that wisdom exists. But whether it is one and common to all men, or whether each individual has his own wisdom as he has his own soul or mind, we do not yet know.

Evodius: Yes.

10. The rules of wisdom are the same for all wise men.

AUGUSTINE: How, then, do we see the truth of what we are maintaining: that wisdom and wise men exist, and that all men wish to be happy? I do not doubt that you see this and see that it is true. Do you see that this is true in the same way that you see your own thoughts, of which I am completely ignorant, unless you disclose them to me? Or do you see it in the same way that you understand, that is, in such a way that I too can see the truth, even though you do not disclose it to me?

EVODIUS: I do not doubt that you can see the truth also, even though I might not want you to.

AUGUSTINE: Is not the one truth which we both see in our individual minds common to both of us?

EVODIUS: Clearly.

AUGUSTINE: Likewise, I believe, you do not deny the truth that we should seek after wisdom.

EVODIUS: I do not doubt it.

AUGUSTINE: Can we deny that this fact is true and one, yet common for all who know it? Each man sees it with his own mind, not with mine, yours, or anyone else's; yet what is seen, is present for all to see in common. We cannot deny this, can we?

EVODIUS: Of course not.

AUGUSTINE: Won't you also admit the following to be absolutely true: that we should live justly; that the worse should be subordinate to the better; that equals should be compared with equals and to each should be given his own; and that each of these truths is present for you, me, and all to see in common?

EVODIUS: Yes.

AUGUSTINE: Will you deny that the incorrupt is better than the corrupt, the eternal better than the temporal, the inviolable better than the violable?

EVODIUS: Who can deny this?

AUGUSTINE: Can anyone call truth his own, when it is present unchangingly, for all to meditate upon who have the power to meditate?

EVODIUS: No one can truly call truth his own. Truth is one and common to all, just as much as it is true.

AUGUSTINE: Likewise, who can deny that the spirit should be turned away from corruption and toward incorruption, and that incorruption, not corruption, should be loved? When a man grants something to be true, does he not also understand that it is changeless, and does he not see that it is present in common for all minds that have the power to behold it?

EVODIUS: True.

AUGUSTINE: Will anyone doubt that the life which cannot be moved by any opposition from a sure and honest judgment is better than the one which is easily broken and overcome by the troubles of this life?

EVODIUS: Who would doubt it?

AUGUSTINE: I shall not ask any more questions of this kind. It is sufficient that you see and grant, as I do, that it is certain that these judgments are rules and, as it were, lights of virtue; and that true and unchangeable things, whether individually or all together, are present in common for all men to meditate upon who have the power to perceive with mind and reason. I do ask this however: Do you think that these things are a part of wisdom? I believe that you think that the man who has gained wisdom is wise.

EVODIUS: Yes.

AUGUSTINE: Could a man who lives justly live this way if he did not see which are the inferior things that he subordinates to superior ones, or the equals that he joins to equals, or the particular things that he assigns to their own particular places?

EVODIUS: He could not.

AUGUSTINE: You won't deny, will you, that the man who sees these things sees wisely?

EVODIUS: No.

AUGUSTINE: Likewise, doesn't the man who lives prudently choose incorruption and judge that incorruption is to be preferred to corruption?

EVODIUS: Most clearly.

AUGUSTINE: Therefore, when he chooses to turn his spirit to that which no one doubts should be chosen, it cannot be denied, can it, that he chooses wisely?

EVODIUS: Of course not.

AUGUSTINE: When, therefore, he turns his mind to a wise choice, he does so wisely.

EVODIUS: Certainly.

AUGUSTINE: And he acts wisely who is not turned by fear or punishment from what he chooses or turns to wisely.

EVODIUS: Without a doubt.

AUGUSTINE: It is very clear, then, that all that we have called the rules and lights to virtue are a part of wisdom, inasmuch as the more a man uses them in leading his life, the more wisely he acts and lives. Moreover, whatever is done wisely cannot rightly be said to be separate from wisdom.

EVODIUS: Yes.

AUGUSTINE: The true and immutable rules of wisdom are as true and immutable as the rules of number, whose order and truth, you have said, are unchangeably present and common to all who see them. When asked about a few of these rules of wisdom individually, you replied that they were evidently true, and you admitted that they are present and common for all to see who have the power to see them.

11. How are the rules of number and wisdom related?

EVODIUS: I cannot doubt this. But I would very much like to know whether these two things, wisdom and number, are members of any single class. You recall that they have been placed together in the Holy Scriptures. Does one depend on the other, or is the one included in the other? Does number, for example, depend upon wisdom, or is it included in wisdom? I do not dare to say that wisdom depends upon number, or is included in number; this could hardly be the case, since I have known many accountants and men skilled in numbers (whatever name is applied to men who use numbers well and accurately), yet I have known few wise men—perhaps none. Wisdom seems by far more worthy than number.

AUGUSTINE: You have mentioned something at which I too often wonder. When I think about the unchanging truth of numbers, and when I consider the province of numbers—their room or sanctuary, as it were, or whatever suitable name can be found by which we may designate the home or seat of numbers—I am far removed from my body. I may, perhaps, find something about which I can think, but it is nothing that I can express in words; as though exhausted, I return to familiar things, so as to be able to speak, and I speak of objects before my eyes, objects that it is usual to speak of. The same thing happens to me when I think as carefully and intently as I can about wisdom. Besides, I am very much amazed because these two things lie in the most secret and yet most certain truth—even by the testimony of the Scriptures, where number and wisdom are placed together. I wonder greatly, as I said before, why number is generally regarded as of little value while wisdom is thought precious. Yet number and wisdom are somehow one and the same thing, since the Divine Writings say of wisdom that it "reaches from end to end powerfully and disposes all things sweetly" [Wisd. of Sol. 8:1]. The power that "reaches from end to end powerfully" is perhaps called "number"; while the power which "disposes all things sweetly" is now thought of as wisdom proper, though both of these belong to the same wisdom. Because wisdom gave numbers to all objects, even the lowliest objects that have been placed at the very end; because all objects, even the least ones, have their own numbers; because, moreover, wisdom did not grant, either to corporeal objects or to all spirits, the power to know, but granted it only to rational beings, as if it made in them a home for itself, from which it could arrange everything, including even the least object to which it has assigned number; because we easily make judgments about corporeal objects as things which have been placed in a lower order than ours and which we see are beneath us, even though numbers have been stamped upon them—for these reasons, we consider these numbers to be inferior to ourselves and therefore regard them as baser.

But when we begin, as it were, to ascend along the path, we discover that numbers transcend our minds and remain unchangeable in their own truth. Because few men can know, but even stupid men can count, men admire wisdom and despise numbers. Yet the further removed learned students are from the filth of the earth, the more clearly do they apprehend both numbers and wisdom in truth itself, and they hold both of them to be precious. For them, not only do silver, gold, and the other things for which we strive bear no comparison with this truth, but even they themselves appear worthless when compared to it. Therefore, do not marvel that, while wisdom has appeared precious to men, number has seemed base: it has seemed so because men can count more easily than they can know. You see that men consider gold more precious than the golden light of a lamp, in comparison with which gold is to be scorned. Yet the lesser object receives more honor because even a beggar may light a lamp for himself, while few men have gold. The comparison suggests that wisdom, since it is rare, is inferior to number—which is impossible, since they are identical; but it requires an eye capable of discerning it. Brightness and heat are perceived consubstantially, so to speak, in the one fire; they cannot be separated. Yet the heat is communicated to objects which are placed near to the fire, while brightness is diffused far and wide. In the same way, the power of intelligence, which lies in wisdom, warms things (such as rational souls) that lie near it. But the power of intelligence does not affect things that are farther away, (for instance, corporeal objects) with the heat of knowing; it floods them, rather, with the light of numbers. This comparison may be somewhat obscure to you, for no analogy from visible things can be made applicable in every respect to that which is invisible.

Yet attend to the following point which is sufficient for our question and is clear enough, even to humble minds like ours. Although it is not clear to us whether number is a part of or separate from wisdom, or whether wisdom is a part of or separate from number, or whether they are the same, it is clear that both are true, and immutably true.

12. One immutable truth, common to all who know, exists, and is more excellent than the minds that know it.

AUGUSTINE: You will not deny, therefore, that immutable truth, comprising everything that is immutably true, exists; and you cannot say that immutable truth is yours, or mine, or anyone else's. It is present and shows itself as a kind of miraculously secret, yet public, light for all who see what is immutably true. Who would say, then, that anything which is present for all who think and know belongs exclusively to the nature of any one of these?

You remember, I imagine, that we have already given some discussion to the senses of the body. The objects which we perceive in common by means of the sense of the eyes or ears—colors and sounds, for example, which you and I can see and hear at the same time—these objects do not belong to the nature of our eyes or ears, but are common for both of us to perceive. You will not, therefore, say that the objects which you and I perceive together, each with our own mind, belong to the natures of either of us. We cannot say that the object seen by the eyes of two people belongs to either of the two. It is, instead, some third object, upon which the sight of each of the two is directed.

EVODIUS: This is evidently the case.

AUGUSTINE: Do you think that the truth of which we have been talking for so long, and in which, though it is one, we see so many things—do you think that this truth is more excellent than our minds, or equally so, or less? If it were less excellent, we would make judgments *about* it, not *according* to it. In the same way, we make judgments about corporeal objects because they are below us, and we say not only that they are or are not this way, but also that they ought to be this way, or ought not to be. It is likewise concerning our spirits: we know not only that the spirit *is*, but often also that it *ought to be*, such and such. When we speak about corporeal objects, we make the following judgments: this is less bright than it should be; or, it is not so square; and so forth. We speak, however, the following way, according to the nature of our character [morum ratio], about spirits: this is less apt than it ought to be; or, less gentle; or, less forceful. We make these judgments according to the inner rules of truth which we perceive in common. But no one makes judgments about the rules themselves. When a man says that the eternal is more powerful than the temporal, and that seven plus three are ten, he does not say that it ought to be so; he knows it is this way, and does not correct it as an examiner would, but he rejoices as if he has made a discovery.

If truth were equal to our minds, it would be subject to change. Our minds sometimes see more and sometimes less, and because of this we acknowledge that they are mutable. Truth, remaining in itself, does not gain anything when we see it, or lose anything when we do not see it. It is whole and uncorrupted. With its light, truth gives joy to the men who turn to it, and punishes with blindness those who turn away from it.

What of the fact that in accordance with truth we make judgments about our minds, yet we cannot make judgments about the truth? We say that a mind knows less than it ought to, or as much as it should. Moreover, the nearer the mind can get to immutable truth and the more closely it can cling to the truth, the more the mind ought to know. Therefore, if truth is neither inferior nor equal to our minds it follows that it is superior to them, and more excellent.

13. Man's enjoyment of the truth.

AUGUSTINE: But I promised, if you remember, that I would show you something higher than our mind and reason. Behold, it is truth itself. If you can, embrace it, enjoy it; "Be glad in the Lord, and He will grant you the prayers of your heart" [Ps. 36:4]. What more do you ask than that you be happy? And what is more blessed than the man who enjoys unshaken, immutable, and most excellent truth? Men declare that they are happy when they embrace beautiful bodies that they have ardently desired, whether of their wives or of prostitutes; do we doubt that we are happy in the embrace of truth? Men exclaim how happy they are when, with throats parched from the heat, they come to a flowing and healthful spring; or when they are hungry and find a plentiful supper or dinner prepared. Shall we deny that we are happy when we are given the food and drink of truth? We usually hear voices of men declaring that they are happy if they rest among roses and other flowers or if they enjoy fragrant perfumes. What is more fragrant or more pleasant than the breath of truth? Do we hesitate to say that we are happy when we breathe the truth? Many think that the life lived amid the music of voice, stringed instrument, or flute is happy, and when they lack this, they think themselves unhappy; when they have it, they are elated with joy. Do we ask for any other happy life, when, so to speak, the silent eloquence of truth glides noiselessly into our minds? Do we not then enjoy a happiness that is sure, and near at hand? Men think themselves happy and want to live forever when they are delighted by the brightness of gold, silver, gems, colors; or by the light of their eyes themselves; or by the fires of the earth, the stars, the moon, or the sun. They are delighted by brightness and joy, as long as trouble or poverty do not separate them from this happiness. Are we afraid to place the happy life in the light of truth?

Furthermore, because the highest good is known and grasped by truth, and because this truth is wisdom, let us, by our wisdom, see and grasp the highest good, and enjoy it. Happy indeed is the man who enjoys the highest good. It is this truth that reveals all true goods, and every man in accordance with his capacity chooses them, either individually or together, for his enjoyment. Men choose by the light of the sun what they wish to see, and they rejoice in the sight. If they are by chance endowed with strong, keen, and healthy eyes, they look at nothing more willingly than at the sun which lights up even the other things by which men with weak eyes are delighted. In the same way, when the rapier edge of the mind cuts through the many true and immutable things with its sure reason, it steers toward the very truth, by which all things are revealed; clinging to truth as if forgetful of all else, it enjoys everything at once in its enjoyment of truth. Whatever is delightful in other truths derives its delightfulness from truth itself.

Our freedom then consists in submission to the truth. It is our God Himself who frees us from death, that is, from the state of sin. Truth itself, when it speaks as a man, says to those who believe in Him, "If you remain in My word, you shall be My disciples indeed, and you shall know the truth and the truth will make you free" [John 8:31–32]. The soul enjoys nothing with freedom, unless it enjoys it securely.

14. Truth, available in common to all men, is the private property of no man.

AUGUSTINE: No one, however, securely possesses those goods which he can lose although he does not wish to. And no one can lose truth and wisdom against his will, for no one can be physically separated from them. That which is called separation from truth and wisdom is the perverse will which loves inferior things. No one wills a thing unwillingly. We possess in the truth, therefore, what we all may enjoy, equally and in common; in it are no defects or limitations. For truth receives all its lovers without arousing their envy. It is open to all, yet it is always chaste. No one says to the other, "Get back! Let me approach too! Hands off! Let me also embrace it!" All men cling to truth, and touch it. The food of truth can never be stolen. There is nothing that you can drink of it which I cannot drink too. You do not turn anything to your private advantage by communion with truth. Whatever you may take from truth and wisdom, they still remain complete for me. I need not wait for you to return the source of your inspiration in order that I too can be inspired by truth. No part of truth is ever made the private property of anyone; rather, it is entirely common to all at the same time. The objects, therefore, that we touch, taste, or smell, are less like truth than are the things we see and hear. This is because every word is heard in its entirety by all who hear it, and at the same time by each individual; and every sight which lies before the eyes is seen as much by one individual as by another at the same time.

There is, however, a very great difference despite these similarities. No voice whatsoever sounds in its entirety at one time, for it is extended and produced in time so that one part sounds earlier and another later. Also, every visible sight swells out, as it were, in space, and is not complete in any one spot. These objects may all be taken away although we may not want them to be, and we are prevented by certain limitations from being able to enjoy them. If someone's sweet singing could be eternal, men would come eagerly in crowds to hear him; the larger the crowd, the more each would fight for a place nearer to the singer. In hearing him, they could retain nothing permanent, but would be touched by fleeting notes. Moreover, if I wished to look upon the sun and could do so continuously, it would only leave me at sunset or be veiled by a cloud, and I would, though unwillingly, lose the pleasure of seeing the sun because of the many obstacles. Finally, if the sweetness of light or of sound were forever present for me to see or hear, what advantage would this be to me, since I would share this in common with brutes? When the will to enjoy is continually present, the beauty of truth and wisdom does not shut out those who have come to hear because of the large crowd; it does not pass with time, and does not move in space. It is not cut short by night or shadows. It does not depend on the senses of the body. It is near to all men who have chosen it and love it. It is eternal for all. It is in no one place, yet it is never away. Without, it advises; within, it teaches. It changes for the better all who behold it, and is not changed for the worse by anyone. No man passes judgment on truth, and no man judges well without it. For this reason it is clear that the beauty of truth and wisdom is, without doubt, superior to our minds, which become wise only through this beauty and which make judgments, not about it but through it, on other things.

15. God, that which is more excellent than reason, demonstrably exists.

AUGUSTINE: You granted, moreover, that if I showed you something higher than our minds, you would admit, assuming that nothing existed which was still higher, that God exists. I accepted your condition and said that it was enough to show this. For if there is something more excellent than truth, this is God. If there is not, then truth itself is God. Whether or not truth is God, you cannot deny that God exists, and this was the question with which we agreed to deal. If it disturbs you that we accept on faith that God is the "Father of Wisdom" in the Sacred Teaching of Christ, remember that we also accept on faith that wisdom born of the eternal is equal to the Father. This is not the question at hand, but it is to be maintained with unshakable faith. For God exists, truly and in the highest degree. This indubitable fact we maintain, I think, not only by faith, but also by a sure though somewhat tenuous form of reasoning, which is sufficient for the immediate question. Thus we can explain the other points pertinent to our discussion, unless you have some objection to raise about the preceding parts.

EVODIUS: I can scarcely find words for the unbelievable joy that fills me. I accept these arguments, crying out that they are most certain. And my inner voice shouts, for truth itself to hear, that I cling to this: not only does good exist, but indeed the highest good—and this is the source of happiness.

AUGUSTINE: Fine. I too am happy. But, I ask you, we are not now wise and happy, are we? Rather, do we not strive toward attaining this goal?

EVODIUS: I think that we are striving toward the goal.

AUGUSTINE: How do you understand that these are certain truths, so that you cry out that you are happy? You admit that this joy comes from wisdom. Can a foolish man know wisdom?

EVODIUS: Not so long as he is foolish.

AUGUSTINE: Then you are wise, or else you do not yet know wisdom.

EVODIUS: I am not yet wise, but I would not say that I am foolish insofar as I know wisdom, for I cannot deny that the things I know are certain, and that they belong to wisdom.

AUGUSTINE: Please tell me, don't you admit that the man who is not just is unjust? And he who is not prudent is imprudent? He who is not temperate is intemperate? Or do you have any doubts about this?

EVODIUS: I admit that, when a man is not just, he is unjust. I would also give the same answer in regard to the prudent or the temperate man.

AUGUSTINE: Why, then, is a man not foolish when he is not wise?

EVODIUS: I admit this too. When someone is not wise, he is foolish.

AUGUSTINE: Now which of these are you?

EVODIUS: Whichever you want to call me. I do not dare say that I am wise; and from what I have just admitted I must indubitably conclude that I am foolish.

AUGUSTINE: Therefore, the foolish man knows wisdom. As we have already said, he would not be sure that he wanted to be wise and that he ought to be wise, unless the idea of wisdom *[notio sapientiæ]* was inherent in his mind. So it is with those individual things that belong to wisdom itself, about which I have just questioned you, and in the knowledge of which you rejoice.

EVODIUS: It is as you say.

16. Wisdom shows itself to the seeker in the guise of numbers embodied in all things of this world.

AUGUSTINE: When we are eager to be wise, we simply, and as quickly as we can, find some means of concentrating our whole soul on the object; when it is attained by the mind, we fix it there firmly, not so that the soul may rejoice in its own private pleasure—which involves only fleeting pleasures—but so that the soul, free of all inclination toward the things of time and space, may grasp that which is one, the same, and eternal. As the soul is the whole life of the body, so God is the happy life of the soul. This is the undertaking in which we are engaged, and toward which we will strive until we have completed it. It has been granted to us to enjoy these true and certain goods which gleam before us, however obscured they may have been until this stage of our journey. Is this not what was written of wisdom's treatment of its lovers, when they approach and seek it? It is said, "In the ways it will show itself to them joyfully and in all providence it will meet them" [Wisd. of Sol. 6:17]. Wherever you turn, wisdom speaks to you through the imprint it has stamped upon its works. When you begin to slip toward outward things, wisdom calls you back, by means of their very forms, so that when something delights you in body and entices you through the bodily senses, you may see that it has number and may ask whence it comes. Thus you return to yourself: you know that you cannot approve or disapprove of what you touch with the bodily senses, unless you have within you certain laws of beauty to which you refer the beautiful objects that you perceive outside of you.

Look at the sky, the earth, and the sea, and at whatever in them shines from above or crawls, flies, or swims below. These have form because they have number. Take away these forms and there will be nothing. Whence are these except from number? Indeed, they exist only insofar as they have number.

In art, the makers of all bodily forms have numbers by which they organize their works. They move their hands and instruments in producing their works until what has been formed externally achieves completion by corresponding as closely as possible to the inward light; and when it has been communicated by the intermediaries of the senses, it delights the inner judge who gazes upward upon numbers. Ask next what moves the limbs of the artist himself, and it will be number, for his limbs also are moved according to number. If you take the work from his hands and take the purpose of creating the work from his spirit, and if you say that pleasure causes the motion of the limbs, it will be called "dancing." If you ask what is pleasant in dancing, number will answer you, "Behold, it is I." Look closely at the beauty of the graceful body and you will see that numbers are held in space. Then look closely at the beauty of motion in a body and you will see that numbers are involved in time. Enter into the art from which the numbers come, and ask there for time and space. Neither will exist; yet number lives there. Number has no location in space *[regio spatiorum]*, no duration of time. Nevertheless, when the men who wish to become artists adapt themselves to the art to be learned, they move their bodies through time and space. They move their spirits through time; indeed, their skill increases with the passage of time.

Go beyond even the spirit of an artist, that you may see eternal number. Then wisdom will shine upon you from its inner abode and from the shrine of truth. If your sight is still too weak and is repelled from this vision, turn the eye of your mind to the road where wisdom used to reveal itself for your delight. Then remember that you have postponed a vision which you may seek again when you are stronger and sounder.

Woe to men who forsake you as their leader, O Wisdom, and wander from your footsteps! Woe to those who love not you, but the signs you show, and who forget your meaning! O sweetest light of the purified mind! Wisdom! You do not cease to suggest to us what you are. Your beckoning is all the beauty of creation.

By the very beauty of his work the artist somehow beckons the spectator, instead of fixing his eyes wholly on the beauty of the work he has made, to pass over this beauty and to look in fondness at him who made it. In the same way, the men who love not you, but what you make, are like those who hear an eloquent wise man and, while they listen avidly to the sweetness of his voice and the formation of his well-placed syllables, lose what is most important—the meaning of the ideas, of which the words were merely signs.

Woe to the men who turn from your light and cling complacently to their own darkness! When they turn their back to you, they are fixed in the work of flesh, as in their own shadows; yet even there, they receive what delights them from the encompassing brightness of your light. But love of the shadow causes the soul's eye to become too lazy and weak to endure the splendor of the sight of you. Besides, the more willingly and more indulgently a man follows and accepts something very weak, the more he becomes covered with darkness, and gradually he becomes unable to see what is supreme. He begins to think that some evil is deceiving him in his blindness, or attracts him in his poverty, or has captured and is torturing him. Yet he is really suffering deservedly because he has turned from the light of wisdom; what is just cannot be evil.

Therefore, Evodius, if you look at something mutable, you cannot grasp it either with the bodily senses or the consideration of the mind, unless it possesses some numerical form. If this form is removed, the mutable dissolves into nothing; do not, then, doubt that there is some eternal and immutable Form which prevents mutable objects from being destroyed and allows them to complete their temporal course, as it were, by measured movements and in a distinct variety of forms. This eternal Form is neither contained by nor, as it were, spread out in space, neither prolonged nor changed by time. Through eternal Form every temporal thing can receive its form and, in accordance with its kind, can manifest and embody number in space and time.

17. All good things come from God.

AUGUSTINE: Just as we say that something which can be changed is "changeable," so I call that which can receive form "formable," and say that everything that is changeable must also be formable. Nothing can give itself form, since nothing can give to itself what it does not have. And surely a thing receives form so that it may have form. Therefore, if anything whatever has a form, it does not need form. But, if something does not have form, it cannot receive from itself what it does not have. Nothing, therefore, as we said, can give itself form.

What more should we say concerning the mutability of body and spirit? Enough has been said above. We have established that body and spirit are given form by an immutable and eternal Form. To this Form it has been said, "Thou shalt change them and they will be changed; but thou art the same, and thy years fail not" [Ps. 101:27–28]. The speech of the prophet has used "years without fail" to mean "eternity." Concerning this Form, it has been said also that it is "permanent in itself, it renews all things" [Wisd. of Sol. 7:27].

We understood from this that everything is governed by providence. If all existing things cease to exist when form is completely taken away, immutable Form itself—through which all mutable things subsist, so that they manifest and embody number appropriate to their forms—this immutable Form is their providence, for if it did not exist, they would not exist either.

As he gazes attentively at the whole of creation, he who travels the road to wisdom perceives how delightfully wisdom reveals itself to him on the way, and meets him in all providence. The more beautiful is the road to the wisdom toward which he hastens, the more ardently he burns to complete the journey.

If you can find any other kind of creature except (1) that which exists and does not live, or (2) that which lives and does not understand, or (3) that which exists, lives, and understands—only then can you tell me that there exists some good which does not come from God. These three kinds of things can be expressed as well by the two terms, "body" and "life," for what only lives, but does not understand—for example, a beast—and what understands—for example, man—are both properly spoken of as "life." These two, therefore, body and life, which are considered creatures (for one even speaks of the life of the Creator, and this is the highest life)—these two creatures, body and life, since, as we have shown above, they are both formable, and since they dissolve into nothing if form is completely lost, prove that they exist as a result of that Form which is always of the same nature. Therefore, all good things, whether great or small, can come only from God.

What is greater in creatures than life that has understanding? What can be less than body? No matter how much creatures may lack, and however much they tend toward nonexistence by virtue of their deficiency, nevertheless some form remains in them, so that they somehow exist. Moreover, whatever form remains in a deficient object comes from that Form which knows no lack and which does not allow the motions of things, whether they be growing or decaying, to exceed the laws of their own numbers.

Therefore, whatever we find to be praiseworthy in nature, whether we judge that its value be great or small, must be referred to the most excellent and ineffable praise of the Creator. Do you have any objections to raise on these points?

18. Freedom of the will, though it may be abused, is good and divinely given, since without it no one could live rightly.

Evodius: I admit that I am quite convinced—insofar as it can be proved in this life among such as we—that God exists and that all goods are from God, since all things that exist are from God, whether they understand, live, and exist, or whether they live and exist only, or whether they merely exist. Now let us turn to a third question: whether we can establish that free will is to be numbered among the goods. When this has been proven, I will grant without hesitation that God gave us free will, and that He was right to have given it.

Augustine: You have remembered well the points we proposed to discuss, and have seen clearly that the second question has already been answered. But you should also have seen that the third question, too, is already solved.

You said you thought that free choice of the will ought not to have been given because through it man sins. To this opinion I replied that no righteous act could be performed except by free choice of the will, and I asserted that God gave it for this reason. You replied that free will ought to have been given as justice was given, so that no one could make evil use of it. This answer of yours forced us to go into a long circuitous course of argument, by which we proved that both greater and lesser goods came only from God. This could not be proved conclusively until we had met the wicked and foolish objections of the fool who "hath said in his heart, 'There is no God'" [Ps. 52:1]. Whatever reasoning we performed, within our limited means, concerning such a great question was directed toward what was obvious, with God

Himself assisting us in so perilous a course. These two facts, nevertheless, that God exists and that all goods come from Him, were thus discussed—even though we previously believed them in firm faith—in such a way that this third question, that free will is to be numbered among the goods, might also appear in the clearest light.

In the previous argument, we proved and established that the nature of the body is on a lower plane than that of the spirit, and because of this, the spirit is a greater good than the body. If, therefore, we find among the goods of the body some that a man can use wrongly, but that we cannot say ought not to have been given to man, since we have agreed that they are goods, why should we wonder if there are in the spirit certain goods, of which we can make wrong use, but which, because they are goods, could not have been given by anyone but Him from whom all good things proceed?

Indeed, you see how great a good is wanting to any body that has no hands; yet he who works cruel or shameful deeds with his hands uses them for evil. Should you see someone without feet, you would acknowledge what an important good was lacking to make his body complete. Yet you would not deny that the man who made evil use of his feet, either for injuring another or for dishonoring himself, was using his feet wrongfully.

With our eyes we see light and distinguish the forms of bodies. The faculty of sight is the fairest in our body, and therefore the eyes are placed, as it were, in the highest position, the place of honor. We use our eyes for keeping safe and for serving life in many other ways. Yet many men commit many shameful deeds by means of their eyes, and force their eyes into the service of lust. You see what a great good the face would lack if there were no eyes; but when we possess them, who gave them but God, the Giver of all good things?

Just as you approve those goods of the body and, disregarding the people who make evil use of them, you praise Him who gave them, so you should admit that free will, without which no one can live rightly, is good and divinely given; and you should grant that those who make evil use of free will ought to be condemned, rather than saying that He who gave it ought not to have given it.

EVODIUS: First, however, I wish that you would prove to me that free will is a good. Then I will grant that God gave it to us, since I acknowledge that all goods proceed from God.

AUGUSTINE: Did I not prove this to you in the great toils of our earlier discussion, when you agreed that every type and form of body is derived from the Form which is supreme over all things, that is, from Truth, and when you acknowledged also that it is a good? For the Truth itself speaks out in the Gospel that even the hairs of our head are numbered [Matt. 10:30]. Have you forgotten what we said about the supremacy of number and its power which extends for ever and ever? What perversity that is! To count the hairs of our head, however scant and useless they may be, among the goods and to find that they can be attributed to no other cause than to God, the Cause of all goods, since the greatest and the least come from Him; yet to hesitate on the question of free will, without which even men who lead the most evil lives agree that they cannot live rightly!

Tell me now, please, which you think is better in us: that without which we can live rightly or that without which we cannot live rightly?

EVODIUS: Please excuse me; I am ashamed of my blindness. Who would doubt that the more excellent thing by far is that without which there is no righteous life?

AUGUSTINE: You will not deny then that a blind man can live rightly?

EVODIUS: May I never be so foolish!

AUGUSTINE: Since, then, you admit that the eye in the body is a good although its loss will not prevent us from living rightly, will you think that free will is not a good when no one can live rightly without it?

Look at justice, which no one uses wrongly. This is numbered among the highest goods of the mind and among all the virtues of the soul, upon which an upright and righteous life depends. No one uses wisdom, courage, or temperance for evil; for in these as in justice, which you have just mentioned, right reason [recta ratio] prevails, and without it virtues cannot exist. No one can use right reason for evil.

19. Of the three classes of goods, great, intermediate, and lowest, freedom of the will is an intermediate good.

AUGUSTINE: These are great goods. Yet remember that not only the great goods but also the least ones can be from no one other than Him from whom all goods proceed, namely from God. Our previous argument proved that, and you have already gladly given your assent to it.

Therefore the virtues, by which men live rightly, are great goods, while all kinds of physical beauty [species], without which men can live rightly, are the lowest goods. The powers of the spirit, without which no one can live rightly, are the intermediate goods [media bona] between these two. No one uses the virtues for evil. However the other goods, the lowest and the intermediate ones, can be used not only for good, but also for evil. No one uses virtues for evil because the very action of a virtue is the good use of those things that we can also use for evil. Moreover, no one can make wrong use of using a thing rightly. Therefore, the abundant generosity of God's goodness is responsible not only for the great goods, but for the intermediate and lowest goods as well. His goodness ought to be praised more in the case of the greatest goods than in that of the intermediate ones, and more in the case of the intermediate goods than the lowest; but more in all goods than if He had not bestowed all.

EVODIUS: I agree. But the following troubles me, since it involves free will, and we see that free will uses some things for good and some for evil: how is free will to be counted among those goods which we use?

AUGUSTINE: In the same way as we know by reason everything that we know, and nevertheless even reason itself is numbered among the things that we know by reason. Have you forgotten that when we asked what is known by reason, you admitted that reason was known by reason? Do not wonder, then, that we can use the free will by means of itself, if we use other things through our free will. As reason, knowing other things, also knows itself, so the free will, which makes use of other things, also makes use of itself. So also memory grasps not only all the other things which we remember, but also retains itself in us, because we do not forget that we have a memory. It remembers not only other things, but also itself; through memory, in other words, we remember ourselves, other things, and memory itself.

When the will, which is an intermediate good, clings to immutable good, and this good is not private but is common to all (like truth, about which we have said much, though nothing really worthy of it), then man leads a happy life. The happy life—that disposition of the spirit which clings to immutable goods—is man's proper and primary good. In this good lie all the virtues that man cannot use for evil. For although these goods are great and most important in man, it is known that they belong to each man, and are not common. But it is by clinging to truth and wisdom, which are common to all, that all men may become wise and happy.

Moreover, one man does not become happy because of another man's happiness. This is because even when he seeks to be happy by imitating another, he desires to become happy through that by which he saw the other man made happy, that is, by immutable truth, which is common to all.

No one becomes prudent through another's prudence, or brave through another's courage, or temperate through another's temperance. So too, no one becomes just through the justice of another. Instead, man obtains virtues by adapting his spirit to the immutable rules and lights of those virtues which dwell incorruptible in truth itself and in common wisdom, to which the virtuous man has adapted himself and fitted his spirit. The man seeking virtue has determined to imitate this spirit, because it is endowed with virtue. Therefore the will, clinging to common and immutable goods, obtains the first and great goods of man, although it is itself only an intermediate good. The will, however, commits sin when it turns away from immutable and common goods, toward its private good, either something external to itself or lower than itself. It turns to its own private good when it desires to be its own master; it turns to external goods when it busies itself with the private affairs of others or with whatever is none of its concern; it turns to goods lower than itself when it loves the pleasures of the body. Thus a man becomes proud, meddlesome, and lustful; he is caught up in another life which, when compared to the higher one, is death. Yet he is ruled by the administration of divine providence, which places everything in its proper order *[ordinat]* and gives to each what is his own. So it follows that (1) neither the goods desired by sinners, nor the free will itself which we found to have been numbered among certain intermediate goods, are evil in any way, and that (2) evil is a turning away from immutable goods and a turning toward changeable goods. This turning away *[aversio]* and turning toward *[conversio]* result in the just punishment of unhappiness, because they are committed, not under compulsion, but voluntarily.

20. The movement of the will from immutable to transient goods, since it is evil, is not from God.

AUGUSTINE: Because the will is moved when it turns from an immutable good to a changeable one, you may perhaps ask how this movement arises. For the movement itself is certainly evil, although the free will must be numbered among the goods, because without it no one can live rightly. Even if this movement, that is, the turning of the will from the Lord God, is without doubt a sin, we cannot say, can we, that God is the cause of sin? This movement will not be from God, but what then is its origin? If I should answer your question by saying that I do not know, you would perhaps be disappointed; yet that would be the truth, for that which is nothing cannot be known. Only hold to your firm faith, since no good thing comes to your perception, understanding, or thought which is not from God. Nothing of any kind can be discovered which is not from God. Wherever you see measure, number, and order, you cannot hesitate to attribute all these to God, their Maker. When you remove measure, number, and order, nothing at all remains. Even if the beginning of some form were to remain, where you do not find order or measure or number (since wherever these exist, form is complete), you must remove even that very beginning of form which seems to be the artisan's raw material. If the completion of form *[formæ perfectio]* is a good, there is some good even in the rudimentary beginning of form. Thus, if all good is completely removed, no vestige of reality persists; indeed, nothing remains. Every good is from God. There is nothing of any kind that is not from God. Therefore, since the movement of turning away from good, which we admit to be sin, is a defective movement *[defectivus motus]* and since, moreover, every defect comes from nothing, see where this movement belongs: you may be sure that it does not belong to God.

Yet since this defect *[defectus]* is voluntary, it lies within our power. You must not be willing to fear this defect, for if you do not desire it, it will not exist. What greater security can there be than to live a life where what you do not will cannot happen to you? Since a man cannot rise of his own will as he fell by his own will, let us hold with firm faith the right hand of God, Jesus Christ our Lord, which is stretched out to us. Let us wait for Him with steadfast hope; let us love Him with burning love.

If, however—though I myself do not think it necessary—you think that we ought to examine the question of the origin of sin more carefully, let us put it off for some other discussion.

EVODIUS: I follow your will gladly. Let us postpone to some other time the points suggested in this discussion. I will not, however, grant to you that enough has been said on the subject.

CONFESSIONS (in part)

BOOK VIII—CONVERSION

5, 10. . . . It was no iron chain imposed by anyone else that fettered me, but the iron of my own will. The enemy had my power of willing in his clutches, and from it had forged a chain to bind me. The truth is that disordered lust springs from a perverted will; when lust is pandered to, a habit is formed; when habit is not checked, it hardens into compulsion. These were like interlinking rings forming what I have described as a chain, and my harsh servitude used it to keep me under duress.

A new will had begun to emerge in me, the will to worship you disinterestedly and enjoy you, O God, our only sure felicity; but it was not yet capable of surmounting that earlier will strengthened by inveterate custom. And so the two wills fought it out—the old and the new, the one carnal, the other spiritual—and in their struggle tore my soul apart.

*   *   *

8, 19. Within the house of my spirit the violent conflict raged on, the quarrel with my soul that I had so powerfully provoked in our secret dwelling, my heart, and at the height of it I rushed to Alypius with my mental anguish plain upon my face. "What is happening to us?" I exclaimed. "What does this mean? What did you make of it? The untaught are rising up and taking heaven by storm, while we with all our dreary teachings are still groveling in this world of flesh and blood! Are we ashamed to follow, just because they have taken the lead, yet not ashamed of lacking the courage even to fol-

Saint Augustine, *Confessions*, Book VIII (5, 8–12) and XI (14–28), translated by Maria Boulding (New York: New City Press, 1997). ©1997 by the Augustinian Heritage Institute.

low?" Some such words as these I spoke, and then my frenzy tore me away from him, while he regarded me in silent bewilderment. Unusual, certainly, was my speech, but my brow, cheeks and eyes, my flushed countenance and the cadences of my voice expressed my mind more fully than the words I uttered.

Adjacent to our lodgings was a small garden. We were free to make use of it as well as of the house, for our host, who owned the house, did not live there. The tumult in my breast had swept me away to this place, where no one would interfere with the blazing dispute I had engaged in with myself until it should be resolved. What the outcome would be you knew, not I. All I knew was that I was going mad, but for the sake of my sanity, and dying that I might live, aware of the evil that I was but unaware of the good I was soon to become. So I went out into the garden and Alypius followed at my heels; my privacy was not infringed by his presence, and, in any case, how could he abandon me in that state? We sat down as far as possible from the house. I was groaning in spirit and shaken by violent anger because I could form no resolve to enter into a covenant with you, though in my bones I knew that this was what I ought to do, and everything in me lauded such a course to the skies. It was a journey not to be undertaken by ship or carriage or on foot, nor need it take me even that short distance I had walked from the house to the place where we were sitting; for to travel—and more, to reach journey's end—was nothing else but to want to go there, but to want it valiantly and with all my heart, not to whirl and toss this way and that a will half crippled by the struggle, as part of it rose up to walk while part sank down.

20. While this vacillation was at its most intense many of my bodily gestures were of the kind that people sometimes want to perform but cannot, either because the requisite limbs are missing, or because they are bound and restricted, or paralyzed through illness, or in some other way impeded. If I tore out my hair, battered my forehead, entwined my fingers and clasped them round my knee, I did so because I wanted to. I might have wanted to but found myself unable, if my limbs had not been mobile enough to obey. So then, there were plenty of actions that I performed where willing was not the same thing as being able; yet I was not doing the one thing that was incomparably more desirable to me, the thing that I would be able to do as soon as I willed, because as soon as I willed—why, then, I would be willing it! For in this sole instance the faculty to act and the will to act precisely coincide, and the willing is already the doing. Yet this was not happening. My body was more ready to obey the slightest whim of my soul in the matter of moving my limbs, than the soul was to obey its own command in carrying out this major volition, which was to be accomplished within the will alone.

9, 21. How did this bizarre situation arise, how develop? May your mercy shed light on my inquiry, so that perhaps an answer may be found in the mysterious punishments meted out to humankind, those utterly baffling pains that afflict the children of Adam. How then did this bizarre situation arise, how develop? The mind commands the body and is instantly obeyed; the mind commands itself, and meets with resistance. When the mind orders the hand to move, so smooth is the compliance that command can scarcely be distinguished from execution; yet the mind is mind, while the hand is body. When the mind issues its command that the mind itself should will something (and the mind so commanded is no other than itself), it fails to do so. How did this bizarre situation arise, how develop? As I say, the mind commands itself to will something: it would not be giving the order if it did not want this thing; yet it does not do what it commands.

Evidently, then, it does not want this thing with the whole of itself, and therefore the command does not proceed from an undivided mind. Inasmuch as it issues the command, it does will it, but inasmuch as the command is not carried out, it does not will it. What the will is ordering is that a certain volition should exist, and this volition is not some alien thing, but its very self. Hence it cannot be giving the order with its whole self. It cannot be identical with that thing which it is commanding to come into existence, for if it were whole and entire it would not command itself to be, since it would be already.

This partial willing and partial non-willing is thus not so bizarre, but a sickness of the mind, which cannot rise with its whole self on the wings of truth because it is heavily burdened by habit. There are two wills, then, and neither is the whole: what one has the other lacks.

10, 22. Some there are who on perceiving two wills engaged in deliberation assert that in us there are two natures, one good, the other evil, each with a mind of its own. Let them perish from your presence, O God, as perish all who talk wildly and lead our minds astray. They are evil themselves as long as they hold these opinions, yet these same people will be good if they embrace true opinions and assent to true teaching, and so merit the apostle's commendation, You were darkness once, but now you are light in the Lord. The trouble is that they want to be light not in the Lord but in themselves, with their notion that the soul is by nature divine, and so they have become denser darkness still, because by their appalling arrogance they have moved further away from you, the true Light, who enlighten everyone who comes into the world. I warn these people, Take stock of what you are saying, and let it shame you; but once draw near to him and be illumined, and your faces will not blush with shame.

When I was making up my mind to serve the Lord my God at last, as I had long since purposed, I was the one who wanted to follow that course, and I was the one who wanted not to. I was the only one involved. I neither wanted it wholeheartedly nor turned from it wholeheartedly. I was at odds with myself, and fragmenting myself. This disintegration was occurring without my consent, but what it indicated was not the presence in me of a mind belonging to some alien nature but the punishment undergone by my own. In this sense, and this sense only, it was not I who brought it about, but the sin that dwelt within me as penalty for that other sin committed with greater freedom;* for I was a son of Adam.

23. Moreover, if we were to take the number of conflicting urges to signify the number of natures present in us, we should have to assume that there are not two, but many. If someone is trying to make up his mind whether to go to a Manichean conventicle or to the theater, the Manichees declare, "There you are, there's the evidence for two natures: the good one is dragging him our way, the bad one is pulling him back in the other direction. How else explain this dithering between contradictory wills?" But I regard both as bad, the one that leads him to them and the one that lures him back to the theater. They, on the contrary, think that an inclination toward them can only be good.

But consider this: suppose one of our people is deliberating, and as two desires clash he is undecided whether to go to the theater or to our church, will not our opponents too be undecided what attitude to take? Either they will have to admit that it is good will that leads a person to our church, just as good as that which leads to theirs the people who are initiated into their sacred rites and trapped there—and this they are unwilling to admit; or they will conclude that two evil natures and two bad minds are

---

*[That is, by Adam. Augustine uses the comparative to suggest a relative freedom enjoyed by Adam, superior to our own but short of perfect freedom. He was to spell out the distinction later in *Correction and Grace* XII, 33 between *posse non peccare* (the ability not to sin, Adam's privilege), and *non posse peccare* (the perfection of freedom in heaven)].

pitted against each other within one person, in which case their habitual assertion of one good and one evil nature will be erroneous; or, finally, they will be brought round to the truth and no longer deny that when a person is deliberating there is but one soul, thrown into turmoil by divergent impulses.

24. When, therefore, they observe two conflicting impulses within one person, let them stop saying that two hostile minds are at war, one good, the other evil, and that these derive from two hostile substances and two hostile principles. For you are true, O God, and so you chide and rebuke them and prove them wrong. The choice may lie between two impulses that are both evil, as when a person is debating whether to murder someone with poison or a dagger; whether to annex this part of another man's property or that, assuming he cannot get both; whether to buy himself pleasure by extravagant spending or hoard his money out of avarice; whether to go to the circus or the theater if both performances are on the same day—and I would even add a third possibility: whether to go and steal from someone else's house while he has the chance, and a fourth as well: whether to commit adultery while he is about it. All these impulses may occur together, at exactly the same time, and all be equally tempting, but they cannot all be acted upon at once. The mind is then rent apart by the plethora of desirable objects as four inclinations, or even more, do battle among themselves; yet the Manichees do not claim that there are as many disparate substances in us as this.

The same holds true for good impulses. I would put these questions to them: Is it good to find delight in a reading from the apostle? To enjoy the serenity of a psalm? To discuss the gospel? To each point they will reply, "Yes, that is good." Where does that leave us? If all these things tug at our will with equal force, and all together at the same time, will not these divergent inclinations put a great strain on the human heart, as we deliberate which to select? All are good, but they compete among themselves until one is chosen, to which the will, hitherto distracted between many options, may move as a united whole. So too when the joys of eternity call us from above, and pleasure in temporal prosperity holds us fast below, our one soul is in no state to embrace either with its entire will. Claimed by truth for the one, to the other clamped by custom, the soul is torn apart in its distress.

11, 25. Such was the sickness in which I agonized, blaming myself more sharply than ever, turning and twisting in my chain as I strove to tear free from it completely, for slender indeed was the bond that still held me. But hold me it did. In my secret heart you stood by me, Lord, redoubling the lashes of fear and shame in the severity of your mercy, lest I give up the struggle and that slender, fragile bond that remained be not broken after all, but thicken again and constrict me more tightly. "Let it be now," I was saying to myself. "Now is the moment, let it be now," and merely by saying this I was moving toward the decision. I would almost achieve it, but then fall just short; yet I did not slip right down to my starting-point, but stood aside to get my breath back. Then I would make a fresh attempt, and now I was almost there, almost there . . . I was touching the goal, grasping it . . . and then I was not there, not touching, not grasping it. I shrank from dying to death and living to life, for ingrained evil was more powerful in me than new-grafted good. The nearer it came, that moment when I would be changed, the more it pierced me with terror. Dismayed, but not quite dislodged, I was left hanging.

26. The frivolity of frivolous aims, the futility of futile pursuits, these things that had been my cronies of long standing, still held me back, plucking softly at my garment of flesh and murmuring in my ear, "Do you mean to get rid of us? Shall we never be your companions again after that moment . . . never . . . never again? From

that time onward so-and-so will be forbidden to you, all your life long." And what was it that they were reminding me of by those words, "so-and-so," O my God, what were they bringing to my mind? May your mercy banish such memories far from me! What foul deeds were they not hinting at, what disgraceful exploits! But now their voices were less than half as loud, for they no longer confronted me directly to argue their case, but muttered behind my back and slyly tweaked me as I walked away, trying to make me look back. Yet they did slow me down, for I could not bring myself to tear free and shake them off and leap across to that place whither I was summoned, while aggressive habit still taunted me: "Do you imagine you will be able to live without these things?"

27. The taunts had begun to sound much less persuasive, however; for a revelation was coming to me from that country toward which I was facing, but into which I trembled to cross. There I beheld the chaste, dignified figure of Continence. Calm and cheerful was her manner, though modest, pure and honorable her charm as she coaxed me to come and hesitate no longer, stretching kindly hands to welcome and embrace me, hands filled with a wealth of heartening examples. A multitude of boys and girls were there, a great concourse of youth and persons of every age, venerable widows and women grown old in their virginity, and in all of them I saw this that this same Continence was by no means sterile, but the fruitful mother of children conceived in joy from you, her Bridegroom. She was smiling at me, but with a challenging smile, as though to say, "Can you not do what these men have done, these women? Could any of them achieve it by their own strength, without the Lord their God? He it was, the Lord their God, who granted me to them. Why try to stand by yourself, only to lose your footing? Cast yourself on him and do not be afraid: he will not step back and let you fall. Cast yourself upon him trustfully; he will support and heal you." And I was bitterly ashamed, because I could still hear the murmurs of those frivolities, and I was still in suspense, still hanging back. Again she appealed to me, as though urging, "Close your ears against those unclean parts of you which belong to the earth and let them be put to death. They tell you titillating tales, but have nothing to do with the law of the Lord your God."

All this argument in my heart raged only between myself and myself. Alypius stood fast at my side, silently awaiting the outcome of my unprecedented agitation.

12, 28. But as this deep meditation dredged all my wretchedness up from the secret profundity of my being and heaped it all together before the eyes of my heart, a huge storm blew up within me and brought on a heavy rain of tears. In order to pour them out unchecked with the sobs that accompanied them I arose and left Alypius, for solitude seemed to me more suitable for the business of weeping. I withdrew far enough to ensure that his presence—even his—would not be burdensome to me. This was my need, and he understood it, for I think I had risen to my feet and blurted out something, my voice already choked with tears. He accordingly remained, in stunned amazement, at the place where we had been sitting. I flung myself down somehow under a fig-tree and gave free rein to the tears that burst from my eyes like rivers, as an acceptable sacrifice to you. Many things I had to say to you, and the gist of them, though not the precise words, was: "O Lord, how long? How long? Will you be angry for ever? Do not remember our age-old sins." For by these I was conscious of being held prisoner. I uttered cries of misery: "Why must I go on saying, 'Tomorrow . . . tomorrow'? Why not now? Why not put an end to my depravity this very hour?"

29. I went on talking like this and weeping in the intense bitterness of my broken heart. Suddenly I heard a voice from a house nearby—perhaps a voice of some boy or

girl, I do not know—singing over and over again, "Pick it up and read, pick it up and read." My expression immediately altered and I began to think hard whether children ordinarily repeated a ditty like this in any sort of game, but I could not recall ever having heard it anywhere else. I stemmed the flood of tears and rose to my feet, believing that this could be nothing other than a divine command to open the Book and read the first passage I chanced upon; for I had heard the story of how Antony had been instructed by a gospel text. He happened to arrive while the gospel was being read, and took the words to be addressed to himself when he heard, "Go and sell all you possess and give the money to the poor: you will have treasure in heaven. Then come, follow me" [Matt. 19:21]. So he was promptly converted to you by this plainly divine message. Stung into action, I returned to the place where Alypius was sitting, for on leaving it I had put down there the book of the apostle's letters. I snatched it up, opened it and read in silence the passage on which my eyes first lighted: "Not in dissipation and drunkenness, nor in debauchery and lewdness, nor in arguing and jealousy; but put on the Lord Jesus Christ, and make no provision for the flesh or the gratification of your desires" [Rom. 13:13–14]. I had no wish to read further, nor was there need. No sooner had I reached the end of the verse than the light of certainty flooded my heart and all dark shades of doubt fled away.

30. I closed the book, marking the place with a finger between the leaves or by some other means, and told Alypius what had happened. My face was peaceful now. He in return told me what had been happening to him without my knowledge. He asked to see what I had read: I showed him, but he looked further than my reading had taken me. I did not know what followed, but the next verse was, "Make room for the person who is weak in faith." He referred this text to himself and interpreted it to me. Confirmed by this admonition he associated himself with my decision and good purpose without any upheaval or delay, for it was entirely in harmony with his own moral character, which for a long time now had been far, far better than mine.

We went indoors and told my mother, who was overjoyed. When we related to her how it had happened she was filled with triumphant delight and blessed you, who have power to do more than we ask or understand, for she saw that you had granted her much more in my regard than she had been wont to beg of you in her wretched, tearful groaning. Many years earlier you had shown her a vision of me standing on the rule of faith; and now indeed I stood there, no longer seeking a wife or entertaining any worldly hope, for you had converted me to yourself. In so doing you had also converted her grief into a joy far more abundant than she had desired, and much more tender and chaste than she could ever have looked to find in grandchildren from my flesh.

*   *   *

BOOK XI—TIME AND ETERNITY

14, 17. There was therefore never any time when you had not made anything, because you made time itself. And no phases of time are coeternal with you, for you abide, and if they likewise were to abide, they would not be time. For what is time? Who could find any quick or easy answer to that? Who could even grasp it in his thought clearly

God in Act of Creation, from a thirteenth-century French Bible. In the *Confessions,* Augustine argues that God created the world *ex nihilo* (out of nothing) and that God is outside of time. *(Corbis-Bettmann)*

enough to put the matter into words? Yet is there anything to which we refer in conversation with more familiarity, any matter of more common experience, than time? And we know perfectly well what we mean when we speak of it, and understand just as well when we hear someone else refer to it. What, then, is time? If no one asks me, I know; if I want to explain it to someone who asks me, I do not know. I can state with confidence, however, that this much I do know: if nothing passed away there would be no past time; if there was nothing still on its way there would be no future time; and if nothing existed, there would be no present time.

Now, what about those two times, past and future: in what sense do they have real being, if the past no longer exists and the future does not exist yet? As for present time, if that were always present and never slipped away into the past, it would not be time at all; it would be eternity. If, therefore, the present's only claim to be called "time" is that it is slipping away into the past, how can we assert that this thing *is,* when its only title to being is that it will soon cease to be? In other words, we cannot really say that time exists, except because it tends to non-being.*

15, 18. Nonetheless we speak of a long time or a short time, and we do so only of time past or time in the future. For example, we call a hundred years ago a long time in the past, and likewise a hundred years hence a long time in the future; but we call—say—ten days ago a short time past, and ten days hence a short time in the future. But on what grounds can something that does not exist be called long or short? The past no longer exists and the future does not exist yet. We ought not, therefore, to say, "That is a long time," but, when speaking of the past, we should say, "That was long," and of the future, "That will be long."

O my Lord, my light, will your truth not deride us humans for speaking so? This long time in the past: was it long when it was already past, or earlier than that, when it was still present? If the latter, yes, then it might have been long, because there was something to be long; but if it was already past it no longer existed, and therefore could not have been long, since it was not in existence at all. We ought not, therefore, to say, "That era in the past was a long one," for we shall not find anything that was long, for since that point at which it became past time it has no longer had any being. Rather, we ought to say, "That era of time was long while present," because while it was present it was long. It had not yet passed away and so passed out of existence, and so there was something there which could be long. But when it passed away it ceased to be long at that very point when it ceased to be at all.

19. Now, human mind, let us consider whether present time can be long, as you seem to think it can, since you have been granted the power to be aware of duration and to measure it. Answer my questions, then. Is the present century a long period of time? Before you say yes, reflect whether a hundred years can be present. If the first of them is running its course, that year is present, but ninety-nine others are future and therefore as yet have no being. If the second year is running its course, one year is already past, another is present, and the remainder are still to come. In the same fashion we may represent any one of the intervening years of the century as present, and always the years that preceded it will be past, and those that follow it future. Evidently, then, a hundred years cannot be present.

*[This is the heart of the matter for Augustine. He pursues the argument relentlessly throughout the rest of this Book XI, revealing time as something elusive that slips the more swiftly through our fingers the more we try to analyze it or justify our habit of measuring it. The inexorable rush of time toward non-being reveals the fragility of time-bound, time-conditioned creatures, whose only refuge from their native nothingness is the eternity of God.]

Well then, consider whether the one current year at least can be present. If we are in the first month of it, the other months are in the future; if we are in the second, the first month is already past and the rest do not yet exist. Even the current year, then, is not present in its totality, and if it is not present in its totality, the year is not present; for a year consists of twelve months, and while any one of them is current that one is present, but the others are either past or future.

But we must go further, and notice that the current month is not in fact present, because only one day of it is: if we are on the first day, the rest are future; if on the last, the others are past; if on any day in the middle, we shall be midway between past and future days.

20. Look where this leaves us. We saw earlier that present time was the only one of the three that might properly be called long, and now this present time has been pared down to the span of a bare day. But let us take the discussion further, because not even a single day is present all at once. It is made up of night hours and day hours, twenty-four in all. From the standpoint of the first hour all the rest are still future; the last hour looks to all those already past; and any one we pick in between has some before it, others to follow. Even a single hour runs its course through fleeing minutes: whatever portion of it has flown is now past, and what remains is future. If we can conceive of a moment in time which cannot be further divided into even the tiniest of minute particles, that alone can be rightly termed the present; yet even this flies by from the future into the past with such haste that it seems to last no time at all. Even if it has some duration, that too is divisible into past and future; hence the present is reduced to vanishing-point.

What kind of time, then, can be referred to as "a long time"? Future time, perhaps? Then we must not say, "That is a long time," because there is as yet nothing to be long; we will have to say, "That will be long." But when will it be so? If at the point of speaking that period is still in the future, it will not be long, because nothing yet exists to be long; if, however, at the moment when we speak it has begun to exist by emerging from the non-existent future, and so has become present, so that there is something in existence to be long, then this present time proclaims itself incapable of being long for the reasons already discussed.

16, 21. All the same, Lord, we are conscious of intervals of time, and we compare them with each other and pronounce some longer, others shorter. We also calculate by how much this period of time is longer or shorter than that other, and we report that the one is twice or three times as long as the other, or that it is the same length. But when we measure periods of time by our awareness of them, what we measure is passing time. Could anyone measure past periods that no longer exist, or future periods that do not yet exist? Only someone who is bold enough to claim that what has no being can be measured. So then, while time is passing it can be felt and measured, but once past it cannot, because it no longer exists.

17, 22. I am asking questions, Father, not making assertions: rule me, O my God, and shepherd me. For who would make so bold as to tell me that there are not really three tenses or times—past, present and future—as we learned as children and as we in our turn have taught our children, but that there is only present, since the other two do not exist? Or is the truth perhaps that they do exist, but that when a future thing becomes present it emerges from some hiding-place, and then retreats into another hiding-place when it moves from the present into the past? Where, otherwise, did soothsayers see future events, if they do not yet exist? What has no being cannot be seen. Nor would people who tell stories about the past be telling true tales if they had no vision of those past events in their minds; and if the events in question were non-existent they could not be seen. The future and the past must exist, then?

18, 23. Allow me, Lord, to press the question further: O my hope, do not let me lose the thread. If future and past things do exist, I want to know where they are. If this is not yet within my compass, I do know at any rate that, wherever they are, they are not there as future or past, but as present. For if in that place too future things are future, they are not there yet; and if there too past things are past, they are there no longer. Clearly, then, wherever they are and whatever they are, they can only be present. Nonetheless, when a true account is given of past events, what is brought forth from the memory is not the events themselves, which have passed away, but words formed from images of those events which as they happened and went on their way left some kind of traces in the mind through the medium of the senses. This is the case with my childhood, which no longer exists: it belongs to past time which exists no longer, but when I recall it and tell the story I contemplate the image of it which is still in my memory.

Whether something similar occurs in the prediction of future events, in that the seer has a presentiment of images which exist already, I confess, O my God, that I do not know. But this I undoubtedly do know, that we often plan our future actions beforehand, and that the plans in our mind are present to us, though the action we are planning has as yet no being, because it is future. When we set about it, and begin to do what we were planning, then the action will have real being, because then it will be not future but present.

24. However the mysterious presentiment of future events may be explained, only what exists can be seen. But what already exists is not future but present. Therefore when it is claimed that future events are seen, it is not that these things are seen in themselves, because they have as yet no existence, being still future. It may be, however, that their causes, or signs of them, are seen, because these already exist; hence they are not future but present to the people who discern them, and from them future events may take shape in the mind and can be foretold. These ideas in the mind also exist already, and can be inwardly contemplated by people who predict the future.

Let me take an example from a wealth of such occurrences. I watch the dawn, and I give advance notice that the sun is about to rise. What I am looking at is present; what I foretell is future. Not that the sun is future, of course—no, that exists already, but its rising is future; it has not yet happened, yet unless I could imagine the sunrise in my mind, as I do now while I speak of it, I would be unable to forecast it. The dawn, which I am watching in the sky, is not the sunrise, but only precedes it; and similarly the picture I have in my mind is not the sunrise either. But these two realities are present and open to observation, so that the future event can be announced before its time.

We must conclude, then, that future events have no being as yet, and if they have no being yet they do not exist, and if they do not exist it is absolutely impossible for anyone to see them. But they can be predicted on the basis of other things which are already present and hence can be seen.

19, 25. You are the king of your creation; tell me, then: how do you instruct people's minds about the future? You did so teach the prophets. What method can you adopt for teaching what is future, when to you nothing is future at all? Would it be better to say that you teach what is present but has a bearing on the future? Yes, because what does not exist obviously cannot be taught. This method of yours is far above the reach of my mind; it is too much for me and of myself I cannot see it, but I will see it with your help, when you grant me this gift, O gracious light of my secret eyes.

20, 26. What is now clear and unmistakable is that neither things past nor things future have any existence, and that it is inaccurate to say, "There are three tenses or times: past, present and future," though it might properly be said, "There are three tenses or times: the present of past things, the present of present things, and the present of future things." These are three realities in the mind, but nowhere else as far as I can see, for the present of past things is memory, the present of present things is attention, and the present of future things is expectation. If we are allowed to put it that way, I do see three tenses or times, and admit that they are three. Very well, then, let the phrase pass: "There are three tenses or times: past, present and future," as common usage improperly has it: let people go on saying this. I do not mind, nor will I put up any opposition or offer correction, provided we understand what we are saying, and do not assert that either the future or the past exists now. There are few things, in fact, which we state accurately; far more we express loosely, but what we mean is understood.

21, 27. I said just now* that we measure periods of time as they pass, so as to declare this interval twice as long as that, or this equal to that, and report anything else about segments of time that our measurements have revealed. It follows, then, that we measure these intervals of time as they are passing by, as I remarked, and if anyone asks me, "How do you know that?" I must be allowed to reply, "I know it because we do in fact measure them; but what does not exist we cannot measure, and past and future do not exist." But how can we measure present time, when it has no extension?** We can only hope to measure it as it passes by, because once it has passed by there will be no measuring; it will not exist to be measured.

But when it is measured, where does it come from, by what path does it pass, and whither go? Where from, if not from the future? By what path, if not the present? Whither, if not into the past? It comes, then, from what is not yet real, travels through what occupies no space, and is bound for what is no longer real. But what are we trying to measure, if not time that does have some extension? We speak of "half as long," "double the time," "three times as long," "equal in length," and make similar statements about time only in reference to extended time, or duration. Where then is this duration which will give us a chance to measure passing time? In the future, whence it has come to pass us by? But we do not measure what does not yet exist. In the present, perhaps, through which it passes on its way? But where there is no extension we cannot measure. In the past, then, to which it has gone? But we cannot measure what no longer exists.

22, 28. My mind is on fire to solve this most intricate enigma. O Lord, my God, my good Father, through Christ I beg you not to shut against me the door to these truths, so familiar yet so mysterious. Do not slam the door in the face of my desire, nor forbid me entrance to that place where I may watch these things grow luminous as your mercy sheds its light upon them, Lord. To whom should I put my questions about them? And to whom should I confess my stupidity with greater profit than to you, who do not weary of my intense, burning interest in your scriptures? Give me what I love; for I love indeed, and this love you have given me. Give this to me, Father, for you truly know how to give good gifts to your children; give me this gift, for I have only just begun to understand, and the labor is too much for me until you open the door. Through Christ I implore you, in the name of that holy of holies, let no noisy person stand in my way. I too have believed, and so I too speak. This is my hope, for this I live: to contemplate the delight of the Lord. See how old you have made my days; they are slipping away and I know not how.

We speak of one time and another time, of this period of time or that; we ask, "How long did that man speak?" or "How long did he take to do it?" We say, "What a long time it is since I saw so-and-so," and "This syllable has twice the length of that

---

*[That is, in XI, 16, 21.]
**[That is, the ideal present is a point, which has position but no magnitude.]

short one." We say these things and listen to them, we are understood and we understand. They are perfectly plain and fully familiar, yet at the same time deeply mysterious, and we still need to discover their meaning.

23, 29. I was once told by a certain learned man that the movements of the sun, moon and stars themselves constitute time. I did not agree with him. Why, in that case, should not the movements of all corporeal things constitute time? Suppose the luminaries of heaven were to halt, but a potter's wheel went on turning, would there not still be time by which we could measure those rotations, and say either that all of them took the same time, or (if the speed of the wheel varied) that some were of longer duration, others shorter? And when we said this, would we too not be speaking within time; and in the words we used, would there not be some long syllables and some short; and why could that be said of them, unless because some of them had taken a longer time to pronounce than others?

Through this small thing, O God, grant our human minds insight into the principles common to small things and great. The stars and the other luminaries in the sky are there to mark our times and days and years. Yes, granted; but as I would not assert that the revolution of that little wooden wheel itself constituted a day, so my learned informant on the other hand had no business to say that its gyrations did not occupy a space of time.

30. I want to know the essence and nature of time, whereby we measure the movement of bodies and say, for instance, that one movement lasts twice as long as another. Now I have a question to ask. Taking the word "day" to apply not only to the period of sunlight on earth—day as opposed to night, that is—but to the sun's whole course from the east and back to the east again, in the sense that we say, "So many days elapsed," meaning to include the nights, and not reckoning the nights as extra time over and above the days; taking it, then, that the movement of the sun in its circular course from the east back to the east completes a day, this is my question: is it the movement itself that constitutes a day? Or the time it takes? Or both? If the movement constitutes a day, then it would still be one day if the sun were to achieve its circuit in an interval of time equivalent to a single hour. If it is the time it takes, there would not be a day if the space between one sunrise and the next were as short as an hour; the sun would have to go round twenty-four times to make up a day. If both were required complete circuit of the sun and the customary duration of this—we could not call it a day if the sun traveled through its whole circuit in the space of an hour, nor could we if the sun stopped and as much time elapsed as it usually takes to run its whole course from morning to morning.

My question now is not, therefore, what is it that we call a day, but what is time itself, the time whereby we would be able to measure the sun's revolution and say that it had been completed in only half the usual time, if the circuit had occupied only that space of time represented by twelve hours? We could compare the two periods in terms of time and say that one was twice the length of the other, and this would still be possible even if the sun sometimes took the single period, and sometimes the double, to circle from the east and back to the east again. Let no one tell me, then, that time is simply the motion of the heavenly bodies. After all, at the prayer of a certain man the sun halted so that he could press home the battle to victory. The sun stood still, but time flowed on its way, and that fight had all the time it needed to be carried through to the finish.

I see, therefore, that time is a kind of strain or tension. But do I really see it? Or only seem to see? You will show me, O Light, O Truth.

24, 31. Are you commanding me to agree with someone who says that time is the motion of a body? You do not so command me. No corporeal object moves except within time: this is what I hear; this is what you tell me. But that a corporeal object's movement is itself time I do not hear; this you do not say. When a body moves, I measure in terms of time how long it is in motion, from the moment when it begins until its motion ceases. If I did not notice when it began, and it continues to move without my seeing when it stops, I cannot measure the time, except perhaps the interval between the moment when I began to watch and that when I ceased to observe it. If my observation is prolonged, I can only say that the process went on for a long time; I cannot say exactly how long, because when we add a definite indication of a length of time we do so by reference to some agreed standard. "This is as long as that," we say; or "This is twice as long as that other," or something similar. If, on the other hand, we have been able to note the position of some corporeal object when it moves (or when parts of it move, if, for example, it is being turned on a lathe), and we have observed its starting-point and its point of arrival, then we are able to state how much time has elapsed while the movement of the object was effected from the one place to the other, or how long it has taken to revolve on its axis.

Therefore if the motion of an object is one thing, and the standard by which we measure its duration another, is it not obvious which of the two has the stronger claim to be called time? Moreover, if the motion is irregular, so that the object is sometimes moving and sometimes stationary, we measure not only its motion but also its static periods in terms of time, and say, "Its stationary periods were equivalent in length to its phases of motion," or "It was stationary for two or three times as long as it was in motion," or whatever else our calculation has ascertained or estimated roughly—more or less, as we customarily say. Clearly, then, time is not the movement of any corporeal object.

25, 32. I confess to you, Lord, that even today I am still ignorant of what time is; but I praise you, Lord, for the fact that I know I am making this avowal within time, and for my realization that within time I am talking about time at such length, and that I know this "length" itself is long only because time has been passing all the while. But how can I know that, when I do not know what time is? Or perhaps I simply do not know how to articulate what I know? Woe is me, for I do not even know what I do not know!

Behold me here before you, O my God; see that I do not lie. As I speak, this is the true state of my heart. You, you alone, will light my lamp, O Lord; O my God, you will illumine my darkness.

26, 33. Am I not making a truthful confession to you when I praise you for my ability to measure time? But this must mean, O my God, that though I can measure it, I do not know what I am measuring! I measure the movement of a body in terms of time, but surely I am by that same calculation measuring time itself? Would it be possible for me to measure a body's motion, to calculate how long it lasts and how long the object takes to travel from here to there, without also measuring the time within which the motion occurs? With what, then, do I measure time itself? Do we measure a longer time by the standard of a shorter, as we use the cubit to measure the span of a crossbeam? That indeed seems to be how we measure the quantity of a long syllable by that of a short syllable, and decide that the former is twice as long. Similarly we measure the length of poems by the length of their lines, and the length of the lines by the length of the feet, and the length of each foot by the length of its syllables, and the length of a long syllable by that of a short syllable. We do not reckon by the number of pages— that would be to impose a spatial, not a temporal standard—but by the pronunciation as voices recite them and die away. We declare, "That is a lengthy poem, for it consists of so many lines; the lines are long, since each is composed of so many feet; the feet are long, since each extends over so many syllables; and a syllable is long, when it is twice the quantity of a short one."

But the mensuration of time by these methods yields no result that is absolute, since it may happen that the sound of a shorter line, spoken with a drawl, actually lasts longer than that of a longer one hurried over. The same holds for the whole poem, a foot, and a syllable.

I have therefore come to the conclusion that time is nothing other than tension: but tension of what, I do not know, and I would be very surprised if it is not tension of consciousness itself. What am I measuring, I beg you to tell me, my God, when I say in imprecise terms, "This is longer than that," or even, precisely, "This is twice that"? That I am measuring time, I know; but I am not measuring future time, because it does not yet exist, not present time, which is a point without extension, nor past time, which exists no more. What, then, am I measuring? Time as it passes by, but not once it has passed? That was what I said earlier.

27, 34. Stick to it, now, my mind, and pay close attention. God is our ally; and he made us, not we ourselves. Mark where truth brightens to the dawn!

Suppose now that a physical voice begins to sound . . . and goes on sounding . . . and is still sounding . . . and now stops. Now there is silence, and that voice is past and is a voice no longer. Before it sounded forth it was a future thing, so it could not be measured because it did not yet exist; neither can it be now, because it exists no more. Perhaps, then, it could be measured while it was sounding forth, because something did then exist that could be measured? But at that time it was not standing still; it was but a fleeting thing that was speeding on its way. Was it therefore any more measurable while sounding than before or after? Only as something transient was it extended over a period of time whereby it might be measured—only as transient, because the present moment has no duration. If it is argued that the sound could, nevertheless, be measured while it lasted, consider this: another voice begins to sound and is still sounding in a continuous, steady tone. Let us measure it, then, while it is sounding, for once it has fallen silent it will be a thing of the past, and nothing measurable will then exist. By all means let us measure it now, and state how long it lasts.

Ah, but it is still sounding, and there is no way of timing it except from its beginning, when the sound originated, to its end, when it ceases. Obviously we measure any interval of time from some inception to some ending. Hence the sound of a voice which has not yet finished cannot be measured in such a way that anyone can say how long or how short it is, nor can it be declared to be of the same length as something else, or half the length, or twice the length, or anything of the kind. But once finished, it will not exist. So by what criteria will it then be subject to measurement?

All the same we do measure periods of time, not periods which as yet have no being, nor those which have ceased to be, nor those which have no duration, nor those which have no terminus. We measure neither future nor past nor present nor passing time. Yet time we do measure.

35. Take the line, *Deus, creator omnium.** This line consists of eight syllables, short and long alternating. The four short ones—the first, third, fifth and seventh—are thus half the length of the four long ones—the second, fourth, sixth and eighth. Each of these latter lasts twice as long as each of the former; I have only to pronounce the line to report that this is the case, insofar as clear sense-perception can verify it. Relying on this unmistakable evidence of my ear I measure each long syllable by the criterion of a

---

*[Ambrose's evening hymn: "God, Creator of all."]

short one, and perceive that it is twice the quantity. But the syllables make themselves heard in succession; and if the first is short and the second long, how am I to hold on to the short one, how am I to apply it to the long one as a measuring-rod in order to discover that the long one has twice the quantity, when the long one does not begin to sound until the short one has ceased? Am I to measure the long one while it is present? Impossible, because I cannot measure something unfinished. But its completion is its passing away, so what now exists for me to measure? Where is the short syllable I was going to use as a standard? What has become of the long one I want to measure? Both have made their sound, and flown away, and passed by, and exist no more; yet I do my calculation and confidently assert that insofar as the testimony of my trained ear can be trusted, the short is half the long, the long twice the short; and obviously I am speaking about a space of time. I can only do this because the syllables have passed away and are completed. Evidently, then, what I am measuring is not the syllables themselves, which no longer exist, but something in my memory, something fixed and permanent there.

36. In you, my mind, I measure time. Do not interrupt me by clamoring that time has objective existence, nor hinder yourself with the hurly-burly of your impressions. In you, I say, do I measure time. What I measure is the impression which passing phenomena leave in you, which abides after they have passed by: that is what I measure as a present reality, not the things that passed by so that the impression could be formed. The impression itself is what I measure when I measure intervals of time. Hence either time is this impression, or what I measure is not time.

What about when we measure silences, and say that this silent pause lasted as long as that sound? Do we not strain our thought to retain the feeling of a sound's duration, as though it were still audible, so as to be able to estimate the intervals of silence in relation to the whole space of time in question? Without any articulate word or even opening our mouths we go over in our minds poems, their lines, a speech, and we assess their developmental patterns and the time they occupied in relation to one another; and our estimate is no different from what it would have been if we had been reciting them aloud.

Suppose a person wishes to utter a fairly long sound, and has determined beforehand in his own mind how long it is to be. He must have first thought through that period of time in silence and committed the impression of it to memory; then he begins to utter the sound, which continues until it reaches the predetermined end. Or rather, it does not "continue," because the sound is evidently both something already heard and something still to be heard, for the part of it already completed is sound that has been, but the part that remains is sound still to be. Thus it is carried through as our present awareness drags what is future into the past. As the future dwindles the past grows, until the future is used up altogether and the whole thing is past.

28, 37. But how can a future which does not yet exist dwindle or be used up, and how can a past which no longer exists grow? Only because there are three realities in the mind which conducts this operation. The mind expects, and attends, and remembers, so that what it expects passes by way of what it attends to into what it remembers. No one, surely, would deny that the future is as yet non-existent? Yet an expectation of future events does exist in the mind. And would anyone deny that the past has ceased to be? Yet the memory of past events still lives on in the mind. And who would deny that the present has no duration, since it passes in an instant? Yet our attention does endure, and through our attention what is still to be makes its way into the state where it is no more. It is not, therefore, future time which is long, for it does not exist; a long future is simply an expectation of the future which represents it as long. Nor is the past a long period of time, because it does not exist at all; a long past is simply a memory of the past which represents it as long.

38. Suppose I have to recite a poem I know by heart. Before I begin, my expectation is directed to the whole poem, but once I have begun, whatever I have plucked away from the domain of expectation and tossed behind me to the past becomes the business of my memory, and the vital energy of what I am doing is in tension between the two of them: it strains toward my memory because of the part I have already recited, and to my expectation on account of the part I still have to speak. But my attention is present all the while, for the future is being channeled through it to become the past. As the poem goes on and on, expectation is curtailed and memory prolonged, until expectation is entirely used up, when the whole completed action has passed into memory.

What is true of the poem as a whole is true equally of its individual stanzas and syllables. The same is true of the whole long performance, in which this poem may be a single item. The same thing happens in the entirety of a person's life, of which all his actions are parts; and the same in the entire sweep of human history, the parts of which are individual human lives.

CITY OF GOD (in part)

BOOK VIII

CHAPTER 1

I must now turn to a matter which calls for much deeper thought than was needed to resolve the issues raised in the previous Books. I mean natural theology. Unlike the poetical theology of the stage which flaunts the crimes of the gods and the political theology of the city which publicizes their evil desires, and both of which reveal them as dangerous demons rather than deities, natural theology cannot be discussed with men in the street but only with philosophers, that is, as the name implies, with lovers of wisdom.

I may add that, since divine truth and scripture clearly teach us that God, the Creator of all things, is Wisdom, a true philosopher will be a lover of God. That does not mean that all who answer to the name are really in love with genuine wisdom, for it is one thing to be and another to be called a philosopher. And, therefore, from all the philosophers whose teachings I have learned from books I shall select only those with whom it would not be improper to discuss this subject.

I shall not bother in this work to refute all the errors of all the philosophers, but only such as pertain to theology—which term from its Greek derivation I take to mean a study of the divine nature. My only purpose is to challenge the opinions of those

St. Augustine, *City of God,* Books VIII, 1–12; XI, 26; XII, 1–9; XIX, 11–17 from *Fathers of the Church; Writings of Saint Augustine; Saint Augustine: City of God,* translated by Gerald G. Walsh, Daniel J. Honan, and Grace Monahan (Washington, DC: The Catholic University of America Press, 1952, 1954). Reprinted by permission.

philosophers who, while admitting that there is a God who concerns himself with human affairs, claim that, since the worship of this one unchangeable God is not sufficient to attain happiness even after death, lesser gods, admittedly created and directed by this supreme God, should also be reverenced.

I must say that such philosophers were nearer to the truth than Varro was. His idea of natural theology embraced at most the universe and the world-soul. They, on the contrary, acknowledged a God who transcends the nature of every kind of soul, a God who created the visible cosmos of heaven and earth, and the spirit of every living creature, and who, by the communication of His own immutable and immaterial light, makes blessed the kind of rational and intellectual soul which man possesses.

Even the most superficial student will recognize in these men the Platonic philosophers, so named after their master, Plato. I shall speak briefly about Plato's ideas, in so far as they are relevant to the matter in hand, but first I must review the opinions of his predecessors in the field of philosophy.

CHAPTER 2

The legacy of literature written in the universally admired Greek language records two schools of philosophy. They are, first, the Italian, established in that part of Italy formerly known as Magna Graecia; and second, the Ionian, in that country which is now called Greece. Pythagoras of Samos is said to be the founder of the Italian school and also the originator of the word philosophy. Before his time, any person of outstanding achievement was called a sage. But when Pythagoras, who considered it arrogance to call one's self wise, was asked his profession, he replied that he was a philosopher, that is to say, a man in pursuit of, or in love with, wisdom.

Thales of Miletus, who initiated the Ionian School, was one of the celebrated Seven Wise Men. While the remaining six were distinguished by balanced lives and moral teachings, Thales took up the study of nature and committed the results of his researches to writing. He won particular applause by his mastery of astronomical calculations and by his predictions of solar and lunar eclipses. His deliberate purpose in this was to found a school that would survive him. His main theory was that the primary stuff of all things is water, and that from this principle originated the elements, the cosmos and everything which the world produced. As far as he was concerned, nothing of all this universe, so marvelous to gaze upon, was directed by divine intelligence.

His disciple and successor, Anaximander, proposed a new cosmological theory. For him, there could be no one ultimate element of all things such as water; rather, each thing is derived from principles of its own. Hence, he held, the number of principles is infinite, and from these arise uncounted worlds and all that they produce. And, in an endless succession of dissolution and becoming, no one world endures longer than its period permits. Like Thales, he found no place for any divine direction in the processes of nature.

Anaximander's disciple, Anaximenes, believed that all cosmic energy is derived from air, which he considered infinite. He neither denied nor ignored the gods; nevertheless, he taught that they were creatures of the air and not its creators. His pupil, Anaxagoras, realizing that divine spirit was the cause of all visible things, held that the divine mind, using infinite matter, consisting of unlike particles, made each particular thing out of its own kind of like particles.

Diogenes, another follower of Anaximenes, held that air was the ultimate element of all things, but that nothing could be produced from it without the agency of the divine reason, which permeated it. Anaxagoras was followed by his pupil Archelaus. He, too, asserted that everything in the universe was composed of like particles, which, however, were informed by intelligence. This mind, by causing the conjunction and dissolution of the eternal bodies or particles, was the source of all movements. Archelaus is said to have taught Socrates, the master of Plato. This brief review has been but a preparation for the discussion of Plato's philosophy.

Chapter 3

To Socrates goes the credit of being the first one to channel the whole of philosophy into an ethical system for the reformation and regulation of morals. His predecessors without exception had applied themselves particularly to physics or natural science. I do not think that it can be definitely decided just why Socrates chose to follow this course. It has been suggested that he did so because he had become wearied of obscure and uncertain investigations, and preferred to turn his mind to a clean-cut objective, to that secret of human happiness which seems to have been the sole purpose of all philosophical research. Others have claimed, more kindly, that he did not think it right for minds darkened with earthly desires to reach out beyond their limits to the realm of the divine.

Socrates realized that his predecessors had been seeking the origin of all things, but he believed that these first and highest causes could be found only in the will of the single and supreme Divinity and, therefore, could be comprehended only by a mind purified from passion. Hence his conclusion, that he must apply himself to the acquisition of virtue, so that his mind, freed from the weight of earthly desires, might, by its own natural vigor, lift itself up to eternal realities and, with purified intelligence, contemplate the very nature of that immaterial and immutable light in which the causes of all created natures abidingly dwell. Nevertheless, with his marvelous combination of wit and words, pungency and politeness, and with his trick of confessing ignorance and concealing knowledge he used to tease and poke fun at the folly of ignoramuses who talked as though they knew the answers to those moral problems in which he seemed wholly absorbed.

The result was that he incurred their enmity. He was falsely accused and condemned to death. However, the very city of Athens that had publicly condemned him began publicly to mourn his loss, and the wrath of the people was so turned against his two accusers that one of them was killed by an angry mob and the other escaped a similar death only by voluntary and perpetual exile.

Socrates was thus so highly distinguished both in life and in death that he left behind him numerous disciples. They rivaled one another in zealous discussions of those ethical problems where there is question of the supreme good and, hence, of human happiness.

In his discussions, Socrates had a way of proposing and defending his theories and then demolishing them. No one could make out exactly what he believed. Consequently, each of his followers picked what he preferred and sought the supreme good in his heart's desire.

Now the truth is that the supreme good is that which, when attained, makes all men happy. Yet, so varied in regard to this good were the views of the Socratics that it seems hardly credible that all of them were followers of one and the same master.

Some, like Aristippus, claimed that pleasure was the highest good; others, like Antisthenes, virtue. The men and their views are so numerous and varied that it would be irksome to mention them all.

CHAPTER 4

Of the pupils of Socrates, Plato was so remarkable for his brilliance that he has deservedly outshone all the rest. He was born in Athens of a good family and by his marvelous ability easily surpassed all his fellow disciples. Realizing, however, that neither his own genius nor Socratic training was adequate to evolve a perfect system of philosophy, he traveled far and wide to wherever there was any hope of gaining some valuable addition to knowledge. Thus, in Egypt he mastered the lore which was there esteemed. From there he went to lower Italy, famous for the Pythagorean School, and there successfully imbibed from eminent teachers all that was then in vogue in Italian philosophy.

However, Plato's special affection was for his old master—so much so that in practically all the Dialogues he makes Socrates, with all his charm, the mouthpiece not only of his own moral arguments but of all that Plato learned from others or managed to discover himself.

Now, the pursuit of wisdom follows two avenues—action and contemplation. Thus, one division of philosophy may be called active; the other part, contemplative. The former deals with the conduct of life; that is to say, with the cultivation of morals. Contemplative philosophy considers natural causality and truth as such. Socrates excelled in practical wisdom; Pythagoras favored contemplation, and to this he applied his whole intelligence.

It is to Plato's praise that he combined both in a more perfect philosophy, and then divided the whole into three parts: first, moral philosophy which pertains to action; second, natural philosophy whose purpose is contemplation; third, rational philosophy which discriminates between truth and error. Although this last is necessary for both action and contemplation, it is contemplation especially which claims to reach a vision of the truth. Hence, this threefold division in no way invalidates the distinction whereby action and contemplation are considered the constituent elements of the whole of philosophy. Just what Plato's position was in each of these three divisions—that is to say, just what he knew or believed to be the end of all action, the cause of all nature, the light of all reason—I think it would be rash to affirm and would take too long to discuss at length.

Plato was so fond of following the well-known habit of his master of dissimulating his knowledge or opinions that in Plato's own works (where Socrates appears as a speaker) it is difficult to determine just what views he held even on important questions. However, of the views which are set forth in his writings, whether his own or those of others which seemed to have pleased him, a few must be recalled and included here. In some places, Plato is on the side of the true religion which our faith accepts and defends. At other times he seems opposed; for example, on the respective merits of monotheism and polytheism in relation to genuine beatitude after death.

Perhaps this may be said of the best disciples of Plato—of those who followed most closely and understood most clearly the teachings of a master rightly esteemed above all other pagan philosophers—that they have perceived, at least, these truths about God: that in Him is to be found the cause of all being, the reason of all thinking, the rule of all living. The first of these truths belongs to natural, the second to rational, the third to moral philosophy.

Now, if man was created so that by his highest faculty he might attain to the highest of all realities, that is, to the one, true and supreme God, apart from whom no nature exists, no teaching is true, no conduct is good, then let us seek Him in whom all we find is real, know Him in whom all we contemplate is true, love Him in whom all things for us are good.

CHAPTER 5

If, then, Plato defined a philosopher as one who knows, loves and imitates the God in whom he finds his happiness, there is little need to examine further. For, none of the other philosophers has come so close to us as the Platonists have, and, therefore, we may neglect the others. Take for example, the theology of the stage. It beguiles the minds of the pagans with the crimes of the gods. Or, take political theology, according to which impure demons under the name of gods seduce the populace who are slaves of earthly pleasures, and demand human errors as divine honors for themselves. They excite in their worshipers an impure passion to watch the demons sinning on the stage as though this were an act of worship, and they are even more satisfied than the spectators with the plays that exhibit their human passions. Proper as such rites may seem in places of worship, they are debased by connection with the obscenity of the theatres; while the filth of the stage loses its foulness by comparison with the rites that take place in the temples.

Nor is the theology of Varro any better in its interpretation of these rites as symbolic of heaven and earth and the origins and movements of mortal affairs. The fact is, they do not denote what he tries to insinuate. His fancy gets the better of the truth. And, even were he right, it would still be wrong for a rational soul to worship as a god something which, in the order of nature, is in a lower category or to submit as to gods to those very things over which the true God has put men in charge.

Finally, the Platonic theology is superior to those revealing writings about the sacred rites which Numa Pompilius had buried with himself in order to hide them and which, when turned up by a plough, the Senate ordered to be burned. And to do justice to Numa, we should include in this class the letter that Alexander of Macedon wrote to his mother, telling her what had been revealed to him by Leo, an Egyptian high priest, to the effect that all the gods, major as well as minor, were nothing more than mortal men—not only Picus and Faunus, Aeneas and Romulus, Hercules and Aesculapius, Bacchus, son of Semele, the twin sons of Tyndareus, and such like mortals who are reckoned as gods, but even the greater gods whom Cicero in his Tusculan Disputations alludes to without mentioning their names; that is, Jupiter, Juno, Saturn, Vulcan, Vesta, and many others whom Varro attempts to identify with the parts or elements of the world. Fearful that he had revealed a great mystery, Leo begged Alexander to have his mother burn the message conveyed to her.

Certainly, all such fancies of both the mythical and civil theologies should yield to the Platonists who acknowledged the true God as the author of being, the light of truth and the giver of blessedness. So, too, those philosophers, the materialists who believe that the ultimate principles of nature are corporeal, should yield to those great men who had knowledge of so great a God. Such were Thales, who found the cause and principle of things in water, Anaximenes in air, the Stoics in fire, Epicurus in atoms, that is, minute indivisible and imperceptible corpuscles. And so of the rest, whose names it is needless to mention, who maintained that bodies, simple or compound, animate or inanimate, but nevertheless material, were the root of all reality.

The Epicureans, for example, believed that life could be produced from lifeless matter. Others taught that both animate and inanimate things derive from a living principle but that this principle must be as material as the things themselves. The Stoics claimed that fire, one of the four material elements of this visible world, had life and intelligence, that it was the creator of the universe and all within it; in fact, that it was God.

Now, philosophers of this type could think only about such matters as their sense-bound minds suggested to them. Yet they have within themselves something they have never seen and they can see in their imagination, without looking at it, an external object which they have previously seen. Now, whatever can be so imagined in the mind's eye is certainly not a body but only the likeness of a body, and that power of the mind which can perceive this likeness is itself neither a body nor an image of a body. Moreover, that faculty which perceives and judges whether this likeness is beautiful or ugly is certainly superior to the object judged.

Now, this faculty is a man's reason, the essence of his rational soul, which is certainly not material, since the likeness of a body which is seen and judged in the mind of a thinking person is not material. The soul, then, cannot be one of the four elements out of which the visible, material cosmos is composed—earth, water, air, and fire. And if our mind is not material, how can God the Creator of the soul be material?

As I said before, let all such philosophers give place to the Platonists. That goes for those, too, who were ashamed to acknowledge a material god, yet thought that men's souls were of the same nature as His—so little were they moved by the fact of a mutability in the soul that it would be unthinkable to attribute to the nature of God. Their answer to this difficulty was that the soul is unalterable in itself but is affected by the body. They might as well have said that the flesh is wounded because of the body, but in itself is invulnerable. The fact is that what is immutable can be changed by nothing. But, if a thing can be changed by a body, it can be changed by something and, therefore, cannot rightly be called immutable.

CHAPTER 6

The Platonic philosophers, then, so deservedly considered superior to all the others in reputation and achievement, well understood that no body could be God and, therefore, in order to find Him, they rose beyond all material things. Convinced that no mutable reality could be the Most High, they transcended every soul and spirit subject to change in their search for God. They perceived that no determining form by which any mutable being is what it is—whatever be the reality, mode or nature of that form—could have any existence apart from Him who truly exists because His existence is immutable.

From this it follows that neither the whole universe, with its frame, figures, qualities and ordered movement, all the elements and bodies arranged in the heavens and on earth, nor any life—whether merely nourishing and preserving as in trees, or both vegetative and sensitive as in animals, or which is also intellectual as in man, or which needs no nourishment but merely preserves, feels and knows as in angels can have existence apart from Him whose existence is simple and indivisible. For, in God, being is not one thing and living another—as though He could be and not be living. Nor in God is it one thing to live and another to understand—as though He could live without understanding. Nor in Him is it one thing to know and another to be blessed—as though He could know and not be blessed. For, in God, to live, to know, to be blessed is one and the same as to be.

The Platonists have understood that God, by reason of His immutability and simplicity, could not have been produced from any existing thing, but that He Himself made all those things that are. They argued that whatever exists is either matter or life;

that life is superior to matter; that the appearance of a body is sensible, whereas the form of life is intelligible. Hence, they preferred intelligible form to sensible appearance. We call things sensible which can be perceived by sight and bodily touch.

If there is any loveliness discerned in the lineaments of the body, or beauty in the movement of music and song, it is the mind that makes this judgment. This means that there must be within the mind a superior form, one that is immaterial and independent of sound and space and time. However, the mind itself is not immutable, for, if it were, all minds would judge alike concerning sensible forms. Actually, a clever mind judges more aptly than the stupid one; a skilled one better than one unskilled; an experienced one better than one inexperienced. Even the same mind, once it improves, judges better than it did before.

Undoubtedly, anything susceptible of degrees is mutable, and for this reason, the most able, learned and experienced philosophers readily concluded that the first form of all could not be in any of these things in which the form was clearly mutable. Once they perceived various degrees of beauty in both body and mind, they realized that, if all form were lacking, their very existence would end. Thus, they argued that there must be some reality in which the form was ultimate, immutable and, therefore, not susceptible of degrees. They rightly concluded that only a reality unmade from which all other realities originate could be the ultimate principle of things.

So that what is known about God, God Himself manifested to them, since "his invisible attributes are clearly seen by them—his everlasting power also and divinity— being understood through the things that are made" (Rom. 1:19–20). By Him, also all visible and temporal things were created. Enough has been said, I think, concerning what the Platonists call physical or natural philosophy.

CHAPTER 7

As for the second part of philosophy, logic or rational philosophy, the Platonists are beyond all comparison with those who taught that the criterion of truth is in the bodily senses, and who would have us believe that all knowledge is to be measured and ruled by such doubtful and deceitful testimony. I mean the Epicureans and even the Stoics. For all their passion for adroitness in disputation or, as they would say, dialectics, even this was reckoned a matter of sense perception. They maintained that it was by sensation that the mind conceived those notions (or *ennoíai* as they would say) which are needed for clear definitions and, hence, for the unification and communication of the whole system of learning and teaching.

When these philosophers quote their famous dictum that only the wise are beautiful, I often wonder by just what bodily senses they have perceived that beauty, by what kind of fleshy eyes they could have possibly beheld the form and fairness of wisdom.

Certainly, the Platonists, whom we rightly prefer to all others, were able to distinguish what is apprehended by the mind from what is experienced by the senses, without either denying or exaggerating the faculties of sense. As for that light of our minds by which all can be learned, that, they declared, was the very God by whom all things were made.

CHAPTER 8

The final division is moral philosophy or, to use the Greek name, ethics. It deals with the supreme good, by reference to which all our actions are directed. It is the good we seek for itself and not because of something else and, once it is attained, we seek nothing further to make us happy. This, in fact, is why we call it our end, because other things are desired on account of this summum bonum, while it is desired purely for itself.

Now, some philosophers maintained that this happiness-giving good for man arises from the body; others claimed that it has its source in the soul; while a third group held that it derives from both.

All philosophers have realized that man is made up of body and soul and, therefore, that the possibility of his well-being must proceed either from one of these constituents or from both together, the final good, whereby man would be happy, being the one to which all human actions would be referred and beyond which they would seek nothing to which it might be referred.

Hence, those who are said to have added to the list of goods the "extrinsic" good—such as honor, glory, wealth and so on—did not mean this as though it were a supreme good to be sought for its own sake, but merely as a relative good and one that was good for good men but bad for the wicked.

Thus, those who sought for human good either in man's body or in his mind or in both did not think they had to search outside of man himself to find it. Only those who looked to the body sought it in man's lower nature; those who looked to the soul, in man's higher nature; and the others, in man as a whole; but in every case they sought it only in man himself.

This threefold division of opinion concerning the summum bonum resulted, not in three, but in a multitude of philosophical sects and dissensions because of the varying views as to what constituted the good of the body, the good of the soul and the good of the whole man.

The definers of all these defective conclusions should yield to those philosophers who taught that man is never fully blessed, in the enjoyment of either corporal or spiritual good, but only by a fruition in God. This joy in God is not like any pleasure found in physical or intellectual satisfaction. Nor is it such as a friend experiences in the presence of a friend. But, if we are to use any such analogy, it is more like the eye rejoicing in light. Elsewhere, with God's help I shall try to explain the nature of this analogy. For the moment, let it suffice to recall the doctrine of Plato that a virtuous life is the ultimate end of man and that only those attain to it who know and imitate God and find their blessedness wholly in this. Consequently, Plato did not hesitate to say that to philosophize is to love that God whose nature is incorporeal.

From this we infer that the pursuer of wisdom, that is, the philosopher, will only be truly happy when he begins to rejoice in God. Certainly, not every one who delights in what he loves is always blessed, for many are unhappy in loving things they should not love and still more wretched once they begin to enjoy them. On the other hand, no one is really happy until his love ends in fruition. For, even those who love what they should not love do not consider loving but only fruition as the source of their satisfaction.

Who, then, but the very sorriest of persons would deny that a man is really happy who finds fruition in what he loves when what he loves is his true and highest good? Now, for Plato, this true and highest good was God, and, therefore, he calls a philosopher a lover of God, implying that philosophy is a hunt for happiness which ends only when a lover of God reaches fruition in God.

CHAPTER 9

Philosophers, therefore, of whatever sort who have believed that the true and supreme God is the cause of created things, and the light by which they are known and the good toward which our actions are directed, and that He is the source from which our nature has its origin, our learning truth, our life its happiness—all these we prefer to others and recognize them as our neighbors. It does not matter whether they call themselves—as, perhaps, they should—Platonists, or whether they give their school some other name. Nor need we enquire whether it was only the leaders of the Ionian School—like Plato and his best disciples—who were teachers of these truths, or whether we should include the Italians on account of Pythagoras and the Pythagoreans and, perhaps, others of similar views. For all I know, there may have been men reckoned as wise men or philosophers in other parts of the world who shared these views and doctrines—Atlantic Libyans, Egyptians, Indians, Persians, Chaldeans, Scythians, Gauls, and Spaniards.

CHAPTER 10

Doubtless, it could happen that a Christian, well versed in ecclesiastical literature, might not be familiar with the name of Platonists nor even know that among Greek-speaking people two distinct schools of philosophy have flourished: the Ionian and the Italian. Nevertheless, he is not so naive as not to know that philosophers look upon themselves as the lovers, if not the possessors, of wisdom; and he is on his guard against materialistic philosophers, who give no thought to the Creator of the world.

The Christian heeds carefully the apostolic admonition which says: "See to it that no one deceives you by philosophy and vain deceit . . . according to the elements of the world" (Col. 2:8). But the same Apostle tells him not to decry all as materialistic philosophers, for of some he says: "What may be known about God is manifest to them. For God has manifested it to them. For since the creation of the world his invisible attributes are clearly seen—his everlasting power also and divinity—being understood through the things that are made" (Rom. 1:19–20). And again, speaking to the Athenians, after the magnificent remark about God which so few can appreciate, namely, that "in Him we live and move and have our being," he went on to add: "as indeed some of your own (poets) have said" (Acts 17:28).

The Christian knows, of course, how to distrust the doctrines of even these latter where they are wrong. Thus, the very Scripture which says that God manifested His invisible attributes to be seen and understood also says that they failed to worship the true God rightly because they rendered to creatures divine honors that were due to Him alone. "Although they knew God, they did not glorify him as God or give thanks, but became vain in their reasonings, and their senseless minds have been darkened. For while professing to be wise, they have become fools, and they have changed the glory of the incorruptible God for an image made like to corruptible man and to birds and fourfooted beasts and creeping things" (Rom. 1:21–23). Here the Apostle has in mind the Romans, Greeks and Egyptians, all boastful of their renown for wisdom.

This is a matter that I intend to debate with these philosophers later on. Yet we prefer them to all others inasmuch as they agree with us concerning one God, the Creator of the universe, who is not only incorporeal, transcending all corporeal beings, but also incorruptible, surpassing every kind of soul—our source, our light, our goal.

Now, it may happen that the Christian has not studied the works of these philosophers, nor learned to use their terms in disputation. He may not designate that part of philosophy which treats of the investigation of nature as natural (if he speaks Latin) or as physical (if Greek); nor that part which seeks the ways by which truth may be perceived as rational or logical; nor that part which treats of conduct, with the highest good which is to be sought and the supreme evil to be avoided, as moral or ethics. Nevertheless, he knows that from the one, true and infinitely good God we have a nature by which we were made in His image, faith by which we know God and ourselves, and grace whereby we reach beatitude in union with God.

This, then, is the reason for preferring the Platonists to all other philosophers. While the others consumed time and talent in seeking the causes of things, and the right ways of learning and living, the Platonists, once they knew God, discovered where to find the cause by which the universe was made, the light by which all truth is seen, the fountain from which true happiness flows.

If philosophers, then, whether Platonists or wise men of any nation whatsoever, hold these truths concerning God, they agree with us. However, I have preferred to plead this cause with the Platonists because I know their writings better. The Greeks, whose language is universally esteemed, have eloquently eulogized these writings. The Latins, captivated either by their fascination or their fame, have gladly studied them, and, by translating them into our own language, have added to them new light and luster.

CHAPTER 11

Some of our fellow Christians are astonished to learn that Plato had such ideas about God and to realize how close they are to the truths of our faith. Some even have been led to suppose that he was influenced by the Prophet Jeremiah during his travels in Egypt or, at least, that he had access to the scriptural prophecies; and this opinion I followed in some of my writings.

However, a careful calculation of dates according to historical chronology shows that Plato was born almost one hundred years after Jeremiah prophesied, and that nearly sixty years intervened between Plato's death at the age of eighty-one and the time when the Septuagint translation was begun. Ptolemy, King of Egypt, it will be remembered, asked that the Hebraic prophecies be sent to him from Judea and he arranged to have them translated and safeguarded by seventy Hebrew scholars who were also experts in Greek.

Therefore, it follows that, while journeying in Egypt, Plato could not have seen Jeremiah who was long since dead, nor could he have read the Scriptures which had not yet been rendered into Greek, his native tongue. Of course, it is just possible that Plato, who was an indefatigable student and who used an interpreter to delve into Egyptian literature, may have done the same with the Scriptures. I do not mean to suggest that he undertook a translation of them. That was a feat which Ptolemy alone could accomplish by virtue of his liberality and of others' respect for his kingly power. But Plato could have learned from conversation the content of the Scriptures, without fully understanding their meaning.

Certain evidence favors this belief. For example, the first book of Genesis begins: "In the beginning God created the heavens and the earth; the earth was waste and void; darkness covered the abyss, and the spirit of God was stirring above the waters" (Gen. 1:1–2). Plato in the *Timaeus* (31b), which deals with the origin of the world, says that in this work God first united earth and fire. Now it is clear that Plato locates fire in the heavens. His statement, therefore, bears a certain resemblance to the words: "In the beginning God created the heavens and the earth."

Plato also mentions two intermediary elements, water and air, by means of which the extremes, earth and fire, were united. This idea, perhaps, originated from his interpretation of the verse: "the spirit of God was stirring above the waters." Paying little attention to the meaning which Scripture habitually ascribes to spirit and remembering that air is often called breath or spirit, Plato could easily have assumed that all four elements were mentioned in this text.

Then, too, Plato's definition of a philosopher—one who loves God—contains an idea which shines forth everywhere in Scripture. But the most palpable proof to my mind that he was conversant with the sacred books is this, that when Moses, informed by an angel that God wished him to deliver the Hebrews from Egypt, questioned the angel concerning the name of the one who had sent him, the answer received was this: "I AM WHO AM. Thus shalt thou say to the children of Israel: He who is, hath sent me to you" (Exod. 3:14), as though, in comparison with Him who, being immutable, truly is, all mutable things are as if they were not. Now, Plato had a passionate perception of this truth and was never tired of teaching it. Yet, I doubt whether this idea can be found in any of the works of Plato's predecessors except in the text: "I AM WHO AM, and you shall say to them: He who is hath sent me to you."

CHAPTER 12

Whether, then, Plato got his ideas from the works of earlier writers or, as seems more likely, in the way described in the words of the Apostle: "Because that which is known of God is manifest in them. For God hath manifested it unto them. For the invisible things of him, from the creation of the world, are clearly seen, being understood by the things that are made: His eternal power also and divinity" (Rom. 1:19–20), it seems to me that I have sufficiently justified my choice of the Platonic philosophers for the purpose of discussing this present problem in natural theology. The question is this: In order to secure happiness after death, should man worship a single God or many?

The main reason for selecting the Platonists is the superiority of their conceptions concerning one God, Creator of heaven and earth, and, hence, their greater reputation in the judgment of posterity. It is true that Aristotle, a disciple of Plato, was a man of extraordinary genius and wide reputation (though in literary style inferior to Plato) who easily surpassed many others, and no less true that the Peripatetic school (so called from Aristotle's custom of teaching while walking) attracted many disciples even while his teacher, Plato, was alive. So, too, after the death of Plato, a son of his sister, Speusippus, and Xenocrates, Plato's favorite pupil, succeeded him in his Academy and, for this reason, they and their successors are called Academics. Nevertheless, the very best of the Platonists are those relatively recent philosophers who, refusing to be styled either Peripatetics or Academics, have called themselves Platonists. Among these last are those highly distinguished Greek scholars, Plotinus, Iamblichus and Porphyry. A hardly less notable Platonist was the African Apuleius, who was a master of both Greek and Latin. All of these and many others of the same school, not to mention Plato himself, believed in polytheistic worship.

*   *   *

BOOK XI

CHAPTER 26

We ourselves can recognize in ourselves an image of God, in the sense of an image of the Trinity. Of course, it is merely an image and, in fact, a very remote one. There is no question of identity nor of co-eternity nor, in one word, of consubstantiality with Him. Nevertheless, it is an image which by nature is nearer to God than anything else in all creation, and one that by transforming grace can be perfected into a still closer resemblance.

For, we are, and we know that we are, and we love to be and to know that we are. And in this trinity of being, knowledge, and love there is not a shadow of illusion to disturb us. For, we do not reach these inner realities with our bodily senses as we do external objects, as, for example, color by seeing, sound by hearing, odor by smelling, flavor by tasting, hard or soft objects by touching. In the case of such sensible things, the best we can do is to form very close and immaterial images which help us to turn them over in our minds, to hold them in our memory, and thus to keep our love for them alive. But, without any illusion of image, fancy, or phantasm, I am certain that I am, that I know that I am, and that I love to be and to know.

In the face of these truths, the quibbles of the skeptics lose their force. If they say; "What if you are mistaken?"—well, if *I* am mistaken, I am. For, if one does not exist, he can by no means be mistaken. Therefore, I am, if I am mistaken. Because, therefore, I am, if I am mistaken, how can I be mistaken that I am, since it is certain that I am, if I am mistaken? And because, if I could be mistaken, I would have to be the one who is mistaken, therefore, I am most certainly not mistaken in knowing that I am. Nor, as a consequence, am I mistaken in knowing that I know. For, just as I know that I am, I also know that I know. And when I love both to be and to know, then I add to the things I know a third and equally important knowledge, the fact that I love.

Nor am I mistaken that I love, since I am not mistaken concerning the objects of my love. For, even though these objects were false, it would still be true that I loved illusions. For, if this were not true, how could I be reproved and prohibited from loving illusions? But, since these objects are true and certain, who can doubt that, when they are loved, the loving of them is also true and certain? Further, just as there is no one who does not wish to be happy, so there is no one who does not wish to exist. For, how can anyone be happy if he does not exist?

*   *   *

BOOK XII

CHAPTER 1

In the previous book we saw something of the beginning of the two cities, so far as angels are concerned. In the same way, we must now proceed to the creation of men and see the beginning of the cities so far as it concerns the kind of rational creatures who are mortal. First, however, a few remarks about the angels must be made in order to make it as clear as I can how there is no real difficulty or impropriety in speaking of a single society composed of both men and angels; and why, therefore, it is right to say that there are not four cities or societies, namely, two of angels and two of men, but only two, one of them made up of the good—both angels and men—and the other of those who are evil.

There is no reason to doubt that the contrary dispositions which have developed among these good and bad angels are due, not to different natures and origins, for God the Author and Creator of all substances has created them both, but to the dissimilar choices and desires of these angels themselves. Some, remaining faithful to God, the common good of all, have lived in the enjoyment of His eternity, truth, and love, while others, preferring the enjoyment of their own power, as though they were their own good, departed from the higher good and common blessedness for all and turned to goods of their own choosing.

Preferring the pomp of pride to this sublimity of eternity, the craftiness of vanity to the certainty of truth, and the turmoil of dissension to the union of love, they became proud, deceitful, and envious.

Since the happiness of all angels consists in union with God, it follows that their unhappiness must be found in the very contrary, that is, in not adhering to God. To the question: "Why are the good angels happy?" the right answer is: "Because they adhere to God." To the question: "Why are the others unhappy?" the answer is: "Because they do not adhere to God." In fact, there is no other good which can make any rational or intellectual creature happy except God. Not every creature has the potentialities for happiness. Beasts, trees, stones, and such things neither acquire nor have the capacity for this gift. However, every creature which has this capacity receives it, not from it-self, since it has been created out of nothing, but from its Creator. To possess Him is to be happy; to lose Him is to be in misery. And, of course, that One whose beatitude depends upon Himself as His own good and not on any other good can never be unhappy since He can never lose Himself.

Thus, there can be no unchangeable good except our one, true, and blessed God. All things which He has made are good because made by Him, but they are subject to change because they were made, not out of Him, but out of nothing. Although they are not supremely good, since God is a greater good than they, these mutable things are, none the less, highly good by reason of their capacity for union with and, therefore, beatitude in the Immutable Good which is so completely their good that, without this good, misery is inevitable.

But it does not follow that other creatures in the universe are better off merely because they are incapable of misery. That would be like saying that other members of the body are better than the eyes because they can never become blind. A sentient nature even in pain is better than a stone that cannot suffer. In the same way, a rational nature even in misery is higher than one which, because it lacks reason or sensation, cannot suffer misery.

This being the case, it is nothing less than a perversion of the nature of the angels if they do not adhere to God. For, remember, their nature is so high in the order of creation that, mutable as it is, it can attain beatitude by adhering to the immutable and supreme Good, which is God, and that, unless it achieves beatitude, this nature fails to satisfy its inmost exigencies, and, finally, that nothing but God can satisfy these needs of the angelic nature.

Now, this perversion, like every imperfection in a nature, harms nature and, therefore, is contrary to the nature. It follows, therefore, that what makes the wicked angels differ from the good ones is not their nature but a perversion or imperfection; and this very blemish is a proof of how highly to be esteemed is the nature itself. Certainly, no blemish in a thing ought to be blamed unless we are praising the thing as a whole, for the whole point of blaming the blemish is that it mars the perfection of something we would like to see praised.

For example, when we say that blindness is a defect of the eyes, we imply that it is the very nature of the eyes to see, and when we say that deafness is a malady of the ears, we are supposing that it is their nature to hear. So, too, when we say that it is a failure in an angel not to attain union with God, we openly proclaim that they were meant by nature to be one with God.

Of course, no one can fully comprehend or properly express the ineffable union of being one with God in His life, in His wisdom, in His joy, and all this without a shadow of death or darkness or disturbance. One thing is certain. The very failure of the bad angels to cling to God—a desertion that damaged their nature like a disease—is itself proof enough that the nature God gave them was good—so good that not to be one with God was for them a disaster.

CHAPTER 2

This explanation just given seemed to me necessary to forestall the objection that the apostate spirits might have received from some principle other than God a nature different from that of the other angels. The malice of this mistake can be more easily and speedily removed the more clearly one grasps what God meant by the words, "I AM WHO AM" (Exod. 3:14), spoken through the medium of an angel at the time when Moses was being sent to the children of Israel.

Since God is supreme being, that is, since He supremely is and, therefore, is immutable, it follows that He gave "being" to all that He created out of nothing; not, however, absolute being. To some things He gave more of being and to others less and, in this way, arranged an order of natures in a hierarchy of being. (This noun, "being," is derived from the verb "to be," just as "wisdom" is from the verb "to be wise." In Latin, *essentia*, "being," is a new word, not used by the ancient writers, recently adopted in order to find an equivalent of the Greek, ⟨ousía⟩, of which *essentia* is the exact translation.)

Consequently, no nature—except a non-existent one—can be contrary to the nature which is supreme and which created whatever other natures have being. In other words, nonentity stands in opposition to that which is. Therefore, there is no being opposed to God who is the Supreme Being and Source of all beings without exception.

CHAPTER 3

In Scripture, those who oppose God's rule, not by nature but by sin, are called His enemies. They can do no damage to Him, but only to themselves; their enmity is not a power to harm, but merely an inclination to oppose Him. In any case, God is immutable and completely invulnerable. Hence, the malice by which His so-called ene-

mies oppose God is not a menace to Him, but merely bad for themselves—an evil because what is good in their nature is wounded. It is not their nature, but the wound in
their nature, that is opposed to God—as evil is opposed to good.

No one will deny that God is supremely good. Thus, any lack of goodness is opposed to God as evil is opposed to good. At the same time, the nature itself is not less
good because the lack of goodness is evil and, therefore, the evil of lacking some
goodness is opposed to this good, which is the goodness of the nature. Note that in respect to God the contrast is merely that of evil to good, but in respect to the nature
which suffers a lack of something good, the lack is not only evil but also harmful. No
evils, of course, can be harmful to God, but only to mutable and corruptible natures—
and, even then, the harm done bears witness to the goodness of the natures which suffer, for, unless they were good, they could not suffer the wounds of a lack of goodness.

Just consider the harm done by these wounds—the loss of integrity, of beauty, of
health, of virtue, or of any other natural good which can be lost or lessened by sin or
sickness. If a nature has nothing of goodness to lose, then there is no harm done by
lacking this nothing and, consequently, there is nothing wrong. For, there is no such
thing as something wrong that does no harm.

The conclusion is that, although no defect can damage an unchangeable good, no
nature can be damaged by a defect unless that nature itself is good—for the simple reason
that a defect exists only where harm is done. To put the matter in another way: a defect
can never be found in the highest good, nor ever apart from some kind of good.

Thus, good things without defects can sometimes be found; absolutely bad
things, never—for even those natures that were vitiated at the outset by an evil will are
only evil in so far as they are defective, while they are good in so far as they are natural. And when a vitiated nature is being punished, in addition to the good of being
what it is, it is a good for it not to go unpunished, since this is just and whatever is just
is certainly good. No one is punished for natural defects, but only for deliberate faults.
And even for a vice to develop, by force of habit and overindulgence, into a strong natural defect, the vice must have begun in the will. But here, of course, I am speaking of
the vices of that nature which has a mind illumined by an immaterial light in virtue of
which it can distinguish what is just from what is unjust.

CHAPTER 4

Of course, in the case of beasts, trees, and other mutable and mortal creatures which
lack not merely an intellect, but even sensation or life itself, it would be ridiculous to
condemn in them the defects which destroy their corruptible nature. For, it was by the
will of the Creator that they received that measure of being whereby their comings and
goings and fleeting existences should contribute to that special, if lowly, loveliness of
our earthly seasons which chimes with the harmony of the universe. For, there was
never any need for the things of earth either to rival those of heaven or to remain uncreated merely because the latter are better.

It is, in fact, the very law of transitory things that, here on earth where such
things are at home, some should be born while others die, the weak should give way to
the strong and the victims should nourish the life of the victors. If the beauty of this
order fails to delight us, it is because we ourselves, by reason of our mortality, are so
enmeshed in this corner of the cosmos that we fail to perceive the beauty of a total pattern in which the particular parts, which seem ugly to us, blend in so harmonious and
beautiful a way. That is why, in those situations where it is beyond our power to under-

stand the providence of God, we are rightly commanded to make an act of faith rather than allow the rashness of human vanity to criticize even a minute detail in the masterpiece of our Creator.

Although these defects in the things of earth are involuntary and unpunishable, yet, like voluntary ones, when properly contemplated, they reveal the excellence in the natures themselves, all of which have God for their Author and Creator. For, in both cases, what we dislike is the lack by defect of something which we like in the nature as a whole. Sometimes, of course, natures themselves are displeasing to men because they happen to be harmful. It is a case of regarding only their utility, not the things themselves, as with the plague of frogs and flies which scourged the pride of the Egyptians. But, with such reasoning, fault could be found even with the sun, since criminals and debtors have sometimes been judicially condemned to solar exposure. It is not by our comfort or inconvenience, but by the nature considered in itself, that glory is given to its Creator. So, even the nature of unquenchable fire is, without doubt, worthy of praise, although it is to serve as a punishment for the damned. Is there anything, in fact, more beautiful than a leaping, luminous flame of fire? Or anything more useful, when it warms us, heals us, cooks our food? Yet, nothing is more painful when it burns us. Thus, the same thing applied in one way is harmful, but when properly used is extremely beneficial. It is all but impossible to enumerate all the good uses to which fire is put throughout the world.

We should pay no attention to those who praise fire for its light but condemn its heat—on the principle that a thing should be judged not by its nature, but by our comfort or inconvenience. They like to see it, but hate to be burnt. What they forget is that the same light which they like is injurious and unsuitable for weak eyes, and that the heat which they hate is, for some animals, the proper condition for a healthy life.

CHAPTER 5

All natures, then, are good simply because they exist and, therefore, have each its own measure of being, its own beauty, even, in a way, its own peace. And when each is in the place assigned by the order of nature, it best preserves the full measure of being that was given to it. Beings not made for eternal life, changing for better or for worse according as they promote the good and improvement of things to which, by the law of the Creator, they serve as means, follow the direction of Divine Providence and tend toward the particular end which forms a part of the general plan for governing the universe. This means that the dissolution which brings mutable and mortal things to their death is not so much a process of annihilation as a progress toward something they were designed to become.

The conclusion from all this is that God is never to be blamed for any defects that offend us, but should ever be praised for all the perfection we see in the natures He has made. For God is Absolute Being and, therefore, all other being that is relative was made by Him. No being that was made from nothing could be on a par with God, nor could it even be at all, were it not made by Him.

CHAPTER 6

It follows that the true cause of the good angels' beatitude lies in their union with Absolute Being. And if we seek the cause of the bad angels' misery, we are right in finding it in this, that they abandoned Him whose Being is absolute and turned to themselves whose being is relative—a sin that can have no better name than pride. "For pride is the beginning of all sin" (Eccli. 10:15). They refused to reserve their strength for Him. They might have had more of being if they had adhered to Him whose Being is supreme, but, by preferring themselves to Him, they preferred what was less in the order of being.

Such was the first defect, the first lack, the first perversion of that nature which, being created, could not be absolute, and yet, being created for beatitude, might have rejoiced in Him who is Absolute Being; but which, having turned from Him, was doomed, not to be nothing but to have so much less of being that it was bound to be wretched.

If one seeks for the efficient cause of their evil will, none is to be found. For, what can make the will bad when it is the will itself which makes an action bad? Thus, an evil will is the efficient cause of a bad action, but there is no efficient cause of an evil will. If there is such a cause, it either has or has not a will. If it has, then that will is either good or bad. If good, one would have to be foolish enough to conclude that a good will makes a bad will. In that case, a good will becomes the cause of sin—which is utterly absurd. On the other hand, if the hypothetical cause of a bad will has itself a bad will, I would have to ask what made this will bad, and, to put an end to the inquiry: What made the first bad will bad? Now, the fact is that there was no first bad will that was made bad by any other bad will—it was made bad by itself. For, if it were preceded by a cause that made it evil, that cause came first. But, if I am told that nothing made the will evil but that it always was so, then I ask whether or not it existed in some nature.

If this evil will existed in no nature, then it did not exist at all. If it existed in some nature, then it vitiated, corrupted, injured that nature and, therefore, deprived it of some good. An evil will could not exist in an evil nature but only in a good one, mutable enough to suffer harm from this deprivation. For, if no harm were done, then there was no deprivation and, consequently, no right to call the will evil. But, if harm was done, it was done by destroying or diminishing what was good. Thus, an evil will could not have existed from all eternity in a nature in which a previously existing good had to be eliminated before the evil will could harm the nature. But, if it did not exist from all eternity, who, then, caused this evil will?

The only remaining suggestion is that the cause of the evil will was something which had no will. My next question is whether this "something" was superior, inferior, or equal to the will. If superior, then it was better. So, then, how can it have had no will and not rather a good will? If equal, the case is the same: for, as long as two wills are equally good, one cannot produce an evil will in the other. The supposition remains, then, that it was an inferior thing without a will which produced the evil will of the angelic nature which first sinned.

But that thing itself, whatever it was, even though it was low to the lowest point of earthliness, was, without doubt good since it was a nature and a being having its own character and species in its own genus and order. How, then, can a good thing be the efficient cause of an evil will? How, I ask, can good be the cause of evil? For, when the will, abandoning what is above it, turns itself to something lower, it becomes evil because the very turning itself and not the thing to which it turns is evil. Therefore, an inferior being does not make the will evil but the will itself, because it is a created will, wickedly and inordinately seeks the inferior being.

Take the case of two men whose physical and mental make-up is exactly the same. They are both attracted by the exterior beauty of the same person. While gazing at this loveliness, the will of one man is moved with an illicit desire; the will of the other remains firm in its purity. Why did the will become evil in one case and not in the other? What produced the evil will in the man in whom it began to be evil? The physical beauty of the person could not have been the cause, since that was seen by both in exactly the same way and yet both wills did not become evil. Was the cause the flesh of one of those who looked? Then why not the flesh of the other, also? Or was the cause the mind of one of them? Again, why not the mind of both? For the supposition is that both are equally constituted in mind and body. Must we say, then, that one was tempted by a secret suggestion of the Devil, as if it were not rather by his own will that he consented to this suggestion or enticement or whatever it was?

If so, then what was it in him that was the cause of his consent, of the evil will to follow the evil suggestion? To settle this difficulty, let us suppose that the two men are tempted equally, that one yields and consents to the temptation, that the other remains as he was before. The obvious conclusion is that one was unwilling, the other willing, to fail in chastity. And what else could be the cause of their attitudes but their own wills, since both men have the same constitution and temperament? The beauty which attracted the eyes of both was the same; the secret suggestion by which both were tempted was the same. However carefully they examine the situation, eager to learn what is was that made one of the two evil, no cause is apparent.

For, suppose we say that the man himself made his will evil. Very well, but what was the man himself before he made his will evil? He was a good nature, created by God, the immutable God.

Take a person who says that the one who consents to the temptation and enticement made his own will evil although previously he had been entirely good. Recall the facts. The one consents, while the other does not, to a sinful desire concerning a beautiful person; the beauty was seen by both equally, and before the temptation both men were absolutely alike in mind and body. Now, the person who talks of a man making his own will evil must ask why the man made his will evil, whether because he is a nature or because he is nature made out of nothing? He will learn that the evil arises not from the fact that the man is a nature, but from the fact that the nature was made out of nothing.

For, if a nature is the cause of an evil will, then we are compelled to say that evil springs from good and that good is the cause of evil—since a bad will comes from a good nature. But how can it come about that a good, though mutable, nature, even before its will is evil, can produce something evil, namely, this evil will itself?

CHAPTER 7

No one, therefore, need seek for an efficient cause of an evil will. Since the "effect" is, in fact, a deficiency, the cause should be called "deficient." The fault of an evil will begins when one falls from Supreme Being to some being which is less than absolute. Trying to discover causes of such deficiencies—causes which, as I have said, are not efficient but deficient—is like trying to see darkness or hear silence. True, we have some knowledge of both darkness and silence: of the former only by the eyes; of the latter only by the ears. Nevertheless, we have no sensation but only the privation of sensation.

So there is no point in anyone trying to learn from me what I know I do not know—unless, perhaps, he wants to know how not to know what, as he ought to know, no one can know. For, things we know, not by sensation, but by the absence of sensation, are known—if the word says or means anything—by some kind of "unknowing," so that they are both known and not known at the same time. For example, when the vision of the eye passes from sensation to sensation, it sees darkness only when it begins not to see. So, too, no other sense but the ear can perceive silence, yet silence can only be heard by not being heard.

So, too, it is only the vision of the mind that discerns the species intellegibilis when it understands intelligible realities. But, when the realities are no longer intelligible, the mind, too, knows by "unknowing." For "who can understand sins?" (Ps. 18:13).

CHAPTER 8

This I know, that the nature of God can never and nowhere be deficient in anything, while things made out of nothing can be deficient. In regard to these latter, the more they have of being and the more good things they do or make—for then they are doing or making something positive—the more their causes are efficient; but in so far as they fail or are defective and, in that sense, "do evil"—if a "defect" can be "done"—then their causes are "deficient." I know, further, that when a will "is made" evil, what happens would not have happened if the will had not wanted it to happen. That is why the punishment which follows is just, since the defection was not necessary but voluntary. The will does not fall "into sin"; it falls "sinfully." Defects are not mere relations to natures that are evil; they are evil in themselves because, contrary to the order of natures, there is a defection from Being that is supreme to some lesser being.

Thus, greed is not a defect in the gold that is desired but in the man who loves it perversely by falling from justice which he ought to esteem as incomparably superior to gold; nor is lust a defect in bodies which are beautiful and pleasing: it is a sin in the soul of the one who loves corporal pleasures perversely, that is, by abandoning that temperance which joins us in spiritual and unblemishable union with realities far more beautiful and pleasing; nor is boastfulness a blemish in words of praise: it is a failing in the soul of one who is so perversely in love with other peoples' applause that he despises the voice of his own conscience; nor is pride a vice in the one who delegates power, still less a flaw in the power itself: it is a passion in the soul of the one who loves his own power so perversely as to condemn the authority of one who is still more powerful.

In a word, anyone who loves perversely the good of any nature whatsoever and even, perhaps, acquires this good makes himself bad by gaining something good and sad by losing something better.

CHAPTER 9

There is, then, no natural efficient cause of an evil will or, if I may use the word, no essential cause. The reason for this is that it is the evil will itself that starts that evil in mutable spirits, which is nothing but a weakening and worsening of the good in their nature. What "makes" the will evil is, in reality, an "unmaking," a desertion from God. The very defection is deficient—in the sense of having no cause. However, in saying that there is no efficient cause even of a good will, we must beware of believing that the good will of the good angels was uncreated and co-eternal with God. But, if good angels were created, how can we say that their good will was not created? The fact is, it was created; the only question is whether it was created simultaneously with the creation of the angels or whether they first existed without a good will. If simultaneously, then, undoubtedly, it was created by Him who created the angels, so that, as soon as they were created, they adhered to Him who created them by means of that love with which they were created. Thus, the reason why the bad were separated from the society of good angels was that the good persevered in the same good will, whereas the others changed themselves into bad angels by defection from good will. The only thing that "made" their will bad was that they fell away from a will which was good. Nor would they have fallen away, had they not chosen to fall away.

In the hypothesis, however, that the good angels, existing at first without a good will, produced it in themselves without the help of God, they must have made themselves better than what they were when God created them. This is nonsense. For, without a good will, what could they be but evil? Or, if we may not say evil, since their will was not yet evil—for they could hardly fall away from what they had not yet begun to have—at least, they certainly were not good angels—not as good as they were to become when they came to possess a good will.

So much for the hypothesis. Since they could not make themselves better than God made them—for no one can make anything better than God can—then it follows that, without the co-operation of their Creator, they could never have come into possession of that good will which made them better.

Now, it is true that their good will was not only the cause of their turning and adhering to Him, who is Perfect Being, rather than to themselves, whose being was less than perfect, but also the reason why they had more of being than before and could live wisely and happily in union with God. Nevertheless, this merely shows that any will, however good, would have been destitute and destined to remain in hopeless desire, did not He who had created their good nature out of nothing, and had given it a capacity for union with Himself, first awaken in the will a greater longing for this union and then fill the will with some of His very Being in order to make it better.

This raises another issue. For, if the good angels did something themselves to bring about their good will, did they do this with or without a will? If without, then, of course, they were not the agents. If with a will, was it an evil or a good one? If evil, how could it produce a good will? If good, well, then, they had a good will already. And who made this but God Himself who created them with a good will (that is, with the unblemished love by which they could adhere to Him) and who at the same time created their nature and enriched it with grace?

Thus, we are compelled to believe that the holy angels never existed without a good will, that is, without the love of God. But what of those angels who were created good and became evil by their own bad will for which their good nature is not responsible except in so far as there was a deliberate defection from good—for it is never good, but a defection from good, that is the cause of evil? These angels either received less grace of divine love than those who persevered in grace, or, if both were created equally good, then, while the former were falling by bad will, the latter were increasingly aided to reach that plenitude of beatitude which made them certain that they would never fall—a matter which I discussed in the preceding Book.

Thus with our praise to our Creator, we should all proclaim that, not only of holy men, but also of holy angels, it may be said that "the charity of God is poured forth" in them "by the Holy Spirit who has been given" to them (Rom. 5:5). Nor is it the good only of men, but first and foremost that of angels, which is referred to in the words: "It is good for me to adhere to my God" (Ps. 72:28).

And they who share this common good are in a holy communion both with Him to whom they adhere and one with another, and they form a single community, one City of God, which is also His living sacrifice and His living temple.

This ends the discussion of the origin of this City in so far as it concerns the angels. I must now turn to the rise of that part of the City which is made up of mortal men, created by the same God, who will one day be united to the immortal angels and who, at present, are either sojourning on earth or, if dead, are resting in the hidden sanctuaries where the souls of the departed have their abode.

It was from one man, the first whom God created, that the whole human race took its start. This is the faith revealed in Holy Scripture, a faith that has gained marvelous and merited authority throughout the world and among all peoples—as, along with other truths, Scripture itself divinely predicted would be the case.

*   *   *

Book XIX

Chapter 11

Thus, we may say of peace what we have said of eternal life—that it is our highest good; more particularly because the holy Psalmist was addressing the City of God (the nature of which I am trying, with so much difficulty, to make clear) when he said: "Praise the Lord, O Jerusalem; praise thy God, O Zion. Because he hath strengthened the bolts of thy gates, he hath blessed thy children within thee. He hath placed peace in thy borders" (Ps. 146:12–14). For, when the bolts of that city's gates will have been strengthened, none will enter in and none will issue forth. Hence, its borders (fines) must be taken to mean that peace which I am trying to show is our final good. Note, too, that Jerusalem, the mystical name which symbolizes this City, means, as I have already mentioned, "the vision of peace."

However, the word "peace" is so often applied to conditions here on earth, where life is not eternal, that it is better, I think, to speak of "eternal life" rather than of "peace" as the end or supreme good of the City of God. It is in this sense that St. Paul says: "But now being made free from sin, and become servants of God, you have your fruit unto sanctification, and the end life everlasting" (Rom. 6:22).

It would be simplest for all concerned if we spoke of "peace in eternal life," or of "eternal" or of "eternal life in peace," as the end or supreme good of this City. The trouble with the expression "eternal life" is that those unfamiliar with the Scriptures might take this phrase to apply also to the eternal loss of the wicked, either because, as philosophers, they accept the immortality of the soul, or even because, as Christians, they know by faith that the punishment of the wicked has no end and, therefore, that they could not be punished forever unless their life were eternal.

The trouble with "peace" is that, even on the level of earthly and temporal values, nothing that we can talk about, long for, or finally get, is so desirable, so welcome, so good as peace. At any rate, I feel sure that if I linger a little longer on this topic of peace I shall tire very few of my readers. After all, peace is the end of this City which is the theme of this work; besides, peace is so universally loved that its very name falls sweetly on the ear.

Chapter 12

Any man who has examined history and human nature will agree with me that there is no such thing as a human heart that does not crave for joy and peace. One has only to think of men who are bent on war. What they want is to win, that is to say, their battles are but bridges to glory and to peace. The whole point of victory is to bring opponents to their knees—this done, peace ensues. Peace, then, is the purpose of waging war; and this is true even of men who have a passion for the exercise of military prowess as rulers and commanders.

What, then, men want in war is that it should end in peace. Even while waging a war every man wants peace, whereas no one wants war while he is making peace. And even when men are plotting to disturb the peace, it is merely to fashion a new peace nearer to the heart's desire; it is not because they dislike peace as such. It is not that they love peace less, but that they love their kind of peace more. And even when a secession is successful, its purpose is not achieved unless some sort of peace remains among those who plotted and planned the rebellion. Take even a band of highwaymen. The more violence and impunity they want in disturbing the peace of other men, the more they demand peace among themselves. Take even the case of a robber so powerful that he dispenses with partnership, plans alone, and single-handed robs and kills his victims. Even he maintains some kind of peace, however shadowy, with those he cannot kill and whom he wants to keep in the dark with respect to his crimes. Certainly in his own home he wants to be at peace with his wife and children and any other members of his household. Of course, he is delighted when his every nod is obeyed; if it is not obeyed, he rages, and scolds, and demands peace in his own home and, if need be, gets it by sheer brutality. He knows that the price of peace in domestic society is to have everyone subject in the home to some head—in this instance, to himself.

Suppose, now, a man of this type were offered the allegiance of a larger society, say of a city or of a nation, with the pledge that he would be obeyed as he looks to be obeyed under his own roof. In this case, he would no longer hide himself away in a darksome robber's den; he would show himself off as a high and mighty king—the same man, however, with all of his old greed and criminality. Thus it is that all men want peace in their own society, and all want it in their own way. When they go to war what they want is to make, if they can, their enemies their own, and then to impose on them the victor's will and call it peace.

Now let us imagine a man like the one that poetry and mythology tell us about, a being so wild and anti-social that it was better to call him half-human than fully a man. He was called Cacus, which is Greek for "bad." His kingdom was the solitude of a dreadful cave and it was his extraordinary wickedness that gave him his name. He had no wife to exchange soft words with him; no tiny children to play with; no bigger ones to keep in order; no friend whose company he could enjoy, not even his father, Vulcan—than whom he was at least this much luckier that he had never begotten a monster like himself! There was no one to whom he would give anything, but whenever and from whomsoever he could he would take whatever he wanted and whenever he wanted it.

Nevertheless, all alone as he was in a cave that was always "warm with the blood of some recent victim," his sole longing was for peace in which no force would do him harm and no fear disturb his rest. Even with his own body he wanted to be at peace, and he was at ease only when peace was there. Even when he was bidding his members to obey him and was seizing, killing, and devouring his victims, his purpose was peace—the speediest possible peace with his mortal nature, driven by its needs to rebellion, and with his hunger, in sedition, clamoring for the breakup of the union of body and soul. Brutal and wild as he was and brutal and wild as were his ways, what he wanted was to have his life and limbs in peace. So much so that, had he been as willing to be at peace with his neighbors as he was active in procuring peace within himself and in his cave, no one would have called him wicked, nor a monster, nor even subhuman; or, at least, despite the shape of his body and the smoke and fire that issued from his mouth and kept all neighbors at a distance, people would have said that what looked like injustice, greed, and savagery were merely means to self-preservation. The truth is, of course, that there never existed any such being, or at least, none just like the foil the poets' fancy invented to glorify Hercules at the expense of Cacus. As is the case with most poetic inventions, we need not believe that any such creature, human or subhuman, ever lived.

I turn now to real wild beasts (from which category the animal part of the so-called half-beast, Cacus, was borrowed). They, too, keep their own particular genus in a kind of peace. Their males and females meet and mate, foster and feed their young, even though many of them by nature are more solitary than gregarious, like lions, foxes, eagles, and owls—as contrasted with deer, pigeons, starlings, and bees. Even a tigress purrs over her cubs and curbs all her fierceness when she fondles them. Even a falcon which seems so lonely when hovering above its prey mates and builds a nest, helps to hatch the eggs and feed the young, and makes every effort to maintain with the mother falcon a peaceful domestic society.

It is even more so with man. By the very laws of his nature, he seems, so to speak, forced into fellowship and, as far as in him lies, into peace with every man. At any rate, even when wicked men go to war they want peace for their own society and would like, if possible, to make all men members of that society, so that every one and every thing might be at the service of one head. Of course, the only means such a conqueror knows is to have all men so fear or love him that they will accept the peace which he imposes. For, so does pride perversely copy God. Sinful man hates the equality of all men under God and, as though he were God, loves to impose his sovereignty on his fellow men. He hates the peace of God which is just and prefers his own peace which is unjust. However, he is powerless not to love peace of some sort. For, no man's sin is so unnatural as to wipe out all traces whatsoever of human nature. Anyone, then, who is rational enough to prefer right to wrong and order to disorder can see that the kind of peace that is based on injustice, as compared with that which is based on justice, does not deserve the name of peace.

Of course, even disorder, in whole or in part, must come to some kind of terms either with the situation in which it finds itself or with the elements out of which it takes its being—otherwise it would have no being at all.

Take a man hanging upside down. Certainly his members are in disorder and the posture of the body as a whole is unnatural. The parts which nature demands should be above and below have become topsy-turvy. Such a position disturbs the peace of the body and is therefore painful. Nevertheless, the soul remains at peace with the body and continues to work for its welfare. Otherwise, the man would not live to feel the agony. And even if the soul is driven from the body by excess of pain, nevertheless, so long as the limbs hold together, some kind of peace among these parts remains. Otherwise, there would be no corpse to go on dangling there. Further, the fact that by gravity the corpse, made out of earth, tends to fall to the ground and pulls at the noose that holds it up proves that there is some order in which it seeks peace, and that its weight is, as it were, crying out for a place where it can rest. Lifeless and insensible though the body now is, it does not renounce that appropriate peace in the order of nature which it either has or seeks to have.

So, too, when a corpse is treated to embalming, to prevent dissolution and decay, there is a kind of peace which holds the parts together while the whole is committed to the earth, its proper resting place, and, therefore, a place with which the body is at peace. If, on the other hand, embalming is omitted and nature is allowed to take its course, the corpse remains a battleground of warring exhalations (that attack our senses with the stench we smell) only until such time as they finally fall in with the elements of this world and, slowly, bit by bit, become indistinguishable in a common peace.

Even afterward, however, the law and ordering of the Creator who is supreme in the whole cosmos and the regulator of its peace are still in control. Even when tiny bacteria spring from the corpse of a larger animal, it is by the same law of the Creator that all these minute bodies serve in peace the organic wholes of which they are parts. Even when the flesh of dead animals is eaten by other animals, there is no change in the universal laws which are meant for the common good of every kind of life, the common good that is effected by bringing like into peace with like. It makes no difference what disintegrating forces are at work, or what new combinations are made, or even what changes or transformations are effected.

CHAPTER 13

The peace, then, of the body lies in the ordered equilibrium of all its parts; the peace of the irrational soul, in the balanced adjustment of its appetites; the peace of the reasoning soul, in the harmonious correspondence of conduct and conviction; the peace of body and soul taken together, in the well-ordered life and health of the living whole. Peace between a mortal man and his Maker consists in ordered obedience, guided by faith, under God's eternal law; peace between man and man consists in regulated fellowship. The peace of a home lies in the ordered harmony of authority and obedience between the members of a family living together. The peace of the political community is an ordered harmony of authority and obedience between citizens. The peace of the heavenly City lies in a perfectly ordered and harmonious communion of those who find their joy in God and in one another in God. Peace, in its final sense, is the calm that comes of order. Order is an arrangement of like and unlike things whereby each of them is disposed in its proper place.

This being so, those who are unhappy, in so far as they are unhappy, are not in peace, since they lack the calm of that Order which is beyond every storm; nevertheless, even in their misery they cannot escape from order, since their very misery is related to responsibility and to justice. They do not share with the blessed in their tranquility, but this very separation is the result of the law of order. Moreover, even the miserable can be momentarily free from anxiety and can reach some measure of adjustment to their surroundings and, hence, some tranquility of order and, therefore, some slender peace. However, the reason why they remain unhappy is that, although they may be momentarily free from worry and from pain, they are not in a condition where they must be free both from worry and pain. Their condition of misery is worse when such peace as they have is not in harmony with that law which governs the order of nature. Their peace can also be disturbed by pain and in proportion to their pain; yet, some peace will remain, so long as the pain is not too acute and their organism as a whole does not disintegrate.

Notice that there can be life without pain, but no pain without some kind of life. In the same way, there can be peace without any kind of war, but no war that does not suppose some kind of peace. This does not mean that war as war involves peace; but war, in so far as those who wage it or have it waged upon them are beings with organic natures, involves peace—for the simple reason that to be organic means to be ordered and, therefore, to be, in some sense, at peace.

Similarly, there can be a nature without any defect and, even, a nature in which there can be no kind of evil whatever, but there can be no nature completely devoid of good. Even the nature of the Devil, in so far as it is a nature, is not evil; it was perversity—not being true to itself—that made it bad. The Devil did not "stand in the truth" (John 8:44) and, therefore, did not escape the judgment of truth. He did not stand fast in the tranquility of order—nor did he, for all that, elude the power of the Ordainer. The goodness which God gave to his nature does not withdraw him from the justice of God by which that nature is subject to punishment. Yet, even in that punishment, God does not hound the good which He created, but only the evil which the Devil committed. So it is that God does not take back the whole of His original gift. He takes a part and leaves a part; He leaves a nature that can regret what God has taken back. Indeed, the very pain inflicted is evidence of both the good that is lost and the good that is left. For, if there were no good left, there would be no one to lament the good that has been lost.

A man who sins is just that much worse if he rejoices in the loss of holiness; but one who suffers pain, and does not benefit by it, laments, at least, the loss of his health. Holiness and health are both good things and, because the loss of any good is more a cause for grief than for gladness (unless there be some higher compensation—the soul's holiness, to be sure, is preferable to the body's health), it is more in accordance with nature that a sinner grieve over his punishment than that he rejoice over his offense. Consequently, just as a man's happiness in abandoning the good of wrong-doing betrays his bad will, so his sorrowing for the good he has lost when in pain bears witness to the good of his nature. For, anyone who grieves over the loss of peace to his nature does so out of some remnant of that peace wherewith his nature loves itself. This is what happens—deservedly, too—in eternal punishment. In the midst of their agonies the evil and the godless weep for the loss of their nature's goods, knowing, meanwhile, that God whose great generosity they condemned was perfectly just when He took these goods away.

God, the wise Creator and just Ordainer of all natures, has made the mortal race of man the loveliest of all lovely things on earth. He has given to men good gifts suited to their existence here below. Among these is temporal peace, according to the poor limits of mortal life, in health, security, and human fellowship; and other gifts, too, needed to preserve this peace or regain it, once lost—for instance, the blessings that lie all around us, so perfectly adapted to our senses: daylight, speech, air to breathe, water to drink, everything that goes to feed, clothe, cure, and beautify the body. These good gifts are granted, however, with the perfectly just understanding that whoever uses the goods which are meant for the mortal peace of mortal men, as these goods should be used, will receive more abundant and better goods—nothing less than immortal peace and all that goes with it, namely, the glory and honor of enjoying God and one's neighbor in God everlastingly; but that whoever misuses his gifts on earth will both lose what he has and never receive the better gifts of heaven.

Chapter 14

In the earthly city, then, temporal goods are to be used with a view to the enjoyment of earthly peace, whereas, in the heavenly City, they are used with a view to the enjoyment of eternal peace. Hence, if we were merely unthinking brutes, we would pursue nothing beyond the orderly interrelationship of our bodily part and the appeasing of our appetites, nothing, that is, beyond the comfort of the flesh and plenty of pleasures, so that the peace of body might contribute to peace of the soul. For, if order in the body be lacking, the peace of an irrational soul is checked, since it cannot attain the satisfaction of its appetites. Both of these forms of peace meanwhile subserve that other form of peace which the body and soul enjoy between them, the peace of life and health in good order.

For, just as brutes show that they love the peace or comfort of their bodies by shunning pain, and the peace of their souls by pursuing pleasure to satisfy their appetites, so, too, by running from death, they make clear enough how much they love the peace which keeps body and soul together.

Because, however, man has a rational soul, he makes everything he shares with brutes subserve the peace of his rational soul, so that he first measures things with his mind before he acts, in order to achieve that harmonious correspondence of conduct and conviction which I called the peace of the rational soul. His purpose in desiring not to be vexed with pain, nor disturbed with desire, nor disintegrated by death is that he may learn something profitable and so order his habits and way of life. However, if the infirmity of his human mind is not to bring him in his pursuit of knowledge to some deadly error, he needs divine authority to give secure guidance, and divine help so that he may be unhampered in following the guidance given.

And because, so long as man lives in his mortal body and is a pilgrim far from the Lord, he walks, not by vision, but by faith. Consequently, he refers all peace of body or soul, or their combination, to that higher peace which unites a mortal man with the immortal God and which I defined as "ordered obedience guided by faith, under God's eternal law."

Meanwhile, God teaches him two chief commandments, the love of God and the love of neighbor. In these precepts man finds three beings to love, namely, God, himself, and his fellow man, and knows that he is not wrong in loving himself so long as he loves God. As a result, he must help his neighbor (whom he is obliged to love as himself) to love God. Thus, he must help his wife, children, servants, and all others whom he can influence. He must wish, moreover, to be similarly helped by his fellow man, in case he himself needs such assistance. Out of all this love he will arrive at peace, as much as in him lies, with every man—at that human peace which is regulated fellowship. Right order here means, first, that he harm no one, and, second, that he help whomever he can. His fundamental duty is to look out for his own home, for both by natural and human law he has easier and readier access to their requirements.

St. Paul says: "But if any does not take care of his own, and especially of his household, he has denied the faith and is worse than an unbeliever" (I Tim. 5:8). From this care arises that peace of the home which lies in the harmonious interplay of authority and obedience among those who live there. For, those who have the care of the others give the orders—a man to his wife, parents to their children, masters to their servants. And those who are cared for must obey—wives their husbands, children their parents, servants their masters. In the home of a religious man, however, of a man living by faith and as yet a wayfarer from the heavenly City, those who command serve those whom they appear to rule—because, of course, they do not command out of lust to domineer, but out of a sense of duty—not out of pride like princes but out of solicitude like parents.

CHAPTER 15

This family arrangement is what nature prescribes, and what God intended in creating man: "let them have dominion over the fish of the sea, the birds of the air, the cattle, over all the wild animals and every creature that crawls on the earth" (Gen. 1:26). God wanted rational man, made to His image, to have no dominion except over irrational nature. He meant no man, therefore, to have dominion over man, but only man over beast. So it fell out that those who were holy in primitive times became shepherds over sheep rather than monarchs over men, because God wishes in this way to teach us that the normal hierarchy of creatures is different from that which punishment for sin has made imperative. For, when subjection came, it was merely a condition deservedly imposed on sinful man. So, in Scripture, there is no mention of the word "servant" until holy Noah used it in connection with the curse on his son's wrong-doing. It is a designation that is not natural, but one that was deserved because of sin.

The Latin word for "slave" is *servus* and it is said that this word is derived from the fact that those who, by right of conquest, could have been killed were sometimes kept and guarded, *servabantur,* by their captors and so became slaves and were called *servi*. Now, such a condition of servitude could only have arisen as a result of sin, since whenever a just war is waged the opposing side must be in the wrong, and every victory, even when won by wicked men, is a divine judgment to humble the conquered and to reform or punish their sin. To this truth Daniel, the great man of God, bore witness. When he was languishing in the Babylonian captivity he confessed to God his sins and those of his people and avowed, with pious repentance, that these sins were the cause of the captivity. It is clear, then, that sin is the primary cause of servitude, in the sense of a social status in which one man is compelled to be subjected to another man. Nor does this befall a man, save by the decree of God, who is never unjust and who knows how to impose appropriate punishments on different sinners.

Our heavenly Master says: "everyone who commits sin is a slave of sin" (John 8:34). So it happens that holy people are sometimes enslaved to wicked masters who are, in turn, themselves slaves. For, "by whatever a man is overcome, of this also he is a slave" (II Pet. 2:19). Surely it is better to be the slave of a man than the slave of passion as when, to take but one example, the lust for lordship raises such havoc in the hearts of men. Such, then, as men now are, is the order of peace. Some are in subjection to others, and, while humility helps those who serve, pride harms those in power. But, as men once were, when their nature was as God created it, no man was a slave either to man or to sin. However, slavery is now penal in character and planned by that law which commands the preservation of the natural order and forbids its disturbance. If no crime had ever been perpetrated against this law, there would be no crime to repress with the penalty of enslavement.

It is with this in mind that St. Paul goes so far as to admonish slaves to obey their masters and to serve them so sincerely and with such good will that, if there is no chance of manumission, they may make their slavery a kind of freedom by serving with love and loyalty, free from fear and feigning, until injustice becomes a thing of the past and every human sovereignty and power is done away with, so that God may be all in all.

CHAPTER 16

Our holy Fathers in the faith, to be sure, had slaves, but in the regulation of domestic peace it was only in matters of temporal importance that they distinguished the position of their children from the status of their servants. So far as concerns the worship of God—from whom all must hope for eternal blessings—they had like loving care for all the household without exception. This was what nature demanded, and it was from this kind of behavior that there grew the designation "father of the family," which is so widely accepted that even wicked and domineering men love to be so called.

Those who are true fathers are as solicitous for every one in their households as for their own children to worship and to be worthy of God. They hope and yearn for all to arrive in that heavenly home where there will be no further need of giving orders to other human beings, because there will be no longer any duty to help those who are happy in immortal life. In the meantime, fathers ought to look upon their duty to command as harder than the duty of slaves to obey.

Meanwhile, in case anyone in the home behaves contrary to its peace, he is disciplined by words or whipping or other kind of punishment lawful and licit in human society, and for his own good, to readjust him to the peace he has abandoned. For, there is no more benevolence and helpfulness in bringing about the loss of a greater good than there is innocence and compassion in allowing a culprit to go from bad to worse. It is the duty of a blameless person not just to do no wrong, but to keep others from wrong-doing and to punish it when done, so that the one punished may be improved by the experience and others be warned by the example.

Now, since every home should be a beginning or fragmentary constituent of a civil community, and every beginning related to some specific end, and every part to the whole of which it is a part, it ought to follow that domestic peace has a relation to political peace. In other words, the ordered harmony of authority and obedience between those who live together has a relation to the ordered harmony of authority and obedience between those who live in a city. This explains why a father must apply certain regulations of civil law to the governance of his home, so as to make it accord with the peace of the whole community.

CHAPTER 17

While the homes of unbelieving men are intent upon acquiring temporal peace out of the possessions and comforts of this temporal life, the families which live according to faith look ahead to the good things of heaven promised as imperishable, and use material and temporal goods in the spirit of pilgrims, not as snares or obstructions to block their way to God, but simply as helps to ease and never to increase the burdens of this corruptible body which weighs down the soul. Both types of homes and their masters have this in common, that they must use things essential to this mortal life. But the respective purposes to which they put them are characteristic and very different.

So, too, the earthly city which does not live by faith seeks only an earthly peace, and limits the goal of its peace, of its harmony of authority and obedience among its citizens, to the voluntary and collective attainment of objectives necessary to mortal existence. The heavenly City, meanwhile—or, rather, that part that is on pilgrimage in mortal life and lives by faith—must use this earthly peace until such time as our mortality which needs such peace has passed away. As a consequence, so long as her life in the earthly city is that of a captive and an alien (although she has the promise of ultimate delivery and the gift of the Spirit as a pledge), she has no hesitation about keeping in step with the civil law which governs matters pertaining to our existence here below. For, as mortal life is the same for all, there ought to be common cause between the two cities in what concerns our purely human living.

Now comes the difficulty. The city of this world, to begin with, has had certain "wise men" of its own mold, whom true religion must reject, because either out of their own daydreaming or out of demonic deception these wise men came to believe that a multiplicity of divinities was allied with human life, with different duties, in some strange arrangement, and different assignments: this one over the body, that one over the mind; in the body itself, one over the head, another over the neck, still others, one for each bodily part; in the mind, one over the intelligence, another over learning, another over temper, another over desire; in the realities, related to life, that lie about us, one over flocks and one over wheat, one over wine, one over oil, and another over forests, one over currency, another over navigation, and still another over warfare and victory, one over marriage, a different one over fecundity and childbirth, so on and so on.

The heavenly City, on the contrary, knows and, by religious faith, believes that it must adore one God alone and serve Him with that complete dedication which the Greeks call latreía and which belongs to Him alone. As a result, she has been unable to share with the earthly city a common religious legislation, and has had no choice but to dissent on this score and so to become a nuisance to those who think otherwise. Hence, she has had to feel the weight of their anger, hatred, and violence, save in those instances when, by sheer numbers and God's help, which never fails, she has been able to scare off her opponents.

So long, then, as the heavenly City is wayfaring on earth, she invites citizens from all nations and all tongues, and unites them into a single pilgrim band. She takes no issue with that diversity of customs, laws, and traditions whereby human peace is sought and maintained. Instead of nullifying or tearing down, she preserves and appropriates whatever in the diversities of diverse races is aimed at one and the same objective of human peace, provided only that they do not stand in the way of the faith and worship of the one supreme and true God.

Thus, the heavenly City, so long as it is wayfaring on earth, not only makes use of earthly peace but fosters and actively pursues along with other human beings a common platform in regard to all that concerns our purely human life and does not interfere with faith and worship. Of course, though, the City of God subordinates this earthly peace to that of heaven. For this is not merely true peace, but, strictly speaking, for any rational creature, the only real peace, since it is, as I said, "the perfectly ordered and harmonious communion of those who find their joy in God and in one another in God."

When this peace is reached, man will be no longer haunted by death, but plainly and perpetually endowed with life, nor will his body, which now wastes away and weighs down the soul, be any longer animal, but spiritual, in need of nothing, and completely under the control of our will.

This peace the pilgrim City already possesses by faith and it lives holily and according to this faith so long as, to attain its heavenly completion, it refers every good act done for God or for his fellow man. I say "fellow man" because, of course, any community life must emphasize social relationships.

EARLY MEDIEVAL PHILOSOPHY

◀O▶

The philosophical questions of the early Middle Ages tended to focus on what is real and how it is known. Such questions by Christians, of course, included queries about the nature of God, about God's relation to the created order (including the problem of evil), and about the status of universals. Questions about knowledge probed the relation between faith and reason, especially the limits of reason in knowing the divine. Late medieval thinkers added questions about the nature of humankind and the role of society, and they philosophized in quite different ways. But the issues of early medieval thought and the categories established to examine those issues were critical for centuries.

For the most part, the early medieval philosophers worked within the broad framework of Platonic thought, whereas later medieval thinkers tended to adopt Aristotelian categories. Augustine (as either the last classical thinker or the first medieval one), Boethius, John Scotus Eriugena, and Anselm all used Neoplatonic concepts. It was only later that thinkers such as Abelard, John of Salisbury, and, especially, Thomas Aquinas adapted the works of Aristotle. On the other hand, most medieval mystics, whether from the early or later Middle Ages, used Neoplatonic categories.

* * *

Étienne Gilson's *History of Christian Philosophy in the Middle Ages* (New York: Random House, 1955) is the classic study of medieval philosophy. Several of his other works, including *Reason and Revelation in the Middle Ages* (New York: Scribner's, 1936) and *The Spirit of Mediæval Philosophy,* translated by

A.H.C. Downes (New York: Scribner's, 1936), are worth noting. Maurice De Wulf's work, particularly *History of Mediaeval Philosophy* (New York: Dover, 1952), has also been influential. Anne Fremantle, *The Age of Belief: The Medieval Philosophers* (New York: New American Library, 1954) provides a helpful short guide with brief passages from medieval philosophers, whereas Armand A. Maurer, *Medieval Philosophy* (New York: Random House, 1962); A.H. Armstrong, ed., *The Cambridge History of Later Greek and Early Medieval Philosophy* (Cambridge: Cambridge University Press, 1967); Michael Haren, *Medieval Thought: The Western Intellectual Tradition from Antiquity to the Thirteenth Century* (New York: St. Martin's Press, 1985); B.B. Price, *Medieval Thought* (Oxford: Blackwell, 1992); David Luscombe, *Medieval Thought* (Oxford: Oxford University Press, 1997); and John Marenbon, *Routledge History of Philosophy, Volume III: Medieval Philosophy* (New York: Routledge, 1998) provide more extensive works.

For books specifically on the early medieval period, see Frederick Copleston, *A History of Philosophy, Volume II: Medieval Philosophy, Part I: Augustine to Bonaventure* (1950; reprinted Garden City, NY: Image Doubleday, 1962), and John Marenbon, *Early Medieval Philosophy (480–1150): An Introduction* (London: Routledge & Kegan Paul, 1983).

BOETHIUS
ca. A.D. 480–ca. A.D. 524

Anicius Manlius Severinus Boethius was the son of a Roman high-government official. Possibly educated in Athens or Alexandria, Boethius had a special interest in the writings of Plato and Aristotle. His intention was to translate all their works into Latin and provide full commentary. He hoped to show the essential unity between Plato and Aristotle, but he finished only Aristotle's logical works. In 510, Boethius became consul and first minister to King Theodoric, the Ostrogothic ruler of Italy. Boethius served the next twelve years in government, wrote commentaries on Porphyry and Cicero, and began his work on Plato and Aristotle. Boethius's sons were named consuls in 522, and Boethius was made the important "master of the offices." But within a year, tragedy struck. Boethius was accused of treason, imprisoned, and executed sometime around 524. The specific charges are not known, but religious differences were probably involved. Theodoric followed the teachings of Arius (ca. A.D. 256–336) that Jesus Christ was neither coeternal with God the Father nor of the same substance. Boethius, as a Catholic, accepted the conclusions of the Council of Nicea (A.D. 325), which condemned Arian theology.

Our first selection, translated by Richard McKeon, is from Boethius's commentary on Porphyry's introduction to Aristotle's *Categories*. (Such commentary on a commentary was quite common in the early Middle Ages as philosophers grappled with the few classical texts that were available.) In the piece excerpted here, Boethius raises the question of the ontological status of universals, an issue that would vex philosophers for the next thousand years. Do universals, such as genera and species, subsist in themselves apart from the mind?

If so, what kind of existence do they have? After summarizing the issues, Boethius presents a review of Plato's and Aristotle's answers—though he does not give an answer of his own.

While in prison, Boethius wrote his most famous work, *The Consolation of Philosophy*. Written as a dialogue between Boethius and Lady Philosophy, it begins with Boethius protesting innocence and complaining of God's injustice and fortune's caprice. Using arguments rooted in both Stoic and Platonic thought, Philosophy replies that fortune is indeed fickle, but that the highest Good is found not in circumstances but in God. The selection given here, translated by Richard Green, is from the final book of the *Consolation* and examines how God's foreknowledge is compatible with free will. Boethius asks how one could be free to perform an action if God knew *beforehand* what one would do. Using a conception of time similar to Augustine's in Book XI of the *Confessions,* Lady Philosophy explains that God is completely outside time. This means that God "sees all things in his eternal present as you see some things in your temporal present. . . . This divine foreknowledge does not change the nature and properties of things; it simply sees things present before it as they will later turn out to be in what we regard as the future." For example, just as I know what my son is doing now even though his action is free, so God can know what I will do tomorrow though I act freely—because for God tomorrow *is* now.

It may seem odd that a devout Catholic presented his final thoughts in Neoplatonic and Stoic terms, without any specifically Christian references. Yet Boethius's *magnum opus* was a source of great comfort to Christians in the Middle Ages for, as Étienne Gilson points out, "even when he is speaking only as a philosopher, Boethius thinks as a Christian."

*   *   *

For background work on Boethius, see Howard Rollin Patch, *The Tradition of Boethius: A Study of His Importance in Medieval Culture* (New York: Oxford University Press, 1935) and Helen Marjorie Barrett, *Boethius: Some Aspects of His Times and Work* (Cambridge: Cambridge University Press, 1940). Henry Chadwick, *Boethius: The Consolations of Music, Logic, Theology, and Philosophy* (Oxford: Clarendon Press, 1981) and Edmund Reiss, *Boethius* (Boston: Twayne, 1982) study Boethius's writings, whereas Ralph M. McInerny, *Boethius and Aquinas* (Washington, DC: Catholic University of America Press, 1990) shows his influence on Thomas Aquinas. For collections of essays, see Michael Masi, ed., *Boethius and the Liberal Arts: A Collection of Essays* (Las Vegas, NV: Peter Lang, 1981), and Margaret Gibson, ed., *Boethius, His Life, Thought, and Influence* (Oxford: Blackwell, 1981).

In recent years, there has been renewed interest in the problems posed by Boethius's conception of God's timelessness and foreknowledge. Paul Helm, *Eternal God: A Study of God Without Time* (Oxford: Clarendon Press, 1988), for example, argues in favor of Boethius's position, whereas Richard Swinburne, *The Coherence of Theism* (Oxford: Clarendon Press, 1977) and Stephen T. Davis, *Logic and the Nature of God* (Grand Rapids, MI: Eerdmans, 1983) oppose it. Much of the most interesting work in this area is found only in journals such as the *Journal of Philosophy* and *Faith and Philosophy*.

THE SECOND EDITION OF THE COMMENTARIES ON THE ISAGOGE OF PORPHYRY (in part)

BOOK I

10. . . . The mind, whatever it understands, either conceives by understanding and describes to itself by reason that which is established in the nature of things, or else depicts to itself in vacant imagination that which is not. It is inquired therefore of which sort the understanding of genus and of the rest is: whether we understand species and genera as we understand things which are and from which we derive a true understanding, or whether we deceive ourselves, since we form for ourselves, by the empty cogitation of the mind, things which are not. But even if it should be established that they are, and if we should say that the understanding of them is conceived from things which are, then another greater, and more difficult question would occasion doubt, since the most grave difficulty is revealed in distinguishing and understanding the na-

Theodoric exiles Boethius from Rome to Padua, 1521, woodcut. Boethius was consul and first minister to King Theodoric, the Ostrogothic ruler of Italy. But in 522 Boethius was accused of treason, imprisoned, and executed sometime around 524. The specific charges are not known, but probably involved religious differences between the Catholic Boethius and the Arian Theodoric. *(Library of Congress/Instructional Resources Corp.)*

ture of genus itself. For since it is necessary that everything which is, be either corporeal or incorporeal, genus and species will have to be in one of these. Of what sort then will that which is called genus be, corporeal or incorporeal? Nor in fact can attention be turned seriously to what it is, unless it is known in which of these classes it must be placed. But even when this question has been solved, all ambiguity will not be avoided. For there remains something which, should genus and species be called incorporeal, besets the understanding and detains it, demanding that it be resolved, to wit, whether they subsist in bodies themselves, or whether they seem to be incorporeal subsistences beyond bodies. Of course, there are two forms of the incorporeal, so that some things can be outside bodies and perdure [persist] in their incorporeality separated from bodies, as God, mind, soul; but others, although they are incorporeal, nevertheless can not be apart from bodies, as line, or surface, or number, or particular qualities, which, although we pronounce them to be incorporeal because they are not at all extended in three dimensions, nevertheless are in bodies in such fashion that they can not be torn from them or separated. Or if they have been separated from bodies, they in no manner continue to be. These questions although they are difficult, to the point that even Porphyry for the time refused to solve them, I shall nevertheless take up, that I may neither leave the mind of the reader uneasy, nor myself consume time and energy in these things which are outside the sequence of the task I have undertaken. First of all I shall state a few things concerning the ambiguity of the question, and then I shall attempt to remove and untie that knot of doubt.

Genera and species either are and subsist or are formed by the understanding and thought alone. But genera and species can not be. This moreover is understood from the following considerations. For anything that is common at one time to many can not be one; indeed, that which is common is of many, particularly when one and the same thing is completely in many things at one time. Howsoever many species indeed there are, there is one genus in them all, not that the individual species share, as it were, some part of it, but each of them has at one time the whole genus. It follows from this that the whole genus, placed at one time in many individuals, can not be one; nor in fact can it happen that, since it is, wholly in many at one time, it be one in number in itself. But if this is so, no genus can possibly be one, from which it follows that it is absolutely nothing; for everything which is, is because it is one. And the same thing may properly be said of species. Yet if there are genus and species, but they are multiplex and not one in number, there will be no last genus, but it will have some other genus superposed on it, which would include that multiplicity in the word of its single name. For as the genera of many animals are sought for the following reason, that they have something similar, yet are not the same, so too, since the genus, which is in many and is therefore multiplex, has the likeness of itself, which is the genus, but is not one, because it is in many, another genus of this genus must likewise be looked for, and when that has been found, for the reason which has been mentioned above, still a third genus is to be sought out. And so reason must proceed *in infinitum,* since no end of the process occurs. But if any genus is one in number, it can not possibly be common to many. For a single thing, if it is common, is common by parts, and then it is not common as a whole, but the parts of it are proper to individual things, or else it passes at different times into the use of those having it, so that it is common as a servant or a horse is; or else it is made common to all at one time, not however that it constitutes the substance of those to which it is common, but like some theatre or spectacle, which is common to all who look on. But genus can be common to the species according to none of these modes; for it must be common in such fashion that it is in the individuals wholly and at one time, and that it is able to constitute and form the substance of those things to which it is common. For this reason, if it is neither one, because it is common, nor many, because still another genus must be sought for that multitude, it will be seen that genus absolutely is not, and the same conclusion must be applied to the others. But if genera and species and the others are grasped only by understandings, since every idea is made either from the subject thing as the thing is constituted itself or as the thing is not constituted—for an idea can not be made from no subject—if the idea of genus and species and the others comes from the subject thing as the thing itself is constituted which is understood, then they are not only placed in the understanding but are placed also in the truth of things. And again it must be sought out what their nature is which the previous question investigated. But if the idea of genus and the rest is taken from the thing not as the thing is constituted which is subject to the idea, the idea must necessarily be vain, which is taken from the thing but not as the thing is constituted; for that is false which is understood otherwise than the thing is. Thus, therefore, since genus and species neither are nor, when they are understood, is the idea of them true, it is not uncertain that all this must be set forth relative to the care which is needed for investigating concerning the five predicables aforementioned, seeing that the inquiry is neither concerning the thing which is, nor concerning that of which something true can be understood or adduced.

11. This for the present is the question with regard to the aforementioned predicables, which we solve, in accord with Alexander, by the following reasoning. We say that it is not necessary that every idea which is formed from a subject but not as the subject itself is constituted, seem false and empty. For false opinion, but not understanding, is in only those ideas which are made by composition. For if any one composes and joins by the understanding that which nature does not suffer to be joined, no one is unaware that that is false, as would be the case should one join by the imagination horse and man and construct a centaur. But if it be done by division and by abstraction, the thing would not be constituted as the idea is, yet for all that, the idea is still not in the least false; for there are many things which have their being in others, from which either they can not at all be separated, or if they should be separated they subsist by no reason. And in order that this be shown to us in a well known example, the line is something in a body, and it owes to the body that which it is, namely, it retains its being through body. Which is shown thus: if it should be separated from body, it does not subsist; for who ever perceived with any sense a line separated from body? But when the mind receives from the senses things confused and intermingled with each other, it distinguishes them by its own power and thought. For sense transmits to us, besides bodies themselves, all incorporeal things of this sort which have their being in bodies, but the mind which has the power to compound that which is disjoined and to resolve that which is composite, so distinguishes the things which are transmitted by the senses, confused with and joined to bodies, that it may contemplate and see the incorporeal nature in itself and without the bodies in which it is concrete. For the characteristics of incorporeal things mixed with bodies are diverse even when they are separated from body. Genera therefore and species and the others are found either in incorporeal things or in those which are corporeal. And if the mind finds them in incorporeal things, it has in that instance an incorporeal understanding of a genus, but if it has perceived the genera and species of corporeal things, it bears off, as is its wont, the nature of incorporeals from bodies, and beholds it alone and pure as the form itself is in itself. So when the mind receives these incorporeals intermixed with bodies, separating them, it looks upon them and contemplates them. No one, therefore, may say that we think about the line falsely because we seize it by the mind as if it were outside bodies, since

it can not be outside bodies. For not every idea which is taken from subject things otherwise than the things are themselves constituted, must be considered to be false but, as has been said above, that only is false which does this by composition, as when one thinks, joining man and horse, that there is a centaur; but that which accomplishes it by divisions, and abstractions, and assumptions from the things in which they are, not only is not false, but it alone can discover that which is true with respect to the characteristic of the thing. Things of this sort therefore are in corporeal and sensible things, but they are understood without sensible things, in order that their nature can be perceived and their characteristic comprehended. Since genera and species are thought, therefore their likeness is gathered from the individuals in which they are, as the likeness of humanity is gathered from individual men unlike each other, which likeness conceived by the mind and perceived truly is made the species; again when the likeness of these diverse species is considered, which can not be except in the species themselves or in the individuals of the species, it forms the genus.

Consequently, genera and species are in individuals, but they are thought universals; and species must be considered to be nothing other than the thought collected from the substantial likeness of individuals unlike in number, and genus the thought collected from the likeness of species. But this likeness when it is in individual things is made sensible, when it is in universals it is made intelligible; and in the same way when it is sensible, it remains in individuals, when it is understood, it is made universal. Therefore, they subsist in sensibles, but they are understood without bodies. For there is nothing to prevent two things which are in the same subject from being different in reason, like a concave and a convex line, which things, although they are defined by diverse definitions and although the understanding of them is diverse, are nevertheless always found in the same subject; for it is the same line which is convex and concave. So too for genera and species, that is, for singularity and universality, there is only one subject, but it is universal in one manner when it is thought, and singular in another when it is perceived in those things in which it has its being.

Once these distinctions are made, therefore, the whole question, I believe, is solved. For genera and species subsist in one manner, but are understood in another; and they are incorporeal, but they subsist in sensible things joined to sensible things. They are understood, to be sure, as subsisting through themselves and not as having their being in others. Plato, however, thinks that genera, and species, and the rest not only are understood as universals, but also are and subsist without bodies; whereas Aristotle thinks that they are understood as incorporeal and universal, but subsist in sensibles; we have not considered it proper to determine between their opinions, for that is of more lofty philosophy. But we have followed out the opinion of Aristotle very diligently for this reason, not in the least because we approved of it, but because this book has been written for the *Categories,* of which Aristotle is the author.

THE CONSOLATION OF PHILOSOPHY
(in part)

BOOK V

1. *Philosophy discusses the question of chance.* When Philosophy had finished her song and was about to turn to the discussion of other matters, I interrupted saying, "Your exhortation is a worthy one and your authority is great, but I know from experience that you are right in saying that the question of Providence involves many other problems. I should like to know whether there is any such thing as chance, and, if so, what it may be."

"I have been trying, as quickly as possible, to carry out my promise to show you the way back to your true country. These other questions are somewhat beside the main point of my argument, even though they are quite important in themselves. I shouldn't want you to become so wearied by side trips that you would not be able to complete the main journey."

"Please do not worry about that," I said. "For it would comfort me to understand the things in which I take the greatest pleasure. When every part of your argument is convincingly established, none of its implications will cause any doubt."

"I will do as you ask," she replied, and took up her explanation again.

"If chance is defined as an event produced by random motion and without any sequence of causes, then I say that there is no such thing as chance; apart from its use in the present context, I consider it an empty word. For what room can there be for random events since God keeps all things in order? The commonplace that nothing can come from nothing is true; and the old philosophers never denied it, though they did not apply it to the effective cause of things but only to the material subject as a kind of foundation of all their reasoning about nature. But if anything should happen without cause, it would seem to come from nothing. And if this cannot be, chance as we defined it a moment ago is impossible."

"Then is there nothing which can rightly be called chance?" I asked. "Does nothing happen fortuitously? Or is there something to which those words refer, even if it is not rightly understood by ordinary people?"

"My true follower, Aristotle, gave a brief and sound definition of chance in his *Physics.*"*

"What did he say?" I asked.

"Whenever anything is done for one reason, but something other than what was intended happens on account of other reasons, it is called chance. For example, when a man digs the earth with the intention of cultivating it, and finds a treasure of buried gold, this is thought to happen by chance. But it does not come from nothing since the event has its own causes whose unforeseen and unexpected concurrence seems to have produced an effect by chance. For, if the farmer had not dug the ground, and if someone had not buried his gold in that spot, the treasure would not have been found. These

---

*Physics II.4–5; cf. *Metaphysics* IV.30.

Boethius, *The Consolation of Philosophy,* Book V (prose), translated by Richard Green (New York: Macmillan/Library of the Liberal Arts, 1962).

are the causes of the fortunate accident which is brought about by the coincidence of causes and not by the intention of the one performing the action. For neither the man who buried the gold, nor the man who was cultivating the field, intended that the money should be found; but, as I said, it happened coincidentally that the farmer dug where the other had buried the money.

"Therefore, we can define chance as an unexpected event brought about by a concurrence of causes which had other purposes in view. These causes come together because of that order which proceeds from inevitable connection of things, the order which flows from the source which is Providence and which disposes all things, each in its proper time and place.

2. *Philosophy argues that rational natures must necessarily have free will.* "I have listened carefully and agree that chance is as you say. But, within this series of connected causes, does our will have any freedom, or are the motions of human souls also bound by the fatal chain?"

"There is free will," Philosophy answered, "and no rational nature can exist which does not have it. For any being, which by its nature has the use of reason, must also have the power of judgment by which it can make decisions and, by its own resources, distinguish between things which should be desired and things which should be avoided. Now everyone seeks that which he judges to be desirable, but rejects whatever he thinks should be avoided. Therefore, in rational creatures there is also freedom of desiring and shunning.

"But I do not say that this freedom is the same in all beings.

In supreme and divine substances there is clear judgment, uncorrupted will, and effective power to obtain what they desire. Human souls, however, are more free while they are engaged in contemplation of the divine mind, and less free when they are joined to bodies, and still less free when they are bound by earthly fetters. They are in utter slavery when they lose possession of their reason and give themselves wholly to vice. For when they turn away their eyes from the light of supreme truth to mean and dark things, they are blinded by a cloud of ignorance and obsessed by vicious passions. By yielding and consenting to these passions, they worsen the slavery to which they have brought themselves and are, as it were, the captives of their own freedom. Nevertheless, God, who beholds all things from eternity, foresees all these things in his providence and disposes each according to its predestined merits."

3. *Boethius contends that divine foreknowledge and freedom of the human will are incompatible.* "Now I am confused by an even greater difficulty," I said.

"What is it?" Philosophy answered, "though I think I know what is bothering you."

"There seems to be a hopeless conflict between divine foreknowledge of all things and freedom of the human will. For if God sees everything in advance and cannot be deceived in any way, whatever his Providence foresees will happen, must happen. Therefore, if God foreknows eternally not only all the acts of men, but also their plans and wishes, there cannot be freedom of will; for nothing whatever can be done or even desired without its being known beforehand by the infallible Providence of God. If things could somehow be accomplished in some way other than that which God foresaw, his foreknowledge of the future would no longer be certain. Indeed, it would be merely uncertain opinion, and it would be wrong to think that of God.

"I cannot agree with the argument by which some people believe that they can solve this problem. They say that things do not happen because Providence foresees that they will happen, but, on the contrary, that Providence foresees what is to come because it will happen, and in this way they find the necessity to be in things, not in Providence. For, they say, it is not necessary that things should happen because they are foreseen, but only that things which will happen be foreseen—as though the problem were whether divine Providence is the cause of the necessity of future events, or the necessity of future events is the cause of divine Providence. But our concern is to prove that the fulfillment of things which God has foreseen is necessary, whatever the order of causes, even if the divine foreknowledge does not seem to make the occurrence of future events necessary. For example, if a man sits down, the opinion that he is sitting must be true; and conversely, if the opinion that someone is sitting be true, then that person must necessarily be sitting. Therefore, there is necessity in both cases: the man must be sitting and the opinion must be true. But the man is not sitting because the opinion is true; the opinion is true because the sitting came before the opinion about it. Therefore, even though the cause of truth came from one side, necessity is common to both.

"A similar line of reasoning applies to divine foreknowledge and future events. For even though the events are foreseen because they will happen, they do not happen because they are foreseen. Nevertheless, it is necessary either that things which are going to happen be foreseen by God, or that what God foresees will in fact happen; and either way the freedom of the human will is destroyed. But of course it is preposterous to say that the outcome of temporal things is the cause of eternal foreknowledge. Yet to suppose that God foresees future events because they are going to happen is the same as supposing that things which happened long ago are the cause of divine Providence. Furthermore, just as when I know that a thing is, that thing must necessarily be; so when I know that something will happen, it is necessary that it happen. It follows, then, that the outcome of something known in advance must necessarily take place.

"Finally, if anyone thinks that a thing is other than it actually is, he does not have knowledge but merely a fallible opinion, and that is quite different from the truth of knowledge. So, if the outcome of some future event is either uncertain or unnecessary, no one can know in advance whether or not it will happen. For just as true knowledge is not tainted by falsity, so that which is known by it cannot be otherwise than as it is known. And that is the reason why knowledge never deceives; things must necessarily be as true knowledge knows them to be. If this is so, how does God foreknow future possibilities whose existence is uncertain? If He thinks that things will inevitably happen which possibly will not happen, He is deceived. But it is wrong to say that, or even to think it. And if He merely knows that they may or may not happen, that is, if He knows only their contingent possibilities, what is such knowledge worth, since it does not know with certainty? Such knowledge is no better than that expressed by the ridiculous prophecy of Tiresias: 'Whatever I say will either be or not be.' Divine Providence would be no better than human opinion if God judges as men do and knows only that uncertain events are doubtful. But if nothing can be uncertain to Him who is the most certain source of all things, the outcome is certain of all things which He knows with certainty shall be.

"Therefore, there can be no freedom in human decisions and actions, since the divine mind, foreseeing everything without possibility of error, determines and forces the outcome of everything that is to happen. Once this is granted, it is clear that the structure of all human affairs must collapse. For it is pointless to assign rewards and punishment to the good and wicked since neither are deserved if the actions of men are not free and voluntary. Punishment of the wicked and recognition of the good, which are now considered just, will seem quite unjust since neither the good nor the wicked are governed by their own will but are forced by the inevitability of predetermination. Vice and virtue will be without meaning, and in their place there will be utter confusion about what is deserved. Finally, and this is the most blasphemous thought of all, it follows that the Author of all good must be made responsible for all human vice since the entire order of human events depends on Providence and nothing on man's intention.

"There is no use in hoping or praying for anything, for what is the point in hope or prayer when everything that man desires is determined by unalterable process? Thus man's only bonds with God, hope and prayer, are destroyed. We believe that our just humility may earn the priceless reward of divine grace, for this is the only way in which men seem able to communicate with God; we are joined to that inaccessible light by supplication before receiving what we ask. But if we hold that all future events are governed by necessity, and therefore that prayer has no value, what will be left to unite us to the sovereign Lord of all things? And so mankind must, as you said earlier, be cut off from its source and dwindle into nothing."

4. *Philosophy begins her argument that divine Providence does not preclude freedom of the will by stressing the difference between divine and human knowledge.* "This is an old difficulty about Providence," Philosophy answered. "It was raised by Cicero in his book on divination,* and has for a long time been a subject of your own investigation, but so far none of you has treated it with enough care and conviction. The cause of the obscurity which still surrounds the problem is that the process of human reason cannot comprehend the simplicity of divine foreknowledge. If in any way we could understand that, no further doubt would remain. I shall try to make this clear after I have explained the things which trouble you.

"First, let me ask why you regard as inconclusive the reasoning of those who think that foreknowledge is no hindrance to free will because it is not the cause of the necessity of future things. For do you have any argument for the necessity of future events other than the principle that things which are known beforehand must happen? If, as you have just now conceded, foreknowledge does not impose necessity on future events, why must the voluntary outcome of things be bound to predetermined results? For the sake of argument, so that you may consider what follows from it, let us suppose that there is no foreknowledge. Then would the things which are done by free will be bound by necessity in this respect?"

"Not at all."

"Then, let us suppose that foreknowledge exists but imposes no necessity on things. The same independence and absolute freedom of will would remain.

"But you will say that even though foreknowledge does not impose necessity on future events, it is still a sign that they will necessarily happen. It must follow then that even if there were no foreknowledge the outcome of these future things would be necessary. For signs only show what is, they do not cause the things they point to. Therefore we must first prove that nothing happens other than by necessity, in order to demonstrate that foreknowledge is a sign of this necessity. Otherwise, if there is no necessity, then foreknowledge cannot be a sign of something that does not exist. Moreover, it is clear that firmly based proof does not rest on signs and extrinsic arguments but is deduced from suitable and necessary causes. But how can it be that things which are foreseen should not happen? We do not suppose that things will not happen, if Providence has foreknowledge that they will; rather we judge that, although they will

De divinatione II.8ff.

happen, they have nothing in their natures which makes it necessary that they should happen. For we see many things in the process of happening before our eyes, just as the chariot driver sees the results of his actions as he guides his chariot; and this is true in many of our activities. Do you think that such things are compelled by necessity to happen as they do?"

"No. For the results of art would be vain if they were all brought about by compulsion."

"Then, since they come into being without necessity, these same things were not determined by necessity before they actually happened. Therefore, there are some things destined to happen in the future whose outcome is free of any necessity. For everyone, I think, would say that things which are now happening were going to happen before they actually came to pass. Thus, these things happen without necessity even though they were known in advance. For just as knowledge of things happening now does not imply necessity in their outcomes, so foreknowledge of future things imposes no necessity on their outcomes in the future.

"But, you will say, the point at issue is whether there can be any foreknowledge of things whose outcomes are not necessary. For these things seem opposed to each other, and you think that if things can be foreseen they must necessarily happen, and that if the necessity is absent they cannot be foreseen, and that nothing can be fully known unless it is certain. If uncertain things are foreseen as certain, that is the weakness of opinion, not the truth of knowledge. You believe that to judge that a thing is other than it is departs from the integrity of knowledge. Now the cause of this error lies in your assumption that whatever is known, is known only by the force and nature of the things which are known; but the opposite is true. Everything which is known is known not according to its own power but rather according to the capacity of the knower.

"Let me illustrate with a brief example: the roundness of a body is known in one way by the sense of touch and in another by the sight. The sight, remaining at a distance, takes in the whole body at once by its reflected rays; but the touch makes direct contact with the sphere and comprehends it piecemeal by moving around its surface. A man himself is comprehended in different ways by the senses, imagination, reason, and intelligence. The senses grasp the figure of the thing as it is constituted in matter; the imagination, however, grasps the figure alone without the matter. Reason, on the other hand, goes beyond this and investigates by universal consideration the species itself which is in particular things. The vision of intelligence is higher yet, and it goes beyond the bounds of the universe and sees with the clear eye of the mind the pure form itself.

"In all this we chiefly observe that the higher power of knowing includes the lower, but the lower can in no way rise to the higher. For the senses achieve nothing beyond the material, the imagination cannot grasp universal species, reason cannot know simple forms; but the intelligence, as though looking down from on high, conceives the underlying forms and distinguishes among them all, but in the same way in which it comprehends the form itself which cannot be known to any other power. The intelligence knows the objects of the lower kinds of knowledge: the universals of the reason, the figures of the imagination, the matter of the senses, but not by using reason, or imagination, or senses. With a single glance of the mind it formally, as it were, sees all things. Similarly, when reason knows a universal nature, it comprehends all the objects of imagination and the senses without using either. For reason defines the general nature of her conception as follows: man is a biped, rational animal. This is a universal idea, but no one ignores the fact that man is also an imaginable and sensible object which reason knows by rational conception rather than by the imagination and senses. Similarly, although the imagination begins by seeing and forming figures with the senses, nevertheless it can, without the aid of the senses, behold sensible objects by an imaginative rather than a sensory mode of knowing.

"Do you see, then, how all these use their own power in knowing rather than the powers of the objects which are known? And this is proper, for since all judgment is in the act of the one judging, it is necessary that everyone should accomplish his own action by his own power, not by the power of something other than himself.

5. *To understand this mystery, human reason must contemplate the power of the divine intelligence.* "Thus, in the case of sentient bodies external stimuli affect the sense organs, and a physical sensation precedes the activity of the mind, calling the mind to act upon itself and in this way to activate the interior forms which before were inactive. Now if, as I say, in sentient bodies the soul is affected by external bodies but judges these stimuli presented to the body not passively, but by virtue of its own power, how much more do intelligences which are wholly free from all bodily affections use the power of the mind rather than objects extrinsic to themselves in arriving at judgments. According to this principle, various and different substances have different ways of knowing. There are certain immobile living things which are without any means of knowing other than by sense impressions. Shellfish and other forms of marine life which are nourished as they stick to rocks are creatures of this kind. Beasts which have the power of motion, on the other hand, have the impulse to seek and avoid certain things, and they have imagination. But reason is characteristic of the human race alone, just as pure intelligence belongs to God alone.

"It follows, then, that the most excellent knowledge is that which by its own nature knows not only its own proper object but also the objects of all lower kinds of knowledge. What, then, should we think if the senses and imagination were to oppose reason by arguing that the universal, which reason claims to know, is nothing? Suppose they were to argue that whatever can be sensed or imagined cannot be universal; and that therefore either the judgment of reason is true, and there are no objects of sense knowledge, or, since everyone knows that many things can be known by the senses and the imagination, that the conception of reason, which regards whatever is sensible and singular as if it were universal, is vain and empty. And suppose, further, that reason should answer that it conceives sensible and imaginable objects under the aspect of universality, but that the senses and imagination cannot aspire to the knowledge of universality because their knowledge cannot go beyond corporeal figures. Moreover, reason might continue, in matters of knowledge we ought to trust the stronger and more perfect judgment. In such a controversy we who possess the power of reason, as well as of imagination and sense perception, ought to take the side of reason.

"The situation is much the same when human reason supposes that the divine intelligence beholds future events only as reason herself sees them. For you argue that if some things seem not to have certain and necessary outcomes, they cannot be foreknown as certainly about to happen. Therefore, you say that there can be no foreknowledge of these things, or, if we believe that there is such foreknowledge, that the outcome of all things is controlled by necessity. But if we, who are endowed with reason, could possess the intelligence of the divine mind, we would judge that just as the senses and imagination should accede to reason, so human reason ought justly to submit itself to the divine mind. Let us rise, if we can, to the summit of the highest intelligence; for there reason will see what in itself it cannot see: that a certain And definite foreknowledge can behold even those things which have no certain outcome. And this foreknowledge is not mere conjecture but the unrestricted simplicity of supreme knowledge.

6. *Philosophy solves the problem of providence and free will by distinguishing between simple and conditional necessity.* "Since, as we have shown, whatever is known is known according to the nature of the knower, and not according to its own nature, let us now consider as far as is lawful the nature of the Divine Being, so that we may discover what its knowledge is. The common judgment of all rational creatures holds that God is eternal. Therefore let us consider what eternity is, for this will reveal both the divine nature and the divine knowledge.

"Eternity is the whole, perfect, and simultaneous possession of endless life. The meaning of this can be made clearer by comparison with temporal things. For whatever lives in time lives in the present, proceeding from past to future, and nothing is so constituted in time that it can embrace the whole span of its life at once. It has not yet arrived at tomorrow, and it has already lost yesterday; even the life of this day is lived only in each moving, passing moment. Therefore, whatever is subject to the condition of time, even that which—as Aristotle conceived the world to be—has no beginning and will have no end in a life coextensive with the infinity of time, is such that it cannot rightly be thought eternal. For it does not comprehend and include the whole of infinite life all at once, since it does not embrace the future which is yet to come. Therefore, only that which comprehends and possesses the whole plenitude of endless life together, from which no future thing nor any past thing is absent, can justly be called eternal. Moreover, it is necessary that such a being be in full possession of itself, always present to itself, and hold the infinity of moving time present before itself.

"Therefore, they are wrong who, having heard that Plato held that this world did not have a beginning in time and would never come to an end, suppose that the created world is coeternal with its Creator. For it is one thing to live an endless life, which is what Plato ascribed to the world, and another for the whole of unending life to be embraced all at once as present, which is clearly proper to the divine mind. Nor should God be thought of as older than His creation in extent of time, but rather as prior to it by virtue of the simplicity of His nature. For the infinite motion of temporal things imitates the immediate present of His changeless life and, since it cannot reproduce or equal life, it sinks from immobility to motion and declines from the simplicity of the present into the infinite duration of future and past. And, since it cannot possess the whole fullness of its life at once, it seems to imitate to some extent that which it cannot completely express, and it does this by somehow never ceasing to be. It binds itself to a kind of present in this short and transitory period which, because it has a certain likeness to that abiding, unchanging present, gives everything it touches a semblance of existence. But, since this imitation cannot remain still, it hastens along the infinite road of time, and so it extends by movement the life whose completeness it could not achieve by standing still. Therefore, if we wish to call things by their proper names, we should follow Plato in saying that God indeed is eternal, but the world is perpetual.

"Since, then, every judgment comprehends the subjects presented to it according to its own nature, and since God lives in the eternal present, His knowledge transcends all movement of time and abides in the simplicity of its immediate present. It encompasses the infinite sweep of past and future, and regards all things in its simple comprehension as if they were now taking place. Thus, if you will think about the foreknowledge by which God distinguishes all things, you will rightly consider it to be not a foreknowledge of future events, but knowledge of a never changing present. For this reason, divine knowledge is called providence, rather than prevision, because it resides above all inferior things and looks out on all things from their summit.

"Why then do you imagine that things are necessary which are illuminated by this divine light, since even men do not impose necessity on the things they see? Does your vision impose any necessity upon things which you see present before you?"

"Not at all," I answered.

"Then," Philosophy went on, "if we may aptly compare God's present vision with man's, He sees all things in his eternal present as you see some things in your temporal present. Therefore, this divine foreknowledge does not change the nature and properties of things; it simply sees things present before it as they will later turn out to be in what we regard as the future. His judgment is not confused; with a single intuition of his mind He knows all things that are to come, whether necessarily or not. Just as, when you happen to see simultaneously a man walking on the street and the sun shining in the sky, even though you see both at once, you can distinguish between them and realize that one action is voluntary, the other necessary; so the divine mind, looking down on all things, does not disturb the nature of the things which are present before it but are future with respect to time. Therefore, when God knows that something will happen in the future, and at the same time knows that it will not happen through necessity, this is not opinion but knowledge based on truth.

"If you should reply that whatever God foresees as happening cannot help but happen, and that whatever must happen is bound by necessity—if you pin me down to this word 'necessity'—I grant that you state a solid truth, but one which only a profound theologian can grasp. I would answer that the same future event is necessary with respect to God's knowledge of it, but free and undetermined if considered in its own nature. For there are two kinds of necessity: one is simple, as the necessity by which all men are mortals; the other is conditional, as is the case when, if you know that someone is walking, he must necessarily be walking. For whatever is known, must be as it is known to be; but this condition does not involve that other, simple necessity. It is not caused by the peculiar nature of the person in question, but by an added condition. No necessity forces the man who is voluntarily walking to move forward; but as long as he is walking, he is necessarily moving forward. In the same way, if Providence sees anything as present, that thing must necessarily be, even though it may have no necessity by its nature. But God sees as present those future things which result from free will. Therefore, from the standpoint of divine knowledge these things are necessary because of the condition of their being known by God; but, considered only in themselves, they lose nothing of the absolute freedom of their own natures.

"There is no doubt, then, that all things will happen which God knows will happen; but some of them happen as a result of free will. And, although they happen, they do not, by their existence, lose their proper natures by which, before they happened, they were able not to happen. But, you may ask, what does it mean to say that these events are not necessary, since by reason of the condition of divine knowledge they happen just as if they were necessary? The meaning is the same as in the example I used a while ago of the sun rising and the man walking. At the time they are happening, they must necessarily be happening; but the sun's rising is governed by necessity even before it happens, while the man's walking is not. Similarly, all the things God sees as present will undoubtedly come to pass; but some will happen by the necessity of their natures, others by the power of those who make them happen. Therefore, we quite properly said that these things are necessary if viewed from the standpoint of divine knowledge, but if they are considered in themselves, they are free of the bonds of necessity. In somewhat the same way, whatever is known by the senses is singular in itself, but universal as far as the reason is concerned.

"But, you may say, if I can change my mind about doing something, I can frustrate Providence, since by chance I may change something which Providence foresaw. My answer is this: you can indeed alter what you propose to do, but, because the present truth of Providence sees that you can, and whether or not you will, you cannot frustrate the divine knowledge any more than you can escape the eye of someone who is present and watching you, even though you may, by your free will, vary your actions. You may still wonder, however, whether God's knowledge is changed by your decisions, so that when you wish now one thing, now another, the divine knowledge undergoes corresponding changes. This is not the case. For divine Providence anticipates every future action and converts it to its own present knowledge. It does not change, as you imagine, foreknowing this or that in succession, but in a single instant, without being changed itself, anticipates and grasps your changes. God has this present comprehension and immediate vision of all things not from the outcome of future events, but from the simplicity of his own nature. In this way, the problem you raised a moment ago is settled. You observed that it would be unworthy of God if our future acts were said to be the cause of divine knowledge. Now you see that this power of divine knowledge, comprehending all things as present before it, itself constitutes the measure of all things and is in no way dependent on things that happen later.

"Since this is true, the freedom of the human will remains inviolate, and laws are just since they provide rewards and punishments to human wills which are not controlled by necessity. God looks down from above, knowing all things, and the eternal present of his vision concurs with the future character of our actions, distributing rewards to the good and punishments to the evil. Our hopes and prayers are not directed to God in vain, for if they are just they cannot fail. Therefore, stand firm against vice and cultivate virtue. Lift up your soul to worthy hopes, and offer humble prayers to heaven. If you will face it, the necessity of virtuous action imposed upon you is very great, since all your actions are done in the sight of a Judge who sees all things."

JOHN SCOTUS ERIUGENA
ca. A.D. 810–ca. 877

The collapse of the Western Roman Empire led to a period of economic and social anarchy. Living conditions from the end of the sixth to the middle of the eleventh centuries were so primitive that, according to historians, "one can almost speak of five centuries of camping out."* Government was largely tribal in nature, led by warriors who considered loyalty to one's liege lord the primary virtue. The existing social stability, negligible though it was, depended upon exceptional individuals, such as Charlemagne and Alfred the Great. One of the few remaining places for intellectual endeavor was the monastery; and monasteries were often far from population centers, many on the very edges of Europe. It should not be surprising, then, that the one philosopher of note to emerge from this period was a monk from Ireland: John Scotus Eriugena.

John Scotus Eriugena's two last names both mean "from Ireland" (at that time the Irish were called "Scoti," and "Eriugena" means "of the people of Erin [Ireland]"). Eriugena, as he is commonly called, studied Greek in an Irish monastery and eventually became a teacher in the court of the king of the Franks, Charles the Bald. While there, he was embroiled in a controversy on the nature of the Eucharist, and one of his books was burned. Apart from these slim data, we know little about Eriugena's life and cannot even say for certain when or how he died (though 877 is the frequently given date).

In the selection from *The Division of Nature* included here, in the Myra L. Uhfelder translation, Eriugena shows his Neoplatonic roots by giving two ways of

---

*Robert E. Lerner et al., *Western Civilizations,* 11th edition (New York: Norton, 1988), p. 278.

dividing "nature" (meaning all of reality). In the first method, based on the concepts of creating and being created, Eriugena divides nature into four parts. First is "that which creates and is not created" (i.e., God), then "that which is created and also creates" (i.e., Platonic Forms), then "that which is created and does not create" (i.e., the material world), and finally "that which neither creates nor is created" (God again). The first and fourth divisions turn out to be the Creator, whereas the second and third are the creation (immaterial and material, respectively).

The second, and more basic, division of nature is into "things that are" and "things that are not." It might seem that "things that are not" would be sheer nothingness and so not really a part of "nature" at all. But, Eriugena explains, there are several "things" that do not exist in one mode or another. These include (1) anything beyond our faculties of apprehension, (2) the negation of the superior, (3) potential beings, (4) changing particulars, and (5) the sinful nature of humans (who have lost their essential nature). The first of these modes of nonbeing has the dubious distinction of making God one of the "things that are not." Eriugena asserted that indeed "God is not," but he pointed out that this way of thinking and talking is simply the *via negativa*—the negative way of confessing God. There is also a *via affirmativa,* which allows the affirmation of God's essential properties. So, for example, it is correct (using the *via negativa*) to say that "God is not good," whereas it is also correct (using the *via affirmativa*) to say that "God is good." Eriugena resolved this seeming contradiction by claiming that although God is not (literally) good, God is (metaphorically) good—in short, God is *super*good.

Eriugena's fourfold division of reality looks a good deal like Plotinus's emanations and seems to put God and God's creation in the same category ("Nature"). Not surprisingly, Eriugena was accused by the Catholic Church of Neoplatonic pantheism, and his work was eventually condemned as heretical in 1225.

*   *   *

In addition to the appropriate chapters in the surveys of early medieval philosophy previously listed (pages 143–44), the following studies of Eriugena should be consulted for further reading: Henry Bett, *Johannes Scotus Eriugena: A Study in Mediaeval Philosophy* (1925; reprinted New York: Russell and Russell, 1964); John O'Meara, *Eriugena* (Oxford: Clarendon Press, 1988); Dermot Moran, *The Philosophy of John Scotus Eriugena: A Study of Idealism in the Middle Ages* (Cambridge: Cambridge University Press, 1989); and Deidre Carabine, *John Scotus Eriugena* (Oxford: Oxford University Press, 2000). For collections of essays, see F.X. Martin and J.A. Richmond, eds., *From Augustine to Eriugena: Essays on Neoplatonism and Christianity* (Washington, DC: Catholic University of America Press, 1991), and Bernard McGinn and Willemien Otten, *Eriugena: East and West* (Notre Dame, IN: Notre Dame University Press, 1994).

THE DIVISION OF NATURE
(PERIPHYSEON) (in part)

BOOK I

TEACHER: Often I investigate as carefully as I can and reflect that of all things which can either be perceived by the mind or surpass its concentrated efforts the first and highest division is into what has and what does not have being. At such times the general designation of them all occurs to me, ⟨*physis*⟩ in Greek and *natura* in Latin. Or don't you agree?

STUDENT: Yes, I do. Although I am just entering upon the path of reasoning, I find that it is so.

TEACHER: As we have just said, then, "nature" is a general name for all things, whether or not they have being.

STUDENT: It certainly is, for we can think of nothing at all to which such a designation does not apply.

TEACHER: Since we have agreed that this is a generic designation, I should like you to tell how it is divided into species by *differentiae*. Or if you prefer, I shall try to establish the divisions first and your task will be to judge them.

STUDENT: Please begin. I am eager and impatient to hear you give a true account about these matters.

[1] TEACHER: The division of nature seems to me to admit of four species through four *differentiae*. The first is the division into what creates and is not created; the second into what is created and creates; the third, into what is created and does not create; the fourth, into what neither creates nor is created. Of these four, two pairs consist of opposites. The third is the opposite of the first, the fourth of the second. But the fourth is among the things which are impossible, and its *differentiae* is its inability to be. Does such a division seem to you correct or not?

STUDENT: It surely does, but would you please go over it to clarify the opposition of the species just mentioned?

TEACHER: Unless I'm mistaken, you see the opposition of the third species to the first. The first creates and is not created, and its opposite is that which is created and does not create. Likewise the opposition of the second to the fourth, since the second is created and creates; the fourth, which neither creates nor is created, is contrary to it in every respect.

STUDENT: I see that clearly, but I am quite perplexed about the fourth species which you added. As for the other three, I should not venture to have any misgivings; for I judge that the first is understood in the Cause of all things which have and all which do not have being, the second in the primordial causes, the third in those things known by generation in time and place. I see, therefore, that we must have a more detailed discussion about the individual species.

John Scotus Erigena [Eriugena], *Periphyseon: On the Division of Nature,* Book I, 1–7; 11–14, edited and translated by Myra L. Uhfelder, summaries by Jean A. Potter (New York: Macmillan/Library of the Liberal Arts, 1976).

TEACHER: You are quite right. But I leave it to your judgment to determine our order of reasoning; i.e., to decide which species of nature should be discussed first.

STUDENT: I think that it would be proper, before dealing with the others to say what our insight reveals to us about the first.

[2] TEACHER: All right, but I think that first we must talk briefly about the highest and main division of all which, as we said, is the division into the things which have and those which do not have being.

STUDENT: That is a very sound and judicious idea. I see that our reasoning should begin no other way, not only because that is the first *differentia* of all things, but also because it appears, and is, more obscure than the others.

TEACHER: Well, then, the original distinguishing *differentia* of all things demands clear-cut methods of interpretation.

[3] Of these, the first seems to be the one by which reason persuades us that all things subject to corporeal sense or the perception of intelligence can reasonably be said to have being; but all that, by the excellence of their nature, elude not only the *hylion*, i.e., every sense, but also intellect and reason, properly seem not to have being. They are correctly understood only in God, matter, and the reasons and essences of all things created by Him. And that is as it should be; for He Himself, who alone truly has being, is the essence of all things, according to Dionysius the Areopagite, who says: "The being of all things is Superbeing, Divinity." Gregory the Theologian too affirms by many reasons that intellect or reason cannot grasp what any substance or essence is, whether it belongs to visible or to invisible creation. For just as God Himself, in Himself, beyond all creation is grasped by no intellect, so also *ousia* ["*essentia*" or "being"] considered in the innermost recesses of the creation made by Him and existing in Him, is incomprehensible. Besides, whatever in every creature is either perceived by corporeal sense or considered by the intellect is simply some accident, incomprehensible in itself, as has been said, of an essence. By quality, quantity, form, matter, some *differentia,* place, or time we know not *what* it is, but *that* it is. This, then, is the first and highest method of division of what is said to have and what is said not to have being. I believe, however, that that method which it seems, in a way, possible to introduce, namely the one based on privations of states in reference to substances, as sight and blindness in reference to the eyes, must be utterly rejected. For if something wholly lacks being and cannot be and does not surpass intellect because of the supernal height of its existence, I fail to see how it can fit into the divisions of things; unless, perhaps, one should say that the absences and privations of things with being are not absolutely nothing, but that they are contained by some remarkable natural power of those things of which they are the privations, absences, or opposites, so that, in a certain way, they have being.

[4] Let us grant that the second method of being and not-being is the one considered in the orders and *differentiae* of created natures. Beginning from the most exalted intellectual power stationed closest to God, it descends to the extreme of rational and irrational creation. To speak more clearly, I mean from the highest angel to the lowest part of a rational or irrational soul, the vital principle of nutrition and growth (for when the soul is considered as a genus, the part of the soul which nurtures the body and causes it to grow is the lowest). Here each order, including the bottommost order of bodies with which all division is terminated, can be said in a remarkable way to have and not to have being. What is stated affirmatively of the lower is stated negatively of the higher. Likewise what is stated negatively of the lower is stated affirmatively of the higher. In the same way, what is stated affirmatively of the higher is stated negatively of the lower; and what is stated negatively of the higher will be stated affirmatively of

the lower. What is stated affirmatively of a man, that he is still mortal, is stated negatively of an angel. What is stated negatively of a man is stated affirmatively of an angel, and vice versa. For example, if a man is a rational, mortal, visible animal, an angel is surely not a rational, mortal, visible animal. Similarly, if an angel is an essential motion of the intellect focusing on God and the causes of things, surely man is not an essential motion of the intellect focusing on God and the causes of things. The same rule can be observed in all celestial essences until one reaches the highest order of all which is terminated above by the Supreme Negation. Its negative definition affirms that no creature is higher than It. There are three orders called *homotageis* ("of equal rank"). The first of these consists of Cherubim, Seraphim, and Thrones; the second of Virtues, Powers, and Dominations; the third of Principalities, Archangels, and Angels. In descending order, the lowest group of bodies merely negates or affirms what is higher than itself because it has nothing beneath itself to take away or add since it is preceded by all higher orders and does not precede anything lower than itself. Similarly for this reason, every order of rational and intellectual creature is said to have and not to have being. It has being insofar as it is known by higher creatures or by itself; it lacks being insofar as it does not allow itself to be comprehended by its inferiors.

[5] The third method is fittingly observed in the things with which the fullness of this visible world is made complete, and in their prior causes in the innermost recesses of nature. For whatever of the causes themselves is known by generation in time and place in formed matter is said, by human convention, to have being. Whatever, on the other hand, is still contained within the recesses of nature and does not appear in formed matter or in place, time, or the other accidents, is said, by the same human convention, not to have being. Clear examples of this kind abound, particularly in human nature. For God formed all men together in that single first man whom He made in His own image, but He did not bring them forth at the same time into this visible world. Rather, at set times and places in a sequence known to Himself He brings into visible essence the nature which He had formed together. Thus those who now visibly appear in the world and who have appeared are said to have being. Those who still lie hidden, but are destined to be, are said not to have being. This is the difference between the first and third methods. The first is seen generally in all things made once and together in their causes and effects. The third is seen specifically in the things which partly still lie hidden in their causes and partly are revealed in their effects; and of these the fabric of this world is properly woven. To this method belongs the reason which considers the power of seeds, whether in animals, trees, or grasses. The power of the seeds, while it lies still in the secret recesses of nature, is said not to have being because it does not yet appear. Once it has appeared, however, in the birth and growth of animals, flowers, or the fruits of trees and grasses, it is said to be.

[6] The fourth method, according to the plausible theory of philosophers, states that only those things grasped by the intellect alone truly have being; that whatever things are varied, collected, or dissolved through generation, by the expansion or contraction of matter, and by local and temporal motions—e.g., all bodies, which can be born and destroyed—are truly said not to have being.

[7] The fifth method is the one which reason observes only in human nature. When through sin it abandoned the dignity of the divine image in which it had properly subsisted, it deservedly lost its being and therefore is said not to have being. When it is restored by the grace of God's only-begotten Son to the original condition of its substance in which it was created in God's image, it begins to have being and to be alive in Him who was created in God's image. It is evidently to this method that the following statement of the Apostle relates: "And He calls the things which have no being,

just as those which do." [Romans 4:17] That is, God the Father calls those lost in the first man and fallen to a kind of substancelessness to have being through faith in His Son like those already reborn in Christ. This method may also be understood, however, as relating to those whom God daily calls from the hidden recesses of nature, in which they are thought not to have being, into visible appearance in form, matter, and the other things in which the hidden can appear. Perhaps a keener reason can discover something besides these methods, but I think that enough has been said about these matters for the present, unless you disagree.

STUDENT: Quite enough. . . .

*   *   *

TEACHER: . . . Now I think that we should go back to the subject proposed, i.e., the division of nature.

STUDENT: Yes, we must limit our discussion for the sake of reaching some conclusions.

[11] TEACHER: Of the divisions of nature already mentioned, we thought that the first distinction marked the one that creates but is not created. And rightly so, because such a species of nature is correctly predicated only of God, who alone is understood as creating all things without a beginning ⟨*anarchos*⟩, since He alone is the primary Cause of all things made from and through Him; and consequently He is the End of all things which are from Him. Everything aspires to Him. He is, therefore, Beginning, Middle, and End; Beginning, because everything which participates in essence comes from Him; Middle, because in Him and through Him they subsist and move; End, because they move toward Him in their search for rest from their motion and stability for their perfection.

STUDENT: I believe very firmly and understand to the best of my ability that this is correctly predicated only of the Divine Cause of all things, because It alone creates all things which come from It, whereas It is not Itself created by any superior or prior cause. It is Itself the highest and sole Cause of all things which come from It and subsist in It.

[12] I should like your view, however, about the disturbing statement that I often come upon in the works of the holy fathers who have tried to discuss Divine Nature. They say that It not only creates everything with being, but is also Itself created. In their words, It makes and is made, creates and is created. If they are correct, I am at a loss to explain how our reasoning can stand since we say that It only creates but is not Itself created by anything.

TEACHER: You are right in being disturbed. I too am very baffled and should like to learn from you how these evidently opposing points of view can be reconciled and how we are to pursue a valid line of reasoning.

STUDENT: Please begin, because in such matters I look to your opinion and method of reasoning, not my own.

TEACHER: Then first, if you agree, I think that we should consider the name *God,* which is most commonly used in Sacred Scripture. Although Divine Nature is designated by many names—e.g., Goodness, Essence, Truth, and others of the kind—Divine Scripture most often uses the name God.

STUDENT: That is clearly evident.

TEACHER: The etymology of this name is from the Greek, either from the verb ⟨*theoro*⟩, "see," or from the verb ⟨*theo*⟩, "run"; or, as is more likely, since one and the same meaning is inherent, it is correctly said to be derived from both. For when

⟨*Theos*⟩ is derived from ⟨*theoro*⟩, it means "Seer," because He sees in Himself everything endowed with being; whereas He beholds nothing outside Himself since there is nothing outside Himself. When the derivation is from ⟨*theo*⟩, ⟨*Theos*⟩ is correctly understood as "Runner," for He runs into all things and does not stand still at all, but fills everything by running. So it has been written, "His word runs quickly" [Psalms 147:15]. But yet He is wholly unmoved, since in reference to God, motion is most correctly called stable and stability mobile. He stands unchangeably in Himself, never abandoning His natural stability. Yet He moves Himself through all things to bring into being whatever essentially subsists from Him; for by His motion all things are made. Hence there is one and the same meaning in the two interpretations of the name *God*. God's running through everything is the same as His vision of everything; and everything is made by His seeing as by His running.

STUDENT: I am quite convinced about the etymology of the name and approve of it. But I do not understand very well where He, who is everywhere, can go; since nothing can be without Him and nothing extends beyond Him. In fact, He is the Place and Circumscription of all things.

TEACHER: I did not say that God moves outside Himself, but from Himself, in Himself, towards Himself. For we should not believe that there is any motion in Him except the longing of His will, by which He wishes everything to be made. Just so His stability is understood not as a coming to rest after motion, but as the unchangeable resolve of His will, by which He decrees that all things remain fixed in the unchangeable stability of their reasons. For neither stability nor motion is predicated of Him properly, since the opposition of these two is evident, especially because stability is properly the end of motion; and true reasoning forbids that opposites be conceived of or understood in Him. God does not begin to move in order to arrive at a certain stability; but these terms, like many similar ones, are metaphorically transferred from creatures to Creator by a kind of divine metaphor. And yet this metaphor has a rational basis, since God is the Cause of all things stable and in motion. From Him they set out on their course to being, since He is the Beginning of everything; and through Him they are borne toward Him by natural motion in order to stand in Him unchangeably and eternally, since He is the End and Resting Place of all things. Beyond Him they aspire to nothing; in Him they find the beginning and end of their motion. God, then, is called "Runner," not because He runs outside Himself (for He, who fills everything, always stands unchangeably in Himself); but because He makes everything take a course from non-existence to existence.

STUDENT: These statements seem reasonable. Return to the main point.

TEACHER: I wish that you would remind me of the point. In trying to discuss incidental questions, we often forget the main ones.

STUDENT: Didn't we propose to investigate as well as possible why Divine Nature is said by those who discuss It both to create and to be created? No intelligent person doubts that It creates everything; but we thought that we should not pass lightly over the sense in which Divine Nature is said to be created.

TEACHER: That is exactly right. But I think that our previous discussion has opened the door quite a bit to the solution of this problem. We concluded that the motion of the Divine Nature must be understood simply as the resolve of the Divine Will to create what is to be made. Therefore Divine Nature, which is simply Divine Will, is said to be made in all things; for in It being and will are not two different things, but one and the same in creating everything which, it seemed, ought to be made. For example, one might say that the motion of Divine Will is introduced in order for things to have being. It therefore creates all things which It brings about from nothing in order that they may pass from non-being to being; and It is created because nothing has being essentially except Itself, for It is the essence of all things. Just as there is no natural good besides Itself, but everything said to be good is good by participation in the one Highest Good, so everything said to exist exists not in itself but by participation in the Truly Existing Nature. Not only, therefore, as we observed in our previous remarks, is Divine Nature said to be made when God's Word is born, in a remarkable and ineffable manner, in those formed anew by faith, hope, love, and the other virtues; as the Apostle says in speaking of Christ: "He has been made in us wisdom from God, and justice, and redemption"; [I Cor. 1:30] but also because It appears in all things with being, It is, though invisible in Itself, fittingly said to have been made. Our intellect too, before it enters upon reflection and memory, is not unreasonably said not to have being; for it is invisible in itself and known to none except God and ourselves. But when it enters into thoughts and receives form from some *phantasiae,* it is deservedly said to be made. It is made in the memory by receiving certain forms of things, whether of sounds, colors, or other sensible things, although it was without form before it came into the memory. Then it receives a kind of second formation when it is formed by certain symbols of forms or sounds—I refer to letters as the symbols of sounds and figures as the symbols of forms—or other sensible signals for learning, by which it can insinuate itself into the senses of the perceivers. Although this analogy is far removed from Divine Nature, it can nevertheless offer a persuasive illustration, I think, of how Divine Nature, while It creates everything and cannot be created by anything, is, in a marvelous fashion, created in all things which are from It. As we have said, intelligence, resolve, judgment, or whatever term can be applied to that innermost first motion of ours when it enters into thought and receives certain forms of *phantasiae* and then proceeds into the symbols of sounds or sensible motions, is fittingly said to be made, since it is formed in the *phantasiae* though in itself it lacks all sensible form. Similarly Divine Essence, which in Its pure state surpasses all intellect, is rightly said to be created in the things made by, through, in, and directed toward Itself; so that It is recognized in Its creations through the intellect (if the creations are solely intelligible) or the senses (if they are sensibles) of those who search for It with proper zeal.

STUDENT: That point has been discussed enough, I believe.

*   *   *

[13] TEACHER: . . . Please tell me . . . whether you understand that anything is opposite to God or included in the concept of God. I use *opposite* to refer to privation, contrariety, relationship, or absence. By *included* I mean eternally understood with Him but not coessential with Him.

STUDENT: I see your intent clearly, and I should therefore never venture to say either that anything is opposite to Him or that anything of a different essence ⟨*heterousion*⟩ is included in the concept of Him. For things in a relationship of opposites are always so opposed to each other that they begin and cease together, since (1) they are of the same nature: e.g., the simple in relation to the double and 2/3 in relation to 3/2; or (2) they are opposite by negation, as *is, is not*; or (3) they are opposites through their natural qualities: (a) by absence, as in the case of light and darkness; (b) by privation, as in the case of life and death; or (c) by contrariety, as in the case of health and infirmity. These kinds of opposition are rightly attributed to things subject to intellect and sense, and therefore are not in God. Indeed, whatever things are at odds with themselves cannot be eternal. If they were, they would not be at odds with themselves because eternity is like itself and subsists wholly simple and undivided in itself. It is, in fact, the one Beginning and the one End of all things, in no way at odds with itself.

[14] According to the same reasoning, I don't know who would dare to assert that something is coeternal with God which is not coessential with Him. If such a thing can be conceived or discovered, it necessarily follows that there is not a single Beginning of all things, but two or more, quite different from one another, a theory which true reasoning usually rejects without hesitation. Everything properly begins from a single source; nothing from two or more sources.

TEACHER: I agree with your argument. If the divine names mentioned are in direct opposition to other names, then necessarily the things properly signified by them are understood to have contraries. Hence they cannot properly be predicated of God, to whom nothing is opposite, or with whom nothing coeternally different in nature is perceived. Of the names mentioned before and others like them, true reason can find none which does not have another name differing from it, whether in an opposite division or within the same genus. And we must necessarily recognize in things signified what we recognize in their names. But since there are countless terms designating God, which are metaphorically predicated of Him in holy Scripture by transposition from creation to Creator (if indeed anything can be rightly predicated of God, a point to be considered elsewhere), and since they cannot be discovered or collected by our poor rational power, a few designations for the Divine must be stated as an example. God, then, is called *Essence*, but He is not properly essence, for nothing is the opposite of essence. He is rather ⟨*hyperousios*⟩, i.e., "superessential." Likewise He is called Goodness, but He is not properly goodness, to which evil is opposite. Instead He is ⟨*hyperagathos*⟩, "More Than Good," and ⟨*hyperagathotes*⟩, i.e., "More Than Goodness." He is called God, but He is not properly God. Blindness is the opposite of vision, and the non-seer of the seer. He is therefore ⟨*hypertheos*⟩, "More Than Seer," if ⟨*Theos*⟩ is interpreted as "Seer." But if you resort to another etymology of this name and understand the derivation of ⟨*Theos*⟩, "God," not from ⟨*theoro*⟩, "see," but from ⟨*theo*⟩, "run," the result is similar. The non-runner is opposite to the runner as slowness is to swiftness. He will then be ⟨*hypertheos*⟩, i.e., "More Than Runner," as recorded in the passage "His word runs quickly." [Psalms 147:15] We understand this passage as relating to God, the Word, who ineffably runs through all things with being in order that they may have being. We should have a similar kind of understanding about truth. Falsehood is the opposite of truth; hence He is not properly truth, but ⟨*hyperalethes*⟩ and ⟨*hyperaletheia*⟩, i.e., "More Than True" and "More Than Truth." The same principle must be observed in regard to all divine names. He is not properly called eternity, since temporality is opposed to eternity. He is, then, ⟨*hyperaionios*⟩ and ⟨*hyperaionia*⟩, "More Than Eternal" and "More Than Eternity." The same principle applies about wisdom also, so that it cannot be judged as properly predicated of God, since the foolish and folly are the opposite of the wise and wisdom. Accordingly, he is correctly and truly called ⟨*hypersophos*⟩, i.e., "More Than Wise" and ⟨*hypersophia*⟩, "More Than Wisdom." Similarly He is More Than Life, since death is opposed to life. We must have the same kind of understanding about "Light," since darkness opposes light. These illustrations of my point are sufficient, I believe.

ANSELM (AND GAUNILO)
1033–1109

Saint Anselm was born to a noble family in Aosta, in what is now Italy. Following a youth of travel and learning, Anselm joined the Benedictine monastery in the town of Bec, Normandy (in modern France). He remained in this monastery for the next thirty-three years, the last fifteen as abbot. During this time, he wrote a number of books on theological and philosophical topics. In 1093, Anselm was coerced into leaving the monastery to become Archbishop of Canterbury. Most of his sixteen years in Canterbury were spent skirmishing with the king of England for control of the church (a pattern that continued for five centuries until Henry VIII severed the English church from Rome entirely in 1534). Anselm died in 1109 and was canonized in 1494.

Anselm's thought can be summed up in the Augustinian phrase, "faith seeking understanding." Anselm was a deeply devoted Christian who began his thinking with the assumption that the doctrines of Christianity are true. And this faith drove him to seek understanding, to find rational explanations for the Christian teachings he already believed. His writings reflected this yearning to understand rationally particular problems in faith; he wrote a number of short treatises on such subjects as the Incarnation and the Trinity. He believed that he could demonstrate the truth of these revealed doctrines.

Anselm's most famous work is his attempt to prove the existence of God in the *Proslogion* (or *Discourse*) known now as the "ontological argument" (from Immanuel Kant's description). The ontological argument attempts to show that if one can conceive of "something greater than which we can conceive of nothing," one must also acknowledge that this being exists in reality as well as in the understanding. That is, if God is thought of, then God must exist. Recent scholars have pointed out that there are actually two arguments here: one, in Chapter II, that proves that God exists in reality; and another, in Chapters III to IV, that proves that God's existence is necessary.

Anselm's argument was attacked by a fellow monk named Gaunilo. Anselm's exchange with Gaunilo has been preserved and the key sections are reprinted here, along with selections from *Proslogion,* in the John F. Wippel and Allan B. Wolter translation.

Despite the fact that this argument has fascinated thinkers for over nine hundred years, a student's first response to this passage is often one of confusion or simple denial: "He can't do that!" The student is not alone in being confused; the history of the argument is full of misrepresentations and misinterpretations. To be sure, careful thinkers such as Hume and Kant have attacked this argument. But it is notoriously difficult to say exactly what is wrong with Anselm's logic, and many purported refutations have actually been refutations of arguments quite different from Anselm's.

In recent years, there has been renewed interest in the argument, with Charles Hartshorne, Norman Malcom, and Alvin Plantinga claiming that it is successful. There has also been a tradition, beginning with the medieval thinker Bonaventure and continuing through Karl Barth in this century, that claims the *Proslogion*, Chapters II to IV, is not a philosophical argument at all. These theologians are convinced that Anselm is not "proving" anything, that he is simply showing the implications of God's self-revelation.

While the debate continues to rage, one fact is clear: Anselm raised some of the most basic questions in the history of philosophy. Questions about modes of existence, possible beings, necessity and contingency, as well as a range of issues in logic, all emerge in discussions of this provocative passage.

*   *   *

For a study of the complete *Proslogion*, see M.J. Charlesworth, *St. Anselm's Proslogion* (Oxford: Clarendon Press, 1965). For the rest of Anselm's major works see, Anselm of Canterbury, *The Major Works,* edited by Brian Davies and G.R. Evans, (Oxford: Oxford University Press, 1998). For a study of Anselm's life and times, see R.W. Southern's books *Saint Anselm and His Biographer* (Cambridge: Cambridge University Press, 1963) and *Saint Anselm: A Portrait in a Landscape* (Cambridge: Cambridge University Press, 1990); and William H. Shannon, *Anselm: The Joy of Faith* (New York: Crossroads, 1999). Jasper Hopkins, *A Companion to the Study of St. Anselm* (Minneapolis: University of Minnesota Press, 1972), provides a comprehensive discussion of Anselm and his work.

For further reading on the ontological argument, the best source is John Hick and Arthur C. McGill, eds., *The Many-Faced Argument* (New York: Macmillan, 1967). Charles Hartshorne, *Anselm's Discovery: A Re-Examination of the Ontological Argument for God's Existence* (LaSalle, IL: Open Court, 1965); Alvin Plantinga, *The Nature of Necessity* (Oxford: Clarendon Press, 1974)—and his "simplified" version of this difficult work, Alvin Plantinga, *God, Freedom, and Evil* (Grand Rapids, MI: Eerdmans, 1977); and Richard Campbell, *From Belief to Understanding* (Canberra: Australian National University Press, 1976), all defend the argument. For theological interpretations, see Karl Barth, *Anselm: Fides Quaren Intellectum,* translated by Ian W. Robinson (London: SCM Press, 1960). (Key chapters from this work are included in Hick and McGill's *The Many-Faced Argument.*)

PROSLOGION [in part]

PREFACE

Some time ago at the pressing invitation of some brethren I did a small work* as a sample of meditation based on faith. The work was written in the person of one seeking to throw light on an area of ignorance by silently reasoning with himself. Reflecting that what I had woven together was really a chain of many arguments, I began to ask myself whether one might not be able to find a single argument, needing no proof beyond itself, which would suffice by itself to link together such conclusions as that God truly exists, that he is the highest good—needing no other but needed for the existence and well-being of all else-and whatever else we believe to be true of the divine being. Diligently and often did I pursue this quest. Sometimes the solution seemed almost at hand; at other times it simply eluded the grasp of my mind. Finally I decided in despair to cease the search for something so impossible to find. But when I tried to put the matter out of mind lest I waste time that might profitably be spent on other matters in such a fruitless quest, it continued to importune me despite my unwillingness and efforts at resistance. And so it was that one day when I was weary of struggling against this obsession the solution I had despaired of finding suddenly appeared amidst the welter of my conflicting thoughts and I eagerly seized the idea I had been so strenuously fending off.

Thinking that, if I put down in writing what I was so happy to find, others too would find pleasure reading it, I did the following little tract which takes up this and some allied matters from the viewpoint of one who tries to bring his mind to contemplate God and seeks to understand what he believes. . . .

CHAPTER 1

. . . It is not your sublimity, O Lord, I seek to penetrate, for my mind is no match for it, but I do desire to understand something of your truth which I believe and love in my heart. For I seek not to understand that I may believe, but I believe that I may understand. For this too I believe: "Unless I believe, I shall not understand!"

CHAPTER 2

O Lord, who grants understanding to faith, make me, so far as is good for me, to understand that you exist, as we believe, and that you are what we believe you to be. Now we believe you to be something greater than which we can conceive of nothing.**

*[*Monologion* (i.e., a soliloquy)]

**[This complicated formulation is difficult to understand, yet cannot be easily simplified without losing Anselm's meaning. Throughout this reading I have stayed with Wolter's wording. It might help the student to think of the phrase, "something greater than which we can conceive of nothing," as a single entity. For a discussion of this complicated formulation, see M.J. Charlesworth, *St. Anselm's Proslogion* (Oxford: Oxford University Press, 1965).]

From John F. Wippel and Allan B. Wolter, eds., *Medieval Philosophy: From St. Augustine to Nicholas of Cusa* (New York: The Free Press, 1969).

Could it be then that there is no such nature, since "the fool says in his heart, 'There is no God'" [Ps. 13:1]? But surely this same fool, when he hears me say this, "something than which we can conceive of nothing greater," understands what he hears and what he understands is in his understanding even if he does not understand it to exist. For it is one thing for something to be in the understanding and quite another to understand that the thing in question exists. When a painter thinks of the work he will make beforehand, he has it in his understanding, but he does not think that what he has yet to make exists. But once he has painted it, he not only has it in his understanding but he understands that what he has made exists. Even the fool then must be convinced that in his understanding at least there is something than which nothing greater can be conceived, for when he hears this, he understands it and whatever is understood is in the understanding. But surely if the thing be such that we cannot conceive of something greater, it does not exist solely in the understanding. For if it were there only, one could also think of it as existing in reality and this is something greater. If the thing than which none greater can be thought were in the mind alone, then this same thing would both be and not be something than which nothing greater can be conceived. But surely this cannot be. Without doubt then there exists both in the understanding and in reality a being greater than which nothing can be conceived.

CHAPTER 3

So truly does such a thing exist that it cannot be thought of as not existing. For we can think of something as existing which cannot be thought of as not existing, and such a thing is greater than what can be thought not to be. Wherefore, if the thing than which none greater can be thought could be conceived of as not existing, then this very thing than which none greater can be thought is not a thing than which none greater can be thought. But this is not possible. Hence, something greater than which nothing can be conceived so truly exists that it cannot be conceived not to be.

O Lord, our God, you are this being. So truly do you exist that you cannot even be thought of as nonexistent. And rightly so, for if some mind could think of something better than you, then the creature would rise above the Creator and would judge him, which is absurd. It is possible indeed to think of anything other than you as nonexistent. Of all beings then you alone have existence in the truest and highest sense, for nothing else so truly is or has existence in so great a measure. Why then does the fool "say in his heart, 'There is no God,'" when it is so evident to a reasoning mind that of all things you exist in a supreme degree? Why indeed save that he is stupid and a fool!

CHAPTER 4

But how did he come to say in his heart what he could not think? Or why was it he could not think what he said in his heart? For after all, to say in one's heart and to think are the same. And if it be true, or rather, since it is true that be thought it because he said it in his heart, and it is also true that he did not say it in his heart because he could not think it, it follows that there is not just one way to think of something or to say it in one's heart. In one sense, we think of something when we think of the word that signifies that something; in another sense, we think of it when we think of the thing itself. In the first sense, then, God can be thought of as not existing, but in the second sense, he cannot be thought of as not existing. For no one who really understands what God is can think that he does not exist, despite the fact that these words may be said in his heart either without any meaning whatsoever or with some peripheral sense. For God is that than which none greater can be thought, and whoever understands this correctly must understand that he so exists that he cannot even be thought of as nonexistent. Hence, he who understands that God exists in this way cannot think of him as nonexistent.

My thanks to you, good Lord, my thanks to you! For now I understand by your light what I once believed by your grace, so that even if I were to refuse to believe that you exist, I should be unable not to understand this to be true.

GAUNILO AND ANSELM: DEBATE*

GAUNILO

[5.] Now the proof I am given that such a being exists not only in the understanding but also in reality is this. If such were not the case, then whatever really exists would be greater than this thing already proved to exist in the intellect. Hence the latter will not really be greater than everything else. To this I reply. Should one say that there is in the understanding something which cannot be conceived as actual, I would not deny it is in me in this way. But since this does not guarantee it any real existence, I shall not admit it has such until unquestionable proof be given. Now he who says: "This being which is greater than all exists, because otherwise it would not be greater than all" does not pay sufficient attention to what he is saying. For I would still not admit, indeed I would doubt or deny, that this [thing in the understanding] is greater than any real thing. Neither would I grant it any other existence (if it should be called "existence") than you have when the mind, on the basis of a word one only hears, tries to imagine something it has no knowledge of. But how do you prove to me this has any greater claim to real existence because it is assumed to be greater than all other things? For I deny or doubt that it is in my intellect or thought in any greater measure than are many dubious and uncertain things. For you must first assure me that it really exists somewhere and then, from the fact that it is greater than everything else, it will be clear that it also subsists of itself.

ANSELM

[II.] . . . I have said that if it is only in the understanding, it could be conceived to be also existing in reality, and this is greater. If it is only in the understanding, then one and the same thing is such that one both can and cannot conceive of anything greater.

---

*I have followed the procedure of John Hick, *Classical and Contemporary Readings in the Philosophy of Religion* (Englewood Cliffs, NJ: Prentice Hall, 1964) and put the main points of Gaunilo's critique together with Anselm's replies. The numbers before each section refer to the paragraph numbers of Gaunilo's *A Reply to the Foregoing by a Certain Writer on Behalf of the Fool* (in Arabic numbers) and Anselm's *Reply to the Foregoing by the Author of the Book in Question* (in Roman numerals).

Which follows more logically, I ask: that it exists in the intellect alone, but cannot be thought to exist also in reality, or that it can be thought to exist in reality, and one who thinks this thinks of something greater than if it were only in the intellect? What follows more logically than this: if a being than which none greater is conceivable is only in the understanding, then it is not such that none greater can be conceived? But surely in no intellect will you find a thing with both these properties, viz. "greater than which something is conceivable" and "greater than which nothing is conceivable." Does it not follow then that if "a thing greater than which nothing is conceivable" is in any understanding, then such a thing is not only in the understanding? For if it were, it is "a thing greater than which something is conceivable," which is not consistent.

***

[IX.] . . . It is obvious also that in similar fashion it is possible to conceive of and to understand a being whose nonexistence is impossible. He who conceives of this conceives of a greater thing than one whose nonexistence is possible. Consequently when a thing than which no greater is conceivable is conceived, if it is a thing whose nonexistence is possible that one conceives, then it is not that being than which no greater is conceivable. But a thing cannot be simultaneously conceived of and not conceived of. Hence one who conceives of a thing than which no greater is conceivable does not conceive of something whose nonexistence is possible, but of something whose nonexistence is impossible. Consequently, what he conceives of must exist; for anything whose nonexistence is possible is simply not what he conceives of.

GAUNILO

[6.] . . . They say that somewhere in the ocean there is an island, which because of the difficulty, or better, the impossibility of finding what does not exist, some call the lost island. And they say this island is inestimably wealthy, having all kinds of delights and riches in greater abundance even than the fabled "Fortunate Islands." And since it has no possessor or inhabitant, it excels all other inhabited countries in its possessions. Now should someone tell me that there is such an island, I could readily understand what he says, since there is no problem there. But suppose he adds, as though it were already implied: "You can't doubt any more that this island, which is more excellent than any land, really exists somewhere, since you don't doubt that it is in your understanding and that it is more excellent not to be in the understanding only. Hence it is necessary that it really exists, for if it did not, any land which does would excel it and consequently the island which you already understand to be more excellent would not be such." If one were to try to prove to me that this island in truth exists and its existence should no longer be questioned, either I would think he was joking or I would not know whether to consider him or me the greater fool, me for conceding his argument or him for supposing he had established with any certainty such an island's existence without first showing such excellence to be real and its existence indubitable rather than just a figment of my understanding, whose existence is uncertain.

ANSELM

[III.] But you claim our argument is on a par with the following. Someone imagines an island in the ocean which surpasses all lands in its fertility. Because of the difficulty, or

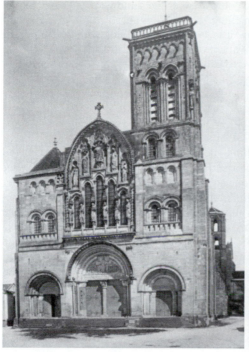

a.   *b.*

The Romanesque Cathedral
a. Exterior view of the Abbey Church of the Madeleine, Vezelay, France, built in the
twelfth century. This church typifies the Romanesque style that flourished from about
1000 to 1200. The rounded arches above the portals are reminiscent of the arches of
Roman construction. The thickness of the stone walls, together with the relatively simple
facade, gives the structure the impression of solidity and solemnity. *(French Government
Tourist Office)*
b. The nave. The rounded interior arches distribute the weight of the roof outward as well
as downward, necessitating thick stone walls. As a result, only a few small windows are
possible in a Romanesque church—adding to the fortress-like feel of the architecture.
(Caisse Nationale des Monuments Historique)

rather impossibility, of finding what does not exist, he calls it "Lost Island." He might
then say you cannot doubt that it really exists, because anyone can readily understand
it from its verbal description. I assert confidently that if anyone finds something for
me, besides that "than which none greater is conceivable," which exists either in reality
or concept alone to which the logic of my argument can be applied, I will find and give
him his "Lost Island," never to be lost again. . . .

GAUNILO

[7.] This then is an answer the fool [in *Proslogion,* Ch. 3] could make to your arguments against him. When he is first assured that this being is so great that its nonexistence is inconceivable, and that this in turn is established for no other reason than that

otherwise it would not excel all things, he could counter the same way and say: "When have I admitted there really is any such thing, i.e. something so much greater than everything else that one could prove to me it is so real, it could not even be conceived as unreal?" What we need at the outset is a very firm argument to show there is some superior being, bigger and better than all else that exists, so that we can go on from this to prove all the other attributes such a bigger and better being has to have.

ANSELM

[III.] . . . It now seems obvious that a thing such that none greater can be conceived cannot be thought of as nonexistent since it exists on such firm grounds of truth. For otherwise it would not exist at all. If anyone says he thinks it does not exist, then I declare that when he thinks this he either thinks of something than which a greater is inconceivable, or else he does not think at all. If he does not think, then neither does he think that what he is not thinking of is nonexistent. But if he does think, then he thinks of something which cannot be thought of as not existing. For if it could be conceived as nonexistent, it could be conceived as having a beginning and an end. Now this is impossible. Hence if anyone thinks of it, he thinks of something that cannot even be conceived to be nonexistent. Now whoever conceives it thus doesn't think of it as nonexistent, for if he did he would conceive what can't be conceived. Nonexistence is inconceivable, then, of something greater than which nothing can be conceived.

GAUNILO

[7.] As for the statement that it is inconceivable that the highest thing of all should not exist, it might be better to say its nonexistence or even its possibility of nonexistence is unintelligible. For according to the true meaning of the word, unreal things are not intelligible, but their existence is conceivable in the way that the fool thinks that God does not exist. I most certainly know I exist, but for all that, I know my nonexistence is possible. As for that supreme being which God is, I understand without doubt both his existence and the impossibility of his nonexistence. But whether I can conceive of my nonexistence as long as I most certainly know I exist, I don't know. But if I am able to, why can I not conceive of the nonexistence of whatever else I know with the same certainty? But if I cannot, then such an inability will not be something peculiar to God [i.e., being such that He cannot be thought not to exist.]

ANSELM

[IV.] You claim moreover that when we say this supreme reality cannot be conceived of as nonexistent, it would be perhaps better to say that its nonexistence or even the possibility of its nonexistence is not understandable. But it is better to say it cannot be conceived. For had I said that the reality itself could not be understood not to exist, perhaps you, who insist that according to proper usage what is false cannot be understood, would object that nothing existing could be understood not to exist. For it is false to claim that what exists does not exist. Hence it would not be peculiar to God to be unable to be understood as nonexistent. If any one of the things that most certainly exist can be understood to be nonexistent, however, then other certain things can also be understood to be nonexistent. But this objection cannot be applied to "conceiving," if this is correctly understood. For though none of the things that exist can be understood not to exist, still they can all be conceived as nonexistent, except the greatest. For all—and only—those things can be conceived as nonexistent which have a beginning or end or consist of parts or do not exist in their entirety in any time or place, as I have said. Only that being which cannot be conceived to be nonexistent must be conceived as having no beginning or end or composition of parts but is whole and entire always and everywhere.

Consequently you must realize that you can conceive of yourself as nonexistent, though you most certainly know that you exist. You surprise me when you say you are not sure of this. For we conceive of many things as nonexistent which we know to exist and of many things as existent which we know do not exist. And we conceive them thus not by judging but by imagining them so. We can indeed conceive of something as existent even while we know it does not exist, because we are able to conceive the one at the same time that we know the other. But we cannot conceive nonexistence while knowing existence, because we cannot conceive existence and nonexistence at the same time. If anyone distinguishes between the two senses of the statement in this fashion, then, he will understand that nothing, as long as it is known to be, can be conceived not to be, and that whatever exists, with the exception of a thing such that no greater is conceivable, can be conceived of as nonexistent even when it is known to exist. This inability to be conceived of as nonexistent, then, is peculiar to God, even though there are many objects which cannot be conceived not to be while they are. As for the way in which God can still be said to be conceived as not existing, I believe this has been explained clearly enough in my little book itself.

PETER ABELARD
ca. 1079–ca. 1142

Peter Abelard (or Pierre Abailard) was born into a noble family of warriors in Le Palais (or Pallet), near Nantes, France. Though he chose to "follow Minerva [the goddess of learning] instead of Mars [the god of war]," this warrior's son was every bit as combative as his ancestors. As he himself put it, "To the prizes of victory in war I preferred the battle of minds in disputation."

Abelard's skill in logical debate, and his lack of prudence in using it, was legendary. While studying dialectics (or logic) with the eminent Parisian teacher William of Champeaux, Abelard humiliated his master in public debate. He forced William to acknowledge that his (William's) position on the question of universals was incorrect. Abelard then compounded the insult by setting up his own school of dialectics and stealing most of William's students. Over the next forty years, Abelard's *curriculum vitae* included dismissal from the theology school of Anselm of Laon, two flights from monasteries where he had enraged the monks (once for proving that the founder of the monastery could not possibly have been Dionysius the Areopagite), and two church condemnations of his writings. Abelard's primary antagonist in later life was Bernard of Clairvaux, a man of deep faith—and of deep suspicions regarding Abelard's intellectualism.

But Abelard's most disastrous adventure took place while he was teaching in Paris in his early thirties. Next door to Abelard's school lived a cathedral official by the name of Fulbert, who had under his care a beautiful and intelligent teenage niece, Heloise. Abelard used his fame to arrange a position tutoring Heloise and, as Abelard later described it, "under the pretext of study we spent our hours in the happiness of love . . . our kisses far outnumbering our reasoned words." When

Heloise became pregnant, Abelard agreed to marry her on the condition that the marriage be kept secret to preserve his career. He was, after all, in holy orders and supposedly celibate. When Fulbert proceeded to publicize the wedding, both Abelard and Heloise vehemently denied their marriage. Fulbert was so enraged by this denial that he hired thugs who castrated Abelard. Abelard retired to a monastery and Heloise joined a convent. While apart, Abelard and Heloise wrote poignant love letters, which are still considered classics. Though they were separated in life, they were eventually buried side by side.

Apart from this ill-starred love affair, Abelard is best known for his work on the problem of universals. Boethius had formulated the question, "Do universals, such as genera and species, subsist in themselves?" Those who said "yes" were called "realists" because they believed universals to be *real* things.* Some, such as William of Champeaux, even went so far as to say that each member of a species has the same essence and that all apparent differences are only accidental. So, for example, the race horse Secretariat and the old nag in the barn share the same essential nature of "horse." The characteristics that differentiate them—size, color, speed, and so on—are merely accidental properties. On the other hand, the "nominalists" went in the opposite direction and denied that universals were anything other than names (*nomina* in Latin). Another of Abelard's former teachers, Roscelin, apparently held that a universal was nothing more than a word or "vocal wind."

Abelard rejected both positions. Abelard argued in public debate that William's extreme realism would mean that the same substance could have contrary accidental properties. The exact same substance, for example, "horse," would have the property of being fast (in the case of Secretariat) and slow (in the case of the old nag). Against the nominalism of Roscelin, Abelard claimed that if a universal is only a word, then it is a "thing" (namely, the "vocal wind" being blown), and a thing cannot be predicated of a thing. But more important, a universal is not just a word; it is a *meaningful* word. The question left unanswered by the extreme nominalist is what that word, or "vocal wind," *means.*

In the selection on universals given here, from A.B. Wolter's translation of *Logica "Ingredientibus,"* Abelard articulates a position similar to that of Aristotle. Abelard argues that universals name real similarities between individuals, though these similarities do not exist as separate things in themselves. The similarities consist not in shared essences but in shared predicates. Secretariat, the old nag, and all other individual horses are not similar "in horse" as if "horse" were a separate thing. Instead they are similar "in *being* a horse"—that is, in sharing the predicate of "horse." Although his student John of Salisbury later classified him as a nominalist, Abelard's position has usually been classified as "conceptualism" or moderate realism.

In his *Ethics,* Abelard argues that morality is concerned with intention. In the passages reprinted here, in J. Ramsay McCallum's translation, Abelard argues that no action is good or bad in itself. Instead, he argues, in anticipation of Immanuel Kant, that an action is good if "it issues from a good intention."

*   *   *

---

*The word "realist" has a quite different meaning today, and we would now probably describe medieval realists as "idealists."

For studies on the problem of universals, see Meyrick Heath Carré, *Realists and Nominalists* (Oxford: Oxford University Press, 1946); Nicholas Wolterstorff, *On Universals: An Essay in Ontology* (Chicago: Chicago University Press, 1970); and Martin M. Tweedale, *Abailard on Universals* (Amsterdam: North Holland, 1976).

For general introductions to Abelard's life and thought, see Joseph McCabe, *Peter Abelard* (1901, reprinted Freeport, NY: Books for Libraries Press, 1971); Ailbe John Luddy, *The Case of Peter Abelard* (Westminster, MD: Newman Bookshop, 1947); Roger B. Lloyd, *Peter Abelard: The Orthodox Rebel* (London: Latimer House, 1947); A. Victor Murray, *Abelard and St. Bernard: A Study in Twelfth Century "Modernism"* (Manchester: Manchester University Press, 1967); Jeffery Garrett Sikes, *Peter Abailard* (1932; reprinted New York: Russell and Russell, 1965); and John Marenbon, *The Philosophy of Peter Abelard* (Cambridge: Cambridge University Press, 1997). Abelard's troubled life has inspired both a novel, Helen Waddell, *Peter Abelard* (New York: Literary Guild, 1933), and an epic poem, Cedric Hubbell Whitman, *Abelard* (Cambridge, MA: Harvard University Press, 1965). For Abelard's description of his misfortunes, see Peter Abelard, *The Letters of Abelard and Heloise,* translated by Betty Radice (Harmondsworth, Middlesex: Penguin Classics, 1974). Étienne Gilson, *Heloise and Abelard,* translated by L.K. Shook (Chicago: Regnery, 1951) provides an essay on this interesting topic.

ON UNIVERSALS (selections)

Porphyry, as Boethius points out [in his Commentary on the *Isagoge*], raises three profitable questions whose answers are shrouded in mystery and though not a few philosophers have attempted to solve them, few have succeeded in doing so. The first is: Do genera and species really exist or are they simply something in the mind? It is as if [Porphyry] were asking whether their existence is a fact or merely a matter of opinion. The second is: Granting they do exist, are they corporeal or incorporeal? The third is: Do they exist apart from sensible things or only in them? For there are two types of incorporeal things. Some, like God or the soul, can subsist in their incorporeality apart from anything sensible. Others are unable to exist apart from the sensible objects in which they are found. A line, for example, is unable to exist apart from some bodily subject.

Porphyry sidesteps answering them with the remark: "For the present I refuse to be drawn into a discussion as to whether genus and species exist in reality or solely and simply in thought; or if they do exist whether they are corporeal or incorporeal, or whether, on the admission they are incorporeal, they are separated from sensibles or exist only in and dependent upon sensible things, and other things of this sort."

"Other things of this sort" can be interpreted in various ways. We could take him to mean: "I refuse to discuss these three questions and other related matters." For other

Reprinted with permission of The Free Press, A Division of Macmillan, Inc., from *Medieval Philosophy: From St. Augustine to Nicholas of Cusa,* translated by A.B. Wolter and edited by John F. Wippel and Allan B. Wolter. Copyright © 1969 by The Free Press.

relevant questions could be raised that pose similar problems. For instance, what is the common basis or reason for applying universal names to things; which boils down to explaining to what extent different things agree; or how should one understand those universal names wherein one seems to conceive of nothing, where the universal term in a word seems to have no referent? And there are many other difficult points. By understanding "other things of this sort" in this way, we can add a fourth question: Do genera and species, as long as they remain such, require that the subject they name have some reality or, if all the things they designate were destroyed, could the universal consist simply in its significance for the mind, as would be the case with the name "rose" when no roses are in bloom which it could designate in general? . . .

Since genera and species are obviously instances of universals and in mentioning them Porphyry touches on the nature of universals in general, we may distinguish the properties common to universals by studying them in these samples. Let us inquire then whether they apply only to *words* or to *things* as well.

Aristotle defines the universal as "that which is of such a nature as to be predicated of many." Porphyry, on the other hand, goes on to define the singular or individual as "that which is predicated of a single individual."

Authorities then seem to apply "universal" to things as much as they do to words. Aristotle himself does this, declaring by way of preface to his definition of the universal, that "some things are universal, others individual. Now by 'universal' I mean that which is of such a nature as to be predicated of many, whereas 'individual' is not something of this kind." Porphyry too, having stated that the species is composed of a genus and difference, proceeds to locate it in the nature of things. From this it is clear that things themselves fall under a universal noun.

Nouns too are called universals. That is why Aristotle says: "The genus specifies the quality with reference to substance, for it signifies what sort of thing it is."

"It seems then that things as well as words are called universals. . . ."

However, things taken either singly or collectively cannot be called universals, because they are not predicable of many. Consequently it remains to ascribe this form of universality to words alone. Just as grammarians call certain nouns proper and others appellative, so dialecticians call certain simple words particulars, that is, individuals, and others universals. A universal word is one which is able to be predicated of many by reason of its intention, such as the noun "man," which can be joined with the names of particular men by reason of the nature of the subject on which they are imposed. A particular word, however, is one which is predicable only of a single subject, as *Socrates* when it is taken as the name of but one individual. For if you take it equivocally, you give it the signification not of one word but of many. For according to Priscian, many nouns can obviously be brought together in a single word. When a universal then is described as "that which is predicable of many," *that which* indicates not only the simplicity of the word as a discrete expression, but also the unity of signification lacking in an equivocal term. . . .

Now that we have defined "universal" and "particular" in regard to words, let us investigate in particular the properties of those which are universal. For questions have been raised about universals, since serious doubts existed as to their meaning because there seemed to be no subject to which they referred. Neither did they express the sense of any one thing. These universal terms then appeared to be imposed on nothing, since it is clear that all things subsisting in themselves are individuals and, as has been shown, they do not share in some one thing by virtue of which a universal name could be given to them. Since it is certain then that (a) universals are not imposed on things by reason of their individual differences, for then they would not be common but singular, (b) nor can they designate things which share in some identical entity, for it is not a thing in which they agree, there seems to be nothing from which universals might derive their meaning, particularly since their sense is not restricted to any one thing. . . . Since "man" is imposed on individuals for an identical reason, viz. because each is a rational, mortal animal, the very generality of the designation prevents one from understanding the term of just one man in the way, for example, that one understands by Socrates just one unique person, which is why it is called a particular. But the common term "man" does not mean just Socrates, or any other man. Neither does it designate a collection, nor does it, as some think, mean just Socrates insofar as he is man. For even if Socrates alone were sitting in this house and because of that the proposition "A man sits in this house" is true, still by the name "man," there is no way of getting to Socrates except insofar as he too is a man. Otherwise, from the proposition itself, "sitting" would be understood to inhere in Socrates, so that from "A man sits in this house," one could infer "Socrates sits in this house." And the same applies to any other individual man. Neither can "A man sits in this house" be understood of a collection, since the proposition can be true if only one man is there. Consequently, there is not a single thing that "man" or any other universal term seems to signify, since there is not a single thing whose sense the term seems to express. Neither does it seem there could be any sense if no subject is thought of. Universals then appear to be totally devoid of meaning.

And yet this is not the case. For universals do signify distinct individuals to the extent of giving names to them, but this significative function does not require that one grasps a sense which arises out of them and which belongs to each of them. "Man," for example, does name individual things, but for the common reason that they are all men. That is why it is called a universal. Also there is a certain sense—common, not proper—that is applicable to those individuals which one conceives to be alike.

But let us look carefully now into some matters we have touched on only briefly, viz. (a) what is the common reason for imposing a universal name on things, (b) what is this intellectual conception of a common likeness, and (c) is a word said to be common because of some common cause by virtue of which all the things it designates are alike, or is it merely because we have a common concept for all of them, or is it for both of these reasons?

Let us consider first the question of the common cause. As we noted earlier, each individual man is a discrete subject since he has as proper to himself not only an essence but also whatever forms [or qualifications] that essence may have. Nevertheless, they agree in this that they are all men. Since there is no man who is not a discrete or distinct individual thing, I do not say they agree "in man," but "in being a man." Now if you consider the matter carefully, man or any other thing is not the same as "to be a man," even as "not to be in a subject" is not a thing, nor is there anything which is "not to undergo contrariety" or "not to be subject to greater or lesser degrees," and still Aristotle says these are points in which all substances agree. Since there is no *thing* in which things could possibly agree, if there is any agreement among certain things, this must not be taken to be some *thing*. Just as Socrates and Plato are alike in being men, so a horse and donkey are alike in not being men. It is for this reason that they are called "nonmen." Different individuals then agree either in being the same or in not being the same, e.g. in being men or white, or in not being men or being white.

Still this agreement among things (which itself is not a thing) must not be regarded as a case of bringing together things which are real on the basis of nothing. In point of fact we do speak of this agreeing with that to the extent of their having the same status, that of man, i.e. the two agree in that they are men. But what we perceive is merely that they are men, and there is not the slightest difference between them, I say, in their being men, even though we may not call this an essence. But "being a man" (which is not a thing) we do call "the status of man" and we have also called it "the common cause for imposing on individuals a universal name." For we frequently give the name "cause" to some characteristic that is not itself a thing as when one says "He was beaten because he did not wish to appear in court." His not wishing to appear in court, cited here as a cause is not a [constitutive] essence [of his being beaten].

We can also designate as "the status of man" those things themselves in a man's nature which the one who imposed the word conceives according to a common likeness.

Having shown how universals signify, namely by functioning as names of things, and having presented what the reason for imposing such general names is, let us indicate just what these universal meanings consist of.

To begin with, let us point out the distinguishing features of all intellectual conception or understanding. Though sense perception as well as intellectual conception are both functions of the soul, there is a difference between the two. Bodies and what inhere in them are objects of sensory knowledge, e.g. a tower or its sensory qualities. In the exercise of this function, however, the soul makes use of corporeal instruments. In understanding or conceiving something intellectually, the soul needs no corporeal organ and consequently no bodily subject in which the thought object inheres is required. It is enough that the mind constructs for itself a likeness of these things and the action called intellection is concerned with this [cognitive content]. Hence, if the tower is removed or destroyed, the sense perception that dealt with it perishes, but the intellectual conception of the tower remains in the likeness preserved in the mind. As the act of sense perception is not the sensed thing itself, so the act of the intellect is not itself the form understood or conceived intellectually. Understanding is an activity of the soul by virtue of which it is said to understand, but the form toward which understanding is directed is a kind of image or construct which the mind fashions for itself at will, like those imaginary cities seen in dreams or the form of a projected building which the architect conceives after the manner of a blueprint. This construct is not something one can call either substance or accident.

Nevertheless, there are those who simply identify it with the act itself through which it is understood or conceived. Thus they speak of the tower building itself, which I think of when the tower is not there and which I conceive to be lofty, square, and situated in a spacious plain, as being the same as thinking of a tower. But we prefer to call the [conceptual] image as such the likeness of the thing.

There is of course nothing to prevent the act of understanding itself from being called in some sense a "likeness" because it obviously conceives what is, properly speaking, a likeness of the thing. Still, as we have said—and rightly so—the two are not the same. For, I ask: "Does the squareness or loftiness represent the actual form or quality possessed by the act of understanding itself when one thinks of the height and the way the tower is put together?" Surely the actual squareness and height are present only in bodies and from an imagined quality no act of understanding or any other real essence can be constructed. What remains then but that the substance, like the quality of which it is the subject, is also fictive? Perhaps one could also say that a mirror or reflected image is not itself a true "thing," since there often appears on the whitish surface of the mirror a color of contrary quality. . . .

Having treated in general the nature of understanding, let us consider how a universal and a particular conception differ. The conception associated with a universal name is an image that is general and indiscriminate, whereas the image associated with a singular word represents the proper and characteristic form, as it were, of a single thing, i.e. it applies to one and only one person. When I hear the word "man," for instance, a certain likeness arises in my mind which is so related to individual men that it is proper to none but common to all. But when I hear "Socrates," a certain form arises in my mind which is the likeness of a particular person. . . . Hence it is correct to say "man" does not rightly signify Socrates or any other man, since by virtue of this name no one in particular is identified; yet it is a name of particular things. "Socrates," on the other hand, must not only name a particular thing, but it must also determine just what thing is its subject. . . . To show what pertains to the nature of all lions, a picture can be constructed which represents nothing that is the peculiar property of only one of them. On the other hand, a picture suited to distinguish any one of them can be drawn by depicting something proper to the one in question, for example, by painting it as limping, maimed, or wounded by the spear of Hercules. Just as one can paint one figure that is general and another that is particular, so too can one form one conception of things that is common and another conception that is proper.

There is some question, however, and not without reason, whether or not this [universal] name also signifies this conceptual form to which the understanding is directed. Both authority and reason, however, seem to be unanimous in affirming that it does.

For Priscian, after first showing how universals were applied commonly to individuals, seemed to introduce another meaning they had, namely the common form. He states that "the general and special forms of things which were given intelligibility in the divine mind before being produced in bodies could be used to reveal what the natural genera and species of things are." In this passage he views God after the fashion of an artist who first conceives in his mind a [model or] exemplar form of what he is to fashion and who works according to the likeness of this form, which form is said to be embodied when a real thing is constructed in its likeness.

It may be all right to ascribe such a common conception to God, but not to man. For those works of God like a man, a soul, or a stone represent general or special states of nature, whereas those of a human artisan like a house or a sword do not. For "house" and "sword" do not pertain to nature as the other terms do. They are the names not of a substance but of something accidental and therefore they are neither genera nor ultimate species. Conceptions by abstraction [of the true nature of things] may well be ascribed to the divine mind but may not be ascribed to that of man, because men, who know things only through the medium of their senses, scarcely ever arrive at such an ideal understanding and never conceive the [underlying] natures of things in their purity. But God knew all things he created for what they were and this even before they actually existed. He can discriminate between these individual states as they are in themselves; senses are no hindrance to him who alone has true understanding of things. Of those things which men have not experienced through the senses, they happen to have opinions rather than understanding, as we learn from experience. For having thought of some city before seeing it, we find on arriving there that it is quite different than we had thought.

And so I believe we have only an opinion about those forms like rationality, mortality, paternity, or what is within. Names for what we experience, however, produce understanding to the extent they can do so, for the one who coined the terms intended that they be imposed in accord with the [true] nature or properties of things, even though he himself was unable to do justice in thought to the nature or property of the thing. It is these common concepts, however, which Priscian calls general and special [i.e. generic and specific], that these general names or the names of species bring to the mind. He says that the universals function as proper names with regard to such conceptions, and although these names refer to the essences named only in an indiscriminate fashion, they direct the mind of the hearer immediately to that common conception in the same way that proper names direct attention to the one thing that they signify.

Porphyry too, in distinguishing between things constituted only in the likeness of matter and form and those actually composed of matter and form, seems to understand this common conception by the former. Boethius also, when he calls the conception gathered from a likeness of many things a genus or a species, seems to have in mind this same common conception. Some think that Plato subscribed to this view, i.e. to these common ideas—which he located in the *nous*—he gave the names of genus and species. On this point, perhaps, Boethius indicates some disagreement between Plato and Aristotle, where he speaks of Plato claiming not only that genera, species, and the rest should be understood to be universals, but also that they have true existence and subsistence apart from bodies, as if to say that Plato understood these common concepts, which he assumed to exist in a bodiless form in the nous, to be universals. He means here by universal "a common likeness of many things" perhaps, rather than "predicable of many" as Aristotle understood the term. For this conception [itself] does not seem to be predicated of many in the way that a name is able to be applied to each of many things.

But his [i.e. Boethius's] statement that Plato thinks universals subsist apart from sensibles can be interpreted in another way, so that there is no disagreement between the philosophers. For Aristotle's statements about universals always subsisting in sensibles is to be understood of the way they actually do exist, because the animal nature (which the universal name "animal" designates and which is called a kind of universal in a transferred sense of the term) is never found to exist in anything which is not sensible. Plato, however, thinks this nature has such a natural subsistence in itself that it would retain its existence if it were not subject to sense [i.e. if it were not clothed with sensible accidents]. Hence what Aristotle denies to be actually the case, Plato, the investigator of the nature, ascribes to a natural capacity. Consequently there is no real disagreement between them.

Reason too seems to agree with these authorities in their apparent claim that the universal names designate these common concepts or forms. For what else does to conceive of them by name mean but that names signify them? But since we hold that these forms conceived are not simply the same as the acts of knowing them, there is in addition to the real thing and the act of understanding a third factor, viz. the signification or meaning of the name. Now while there is no authority for holding this, still it is not contrary to reason.

At this point, let us give an answer to the question we promised earlier to settle, namely whether the ability of universal words to refer to things in general is due to the fact that there is in them a common cause for imposing the words on them, or whether it is due to the fact that a common concept of them exists, or whether it is for both of these reasons. Now there seems to be no ground why it should not be for both of these reasons, but if we understand "common cause" as involving something of the nature of the things, then this seems to be the stronger of the two reasons.

Another point we must clarify is the one noted earlier, namely that these universal conceptions are formed by abstraction, and we must show how one can speak of them as isolated, naked, and pure without their being empty. But first about abstraction. Here we must remember that while matter and form are always fused together, the rational power of the mind is such that it can consider matter alone or form alone or both together. The first two are considerations by way of abstraction, since in order to study its precise nature, they abstract one thing from what does not exist alone. The third type of consideration is by way of synthesis. The substance of man, for instance, is a body, an animal, a man; it is invested with no end of forms. But when I turn my attention exclusively to the material essence of a substance, disregarding all its additional forms or qualifications, my understanding takes the form of a concept by abstraction. If I direct my attention, however, to nothing more than the corporeity of this substance, the resulting concept, though it represents a synthesis when compared with the previous concept (that of substance alone), is still formed by abstraction from the forms other than corporeity, such as animation, sensitivity, rationality, or whiteness, none of which I consider.

Such conceptions by abstraction might appear to be false or empty, perhaps, since they look to the thing in a way other than that in which it exists. For since they consider matter or form exclusively, and neither of these subsists separately, they clearly represent a conception of the thing otherwise than the way it is. Consequently, they seem to be vacuous, yet this is not really the case. For it is only when a thing is considered to have some property or nature which it does not actually possess that the conception which represents the thing otherwise than it is, is indeed empty. But this is not what happens in abstraction. For when I consider this man only in his nature as a substance or a body, but not as an animal, a man, or a grammarian, certainly I do not think of anything that is not in that nature, and still I do not attend to all that it has. And when I say that I attend only to what is in it, "only" refers to my attention and not to the way this characteristic exists, for otherwise my conception would be empty. For the thing does not only have this, but I only consider it as having this. And while I do consider it in some sense to be otherwise than it actually is, I do not consider it to be in a state or condition other than that in which it is, as was pointed out earlier. "Otherwise" means merely that the mode of thought is other than the mode of existing. For the thing in question is thought of not as separated, but separately from the other, even though it does not exist separately. Matter is perceived purely, form simply, even though the former does not exist purely nor the latter simply. Purity and simplicity, in a word, are features of our understanding, not of existence; they are characteristic of the way we think, not of the way things exist. Even the senses often function discriminatively where composite objects are concerned. If a statue is half gold, half silver, I can look separately at the gold and silver combined there, studying first the gold, then the silver exclusively, thus viewing piecemeal what is actually joined together, and yet I do not perceive to be divided what is not divided. In much the same way "understanding by way of abstraction" means "considering separately" but not "considering [it] as separated." Otherwise such understanding would be vacuous. . . .

But let us return to our *universal* conceptions, which must always be produced by way of abstraction. For when I hear "man" or "whiteness" or "white," I do not recall in virtue of the name all the natures or properties in those subjects to which the name refers. "Man" gives rise to the conception, indiscriminate, not discrete, of animal, rational and mortal only, but not of the additional accidents as well. Conceptions of individuals also can be formed by abstraction, as happens for example when one speaks of "this substance," "this body," "this animal," "this white," or "this whiteness." For by "this man," though I consider just man's nature, I do so as related to a certain subject, whereas by "man" I regard this nature simply in itself and not in relation to some one man. That is why a universal concept is correctly described as being *isolated, bare*, and *pure:* i.e. "isolated from sense," because it is not a perception of the thing as sensory; "bare," because it is abstracted from some or from all forms; "pure," because it is unadulterated by any reference to any single individual, since there is not just one thing, be it the matter or the form, to which it points, as we explained earlier when we described such a conception as indiscriminate.

Now that we have considered these matters, let us proceed to answer the questions posed by Porphyry about genera and species. This we can easily do now that we have clarified the nature of universals in general. The point of the first question was whether genera and species exist. More precisely, are they signs of something which really exists or of something that merely exists in thought, i.e. are they simply vacuous, devoid of any real reference, as is the case with words like "chimera" or "goat-stag," which fail to produce any coherent meaning? To this one has to reply that as a matter of fact they do serve to name things that actually exist and therefore are not the subjects of purely empty thoughts. But what they name are the selfsame things named by singular names. And still, there is a sense in which they exist as isolated, bare, and pure only in the mind, as we have just explained. . . .

The second question, viz. "Are they corporeal or incorporeal?" can be taken in the same way, that is, "Granting that they are signs of existing things, are these things corporeal or incorporeal?" For surely everything that exists, as Boethius puts it, is either corporeal or incorporeal, regardless of whether these words mean respectively: (1) a bodily or a bodiless substance, (2) something perceptible to the senses like man, wood, and whiteness, or something imperceptible in this way like justice or the soul. (3) "Corporeal" can also have the meaning of something discrete or individual, so that the question boils down to asking whether genera and species signify discrete individuals or not. A thoroughgoing investigator of truth considers not only what can be factually stated but also such possible opinions as might be proposed. Consequently, even though one is quite certain that only individuals are real, in view of the fact that someone might be of the opinion that there are other things that exist, it is justifiable to inquire about them. Now this third meaning of "corporeal" makes better sense of our question, reducing it to an inquiry as to whether it is discrete individuals or not that are signified. On the other hand, since nothing existing is incorporeal, i.e. nonindividual, "incorporeal" would seem to be superfluous in Boethius's statement that everything existing is either corporeal or incorporeal. Here the order of the questions, it seems, suggests nothing that would be of help except perhaps that corporeal and incorporeal, taken in another sense, do represent divisions of whatever exists and that this might also be the case here. The inquirer in this case would seem to be asking, in effect: "Since I see that some existing things are called corporeal and others incorporeal, I would like to know which of these names we should use for what universals signify?" The answer to this would be: "To some extent, 'corporeal' would be appropriate, since the *significata* are in essence discrete individuals. 'Incorporeal' would be a better description, however, of the way a universal term names things, for it does not point to them in an individual and specific fashion but points only in an indiscriminate way, as we have adequately explained above." Hence universal names are described both as corporeal (because of the nature of the things they point to) and as incorporeal (because of the way these things are signified, for although they name discrete individuals, universals do not name them individually or properly).

The third question ("Do they exist apart from or only in sensible things?") arises from the admission that they are incorporeal, since, as we noted [in the opening paragraph], there is a certain sense in which "existing in the sensible" and "not existing in the sensible" represent a division of the incorporeal. Now universals are said to exist in sensible things to the extent that they signify the inner substance of some-thing which is sensible by reason of its external forms. While they signify this same substance actually existing in sensible garb, they point to what is by its nature something distinct from the sensible thing [i.e. as substance it is other than its accidental garb], as we said above in our reinterpretation of Plato. That is why Boethius does not claim that genera and species exist apart from sensible things, but only that they are understood apart from them, to the extent namely that the things conceived generically or specifically are viewed with reference to their nature in a rational fashion rather than in a sensory way, and they could indeed subsist in themselves [i.e. as individual substances] even if stripped of the exterior or [accidental] forms by which they come to the attention of the senses. For we admit that all genera and species exist in things perceptible to the senses. Since our understanding of them has always been described as something apart from the senses, however, they appeared not to be in sensible things in any way. There was every reason, then, to ask whether they could be in sensibles. And to this question, the answer is that some of them are, but only to the extent, as was explained, that they represent the enduring substrate that lies beneath the sensible.

We can take corporeal and incorporeal in this second question as equivalent to sensible and insensible, so that the sequence of questions becomes more orderly. And since our understanding of universals is derived solely from sense perceptions, as has been said, one could appropriately ask whether universals were sensible or insensible. Now the answer is that some of them are sensible (we refer here to the nature of those things classed as sensible) and the same time not sensible (we refer here to the way they are signified). For while it is sensible things that these universals name, they do not designate these things in the way they are perceived by the senses, i.e. as distinct individuals, and when things are designated only in universal terms the senses cannot pick them out. Hence the question arose: "Do universals designate only sensible things, or is there something else they signify?" And the answer to this is that they signify both the sensible things themselves and also that common concept which Priscian ascribes above all to the divine mind.

As for the fourth question we added to the others, our solution is this. We do not want to speak of there being universal names when the things they name have perished and they can no longer be predicated of many and are not common names of anything, as would be the case when all the roses were gone. Nevertheless, "rose" would still have meaning for the mind even though it names nothing. Otherwise, "There is no rose" would not be a proposition.

ETHICS (in part)

PROLOGUE

In the study of morals we deal with the defects or qualities of the mind which dispose us to bad or good actions. Defects and qualities are not only mental, but also physical. There is bodily weakness; there is also the endurance which we call strength. There is

Abailard's Ethics, "Prologue," 1–3, 10–12, translated by J. Ramsay McCallum (Oxford: Basil Blackwell, 1935). Reprinted by permission.

sluggishness or speed; blindness or sight. When we now speak of defects, therefore, we pre-suppose defects of the mind, so as to distinguish them from the physical ones. The defects of the mind are opposed to the qualities; injustice to justice; cowardice to constancy; intemperance to temperance.

CHAPTER 1: THE DEFECT OF MIND BEARING UPON CONDUCT

Certain defects or merits of mind have no connection with morals. They do not make human life a matter of praise or blame. Such are dull wits or quick insight; a good or a bad memory; ignorance or knowledge. Each of these features is found in good and bad alike. They have nothing to do with the system of morals, nor with making life base or honourable. To exclude these we safeguarded above the phrase "defects of mind" by adding "which dispose to bad actions," that is, those defects which incline the will to what least of all either should be done or should be left undone.

CHAPTER 2: HOW DOES SIN DIFFER FROM A DISPOSITION TO EVIL?

Defect of this mental kind is not the same thing as sin. Sin, too, is not the same as a bad action. For example, to be irascible, that is, prone or easily roused to the agitation of anger is a defect and moves the mind to unpleasantly impetuous and irrational action. This defect, however, is in the mind so that the mind is liable to wrath, even when it is not actually roused to it. Similarly, lameness, by reason of which a man is said to be lame, is in the man himself even when he does not walk and reveal his lameness. For the defect is there though action be lacking. So, also, nature or constitution renders many liable to luxury. Yet they do not sin because they are like this, but from this very fact they have the material of a struggle whereby they may, in the virtue of temperance, triumph over themselves and win the crown. As Solomon says: "Better a patient than a strong man; and the Lord of his soul than he that taketh a city" (Prov. xvi, 32). For religion does not think it degrading to be beaten by man; but it is degrading to be beaten by one's lower self. The former defeat has been the fate of good men. But, in the latter, we fall below ourselves. The Apostle commends victory of this sort; "No one shall be crowned who has not truly striven" (2 Tim. ii, 5). This striving, I repeat, means standing less against men than against myself, so that defects may not lure me into base consent. Though men cease to oppose us, our defects do not cease. The fight with them is the more dangerous because of its repetition. And as it is the more difficult, so victory is the more glorious. Men, however much they prevail over us, do not force baseness upon us, unless by their practice of vice they turn us also to it and overcome us through our own wretched consent. They may dominate our body; but while our mind is free, there is no danger to true freedom. We run no risk of base servitude. Subservience to vice, not to man, is degradation. It is the overlordship of defects and not physical serfdom which debases the soul.

CHAPTER 3: DEFINITION OF "DEFECT" AND OF SIN

Defect, then, is that whereby we are disposed to sin. We are, that is, inclined to consent to what we ought not to do, or to leave undone what we ought to do. Consent of this kind we rightly call sin. Here is the reproach of the soul meriting damnation or being declared guilty by God. What is that consent but to despise God and to violate his laws? God cannot be set at enmity by injury, but by contempt. He is the highest power, and is not diminished by any injury, but He avenges contempt of Himself. Our sin, therefore, is contempt of the Creator. To sin is to despise the Creator; that is, not to do for Him what we believe we should do for Him, or, not to renounce what we think should be renounced on His behalf. We have defined sin negatively by saying that it means not doing or not renouncing what we ought to do or renounce. Clearly, then, we have shown that sin has no reality. It exists rather in *not being* than in *being*. Similarly we could define shadows by saying: The absence of light where light usually is.

Perhaps you object that sin is the desire or will to do an evil deed, and that this will or desire condemns us before God in the same way as the will to do a good deed justifies us. There is as much quality, you suggest, in the good will as there is sin in the evil will; and it is no less "in being" in the latter than in the former. By willing to do what we believe to be pleasing to God we please Him. Equally, by willing to do what we believe to be displeasing to God, we displease Him and seem either to violate or despise His nature.

But diligent attention will show that we must think far otherwise of this point. We frequently err; and from no evil will at all. Indeed, the evil will itself, when restrained, though it may not be quenched, procures the palm-wreath for those who resist it. It provides, not merely the materials for combat, but also the crown of glory. It should be spoken of rather as a certain inevitable weakness than as sin. Take, for example, the case of an innocent servant whose harsh master is moved with fury against him. He pursues the servant, drawing his sword with intent to kill him. For a while the servant flies and avoids death as best he can. At last, forced all unwillingly to it, he kills his master so as not to be killed by him. Let anyone say what sort of evil will there was in this deed. His will was only to flee from death and preserve his own life. Was this an evil will? You reply: "I do not think this was an evil will. But the will that he had to kill the master who was pursuing him was evil." Your answer would be admirable and acute if you could show that the servant really willed what you say that he did. But, as I insisted, he was unwillingly forced to his deed. He protracted his master's life as long as he could, knowing that danger also threatened his own life from such a crime. How, then was a deed done voluntarily by which he incurred danger to his own life?

Your reply may be that the action was voluntary because the man's will was to escape death even though it may not have been to kill his master. This charge might easily be preferred against him. I do not rebut it. Nevertheless, as has been said, that will be which he sought to evade death, as you urge, and not to kill his master, cannot at all be condemned as bad. He did, however, fail by consenting, though driven to it through fear of death, to an unjust murder which he ought rather to have endured than committed. Of his own will, I mean, he took the sword. It was not handed to him by authority. The Truth saith: "Everyone that taketh the sword shall perish by the sword" (Matt. xxvi, 52). By his rashness he risked the death and damnation of his soul. The servant's wish, then, was not to kill his master, but to avoid death. Because he *consented,* however, as he should not have done, to murder, this wrongful consent preceding the crime was sin.

Someone may interpose: "But you cannot conclude that he wished to kill his master because, in order to escape death, he was willing to kill his master. I might say to a man: I am willing for you to have my cape so that you may give me five shillings. Or, I am glad for you to have it at this price. But I do not hand it over because I desire you to have possession of it." No, and if a man in prison desired under duress, to put his son there in his place that he might secure his own ransom, should we therefore admit that he wished to send his son to prison?

It was only with many a tear and groan that he consented to such a course.

The fact is that this kind of will, existing with much internal regret, is not, if I may so say, *will*, but a passive submission of mind. It is so because the man wills one thing on account of another. He puts up with *this* because he really desires *that*. A patient is said to submit to cautery or lancet that he may obtain health. Martyrs endured that they might come to Christ; and Christ, too, that we may be saved by his passion.

Yet we are not bound to admit simply that these people therefore wish for this mental unease. Such unease can only be where something occurs contrary to wish. No man suffers so long as he fulfills his wish and does what he likes to experience. The Apostle says: "I desire to depart and to be with Christ" (Phil. i, 23), that is, to die so that I may attain to him. Elsewhere this apostle says: "We desire not to be despoiled of our garments, but to be clothed from above, that our mortal part may be swallowed up in life." This notion, Blessed Augustine reminds us, was contained in the Lord's address to Peter: "Thou shalt extend thy hands and another shall gird thee, and lead thee whither thou willest not" (John xxi, 18). The Lord also spoke to the Father out of the weakness of the human nature which he had taken upon himself: "If it be possible, let this cup pass from me; nevertheless not as I will, but as thou willest" (Matt. xxvi, 39). His spirit naturally trembled before the great terror of death: and he could not speak of what he knew to be punishment as a matter of his own will. When elsewhere it is written of Him: "He was offered because He himself willed it" (Isaiah liii, 7), it must be understood either of His divine nature, in whose will it was that he should suffer as a man, or "He himself willed it" must be taken according to the Psalmist's phrase: "Whatsoever he willed, that he did" (Ps. cxiii, 3).

Sin, therefore, is sometimes committed without an evil will. Thus sin cannot be defined as "will." True, you will say, when we sin under constraint, but not when we sin willingly, for instance, when we will to do something which we know ought not to be done by us. There the evil will and sin seem to be the same thing. For example a man sees a woman; his concupiscence is aroused; his mind is enticed by fleshly lust and stirred to base desire. This wish, this lascivious longing, what else can it be, you say, than sin?

I reply: What if that wish may be bridled by the power of temperance? What if its nature is never to be entirely extinguished but to persist in struggle and not fully fail even in defeat? For where is the battle if the antagonist is away? Whence the great reward without grave endurance? When the fight is over nothing remains but to reap the reward. Here we strive in contest in order elsewhere to obtain as victors a crown. Now, for a contest, an opponent is needed who will resist, not one who simply submits. This opponent is our evil will over which we triumph when we subjugate it to the divine will. But we do not entirely destroy it. For we needs must ever expect to encounter our enemy. What achievement before God is it if we undergo nothing contrary to our own will, but merely practice what we please? Who will be grateful to us if in what we say we do for him we merely satisfy our own fancy?

You will say, what merit have we with God in acting willingly or unwillingly? Certainly none: I reply. He weighs the intention rather than the deed in his recompense. Nor does the deed, whether it proceed from a good or an evil will, add anything to the merit, as we shall show shortly. But when we set His will before our own so as to follow His and not ours, our merit with God is magnified, in accordance with that perfect word of Truth: "I came not to do mine own will, but the will of Him that sent me" (John vi, 38). To this end He exhorts us: "If anyone comes to me, and does not hate father, and mother . . . yea his own soul also, he is not worthy of me" (Luke xiv, 26). That is to say, "unless a man renounces his parents' influence and his own will and submits himself to my teaching, he is not worthy of me." Thus we are bidden to hate our father, not to destroy him. Similarly with our own will. We must not be led by it; at the same time, we are not asked to root it out altogether.

When the Scripture says: "Go not after your own desires" (Eccles. xviii, 30) and: "Turn from your own will" (*ibid.*), it instructs us not to fulfil our desires. Yet it does not say that we are to be wholly without them. It is vicious to give in to our desires; but not to have any desires at all is impossible for our weak nature.

The sin, then, consists not in desiring a woman, but in consent to the desire, and not the wish for whoredom, but the consent to the wish is damnation.

Let us see how our conclusions about sexual intemperance apply to theft. A man crosses another's garden. At the sign of the delectable fruit his desire is aroused. He does not, however, give way to desire so as to take anything by theft or rapine, although his mind was moved to strong inclination by the thought of the delight of eating. Where there is desire, there, without doubt, will exists. The man desires the eating of that fruit wherein he doubts not that there will be delight. The weakness of nature in this man is compelled to desire the fruit which, without the master's permission, he has no right to take. He conquers the desire, but does not extinguish it. Since, however, he is not enticed into consent, he does not descend to sin.

What, then, of your objection? It should be clear from such instances, that the wish or desire itself of doing what is not seemly is never to be called sin, but rather, as we said, the consent is sin. We consent to what is not seemly when we do not draw ourselves back from such a deed, and are prepared, should opportunity offer, to perform it completely. Whoever is discovered in this intention, though his guilt has yet to be completed in deed, is already guilty before God in so far as he strives with all his might to sin, and accomplishes within himself, as the blessed Augustine reminds us, as much as if he were actually taken in the act.

But while wish is not sin, and, as we have said, we sometimes commit sin unwillingly, there are nevertheless those who assert that every sin is voluntary. In this respect they discover a certain difference between sin and will. Will is one thing, they say, but a voluntary act is another. They mean that there is a distinction between will and what is done willingly. If, however, we call sin what we have already decided that it essentially is, namely, contempt of God or consent to that which we believe should not, for God's sake, be done how can we say that sin is voluntary? I mean, how can we say that we wish to despise God? What is sin but sinking below a standard, or becoming liable to damnation? For although we desire to do what we know deserves punishment, yet we do not desire to be punished. Thus plainly we are reprobate. We are willing to do wrong; but we are unwilling to bear the just punishment of wrongdoing. The punishment which is just displeases: the deed which is unjust pleases. Often we woo a married woman because of her charm. Our wish is not so much to commit adultery as a longing that she were unmarried. On the other hand, many covet the wives of influential men for the sake of their own fame, and not for the natural attractiveness of these ladies. Their wish is for adultery rather than sexual relationship, the major in preference to the minor excess. Some, too, are ashamed altogether of being betrayed into any consent to concupiscence or evil will; and thus from the weakness of the flesh are compelled to wish what they least of all wish to wish.

How, then, a wish which we do not wish to have can be called voluntary, as it is according to those thinkers I have mentioned, so that all sin becomes a matter of voluntary action, I assuredly do not understand, unless by voluntary is meant that no action is determined, since a sin is never a predestined event. Or perhaps we are to take "voluntary" to be that which proceeds from some kind of will. For although the man who slew his master had no will to perform the actual murder, nevertheless he did it from some sort of will, because he certainly wished to escape or defer death.

Some are intensely indignant when they hear us assert that the act of sinning adds nothing to guilt or damnation before God. Their contention is that in this act of sinning a certain delight supervenes, which increases the sin, as in sexual intercourse or indulgence in food which we referred to above. Their statement is absurd unless they can prove that physical delight of this kind is itself sin, and that such pleasure cannot be taken without a sin being thereby committed. If it be as they suppose, then no one is permitted to enjoy physical pleasure. The married do not escape sin when they employ their physical privilege; nor yet the man who eats with relish his own fruits.

Invalids, too, who are treated to more delicate dishes to aid their recovery of strength would likewise be guilty, since they are not able to eat without a sense of delight and should this be lacking, the food does them no good. Finally, God, the Creator of nourishment and of the bodies which receive it, would not be without guilt for having instilled savours which necessarily involve in sin those who ignorantly use them. Yet how should He supply such things for our consumption, or permit them to be consumed, if it were impossible for us to eat them without sin? How, again, can it be said that there is sin in doing what is allowed? In regard to those matters which once were unlawful and forbidden, if they are later allowed and made lawful, they can be done entirely without sin. For instance, the eating of pork and many other things once out of bounds to the Jew are now free to us Christians. When, therefore, we see Jews turned Christian gladly eating food of this sort which the law had prohibited, how can we defend their rectitude except by affirming that this latitude has now been conceded to them by God?

Well, in what was formerly a food restriction and is now food freedom, the concession of freedom excludes sin and eliminates contempt of God. Who then shall say that a man sins in respect of a matter which the divine permission has made lawful for him? If the marriage-bed or the eating of even delicate food was permitted from the first day of our creation, when we lived in Paradise without sin, who can prove that we transgress in these enjoyments, so long as we do not pass the limits of the permission? Another objection is that matrimonial intercourse and the eating of tasty food are only allowed on condition of being taken without pleasure. But, if this is so, then they are allowed to be done in a way in which they never can be done. That concession is not reasonable which concedes that a thing shall be so done as it is certain that it cannot be done. By what reasoning did the law aforetime enforce matrimony so that each might leave his seed to Israel? Or, how did the Apostle oblige wives to fulfil the mutual debt if these acts could not be done without sinning? How can he refer to this debt when already it is of necessity sin? Or how should a man be compelled to do what he will grieve God by doing? Hence, I think that it is plain that no natural physical delight can be set down as sin, nor can it be called guilt for men to delight in what, when it is done, must involve the feeling of delight.

For example, if anyone obliged a monk, bound in chains, to lie among women, and the monk by the softness of the couch and by contact with his fair flatterers is allured into delight, though not into consent, who shall presume to designate guilt the delight which is naturally awakened?

You may urge, with some thinkers, that the carnal pleasure, even in lawful intercourse, involves sin. Thus David says: "Behold in sin was I conceived" (Ps. 1, 7). And the Apostle, when he had said: "Ye return to it again" (1 Cor. vii, 5), adds, nevertheless, "This I say by way of concession, not of command" (*ibid.*, v, 6.). Yet authority rather than reason, seems to dictate the view that we should allow simple physical delight to be sin. For, assuredly, David was conceived not in fornication, but in matrimony: and concession, that is forgiveness, does not, as this standpoint avers, condone when there is no guilt to forgive. As for what David meant when he says that he had been conceived "in iniquity" or "in sin" and does not say "whose" sin, he referred to the general curse of original sin, wherein from the guilt of our first parents each is subject to damnation, as it is elsewhere stated: "None are pure of stain, not the infant a day old, if he has life on this earth." As the blessed Jerome reminds us and as manifest reason teaches, the soul of a young child is without sin. If, then, it is pure of sin, how is it also impure by sinful corruption? We must understand the infant's purity from sin in reference to its personal guilt. But its contact with sinful corruption, its "stain," is in reference to penalty owed by mankind because of Adam's sin. He who has not yet perceived by reason what he ought to do cannot be guilty of contempt of God. Yet he is not free from the contamination of the sin of his first parents, from which he contracts the penalty, though not the guilt, and bears in penalty what they committed in guilt. When, therefore, David says that he was conceived in iniquity or sin, he sees himself subject to the general sentence of damnation from the guilt of his racial parents, and he assigns these sins, not to his father and mother but to his first parents.

When the Apostle speaks of indulgence, he must not be understood as some would wish to understand him, to mean permission to be equivalent to pardon for sin. His statement is: "By way of indulgence not of command." He might equally have said: "By permission, not by force." If husband and wife wish and decide upon mutual agreement they can abstain altogether from intercourse, and may not be compelled to it by command. But should they not so decide they have indulgence, that is, permission to substitute a less perfect for a more perfect rule of life. The Apostle, in this passage, did not therefore refer to pardon for sin, but to the permission of a less strict life for the avoidance of fornication. He meant that this lower level might elude the peaks of sin, and by its inferior standing escape the greater guilt.

We come, then, to this conclusion, that no one who sets out to assert that all fleshly desire is sin may say that the sin itself is increased by the doing of it. For this would mean extending the consent of the soul into the exercise of the action. In short, one would be stained not only by consent to baseness, but also by the mire of the deed, as if what happens externally in the body could possibly soil the soul. Sin is not, therefore, increased by the doing of an action: and nothing mars the soul except what is of its own nature, namely consent. This we affirmed was alone sin, preceding action in will, or subsequent to the performance of action. Although we wish for, or do, what is unseemly, we do not therefore sin. For such deeds not uncommonly occur without there being any sin. On the other hand, there may be consent without the external effects, as we have indicated. There was wish without consent in the case of the man who was attracted by a woman whom he caught sight of, or who was tempted by his neighbour's fruit, but who was not enticed into consent. There was evil consent without evil desire in the servant who unwillingly killed his master.

Certain acts which ought not to be done often are done, and without any sin, when, for instance, they are committed under force or ignorance. No one, I think, ignores this fact. A woman under constraint of violence, lies with another's husband. A man, taken by some trick, sleeps with one whom he supposed to be his wife, or kills a man, in the belief that he himself has the right to be both judge and executioner. Thus to desire the wife of another or actually to lie with her is not sin. But to consent to that desire or to that action is sin. This consent to covetousness the law calls covetousness in saying: "Thou shalt not covet" (Deut. v, 21). Yet that which we cannot avoid ought not to be forbidden, nor that wherein, as we said, we do not sin. But we should be cautioned about the consent to covetousness. So, too, the saying of the Lord must be understood: "Whosoever shall look upon a woman to desire her" (Matt. v, 28). That is, whosoever shall so look upon her as to slip into consent to covetousness, "has already committed adultery with her in his heart" (Matt. v, 28), even though he may not have committed adultery in deed. He is guilty of sin, though there be no sequel to his intention.

Careful account will reveal that wherever actions are restricted by some precept or prohibition, these refer rather to will and consent than to the deeds themselves. Otherwise nothing relative to a person's moral merit could be included under a precept. Indeed, actions are so much the less worth prescribing as they are less in our power to do. At the same time, many things we are forbidden to do for which there exists in our will both the inclination and the consent.

The Lord God says: "Thou shalt not kill. Thou shalt not bear false witness" (Deut. v, 17, 20). If we accept these cautions as being only about actions, as the words suggest, then guilt is not forbidden, but simply the activity of guilt. For we have seen that actions may be carried out without sin, as that it is not sin to kill a man or to lie with another's wife. And even the man who desires to bear false testimony, and is willing to utter it, so long as he is silent for some reason and does not speak, is innocent before the law, that is, if the prohibition in this matter be accepted literally of the action. It is not said that we should not *wish* to give false witness, or that we should not *consent* in bearing it, but simply that we should not bear false witness.

Similarly, when the law forbids us to marry or have intercourse with our sisters, if this prohibition relates to deed rather than to intention, no one can keep the commandment, for a sister unless we recognize her, is just a woman. If a man, then, marries his sister in error, is he a transgressor for doing what the law forbade? He is not, you will reply, because, in acting ignorantly in what he did, he did not consent to a transgression. Thus a transgressor is not one who *does* what is prohibited. He is one who *consents* to what is prohibited. The prohibition is, therefore, not about action, but about consent. It is as though in saying: "Do not do this or that," we meant: "Do not consent to do this or that," or "Do not wittingly do this."

Blessed Augustine, in his careful view of this question, reduces every sin or command to terms of charity and covetousness, and not to works. "The law," he says, "inculcates nothing but charity, and forbids nothing but covetousness." The Apostle, also, asserts: "All the law is contained in one word: thou shalt love thy neighbour as thyself" (Rom. xiii, 8, 10), and again, "Love is the fulfilling of the law" (*ibid*.).

Whether you actually give alms to a needy person, or charity makes you ready to give, makes no difference to the merit of the deed. The will may be there when the opportunity is not. Nor does it rest entirely with you to deal with every case of need which you encounter. Actions which are right and actions which are far from right are done by good and bad men alike. The intention alone separates the two classes of men.

Augustine reminds us that in the self-same action we find God the Father, the Lord Jesus Christ, and also Judas the betrayer. The betrayal of the Son was accomplished by God the Father, and by the Son, and by the betrayer. For "the Father delivered up the Son, and the Son Himself" (Rom. viii, 32; Gal. ii, 22), as the Apostle says, and Judas delivered up his Master. The traitor, therefore, did the same thing as God Himself. But did Judas do anything well? No. Good certainly came of his act; but his act was not well done, nor was it destined to benefit him.

God considers not the action, but the spirit of the action. It is the intention, not the deed wherein the merit or praise of the doer consists. Often, indeed, the same action is done from different motives: for justice sake by one man, for an evil reason by another. Two men, for instance, hang a guilty person. The one does it out of zeal for justice; the other in resentment for an earlier enmity. The action of hanging is the same. Both men do what is good and what justice demands. Yet the diversity of their intentions causes the same deed to be done from different motives, in the one case good, in the other bad.

Everyone knows that the devil himself does nothing without God's permission, when he either punishes a wicked man according to his deserts, or is allowed to afflict a just man for moral cleansing or for an example of endurance. Since, however, in doing what God permits the devil moves at the spur of his own malice, the power which he has may be called good, or even just, while his will is for ever unjust. He receives, that is, the power from God, but his will is of himself.

Who, among the elect, can ever emulate the deeds of hypocrites? Who, for the love of God, ever endures or undertakes so much as they do from thirst for human praise? Who does not agree that sometimes what God forbids may rightly be done, while, contrarily, He may counsel certain things which of all things are least convenient? We note how He forbade certain miracles, whereby He had healed infirmities, to be made public. He set an example of humility lest any man should claim glory for the grace bestowed on him. Nevertheless, the recipients of those benefits did not cease to broadcast them, to the praise of Him who had done such things, and yet had forbidden them to be revealed. Thus we read: "As much as He bade them not to speak, so much the more did they publish abroad, etc." Will you judge these men guilty of a fault who acted contrary to the command which they had received, and did so wittingly? Who can acquit them of wrong-doing, unless by finding that they did not act out of contempt for the One who commanded, but decided to do what was to His honour? How, then, did the matter stand? Did Christ command what ought not to have been commanded? Or, did the newly-healed men disobey when they should have obeyed? The command was a good thing; yet it was not good for it to be obeyed.

In the case of Abraham, also, you will accuse God for first enjoining the sacrifice of Abraham's son, and then revoking the command. Has, then, God never *wisely commanded* anything which, *if it had come about,* would not have been good? If good, you will object, why was it afterwards forbidden? But conceive that it was good for the same thing to be prescribed and also to be prohibited. God, we know, permits nothing, and does not himself consent to achieve anything apart from rational cause. Thus it is the pure intention of the command, not the execution of the action which justifies God in wisely commanding what would not in actual fact be good. God did not intend Abraham to sacrifice his son, or command this sacrifice to be put into effect. His aim was to test Abraham's obedience, constancy of faith, and love towards Him, so that these qualities should be left to us as an example. This intention the Lord God plainly asserts afterwards in saying: "Now know I that thou fearest the Lord" (Gen. xxii, 12). It is as if he frankly said: "I commanded you: you showed yourself ready to obey Me. Both these things were done so that others might know what I had Myself known of you from the beginning." There was a right intention on God's part; but it was not right for it to be put in practice. The prohibition, too, in the case of the miracles of healing was right. The object of this prohibition was not for it to be obeyed, but for an example to be given to our weak spirit in avoiding empty applause. God, in the one case enjoined an action which, if obeyed, would not have been good. In the other case, He forbade what was worth putting into fact, namely, a knowledge of Christ's miracles. The intention excuses Him in the first matter, just as the intention excuses the men who, in the second instance, were healed and did not carry out his injunction. They knew that the precept was not given to be practised, but in order that the aforenamed example of moderation in a successful miracle might be set. In keeping, then, the spirit of the command they showed, by actually disobeying no contempt for Him with whose intention they knew that they were acting.

A scrutiny of the deed rather than of the intention will reveal, then, cases where men frequently not only wish to go against God's bidding, but carry their wish knowingly into effect, and do so without any guilt of sin. An action or a wish must not be called bad because it does not in actual fact fall in with God's command. It may well be that the doer's intention does not at all differ from the will of his divine superior. The intention exonerates Him who gave a practically unseemly command: the intention excuses the man who, out of kindness, disobeyed the command to conceal the miracle.

Briefly to summarize the above argument: Four things were postulated which must be carefully distinguished from one another.

1. Imperfection of soul, making us liable to sin.
2. Sin itself, which we decided is consent to evil or contempt of God.
3. The will or desire of evil.
4. The evil deed.

To wish is not the same thing as to fulfil a wish. Equally, to sin is not the same as to carry out a sin. In the first case, we sin by consent of the soul: the second is a matter of the external effect of an action, namely, when we fulfil in deed that whereunto we have previously consented. When, therefore, temptation is said to proceed through three stages, suggestion, delight, consent, it must be understood that, like our first parents, we are frequently led along these three paths to the commission of sin. The devil's persuasion comes *first* promising from the taste of the forbidden fruit immortality. Delight follows. When the woman sees the beautiful tree, and perceives that the fruit is good, her appetite is whetted by the anticipated pleasure of tasting. This desire she ought to have repressed, so as to obey God's command. But in consenting to it, she was drawn *secondly* into sin. By penitence she should have put right this fault, and obtained pardon. Instead, she *thirdly* consummated the sin by the deed. Eve thus passed through the three stages to the commission of sin.

By the same avenues we also arrive not at sin, but at the action of sin, namely, the doing of an unseemly deed through the suggestion or prompting of something within us. If we already know that such a deed will be pleasant, our imagination is held by anticipatory delight and we are tempted thereby in thought. So long as we give consent to such delight, we sin. Lastly, we pass to the third stage, and actually commit the sin.

It is agreed by some thinkers that carnal suggestion, even though the person causing the suggestion be not present, should be included under sinful suggestion. For example, a man having seen a woman falls into a sensual desire of her. But it seems that this kind of suggestion should simply be called delight. This delight, and other delights of the like kind, arise naturally and, as we said above, they are not sinful. The Apostle calls them "human temptations." "No temptation has taken you yet which was not common to men. God is faithful, and will not suffer you to be tempted above what you are able; but will, with the temptation make a way of escape, that you may be able to bear it." By temptation is meant, in general, any movement of the soul to do something unseemly, whether in wish or consent. We speak of human temptation without which it is hardly or never possible for human weakness to exist. Such are sexual desire, or the pleasures of the table. From these the Psalmist asks to be delivered when he says: "Deliver me from my wants, O Lord" (Ps. xxiv, 17); that is, from the temptations of natural and necessary appetites that they may not influence him into sinful consent. Or, he may mean: "When this life is over, grant me to be without those temptations of which life has been full."

When the Apostle says: "No temptation has taken you but what is human," his statement amounts to this: Even if the soul be stirred by that delight which is, as we said, human temptation, yet God would not lead the soul into that consent wherein sin consists. Someone may object: But by what power of our own are we able to resist those desires? We may reply: "God is faithful, who will not allow you to be tempted," as the Scripture says. In other words: We should rather trust him than rely upon ourselves. He promises help, and is true to his promises. He is faithful, so that we should have complete faith in him. Out of pity God diminishes the degree of human temptation, "does not suffer us to be tempted above what we are able," in order that it may not drive us to sin at a pace we cannot endure, when, that is, we strive to resist it. Then, too, God turns the temptation to our advantage: for He trains us thereby so that the recurrence of temptation causes us less care, and we fear less the onset of a foe over whom we have already triumphed, and whom we know how to meet.

Every encounter, not as yet undertaken, is for that reason, to us, a matter of more anxiety and dismay. But when such an encounter comes to those accustomed to victory, its force and terror alike vanish.

*   *   *

CHAPTER 10: A NUMBER OF GOOD THINGS IS NOT BETTER THAN ONE OF THESE GOOD THINGS

The number of actions is of no importance for their intention. For to speak of good intention and good action, that is action proceeding from good intention, is to refer merely to the goodness of the intention. We cannot retain the term good in this same sense and talk of many "goods."

When we say that a man is simple, and speech simple, we do not therefore allow that there exist many "simples" just because this word "simple" is employed in the first instance of a man, and in the second instance of speech. No one can then compel us to concede that when the good act is added to the good intention, good is added to good, as though there could be many goods in proportion to whose number recompense ought to be increased. As we have said, we cannot call those actions "additional goods," for the word "good" does not properly apply to them.

CHAPTER 11: THE GOOD ACTION SPRINGS FROM THE GOOD INTENTION

We call the intention good which is right in itself, but the action is good, not because it contains within it some good, but because it issues from a good intention. The same act may be done by the same man at different times. According to the diversity of his intention, however, this act may be at one time good, at another bad. So goodness and badness vary. Compare the proposition: "Socrates sits." One conceives this statement either truly or falsely according as Socrates actually does sit, or stands. This alternation in truth and falsity, Aristotle affirms, comes about not from any change in the circumstances which compose the true or false situation, but because the subject-matter of the statement (that is, Socrates) moves in itself, I mean changes from sitting to standing or vice versa.*

CHAPTER 12: WHAT ARE THE GROUNDS OF GOOD INTENTIONS?

Good or right intention is held by some to be when anyone believes that he acts well, and that what he does pleases God. An example is supplied by those who persecuted the martyrs. About them the Gospel Truth says: "The hour comes when everyone who kills you will think that he is obedient to God" (John xvi, 2). In sympathy with the ignorance of such the Apostle exclaims: "I bear this testimony on their behalf, that they are zealous for God but not according to knowledge." That is to say, they are fervently eager to do what they believe pleases God. Since, however, in this desire or keenness of mind they are deceived, their intention is a mistake. The eye of the heart is not so simple as to be capable of seeing clearly and to guard itself from error. For this reason the Lord, when he distinguished works according to right and wrong intention, spoke of the eye of the mind, that is the intention, as either *single,* pure, as it were, from spot, so that it could see clearly, or, on the contrary, as *clouded.* "If thine eye be single, thy whole body shall be full of light." This means that, provided the intention was right, all the acts proceeding from the intention which can possibly be foreseen in the manner of mortal affairs, will be worthy of the light, that is to say, good. And, contrarily, from wrong intention arise dark deeds.

The intention, therefore, must not be called good, merely because it seems good, but over and above this, because it is such as it is estimated to be. I mean that, if it thinks to please God in what it aims as its aim therein should not be mistaken. Otherwise the heathen, just like us, could count their good works, since they no less than we believe themselves either to be saved or to please God by their deeds.

---

*We may do the same action twice, just as we may say "Socrates sits" twice. But just as the same statement will be true when Socrates sits and false when he stands, so the same action will be good when the intention is good, and bad when the intention is bad.

HILDEGARD OF BINGEN
1098–1179

The monasteries and convents were as important to the intellectual life of twelfth-century Europe as were the developing universities. Those religious houses contained both scholars seeking the reconciliation of faith and reason and contemplatives who emphasized the nonrational and mystical elements of Christianity. For example, both the academic Peter Abelard and the mystic St. Bernard of Clairvaux, his adversary, were monks. The cloister was also one of the few places where women could get an education, write, and assume positions of intellectual leadership. Among the leading nuns who wrote during this period was the mystic, Hildegard of Bingen.

Hildegard was born in Bermersheim, near Mainz, Germany. As their tenth and last child, her parents gave her as a "tithe" (literally a "tenth") to the church when she was eight years old. She took the vows of the Order of St. Benedict at around fifteen and spent her next two decades as a devoted Benedictine nun at Disibodenberg. In 1137, Hildegard became the abbess of her convent and soon thereafter began her writing career. Over the next forty-two years, Hildegard not only wrote, she also founded two new convents, worked for social and church reform, and preached throughout the Rhine River basin. Sought out for advice by kings and popes as well as by common people, she wrote numerous letters of counsel and warning. Hildegard was fearlessly direct in these letters, as the opening lines of her letter to Pope Anastasius IV indicate:

So it is, O man, that you who sit in the chief seat of the Lord, hold him in contempt when you embrace evil, since you do not reject [evil] but kiss it, by silently tolerating it in depraved men. . . . Beware, therefore, of wanting to associate yourself with the ways of the pagans, lest you fall.*

In addition to letters, Hildegard's works include an explication of the Rule of St. Benedict (a list of rules used to govern monastic life), commentaries on the Gospels, scientific and medical treatises, poetry, songs, and the earliest known morality play. But Hildegard is best known for her visionary trilogy, *Scivias.*

Perhaps from as early as age three, Hildegard had visions, and she continued to have them throughout her life. As she explained in her preface to the *Scivias,* these visions did not come to her while sleeping or in a trance, "but by God's will [I] beheld them wide awake and clearly, with the mind, eyes, and ears of the inner person." In the passage from this work, reprinted here as translated by Mother Columba Hart and Jane Bishop, Hildegard relates a vision of a fetus receiving a soul. She goes on to discuss the relation between the body and the soul, as well as the interrelations among the various parts of the soul: senses, intellect, will, reason. She ends this interesting discussion with a pictorial analogy that illustrates her visual style.

*   *   *

For an overview of mysticism, begin with the classic by Evelyn Underhill, *Mysticism: A Study in the Nature and Development of Man's Spiritual Consciousness*, 12th edition (London: Methuen, 1930). W.T. Stace, *Mysticism and Philosophy* (London: Macmillan, 1960); M.D. Knowles, *The Nature of Mysticism* (New York: Hawthorn Books, 1966); Georgia Harkness, *Mysticism: Its Meaning and Message* (Nashville, TN: Abingdon Press, 1973); and S.T. Katz, *Mysticism and Philosophical Analysis* (New York: Oxford University Press, 1978) also give good general introductions. Paul E. Szarmach, *An Introduction to the Medieval Mystics of Europe* (Albany, NY: SUNY Press, 1984) provides sketches of virtually every major medieval mystic.

For a study of Hildegard of Bingen's life and thought, see Sabina Flanagan, *Hildegard of Bingen, 1098–1179: A Visionary Life* (London: Routledge, 1989); and Renate Craine, *Hildegard: Prophet of the Cosmic Christ* (New York: Crossroads, 1997). Surveys with sections on Hildegard include Lina Eckenstein, *Women under Monasticism* (New York: Russell and Russell, 1963); Peter Dronke, *Women Writers of the Middle Ages* (Cambridge: Cambridge University Press, 1984); Margaret Alic, *Hypatia's Heritage: A History of Women in Science from Antiquity through the Nineteenth Century* (Boston: Beacon Press, 1986); and Elisabeth Gössmann, "Hildegard of Bingen" in Mary Ellen Waithe, *A History of Women Philosophers, Volume II: Medieval, Renaissance and Enlightenment Women Philosophers, 500–1600* (Dordrecht, The Netherlands: Kluwer Academic, 1989).

*Hildegard of Bingen, *Mystical Writings,* edited by Fiona Bowie and Oliver Davies, translated by Robert Carver (New York: Crossroads, 1990), p. 134. Portentously, Pope Anastasius IV died soon after this letter was sent.

SCIVIAS (in part)

BOOK I, VISION FOUR

16: AN INFANT IS VIVIFIED IN THE WOMB AND CONFIRMED
BY A SOUL ON LEAVING IT

And you see the image of a woman who has a perfect human form in her womb. This
means that after a woman has conceived by human semen, an infant with all its members whole is formed in the secret chamber of her womb. And behold! *By the secret
design of the Supernal Creator that form moves with vital motion;* for, by God's secret
and hidden command and will, fitly and rightly at the divinely appointed time the infant in the maternal womb receives a spirit, and shows by the movements of its body
that it lives, just as the earth opens and brings forth the flowers of its use when the dew
falls on it. *So that a fiery globe which has no human lineaments possesses the heart of
that form;* that is, the soul, burning with a fire of profound knowledge, which discerns
whatever is within the circle of its understanding, and, without the form of human
members, since it is not corporeal or transitory like a human body, gives strength to the
heart and rules the whole body as its foundation, as the firmament of Heaven contains
the lower regions and touches the higher. *And it also touches the person's brain;* for in
its powers it knows not only earthly but also heavenly things, since it wisely knows
God; *and it spreads itself through all the person's members;* for it gives vitality to the
marrow and veins and members of the whole body, as the tree from its root gives sap
and greenness to all the branches. *But then this human form, in this way vivified, comes
forth from the woman's womb, and changes its color according to the movement the
globe makes in that form;* which is to say that after the person has received the vital
spirit in the maternal womb and is born and begins his actions, his merits will be according to the works his soul does with the body, for he will put on brightness from the
good ones and darkness from the evil ones.

17: HOW THE SOUL SHOWS ITS POWERS ACCORDING
TO THE POWERS OF THE BODY

The soul now shows its powers according to the powers of the body, so that in a person's infancy it produces simplicity, in his youth strength, and in adulthood, when all
the person's veins are full, it shows its strongest powers in wisdom; as the tree in its
first shoots is tender and then shows that it can bear fruit, and finally, in its full utility,
bears it. But then in human old age, when the marrow and veins start to incline to
weakness, the soul's powers are gentler, as if from a weariness at human knowledge;
as when winter approaches the sap of the tree diminishes in the branches and the
leaves, and the tree in its old age begins to bend.

Hildegard of Bingen, *Scivias,* Book I, Vision 4, Chapters 16–26, translated by Mother Columba Hart and
Jane Bishop (New York: Paulist Press, 1990). Copyright © Abbey of Regina Laudis: Benedictine Congrega-
tion Regina Laudis of the Strict Observance, Inc. Reprinted by permission.

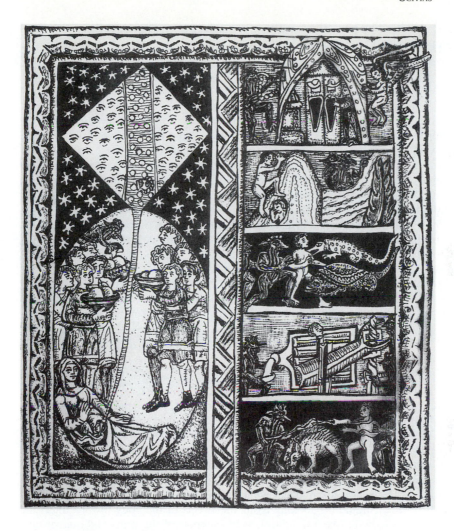

Body and Soul, from an early edition of *Scivias.* One of the souls in heaven (represented by the eyes) is entering the fetus in the womb. As Hildegard writes, ". . . at the divinely appointed time the infant in the maternal womb receives a spirit, and shows by the movements of its body that it lives." *(From "Hildegard of Bingen," Paulist Press, New York, page 107. Illustration by Mother Placid Dempsey)*

18: A PERSON HAS THREE PATHS WITHIN HIMSELF

But a person has within himself three paths. What are they? The soul, the body and the senses; and all human life is led in these. How? The soul vivifies the body and conveys the breath of life to the senses; the body draws the soul to itself and opens the senses; and the senses touch the soul and draw the body. For the soul gives life to the body as fire gives light to darkness, with two principal powers like two arms, intellect and will; the soul has arms not so as to move itself, but so as to show itself in these powers as the sun shows itself by its brilliance. Therefore, O human, who are not just a bundle of marrow, pay attention to scriptural knowledge!

19: ON THE INTELLECT

The intellect is joined to the soul like an arm to the body. For as the arm, joined to the hand with its fingers, branches out from the body, so the intellect, working with the other powers of the soul, by which it understands human actions, most certainly proceeds from the soul. For before all the other powers of the soul it understands whatever is in human works, whether good or evil, so that through it, as through a teacher, everything is understood; for it sifts things as wheat is purified of any foreign matter, inquiring whether they are useful or useless, lovable or hateful, pertinent to life or death. Thus, as food without salt is tasteless, the other powers of the soul without intellect are insipid and undiscerning. But the intellect is also to the soul as the shoulder is to the body, the very core of the other powers of the soul; as the bodily shoulder is strong, so it understands the divinity and the humanity in God, which is the joint of the arm, and it has true faith in its work, which is the joint of the hand, with which it chooses among the various works wisely as if with fingers. But it does not work in the same way as the other powers of the soul. What does this mean?

20: ON THE WILL

The will activates the work, and the mind receives it, and the reason produces it. But the intellect understands the work, knowing good and evil, just as the angels, who have intellect, love good and despise evil. And where the heart is in the body, there the intellect is in the soul, exercising its power in that part of the soul as the will does in another part. How? Because the will has great power in the soul. How? The soul stands in a corner of the house, that is, by the prop of the heart, like a man who stands in a corner of his house, so that looking through the whole house he may command all its contents, lifting his right arm to point out what is useful in the house and turning to the East. Thus the soul should do, looking along the streets of the body toward the rising sun. Thus it puts its will, like a right arm, as the support of the veins and marrow and the movement of the whole body; for the will does every work, whether it be good or bad.

21: ANALOGY OF FIRE AND BREAD

For the will is like a fire, baking each deed as if in a furnace. Bread is baked so that people may be nourished by it and be able to live. So too the will is the strength of the whole work, for it starts by kneading it and when it is firm adds the yeast and pounds it severely; and, thus preparing the work in contemplation as if it were bread, it bakes it in perfection by the full action of its ardor, and so makes a greater food for humans in the work they do than in the bread they eat. A person stops eating from time to time, but the work of his will goes on in him till his soul leaves his body. And in whatever differing circumstances the work is performed, whether in infancy, youth, adulthood or bent old age, it always progresses in the will and in the will comes to perfection.

22: How in the Will's Tabernacle All Powers Are Activated and Come Together

But the will has in the human breast a tabernacle, the mind, upon which the intellect and that same will and a sort of force of the soul all breathe in strength. And all these are activated and come together in the same tabernacle. How? If anger arises, gall is produced and brings the anger to its height by filling the tabernacle with smoke. If wicked delight rises up, the flame of lust touches its structure, and so the wantonness that pertains to that sin is elevated and in that tabernacle united with it. But there is another, lovely kind of joy, which is kindled in that tabernacle by the Holy Spirit, and the rejoicing soul receives it faithfully and perfects good works in the desire of Heaven. And there is a kind of sadness that engenders in the tabernacle, out of those humors that surround the gall, the sloth which produces disdain, obduracy and stubbornness in people and depresses the soul, unless the grace of God comes quickly to rescue it.

But since in that tabernacle there occur contrary conditions, it is often disturbed by hatred and other deadly emotions, which kill the soul and try to lay it waste in perdition. But when the will wills, it can move the implements in the tabernacle and in its burning ardor dispose of them, whether they are good or evil. But if these implements please the will, it bakes its food there and offers it to people to enjoy. So in that tabernacle a great throng of good and evil things arises, like an army gathered in some place of assembly; when the commander of an army arrives, if the army pleases him he accepts it, but if it displeases him he orders it to disband. The will does the same. How? If good or evil arises in the breast, the will either carries it out or ignores it.

23: On the Reason

But both in the intellect and in the will reason stands forth as the loud sound of the soul, which makes known every work of God or Man. For sound carries words on high, as the wind lifts the eagle so that it can fly. Thus the soul utters the sound of reason in the hearing and the understanding of humanity, that its powers may be understood and its every work brought to perfection. But the body is the tabernacle and support of all the powers of the soul, since the soul resides in the body and works with the body, and the body with it, whether for good or for evil.

24: On the Senses

It is the senses on which the interior powers of the soul depend, so that these powers are known through them by the fruits of each work. The senses are subject to these powers, since they guide them to the work, but the senses do not impose work on the powers, for they are their shadow and do what pleases them. The exterior human being awakens with senses in the womb of his mother before he is born, but the other powers of the soul still remain in hiding. What is this? The dawn announces the daylight; just so the human senses manifest the reason and all the powers of the soul. And as on the two commandments of God hang all the Law and the prophets, so also on the soul and its powers depend the human senses. What does this mean?

The Law is ordained for human salvation, and the prophets show forth the hidden things of God; so also human senses protect a person from harmful things and lay bare the soul's interior. For the soul emanates the senses. How? It vivifies a person's face and glorifies him with sight, hearing, taste, smell and touch, so that by this touch he becomes watchful in all things. For the senses are the sign of all the powers of the soul, as the body is the vessel of the soul. What does this mean? A person is recognized by his face, sees with his eyes, hears with his ears, opens his mouth to speak, feels with his hands, walks with his feet; and so the senses are to a person as precious stones and as a rich treasure sealed in a vase. But as the treasure within is known when the vase is seen, so also the powers of the soul are inferred by the senses.

25: THAT THE SOUL IS THE MISTRESS AND THE FLESH THE HANDMAID

The soul is the mistress, the flesh the handmaid. How? The soul rules the body by vivifying it, and the body is ruled by this vivification, for if the soul did not vivify the body it would fall apart and decay. But when a person does an evil deed and the soul knows it, it is as bitter for the soul as poison is for the body when it knowingly takes it. But the soul rejoices in a sweet deed as the body delights in sweet food. And the soul flows through the body like sap through a tree. What does this mean? By the sap, the tree grows green and produces flowers and then fruit. And how is this fruit matured? By the air's tempering. How? The sun warms it, the rain waters it, and thus by the tempering of the air it is perfected. What does this mean? The mercy of God's grace, like the sun, will illumine the person, the breath of the Holy Spirit, like the rain, will water him, and so discernment, like the tempering of the air, will lead him to the perfection of good fruits.

26: ANALOGY OF A TREE TO THE SOUL

The soul in the body is like sap in a tree, and the soul's powers are like the form of the tree. How? The intellect in the soul is like the greenery of the tree's branches and leaves, the will like its flowers, the mind like its bursting firstfruits, the reason like the perfected mature fruit, and the senses like its size and shape. And so a person's body is strengthened and sustained by the soul. Hence, O human, understand what you are in your soul, you who lay aside your good intellect and try to liken yourself to the brutes.

JOHN OF SALISBURY
ca. 1120–1180

Born into a family of humble means in Old Sarum (Salisbury), England, John of Salisbury first studied with a rural priest. In 1136, John went to Paris where he spent the next twelve years studying with such renowned teachers as Peter Abelard. After his training, John was ordained to the priesthood. He served first in the papal court in Rome for five or six years before being sent home to England in 1154 to become the secretary of and trusted advisor to Theobald, Archbishop of Canterbury. For the next seven years, he assisted in Theobald's struggle for the independence of the church from the government of King Henry II.

When Thomas Becket, the king's former chancellor, was made archbishop in 1161, after Theobald's death, John continued his service as secretary and advisor. Many scholars believe that John may have shared responsibility for the transformation of Becket from king's counselor to church defender. As the conflict between King Henry and the church intensified, it was John who was attacked first. Accused by the king of going over his head by encouraging appeals to Rome, John was forced into exile in 1163. For the next seven years, John worked for Becket's interests with King Louis VII of France and other leaders. When Becket himself was banished from England, he joined John in exile. When Henry allowed Becket to return to Canterbury, John joined him again. John was at Canterbury Cathedral on the night of December 29, 1170, when Henry's knights murdered Becket. Returning again to France, John was made Bishop of Chartres by King Louis VII in 1176, and he served in that position until his death four years later.

Whereas John of Salisbury wrote on a number of topics, he is best known for the *Metalogicon* and the *Policratus,* two works addressed in 1159 to then Chancellor Thomas Becket. The *Metalogicon* is a treatise on education, which argues against technical logic in favor of the civilizing effects of what we would call the liberal arts. In this work, John criticizes the obsession of his age with the problem of universals. His criticism includes a brief and interesting summary of the various positions taken on this important question. This treatise is reprinted here in the Daniel D. McGarry translation.

John's other major work, the *Policratus* or *Statesman,* is typical of twelfth-century political theory. John clearly asserts the superiority of the church over the state, claiming that the role of the state is to carry out duties beneath the dignity of the church. In the selection given here, translated by Eugene Fairweather, John holds that, unlike the tyrant, the prince rules by law and recognizes that he is a servant of law. Furthermore, the true prince is also the servant of the church and of her priesthood. Given this emphasis on the power of the church over the state—and given that the *Policratus* ends with a section condoning the assassination of a political tyrant—it is not difficult to see why John was exiled by King Henry II.

*   *   *

For studies of John of Salisbury, see Clement C.J. Webb, *John of Salisbury* (London: Methuen, 1932) and Hans Liebeschutz, *Mediaeval Humanism in the Life and Writings of John of Salisbury* (London: Warburg Institute, University of London, 1950). Roger Lloyd, *The Golden Middle Age* (1939; reprinted Freeport, NY: Books for Libraries Press, 1969) discusses John of Salisbury in the context of twelfth-century education.

For works on the problem of universals, see the suggested readings in the introduction to Peter Abelard (page 177). For primary source readings in medieval political thought, see Ralph Lerner and Muhsin Mahdi, eds., *Medieval Political Philosophy: A Sourcebook* (New York: The Free Press, 1963); and for secondary works consult R.W. Carlyle, *A History of Mediaeval Political Theory in the West,* six volumes (New York: Barnes & Noble, 1927–1936); Otto Friedrich von Gierke, *Political Theories of the Middle Age,* translated by Frederic William Maitland (Boston: Beacon Press, 1958); John B. Morrall, *Political Thought in Medieval Times* (London: Hutchinson, 1958); Walter Ullmann, *A History of Political Thought: The Middle Ages* (Harmondsworth, Middlesex: Penguin Books, 1965); and J.H. Burns, ed., *The Cambridge History of Medieval Political Thought ca. 350–ca. 1450* (Cambridge: Cambridge University Press, 1988).

METALOGICON (in part)

BOOK II

CHAPTER 17: IN WHAT A PERNICIOUS MANNER LOGIC IS SOMETIMES TAUGHT; AND THE IDEAS OF MODERNS ABOUT [THE NATURE OF] GENERA AND SPECIES

To show off their knowledge, our contemporaries dispense their instruction in such a way that their listeners are at a loss to understand them. They seem to have the impression that every letter of the alphabet is pregnant with the secrets of Minerva. They analyze and press upon tender ears everything that anyone has ever said or done. Falling into the error condemned by Cicero, they frequently come to be unintelligible to their hearers more because of the multiplicity than the profundity of their statements. "It is indeed useful and advantageous for disputants," as Aristotle observes, "to take cognizance of several opinions on a topic." From the mutual disagreement thus brought into relief, what is seen to be poorly stated may be disproved or modified. Instruction in elementary logic does not, however, constitute the proper occasion for such procedure. Simplicity, brevity, and easy subject matter are, so far as is possible, appropriate in introductory studies. This is so true that it is permissible to expound many difficult points in a simpler way than their nature strictly requires. Thus, much that we have learned in our youth must later be amended in more advanced philosophical studies. Nevertheless, at present, all are here [in introductory logical studies] declaiming on the nature of universals, and attempting to explain, contrary to the intention of the author, what is really a most profound question, and a matter [that should be reserved] for more advanced studies. One holds that universals are merely word sounds, although this opinion, along with its author Roscelin, has already almost completely passed into oblivion. Another maintains that universals are word concepts, and twists to support his thesis everything that he can remember to have ever been written on the subject. Our Peripatetic of Pallet, Abelard, was ensnared in this opinion. He left many, and still has, to this day, some followers and proponents of his doctrine. They are friends of mine, although they often so torture the helpless letter that even the hardest heart is filled with compassion for the latter. They hold that it is preposterous to predicate a thing concerning a thing, although Aristotle is author of this monstrosity. For Aristotle frequently asserts that a thing is predicated concerning a thing, as is evident to anyone who is really familiar with his teaching. Another is wrapped up in a consideration of acts of the [intuitive] understanding, and says that genera and species are nothing more than the latter. Proponents of this view take their cue from Cicero and Boethius, who cite Aristotle as saying that universals should be regarded as and called "notions." "A notion," they tell us, "is the cognition of something, derived from its previously perceived form, and in need of unravelment." Or again [they say]: "A notion is an act of the [intuitive] understanding, a simple mental comprehension." They accordingly distort everything written, with an eye to making acts of [intuitive] understanding or

John of Salisbury, *The Metalogicon of John Salisbury: A Twelfth-Century Defense of the Verbal and Logical Arts of the Trivium,* Book II, Chapter 17, translated by Daniel D. McGarry (Berkeley: University of California Press, 1955).

"notions" include the universality of universals. Those who adhere to the view that universals are things, have various and sundry opinions. One, reasoning from the fact that everything which exists is singular in number, concludes that either the universal is numerically one, or it is non-existent. But since it is impossible for things that are substantial to be non-existent, if those things for which they are substantial exist, they further conclude that universals must be essentially one with particular things. Accordingly, following Walter of Mortagne, they distinguish [various] states [of existence], and say that Plato is an individual in so far as he is Plato; a species in so far as he is a man; a genus of a subaltern [subordinate] kind in so far as he is an animal; and a most general genus in so far as he is a substance. Although this opinion formerly had some proponents, it has been a long time since anyone has asserted it. Walter now upholds [the doctrine of] ideas, emulating Plato and imitating Bernard of Chartres, and maintains that genus and species are nothing more nor less than these, namely, ideas. "An idea," according to Seneca's definition, "is an eternal exemplar of those things which come to be as a result of nature." And since universals are not subject to corruption, and are not altered by the changes that transform particular things and cause them to come and go, succeeding one another almost momentarily, ideas are properly and correctly called "universals." Indeed, particular things are deemed incapable of supporting the substantive verb, [i.e., of being said "to be"], since they are not at all stable, and disappear without even waiting to receive names. For they vary so much in their qualities, time, location, and numerous different properties, that their whole existence seems to be more a mutual transition than a stable status. In contrast, Boethius declares: "We say that things 'are' when they may neither be increased nor diminished, but always continue as they are, firmly sustained by the foundations of their own nature." These [foundations] include their quantities, qualities, relations, places, times, conditions, and whatever is found in a way united with bodies. Although these adjuncts of bodies may seem to be changed, they remain immutable in their own nature. In like manner, although individuals [of species] may change, species remain the same. The waves of a stream wash on, yet the same flow of water continues, and we refer to the stream as the same river. Whence the statement of Seneca, which, in fact, he has borrowed from another: "In one sense it is true that we may descend twice into the same river, although in another sense this is not so." These "ideas," or "exemplary forms," are the original plans of all things. They may neither be decreased nor augmented; and they are so permanent and perpetual, that even if the whole world were to come to an end, they could not perish. They include all things, and, as Augustine seems to maintain in his book *On Free Will,* their number neither increases nor diminishes, because the ideas always continue on, even when it happens that [particular] temporal things cease to exist. What these men promise is wonderful, and familiar to philosophers who rise to the contemplation of higher things. But, as Boethius and numerous other authors testify, it is utterly foreign to the mind of Aristotle. For Aristotle very frequently opposes this view, as is clear from his books. Bernard of Chartres and his followers labored strenuously to compose the differences between Aristotle and Plato. But I opine that they arrived on the scene too late, so that their efforts to reconcile two dead men, who disagree as long as they were alive and could do so, were in vain. Still another, in his endeavor to explain Aristotle, places universality in "native forms," as does Gilbert, Bishop of Poitiers, who labors to prove that "native forms" and universals are identical. A "native form" is an example of an original [exemplar]. It [the native form, unlike the original] inheres in created things, instead of subsisting in the divine mind. In Greek it is called the *idos,* since it stands in relation to the idea as the example does to its exemplar. The native form is sensible in things that are perceptible by the senses; but insensible as conceived in the mind. It is singular in individuals, but universal in all [of a kind]. Another, with Joscelin, Bishop of Soissons, attributes universality to collections of things, while denying it to things as individuals. When Joscelin tries to explain the authorities, he has his troubles and is hard put, for in many places he cannot bear the gaping astonishment of the indignant letter. Still another takes refuge in a new tongue, since he does not have sufficient command of Latin. When he hears the words "genus" and "species," at one time he says they should be understood as universals, and at another that they refer to the *maneries* [ways, modes, or manners] of things. I know not in which of the authors he has found this term or this distinction, unless perhaps he has dug it out of lists of abstruse and obsolete words, or it is an item of jargon [in the baggage] of present-day doctors. I am further at a loss to see what it can mean here, unless it refers to collections of things, which would be the same as Joscelin's view, or to a universal thing, which, however, could hardly be called a *maneries*. For a *maneries* may be interpreted as referring to both [collections and universals], since a number of things, or the status in which a thing of such and such a type continues to exist may be called a *maneries*. Finally, there are some who fix their attention on the status of things, and say that genera and species consist in the latter.

STATESMAN (POLICRATUS) (in part)

CHAPTER 1: THE DIFFERENCE BETWEEN A PRINCE AND A TYRANT, AND WHAT A PRINCE IS

This, then, is the sole (or at least the greatest) difference between a tyrant and a prince, that the latter conforms to the law, and rules the people, whose servant he believes himself to be, by its judgment. Also, when he performs the duties of the commonwealth and undergoes its burdens, he claims for himself the first place by privilege of law, and is set before others in so far as universal burdens hang over the prince, while individuals are bound to individual concerns. On this account, the power over all his subjects is rightly conferred on him, so that, in seeking and accomplishing the welfare of each and all, he may be self-sufficient and the state of the human commonwealth may be best disposed, while one is the member of another. In this, indeed, we follow nature, the best guide for living, which arranged all the senses of its microcosm—that is, its little world, man—in the head, and subjected all the members to the latter so that they all are rightly moved, as long as they follow the decision of a sound head. Therefore, the princely crown is exalted and shines with privileges as many and as great as it has believed to be necessary for itself. And this is done rightly, because nothing is more beneficial for the people than for the prince's necessity to be met—when his will is not opposed to justice, to be sure. Therefore (as many define him) the prince is the public ruler and a kind of image of the divine Majesty on earth. Beyond doubt, it is shown that something great in the way of divine power indwells princes, when men submit their necks to their nods and very often fearlessly yield their

From *A Scholastic Miscellany: Anselm to Ockham,* Chapters 1–3, edited and translated by Eugene R. Fairweather (Volume X: The Library of Christian Classics). First published in 1940 by SCM Press Ltd., London and The Westminster Press, Philadelphia. Used by permission of Westminster/John Knox Press.

necks to be smitten, and each for whom he is a matter of dread fears him by divine instigation. I do not think that this could happen, save by the act of the divine pleasure. For all
power is from the Lord God, and it has been with him always, and is with him eternally.
Therefore, what the prince can do comes from God in such a way that the power does not
depart from the Lord, but he exercises it by a hand that is subject to him, and that follows
in all things the instruction of his clemency or justice. Thus "he that resisteth the power resisteth the ordinance of God," with whom rests the authority to confer it and (when he
wills) to take it away or lessen it. For when a mighty one decides to rage against his subjects, this involves not just himself but also the divine dispensation, by which those who
are subject to it are punished or vexed for God's good pleasure. So, for instance, during the
depredations of the Huns, Attila was asked, by the devout bishop of a certain city, who he
was, and replied, "I am Attila, the scourge of God." It is written that, when the bishop had
reverenced the divine Majesty in him, he said, "Welcome to the servant of God," and, repeating, "Blessed is he that cometh in the name of the Lord," opened the doors of the
church and admitted the persecutor, and through him attained to the palm of martyrdom.
For he did not dare to shut out the scourge of God, knowing as he did that it is the beloved
son that is scourged, and that the very power of the scourge comes from the Lord alone. If,
then, the power is to be reverenced in this way by the good, even when it brings misfortune
to the elect, who will not reverence it? After all, it was instituted by the Lord "for the punishment of evildoers, and for the praise of the good," and it serves the laws with the readi-
est devotion. For, as the emperor says, it is a statement worthy of the majesty of the ruler
that the prince should acknowledge that he is bound by laws, because the authority of the
prince depends on the authority of the law, and it is certainly a greater thing for the realm
when sovereignty is set under the laws, so that the prince understands that nothing is permitted to him if it is at variance with justice and equity.

CHAPTER 2: WHAT LAW IS, AND THAT THE PRINCE, ALTHOUGH HE IS RELEASED FROM THE OBLIGATIONS OF LAW, IS STILL THE BONDSERVANT OF LAW AND EQUITY, AND BEARS A PUBLIC CHARACTER, AND SHEDS BLOOD BLAMELESSLY

Princes should not think that anything is taken away from them in all this, unless they believe that the statutes of their own justice are to be preferred to the justice of God, whose
justice is justice forever, and his law equity. Besides, as legal experts affirm, equity is the
fitness of things, which makes everything equal by reason and desires equal laws for unequal things; it is equitable toward all and assigns to each what belongs to him. But law
is its interpreter, in so far as the will of equity and justice has been made known to it.
Therefore, Chrysippus claimed that law has power over all things human and divine, and
on that account is superior to all goods and evils and is the chief and guide of things and
men alike. Papinian, a really great expert in the law, and Demosthenes, the powerful or-
ator, seem to uphold the law and to subject the obedience of all men to it, inasmuch as in
truth all law is the device and gift of God, the doctrine of wise men, the corrector of inclinations to excess, the settlement of the state, and the banishment of all crime, so that all
who are engaged in the whole world of political affairs must live according to it. Thus all
are closely bound by the necessity of maintaining the law, unless there may perhaps be
someone to whom license seems to have been conceded for wickedness. Nevertheless, the
prince is said to be released from legal obligations, not because evil actions are allowed
him, but because he should be one who cherishes equity, not from fear of punishment but
from love of justice, and in everything puts others' advantage before his personal desires.

But who will speak of the desires of the prince in connection with public business, since in this area he is permitted to desire nothing for himself save what law or equity suggests or the nature of the common welfare determines? For in these things his will ought to have the effect of a judgment, and it is quite right that what pleases him in such matters should have the force of law, in so far as his sentence is not in disagreement with the intention of equity. "Let my judgment," the psalmist says, "come forth from thy countenance; let thine eyes behold the thing that is equitable," for an uncorrupt judge is he whose sentence is the image of equity, because of assiduous contemplation. The prince, then, is the servant of the public welfare and the bondservant of equity, and in that sense plays a public role, because he both avenges the injuries and losses of all and punishes all crimes with impartial justice. Moreover, his rod and staff, applied with wise moderation, bring the agreements and the errors of all into the way of equity, so that the spirit rightly gives thanks to the princely power, when it says, "Thy rod and thy staff, they have comforted me." It is true also that his shield is strong, but it is the shield of the weak and it effectively intercepts the darts aimed at the innocent by the malicious. His function also is of the utmost benefit to those who have the least power, and is most strongly opposed to those who desire to do harm. Therefore, "he beareth not the sword in vain," when he sheds blood by it, but blamelessly, so that he is not a man of blood, but often kills men without thereby incurring the name or the guilt of a homicide. For if the great Augustine is to be believed, David was called a "man of blood," not because of his wars but on account of Uriah. And it is nowhere written that Samuel was a man of blood or a homicide, even though he slew Agag, the very rich king of Amalek. In fact, the princely sword is the "sword of the dove," which strives without animosity, smites without fury, and, when it goes into combat, conceives no bitterness whatsoever. For, just as the law proceeds against crimes without any hatred of persons, so the prince also punishes offenders most rightly, not by any impulse of anger but by the decision of a mild law. For though the prince may seem to have his own "lictors," [attendants who carried the symbols of power] we should believe that in fact he is his only (or his foremost) lictor, but that it is lawful for him to smite by the hand of a substitute. For if we consult the Stoics, who diligently search out the origins of names, we shall learn that he is called a "lictor"—as it were, a "striker of the law"—inasmuch as it pertains to his office to smite him who, in the law's judgment, is to be smitten. On this account also, when the guilty were threatened with the sword, it used to be said in ancient days to the officials by whose hand the judge punished evildoers, "Comply with the decision of the law," or "Fulfill the law," so that the mildness of the words might in fact modify the sadness of the event.

CHAPTER 3: THAT THE PRINCE IS THE SERVANT OF PRIESTS
AND BENEATH THEM, AND WHAT IT MEANS TO CARRY OUT
THE PRINCELY OFFICE FAITHFULLY

The prince, therefore, receives this sword from the hand of the Church, even though, to be sure, the latter does not possess the sword of blood. Nevertheless, she does possess it as well, but makes use of it by the hand of the prince, to whom she has conceded the power of keeping bodies under restraint, although she has retained authority in spiritual matters for her pontiffs. Thus the prince is in fact the servant of the priesthood, and exercises that part of the sacred duties which seems unworthy of the hands of the priesthood. For while every duty imposed by the sacred laws is a matter of religion and piety, the function of punishing crimes, which seems to constitute a kind of image of the hangman's office, is lower than others. It was on account of this inferiority that Constantine, the most faithful emperor of the Romans, when he had convoked the council of priests

Murder of Thomas Becket, from an English Psalter, ca. 1200. Infuriated by his former chancellor's defiance of the crown in favor of the church, King Henry II made remarks that led some of his knights to kill Becket. The priest shown in the background may well have been John of Salisbury who, as Becket's secretary and advisor, was at Canterbury Cathedral when Becket was murdered. *(The Walters Art Gallery, Baltimore)*

at Nicaea, did not dare to take the first place or mingle with the assemblies of the presbyters, but occupied the lowest seat. Indeed, he reverenced the conclusions which he heard approved by them as if he supposed that they proceeded from the judgment of the divine Majesty. As for the written accusations, stating the offenses of the priests, which they had drawn up against one another and presented to the emperor, he received them and put them away, still unopened, in his bosom. Moreover, when he had recalled the council to charity and concord, he said that it was unlawful for him (as a man, and as one who was subject to the judgment of priests) to consider the cases of the gods, who can be judged by God alone. And he committed the books which he had received to the fire, without looking at them, because he was afraid to disclose the crimes or vices of the Fathers, lest he bring on himself the curse of Ham, the rejected son, who failed to cover what he should have respected in his father. For the same reason, he is said (in the writings of Nicholas, the Roman Pontiff) to have stated: "Truly, if with my own eyes I had seen a priest of God, or anyone who had been clothed in the monastic habit, committing sin, I should have spread out my cloak and covered him, lest he be seen by anyone." Theodosius also, the great emperor, when he was suspended from the use of the regalia and the badges of sovereignty by the bishop of Milan, because of a crime that was real enough, but not quite that serious, patiently and solemnly did the penance imposed on him for homicide. Certainly, to appeal to the testimony of the doctor of the Gentiles, he who blesses is greater than he who is blessed, and he who possesses the authority to confer a dignity surpasses in the privilege of honor him on whom the dignity itself is conferred. Besides, according to the very nature of law, it pertains to the same person to will and not to will, and it is he who has the right to confer who also has the right to take away. Did not Samuel bring sentence of deposition against Saul on account of his disobedience, and substitute the lowly son of Jesse for him in the highest place in the kingdom? But if he who is set up as prince has faithfully performed the function he received, he is to be shown great honor and great reverence, in proportion to the superiority of the head over all the members of the body. Now he performs his task faithfully when, mindful of his rank, he remembers that he bears in himself the totality of his subjects, and knows that he owes his own life not to himself but to others, and as it were distributes it among them with due charity. He owes his entire self then, to God, most of himself to his fatherland, much to his kinsfolk and neighbors, and least (but still something) to strangers. He is debtor, then, to the wise and the unwise, to the small and the great. In fact, this concern is common to all who are set over others, both to those who bear the care of spiritual things and to those who exercise worldly jurisdiction. On this account we read of Melchizedek, who is the first king and priest referred to in Scripture—not to mention, for the present, the mystery by which he prefigures Christ, who was born in heaven without a mother and on earth without a father—we read, I say, that he had neither father nor mother. It is not that he lacked either, but that flesh and blood do not by their nature bring forth kingship and priesthood, since in the creation of either respect of parents should not carry weight without regard for meritorious virtue, but the wholesome desires of faithful subjects should have priority. Thus, when anyone reaches the pinnacle of either kingship or priesthood, he should forget the affection of the flesh and do only what the welfare of his subjects demands. Let him be, therefore, the father and husband of his subjects, or, if he knows a more tender affection, let him practice it; let him strive to be loved more than he is feared, and let him show himself to them in such a light that out of sheer devotion they may put his life before their own and reckon his safety to be a kind of public life. Then everything will go well with him, and if need be a few guards will prevail by their obedience against countless enemies. For "love is strong as death," and a wedge which the cords of love hold together is not easily broken.

ISLAMIC AND JEWISH PHILOSOPHY IN THE MIDDLE AGES

◄──○►───

When Emperor Justinian closed the schools in Athens in A.D. 529, many of the teachers moved east to Syria, taking their books with them. There the works of Aristotle and many of the Neoplatonists were translated into Syriac and, later, into Arabic. These works were to return to Western Europe centuries later in the hands of Islamic and Jewish philosophers.

The religion of Islam began with Muhammad (A.D. 571–632), an Arab from the town of Mecca in what is now Saudi Arabia. Repelled by the polytheism of his day and believing himself to be called as a prophet, Muhammad taught that there is no God but Allah. According to Islam, over a period of twenty-three years, Muhammad received messages from Allah, which he wrote down in the *Qur'ān* (or Koran). These sacred writings taught an uncomplicated message of submission (which is what the word "Islam" means), submission to the will of Allah, expressed in a life of obedience and in deeds such as prayer, almsgiving, periods of fasting, and a once-in-a-lifetime Hajj or pilgrimage to Mecca. Through the work of Muhammad and his immediate successors, Islam spread quickly throughout the Arabian peninsula. Within a century, Islam was the dominant religion in the Middle East, Northern Africa, and even European Spain. Throughout this expansion, Islam was relatively tolerant of Christianity and Judaism, holding that the adherents of these monotheistic religions were also "people of the Book."

The Islamic culture of this period was quite sophisticated and cosmopolitan—especially when compared to that of Western Europe. When Western Europe was largely illiterate, the Muslims (adherents of Islam) were making advances in astronomy, mathematics, and medicine. There was also a group of Muslim thinkers known as *falyasufs* ("philosophers") who studied and applied the manuscripts of Aristotle and the Neoplatonists that had come through Syria. As Islamic thinkers worked with these texts, they encountered the problems their colleagues in the West knew well: how to reconcile philosophy with sacred texts; how to combine reason and faith. The *falyasufs* were centered in two different regions and times. An early group, around Baghdad, included al-Kindī (ca. 800–870), al-Fārābī (870–950), Ibn-Sīnā, or Avicenna, his Latin name (980–1037) and al-Ghazālī (1058–1111). A later group in Spain included Ibn Bājjah (d. 1138), Ibn Tufayl (ca. 1100–1185), and Ibn Rushd, or Averroës (1126–1198).

During the early years of Islam, Jewish philosophy coexisted and interacted freely with Islamic thought. Jewish thinkers such as Saadia ben Joseph al-Fayyumi (882–942) and Isaac Israeli (ca. 855–955) in the East, and later Solomon Ibn-Gabirol (ca. 1021–1070) and Judah Halevi (ca. 1075–1141) in Spain, worked with the same categories and used many of the same texts as their Islamic neighbors. Jews mixed socially with Muslims, often even serving as advisors to Muslim rulers. Moses Maimonides of Spain (1135–1204), the greatest of the medieval Jewish thinkers, even served the powerful sultan Saladin.

It was through Islamic and Jewish philosophers that Aristotle was reintroduced to the Western Europe, an event that radically changed the course of medieval philosophy.

*   *   *

For general surveys, see De Lacy Evans O'Leary, *Arabic Thought and Its Place in History* (London: K. Paul, Trench, Trubner, 1939); T.J. de Boer, *The History of Philosophy in Islam*, translated by Edward R. Jones (New York: Dover, 1967); Majid Fakhry, *A History of Islamic Philosophy* (New York: Columbia University Press, 1970); Isaac Husik, *A History of Mediaeval Jewish Philosophy* (1916; reprinted New York: Atheneum, 1976); Colette Sirat, *A History of Jewish Philosophy in the Middle Ages* (Cambridge: Cambridge University Press, 1985); Oliver Leeman, *An Introduction to Medieval Islamic Philosophy* (Cambridge: Cambridge University Press, 1985); and Dan Cohn-Sherbok, *Medieval Jewish Philosophy: An Introduction* (Richmond, Surrey, UK: Curzon Press, 1997). A.J. Arberry, *Revelation and Reason in Islam* (London: George Allen & Unwin, 1957); F.E. Peters, *Aristotle and the Arabs: The Aristotelian Tradition in Islam* (New York: New York University Press, 1968); I.R. Netton, *Muslim Neoplatonists* (London: George Allen & Unwin, 1982); Herbert Davidson, *Proofs for Eternity, Creation, and the Existence of God in Medieval Islamic and Jewish Philosophy* (New York: Oxford University Press, 1987); and Mehdi Ha'iri Yazdi, *The Principles of Epistemology in Islamic Philosophy* (Albany, NY: SUNY Press, 1992) provide studies of particular areas. For collections of essays, see Parviz Morewedge, ed., *Neoplatonism and Islamic Thought* (Albany, NY: SUNY Press, 1992), Lenn E. Goodman, ed., *Neoplatonism and Jewish Thought* (Albany, NY: SUNY Press, 1992); and Richard G. Hovannisian and Georges Sabagh, eds., *Religion and Culture in Medieval Islam* (Cambridge: Cambridge University Press, 1999).

AVICENNA
A.D. 980–1037

Abū 'Alī al-Husayn Ibn 'Abd-Allāh Ibn Sīnā, better known as Avicenna, was a Persian born near the capital of the Samānid dynasty, Bukhārā (today part of Uzbekistan). As a boy, Avicenna showed exceptional intellectual abilities. By the age of ten, he had learned Arabic and studied the *Qur'ān*; by age 16, he had finished his study of medicine; and by age 18, he had read and mastered all the philosophy available. Only with Aristotle's *Metaphysics* did he meet his match. He claimed he read it forty times without comprehension before finding al-Fārābī's clarifying commentary. Beginning at age 18, Avicenna became a physician and aide to a series of princes and ministers. His associations often proved short-lived, and his fortunes waxed and waned with those of his patrons. During this time, he wrote extensively on varied topics, including a medical book, *The Canon of Medicine,* which served as a reference work in Western Europe clear into the seventeenth century. He died at the age of 58, reportedly from a profligate life.

Using Aristotelian categories, Avicenna held that the study of "Being" is the proper study of metaphysics, and that this study applies in its fullest sense only to Allah. Only God has existence as a part of His nature. We could, for example, describe the characteristics of a given species without knowing whether such creatures actually exist; their existence is only possible, not necessary. But God's essence includes *necessary* existence. This means that whatever is a part of God's essence is also necessary, and so all of God's attributes are necessary. By implication, then, God did not freely choose to create the world, since a necessary attribute of being God is being Creator. And if being Creator is a necessary

219

attribute of the eternal God, then the world must have existed eternally and everything in the world must be exactly as it is, by necessity.

Using Neoplatonic categories, Avicenna explained that God did not create the world directly but through a series of intermediate Intelligences. The last of these Intelligences, "Active Intelligence" (associated with the moon), "created" the physical world by putting form onto matter. Our individual souls are also emanations from Active Intelligence, and Active Intelligence "imprints" forms into our souls, giving us the rational principles that are the basis of our knowledge.

Although Avicenna used Aristotle's division of the soul into vegetative, animal, and rational parts, he held that the individual soul is separate from the body and that it is immortal—a view never explicitly stated by Aristotle. Because the soul can conceive of itself apart from a body, the soul must not be a material thing (thus anticipating Descartes' "I think, therefore I am" by six hundred years).

These three beliefs—that God acts out of necessity, that God emanates through intermediate Intelligences, and that the soul is immortal apart from the body—are all contrary to the teachings of the *Qur'ān*. Avicenna dealt with this problem by explaining that the *Qur'ān* uses symbolic or metaphorical language and that only the multitude took it literally.

In the "Essay on the Secret of Destiny," given here in the George F. Hourani translation, Avicenna discusses why it is necessary that there be evil in the world, discusses the nature of rewards and punishments, and affirms his belief in the immortality of the soul. The selection from *Concerning the Soul,* translated by Fazlur Rahman, explains how Active Intelligence imparts knowledge of the "middle terms" (universals) through intuition.

*   *   *

For translations and commentary on two of Avicenna's major works, see Avicenna, *Avicenna on Theology,* translated by Arthur J. Arberry (London: Murray, 1951), and Parviz Morewedge, *The "Metaphysica" of Avicenna* (London: Routledge & Kegan Paul, 1973).

Lenn E. Goodman, *Avicenna* (London: Routledge, 1992) provides a good overview of Avicenna's thought. For information on Avicenna, the person, see Soheil Muhsin Afnan, *Avicenna: His Life and Works* (London: George Allen & Unwin, 1958), or his autobiography, *Avicenna, The Life of Ibn Sina,* translated by William E. Gohlman (Albany, NY: SUNY Press, 1974). E.G. Brown, *Arabian Medicine* (Cambridge: Cambridge University Press, 1921), and Henri Corbin, *Avicenna and the Visionary Recital,* translated by W.R. Trask (New York: Pantheon, 1960) provide specialized studies, whereas Seyyed Hossein Nasr, *Three Muslim Sages: Avicenna, Suhrawardi, Ibn Arabi* (Cambridge, MA: Harvard University Press, 1964); David B. Burrell, *Knowing the Unknowable God: Ibn-Sina, Maimonides, Aquinas* (Notre Dame, IN: University of Notre Dame Press, 1986); and Herbert A. Davidson, *Alfarabi, Avicenna, and Averroes: Their Cosmologies, Theories of Active Intellect and Theories of the Human Intellect* (Oxford: Oxford University Press, 1992) offer comparisons to other thinkers.

ESSAY ON THE SECRET OF DESTINY

In the name of God, the Merciful, the Compassionate.

Someone asked the eminent *shaykh* Abū 'Alī b. Sīnī (may God the Exalted have mercy on him) the meaning of the Sūfī saying, "He who knows the secret of destiny is an atheist." In reply he stated that this matter contains the utmost obscurity, and is one of those matters which may be set down only in enigmatic form and taught only in a hidden manner, on account of the corrupting effects its open declaration would have on the general public. The basic principle concerning it is found in a Tradition of the Prophet (God bless and safeguard him): "Destiny is the secret of God; do not declare the secret of God." In another Tradition, when a man questioned the Prince of the Believers, "Alī (may God be pleased with him)," he replied, "Destiny is a deep sea; do not sail out on it." Being asked again he replied, "It is a stony path; do not walk on it." Being asked once more he said, "It is a hard ascent; do not undertake it." The shaykh said: Know that the secret of destiny is based upon certain premisses, such as [1] the world order, [2] the report that there is Reward and Punishment, and [3] the affirmation of the resurrection of souls.

[1] The first premiss is that you should know that in the world as a whole and in its parts, both upper and earthly, there is nothing which forms an exception to the facts that God is the cause of its being and origination and that God has knowledge of it, controls it, and wills its existence; it is all subject to His control, determination, knowledge, and will. This is a general and superficial account, although in these assertions we intend to describe it truly, not as the theologians understand it; and it is possible to produce proofs and demonstrations of that. Thus, if it were not that this world is composed of elements which give rise to good and evil things in it and produce both righteousness and wickedness in its inhabitants, there would have been no completion of an order for the world. For if the world had contained nothing but pure righteousness, it would not have been this world but another one, and it would necessarily have had a composition different from the present composition; and likewise if it had contained nothing but sheer wickedness, it would not have been this world but another one. But whatever is composed in the present fashion and order contains both righteousness and wickedness.

[2] The second premiss is that according to the ancients Reward is the occurrence of pleasure in the soul corresponding to the extent of its perfection, while Punishment is the occurrence of pain in the soul corresponding to the extent of its deficiency. So the soul's abiding in deficiency is its "alienation from God the Exalted," and this is "the curse," "the Penalty," [God's] "wrath" and "anger," and pain comes to it from that deficiency; while its perfection is what is meant by [God's] "satisfaction" with it, its "closeness" and "nearness" and "attachment." This, then, and nothing else is the meaning of "Reward" and "Punishment" according to them.

[3] The third premiss is that the resurrection is just the return of human souls to their own world: this is why God the Exalted has said, "O tranquil soul, return to your Lord satisfied and satisfactory."

From Avicenna, "Essay on the Secret of Destiny," translated by George F. Hourani, in John F. Wippel and Allan B. Wolter, eds., *Medieval Philosophy* (New York: The Free Press, 1969), pp. 229–232. Originally published in the *Bulletin of the School of Oriental and African Studies* (University of London), Vol. 29, Pt. 1, 1966, pp. 31–33. Reprinted by permission.

These are summary statements, which need to be supported by their proper demonstrations.

[a] Now, if these premises are established, we say that the apparent evils which befall this world are, on the principles of the Sage [i.e., Aristotle], not purposed for the world—the good things alone are what is purposed, the evil ones are a privation, while according to Plato both are purposed as well as willed; *[b]* and that the commanding and forbidding of acts to responsible beings, by revelation in the world, are just a stimulant to him of whom it was foreknown [by God] that there would occur in him [performance of] the commandments, or (in the case of a prohibition) a deterrent to him of whom it was foreknown that he would refrain from what is forbidden. Thus the commandment is a cause of the act's proceeding from him of whom it is foreknown that it will proceed, and the prohibition is a cause of intimidation to him who refrains from something bad because of it. Without the commandment the former would not have come to desire the act; without the prohibition the latter would not have been scared. It is as if one were to imagine that it would have been possible for 100% of wickedness to befall in the absence of any prohibition, and that with the presence of the prohibitions 50% of wickedness has befallen, whereas without prohibitions 100% would have befallen. Commandments must be judged in the same way: had there been no commandments nothing of righteousness would have befallen, but with the advent of the commandments 50% of righteousness has occurred.

[c] As for praise and blame, these have just two objects. One is to incite a doer of good to repeat the like act which is willed to proceed from him; the second is to scare the one from whom the act has occurred from repeating the like of it, and [ensure] that the one from whom that act has [not] occurred will abstain from doing what is not willed to proceed from him, though it is in his capacity to do it.

[d] It is not admissible that Reward and Punishment should be such as the theologians suppose: chastisement of the fornicator, for example, by putting him in chains and shackles, burning him in the fire over and over again, and setting snakes and scorpions upon him. For this is the behaviour of one who wills to slake his wrath against his enemy, through injury or pain which he inflicts on him out of hostility against him; and that is impossible in the character of God the Exalted, for it is the act of one who wills that the very being who models himself on him should refrain from acts like his or be restrained from repeating such acts. And it is not to be imagined that after the resurrection there are obligations, commandments, and prohibitions for anyone, so that by witnessing Reward and Punishment they should be scared or refrain from what is proscribed to them and desire what is commanded to them. So it is false that Reward and Punishment are as they have imagined them.

[e] As for the [system of] penalties ordained by the divine Law for those who commit transgressions, it has the same effect as the prohibitions in serving as a restraint upon him who abstains from transgression, whereas without it is imaginable that the act might proceed from him. There may also be a gain to the one who is subject to penalty, in preventing him from further wickedness, because men must be bound by one of two bonds, either the bond of the divine Law or the bond of reason, that the order of the world may be completed. Do you not see that if anyone were let loose from both bonds the load of wickedness he would commit would be unbearable, and the order of the world's affairs would be upset by the dominance of him who is released from both bonds? But God is more knowing and wiser.

CONCERNING THE SOUL (in part)

CHAPTER 1: THE VEGETATIVE SOUL

When the elements are mixed together in a more harmonious way, i.e. in a more balanced proportion than in the cases previously mentioned, other beings also come into existence out of them due to the powers of the heavenly bodies. The first of these are plants. Now some plants are grown from seed and set aside a part of the body bearing the reproductive faculty, while others grow from spontaneous generation without seeds.

Since plants nourish themselves they have the faculty of nutrition. And because it is of the nature of plants to grow, it follows that they have the faculty of growth. Again, since it is the nature of certain plants to reproduce their like and to be reproduced by their like, they have a reproductive faculty. The reproductive faculty is different from the faculty of nutrition, for unripe fruits possess the nutritive but not the reproductive faculty; just as they possess the faculty of growth, but not that of reproduction. Similarly, the faculty of nutrition differs from that of growth. Do you not see that decrepit animals have the nutritive faculty but lack that of growth?

The nutritive faculty transmits food and replaces what has been dissolved with it; the faculty of growth increases the substance of the main structural organs in length, breadth, and depth, not haphazard but in such a way that they can reach the utmost perfection of growth. The reproductive faculty gives the matter the form of the thing; it separates from the parent body a part in which a faculty derived from its origin inheres and which, when the matter and the place which are prepared to receive its activity are present, performs its functions.

It will be evident from the foregoing that all vegetable, animal, and human functions are due to faculties over and above bodily functions, and even over and above the nature of the mixture itself.

After the plant comes the animal, which emerges from a compound of elements whose organic nature is much nearer to the mean than the previous two and is therefore prepared to receive the animal soul, having passed through the stage of the vegetable soul. And so the nearer it approaches the mean the greater is its capacity for receiving yet another psychical faculty more refined than the previous one.

The soul is like a single genus divisible in some way into three parts. The first is the vegetable soul, which is the first entelechy of a natural body possessing organs in so far as it is reproduced, grows, and assimilates nourishment. Food is a body whose function it is to become similar to the nature of the body whose food it is said to be, and adds to that body either in exact proportion or more or less what is dissolved.

The second is the animal soul, which is the first entelechy of a natural body possessing organs in so far as it perceives individuals and moves by volition.

The third is the human soul, which is the first entelechy of a natural body possessing organs in so far as it acts by rational choice and rational deduction, and in so far as it perceives universals.

The vegetable soul has three faculties. First, the nutritive faculty which transforms another body into a body similar to that in which it is itself present, and replaces what has

Avicenna, *Concerning the Soul from Avicenna's Psychology,* translated by Fazlur Rahman (London: Geoffrey Cumberlege, Oxford University Press, 1952). Reprinted by permission of Oxford University Press.

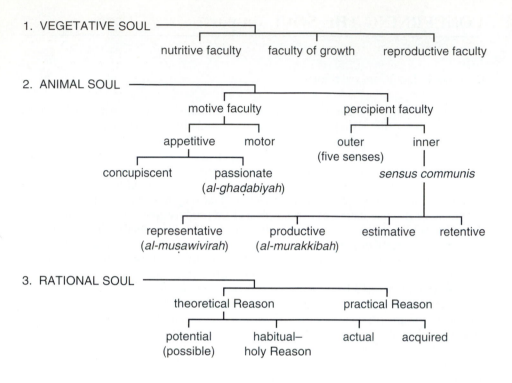

been dissolved. Secondly, the faculty of growth which increases every aspect of the body in which it resides, by length, breadth, and depth in proportion to the quantity necessary to make it attain its perfection in growth. Thirdly, the reproductive faculty which takes from the body in which it resides a part which is potentially similar to it and acts upon it with the help of other similar bodies, generating and mixing them so as to render that part actually similar to the body (to which it had been only potentially similar).

CHAPTER 2: THE ANIMAL SOUL

The animal soul, according to the primary division, has two faculties—the motive and the perceptive. The motive faculty again is of two kinds: either it is motive in so far as it gives an impulse, or in so far as it is active. Now the motive faculty, in so far as it provides the impulse, is the faculty of appetence. When a desirable or repugnant image is imprinted on the imagination of which we shall speak before long, it rouses this faculty to movement. It has two subdivisions: one is called the faculty of desire which provokes a movement (of the organs) that brings one near to things imagined to be necessary or useful in the search for pleasure. The second is called the faculty of anger, which impels the subject to a movement of the limbs in order to repulse things imagined to be harmful or destructive, and thus to overcome them. As for the motive faculty in its active capacity, it is a power which is distributed through the nerves and muscles, and its function is to contract the muscles and to pull the tendons and ligaments towards the starting-point of the movement, or to relax them or stretch them so that they move away from the starting-point.

The perceptive faculty can be divided into two parts, the external sense and the internal sense. The external senses are the five or eight senses. One of them is sight, which is a faculty located in the concave nerve; it perceives the image of the forms of coloured bodies imprinted on the vitreous humour. These forms are transmitted through actually transparent media to polished surfaces. The second is the sense of hearing, which is a faculty located in the nerves distributed over the surface of the ear-hole; it perceives the form of what is transmitted to it by the vibration of the air which is compressed between two objects, one striking and the other being struck, the latter offering it resistance so as to set up vibrations in the air which produce the sound. This vibration of the air outside reaches the air which lies motionless and compressed in the cavity of the ear, moving it in a way similar to that in which it is itself moved. Its waves touch that nerve, and so it is heard.

The third sense is that of smell, a faculty located in the two protuberances of the front part of the brain which resemble the two nipples of the breasts. It perceives the odour conveyed to it by inhaled air, which is either mixed with the vapour in the air or is imprinted on it through qualitative change in the air produced by an odorous body.

The fourth sense is that of taste, a faculty located in the nerves distributed over the tongue, which perceives the taste dissolved from bodies touching it and mingling with the saliva it contains, thus producing a qualitative change in the tongue itself.

The fifth sense is that of touch, which is a faculty distributed over the entire skin and flesh of the body. The nerves perceive what touches them and are affected when it is opposed to them in quality, and changes are then wrought in their constitution or structure.

Probably this faculty is not one species but a genus including four faculties which are all distributed throughout the skin. The first of them judges the opposition between hot and cold; the second that between dry and moist; the third that between hard and soft; and the fourth that between rough and smooth. But their coexistence in the same organ gives the false impression that they are essentially one.

The forms of all the sensibles reach the organs of sense and are imprinted on them, and then the faculty of sensation perceives them. This is almost evident in touch, taste, smell, and hearing. But concerning sight, a different view has been maintained, for some people have thought that something issues from the eye, meets the object of sight, takes its form from without—and that this constitutes the act of seeing. They often call the thing which according to them issues from the eye, light.

But true philosophers hold the view that when an actually transparent body, i.e., a body which has no colour, intervenes between the eye and the object of sight, the exterior form of the coloured body on which light is falling is transmitted to the pupil of the eye and so the eye perceives it.

This transmission is similar to the transmission of colours by means of light being refracted from a coloured thing and giving its colour to another body. The resemblance is not complete, however, for the former is more like an image in a mirror.

The absurdity of the view that light issues from the eye is shown by the following consideration. What emanates is either a body or a non-body. If it is not a body it is absurd to attribute motion and change of place to it, except figuratively in that there may be a power in the eye which transforms the air and other things it encounters into some sort of quality, so that it may be said that this quality "came out of the eye." Likewise, it is absurd to hold the view that it is a body, because if so then either—

(1) it will remain intact, issuing from the eye and reaching to the sphere of the fixed stars. In this case there will have emerged from the eye, despite its smallness, a conical body of immense size, which will have compressed the air and repulsed all the heavenly bodies, or it will have traversed an empty space. Both these views are manifestly absurd. Or—

(2) it will be dispersed, diffused and split up. In that case the percipient animal will of necessity feel something being detached from him and then dispersed and diffused; also, he will perceive the spots where that ray falls to the exclusion of the spots where it does not fall, so that he will only partially perceive the body, sensing some points here and there but missing the major part. Or—

(3) this emanating body is united with the air and the heavens and becomes one with them, so that the uniform whole is like one organ of the animal. In this case the uniform whole in its entirety will possess sensation. This is a most peculiar change indeed! It follows necessarily that if many eyes cooperate, it will be more powerful. Thus a man when in the company of others would have keener sight than when alone, for many people can effect a more powerful change than a single person. Again, this emanating body will necessarily be either simple or composite, and its composite nature will also be of a particular kind. Its motion then must be either voluntary or natural. But we know that this movement is not voluntary and by choice, although the opening and closing of the eyelids are voluntary. The only remaining alternative is that the movement is natural. But the simple natural movement will be only in one direction, not in many; and so the composite movement will also be, according to the dominant element, only in one direction, not in many. But it is not so with this movement according to those who support the theory of the "issuing body."

Again, if the sensed object is seen through the base of the conical emanating body which touches it, and not through the angle, it will necessarily follow that the shape and magnitude of the object perceived at a distance will also be perceptible as well as its colour. This is because the percipient subject comes in contact with it and encompasses it. But if it is perceived through the angle, I mean the section between the vitrium and the hypothetical cone, then the remoter the object the smaller will be the angle and also the common section, and consequently the form imprinted on it will also be smaller and will be so perceived. Sometimes the angle will be so small that the object will fail to be perceived and so the form will not be seen at all.

As for the second part, namely that the emanating something is not a body but an accident or a quality, this "changing" or "being changed" will inevitably be more powerful with the increase of the percipient subjects. In that case the same absurdity which we mentioned before will arise. Again, the air will either be merely a medium of transmission or percipient in itself. If it is only a medium of transmission and not percipient, then, as we maintain, perception takes place in the pupil of the eye and not outside it. But if the percipient is the air, then the same absurdity which we have already mentioned will be repeated; and it will necessarily follow that whenever there is commotion or disturbance in the air, sight will be distorted with the renewal of "change" and the renewed action of the percipient in perceiving one thing after another, just as when a man runs in calm air his perception of minute things is confused. All this shows that sight is not due to something issuing from us towards the sensed object. It must therefore be due to something coming towards us from the sensed object; since this is not the body of the object, it must be its form. If this view were not correct, the creation of the eye with all its strata and humours and their respective shape and structure would be useless.

*   *   *

CHAPTER 4: THE RATIONAL SOUL

The human rational soul is also divisible into a practical and a theoretical faculty, both of which are equivocally called intelligence. The practical faculty is the principle of movement of the human body, which urges it to individual actions characterized by deliberation and in accordance with purposive considerations. This faculty has a certain correspondence with the animal faculties of appetence, imagination, and estimation, and a certain dual character in itself. Its relationship to the animal faculty of appetence is that certain states arise in it peculiar to man by which it is disposed to quick actions and passions such as shame, laughter, weeping, etc. Its relationship to the animal faculty of imagination and estimation is that it uses that faculty to deduce plans concerning transitory things and to deduce human arts. Finally, its own dual character is that with the help of the theoretical intelligence it forms the ordinary and commonly accepted opinions concerning actions, as, for instance, that lies and tyranny are evil and other similar premises which, in books of logic, have been clearly distinguished from the purely rational ones. This faculty must govern all the other faculties of the body in accordance with the laws of another faculty which we shall mention, so that it should not submit to them but that they should be subordinated to it, lest passive dispositions arising from the body and derived from material things should develop in it. These passive dispositions are called bad morals. But far from being passive and submissive this faculty must govern the other bodily faculties so that it may have excellent morals.

It is also possible to attribute morals to the bodily faculties. But if the latter predominate they are in an active state, while the practical intelligence is in a passive one. Thus the same thing produces morals in both. But if the practical intelligence predominates, it is in an active state while the bodily faculties are in a passive one, and this is morals in the strict sense (even so there would be two dispositions or moral characters); or character is only one with two different relationships. If we examine them more closely the reason why morals are attributed to this faculty is that the human soul, as will be shown later, is a single substance which is related to two planes—the one higher and the other lower than itself. It has special faculties which establish the relationship between itself and each plane: the practical faculty which the human soul possesses in relation to the lower plane, which is the body, and its control and management; and the theoretical faculty in relation to the higher plane, from which it passively receives and acquires intelligibles. It is as if our soul has two faces: one turned towards the body and it must not be influenced by any requirements of the bodily nature; and the other turned towards the higher principles, and it must always be ready to receive from what is There in the Higher Plane and to be influenced by it. So much for the practical faculty.

*   *   *

CHAPTER 6: HOW THE RATIONAL SOUL ACQUIRES KNOWLEDGE

The acquisition of knowledge, whether from someone else or from within oneself, is of various degrees. Some people who acquire knowledge come very near to immediate perception, since their potential intellect which precedes the capacity we have mentioned is the most powerful. If a person can acquire knowledge from within himself, this strong capacity is called "intuition." It is so strong in certain people that they do not need great effort, or instruction and actualization, in order to make contact with the active intelligence. But the primary capacity of such a person for this is so powerful that he might also be said to possess the second capacity; indeed, it seems as though he knows everything from within himself. This is the highest degree of this capacity. In this state the material intelligence must be called "Divine Spirit." It belongs to the genus of *intellectus in habitu,* but is so lofty that not all people share it. It is not unlikely, indeed, that some of these actions attributed to the "Divine Intelligence" because of their powerful and lofty nature overflow into the imagination which symbolizes them in sense-imagery and words in the way which we have previously indicated.

What proves this is the evident fact that the intelligible truths are acquired only when the middle term of a syllogism is obtained. This may be done in two ways: sometimes through intuition, which is an act of mind by which the mind itself immediately perceives the middle term. This power of intuition is quickness of apprehension. But sometimes the middle term is acquired through instruction, although even the first principles of instruction are obtained through intuition, since all knowledge can be reduced ultimately to certain intuitive principles handed down by those who first accepted them to their students.

It is possible that a man may find the truth within himself, and that the syllogism may be effected in his mind without any teacher. This varies both quantitatively and qualitatively; quantitatively, because some people possess a greater number of middle terms which they have discovered themselves; and qualitatively, because some people find the term more quickly than others. Now since these differences are unlimited and always vary in degrees of intensity, and since their lowest point is reached in men who are wholly without intuition, so their highest point must be reached in people who possess intuition regarding all or most problems, or in people who have intuition in the shortest possible time. Thus there might be a man whose soul has such an intense purity and is so firmly linked to the rational principles that he blazes with intuition, i.e. with the receptivity of inspiration coming from the active intelligence concerning everything. So the forms of all things contained in the active intelligence are imprinted on his soul either all at once or nearly so, not that he accepts them merely on authority but on account of their logical order which encompasses all the middle terms. For beliefs accepted on authority concerning those things which are known only through their causes possess no rational certainty. This is a kind of prophetic inspiration, indeed its highest form and the one most fitted to be called Divine Power; and it is the highest human faculty.

The Hierarchy of Faculties

It should be seen how some of these faculties govern others. You will find the acquired intellect to be the governor whom all the rest serve. It is the ultimate goal. The *intellectus in habitu* serves the *intellectus in actu,* and is in turn served by the material intellect with all its capacities. The practical intellect serves them all, for attachment to the body, as will shortly become clear, exists for the sake of the perfection and purification of the theoretical intellect, and the practical intellect governs this relationship. It is served by the faculty of estimation which, in its turn, is served by two faculties: an anterior and a posterior. The posterior conserves what is brought to it by estimation, while the anterior is the totality of animal faculties. The faculty of representation is served by two faculties of different origins: the appetitive faculty

serves it by obeying it, for the representative faculty impels the appetitive to movement, and the faculty of imagination serves it by accepting the combination and separation of its images. In their turn those two are the governors of two groups. The faculty of imagination is served by *fantasia* or *sensus communis,* which is itself served by
the five senses, while the appetitive faculty is served by desire and anger. These last
two are served by the motive faculty distributed through the muscles. Here the animal
faculties come to an end.

The animal faculties in their entirety are served by the vegetable faculties, of
which the reproductive is the first in rank and the highest one. The faculty of growth
serves the reproductive, and the nutritive faculty serves them both. The four "natural"
faculties—of digestion, retention, assimilation, and excretion—are subservient to all
these. The digestive faculty is served on the one hand by the retentive and the assimila-
tive, and on the other by the excretive. The four physical qualities serve these, with
cold subservient to heat, while dryness and moisture serve them both. This is the last
degree of the faculties.

*　　*　　*

CHAPTER 12: CONCERNING THE TEMPORAL ORIGIN OF THE SOUL

We say that human souls are of the same species and concept. If they existed before
the body, they would either be multiple entities or one single entity. But it is impossible for them to be either the one or the other, as will be shown later, therefore it is impossible for them to exist before the body. We now begin with the explanation of the
impossibility of its numerical multiplicity and say that the mutual difference of the
souls before [their attachment to] bodies is either due to their quiddity and form; or to
the element and matter which is multiple in space, a particular part of which each matter occupies; or to the various times peculiar to every soul when it becomes existent in
its matter; or to the causes which divide their matter. But their difference is not due to
their quiddity or form, since their form is one, therefore their difference is due to the
recipient of the quiddity or to the body to which the quiddity is specifically related. Before its attachment to the body the soul is quiddity pure and simple; thus it is impossible for one soul to be numerically different from another, or for the quiddity to admit
of essential differentiation. This holds absolutely true in all cases; for the multiplicity
of the species of those things whose essences are pure concepts is only due to the sub-
strata which receive them and to what is affected by them, or due only to their times.
But when they are absolutely separate, i.e. when the categories we have enumerated
are not applicable to them, they cannot be diverse. It is therefore impossible for them
to have any kind of diversity or multiplicity among them. Thus it is untrue that before
they enter bodies souls have numerically different essences.

I say that it is also impossible for souls to have numerically one essence, for
when two bodies come into existence two souls also come into existence in them. Then
either—

1. these two souls are two parts of the same single soul, in which case one single thing which does not possess any magnitude and bulk would be potentially divisible. This is manifestly absurd according to the principles established in physics. Or—

2. a soul which is numerically one would be in two bodies. This also does not require much effort to refute.

It is thus proved that the soul comes into existence when ever a body does so fit to be used by it. The body which thus comes into being is the kingdom and instrument of the soul. In the very disposition of the substance of the soul which comes into existence together with a certain body—a body, that is to say, with the appropriate qualities to make it suitable to receive the soul which takes its origin from the first principles—there is a natural yearning to occupy itself with that body, to use it, control it, and be attracted by it. This yearning binds the soul specially to this body, and turns it away from other bodies different from it in nature so that the soul does not contact them except through it. Thus when the principle of its individualization, namely, its peculiar dispositions, occurs to it, it becomes an individual. These dispositions determine its attachment to that particular body and form the relationship of their mutual suitability, although this relationship and its condition may be obscure to us. The soul achieves its first entelechy through the body; its subsequent development, however, does not depend on the body but on its own nature.

But after their separation from their bodies the souls remain individual owing to the different matters in which they had been, and owing to the times of their birth and their different dispositions due to their bodies which necessarily differ because of their peculiar conditions.

*   *   *

CHAPTER 13: THE SOUL DOES NOT DIE WITH THE DEATH OF THE BODY; IT IS INCORRUPTIBLE

We say that the soul does not die with the death of the body and is absolutely incorruptible. As for the former proposition, this is because everything which is corrupted with the corruption of something else is in some way attached to it. And anything which in some way is attached to something else is either coexistent with it or posterior to it in existence or prior to it, this priority being essential and not temporal. If, then, the soul is so attached to the body that it is coexistent with it, and this is not accidental but pertains to its essence, then they are essentially interdependent. Then neither the soul nor the body would be a substance; but in fact they are substances. And if this is an accidental and not an essential attachment, then, with the corruption of the one term only the accidental relationship of the other term will be annulled, but its being will not be corrupted with its corruption. If the soul is so attached to the body that it is posterior to it in existence, then, in that case, the body will be the cause of the soul's existence. Now the causes are four; so either the body is the efficient cause of the soul and gives it existence, or it is its receptive and material cause—maybe by way of composition as the elements are for the body or by way of simplicity as bronze is for the statue—or the body is the soul's formal or final cause. But the body cannot be the soul's efficient cause, for body, as such, does not act; it acts only through its faculties. If it were to act through its essence, not through its faculties, every body would act in the same way. Again, the bodily faculties are all of them either accidents or material forms, and it is impossible that either accidents or forms subsisting in matter should produce the being of a self-subsisting entity independent of matter or that of an absolute substance. Nor is it possible that the body should be the receptive and material cause of the soul, for we have clearly shown and proved that the soul is in no way imprinted in the body. The body, then, is not "informed" with the form of the soul, either by way of simplicity or composition so that certain parts of the body are composed and mixed together in a certain way and then the soul is imprinted in them. It is also impossible that the body should be the formal or the final cause of the soul, for the reverse is the more plausible case.

Thus the attachment of the soul to the body is not the attachment of an effect to a necessary cause. The truth is that the body and the temperament are an accidental cause of the soul, for when the matter of a body suitable to become the instrument of the soul and its proper subject comes into existence, the separate causes bring into being the individual soul, and that is how the soul originates from them. This is because it is impossible to bring arbitrarily into being different souls without any specific cause. Besides, the soul does not admit of numerical multiplicity, as we have shown. Again, whenever a new thing comes into being, it must be preceded by a matter which is prepared to receive it or to have a relationship with it, as has been shown in the other sciences. Again, if an individual soul were to come into being without an instrument through which it acts and attains perfection, its being would be purposeless; but there is nothing purposeless in nature. In truth, when the suitability and preparation for such a relationship exist in the instrument, it becomes necessary that such a thing as a soul should originate from the separate causes.

But if the existence of one thing necessitates the existence of another, the corruption of the former does not necessarily entail that of the latter. This happens only where its very being subsists through or in that thing. Many things originating from other things survive the latter's corruption; when their being does not subsist in them, and especially when they owe their existence to something other than what was merely preparatory for the emanation of their being. And the being of the soul does in fact emanate from something different from the body and bodily functions, as we have shown; its source of emanation must be something different from the body. Thus when the soul owes its being to that other thing and only the time of its realization to the body, its being would be independent of the body which is only its accidental cause; it cannot then be said that they have a mutual relationship which would necessitate the body preceding the soul as its necessary cause.

Let us turn to the third division which we mentioned in the beginning, namely, that the attachment of the soul to the body might be in the sense that the soul is prior to the body in existence. Now in that case the priority will be either temporal as well as essential, and so the soul's being could not possibly be attached to the body since it precedes the body in time, or the priority will be only essential and not temporal, for in time the soul will not be separate from the body. This sort of priority means that when the prior entity comes into existence, the being of the posterior entity must follow from it. Then the prior entity cannot exist, if the posterior is supposed to be non-existent. I do not say that the supposition of the non-existence of the posterior necessitates the non-existence of the prior, but that the posterior cannot be non-existent except when first something has naturally happened to the prior which has made it non-existent, too. Thus it is not the supposition of the non-existence of the posterior entity which necessitates the nonexistence of the prior, but the supposition of the non-existence of the prior itself, for the posterior can be supposed to be non-existent only after the prior itself has ceased to exist. This being so, it follows that the cause of non-existence must occur in the substance of the soul necessitating the body's corruption along with it, and that the body cannot be corrupted through a cause special to itself. But in fact the corruption of the body does take place through a cause special to itself, namely, through changes in its composition and its temperament. Thus it is false to hold that the soul is attached to the body as essentially prior to it, and that at the same time the body is indeed corrupted through a cause in itself; so no such relationship subsists between the two.

This being so, all the forms of attachment between the body and the soul have proved to be false and it only remains that the soul, in its being, has no relationship with the body but is related with other principles which are not subject to change or corruption.

As for the proposition that the soul does not admit of corruption at all, I say that there is another conclusive reason for the immortality of the soul. Everything which might be corrupted through some cause has in itself the potentiality of corruption and, before corruption, has the actuality of persistence. But it is absurd that a single thing in the same sense should possess both, the potentiality of corruption and the actuality of persistence; its potentiality of corruption cannot be due to its actual persistence, for the concept of potentiality is contrary to that of actuality. Also, the relation of this potentiality is opposed to the relation of this actuality, for the one is related with corruption, the other with persistence. These two concepts, then, are attributable to two different factors in the concrete thing. Hence we say that the actuality of persistence and the potentiality of corruption may be combined in composite things and in such simple things as subsist in composite ones. But these two concepts cannot come together in simple things whose essence is separate. I say in another absolute sense that these two concepts cannot exist together in a simple thing whose essence is unitary. This is because everything which persists and has the potentiality of corruption also has the potentiality of persistence, since its persistence is not necessary. When it is not necessary, it is possible; and possibility is of the nature of potentiality. Thus the potentiality of persistence is in its very substance. But, of course, it is clear that the actuality of persistence of a thing is not the same as its potentiality of persistence. Thus its actuality of persistence is a fact which happens to the body which has the potentiality of persistence. Therefore that potentiality does not belong to something actual but to something of which actual existence is only an accident and does not constitute its real essence. From this it necessarily follows that its being is composed of a factor the possession of which gives actual existence to it (this factor is the form in every concrete existent), and another factor which attains this actual existence but which in itself has only the potentiality of existence (and this factor is the matter in the concrete existent).

So if the soul is absolutely simple and is not divisible into matter and form, it will not admit of corruption. But if it is composite, let us leave the composite and consider only the substance which is its matter. We say: either that matter will continue to be divisible and so the same analysis will go on being applied to it and we shall then have a regress *ad infinitum,* which is absurd; or this substance and base will never cease to exist. But if so, then our present discourse is devoted to this factor which is the base and origin (i.e. the substance) and not to the composite thing which is composed of this factor and some other. So it is clear that everything which is simple and not composite, or which is the origin and base (i.e. the substance) of the composite thing, cannot in itself possess both the actuality of persistence and the potentiality of corruption. If it has the potentiality of corruption, it cannot possibly have the actuality of persistence, and if it has the actuality of persistence and existence, it cannot have the potentiality of corruption. Obviously, then, the substance of the soul does not have the potentiality of corruption. Of those things which come to be and are corrupted, the corruptible is only the concrete composite. The potentiality of corruption and of persistence at the same time does not belong to something which gives unity to the composite, but to the matter which potentially admits of both contraries. So the corruptible composite as such possesses neither the potentiality of persistence nor that of corruption, let alone both. As to the matter itself, it either has persistence not due to any potentiality, which gives it the capacity for persistence—as some people think—or it has persistence through a potentiality which gives it persistence, but does not have the potentiality of corruption; this latter being something which it acquires. The potentiality of corruption of simple entities which subsist in matter is due to matter and is not in their own substance. The argument which proves that everything which comes to exist passes away on account of the finitude of the potentialities of persistence and corruption is relevant only to those things whose being is composed of matter and form. Matter has the potentiality that this form may persist in it, and at the same time the potentiality that this form may cease to exist in it. It is then obvious that the soul is absolutely incorruptible. This is the point which we wanted to make, and this is what we wanted to prove.

AL-GHAZĀLĪ
1058–1111

Abū Hāmid Muhammad ibn Muhammad Ghazālī, (or al-Ghazālī in Arabic) was born in the village of Ghazāleh, just outside the city of Tūs in what is now northeastern Iran. He received a first-rate education as a young man and in 1091 was appointed the rector of the prestigious Nizāmīya College in Baghdad. For the next five years he taught Islamic law and acted as the defender and definer of Sunnite Muslim orthodoxy for the Baghdad community.

Following the assassination of his patron and the local sultan, al-Ghazālī underwent a profound spiritual crisis. The man who had rationally defined what was and was not "orthodox" found himself skeptical of *all* knowledge. Al-Ghazālī quit his post at the college and spent the next eleven years wandering as a Sufi mystic in Syria, Palestine, and Saudi Arabia. As he explained in his spiritual autobiography, *al-Munquidh mina'l-Dalāl* (*Deliverance from Error* or *The Deliverer from Error*), al-Ghazālī came to doubt both sensory knowledge and the ability of reason to know the world. It was only through the certainty of divine light that he was rescued from spiritual depression. Like Augustine in the Christian world, al-Ghazālī sensed a "light which God infused into his heart, which indeed is the key to most species of knowledge."* Al-Ghazālī concluded that it was only through the grace of Allah that certainty could be found. The proper response to such grace was a humble acceptance of the *Qur'ān* and a life of devotion to Allah. As for the knowledge claims of the philosophers and their rational arguments to support them, they were worthless. In fact, such reliance on reason was downright dangerous to true faith.

*al-Munqidh mina'l-Dalāl, p. 12 as quoted in Majid Fakhry, A History of Islamic Philosophy (New York: Columbia University Press, 1970), p. 246.

Having concluded that the philosophers were wrong, al-Ghazālī set about to refute them on their own ground. In his major work, *Tahāfut al-Falāsifah (The Incoherence of the Philosophers),* al-Ghazālī uses his vast knowledge of philosophy against the philosophers. In our selection from the introduction and the first preface (translated by Sabih Ahmad Kamali), al-Ghazālī explains the goal of his work: it is to show those "idiots" who accept the ancient philosophers the inconsistencies and errors of their systems. He makes clear that one of the biggest "idiots," who uncritically accepted the ancients, is his rival Ibn Sīna [Avicenna].

After a brief return to teaching, al-Ghazālī spent the rest of his life writing and practicing the Sufi disciplines in his hometown of Tūs. Though his life's work was primarily an attack on philosophy, it should be noted that he used philosophical categories to mount his attack and so presaged many later philosophical debates. Some scholars, for instance, see similarities to Kant's critique of metaphysics or to Descartes' methodological doubt. While such connections may be a bit of a stretch, it is clear that al-Ghazālī had an enormous influence in the Sunni Muslim world. His attack on philosophy was essentially successful and, despite the subsequent defense of such Muslim philosophers as Averroës, philosophy declined precipitously in the Middle-Eastern Muslim world.

*   *   *

Several of the books listed in the introduction to Islamic and Jewish philosophy include sections on al-Ghazālī. For book-length studies, consult W. Montgomery Watt, *Muslim Intellectual: A Study of al-Ghazali* (Edinburgh: University Press, 1963); F. Shehadi, *Ghazali's Unique Unknowable God* (Leiden, Netherlands: Brill, 1964); and R.M. Frank, *Al-Ghazali and the Ash'arite School* (Durham, NC: Duke University Press, 1994). Al-Ghazālī's autobiography is translated by R.J. McCarty in *Freedom and Fulfillment: An Annotated Translation of al-Ghazālī's al-Munqidh min al-Dalal and other Relevant Works of al-Ghazālī* (Boston, MA: Twayne, 1980).

THE INCOHERENCE OF THE PHILOSOPHERS (in part)

INTRODUCTION

... I have observed that there is a class of men who believe in their superiority to others because of their greater intelligence and insight. They have abandoned all the religious duties Islam imposes on its followers. They laugh at the positive commandments of religion which enjoin the performance of acts of devotion, and the abstinence from

From al-Ghazālī, *Tahāfut al-Falāsifah (The Incoherence of the Philosophers),* translated by Sabih Ahmad Kamali (Lahore, Pakistan: Pakistan Philosophical Congress, 1963), pp. 1–5. Reprinted by permission.

forbidden things. They defy the injunctions of the Sacred Law. Not only do they over-step the limits prescribed by it, but they have renounced the Faith altogether, by having indulged in diverse speculations, wherein they followed the example of those people who "turn men aside from the path of God, and seek to render it crooked; and who do not believe in the life to come." The heresy of these people has its basis only in an un-critical acceptance—like that of the Jews and the Christians—of whatever one hears from others or sees all around. They could not avoid it; for they were born into an un-Islamic atmosphere, and their ancestors had pursued no better ways. In the second place, such heresy results from theoretical inquiries which are the outcome of stum-bling—sceptically, misguidedly and stupidly—upon fanciful notions. (A similar case is that of the Disputants who discussed the questions concerning faith and belief raised by the People of wilful Innovations.)

The heretics in our times have heard the awe-inspiring names of people like Socrates, Hippocrates, Plato, Aristotle, etc. They have been deceived by the exaggera-tions made by the followers of these philosophers—exaggerations to the effect that the ancient masters possessed extraordinary intellectual powers: that the principles they have discovered are unquestionable: that the mathematical, logical, physical and meta-physical sciences developed by them are the most profound: that their excellent intelli-gence justifies their bold attempts to discover the Hidden Things by deductive meth-ods; and that with all the subtlety of their intelligence and the originality of their accomplishments they repudiated the authority of religious laws: denied the validity of the positive contents of historical religions, and believed that all such things are only sanctimonious lies and trivialities.

When such stuff was dinned into their ears, and struck a responsive chord in their hearts, the heretics in our times thought that it would be an honour to join the company of great thinkers for which the renunciation of their faith would prepare them. Emula-tion of the example of the learned held out to them the promise of an elevated status far above the general level of common men. They refused to be content with the religion followed by their ancestors. They flattered themselves with the idea that it would do them honour not to accept even truth uncritically. But they had actually begun to ac-cept falsehood uncritically. They failed to see that a change from one kind of intellec-tual bondage to another is only a self-deception, a stupidity. What position in this world of God can be baser than that of one who thinks that it is honourable to renounce the truth which is accepted on authority, and then relapses into an acceptance of false-hood which is still a matter of blind faith, unaided by independent inquiry? Such a scandalous attitude is never taken by the unsophisticated masses of men; for they have an instinctive aversion to following the example of misguided genius. Surely, their simplicity is nearer to salvation than sterile genius can be. For total blindness is less dangerous than oblique vision.

When I saw this vein of folly pulsating among these idiots, I decided to write this book in order to refute the ancient philosophers. It will expose the incoherence of their beliefs and the inconsistency of their metaphysical theories. It will bring to light the flimsiest and the obscurest elements of their thought which will provide some amuse-ment for, and serve as a warning to, the intelligent men. (I mean those things which they contributed to beliefs and opinions, and by virtue of which they thought they could be distinguished from the common men.)

Moreover, this book will set forth the doctrines of the ancient philosophers as those doctrines really are. This will serve the purpose of making it clear to the hide-bound atheists of our day that every piece of knowledge, whether ancient or modern, is really a corroboration of the faith in God and in the Last Day. The conflict between faith and knowledge is related only to the details superadded to these two fundamental principles, the two recurring themes in the teachings of all the prophets—i.e., divinely ordained persons the truth of whose mission is evident from the miracles they performed. It was only a few persons having irresponsible views and perverted minds who denied these principles. But in serious discussions no importance can be attached to such persons; and no notice ought to be taken of them. And they must be branded with diabolical perversity and stupid contumacy, so that their example may be a deterrent to people who tend to think that a vainglorious conversion to unoriginal heresy would be an indication of intelligence and good sense. This book is going to demonstrate that the ancient philosophers, whose followers the atheists in our day claim to be, were really untainted with what is imputed to them. They never denied the validity of the religious laws. On the contrary, they did believe in God, and did have faith in His messengers; although in regard to the minor details, they sometimes faltered and went astray, and caused others to go astray, from the even path. We propose to show how they slipped into error and falsehood. But our examination will not obscure their solid achievements which lie beneath the repulsive facade of their thought. Let God be the sustainer and the helper in the investigations we have undertaken.

Now to begin the book, we proceed to the Prefaces which will presage the general trend of the discussion in this book.

PREFACE ONE

Let it be known that it would be tedious to dwell at length upon the differences among the philosophers themselves. For prolixity is their manner, and their disputes are too many, and their opinions are scattered, and their ways are divergent and devious. Therefore, we will confine our attention to the inconsistencies which are found in the theories of the premier philosopher who is called *the* Philosopher, or the First Teacher, for he systematised their sciences, and reformulated them, eliminating all that was redundant in the philosophers' opinions, and retaining only that which was close to the basic principles and tendencies of philosophical thought. This is Aristotle, who refuted all his predecessors—including his own teacher, whom the philosophers call the divine Plato. Having refuted Plato, Aristotle excused himself by saying: "Plato is dear to us. And truth is dear, too. Nay, truth is dearer than Plato."

We have related this story in order to show that in their own view there is nothing fixed and constant in the philosophers' position. They base their judgments on conjecture and speculation, unaided by positive inquiry and unconfirmed by faith. They try to infer the truth of their metaphysical theories from the clarity of the arithmetical and logical sciences. And this method sometimes carries conviction with the weak-minded people. But if their metaphysical theories had been as cogent and definite as their arithmetical knowledge is, they would not have differed among themselves on metaphysical questions as they do not differ on the arithmetical.

As far as the translators of Aristotle's works into Arabic are concerned, our problem is even more difficult. For the translations themselves have been subjected to interpolation and changes, which have necessitated further commentaries and interpretations. As a result, the translations are as much in dispute among the philosophers as the original works are. However, the most faithful—as Aristotle's translators—and the most original—as his commentators—among the philosophising Muslims are al-Fārābī Abū Naṣr, and Ibn Sīna [Avicenna]. Therefore, we will confine our attention to what these two have taken to be the authentic expression of the views of their mis-leaders. For what they discarded and refused to follow must undoubtedly have been ut-terly useless, and should not call for an elaborate refutation.

Therefore, let it be known that we propose to concentrate on the refutation of philosophical thought as it emerges from the writings of these two persons. For other-wise, the scattered character of the philosophical theories should have to be reflected in a proportionately loose arrangement of our subject-matter.

AVERROËS
1126–1198

Abū al-Walīd Muhammad Ibn Ahmed Ibn Rushd, better known as Averroës, was born into a prominent family of jurists in Córdoba, Spain. Moving in high society, Averroës made the acquaintance of the sultan of Marrakesh and, through the sultan's favor, became a *qādī,* or judge, serving first in Seville and later in Córdoba. The sultan also expressed an interest in philosophy and commissioned Averroës to write three sets of commentaries (short, intermediate, and long) on each of Aristotle's writings. These commentaries became so influential in Western Europe that Averroës became known simply as "The Commentator." In addition to the thirty-eight commentaries he produced on Aristotle, Averroës also wrote books on politics, religion, logic, astronomy, and medicine. His expertise in medicine led to his being called to Marrakesh to serve as the sultan's personal physician in 1182. He remained in that post until 1195 when he was forced to leave for religious reasons (apparently because of his glorification of Aristotle). He regained his standing and returned to Marrakesh shortly before his death in 1198. Soon after his death, Islamic culture in Spain virtually disappeared; and even though his thought continued to influence Latin Europe, Averroës had surprisingly little impact on the Muslim world.

Through his writings, Averroës sought to counter two misconceptions. First, he wrote his commentaries to rid Aristotle of the misinterpretations of Avicenna and others. For example, Averroës rejected Avicenna's doctrine of the immortality of the soul. Instead he agreed with Aristotle that individual souls cannot exist apart from a body. But in agreement with the teachings of the *Qur'ān,* Averroës also taught that there is a bodily resurrection. According to Averroës, after death we receive new bodies that "emanate from the heavenly bodies." In this way, he denied Avicenna's immortality of the soul and managed to agree with both Aristotle and the *Qur'ān*.

Averroës was opposed to several of Avicenna's teachings, but he was even more opposed to Avicenna's chief critic, al-Ghazālī. Where al-Ghazālī had written *The Incoherence of Philosophy*, Averroës responded with *The Incoherence of the Incoherence*—a play on the title of his predecessor's work. In his rejoinder, Averroës sought to refute al-Ghazālī by dividing people into three classes. The majority of people can understand truth only in imaginative form. For them philosophy would, indeed, be dangerous and they must take the *Qur'ān* literally. A smaller group of people, the theologians, can understand dialectical arguments and draw probable inferences from the *Qur'ān*. But the elite, the philosophers, are capable of understanding truth in its pure, rational form. For them, the *Qur'ān* can be read for its "deeper" allegorical meanings.

As Averroës' teachings reached Christendom, this last (allegorical) conviction was taken to mean he advocated a "double truth": Truth in philosophy might be entirely different—even opposite—from truth in religion. In his rejoinder, Averroës himself denied this in his *Decisive Treatise Determining the Nature of the Connection Between Religion and Philosophy*, given here, complete, in the George F. Hourani translation. In the *Decisive Treatise*, Averroës claims that there is only one truth, but that there are many ways to access this truth. Unfortunately for Averroës' reputation, this work was lost to the West until the Renaissance.

*   *   *

For Averroës' major work in opposition to al-Ghazālī, see Averroës, *Tahafut al-Tahafut (The Incoherence of the Incoherence)*, translated by Simon van den Bergh (London: Luzac, 1954). For a medieval response see Thomas Aquinas, *On The Unity of the Intellect Against the Averroists*, translated by Beatrice H. Zedler (Milwaukee, WI: Marquette University Press, 1968). Oliver Leaman, *Averroës and His Philosophy* (Oxford: Oxford University Press, 1988) provides a general overview of Averroës thought. For more specialized studies, see Barry S. Kogan, *Averroës and the Metaphysics of Causation* (Albany, NY: SUNY Press, 1985), and Herbert A. Davidson, *Alfarabi, Avicenna, and Averroës: Their Cosmologies, Theories of Active Intellect and Theories of the Human Intellect* (Oxford: Oxford University Press, 1992).

THE DECISIVE TREATISE, DETERMINING THE NATURE OF THE CONNECTION BETWEEN RELIGION AND PHILOSOPHY

What is the attitude of the Law to philosophy?

Thus spoke the lawyer, *imām,* judge, and unique scholar, Abul Walīd Muhammad Ibn Ahmad Ibn Rushd:

Praise be to God with all due praise, and a prayer for Muhammad His chosen servant and apostle. The purpose of this treatise is to examine, from the standpoint of the study of the Law, whether the study of philosophy and logic is allowed by the Law, or prohibited, or commanded—either by way of recommendation or as obligatory.

CHAPTER ONE: THE LAW MAKES PHILOSOPHIC STUDIES OBLIGATORY

If teleological study of the world is philosophy, and if the Law commands such a study, then the Law commands philosophy.

We say: If the activity of "philosophy" is nothing more than study of existing beings and reflection on them as indications of the Artisan, i.e. inasmuch as they are products of art (for beings only indicate the Artisan through our knowledge of the art in them, and the more perfect this knowledge is, the more perfect the knowledge of the Artisan becomes), and if the Law has encouraged and urged reflection on beings, then it is clear that what this name signifies is either obligatory or recommended by the Law.

The Law commands such a study.

That the Law summons to reflection on beings, and the pursuit of knowledge about them, by the intellect is clear from several verses of the Book of God, Blessed and Exalted, such as the saying of the Exalted, "Reflect, you have vision": (lix, 2)* this is textual authority for the obligation to use intellectual reasoning, or a combination of intellectual and legal reasoning. Another example is His saying, "Have they not studied the kingdom of the heavens and the earth, and whatever things God has created?" (viii, 185): this is a text urging the study of the totality of beings. Again, God the Exalted has taught that one of those whom He singularly honoured by this knowledge was Abraham, peace on him, for the Exalted said, "So we made Abraham see the king-

---

*[References from the *Qur'ān* are noted in parentheses in the text.]

From *Averroes on the Harmony of Religion and Philosophy,* translated by George F. Hourani (London: Luzac & Co., 1961). Reprinted by permission of the Gibb Memorial Trust.

dom of the heavens and the earth, that he might be" [and so on to the end of the verse] (vi, 75). The Exalted also said, "Do they not observe the camels, how they have been created, and the sky, how it has been raised up?" (lxxxviii, 17–18), and He said, "and they give thought to the creation of the heavens and the earth" (iii, 191), and so on in countless other verses.

This study must be conducted in the best manner, by demonstrative reasoning.

Since it has now been established that the Law has rendered obligatory the study of beings by the intellect, and reflection on them, and since reflection is nothing more than inference and drawing out of the unknown from the known, and since this is reasoning or at any rate done by reasoning, therefore we are under an obligation to carry on our study of beings by intellectual reasoning. It is further evident that this manner of study, to which the Law summons and urges, is the most perfect kind of study using the most perfect kind of reasoning; and this is the kind called "demonstration."

To master this instrument the religious thinker must make a preliminary study of logic, just as the lawyer must study legal reasoning. This is no more heretical in the one case than in the other. And logic must be learned from the ancient masters, regardless of the fact that they were not Muslims.

The Law, then, has urged us to have demonstrative knowledge of God the Exalted and all the beings of His creation. But it is preferable and even necessary for anyone, who wants to understand God the Exalted and the other beings demonstratively, to have first understood the kinds of demonstration and their conditions [of validity], and in what respects demonstrative reasoning differs from dialectical, rhetorical and fallacious reasoning. But this is not possible unless he has previously learned what reasoning as such is, and how many kinds it has, and which of them are valid and which invalid. This in turn is not possible unless he has previously learned the parts of reasoning, of which it is composed, i.e. the premises and their kinds. Therefore he who believes in the Law, and obeys its command to study beings, ought prior to his study to gain a knowledge of these things, which have the same place in theoretical studies as instruments have in practical activities.

For just as the lawyer infers from the Divine command to him to acquire knowledge of the legal categories that he is under obligation to know the various kinds of legal syllogisms, and which are valid and which invalid, in the same way he who would know [God] ought to infer from the command to study beings that he is under obligation to acquire a knowledge of intellectual reasoning and its kinds. Indeed it is more fitting for him to do so, for if the lawyer infers from the saying of the Exalted, "Reflect, you who have vision," the obligation to acquire a knowledge of legal reasoning, how much more fitting and proper that he who would know God should infer from it the obligation to acquire a knowledge of intellectual reasoning!

It cannot be objected: "This kind of study of intellectual reasoning is a heretical innovation since it did not exist among the first believers." For the study of legal reasoning and its kinds is also something which has been discovered since the first believers, yet it is not considered to be a heretical innovation. So the objector should believe the same about the study of intellectual reasoning. (For this there is a reason, which it is not the place to mention here.) But most [masters] of this religion support intellectual reasoning, except a small group of gross literalists, who can be refuted by [sacred] texts.

Since it has now been established that there is an obligation of the Law to study intellectual reasoning and its kinds, just as there is an obligation to study legal reasoning, it is clear that, if none of our predecessors had formerly examined intellectual reasoning and its kinds, we should be obliged to undertake such an examination from the beginning, and that each succeeding scholar would have to seek help in that task from his predecessor in order that knowledge of the subject might be completed. For it is difficult or impossible for one man to find out by himself and from the beginning all that he needs of that subject, as it is difficult for one man to discover all the knowledge that he needs of the kinds of legal reasoning; indeed this is even truer of knowledge of intellectual reasoning.

But if someone other than ourselves has already examined that subject, it is clear that we ought to seek help towards our goal from what has been said by such a predecessor on the subject, regardless of whether this other one shares our religion or not. For when a valid sacrifice is performed with a certain instrument, no account is taken, in judging the validity of the sacrifice, of whether the instrument belongs to one who shares our religion or to one who does not, so long as it fulfils the conditions for validity. By "those who do not share our religion" I refer to those ancients who studied these matters before Islam. So if such is the case, and everything that is required in the study of the subject of intellectual syllogisms has already been examined in the most perfect manner by the ancients, presumably we ought to lay hands on their books in order to study what they said about that subject; and if it is all correct we should accept it from them, while if there is anything incorrect in it, we should draw attention to that.

After logic we must proceed to philosophy proper. Here too we have to learn from our predecessors, just as in mathematics and law. Thus it is wrong to forbid the study of ancient philosophy. Harm from it is accidental, like harm from taking medicine, drinking water, or studying law.

When we have finished with this sort of study and acquired the instruments by whose aid we are able to reflect on beings and the indications of art in them (for he who does not understand the art does not understand the product of art, and he who does not understand the product of art does not understand the Artisan), then we ought to begin the examination of beings in the order and manner we have learned from the art of demonstrative syllogisms.

And again it is clear that in the study of beings this aim can be fulfilled by us perfectly only through successive examinations of them by one man after another, the later ones seeking the help of the earlier in that task, on the model of what has happened in the mathematical sciences. For if we suppose that the art of geometry did not exist in this age of ours, and likewise the art of astronomy, and a single person wanted to ascertain by himself the sizes of the heavenly bodies, their shapes, and their distances from each other, that would not be possible for him—e.g. to know the proportion of the sun to the earth or other facts about the sizes of the stars—even though he were the most intelligent of men by nature, unless by a revelation or something resembling revelation. Indeed if he were told that the sun is about 150 or 160 times as great as the earth, he would think this statement madness on the part of the speaker, although this is a fact which has been demonstrated in astronomy so surely that no one who has mastered that science doubts it.

But what calls even more strongly for comparison with the art of mathematics in this respect is the art of the principles of law; and the study of law itself was completed only over a long period of time. And if someone today wanted to find out by himself all the arguments which have been discovered by the theorists of the legal schools on controversial questions, about which debate has taken place between them in most countries of Islam (except the West), he would deserve to be ridiculed, because such a task is impossible for him, apart from the fact that the work has been done already. Moreover, this is a situation that is self-evident not in the scientific arts alone but also in the practical arts; for there is not one of them which a single man can construct by himself. Then how can he do it with the art of arts, philosophy? If this is so, then whenever we find in the works of our predecessors of former nations a theory about beings and a reflection on them conforming to what the conditions of demonstration require, we ought to study what they said about the matter and what they affirmed in their books. And we should accept from them gladly and gratefully whatever in these books accords with the truth, and draw attention to and warn against what does not accord with the truth, at the same time excusing them.

From this it is evident that the study of the books of the ancients is obligatory by Law, since their aim and purpose in their books is just the purpose to which the Law has urged us, and that whoever forbids the study of them to anyone who is fit to study them, i.e. anyone who unites two qualities, (1) natural intelligence and (2) religious integrity and moral virtue, is blocking people from the door by which the Law summons them to knowledge of God, the door of theoretical study which leads to the truest knowledge of Him; and such an act is the extreme of ignorance and estrangement from God the Exalted.

And if someone errs or stumbles in the study of these books owing to a deficiency in his natural capacity, or bad organization of his study of them, or being dominated by his passions, or not finding a teacher to guide him to an understanding of their contents, or a combination of all or more than one of these causes, it does not follow that one should forbid them to anyone who is qualified to study them. For this manner of harm which arises owing to them is something that is attached to them by accident, not by essence; and when a thing is beneficial by its nature and essence, it ought not to be shunned because of something harmful contained in it by accident. This was the thought of the Prophet, peace on him, on the occasion when he ordered a man to give his brother honey to drink for his diarrhoea, and the diarrhoea increased after he had given him the honey: when the man complained to him about it, he said, "God spoke the truth; it was your brother's stomach that lied." We can even say that a man who prevents a qualified person from studying books of philosophy, because some of the most vicious people may be thought to have gone astray through their study of them, is like a man who prevents a thirsty person from drinking cool, fresh water until he dies of thirst, because some people have choked to death on it. For death from water by choking is an accidental matter, but death by thirst is essential and necessary.

Moreover, this accidental effect of this art is a thing which may also occur accidentally from the other arts. To how many lawyers has law been a cause of lack of piety and immersion in this world! Indeed we find most lawyers in this state, although their art by its essence calls for nothing but practical virtue. Thus it is not strange if the same thing that occurs accidentally in the art which calls for practical virtue should occur accidentally in the art which calls for intellectual virtue.

For every Muslim the Law has provided a way to truth suitable to his nature, through demonstrative, dialectical or rhetorical methods.

Since all this is now established, and since we, the Muslim community, hold that this divine religion of ours is true, and that it is this religion which incites and summons us to the happiness that consists in the knowledge of God, Mighty and Majestic, and of His creation, that [end] is appointed for every Muslim by the method of assent which his temperament and nature require. For the natures of men are on different levels with respect to [their paths to] assent. One of them comes to assent through demonstration; another comes to assent through dialectical arguments, just as firmly as the demonstrative man through demonstration, since his nature does not contain any greater capacity; while another comes to assent through rhetorical arguments, again just as firmly as the demonstrative man through demonstrative arguments.

Thus since this divine religion of ours has summoned people by these three methods, assent to it has extended to everyone, except him who stubbornly denies it with his tongue or him for whom no method of summons to God the Exalted has been appointed in religion owing to his own neglect of such matters. It was for this purpose that the Prophet, peace on him, was sent with a special mission to "the white man and the black man" alike; I mean because his religion embraces all the methods of summons to God the Exalted. This is clearly expressed in the saying of God the Exalted, "Summon to the way of your Lord by wisdom and by good preaching, and debate with them in the most effective manner" (xvi, 125).

CHAPTER TWO: PHILOSOPHY CONTAINS NOTHING OPPOSED TO ISLAM

Demonstrative truth and scriptural truth cannot conflict.

Now since this religion is true and summons to the study which leads to knowledge of the Truth, we the Muslim community know definitely that demonstrative study does not lead to [conclusions] conflicting with what Scripture has given us; for truth does not oppose truth but accords with it and bears witness to it.

If the apparent meaning of Scripture conflicts with demonstrative conclusions it must be interpreted allegorically, i.e. metaphorically.

This being so, whenever demonstrative study leads to any manner of knowledge about any being, that being is inevitably either unmentioned or mentioned in Scripture. If it is unmentioned there is no contradiction, and it is in the same case as an act whose category is unmentioned, so that the lawyer has to infer it by reasoning from Scripture. If Scripture speaks about it, the apparent meaning of the words inevitably either accords or conflicts with the conclusions of demonstration about it. If this [apparent meaning] accords there is no argument. If it conflicts there is a call for allegorical interpretation of it. The meaning of "allegorical interpretation" is: extension of the significance of an expression from real to metaphorical significance, without forsaking therein the standard metaphorical practices of Arabic, such as calling a thing by the name of something resembling it or a cause or consequence or accompaniment of it, or other things such as are enumerated in accounts of the kinds of metaphorical speech.

If the lawyer can do this, the religious thinker certainly can. Indeed these allegorical interpretations always receive confirmation from the apparent meaning of other passages of Scripture.

Now if the lawyer does this in many decisions of religious law, with how much more right is it done by the possessor of demonstrative knowledge! For the lawyer has at his disposition only reasoning based on opinion, while he who would know [God] [has at his disposition] reasoning based on certainty. So we affirm definitely that whenever the conclusion of a demonstration is in conflict with the apparent meaning of Scripture, that apparent meaning admits of allegorical interpretation according to the rules for such interpretation in Arabic. This proposition is questioned by no Muslim and doubted by no believer. But its certainty is immensely increased for those who have had close dealings with this idea and put it to the test, and made it their aim to reconcile the assertions of intellect and tradition. Indeed we may say that whenever a statement in Scripture conflicts in its apparent meaning with a conclusion of demonstration, if Scripture is considered carefully, and the rest of its contents searched page by page, there will invariably be found among the expressions of Scripture something which in its apparent meaning bears witness to that allegorical interpretation or comes close to bearing witness.

All Muslims accept the principle of allegorical interpretation; they only disagree about the extent of its application.

In the light of this idea the Muslims are unanimous in holding that it is not obligatory either to take all the expressions of Scripture in their apparent meaning or to extend them all from their apparent meaning by allegorical interpretation. They disagree [only] over which of them should and which should not be so interpreted: the Ash'arites for instance give an allegorical interpretation to the verse about God's directing Himself and the Tradition about His descent, while the Hanbalites take them in their apparent meaning.

The double meaning has been given to suit people's diverse intelligence. The apparent contradictions are meant to stimulate the learned to deeper study.

The reason why we have received a Scripture with both an apparent and an inner meaning lies in the diversity of people's natural capacities and the difference of their innate dispositions with regard to assent. The reason why we have received in Scripture texts whose apparent meanings contradict each other is in order to draw the attention of those who are well grounded in science to the interpretation which reconciles them. This is the idea referred to in the words received from the Exalted, "He it is who has sent down to you the Book, containing certain verses clear and definite" [and so on] down to the words "those who are well grounded in science" (iii, 7).

In interpreting texts allegorically we must never violate Islamic consensus, when it is certain. But to establish it with certainty with regard to theoretical texts is impossible, because there have always been scholars who would not divulge their interpretation of such texts.

It may be objected: "There are some things in Scripture which the Muslims have unanimously agreed to take in their apparent meaning, others [which they have agreed] to interpret allegorically, and others about which they have disagreed; is it permissible, then, that demonstration should lead to interpreting allegorically what they have agreed to take in its apparent meaning, or to taking in its apparent meaning what they have agreed to interpret allegorically?" We reply: If unanimous agreement is established by a method which is certain, such [a result] is not sound; but if [the existence of] agreement on those things is a matter of opinion, then it may be sound. This is why Abū Hāmid, Abul-Ma'ālī, and other leaders of thought said that no one should be definitely called an unbeliever for violating unanimity on a point of interpretation in matters like these.

That unanimity on theoretical matters is never determined with certainty, as it can be on practical matters, may be shown to you by the fact that it is not possible for unanimity to be determined on any question at any period unless that period is strictly limited by us, and all the scholars existing in that period are known to us (i.e. known as individuals and in their total number), and the doctrine of each of them on the question has been handed down to us on unassailable authority, and, in addition to all this, unless we are sure that the scholars existing at the time were in agreement that there is not both an apparent and an inner meaning in Scripture, that knowledge of any question ought not to be kept secret from anyone, and that there is only one way for people to understand Scripture. But it is recorded in Tradition that many of the first believers used to hold that Scripture has both an apparent and an inner meaning, and that the inner meaning ought not to be learned by anyone who is not a man of learning in this field and who is incapable of understanding it. Thus, for example, Bukhārī reports a saying of 'Alī Ibn Abī Tālib, may God be pleased with him, "Speak to people about what they know. Do you want God and His Prophet to be accused of lying?" Other examples of the same kind are reported about a group of early believers. So how can it possibly be conceived that a unanimous agreement can have been handed down to us about a single theoretical question, when we know definitely that not a single period has been without scholars who held that there are things in Scripture whose true meaning should not be learned by all people?

The situation is different in practical matters: everyone holds that the truth about these should be disclosed to all people alike, and to establish the occurrence of unanimity about them we consider it sufficient that the question [at issue] should have been widely discussed and that no report of controversy about it should have been handed down to us. This is enough to establish the occurrence of unanimity on matters of practice, but on matters of doctrine the case is different.

Ghazālī's charge of unbelief against Fārābī and Ibn Sīnā, for asserting the world's eternity and God's ignorance of particulars and denying bodily resurrection, is only tentative, not definite.

You may object: "If we ought not to call a man an unbeliever for violating unanimity in cases of allegorical interpretation, because no unanimity is conceivable in such cases, what do you say about the Muslim philosophers, like Abū Nasr and Ibn Sīnā? For Abū Hāmid called them both definitely unbelievers in the book of his known as *The disintegration*, on three counts: their assertions of the pre-eternity of the world and that God the Exalted does not know particulars" (may He be Exalted far above that [ignorance]!), "and their allegorical interpretation of the passages concerning the resurrection of bodies and states of existence in the next life."

We answer: It is apparent from what he said on the subject that his calling them both unbelievers on these counts was not definite, since he made it clear in *The book of distinction* that calling people unbelievers for violating unanimity can only be tentative.

> *Such a charge cannot be definite, because there has never been a consensus against allegorical interpretation. The* Qur'ān *itself indicates that it has inner meanings which it is the special function of the demonstrative class to understand.*

Moreover, it is evident from what we have said that a unanimous agreement cannot be established in questions of this kind, because of the reports that many of the early believers of the first generation, as well as others, have said that there are allegorical interpretations which ought not to be expressed except to those who are qualified to receive allegories. These are "those who are well grounded in science"; for we prefer to place the stop after the words of God the Exalted "and those who are well grounded in science" (iii, 7), because if the scholars did not understand allegorical interpretation, there would be no superiority in their assent which would oblige them to a belief in Him not found among the unlearned. God has described them as those who believe in Him, and this can only be taken to refer to the belief which is based on demonstration; and this [belief] only occurs together with the science of allegorical interpretation. For the unlearned believers are those whose belief in Him is not based on demonstration; and if this belief which God has attributed to the scholars is peculiar to them, it must come through demonstration, and if it comes through demonstration it only occurs together with the science of allegorical interpretation. For God the Exalted has informed us that those [verses] have an allegorical interpretation which is the truth, and demonstration can only be of the truth. That being the case, it is not possible for general unanimity to be established about allegorical interpretations, which God has made peculiar to scholars. This is self-evident to any fair-minded person.

> *Besides, Ghazālī was mistaken in ascribing to the Peripatetics the opinion that God does not know particulars. Their view is that His knowledge of both particulars and universals differs from ours, in being the cause, not an effect, of the object known. They even hold that God sends premonitions in dreams of particular events.*

In addition to all this we hold that Abū Hāmid was mistaken about the Peripatetic philosophers, in ascribing to them the assertion that God, Holy and Exalted, does not know particulars at all. In reality they hold that God the Exalted knows them in a way which is not of the same kind as our way of knowing them. For our knowledge of them is an effect of the object known, originated when it comes into existence and changing when it changes; whereas Glorious God's Knowledge of existence is the opposite of this: it is the cause of the object known, which is existent being. Thus to suppose the two kinds of knowledge similar to each other is to identify the essences and properties of opposite things, and that is the extreme of ignorance. And if the name of "knowledge" is predicated of both originated and eternal knowledge, it is predicated by sheer homonymy, as many names are predicated of opposite things: e.g. *jalal* of great and small, *sarīm* of light and darkness. Thus there exists no definition embracing both kinds of knowledge at once, as the theologians of our time imagine. We have devoted a separate essay to this question, impelled by one of our friends.

But how can anyone imagine that the Peripatetics say that God the Glorious does not know particulars with His eternal Knowledge, when they hold that true visions in-

The Lion's Court, the Alhambra, Granada, Spain, begun in 1230. This palace of the rulers
is the best example of the Islamic culture that dominated Spain from the early eighth
century until the surrender of Granada in 1492. *(Scala/Art Resource)*

clude premonitions of particular events due to occur in future time, and that this warning foreknowledge comes to people in their sleep from the eternal Knowledge which
orders and rules the universe? Moreover, it is not only particulars which they say God
does not know in the manner in which we know them, but universals as well; for the
universals known to us are also effects of the nature of existent being, while with His
Knowledge the reverse is true. Thus the conclusion to which demonstration leads is
that His Knowledge transcends qualification as "universal" or "particular." Consequently there is no point in disputing about this question, i.e. whether to call them unbelievers or not.

> *On the question of the world, the ancient philosophers agree with the Ash'arites
> that it is originated and coeval with time. The Peripatetics only disagree with the
> Ash'arites and the Platonists in holding that past time is infinite. This difference
> is insufficient to justify a charge of unbelief.*

Concerning the question whether the world is pre-eternal or came into existence,
the disagreement between the Ash'arite theologians and the ancient philosophers is in
my view almost resolvable into a disagreement about naming, especially in the case of
certain of the ancients. For they agree that there are three classes of beings: two extremes and one intermediate between the extremes. They agree also about naming the
extremes; but they disagree about the intermediate class.

[1] One extreme is a being which is brought into existence from something other
than itself and by something, i.e. by an efficient cause and from some matter; and it,

i.e. its existence, is preceded by time. This is the status of bodies whose generation is apprehended by sense, e.g., the generation of water, air, earth, animals, plants, and so on. All alike, ancients and Ash'arites, agree in naming this class of beings "originated." [2] The opposite extreme to this is a being which is not made from or by anything and not preceded by time; and here too all members of both schools agree in naming it "pre-eternal." This being is apprehended by demonstration; it is God, Blessed and Exalted, Who is the Maker, Giver of being and Sustainer of the universe; may He be praised and His Power exalted!

[3] The class of being which is between these two extremes is that which is not made from anything and not preceded by time, but which is brought into existence by something, i.e. by an agent. This is the world as a whole. Now they all agree on the presence of these three characters in the world. For the theologians admit that time does not precede it, or rather this is a necessary consequence for them since time according to them is something which accompanies motion and bodies. They also agree with the ancients in the view that future time is infinite and likewise future being. They only disagree about past time and past being: the theologians hold that it is finite (this is the doctrine of Plato and his followers), while Aristotle and his school hold that it is infinite, as is the case with future time.

Thus it is clear that [3] this last being bears a resemblance both to [1] the being which is really generated and to [2] the pre-eternal Being. So those who are more impressed with its resemblance to the pre-eternal than its resemblance to the originated name it "pre-eternal," while those who are more impressed with its resemblance to the originated name it "originated." But in truth it is neither really originated nor really pre-eternal, since the really originated is necessarily perishable and the really pre-eternal has no cause. Some—Plato and his followers—name it "originated and coeval with time," because time according to them is finite in the past.

Thus the doctrines about the world are not so very far apart from each other that some of them should be called irreligious and others not. For this to happen, opinions must be divergent in the extreme, i.e. contraries such as the theologians suppose to exist on this question; i.e. [they hold] that the names "pre-eternity" and "coming into existence" as applied to the world as a whole are contraries. But it is now clear from what we have said that this is not the case.

> *Anyhow, the apparent meaning of Scripture is that there was a being and time before God created the present being and time. Thus the theologians' interpretation is allegorical and does not command unanimous agreement.*

Over and above all this, these opinions about the world do not conform to the apparent meaning of Scripture. For if the apparent meaning of Scripture is searched, it will be evident from the verses which give us information about the bringing into existence of the world that its form really is originated, but that being itself and time extend continuously at both extremes, i.e. without interruption. Thus the words of God the Exalted, "He it is Who created the heavens and the earth in six days, and His throne was on the water" (xi, 7), taken in their apparent meaning imply that there was a being before this present being, namely the throne and the water, and a time before this time, i.e. the one which is joined to the form of this being, namely the number of the movement of the celestial sphere. And the words of the Exalted, "On the day when the earth shall be changed into other than earth, and the heavens as well" (xiv, 48), also in their apparent meaning imply that there will be a second being after this being. And the words of the Exalted, "Then He directed Himself towards the sky, and it was smoke" (xli, 11), in their apparent meaning imply that the heavens were created from something.

Thus the theologians too in their statements about the world do not conform to the apparent meaning of Scripture but interpret it allegorically. For it is not stated in Scripture that God was existing with absolutely nothing else: a text to this effect is nowhere to be found. Then how is it conceivable that the theologians' allegorical interpretation of these verses could meet with unanimous agreement, when the apparent meaning of Scripture which we have mentioned about the existence of the world has been accepted by a school of philosophers!

On such difficult questions, error committed by a qualified judge of his subject is excused by God, while error by an unqualified person is not excused.

It seems that those who disagree on the interpretation of these difficult questions earn merit if they are in the right and will be excused [by God] if they are in error. For assent to a thing as a result of an indication [of it] arising in the soul is something compulsory, not voluntary: i.e. it is not for us [to choose] not to assent or to assent, as it is to stand up or not to stand up. And since free choice is a condition of obligation, a man who assents to an error as a result of a consideration that has occurred to him is excused, if he is a scholar. This is why the Prophet, peace on him, said, "If the judge after exerting his mind makes a right decision, he will have a double reward; and if he makes a wrong decision he will [still] have a single reward." And what judge is more important than he who makes judgements about being, that it is thus or not thus? These judges are the scholars, specially chosen by God for [the task of] allegorical interpretation, and this error which is forgivable according to the Law is only such error as proceeds from scholars when they study the difficult matters which the Law obliges them to study.

But error proceeding from any other class of people is sheer sin, equally whether it relates to theoretical or to practical matters. For just as the judge who is ignorant of the [Prophet's] way of life is not excused if he makes an error in judgement, so he who makes judgements about beings without having the proper qualifications for [such] judgements is not excused but is either a sinner or an unbeliever. And if he who would judge what is allowed and forbidden is required to combine in himself the qualifications for exercise of personal judgement, namely knowledge of the principles [of law] and knowledge of how to draw inferences from those principles by reasoning, how much more properly is he who would make judgements about beings required to be qualified, i.e. to know the primary intellectual principle and the way to draw inferences from them!

Texts of Scripture fall into three kinds with respect to the excusability of error. [1] Texts which must be taken in their apparent meaning by everyone. Since the meaning can be understood plainly by demonstrative, dialectical and rhetorical methods alike, no one is excused for the error of interpreting these texts allegorically. [2] Texts which must be taken in their apparent meaning by the lower classes and interpreted allegorically by the demonstrative class. It is inexcusable for the lower classes to interpret them allegorically or for the demonstrative class to take them in their apparent meaning. [3] Texts whose classification under the previous headings is uncertain. Error in this matter by the demonstrative class is excused.

In general, error about Scripture is of two types: either error which is excused to one who is a qualified student of that matter in which the error occurs (as the skilful doctor is excused if he commits an error in the art of medicine and the skilful judge if he gives an erroneous judgement), but not excused to one who is not qualified in that subject; or error which is not excused to any person whatever, and which is unbelief if it concerns the principles of religion, or heresy if it concerns something subordinate to the principles.

This [latter] error is that which occurs about [1] matters, knowledge of which is provided by all the different methods of indication, so that knowledge of the matter in question is in this way possible for everyone. Examples are acknowledgement of God, Blessed and Exalted, of the prophetic missions, and of happiness and misery in the next life; for these three principles are attainable by the three classes of indication, by which everyone without exception can come to assent to what he is obliged to know: I mean the rhetorical, dialectical and demonstrative indications. So whoever denies such a thing, when it is one of the principles of the Law, is an unbeliever, who persists in defiance with his tongue though not with his heart, or neglects to expose himself to learning the indication of its truth. For if he belongs to the demonstrative class of men, a way has been provided for him to assent to it, by demonstration; if he belongs to the dialectical class, the way is by dialectic; and if he belongs to the class [which is convinced] by preaching, the way for him is by preaching. With this in view the Prophet, peace on him, said, "I have been ordered to fight people until they say 'There is no god but God' and believe in me"; he means, by any of the three methods of attaining belief that suits them.

[2] With regard to things which by reason of their recondite character are only knowable by demonstration, God has been gracious to those of His servants who have no access to demonstration, on account of their natures, habits or lack of facilities for education: He has coined for them images and likenesses of these things, and summoned them to assent to those images, since it is possible for assent to those images to come about through the indications common to all men, i.e. the dialectical and rhetorical indications. This is the reason why Scripture is divided into apparent and inner meanings: the apparent meaning consists of those images which are coined to stand for those ideas, while the inner meaning is those ideas [themselves], which are clear only to the demonstrative class. These are the four or five classes of beings mentioned by Abū Hāmid in *The book of the distinction*.

[1] But when it happens, as we said, that we know the thing itself by the three methods, we do not need to coin images of it, and it remains true in its apparent meaning, not admitting allegorical interpretation. If an apparent text of this kind refers to principles, anyone who interprets it allegorically is an unbeliever, e.g. anyone who thinks that there is no happiness or misery in the next life, and that the only purpose of this teaching is that men should be safeguarded from each other in their bodily and sensible lives, that it is but a practical device, and that man has no other goal than his sensible existence

If this is established, it will have become clear to you from what we have said that there are [1] apparent texts of Scripture which it is not permitted to interpret allegorically; to do so on fundamentals is unbelief, on subordinate matters, heresy. There are also [2] apparent texts which have to be interpreted allegorically by men of the demonstrative class; for such men to take them in their apparent meaning is unbelief, while for those who are not of the demonstrative class to interpret them allegorically and take them out of their apparent meaning is unbelief or heresy on their part.

Of this [latter] class are the verse about God's directing Himself and the Tradition about His descent. That is why the Prophet, peace on him, said in the case of the black woman, when she told him that God was in the sky, "Free her, for she is a believer." This was because she was not of the demonstrative class; and the reason for his decision was that the class of people to whom assent comes only through the imagination, i.e. who do not assent to a thing except in so far as they can imagine it, find it difficult to assent to the existence of a being which is unrelated to any imaginable thing. This applies as well to those who understand from the relation stated merely [that God has] a place; these are people who have advanced a little in their thought beyond the position of the first class, [by rejecting] belief in corporeality. Thus the [proper] answer to them with regard to such passages is that they belong to the ambiguous texts, and that the stop is to be placed after the words of God the Exalted, "And no one knows the interpretation thereof except God" (iii, 7). The demonstrative class, while agreeing unanimously that this class of text must be interpreted allegorically, may disagree about the interpretation, according to the level of each one's knowledge of demonstration.

There is also [3] a third class of Scriptural texts falling uncertainly between the other two classes, on which there is doubt. One group of those who devote themselves to theoretical study attach them to the apparent texts which it is not permitted to interpret allegorically, others attach them to the texts with inner meanings which scholars are not permitted to take in their apparent meanings. This [divergence of opinions] is due to the difficulty and ambiguity of this class of text. Anyone who commits an error about this class is excused, I mean any scholar.

The texts about the future life fall into [3], since demonstrative scholars do not agree whether to take them in their apparent meaning or interpret them allegorically. Either is permissible. But it is inexcusable to deny the fact of a future life altogether.

If it is asked, "Since it is clear that scriptural texts in this respect fall into three grades, to which of these three grades, according to you, do the descriptions of the future life and its states belong?," we reply: The position clearly is that this matter belongs to the class [3] about which there is disagreement. For we find a group of those who claim an affinity with demonstration saying that it is obligatory to take these passages in their apparent meaning, because there is no demonstration leading to the impossibility of the apparent meaning in them—this is the view of the Ash'arites; while another group of those who devote themselves to demonstration interpret these passages allegorically, and these people give the most diverse interpretations of them. In this class must be counted Abū Hāmid and many of the Sūfīs; some of them combine the two interpretations of the passages, as Abū Hāmid does in some of his books.

So it is likely that a scholar who commits an error in this matter is excused, while one who is correct receives thanks or a reward: that is, if he acknowledges the existence [of a future life] and merely gives a certain sort of allegorical interpretation, i.e. of the mode of the future life not of its existence, provided that the interpretation given does not lead to denial of its existence. In this matter only the negation of existence is unbelief, because it concerns one of the principles of religion and one of those points to which assent is attainable through the three methods common to "the white man and the black man."

The unlearned classes must take such texts in their apparent meaning. It is unbelief for the learned to set down allegorical interpretations in popular writings. By doing this Ghazālī caused confusion among the people. Demonstrative books should be banned to the unqualified, but not to the learned.

But anyone who is not a man of learning is obliged to take these passages in their apparent meaning, and allegorical interpretation of them is for him unbelief because it *leads to* unbelief. That is why we hold that, for anyone whose duty it is to believe in the apparent meaning, allegorical interpretation is unbelief, because it leads to unbelief. Anyone of the interpretative class who discloses such [an interpretation] to him is summoning him to unbelief, and he who summons to unbelief is an unbeliever.

Therefore allegorical interpretations ought to be set down only in demonstrative books because if they are in demonstrative books they are encountered by no one but men of the demonstrative class. But if they are set down in other than demonstrative books and one deals with them by poetical, rhetorical or dialectical methods, as Abū Hāmid does, then he commits an offence against the Law and against philosophy, even though the fellow intended nothing but good. For by this procedure he wanted to increase the number of learned men, but in fact he increased the number of the corrupted not of the learned! As a result, one group came to slander philosophy, another to slander religion, and another to reconcile the [first] two [groups]. It seems that this [last] was one of his objects in his books; an indication that he wanted by this [procedure] to arouse minds is that he adhered to no one doctrine in his books but was an Ash'arite with the Ash'arites, a Sūfī with the Sūfīs and a philosopher with the philosophers, so that he was like the man in the verse:

"One day a Yamani, if I meet a man of Yaman,
And if I meet a Ma'addi, I'm an 'Adnani."

The *imāms* of the Muslims ought to forbid those of his books which contain learned matter to all save the learned, just as they ought to forbid demonstrative books to those who are not capable of understanding them. But the damage done to people by demonstrative books is lighter, because for the most part only persons of superior natural intelligence become acquainted with demonstrative books, and this class of persons is only misled through lack of practical virtue, unorganized reading, and tackling them without a teacher. On the other hand their total prohibition obstructs the purpose to which the Law summons, because it is a wrong to the best class of people and the best class of beings. For to do justice to the best class of beings demands that they should be known profoundly by persons equipped to know them profoundly, and these are the best class of people; and the greater the value of the being, the greater is the injury towards it, which consists of ignorance of it. Thus the Exalted has said, "Associating [other gods] with God is indeed a great wrong" (xxxi, 12).

We have only discussed these questions in a popular work because they were already being publicly discussed.

This is as much as we see fit to affirm in this field of study, i.e. the correspondence between religion and philosophy and the rules for allegorical interpretation in religion. If it were not for the publicity given to the matter and to these questions which we have discussed, we should not have permitted ourselves to write a word on the subject; and we should not have had to make excuses for doing so to the interpretative scholars, because the proper place to discuss these questions is in demonstrative books. God is the Guide and helps us to follow the right course!

Chapter Three: Philosophical Interpretations of Scripture Should Not Be Taught to the Majority. The Law Provides Other Methods of Instructing Them

The purpose of Scripture is to teach true theoretical and practical science and right practice and attitudes.

You ought to know that the purpose of Scripture is simply to teach true science and right practice. True science is knowledge of God, Blessed and Exalted, and the other beings as they really are, and especially of noble beings, and knowledge of happiness and misery in the next life. Right practice consists in performing the acts which bring happiness and avoiding the acts which bring misery; and it is knowledge of these acts that is called "practical science." They fall into two divisions: (1) outward bodily acts; the science of these is called "jurisprudence"; and (2) acts of the soul such as gratitude, patience and other moral attitudes which the Law enjoins or forbids; the science of these is called "asceticism" or "the sciences of the future life." To these Abū Hāmid turned his attention in his book: as people had given up this sort [of act] and become immersed in the other sort, and as this sort [2] involves the greater fear of God, which is the cause of happiness, he called his book *"The revival of the sciences of religion."* But we have digressed from our subject, so let us return to it.

Scripture teaches concepts both directly and by symbols, and uses demonstrative, dialectical and rhetorical arguments. Dialectical and rhetorical arguments are prevalent because the main aim of Scripture is to teach the majority. In these arguments concepts are indicated directly or by symbols, in various combinations in premises and conclusion.

We say: The purpose of Scripture is to teach true science and right practice; and teaching is of two classes, [of] concepts and [of] judgements, as the logicians have shown. Now the methods available to men of [arriving at] judgements are three: demonstrative, dialectical and rhetorical; and the methods of forming concepts are two: either [conceiving] the object itself or [conceiving] a symbol of it. But not everyone has the natural ability to take in demonstrations, or [even] dialectical arguments, let alone demonstrative arguments which are so hard to learn and need so much time [even] for those who are qualified to learn them. Therefore, since it is the purpose of Scriptures simply to teach everyone, Scripture has to contain every method of [bringing about] judgements of assent and every method of forming concepts.

Now some of the methods of assent comprehend the majority of people, i.e. the occurrence of assent as a result of them [is comprehensive]: these are the rhetorical and the dialectical [methods]—and the rhetorical is more comprehensive than the dialectical. Another method is peculiar to a smaller number of people: this is the demonstrative. Therefore, since the primary purpose of Scripture is to take care of the majority (without neglecting to arouse the élite), the prevailing methods of expression in religion are the common methods by which the majority comes to form concepts and judgements.

These [common] methods in religion are of four classes:

One of them occurs where the method is common, yet specialized in two respects: i.e. where it is certain in its concepts and judgements, in spite of being rhetorical or dialectical. These syllogisms are those whose premisses, in spite of being based on accepted ideas or on opinions, are accidentally certain, and whose conclusions are accidentally to be taken in their direct meaning without symbolization. Scriptural texts of this class have no allegorical interpretations, and anyone who denies them or interprets them allegorically is an unbeliever.

The second class occurs where the premisses, in spite of being based on accepted ideas or on opinions, are certain, and where the conclusions are symbols for the things which it was intended to conclude. [Texts of] this [class], i.e. their conclusions, admit of allegorical interpretation.

The third is the reverse of this: it occurs where the conclusions are the very things which it was intended to conclude, while the premisses are based on accepted ideas or on opinions without being accidentally certain. [Texts of] this [class] also, i.e. their conclusions, do not admit of allegorical interpretation, but their premisses may do so.

The fourth [class] occurs where the premisses are based on accepted ideas or opinions, without being accidentally certain, and where the conclusions are symbols for what it was intended to conclude. In these cases the duty of the élite is to interpret them allegorically, while the duty of the masses is to take them in their apparent meaning.

Where symbols are used, each class of men, demonstrative, dialectical and rhetorical, must try to understand the inner meaning symbolized or rest content with the apparent meaning, according to their capacities.

In general, everything in these [texts] which admits of allegorical interpretation can only be understood by demonstration. The duty of the élite here is to apply such interpretation; while the duty of the masses is to take them in their apparent meaning in both respects, i.e. in concept and judgement, since their natural capacity does not allow more than that.

But there may occur to students of Scripture allegorical interpretations due to the superiority of one of the common methods over another in [bringing about] assent, i.e. when the indication contained in the allegorical interpretation is more persuasive than the indication contained in the apparent meaning. Such interpretations are popular; and [the making of them] is possibly a duty for those powers of theoretical understanding have attained the dialectical level. To this sort belong some of the interpretations of the Ash'arites and Mu'tazilites—though the Mu'tazilites are generally sounder in their statements. The masses on the other hand, who are incapable of more than rhetorical arguments, have the duty of taking these [texts] in their apparent meaning, and they are not permitted to know such interpretations at all.

Thus people in relation to Scripture fall into three classes:

One class is these who are not people of interpretation at all: these are the rhetorical class. They are the overwhelming mass, for no man of sound intellect is exempted from this kind of assent.

Another class is the people of dialectical interpretation: these are the dialecticians, either by nature alone or by nature and habit.

Another class is the people of certain interpretation: these are the demonstrative class, by nature and training, i.e. in the art of philosophy. This interpretation ought not to be expressed to the dialectical class, let alone to the masses.

To explain the inner meaning to people unable to understand it is to destroy their belief in the apparent meaning without putting anything in its place. The result is unbelief in learners and teachers. It is best for the learned to profess ignorance, quoting the Qur'ān *on the limitation of man's understanding.*

When something of these allegorical interpretations is expressed to anyone unfit to receive them—especially demonstrative interpretations because of their remoteness from common knowledge—both he who expresses it and he to whom it is expressed are led into unbelief. The reason for that [in the case of the latter] is that allegorical interpretation comprises two things, rejection of the apparent meaning and affirmation of the allegorical one; so that if the apparent meaning is rejected in the mind of someone who can only grasp apparent meanings, without the allegorical meaning being affirmed in his mind, the result is unbelief, if it [the text in question] concerns the principles of religion.

Allegorical interpretations, then, ought not to be expressed to the masses nor set down in rhetorical or dialectical books, i.e. books containing arguments of these two sorts, as was done by Abū Hāmid. They should [not] be expressed to this class; and with regard to an apparent text, when there is a [self-evident] doubt whether it is apparent to everyone and whether knowledge of its interpretation is impossible for them, they should be told that it is ambiguous and [its meaning] known by no one except God; and that the stop should be put here in the sentence of the Exalted, "And no one knows the interpretation thereof except God" (iii, 7). The same kind of answer should also be given to a question about abstruse matters, which there is no way for the masses to understand; just as the Exalted has answered in His saying, "And they will ask you about the Spirit. Say, 'The Spirit is by the command of my Lord; you have been given only a little knowledge'" (xvii, 85).

Certain people have injured the masses particularly, by giving them allegorical interpretations which are false. These people are exactly analogous to bad medical advisers. The true doctor is related to bodily health in the same way as the Legislator to spiritual health, which the Qur'ān *teaches us to pursue. The true allegory is "the deposit" mentioned in the* Qur'ān.

As for the man who expresses these allegories to unqualified persons, he is an unbeliever on account of his summoning people to unbelief. This is contrary to the summons of the Legislator, especially when they are false allegories concerning the principles of religion, as has happened in the case of a group of people of our time. For we have seen some of them thinking that they were being philosophic and that they perceived, with their remarkable wisdom, things which conflict with Scripture in every respect, i.e. [in passages] which do not admit of allegorical interpretation; and that it was obligatory to express these things to the masses. But by expressing those false beliefs to the masses they have been a cause of perdition to the masses and themselves, in this world and the next.

The relation between the aim of these people and the aim of the Legislator [can be illustrated by] a parable of a man who goes to a skilful doctor. [This doctor's] aim is to preserve the health and cure the diseases of all the people, by prescribing for them rules which can be commonly accepted, about the necessity of using the things which will preserve their health and cure their diseases, and avoiding the opposite things. He is unable to make them all doctors, because a doctor is one who knows by demonstrative methods the things which preserve health and cure disease. Now this [man whom we have mentioned] goes out to the people and tells them, "These methods prescribed by this doctor for you are not right"; and he sets out to discredit them, so that they are rejected by the people. Or he says, "They have allegorical interpretations"; but the people neither understand these nor assent to them in practice. Well, do you think that people in this condition will do any of the things which are useful for preserving health and curing disease, or that this man who has persuaded them to reject what they formerly believed in will now be able to use those [things] with them, I mean for preserving health? No, he will be unable to use those [things] with them, nor will they use them, and so they will all perish.

This [is what will happen] if he expresses to them true allegories about those matters, because of their inability to understand them; let alone if he expresses to them false allegories, because this will lead them to think that there are no such things as health which ought to be preserved and disease which ought to be cured—let alone that there are things which preserve health and cure disease. It is the same when someone expresses allegories to the masses, and to those who are not qualified to understand them, in the sphere of Scripture; thus he makes it appear false and turns people away from it; and he who turns people away from Scripture is an unbeliever.

Indeed this comparison is certain, not poetic as one might suppose. It presents a true analogy, in that the relation of the doctor to the health of bodies is [the same as] the relation of the Legislator to the health of souls; i.e. the doctor is he who seeks to preserve the health of bodies when it exists and to restore it when it is lost, while the Legislator is he who desires this [end] for the health of souls. This health is what is called "fear of God." The precious Book has told us to seek it by acts conformable to the Law, in several verses. Thus the Exalted has said, "Fasting has been prescribed for you, as it was prescribed for those who were before you; perhaps you will fear God" (ii, 183). Again the Exalted has said, "Their flesh and their blood shall not touch God, but your fear shall touch him" (xxii, 37); "Prayer prevents immorality and transgression" (xxix, 45); and other verses to the same effect contained in the precious Book. Through knowledge of Scripture and practice according to Scripture the Legislator aims solely at this health; and it is from this health that happiness in the future life follows, just as misery in the future life follows from its opposite.

From this it will be clear to you that true allegories ought not to be set down in popular books, let alone false ones. The true allegory is the deposit which man was charged to hold and which he held, and from which all beings shied away, i.e. that which is mentioned in the words of the Exalted, "We offered the deposit to the heavens, the earth and the mountains" (xxxiii, 72), [and so on to the end of] the verse.

It was due to the wrong use of allegorical interpretation by the Mu'tazilites and Ash'arites that hostile sects arose in Islam.

It was due to allegorical interpretations—especially the false ones—and the supposition that such interpretations of Scripture ought to be expressed to everyone, that the sects of Islam arose, with the result that each one accused the others of unbelief or heresy. Thus the Mu'tazilites interpreted many verses and Traditions allegorically, and expressed their interpretations to the masses, and the Ash'arites did the same, although they used such interpretations less frequently. In consequence they threw people into hatred, mutual detestation and wars, tore the Scriptures to shreds, and completely divided people.

In addition to all this, in the methods which they followed to establish their interpretations they neither went along with the masses nor with the élite: not with the masses, because their methods were [more] obscure than the methods common to the majority, and not with the élite, because if these methods are inspected they are found deficient in the conditions [required] for demonstrations, as will be understood after the slightest inspection by anyone acquainted with the conditions of demonstration. Further, many of the principles on which the Ash'arites based their knowledge are sophistical, for they deny many necessary truths such as the permanence of accidents, the action of things on other things, the existence of necessary causes for effects, of substantial forms, and of secondary causes.

And their theorists wronged the Muslims in this sense, that a sect of Ash'arites called an unbeliever anyone who did not attain knowledge of the existence of the Glorious Creator by the methods laid down by them in their books for attaining this knowledge. But in truth it is they who are the unbelievers and in error! From this point they proceeded to disagree, one group saying "The primary obligation is theoretical study," another group saying "It is belief"; i.e. [this happened] because they did not know which are the methods common to everyone, through whose doors the Law has summoned all people [to enter]; they supposed that there was only one method. Thus they mistook the aim of the Legislator, and were both themselves in error and led others into error.

The proper methods for teaching the people are indicated in the Qur'ān, as the early Muslims knew. The popular portions of the Book are miraculous in providing for the needs of every class of mind. We intend to make a study of its teachings at the apparent level, and thus help to remedy the grievous harm done by ignorant partisans of philosophy and religion.

It may be asked: "If these methods followed by the Ash'arites and other theorists are not the common methods by which the Legislator has aimed to teach the masses, and by which alone it is possible to teach them, then what are those [common] methods in this religion of ours?" We reply: They are exclusively the methods set down in the precious Book. For if the precious Book is inspected, there will be found in it the three methods that are available for all the people, [namely] the common methods for the instruction of the majority of the people and the special method. And if their merits are inspected, it becomes apparent that no better common methods for the instruction of the masses can be found than the methods mentioned in it.

Thus whoever tampers with them, by making an allegorical interpretation not apparent in itself, or [at least] not more apparent to everyone than they are (and that [greater apparency] is something non-existent), is rejecting their wisdom and rejecting their intended effects in procuring human happiness. This is very apparent from [a comparison of] the condition of the first believers with the condition of those who came after them. For the first believers arrived at perfect virtue and fear of God only by using these sayings [of Scripture] without interpreting them allegorically; and anyone of them who did find out an allegorical interpretation did not think fit to express it [to others]. But when those who came after them used allegorical interpretation, their fear of God grew less, their dissensions increased, their love for one another was removed, and they became divided into sects.

So whoever wishes to remove this heresy from religion should direct his attention to the precious Book, and glean from it the indications present [in it] concerning everything in turn that it obliges us to believe, and exercise his judgement in looking at its apparent meaning as well as he is able, without interpreting any of it allegorically, except where the allegorical meaning is apparent in itself, i.e. commonly apparent to everyone. For if the sayings set down in Scripture for the instruction of the people are inspected, it seems that in mastering their meaning one arrives at a point, beyond which none but a man of the demonstrative class can extract from their apparent wording a meaning which is not apparent in them. This property is not found in any other sayings.

For those religious sayings in the precious Book which are expressed to everyone have three properties that indicate their miraculous character: (1) There exist none more completely persuasive and convincing to everyone than they. (2) Their meaning admits naturally of mastery, up to a point beyond which their allegorical interpretation (when they are of a kind to have such an interpretation) can only be found out by the demonstrative class. (3) They contain means of drawing the attention of the people of truth to the true allegorical meaning. This [character] is not found in the doctrines of the Ash'arites nor in those of the Mu'tazilites, i.e. their interpretations do not admit of mastery nor contain [means of] drawing attention to the truth, nor are they true; and this is why heresies have multiplied.

It is our desire to devote our time to this object and achieve it effectively, and if God grants us a respite of life we shall work steadily towards it in so far as this is made possible for us; and it may be that that work will serve as a starting point for our successors. For our soul is in the utmost sorrow and pain by reason of the evil fancies and perverted beliefs which have infiltrated this religion, and particularly such [afflictions] as have happened to it at the hands of people who claim an affinity with philosophy. For injuries from a friend are more severe than injuries from an enemy. I refer to the fact that philosophy is the friend and milk-sister of religion; thus injuries from people related to philosophy are the severest injuries [to religion]—apart from the enmity, hatred and quarrels which such [injuries] stir up between the two, which are companions by nature and lovers by essence and instinct. It has also been injured by a host of ignorant friends who claim an affinity with it: these are the sects which exist within it. But God directs all men aright and helps everyone to love Him; He unites their hearts in the fear of Him, and removes from them hatred and loathing by His grace and His mercy!

Indeed God has already removed many of these ills, ignorant ideas and misleading practices, by means of this triumphant rule. By it He has opened a way to many benefits, especially to the class of persons who have trodden the path of study and sought to know the truth. This [He has done] by summoning the masses to a middle way of knowing God the Glorious, [a way] which is raised above the low level of the followers of authority but is below the turbulence of the theologians; and by drawing the attention of the élite to their obligation to make a thorough study of the principles of religion. God is the Giver of success and the Guide by His Goodness.

Moses Maimonides
1135–1204

Moses ben Maimon, or Maimonides (referred to by Jewish scholars as "Rambam" for "Rabbi Moses ben Maimon"), was born at 1:00 P.M. on March 30, 1135, and died on December 13, 1204. The fact that we have such precise dates indicates the esteem with which he was held in his lifetime. As a boy in Córdoba, Spain, he was taught the Torah and the Talmud by his father, along with philosophy and science. At age 13, Maimonides and his family were forced to flee Spain after a time of peaceful coexistence between Jews and Muslims came to an end. Following a period of travel, which included a stay in Palestine, Maimonides and his family settled in Cairo, Egypt. There, Maimonides and his brother David became jewel merchants. Within a few years, Maimonides lost both his father and David, the latter killed in a shipwreck in the Indian Ocean during a business trip. Maimonides gave up the jewel business and turned to medicine. His expertise as a doctor eventually led to his appointment as a court physician for the ruler Saladin (the same Saladin who defeated Richard the Lionhearted in the Third Crusade). Maimonides' spiritual insights led to his being named the head of the Egyptian Jewish community. While serving both his religion and the state, he still found time to write extensively. His death in 1204 was mourned by Jews throughout the Mediterranean region, and his remains were taken from Cairo to Tiberias, on the Sea of Galilee, where his tomb is still visited today.

Maimonides' philosophical fame rests squarely on his major work, *The Guide for the Perplexed*. This work was written not for the majority of believers, but for those who knew both Jewish Law and Greek philosophy and were perplexed on how to harmonize the two. Though his religion was different, Maimonides faced questions similar to those of his neighboring Muslims and Christians: how to reconcile faith and reason. In the *Guide,* Maimonides asserts that there can be no conflict between faith and reason. Using Aristotle's philosophy (with some Neoplatonic spin), Maimonides believed he could answer a number of philosophical questions about the nature of God and of God's creation in a way that was consistent with sacred writings. Apparent disagreements between philosophy and theology frequently resulted from either taking figurative passages in Scripture literally or misunderstanding difficult philosophical arguments. Occasionally, philosophy is simply incapable of answering a given question and one must accept "the authority of Prophecy, which can teach things beyond the reach of human speculation." But even in such cases, philosophy can still provide general reasons for believing Scripture. For example, philosophy is inconclusive in determining whether or not the world is eternal. But whichever position we assume, says Maimonides, we can use that assumption to prove that God exists (when using arguments that Maimonides collected).

The selections from the *Guide* given here, in the M. Friedländer translation, present Maimonides' discussions of the nature of God, the arguments for God's existence, the temporal creation of the world, and the problem of evil. These passages greatly influenced Thomas Aquinas, and echoes of Maimonides' thought can be heard throughout Thomas's writings.

*   *   *

For selections from Maimonides' writings, see Jacob Samuel Minkin, *The World of Moses Maimonides,* with Selections From His Writings (New York: T. Yoseloff, 1957); Moses Maimonides, *The Guide for the Perplexed,* translated by Shlomo Pines (Chicago: Chicago University Press, 1963); and Moses Maimonides, *Rambam: Readings in the Philosophy of Moses Maimonides,* translated by Lenn Evan Goodman (New York: Viking Press, 1976).

Among the many general introductions to Maimonides' life and thought, more recent helpful studies include Abraham Joshua Heschel, *Maimonides: A Biography*, translated by Joachim Neugroschel (New York: Farrar, Straus & Giroux, 1982), and Oliver Leaman, *Moses Maimonides* (London: Routledge, 1990). For more specialized studies, see Carol Klein, *The Credo of Maimonides: A Synthesis* (New York: Philosophical Library, 1958); Jehuda Melber, *The Universality of Maimonides* (New York: Jonathan David, 1968); Menachem Marc Kellner, *Dogma in Medieval Jewish Thought: From Maimonides to Abravanel* (Oxford: Oxford University Press, 1986); Raymond L. Weiss, *Maimonides' Ethics* (Chicago: University of Chicago Press, 1991); Howard Kreisel, *Maimonides' Political Thought* (Albany, NY: SUNY Press, 1999); and David Hartman, *Maimonides' Torah and Philosophic Quest* (Philadelphia, PA: Jewish Publication Society, 2000). For collections of essays, see Salo Whittmay Baron, ed., *Essays on Maimonides: An Octocennial Volume* (New York: Columbia University Press, 1941); Joseph A. Buijs, ed., Maimonides: *A Collection of Critical Essays* (Notre Dame, IN: University of Notre Dame Press, 1988); and Eric L. Ormsby, ed., *Moses Maimonides and His Time* (Washington, DC: Catholic University of America Press, 1989).

THE GUIDE FOR THE PERPLEXED
(in part)

Part I

Chapter 51

There are many things whose existence is manifest and obvious; some of these are innate notions or objects of sensation, others are nearly so; and in fact they would require no proof if man had been left in his primitive state. Such are the existence of motion, of man's free will, of phases of production and destruction, and of the natural properties perceived by the senses, e.g., the heat of fire, the coldness of water, and many other similar things. False notions, however, may be spread either by a person labouring under error, or by one who has some particular end in view, and who establishes theories contrary to the real nature of things, by denying the existence of things perceived by the senses, or by affirming the existence of what does not exist. Philosophers are thus required to establish by proof things which are self-evident, and to disprove the existence of things which only exist in man's imagination. Thus Aristotle gives a proof for the existence of motion, because it had been denied; he disproves the reality of atoms, because it had been asserted.

To the same class belongs the rejection of essential attributes in reference to God. For it is a self-evident truth that the attribute is not inherent in the object to which it is ascribed, but it is superadded to its essence, and is consequently an *accident*; if the attribute denoted the essence of the object, it would be either mere tautology, as if, e.g., one would say "man is man," or the explanation of a name, as, e.g., "man is a speaking animal"; for the words "speaking animal" include the true essence of man, and there is no third element besides life and speech in the definition of man; when he, therefore, is described by the attributes of life and speech, these are nothing but an explanation of the name "man," that is to say, that the thing which is called man, consists of life and speech. It will now be clear that the attribute must be one of two things, either the essence of the object described—in that case it is a mere explanation of a name, and on that account we might admit the attribute in reference to God, but we reject it from another cause as will be shown—or the attribute is something different from the object described, some extraneous superadded element; in that case the attribute would be an accident, and he who merely rejects the appellation "accidents" in reference to the attributes of God, does not thereby alter their character; for everything superadded to the essence of an object joins it without forming part of its essential properties, and that constitutes an accident. Add to this the logical consequence of admitting many attributes, viz., the existence of many eternal beings. There cannot be any belief in the unity of God except by admitting that He is one simple substance, without any composition or plurality of elements; one from whatever side you view it, and by whatever test you examine it; not divisible into two parts in any way and by any cause, nor capable of any form of plurality either objectively or subjectively, as will be proved in this treatise.

Some thinkers have gone so far as to say that the attributes of God are neither His essence nor anything extraneous to His essence. This is like the assertion of some theorists, that the ideals, i.e., the *universalia,* are neither existing nor non-existent, and like the views of others, that the atom does not fill a definite place, but keeps an atom of space occupied; that man has no freedom of action at all, but has acquirement. Such things are only said; they exist only in words, not in thought, much less in reality. But as you know, and as all know who do not delude themselves, these theories are preserved by a multitude of words, by misleading similes sustained by declamation and invective, and by numerous methods borrowed both from dialectics and sophistry. If after uttering them and supporting them by such words, a man were to examine for himself his own belief on this subject, he would see nothing but confusion and stupidity in an endeavour to prove the existence of things which do not exist, or to find a mean between two opposites that have no mean. Or is there a mean between existence and non-existence, or between the identity and non-identity of two things? But, as we said, to such absurdities men were forced by the great licence given to the imagination, and by the fact that every existing material thing is necessarily imagined as a certain substance possessing several attributes; for nothing has ever been found that consists of one simple substance without any attribute. Guided by such imaginations, men thought that God was also composed of many different elements, viz., of His essence and of the attributes superadded to His essence. Following up this comparison, some believed that God was corporeal, and that He possessed attributes; others, abandoning this theory, denied the corporeality, but retained the attributes. The adherence to the literal sense of the text of Holy Writ is the source of all this error, as I shall show in some of the chapters devoted to this theme.

CHAPTER 52

Every description of an object by an affirmative attribute, which includes the assertion that an object is of a certain kind, must be made in one of the following five ways:—

First. The object is described by its *definition,* as e.g., man is described as a being that lives and has reason; such a description, containing the true essence of the object, is, as we have already shown, nothing else but the explanation of a name. All agree that this kind of description cannot be given of God; for there are no previous causes to His existence, by which He could be defined: and on that account it is a well-known principle, received by all the philosophers, who are precise in their statements, that no definition can be given of God.

Secondly. An object is described by *part of its definition,* as when, e.g., man is described as a living being or as a rational being. This kind of description includes the necessary connection [of the two ideas]; for when we say that every man is rational we mean by it that every being which has the characteristics of man must also have reason. All agree that this kind of description is inappropriate in reference to God; for if we were to speak of a portion of His essence, we should consider His essence to be a compound. The inappropriateness of this kind of description in reference to God is the same as that of the preceding kind.

Thirdly. An object is described by something different from its true essence, by something that does not complement or establish the essence of the object. The description, therefore, relates to a *quality;* but quality, in its most general sense, is an accident. If God could be described in this way, He would be the substratum of accidents: a sufficient reason for rejecting the idea that He possesses quality, since it diverges from the true conception of His essence. It is surprising how those who admit the application of attributes to God can reject, in reference to Him, comparison and qualification. For when they say "He cannot be qualified," they can only mean that He possesses no quality; and yet every positive essential attribute of an object either constitutes its essence,—and in that case it is identical with the essence,—or it contains a quality of the object.

There are, as you know, four kinds of quality; I will give you instances of attributes of each kind, in order to show you that this class of attributes cannot possibly be applied to God. (*a*) A man is described by any of his intellectual or moral qualities, or by any of the dispositions appertaining to him as an animate being, when, e.g., we speak of a person who is a carpenter, or who shrinks from sin, or who is ill. It makes no difference whether we say, a carpenter, or a sage, or a physician; by all these we represent certain physical dispositions; nor does it make any difference whether we say "sin-fearing" or "merciful." Every trade, every profession, and every settled habit of man are certain physical dispositions. All this is clear to those who have occupied themselves with the study of Logic. (*b*) A thing is described by some physical quality it possesses, or by the absence of the same, e.g., as being soft or hard. It makes no difference whether we say "soft or hard," or "strong or weak"; in both cases we speak of physical conditions. (*c*) A man is described by his passive qualities, or by his emotions; we speak, e.g., of a person who is passionate, irritable, timid, merciful, without implying that these conditions have become permanent. The description of a thing by its color, taste, heat, cold, dryness, and moisture, belongs also to this class of attributes. (*d*) A thing is described by any of its qualities resulting from quantity as such; we speak, e.g., of a thing which is long, short, curved, straight, etc.

Consider all these and similar attributes, and you will find that they cannot be employed in reference to God. He is not a magnitude that any quality resulting from quantity as such could be possessed by Him; He is not affected by external influences, and therefore does not possess any quality resulting from emotion. He is not subject to physical conditions, and therefore does not possess strength or similar qualities; He is not an animate being, that He should have a certain disposition of the soul, or acquire certain properties, as meekness, modesty, etc., or be in a state to which animate beings as such are subject, as, e.g., in that of health or of illness. Hence it follows that no attribute coming under the head of quality in its widest sense, can be predicated of God. Consequently, these three classes of attributes, describing the essence of a thing, or part of the essence, or a quality of it, are clearly inadmissible in reference to God, for they imply composition, which, as we shall prove, is out of question as regards the Creator. We say, with regard to this latter point, that He is absolutely One.

Fourthly. A thing is described by its *relation* to another thing, e.g., to time, to space, or to a different individual; thus we say, Zaid, the father of A, or the partner of B, or who dwells at a certain place, or who lived at a stated time. This kind of attribute does not necessarily imply plurality or change in the essence of the object described; for the same Zaid, to whom reference is made, is the partner of Amru, the father of Becr, the master of Khalid, the friend of Zaid, dwells in a certain house, and was born in a certain year. Such relations are not the essence of a thing, nor are they so intimately connected with it as qualities. At first thought, it would seem that they may be employed in reference to God, but after careful and thorough consideration we are convinced of their inadmissibility. It is quite clear that there is no relation between God and time or space. For time is an accident connected with motion, in so far as the latter includes the relation of anteriority and posteriority, and is expressed by number, as is explained in books devoted to this subject; and since motion is one of the conditions to which only material bodies are subject, and God is immaterial, there can be no relation between Him and time. Similarly there is no relation between Him and space. But what we have to investigate and to examine is this: whether some real relation exists between God and any of the substances created by Him, by which He could be described? That there is no correlation between Him and any of His creatures can easily be seen; for the characteristic of two objects correlative to each other is the equality of their reciprocal relation. Now, as God has absolute existence, while all other beings have only possible existence, as we shall show, there consequently cannot be any correlation [between God and His creatures]. That a certain kind of relation does exist between them is by some considered possible, but wrongly. It is impossible to imagine a relation between intellect and sight, although, as we believe, the same kind of existence is common to both; how, then, could a relation be imagined between any creature and God, who has nothing in common with any other being; for even the term existence is applied to Him and other things, according to our opinion, only by way of pure homonymity. Consequently there is no relation whatever between Him and any other being. For whenever we speak of a relation between two things, these belong to the same kind; but when two things belong to different kinds though of the same class, there is no relation between them. We therefore do not say, this red compared with that green, is more, or less, or equally intense, although both belong to the same class—color; when they belong to two different classes, there does not appear to exist any relation between them, not even to a man of ordinary intellect, although the two things belong to the same category; e.g., between a hundred cubits and the heat of pepper there is no relation, the one being a quality, the other a quantity; or between wisdom and sweetness, between meekness and bitterness, although all these come under the head of quality in its more general signification. How, then, could there be any relation between God and His creatures, considering the important difference between them in respect to true existence, the greatest of all differences. Besides, if any relation existed between them, God would be subject to the accident of relation; and although that would not be an accident to the essence of God, it would still be, to some extent, a kind of accident. You would, therefore, be wrong if you applied affirmative attributes in their literal sense to God, though they contained only relations; these, however, are the most appropriate of all attributes, to be employed, in a less strict sense, in reference to God, because they do not imply that a plurality of eternal things exists, or that any change takes place in the essence of God, when those things change to which God is in relation.

Fifthly. A thing is described by its *actions;* I do not mean by "its actions" the inherent capacity for a certain work, as is expressed in "carpenter," "painter," or "smith"—for these belong to the class of qualities which have been mentioned above—but I mean the action the latter has performed—we speak, e.g., of Zaid, who made this door, built that wall, wove that garment. This kind of attribute is separate from the essences of the thing described, and, therefore, appropriate to be employed in describing the Creator, especially since we know that these different actions do not imply that different elements must be contained in the substance of the agent, by which the different actions are produced, as will be explained. On the contrary, all the actions of God emanate from His essence, not from any extraneous thing superadded to His essence, as we have shown.

What we have explained in the present chapter is this: that God is one in every respect, containing no plurality or any element superadded to His essence: and that the many attributes of different significations applied in Scripture to God, originate in the multitude of His actions, not in a plurality existing in His essence, and are partly employed with the object of conveying to us some notion of His perfection, in accordance with what we consider perfection, as has been explained by us. The possibility of one simple substance excluding plurality, though accomplishing different actions, will be illustrated by examples in the next chapter.

CHAPTER 53

The circumstance which caused men to believe in the existence of divine attributes is similar to that which caused others to believe in the corporeality of God. The latter have not arrived at that belief by speculation, but by following the literal sense of certain passages in the Bible. The same is the case with the attributes; when in the books of the Prophets and of the Law, God is described by attributes, such passages are taken in their literal sense, and it is then believed that God possesses attributes; as if He were to be exalted above corporeality, and not above things connected with corporeality, i.e., the accidents, I mean psychical dispositions, all of which are qualities [and connected with corporeality]. Every attribute which the followers of this doctrine assume to be essential to the Creator, you will find to express, although they do not distinctly say so, a quality similar to those which they are accustomed to notice in the bodies of all living beings. We apply to all such passages the principle, "The Torah speaketh in the language of man," and say that the object of all these terms is to describe God as the most perfect being, not as possessing those qualities which are only perfections in relation to created living beings. Many of the attributes express different acts of God, but that difference does not necessitate any difference as regards Him from whom the acts proceed. This fact, viz., that from one agency different effects may result, although that agency has not free will, and much more so if it has free will, I will illustrate by an instance taken from our own sphere. Fire melts certain things and makes others hard, it boils and burns, it bleaches and blackens. If we described the fire as bleaching, blackening, burning, boiling, hardening and melting, we should be correct, and yet he who does not know the nature of fire, would think that it included six different elements, one by which it blackens, another by which it bleaches, a third by which it boils, a fourth by which it consumes, a fifth by which it melts, a sixth by which it hardens things—actions which are opposed to one another, and of which each has its peculiar property. He, however, who knows the nature of fire, will know that by virtue of one quality in action, namely, by heat, it produces all these effects. If this is the case with that which is done by nature, how much more is it the case with regard to beings that act by free will, and still more with regard to God, who is above all description. If we, therefore, perceive in God certain relations of various kinds—for wisdom in us is different from power, and power from will—it does by no means follow that different elements are really contained in Him, that He contains one element by which He knows, another by which He wills, and another by which He exercises power, as is, in fact, the signification of the attributes of God according to the Attributists. Some of them express it plainly, and enumerate the attributes as elements added to the essence. Others, however, are more reserved with regard to this matter, but indicate their opinion, though they do not express it in distinct and intelligible words. Thus, e.g., some of them say: "God is omnipotent by His essence, wise by His essence, living by His essence, and endowed with a will by His essence." (I will mention to you, as an instance, man's reason, which being one faculty and implying no plurality, enables him to know many arts and sciences; by the same faculty man is able to sow, to do carpenter's work, to weave, to build, to study, to acquire a knowledge of geometry, and to govern a state. These various acts resulting from one simple faculty, which involves no plurality, are very numerous; their number, that is, the number of the actions originating in man's reason, is almost infinite. It is therefore intelligible how in reference to God, those different actions can be caused by one simple substance, that does not include any plurality or any additional element. The attributes found in Holy Scripture are either qualifications of His actions, without any reference to His essence, or indicate absolute perfection, but do not imply that the essence of God is a compound of various elements.) For in not admitting the *term* "compound," they do not reject the idea of a compound when they admit a substance with attributes.

There still remains one difficulty which led them to that error, and which I am now going to mention. Those who assert the existence of the attributes do not found their opinion on the variety of God's actions; they say it is true that one substance can be the source of various effects, but His essential attributes cannot be qualifications of His actions, because it is impossible to imagine that the Creator created Himself. They vary with regard to the so-called essential attributes—I mean as regards their number—according to the text of the Scripture which each of them follows. I will enumerate those on which all agree, and the knowledge of which they believe that they have derived from reasoning, not from some words of the Prophets, namely, the following four:—life, power, wisdom, and will. They believe that these are four different things, and such perfections as cannot possibly be absent from the Creator, and that these cannot be qualifications of His actions. This is their opinion. But you must know that wisdom and life in reference to God are not different from each other; for in every being that is conscious of itself, life and wisdom are the same thing, that is to say, if by wisdom we understand the consciousness of self. Besides, the subject and the object of that consciousness are undoubtedly identical [as regards God]; for according to our opinion, He is not composed of an element that apprehends, and another that does not apprehend; He is not like man, who is a combination of a conscious soul and an unconscious body. If, therefore, by "wisdom" we mean the faculty of self-consciousness, wisdom and life are one and the same thing. They, however, do not speak of wisdom in this sense, but of His power to apprehend His creatures. There is also no doubt that power and will do not exist in God in reference to Himself; for He cannot have power or will as regards Himself; we cannot imagine such a thing. They take these attributes as different relations between God and His creatures, signifying that He has power in creating things, will in giving to things existence as He desires, and wisdom in knowing what He created. Consequently, these attributes do not refer to the essence of God, but express relations between Him and His creatures.

Therefore we, who truly believe in the Unity of God, declare, that as we do not believe that some element is included in His essence by which He created the heavens, another by which He created the [four] elements, a third by which He created the ideals, in the same way we reject the idea that His essence contains an element by which He has power, another element by which He has will, and a third by which He has a knowledge of His creatures. On the contrary, He is a simple essence, without any additional element whatever; He created the universe, and knows it, but not by any extraneous force. There is no difference whether these various attributes refer to His actions or to relations between Him and His works; in fact, these relations, as we have also shown, exist only in the thoughts of men. This is what we must believe concerning the attributes occurring in the books of the Prophets; some may also be taken as expressive of the perfection of God by way of comparison with what we consider as perfections in us. . . .

*　　*　　*

CHAPTER 58

This chapter is even more recondite than the preceding. Know that the negative attributes of God are the true attributes: they do not include any incorrect notions or any deficiency whatever in reference to God, while positive attributes imply polytheism, and are inadequate, as we have already shown. It is now necessary to explain how negative expressions can in a certain sense be employed as attributes, and how they are distinguished from positive attributes. Then I shall show that we cannot describe the Creator by any means except by negative attributes. An attribute does not exclusively belong to the one object to which it is related; while qualifying one thing, it can also be employed to qualify other things, and is in that case not peculiar to that one thing. E.g., if you see an object from a distance, and on enquiring what it is, are told that it is a living being, you have certainly learnt an attribute of the object seen, and although that attribute does not exclusively belong to the object perceived, it expresses that the object is not a plant or a mineral. Again, if a man is in a certain house, and you know that something is in the house, but not exactly what, you ask what is in that house, and you are told, not a plant nor a mineral. You have thereby obtained some special knowledge of the thing; you have learnt that it is a living being, although you do not yet know what kind of a living being it is. The negative attributes have this in common with the positive, that they necessarily circumscribe the object to some extent, although such circumscription consists only in the exclusion of what otherwise would not be excluded. In the following point, however, the negative attributes are distinguished from the positive. The positive attributes, although not peculiar to one thing, describe a portion of what we desire to know, either some part of its essence or some of its accidents; the negative attributes, on the other hand, do not, as regards the essence of the thing which we desire to know, in any way tell us what it is, except it be indirectly, as has been shown in the instance given by us.

After this introduction, I would observe that,—as has already been shown— God's existence is absolute, that it includes no composition, as will be proved, and that we comprehend only the fact that He exists, not His essence. Consequently it is a false assumption to hold that He has any positive attribute; for He does not possess existence in addition to His essence; it therefore cannot be said that the one may be described as an attribute [of the other]; much less has He [in addition to His existence] a compound essence, consisting of two constituent elements to which the attribute could refer; still less has He accidents, which could be described by an attribute. Hence it is clear that He has no positive attribute whatever. The negative attributes, however, are those which are necessary to direct the mind to the truths which we must believe concerning God; for, on the one hand, they do not imply any plurality, and, on the other, they convey to man the highest possible knowledge of God; e.g., it has been established by proof that some being must exist besides those things which can be perceived by the senses, or apprehended by the mind; when we say of this being, that it exists, we mean that its non-existence is impossible. We then perceive that such a being is not, for instance, like the four elements, which are inanimate, and we therefore say that it is living, expressing thereby that it is not dead. We call such a being incorporeal, because we notice that it is unlike the heavens, which are living, but material. Seeing that it is also different from the intellect, which, though incorporeal and living, owes its existence to some cause, we say it is the first, expressing thereby that its existence is not due to any cause. We further notice, that the existence, that is the essence, of this being is not limited to its own existence; many existences emanate from it, and its influence is not like that of the fire in producing heat, or that of the sun in sending forth light, but consists in constantly giving them stability and order by well-established rule, as we shall show: we say, on that account, it has power, wisdom, and will, i.e., it is not feeble or ignorant, or hasty, and does not abandon its creatures; when we say that it is not feeble, we mean that its existence is capable of producing the existence of many other things; by saying that it is not ignorant, we mean "it perceives" or "it lives,"—for everything that perceives is living—by saying "it is not hasty, and does not abandon its creatures," we mean that all these creatures preserve a certain order and arrangement; they are not left to themselves; they are not produced aimlessly, but whatever condition they receive from that being is given with design and intention. We thus learn that there is no other being like unto God, and we say that He is One, i.e., there are not more Gods than one.

It has thus been shown that every attribute predicated of God either denotes the quality of an action, or—when the attribute is intended to convey some idea of the Divine Being itself, and not of His actions—the negation of the opposite. Even these negative attributes must not be formed and applied to God, except in the way in which, as you know, sometimes an attribute is negatived in reference to a thing, although that attribute can naturally never be applied to it in the same sense, as, e.g., we say, "This wall does not see." Those who read the present work are aware that, notwithstanding all the efforts of the mind, we can obtain no knowledge of the essence of the heavens—a revolving substance which has been measured by us in spans and cubits, and examined even as regards the proportions of the several spheres to each other and respecting most of their motions—although we know that they must consist of matter and form; but the matter not being the same as sublunary matter, we can only describe the heavens in terms expressing negative properties, but not in terms denoting positive qualities. Thus we say that the heavens are not light, not heavy, not passive and therefore not subject to impressions, and that they do not possess the sensations of taste and smell; or we use similar negative attributes. All this we do, because we do not know their substance. What, then, can be the result of our efforts, when we try to obtain a knowledge of a Being that is free from substance, that is most simple, whose existence is absolute, and not due to any cause, to whose perfect essence nothing can be superadded, and whose perfection consists, as we have shown, in the absence of all defects. All we understand is the fact that He exists, that He is a Being to whom none of His creatures is similar, who has nothing in common with them, who does not include plurality, who is never too feeble to produce other beings, and whose relation to the universe is that of a steersman to a boat; and even this is not a real relation, a real simile, but serves only to convey to us the idea that God rules the universe; that is, that He gives it duration, and preserves its necessary arrangement. This subject will be treated more fully. Praised be He! In the contemplation of His essence, our comprehension and knowledge prove insufficient; in the examination of His works, how they necessarily result from His will, our knowledge proves to be ignorance, and in the endeavor to extol Him in words, all our efforts in speech are mere weakness and failure!

CHAPTER 59

The following question might perhaps be asked: Since there is no possibility of obtaining a knowledge of the true essence of God, and since it has also been proved that the only thing that man can apprehend of Him is the fact that He exists, and that all positive attributes are inadmissible, as has been shown; what is the difference among those who have obtained a knowledge of God? Must not the knowledge obtained by our teacher Moses, and by Solomon, be the same as that obtained by any one of the lowest class of philosophers, since there can be no addition to this knowledge? But, on the other hand, it is generally accepted among theologians and also among philosophers, that there can be a great difference between two persons as regards the knowledge of God obtained by them. Know that this is really the case, that those who have obtained a knowledge of God differ greatly from each other, for in the same way as by each additional attribute an object is more specified, and is brought nearer to the true apprehension of the observer, so by each additional negative attribute you advance toward the knowledge of God, and you are nearer to it than he who does not negative, in reference to God, those qualities which you are convinced by proof must be negatived. There may thus be a man who after having earnestly devoted many years to the pursuit of one science, and to the true understanding of its principles, till he is fully convinced of its truths, has obtained as the sole result of this study the conviction that a certain quality must be negatived in reference to God, and the capacity of demonstrating that it is impossible to apply it to Him. Superficial thinkers will have no proof for this, will doubtfully ask, Is that thing existing in the Creator, or not? And those who are deprived of sight will positively ascribe it to God, although it has been clearly shown that He does not possess it. E.g., while I show that God is incorporeal, another doubts and is not certain whether He is corporeal or incorporeal; others even positively declare that He is corporeal, and appear before the Lord with that belief. Now see how great the difference is between these three men; the first is undoubtedly nearest to the Almighty; the second is remote, and the third still more distant from Him. If there be a fourth person who holds himself convinced by proof that emotions are impossible in God, while the first who rejects the corporeality, is not convinced of that impossibility, that fourth person is undoubtedly nearer the knowledge of God than the first, and so on, so that a person who, convinced by proof, negatives a number of things in reference to God, which according to our belief may possibly be in Him or emanate from Him, is undoubtedly a more perfect man than we are, and would surpass us still more if we positively believed these things to be properties of God. It will now be clear to you, that every time you establish by proof the negation of a thing in reference to God, you become more perfect, while with every additional positive assertion you follow your imagination and recede from the true knowledge of God. Only by such ways must we approach the knowledge of God, and by such researches and studies as would show us the inapplicability of what is inadmissible as regards the Creator, not by such methods as would prove the necessity of ascribing to Him anything extraneous to His essence, or asserting that He has a certain perfection, when we find it to be a perfection in relation to us. The perfections are all to some extent acquired properties, and a property which must be acquired does not exist in everything capable of making such acquisition.

You must bear in mind, that by affirming anything of God, you are removed from Him in two respects; first, whatever you affirm, is only a perfection in relation to us; secondly, He does not possess anything superadded to this essence; His essence includes all His perfections, as we have shown. Since it is a well-known fact that even that knowledge of God which is accessible to man cannot be attained except by negations, and that negations do not convey a true idea of the being to which they refer, all people, both of past and present generations, declared that God cannot be the object of human comprehension, that none but Himself comprehends what He is, and that our knowledge consists in knowing that we are unable truly to comprehend Him. All philosophers say, "He has overpowered us by His grace, and is invisible to us through the intensity of His light," like the sun which cannot be perceived by eyes which are too weak to bear its rays. Much more has been said on this topic, but it is useless to repeat it here. The idea is best expressed in the book of Psalms, "Silence is praise to Thee" (lxv. 2). It is a very expressive remark on this subject; for whatever we utter with the intention of extolling and of praising Him, contains something that cannot be applied to God, and includes derogatory expressions; it is therefore more becoming to be silent, and to be content with intellectual reflection, as has been recommended by men of the highest culture, in the words "Commune with your own heart upon your bed, and be still" (Ps. iv. 4). You must surely know the following celebrated passage in the Talmud—would that all passages in the Talmud were like that!—although it is known to you, I quote it literally, as I wish to point out to you the ideas contained in it: "A certain person, reading prayers in the presence of Rabbi Haninah, said, 'God, the great, the valiant and the tremendous, the powerful, the strong and the mighty.'— The rabbi said to him, 'Have you finished all the praises of your Master?' The three epithets, 'God, the great, the valiant and the tremendous,' we should not have applied to God, had Moses not mentioned them in the Law, and had not the men of the Great Synagogue come forward subsequently and established their use in the prayer; and you say all this! Let this be illustrated by a parable. There was once an earthly king, possessing millions of gold coin; he was praised for owning millions of silver coin; was this not really dispraise to him?" Thus for the opinion of the pious rabbi. Consider, first, how repulsive and annoying the accumulation of all these positive attributes was to him; next, how he showed that if we had only to follow our reason, we should never have composed these prayers, and we should not have uttered any of them. It has, however, become necessary to address men in words that should leave some idea in their minds, and, in accordance with the saying of our Sages, "The Torah speaks in the language of men," the Creator has been described to us in terms of our own perfections; but we should not on that account have uttered any other than the three above-mentioned attributes, and we should not have used them as names of God except when meeting with them in reading the Law. Subsequently, the men of the Great Synagogue, who were prophets, introduced these expressions also into the prayer, but we should not on that account use [in our prayers] any other attributes of God. The principal lesson to be derived from this passage is that there are two reasons for our employing those phrases in our prayers: first, they occur in the Pentateuch; secondly, the Prophets introduced them into the prayer. Were it not for the first reason, we should never have uttered them; and were it not for the second reason, we should not have copied them from the Pentateuch to recite them in our prayers; how then could we approve of the use of those numerous attributes! You also learn from this that we ought not to mention and employ in our prayers all the attributes we find applied to God in the books of the Prophets; for he does not say, "Were it not that Moses, our Teacher, said them, we should not have been able to use them"; but he adds another condition—"and had not the men of the Great Synagogue come forward and established their use in the prayer," because only for that reason are we allowed to use them in our prayers. We cannot approve of what those foolish persons do who are extravagant in praise, fluent and prolix in the prayers they compose, and in the hymns they make in the desire to approach the Creator. They describe God in attributes which would be an offence if applied to a human being; for those persons have no knowledge of these great and important principles, which are not accessible to the ordinary intelligence of man. Treating the Creator as a familiar object, they describe Him and speak of Him in any expressions they think proper; they eloquently continue to praise Him in that manner, and believe that they can thereby influence Him and produce an effect on Him. If they find some phrase suited to their object in the words of the Prophets they are still more inclined to consider that they are free to make use of such texts—which should at least be explained—to employ them in their literal sense, to derive new expressions from them, to form from them numerous variations, and to found whole compositions on them. This license is frequently met with in the compositions of the singers, preachers, and others who imagine themselves to be able to compose a poem. Such authors write things which partly are real heresy, partly contain such folly and absurdity that they naturally cause those who hear them to laugh, but also to feel grieved at the thought that such things can be uttered in reference to God. Were it not that I pitied the authors for their defects, and did not wish to injure them, I should have cited some passages to show you their mistakes; besides, the fault of their compositions is obvious to all intelligent persons. You must consider it, and think thus: If slander and libel is a great sin, how much greater is the sin of those who speak with looseness of tongue in reference to God, and describe Him by attributes which are far below Him; and I declare that they not only commit an ordinary sin, but unconsciously at least incur the guilt of profanity and blasphemy. This applies both to the multitude that listens to such prayers, and to the foolish man that recites them. Men, however, who understand the fault of such compositions, and, nevertheless, recite them, may be classed, according to my opinion, among those to whom the following words are applied: "And the children of Israel used words that were not right against the Lord their God" (2 Kings xvii. 9); and "utter error against the Lord" (Isa. xxxii. 6). If you are of those who regard the honor of their Creator, do not listen in any way to them, much less utter what they say, and still less compose such prayers, knowing how great is the offence of one who hurls aspersions against the Supreme Being. There is no necessity at all for you to use positive attributes of God with the view of magnifying Him in your thoughts, or to go beyond the limits which the men of the Great Synagogue have introduced in the prayers and in the blessings, for this is sufficient for all purposes, and even more than sufficient, as Rabbi Haninah said. Other attributes, such as occur in the books of the Prophets, may be uttered when we meet with them in reading those books; but we must bear in mind what has already been explained, that they are either attributes of God's actions, or expressions implying the negation of the opposite. This likewise should not be divulged to the multitude; but a reflection of this kind is fitted for the few only who believe that the glorification of God does not consist in *uttering* that which is in *reflecting* on that on which man should reflect.

We will now conclude our exposition of the wise words of R. Haninah. He does not employ any such simile as: "A king who possesses millions of gold denarii, and is praised as having hundreds"; for this would imply that God's perfections, although more perfect than those ascribed to man are still of the same kind; but this is not the case, as has been proved. The excellence of the simile consists in the words: "who possesses golden denarii, and is praised as having silver denarii"; this implies that these attributes, though perfections as regards ourselves, are not such as regards God; in reference to Him they would all be defects, as is distinctly suggested in the remark, "Is this not an offence to Him?"

I have already told you that all these attributes, whatever perfection they may denote according to your idea, imply defects in reference to God, if applied to Him in the same sense as they are used in reference to ourselves. Solomon has already given us sufficient instruction on this subject by saying, "For God is in heaven, and thou upon earth; therefore let thy words be few" (Eccles. v. 2).

CHAPTER 60

I will give you in this chapter some illustrations, in order that you may better understand the propriety of forming as many negative attributes as possible, and the impropriety of ascribing to God any positive attributes. A person may know for certain that a "ship" is in existence, but he may not know to what object that name is applied, whether to a substance or to an accident; a second person then learns that the ship is not an accident; a third, that it is not a mineral; a fourth, that it is not a plant growing in the earth; a fifth, that it is not a body whose parts are joined together by nature; a sixth, that it is not a flat object like boards or doors; a seventh, that it is not a sphere; an eighth, that it is not pointed; a ninth, that it is not round-shaped; nor equilateral; a tenth, that it is not solid. It is clear that this tenth person has almost arrived at the correct notion of a "ship" by the foregoing negative attributes, as if he had exactly the same notion as those have who imagine it to be a wooden substance which is hollow, long, and composed of many pieces of wood, that is to say, who know it by positive attributes. Of the other persons in our illustration, each one is more remote from the correct notion of a ship than the next mentioned, so that the first knows nothing about it but the name. In the same manner you will come nearer to the knowledge and comprehension of God by the negative attributes. But you must be careful, in what you negative, to negative by proof, not by mere words, for each time you ascertain by proof that a certain thing, believed to exist in the Creator, must be negatived, you have undoubtedly come one step nearer to the knowledge of God.

   It is in this sense that some men come very near to God, and others remain exceedingly remote from Him, not in the sense of those who are deprived of vision, and believe that God occupies a place, which man can physically approach or from which he can recede. Examine this well, know it, and be content with it. The way which will bring you nearer to God has been clearly shown to you; walk in it, if you have the desire. On the other hand, there is a great danger in applying positive attributes to God. For it has been shown that every perfection we could imagine, even if existing in God in accordance with the opinion of those who assert the existence of attributes, would in reality not be of the same kind as that imagined by us, but would only be called by the same name, according to our explanation; it would in fact amount to a negation. Suppose, e.g., you say He has knowledge, and that knowledge, which admits of no change and of no plurality, embraces many changeable things; His knowledge remains unaltered, while new things are constantly formed, and His knowledge of a thing before it exists, while it exists, and when it has ceased to exist, is the same without the least change: you would thereby declare that His knowledge is not like ours; and similarly that His existence is not like ours. You thus necessarily arrive at some negation, without obtaining a true conception of an essential attribute; on the contrary, you are led to assume that there is a plurality in God, and to believe that He, though one essence, has several unknown attributes. For if you intend to affirm them, you cannot compare them with those attributes known by us, and they are consequently not of the same kind. You are, as it were, brought by the belief in the reality of the attributes, to say that God is one subject of which several things are predicated; though the subject is not like ordinary subjects, and the predicates are not like ordinary predicates. This belief would ultimately lead us to associate other things with God, and not to believe that He is One. For of every subject certain things can undoubtedly be predicated, and although in reality subject and predicate are combined in one thing, by the actual definition they consist of two elements, the notion contained in the subject not being the same as that contained in the predicate. In the course of this treatise it will be proved to you that God cannot be a compound, and that He is simple in the strictest sense of the word.

I do not merely declare that he who affirms attributes of God has not sufficient knowledge concerning the Creator, admits some association with God, or conceives Him to be different from what He is; but I say that he unconsciously loses his belief in God. For he whose knowledge concerning a thing is insufficient, understands one part of it while he is ignorant of the other, as, e.g., a person who knows that man possesses life, but does not know that man possesses understanding; but in reference to God, in whose real existence there is no plurality, it is impossible that one thing should be known, and another unknown. Similarly he who associates an object with [the properties of] another object, conceives a true and correct notion of the one object, and applies that notion also to the other, while those who admit the attributes of God, do not consider them as identical with His essence, but as extraneous elements. Again, he who conceives an incorrect notion of an object, must necessarily have a correct idea of the object to some extent; he, however, who says that taste belongs to the category of quantity has not, according to my opinion, an incorrect notion of taste, but is entirely ignorant of its nature, for he does not know to what object the term "taste" is to be applied.—This is a very difficult subject; consider it well.

According to this explanation you will understand, that those who do not recognize, in reference to God, the negation of things, which others negative by clear proof, are deficient in the knowledge of God, and are remote from comprehending Him. Consequently, the smaller the number of things is which a person can negative in relation to God, the less he knows of Him, as has been explained in the beginning of this chapter; but the man who affirms an attribute of God, knows nothing but the name; for the object to which, in his imagination, he applies that name, does not exist; it is a mere fiction and invention, as if he applied that name to a non-existing being, for there is, in reality, no such object. E.g., some one has heard of the elephant, and knows that it is an animal, and wishes to know its form and nature. A person, who is either misled or misleading, tells him it is an animal with one leg, three wings, lives in the depth of the sea, has a transparent body; its face is wide like that of a man, has the same form and shape, speaks like a man, flies sometimes in the air, and sometimes swims like a fish. I should not say, that he described the elephant incorrectly, or that he has an insufficient knowledge of the elephant, but I would say that the thing thus described is an invention and fiction, and that in reality there exists nothing like it; it is a non-existing being, called by the name of a really existing being, and like the griffin, the centaur, and similar imaginary combinations for which simple and compound names have been borrowed from real things. The present case is analogous; namely, God, praised be His name, exists, and His existence has been proved to be absolute and perfectly simple, as I shall explain. If such a simple, absolutely existing essence were said to have attributes, as has been contended, and were combined with extraneous elements, it would in no way be an existing thing, as has been proved by us; and when we say that that essence, which is called "God," is a substance with many properties by which it can be described, we apply that name to an object which does not at all exist. Consider, therefore, what are the consequences of affirming attributes to God! As to those attributes of

God which occur in the Pentateuch, or in the books of the Prophets, we must assume that they are exclusively employed, as has been stated by us, to convey to us some notion of the perfections of the Creator, or to express qualities of actions emanating from Him.

*   *   *

PART II

INTRODUCTION

Twenty-five of the propositions which are employed in the proof for the existence of God, or in the arguments demonstrating that God is neither corporeal nor a force connected with a material being, or that He is One, have been fully established, and their correctness is beyond doubt. Aristotle and the Peripatetics who followed him have proved each of these propositions. There is, however, one proposition which we do not accept—namely, the proposition which affirms the Eternity of the Universe, but we will admit it for the present, because by doing so we shall be enabled clearly to demonstrate our own theory.

PROPOSITION I: The existence of an infinite magnitude is impossible.

PROPOSITION II: The coexistence of an infinite number of finite magnitudes is impossible.

PROPOSITION III: The existence of an infinite number of causes and effects is impossible, even if these were not magnitudes; if, e.g., one Intelligence were the cause of a second, the second the cause of a third, the third the cause of a fourth, and so on, the series could not be continued ad infinitum.

PROPOSITION IV: Four categories are subject to change:—
    (a.) *Substance.*—Changes which affect the substance of a thing are called genesis and destruction.
    (b.) *Quantity.*—Changes in reference to quantity are increase and decrease.
    (c.) *Quality.*—Changes in the qualities of things are transformations.
    (d.) *Place.*—Change of place is called motion.

    The term "motion" is properly applied to change of place, but is also used in a general sense of all kinds of changes.

PROPOSITION V: Motion implies change and transition from potentiality to actuality.

PROPOSITION VI: The motion of a thing is either essential or accidental; or it is due to an external force, or to the participation of the thing in the motion of another thing. This latter kind of motion is similar to the accidental one. An instance of essential motion may be found in the translation of a thing from one place to another. The accident of a thing, as, e.g., its black color, is said to move when the thing itself changes its place. The upward motion of a stone, owing to a force applied to it in that direction, is an instance of a motion due to an external force. The motion of a nail in a boat may serve to illustrate motion due to the participation of a thing in the motion of another thing; for when the boat moves, the nail is said to move likewise. The same is the case with everything composed of several parts: when the thing itself moves, every part of it is likewise said to move.

PROPOSITION VII: Things which are changeable are, at the same time, divisible. Hence everything that moves is divisible, and consequently corporeal; but that which is indivisible cannot move, and cannot therefore be corporeal.

PROPOSITION VIII: A thing that moves accidentally must come to rest, because it does not move of its own accord; hence accidental motion cannot continue for ever.

PROPOSITION IX: A corporeal thing that sets another corporeal thing in motion can only effect this by setting itself in motion at the time it causes the other thing to move.

PROPOSITION X: A thing which is said to be contained in a corporeal object must satisfy either of the two following conditions: it either exists through that object, as is the case with accidents, or it is the cause of the existence of that object; such is, e.g., its essential property. In both cases it is a force existing in a corporeal object.

PROPOSITION XI: Among the things which exist through a material object, there are some which participate in the division of that object, and are therefore accidentally divisible, as, e.g., its color, and all other qualities that spread throughout its parts. On the other hand, among the things which form the essential elements of an object, there are some which cannot be divided in any way, as, e.g., the soul and the intellect.

PROPOSITION XII: A force which occupies all parts of a corporeal object is finite, that object itself being finite.

PROPOSITION XIII: None of the several kinds of change can be continuous, except motion from place to place, provided it be circular.

PROPOSITION XIV: Locomotion is in the natural order of the several kinds of motion the first and foremost. For genesis and corruption are preceded by transformation, which, in its turn, is preceded by the approach of the transforming agent to the object which is to be transformed. Also, increase and decrease are impossible without previous genesis and corruption.

PROPOSITION XV: Time is an accident that is related and joined to motion in such a manner that the one is never found without the other. Motion is only possible in time, and the idea of time cannot be conceived otherwise than in connection with motion; things which do not move have no relation to time.

PROPOSITION XVI: Incorporeal bodies can only be numbered when they are forces situated in a body; the several forces must then be counted together with substances or objects in which they exist. Hence purely spiritual beings, which are neither corporeal nor forces situated in corporeal objects, cannot be counted, except when considered as causes and effects.

PROPOSITION XVII: When an object moves, there must be some agent that moves it, from without, as, e.g., in the case of a stone set in motion by the hand; or from within, e.g., when the body of a living being moves. Living beings include in themselves, at the same time, the moving agent and the thing moved; when, therefore, a living being dies, and the moving agent, the soul, has left the body, i.e., the thing moved, the body remains for some time in the same condition as before, and yet cannot move in the manner it has moved previously. The moving agent, when included in the thing moved, is hidden from, and imperceptible to, the senses. This circumstance gave rise to the belief that the body of an animal moves without the aid of a moving agent. When we therefore affirm, concerning a thing in motion, that it is its own moving agent, or, as is generally said, that it moves of its own accord, we mean to say that the force which really sets the body in motion exists in that body itself.

PROPOSITION XVIII: Everything that passes over from a state of potentiality to that of actuality, is caused to do so by some external agent; because if that agent existed in the thing itself, and no obstacle prevented the transition, the thing would never be in a state of potentiality, but always in that of actuality. If, on the other hand, while the thing itself contained that agent, some obstacle existed, and at a certain time that obstacle was removed, the same cause which removed the obstacle would undoubtedly be described as the cause of the transition from potentiality to actuality, [and not the force situated within the body]. Note this.

PROPOSITION XIX: A thing which owes its existence to certain causes has in itself merely the possibility of existence; for only if these causes exist, the thing likewise exists. It does not exist if the causes do not exist at all, or if they have ceased to exist, or if there has been a change in the relation which implies the existence of that thing as a necessary consequence of those causes.

PROPOSITION XX: A thing which has in itself the necessity of existence cannot have for its existence any cause whatever.

PROPOSITION XXI: A thing composed of two elements has necessarily their composition as the cause of its present existence. Its existence is therefore not necessitated by its own essence; it depends on the existence of its two component parts and their combination.

PROPOSITION XXII: Material objects are always composed of two elements [at least], and are without exception subject to accidents. The two component elements of all bodies are substance and form. The accidents attributed to material objects are quantity, geometrical form, and position.

PROPOSITION XXIII: Everything that exists potentially, and whose essence includes a certain state of possibility, may at some time be without actual existence.

PROPOSITION XXIV: That which is potentially a certain thing is necessarily material, for the state of possibility is always connected with matter.

PROPOSITION XXV: Each compound substance consists of matter and form, and requires an agent for its existence, viz., a force which sets the substance in motion, and thereby enables it to receive a certain form. The force which thus prepares the substance of a certain individual being, is called the immediate motor. Here the necessity arises of investigating into the properties of motion, the moving agent and the thing moved. But this has already been explained sufficiently; and the opinion of Aristotle may be expressed in the following proposition: Matter does not move of its own accord—an important proposition that led to the investigation of the Prime Motor (the first moving agent).

Of these foregoing twenty-five propositions some may be verified by means of a little reflection and the application of a few propositions capable of proof, or of axioms or theorems of almost the same force, such as have been explained by me. Others require many arguments and propositions, all of which, however, have been established by conclusive proofs partly in the Physics and its commentaries, and partly in the Metaphysics and its commentary. I have already stated that in this work it is not my intention to copy the books of the philosophers or to explain difficult problems, but simply to mention those propositions which are closely connected with our subject, and which we want for our purpose.

To the above propositions one must be added which enunciates that the universe is eternal, and which is held by Aristotle to be true, and even more acceptable than any other theory. For the present we admit it, as a hypothesis, only for the purpose of demonstrating our theory. It is the following proposition:—

PROPOSITION XXVI: Time and motion are eternal, constant, and in actual existence.

In accordance with this proposition, Aristotle is compelled to assume that there exists actually a body with constant motion, viz., the fifth element. He therefore says that the heavens are not subject to genesis or destruction, because motion cannot be generated nor destroyed. He also holds that every motion must necessarily be preceded by another motion, either of the same or of a different kind. The belief that the locomotion of an animal is not preceded by another motion, is not true; for the animal is caused to move, after it had been in rest, by the intention to obtain those very things which bring about that locomotion. A change in its state of health, or some image, or some new idea can produce a desire to seek that which is conducive to its welfare and to avoid that which is contrary. Each of these three causes sets the living being in motion, and each of them is produced by various kinds of motion. Aristotle likewise asserts that everything which is created must, before its actual creation, have existed in potentiâ. By inferences drawn from this assertion he seeks to establish his proposition, viz., the thing that moves is finite, and its path finite; but it repeats the motion in its path an infinite number of times. This can only take place when the motion is circular, as has been stated in Proposition XIII. Hence follows also the existence of an infinite number of things which do not co-exist but follow one after the other.

Aristotle frequently attempts to establish this proposition; but I believe that he did not consider his proofs to be conclusive. It appeared to him to be the most probable and acceptable proposition. His followers, however, and the commentators of his books, contend that it contains not only a probable but a demonstrative proof, and that it has, in fact, been fully established. On the other hand, the Mutakallemim try to prove that the proposition cannot be true, as, according to their opinion, it is impossible to conceive how an infinite number of things could even come into existence successively. They assume this impossibility as an axiom. I, however, think that this proposition is admissible, but neither demonstrative, as the commentators of Aristotle assert, nor, on the other hand, impossible, as the Mutakallemim say. We have no intention to explain here the proofs given by Aristotle, or to show our doubts concerning them, or to set forth our opinions on the creation of the universe. I here simply desire to mention those propositions which we shall require for the proof of the three principles stated above. Having thus quoted and admitted these propositions, I will now proceed to explain what may be inferred from them.

*   *   *

CHAPTER 13

Among those who believe in the existence of God, there are found three different theories as regards the question whether the Universe is eternal or not.

First Theory.—Those who follow the Law of Moses, our Teacher, hold that the whole Universe, i.e., everything except God, has been brought by Him into existence out of non-existence. In the beginning God alone existed, and nothing else; neither angels, nor spheres, nor the things that are contained within the spheres existed. He then produced from nothing all existing things such as they are, by His will and desire. Even time itself is among the things created; for time depends on motion, i.e., on an accident in things which move, and the things upon whose motion time depends are themselves created beings, which have passed from non-existence into existence. We say that God *existed* before the creation of the Universe, although the verb *existed* appears to imply the notion of time; we also believe that He existed an infinite space of time before the Universe was created; but in these cases we do not mean time in its true sense. We only use the term to signify something analogous or similar to time. For time is undoubtedly an accident, and, according to our opinion, one of the created accidents, like blackness and whiteness; it is not a quality, but an accident connected with motion. This must be clear to all who understand what Aristotle has said on time and its real existence.

The following remark does not form an essential part of our present research; it will nevertheless be found useful in the course of this discussion. Many scholars do not know what time really is, and men like Galen were so perplexed about it that they asked whether time has a real existence or not; the reason for this uncertainty is to be found in the circumstance that time is an accident of an accident. Accidents which are directly connected with material bodies, e.g., color and taste, are easily understood, and correct notions are formed of them. There are, however, accidents which are connected with other accidents, e.g., the splendor of color, or the inclination and the curvature of a line; of these it is very difficult to form a correct notion, especially when the accident which forms the substratum for the other accident is not constant but variable. Both difficulties are present in the notion of time: it is an accident of motion, which is itself an accident of a moving object; besides, it is not a fixed property; on the contrary, its true and essential condition is, not to remain in the same state for two consecutive moments. This is the source of ignorance about the nature of time.

We consider time a thing created; it comes into existence in the same manner as other accidents, and the substances which form the substratum for the accidents. For this reason, viz., because time belongs to the things created, it cannot be said that God produced the Universe *in the beginning*. Consider this well; for he who does not understand it is unable to refute forcible objection raised against the theory of *Creatio ex nihilo*. If you admit the existence of time before the Creation, you will be compelled to accept the theory of the Eternity of the Universe. For time is an accident and requires a substratum. You will therefore have to assume that something [beside God] existed before this Universe was created, an assumption which it is our duty to oppose.

This is the first theory, and it is undoubtedly a fundamental principle of the Law of our teacher Moses; it is next in importance to the principle of God's unity. Do not follow any other theory. Abraham, our father, was the first that taught it, after he had established it by philosophical research. He proclaimed, therefore, "the name of the Lord the God of the Universe" (Gen. xxi. 33); and he had previously expressed this theory in the words, "The Possessor of heaven and earth" (*ibid*. xiv. 22).

Second Theory.—The theory of all philosophers whose opinions and works are known to us is this: It is impossible to assume that God produced anything from nothing, or that He reduces anything to nothing; that is to say, it is impossible that an object consisting of matter and form should be produced when that matter is absolutely absent, or that it should be destroyed in such a manner that that matter be absolutely no longer in existence. To say of God that He can produce a thing from nothing or reduce a thing to nothing is, according to the opinion of these philosophers, the same as if we were to say that He could cause one substance to have at the same time two opposite properties, or produce another being like Himself, or change Himself into a body, or produce a square the diagonal of which be equal to its side, or similar impossibilities. The philosophers thus believe that it is no defect in the Supreme Being that He does not produce impossibilities, for the nature of that which is impossible is constant—it does not depend on the action of an agent, and for this reason it cannot be changed. Similarly there is, according to them, no defect in the greatness of God, when He is unable to produce a thing from nothing, because they consider this as one of the impossibilities. They therefore assume that a certain substance has coexisted with God from eternity in such a manner that neither God existed without that substance nor the latter without God. But they do not hold that the existence of that substance equals in rank that of God; for God is the cause of that existence, and the substance is in the same relation to God as the clay is to the potter, or the iron to the smith; God can do with it what He pleases; at one time He forms of it heaven and earth, at another time He forms some other thing. Those who hold this view also assume that the heavens are transient, that they came into existence, though not from nothing, and may cease to exist, although they cannot be reduced to nothing. They are transient in the same manner as the individuals among living beings which are produced from some existing substance, and are again reduced to some substance that remains in existence. The process of genesis and destruction is, in the case of the heavens, the same as in that of earthly beings.

The followers of this theory are divided into different schools, whose opinions and principles it is useless to discuss here; but what I have mentioned is common to all of them. Plato holds the same opinion. Aristotle says in his *Physics* that according to Plato the heavens are transient. This view is also stated in Plato's *Timeus*. His opinion, however, does not agree with our belief; only superficial and careless persons wrongly assume that Plato has the same belief as we have. For whilst we hold that the heavens have been created from absolutely nothing, Plato believes that they have been formed out of something.—This is the second theory.

Third Theory.—viz., that of Aristotle, his followers, and commentators. Aristotle maintains, like the adherents of the second theory, that a corporeal object cannot be produced without a corporeal substance. He goes, however, farther, and contends that the heavens are indestructible. For he holds that the Universe in its totality has never been different, nor will it ever change: the heavens, which form the permanent element in the Universe, and are not subject to genesis and destruction, have always been so; time and motion are eternal, permanent, and have neither beginning nor end; the sublunary world, which includes the transient elements, has always been the same, because the *materia prima* is itself eternal, and merely combines successively with different forms; when one form is removed, another is assumed. This whole arrangement, therefore, both above and here below, is never disturbed or interrupted, and nothing is produced contrary to the laws or the ordinary course of Nature. He further says—though not in the same terms—that he considers it impossible for God to change His will or conceive a new desire; that God produced this Universe in its totality by His will, but not from nothing. Aristotle finds it as impossible to assume that God changes His will or conceives a new desire, as to believe that He is nonexisting, or that His essence is changeable. Hence it follows that this Universe has always been the same in the past, and will be the same eternally.

This is a full account of the opinions of those who consider that the existence of God, the First Cause of the Universe, has been established by proof. But it would be quite useless to mention the opinions of those who do not recognize the existence of God, but believe that the existing state of things is the result of accidental combination and separation of the elements, and that the Universe has no Ruler or Governor. Such is the theory of Epicurus and his school, and similar philosophers, as stated by Alexander [Aphrodisiensis]; it would be superfluous to repeat their views, since the existence of God has been demonstrated whilst their theory is built upon a basis proved to be untenable. It is likewise useless to prove the correctness of the followers of the second theory in asserting that the heavens are transient, because they at the same time believe in the Eternity of the Universe, and so long as this theory is adopted, it makes no difference to us whether it is believed that the heavens are transient, and that only their substance is eternal, or the heavens are held to be indestructible, in accordance with the view of Aristotle. All who follow the Law of Moses, our Teacher, and Abraham, our Father, and all who adopt similar theories, assume that nothing is eternal except God, and that the theory of *Creatio ex nihilo* includes nothing that is impossible, whilst some thinkers even regard it as an established truth.

*   *   *

CHAPTER 17

Everything produced comes into existence from non-existence; even when the substance of a thing has been in existence, and has only changed its form, the thing itself, which has gone through the process of genesis and development, and has arrived at its final state, has now different properties from those which it possessed at the commencement of the transition from potentiality to reality, or before that time. Take, e.g., the human ovum is contained in the female's blood when still included in its vessels; its nature is different from what it was in the moment of conception, when it is met by the semen of the male and begins to develop; the properties of the semen in that moment are different from the properties of the living being after its birth when fully developed. It is therefore quite impossible to infer from the nature which a thing possesses after having passed through all stages of its development, what the condition of the thing has been in the moment when this process commenced; nor does the condition of a thing in this moment show what its previous condition has been. If you make this mistake, and attempt to prove the nature of a thing in potential existence by its properties when actually existing, you will fall into great confusion; you will reject evident truths and admit false opinions. Let us assume, in our above instance, that a man born without defect had after his birth been nursed by his mother only a few months; the mother then died, and the father alone brought him up in a lonely island, till he grew up, became wise, and acquired knowledge. Suppose this man has never seen a woman or any female being; he asks some person how man has come into existence, and how he has developed, and receives the following answer: "Man begins his existence in the womb of an individual of his own class, namely, in the womb of a female, which has a certain form. While in the womb he is very small; yet he has life, moves, receives nourishment, and gradually grows, till he arrives at a certain stage of development. He then leaves the womb and continues to grow till he is in the condition in which you see him." The orphan will naturally ask: "Did this person, when he lived, moved, and grew in the womb, eat and drink, and breathe with his mouth and his nostrils? Did he excrete any substance?" The answer will be, "No." Undoubtedly he will then attempt to refute the statements of that person, and to prove their impossibility, by referring to the properties of a fully developed person, in the following manner: "When any one of us is deprived of breath for a short time he dies, and cannot move any longer: how then can we imagine that any one of us has been inclosed in a bag in the midst of a body for several months and remained alive, able to move? If any one of us would swallow a living bird, the bird would die immediately when it reached the stomach, much more so when it came to the lower part of the belly; if we should not take food or drink with our mouth, in a few days we should undoubtedly be dead: how then can man remain alive for months without taking food? If any person would take food and would not be able to excrete it, great pains and death would follow in a short time, and yet I am to believe that man has lived for months without that function! Suppose by accident a hole were formed in the belly of a person, it would prove fatal, and yet we are to believe that the navel of the fetus has been open! Why should the fetus not open the eyes, spread forth the hands and stretch out the legs, if, as you think, the limbs are all whole and perfect." This mode of reasoning would lead to the conclusion that man cannot come into existence and develop in the manner described.

If philosophers would consider this example well and reflect on it, they would find that it represents exactly the dispute between Aristotle and ourselves. We, the followers of Moses, our Teacher, and of Abraham, our Father, believe that the Universe has been produced and has developed in a certain manner, and that it has been created in a certain order. The Aristotelians oppose us, and found their objections on the properties which the things in the Universe possess when in actual existence and fully developed. We admit the existence of these properties, but hold that they are by no means the same as those which the things possessed in the moment of their production; and we hold that these properties themselves have come into existence from absolute non-existence. Their arguments are therefore no objection whatever to our theory; they have demonstrative force only against those who hold that the nature of things as at present in existence proves the Creation. But this is not my opinion.

I will now return to our theme, viz., to the description of the principal proofs of Aristotle, and show that they prove nothing whatever against us, since we hold that God brought the entire Universe into existence from absolute non-existence, and that He caused it to develop into the present state. Aristotle says that the *materia prima* is eternal, and by referring to the properties of transient beings he attempts to prove this statement, and to show that the *materia prima* could not possibly have been produced. He is right; we do not maintain that the *materia prima* has been produced in the same manner as man is produced from the ovum, and that it can be destroyed in the same manner as man is reduced to dust. But we believe that God created it from nothing, and that since its creation it has its own properties, viz., that all things are produced of it and again reduced to it, when they cease to exist; that it does not exist without Form; and that it is the source of all genesis and destruction. Its genesis is not like that of the things produced from it, nor its destruction like theirs; for it has been created from nothing, and if it should please the Creator, He might reduce it to absolutely nothing. The same applies to motion. Aristotle founds some of his proofs on the fact that motion is not subject to genesis or destruction. This is correct; if we consider motion as it exists at present, we cannot imagine that in its totality it should be subject, like individual motions, to genesis and destruction. In like manner Aristotle is correct in saying that circular motion is without beginning, in so far as seeing the rotating spherical body in actual existence, we cannot conceive the idea that that rotation has ever been absent. The same argument we employ as regards the law that a state of potentiality precedes all actual genesis. This law applies to the Universe as it exists at present, when everything produced originates in another thing; but nothing perceived with our senses or comprehended in our mind can prove that a thing created from nothing must have been previously in a state of potentiality. Again, as regards the theory that the heavens contain no opposites [and are therefore indestructible], we admit its correctness; but we do not maintain that the production of the heavens has taken place in the same way as that of a horse or ass, and we do not say that they are like plants and animals, which are destructible on account of the opposite elements they contain. In short, the properties of things when fully developed contain no clue as to what have been the properties of the things before their perfection. We therefore do not reject as impossible the opinion of those who say that the heavens were produced before the earth, or the reverse, or that the heavens have existed without stars, or that certain species of animals have been in existence, and others not. For the state of the whole Universe when it came into existence may be compared with that of animals when their existence begins; the heart evidently precedes the testicles, the veins are in existence before the bones; although, when the animal is fully developed, none of the parts is missing which is essential to its existence. This remark is not superfluous, if the Scriptural account of the Creation be taken literally; in reality, it cannot be taken literally, as will be shown when we shall treat of this subject.

The principle laid down in the foregoing must be well understood; it is a high rampart erected round the Law and able to resist all missiles directed against it. Aristotle, or rather his followers, may perhaps ask us how we know that the Universe has been created; and that other forces than those it has at present were acting in its Creation, since we hold that the properties of the Universe, as it exists at present, prove nothing as regards its creation? We reply, there is no necessity for this according to our plan; for we do not desire to prove the Creation, but only its possibility; and this possibility is not refuted by arguments based on the nature of the present Universe, which we do not dispute. When we have established the admissibility of our theory, we shall then show its superiority. In attempting to prove the inadmissibility of *Creatio ex nihilo*, the Aristotelians can therefore not derive any support from the nature of the Universe; they must resort to the notion our mind has formed of God. Their proofs include the three methods which I have mentioned above, and which are based on the notion conceived of God. In the next chapter I will expose the weak points of these arguments, and show that they really prove nothing.

*   *   *

PART III

CHAPTER 12

Men frequently think that the evils in the world are more numerous than the good things; many savings and songs of the nations dwell on this idea. They say that a good thing is found only exceptionally, whilst evil things are numerous and lasting. Not only common people make this mistake, but even many who believe that they are wise. Al-Razi wrote a well-known book *On Metaphysics* [or *Theology*]. Among other mad and foolish things, it contains also the idea, discovered by him, that there exists more evil than good. For if the happiness of man and his pleasure in the times of prosperity be compared with the mishaps that befall him,—such as grief, acute pain, defects, paralysis of the limbs, fears, anxieties, and troubles,—it would seem as if the existence of man is a punishment and a great evil for him. This author commenced to verify his opinion by counting all the evils one by one; by this means he opposed those who hold the correct view of the benefits bestowed by God and His evident kindness, viz., that God is perfect goodness, and that all that comes from Him is absolutely good. The origin of the error is to be found in the circumstance that this ignorant man, and his party among the common people, judge the whole universe by examining one single person. For an ignorant man believes that the whole universe only exists for him; as if nothing else required any consideration. If, therefore, anything happens to him contrary to his expectation, he at once concludes that the whole universe is evil. If, however, he would take into consideration the whole universe, form an idea of it, and comprehend what a small portion he is of the Universe, he will find the truth. For it is clear that persons who have fallen into this widespread error as regards the multitude of evils in the world, do not find the evils among the angels, the spheres and stars, the elements, and that which is formed of them, viz., minerals and plants, or in the various species of living beings, but only in some individual instances of mankind. They wonder that a person, who became leprous in consequence of bad food, should be afflicted with so great an illness and suffer such a misfortune; or that he who indulges so much in sensuality as to weaken his sight, should be struck with blindness and the like. What we have, in truth, to consider is this:—The whole mankind at present in existence, and *a fortiori,* every other species of animals, form an infinitesimal portion of the permanent universe. Comp. "Man is like to vanity" (Ps. cxliv. 4); "How much less man, that is a worm; and the son of man, which is a worm" (Job xxv. 6); "How much less in them who dwell in houses of clay" (*ibid.* iv. 19); "Behold, the nations are as a drop of the bucket" (Isa. xl. 15). There are many other passages in the books of the prophets expressing the same idea. It is of great advantage that man should know his station, and not erroneously imagine that the whole universe exists only for him. We hold that the universe exists because the Creator wills it so; that mankind is low in rank as compared with the uppermost portion of the universe, viz., with the spheres and the stars; but, as regards the angels, there cannot be any real comparison between man and angels, although man is the highest of all beings on earth; i.e., of all beings formed of the four elements. Man's existence is nevertheless a great boon to him, and his distinction and perfection is a divine gift. The numerous evils to which individual persons are exposed are due to the defects existing in the persons themselves. We complain and seek relief from our own faults; we suffer from the evils which we, by our own free will, inflict on ourselves and ascribe them to God, who is far from being connected with them! Comp. "Is destruction his [work]? No. Ye [who call yourselves] wrongly his sons, you who are a perverse and crooked generation" (Deut. xxxii. 5). This is explained by Solomon, who says, "The foolishness of man perverteth his way, and his heart fretteth against the Lord" (Prov. xix. 3).

I explain this theory in the following manner. The evils that befall man are of three kinds:—

(1) The first kind of evil is that which is caused to man by the circumstance that he is subject to genesis and destruction, or that he possesses a body. It is on account of the body that some persons happen to have great deformities or paralysis of some of the organs. This evil may be part of the natural constitution of these persons, or may have developed subsequently in consequence of changes in the elements, e.g., through bad air, or thunderstorms, or landslips. We have already shown that, in accordance with the divine wisdom, genesis can only take place through destruction, and without the destruction of the individual members of the species the species themselves would not exist permanently. Thus the true kindness, and beneficence, and goodness of God is clear. He who thinks that he can have flesh and bones without being subject to any external influence, or any of the accidents of matter, unconsciously wishes to reconcile two opposites, viz., to be at the same time subject and not subject to change. If man were never subject to change there could be no generation; there would be one single being, but no individuals forming a species. Galen, in the third section of his book, *The Use of the Limbs,* says correctly that it would be in vain to expect to see living beings formed of the blood of menstruous women and the semen virile, who will not die, will never feel pain, or will move perpetually, or will shine like the sun. This dictum of Galen is part of the following more general proposition:—Whatever is formed of any matter receives the most perfect form possible in that species of matter; in each individual case the defects are in accordance with the defects of that individual matter. The best and most perfect being that can be formed of the blood and the semen is the species of man, for as far as man's nature is known, he is living, reasonable, and mortal. It is therefore impossible that man should be free from this species of evil. You will, nevertheless, find that the evils of the above kind which befall man are very few and rare; for you find countries that have not been flooded or burned for thousands of years; there are thousands of men in perfect health, deformed individuals are a strange and exceptional occurrence, or say few in number if you object to the term exceptional,—they are not one-hundredth, not even one-thousandth part of those that are perfectly normal.

(2) The second class of evils comprises such evils as people cause to each other, when, e.g., some of them use their strength against others. These evils are more numerous than those of the first kind; their causes are numerous and known; they likewise originate in ourselves, though the sufferer himself cannot avert them. This kind of evil is nevertheless not widespread in any country of the whole world. It is of rare occurrence that a man plans to kill his neighbor or to rob him of his property by night. Many persons are, however, afflicted with this kind of evil in great wars; but these are not frequent, if the whole inhabited part of the earth is taken into consideration.

(3) The third class of evils comprises those which every one causes to himself by his own action. This is the largest class, and is far more numerous than the second class. It is especially of these evils that all men complain,—only few men are found that do not sin against themselves by this kind of evil. Those that are afflicted with it are therefore justly blamed in the words of the prophet, "This hath been by your means" (Mal. i. 9); the same is expressed in the following passage, "He that doeth it destroyeth his own soul" (Prov. vi. 32). In reference to this kind of evil, Solomon

says, "The foolishness of man perverteth his way" (*ibid.* xix. 3). In the following passage he explains also that this kind of evil is man's own work, "Lo, this only have I found, that God hath made man upright, but they have thought out many inventions" (Eccles. vii. 29), and these inventions bring the evils upon him. The same subject is referred to in Job (v. 6), "For affliction cometh not forth of the dust, neither doth trouble spring out of the ground." These words are immediately followed by the explanation that man himself is the author of this class of evils, "But man is born unto trouble." This class of evils originates in man's vices, such as excessive desire for eating, drinking, and love; indulgence in these things in undue measure, or in improper manner, or partaking of bad food. This course brings diseases and afflictions upon body and soul alike. The sufferings of the body in consequence of these evils are well known; those of the soul are twofold:—First, such evils of the soul as are the necessary consequence of changes in the body, in so far as the soul is a force residing in the body; it has therefore been said that the properties of the soul depend on the condition of the body. Secondly, the soul, when accustomed to superfluous things, acquires a strong habit of desiring things which are neither necessary for the preservation of the individual nor for that of the species. This desire is without a limit, whilst things which are necessary are few in number and restricted within certain limits; but what is superfluous is without end—e.g., you desire to have your vessels of silver, but golden vessels are still better: others have even vessels of sapphire, or perhaps they can be made of emerald or rubies, or any other substance that could be suggested. Those who are ignorant and perverse in their thought are constantly in trouble and pain, because they cannot get as much of superfluous things as a certain other person possesses. They as a rule expose themselves to great dangers, e.g., by sea-voyage, or service of kings, and all this for the purpose of obtaining that which is superfluous and not necessary. When they thus meet with the consequences of the course which they adopt, they complain of the decrees and judgments of God; they begin to blame the time, and wonder at the want of justice in its changes; that it has not enabled them to acquire great riches, with which they could buy large quantities of wine for the purpose of making themselves drunk, and numerous concubines adorned with various kind of ornaments of gold, embroidery, and jewels, for the purpose of driving themselves to voluptuousness beyond their capacities, as if the whole Universe existed exclusively for the purpose of giving pleasure to these low people. The error of the ignorant goes so far as to say that God's power is insufficient, because He has given to this Universe the properties which they imagine cause these great evils, and which do not help all evil-disposed persons to obtain the evil which they seek, and to bring their evil souls to the aim of their desires, though these, as we have shown, are really without limit. The virtuous and wise, however, see and comprehend the wisdom of God displayed in the Universe. Thus David says, "All the paths of the Lord are mercy and truth unto such as keep His covenant and His testimonies" (Ps. xxv. 10). For those who observe the nature of the Universe and the commandments of the Law, and know their purpose, see clearly God's mercy and truth in everything; they seek, therefore, that which the Creator intended to be the aim of man, viz., comprehension. Forced by the claims of the body, they seek also that which is necessary for the preservation of the body, "bread to eat and garment to clothe," and this is very little; but they seek nothing superfluous; with very slight exertion man can obtain it, so long as he is contented with that which is indispensable. All the difficulties and troubles we meet in this respect are due to the desire for superfluous things; when we seek unnecessary things, we have difficulty even in finding that which is indispensable. For the more we desire to have that which is superfluous, the more we meet with difficulties; our strength and possessions are spent in unnecessary things, and are wanting when required for that which is necessary. Observe how Nature proves the correctness of this assertion. The more necessary a thing is for living beings, the more easily it is found and the cheaper it is; the less necessary it is, the rarer and dearer it is. E.g., air, water, and food are indispensable to man: air is most necessary, for if man is without air a short time he dies; whilst he can be without water a day or two. Air is also undoubtedly found more easily and cheaper [than water]. Water is more necessary than food; for some people can be four or five days without food, provided they have water; water also exists in every country in larger quantities than food, and is also cheaper. The same proportion can be noticed in the different kinds of food; that which is more necessary in a certain place exists there in larger quantities and is cheaper than that which is less necessary. No intelligent person, I think, considers musk, amber, rubies, and emerald as very necessary for man except as medicines; and they, as well as other like substances, can be replaced for this purpose by herbs and minerals. This shows the kindness of God to His creatures, even to us weak beings. His righteousness and justice as regards all animals are well known; for in the transient world there is among the various kinds of animals no individual being distinguished from the rest of the same species by a peculiar property or an additional limb. On the contrary, all physical, psychical, and vital forces and organs that are possessed by one individual are found also in the other individuals. If any one is somehow different it is by accident, in consequence of some exception, and not by a natural property; it is also a rare occurrence. There is no difference between individuals of a species in the due course of Nature; the difference originates in the various dispositions of their substances. This is the necessary consequence of the nature of the substance of that species; the nature of the species is not more favorable to one individual than to the other. It is no wrong or injustice that one has many bags of finest myrrh and garments embroidered with gold, while another has not those things, which are not necessary for our maintenance; he who has them has not thereby obtained control over anything that could be an essential addition to his nature, but has only obtained something illusory or deceptive. The other, who does not possess that which is not wanted for his maintenance, does not miss anything indispensable: "He that gathered much had nothing over, and he that gathered little had no lack: they gathered every man according to his eating" (Exod. xvi. 18). This is the rule at all times and in all places; no notice should be taken of exceptional cases, as we have explained.

In these two ways you will see the mercy of God toward His creatures, how He has provided that which is required, in proper proportions, and treated all individual beings of the same species with perfect equality. In accordance with this correct reflection the chief of the wise men says, "All his ways are judgment" (Deut. xxxii. 4); David likewise says: "All the paths of the Lord are mercy and truth" (Ps. xxv. 10); he also says expressly, "The Lord is good to all; and his tender mercies are over all his works" (*ibid*. cxlv. 9); for it is an act of great and perfect goodness that He gave us existence; and the creation of the controlling faculty in animals is a proof of His mercy towards them, as has been shown by us.

THIRTEENTH-CENTURY PHILOSOPHY

——◄○►——

Thirteenth-century Western European philosophy was shaped by three movements: the rise of the mendicant (or begging) orders, the development of the university, and, most important, the rediscovery of the complete works of Aristotle.

Having survived the collapse of the Roman Empire and having helped fight
back the Islamic expansion in southern Europe, the Catholic church had gained
new influence and power in society at the beginning of the thirteenth century. As
the church grew in temporal authority, spiritual concerns and doctrinal purity
often became less important. Advocating a simple life of obedience, poverty, and
chastity, the Franciscan and Dominican orders sought to reverse this secularizing
trend. Founded by St. Francis of Assisi (1181–1226), the Franciscans fostered
spiritual renewal and often served as dedicated teachers and missionaries. The
Dominicans, founded by St. Dominic (1170–1221), sought doctrinal purity and
became leading university professors throughout the West.

The thirteenth century also witnessed the rise of universities. Usually founded
as schools attached to cathedrals, the universities were corporations of scholars
with a measure of independence from the church. Acting as magnets for scholars, students, and collections of great works, the universities quickly became important, crowded intellectual centers. (The greatest of the early universities, in
Paris, had as many as twenty thousand students in the Middle Ages.)

Among the issues discussed at the emerging universities, none was more controversial than the recently rediscovered books of Aristotle. Although some of
Aristotle's works had been available to Western Europeans, his most important
writings had been preserved only in the Islamic world. Texts brought as loot
from the Crusaders' incursions into Muslim strongholds in Spain and Sicily

found their way to the University of Paris. There, Aristotle's ideas provided fertile ground for many new questions.

But with Aristotle's works came the problems with which Islamic and Jewish thinkers had earlier struggled. Aristotle had taught the eternity of the world and apparently denied life after death—teachings at variance with the Bible as well as with the *Qur'ān*. Fortunately for Christendom, along with Aristotle's works came the commentaries of the great Muslim teachers Avicenna and Averroës. Thirteenth-century Western thinkers were able to appeal not only to Aristotle, but also to his Muslim glosses in their attempts to harmonize Aristotle with Christianity.

In general, the Dominicans, led by St. Thomas Aquinas, were enthusiastic about Aristotelian thought, whereas the Franciscans, led by St. Bonaventure, preferred Augustinian Platonism. But the conflict was in fact much more complicated than such a generalization might indicate. There were numerous variations on Aristotle's thought. Robert Grosseteste and Roger Bacon, used Aristotelian categories when they suited their purposes; but they were actually more Neoplatonic than Aristotelian. Even opponents of Aristotle, such as Bonaventure, used Aristotelian categories in their criticisms of Aristotle. But whether defended or attacked, the spirit of Aristotle ruled Western philosophy in the thirteenth century.

*   *   *

Frederick Copleston, *A History of Philosophy: Volume II, Medieval Philosophy, Part II, Albert the Great to Duns Scotus* (1950; reprinted Garden City, NY: Image Doubleday, 1962); Fernand van Steenberghen, *The Philosophical Movement in the Thirteenth Century* (Edinburgh: Thomas Nelson's Sons, 1955); and Fernand van Steenberghen, *Aristotle in the West: The Origins of Latin Aristotelianism,* translated by Leonard Johnston (Louvain, Belgium: E. Nauwelaerts, 1955) provide overviews of thirteenth-century thought. For general introductions to Scholasticism, see Maurice M.C.J. de Wulf, *An Introduction to Scholastic Philosophy, Medieval and Modern,* translated by P. Coffey (New York: Dover, 1956); and Josef Pieper, *Scholasticism: Personalities and Problems of Medieval Philosophy,* translated by Richard and Clara Winston (New York: Pantheon Books, 1960).

ROBERT GROSSETESTE
ca. 1168–1253

Robert Grosseteste was born to a peasant family at Stradbroke, in Suffolk, England, sometime around 1168. Despite his humble origins, he studied law, medicine, and theology at Oxford University. He may have studied in Paris as well. He served for a time under the Bishop of Hereford, perhaps as a teacher at the Hereford school, after which he returned to teaching at Oxford. King John's troubles with France and with his own nobles led to the closing of Oxford from 1209 to 1214, during which time Grosseteste presumably studied theology in Paris. He returned to England in time to be present at the signing of the Magna Carta in 1215. Sometime after the reopening of Oxford, Grosseteste was made the first chancellor of the university and taught at the Oxford Franciscan house. He remained in that post until 1235 when he was made bishop of Lincoln, then the largest diocese in England. For his last eighteen years, he served in Lincoln and was often called "the Lincolnian" by his contemporaries.

The specifics of Grosseteste's life are sketchy, and we now know that some works attributed to him were written by others. But we also know that he did write the work *On Light,* reprinted here in the Clare C. Riedl translation. In this work, Grosseteste claims that God created light (*lux* or "light at its source") as the first form along with simple unextended matter. This light immediately "multiplied itself by its very nature an infinite number of times on all sides and spread itself out uniformly in every direction." As light spread out in all directions, it drew matter "along with itself into a mass the size of the material universe" forming the perfect outer sphere of "the firmament." After the material universe had been formed in this way, the light (*lumen* or "reflected light") on the periphery was reflected back to the center where it gathered the dense mass of matter inside the firmament and spread it outward in a sphere smaller than the first. This process continued until the thirteen spheres—the nine spheres of the heavens and the four elements of fire, air, water, and earth—had been formed. This process of expansion and reflection managed to combine the cosmologies of Aristotle and Ptolemy with elements of the Neoplatonists' emanation theory.

Although his treatise *On Light* may seem ethereal, Grosseteste was in fact one of the first medieval scientists. He sought to divide complex phenomena into smaller units that could then be examined separately. He attempted to limit possible causes of a given effect in an effort to remove unnecessary variables. He used both working hypotheses and experiments in his scientific investigations. Finally, since he believed that light is the cause of all motion and that light operates according to geometrical rules, he held that all motion can be explained mathematically. These scientific advances proved fruitful in succeeding centuries.

*   *   *

The best general introduction to Grosseteste is the recently updated Richard W. Southern, *Robert Grosseteste: The Growth of an English Mind in Medieval Europe*, 2nd edition (Oxford: Clarendon Press, 1992). Other introductions include James McEvoy, *The Philosophy of Robert Grosseteste* (Oxford: Clarendon Press, 1982); Steven P. Marrone, *William of Auvergne and Robert Grosseteste: New Ideas of Truth in the Early Thirteenth Century* (Princeton, NJ: Princeton University Press, 1983); and James McEvoy, *Robert Grosseteste* (Oxford: Oxford University Press, 2000). S. Harrison Thomson, *The Writings of Robert Grosseteste, Bishop of Lincoln, 1235–1253* (Cambridge: Cambridge University Press, 1940) provides a commentary on Grosseteste's writings; whereas Lee M. Friedman, *Robert Grosseteste and the Jews* (Cambridge, MA: Harvard University Press, 1934) and Alistair Cameron Crombie, *Robert Grosseteste and the Origins of Experimental Science, 1100–1700* (Oxford: Clarendon Press, 1953) have written studies of particular topics. For critical essays, see Daniel Angelo Philip Callus, ed., *Robert Grosseteste: Scholar and Bishop: Essays in Commemoration of the Seventh Centenary of His Death* (Oxford: Clarendon Press, 1955). For general introductions to medieval science, see the suggested readings in the introduction to Roger Bacon (page 300).

ON LIGHT

The first corporeal form which some call corporeity is in my opinion light. For light of its very nature diffuses itself in every direction in such a way that a point of light will produce instantaneously a sphere of light of any size whatsoever, unless some

Robert Grosseteste, *On Light,* translated by Clare C. Riedl (Milwaukee, WI: Marquette University Press, 1942, 1978). Reprinted by permission of Marquette University Press.

opaque object stands in the way. Now the extension of matter in three dimensions is a necessary concomitant of corporeity, and this despite the fact that both corporeity and matter are in themselves simple substances lacking all dimension. But a form that is in itself simple and without dimension could not introduce dimension in every direction into matter, which is likewise simple and without dimension, except by multiplying itself and diffusing itself instantaneously in every direction and thus extending matter in its own diffusion. For the form cannot desert matter, because it is inseparable from it, and matter itself cannot be deprived of form.—But I have proposed that it is light which possesses of its very nature the function of multiplying itself and diffusing itself instantaneously in all directions. Whatever performs this operation is either light or some other agent that acts in virtue of its participation in light to which this operation belongs essentially. Corporeity, therefore, is either light itself or the agent which performs the aforementioned operation and introduces dimensions into matter in virtue of its participation in light, and acts through the power of this same light. But the first form cannot introduce dimensions

The Ptolemaic Conception of the Universe, from *Introductorium*, 1513, woodcut by Jon Glagowczyke. Grosseteste's theory of light combines Ptolemaic cosmology and the Neoplatonists' emanation theory. According to Grosseteste, through a process of multiplication and reflection, light forms thirteen spheres—the nine spheres of the heavens and the four elements of fire, air, water, and earth. (*Library of Congress*)

into matter through the power of a subsequent form. Therefore light is not a form subsequent to corporeity, but it is corporeity itself.

Furthermore, the first corporeal form is, in the opinion of the philosophers, more exalted and of a nobler and more excellent essence than all the forms that come after it. It bears, also, a closer resemblance to the forms that exist apart from matter. But light is more exalted and of a nobler and more excellent essence than all corporeal things. It has, moreover, greater similarity than all bodies to the forms that exist apart from matter, namely, the intelligences. Light therefore is the first corporeal form.

Thus light, which is the first form created in first matter, multiplied itself by its very nature an infinite number of times on all sides and spread itself out uniformly in every direction. In this way it proceeded in the beginning of time to extend matter which it could not leave behind, by drawing it out along with itself into a mass the size of the material universe. This extension of matter could not be brought about through a finite multiplication of light, because the multiplication of a simple being a finite number of times does not produce a quantity, as Aristotle shows in the *De Caelo et Mundo*. However, the multiplication of a simple being an infinite number of times must produce a finite quantity, because a product which is the result of an infinite multiplication exceeds infinitely that through the multiplication of which it is produced. Now one simple being cannot exceed another simple being infinitely, but only a finite quantity infinitely exceeds a simple being. For an infinite quantity exceeds a simple being by infinity times infinity. Therefore, when light, which is in itself simple, is multiplied an infinite number of times, it must extend matter, which is likewise simple, into finite dimensions.

It is possible, however, that an infinite sum of number is related to an infinite sum in every proportion, numerical and non-numerical. And some infinites are larger than other infinites, and some are smaller. Thus the sum of all numbers both even and odd is infinite. It is at the same time greater than the sum of all the even numbers although this is likewise infinite, for it exceeds it by the sum of all the odd numbers. The sum, too, of all numbers starting with one and continuing by doubling each successive number is infinite, and similarly the sum of all the halves corresponding to the doubles is infinite. The sum of these halves must be half of the sum of their doubles. In the same way the sum of all numbers starting with one and multiplying by three successively is three times the sum of all the thirds corresponding to these triples. It is likewise clear in regard to all kinds of numerical proportion that there can be a proportion of finite to infinite according to each of them.

But if we posit an infinite sum of all doubles starting with one, and an infinite sum of all the halves corresponding to these doubles, and if one, or some other finite number, be subtracted from the sum of the halves, then, as soon as this subtraction is made, there will no longer be a two to one proportion between the first sum and what is left of the second sum. Indeed there will not be any numerical proportion, because if a second numerical proportion is to be left from the first as the result of subtraction from the lesser member of the proportion, then what is subtracted must be an aliquot* part or aliquot parts of an aliquot part of that from which it is subtracted. But a finite number cannot be an aliquot part or aliquot parts of an aliquot part of an infinite number. Therefore when we subtract a number from an infinite sum of halves there will not re-

---

*[The part of a number that divides the given number without a remainder.]

main a numerical proportion between the infinite sum of doubles and what is left from the infinite sum of halves.

Since this is so, it is clear that light through the infinite multiplication of itself extends matter into finite dimensions that are smaller and larger according to certain proportions that they have to one another, namely, numerical and non-numerical. For if light through the infinite multiplication of itself extends matter into a dimension of two cubits, by the doubling of this same infinite multiplication it extends it into a dimension of four cubits, and by the dividing in half of this infinite multiplication, it extends it into a dimension of one cubit. Thus it proceeds according to numerical and non-numerical proportions.

It is my opinion that this was the meaning of the theory of those philosophers who held that everything is composed of atoms, and said that bodies are composed of surfaces, and surfaces of lines, and lines of points. This opinion does not contradict the theory that a magnitude is composed only of magnitudes, because for every meaning of the word whole, there is a corresponding meaning of the word part. Thus we say that a half is part of a whole, because two halves make a whole. We say, too, that a side is part of a diameter, but in a different sense, because no matter how many times a side is taken it does not make a diameter, but is always less than the diameter. Again we say that an angle of contingence is part of a right angle because there is an infinite number of angles of contingence in a right angle, and yet when an angle of contingence is subtracted from a right angle a finite number of times the latter becomes smaller. It is in a different sense, however, that a point is said to be part of a line in which it is contained an infinite number of times, for when a point is taken away from a line a finite number of times this does not shorten the line.

To return therefore to my theme, I say that light through the infinite multiplication of itself equally in all directions extends matter on all sides equally into the form of a sphere and, as a necessary consequence of this extension, the outermost parts of matter are more extended and more rarefied than those within, which are close to the center. And since the outermost parts will be rarefied to the highest degree, the inner parts will have the possibility of further rarefaction.

In this way light, by extending first matter into the form of a sphere, and by rarefying its outermost parts to the highest degree, actualized completely in the outermost sphere the potentiality of matter, and left this matter without any potency to further impression. And thus the first body in the outermost part of the sphere, the body which is called the firmament, is perfect, because it has nothing in its composition but first matter and first form. It is therefore the simplest of all bodies with respect to the parts that constitute its essence and with respect to its quantity which is the greatest possible in extent. It differs from the genus body only in this respect, that in it the matter is completely actualized through the first form alone. But the genus body, which is in this and in other bodies and has in its essence first matter and first form, abstracts from the complete actualization of matter through the first form and from the diminution of matter through the first form.

When the first body, which is the firmament, has in this way been completely actualized, it diffuses its light (*lumen*) from every part of itself to the center of the universe. For since light (*lux*) is the perfection of the first body and naturally multiplies itself from the first body, it is necessarily diffused to the center of the universe. And since this light (*lux*) is a form entirely inseparable from matter in its diffusion from the first body, it extends along with itself the spirituality of the matter of the first body. Thus there proceeds from the first body light (*lumen*), which is a spiritual body, or if you prefer, a bodily spirit. This light (*lumen*) in its passing does not divide the body through which it passes, and thus it passes instantaneously from the body of the first heaven to the center of the universe. Furthermore, its passing is not to be understood in the sense of something numerically one passing instantaneously from that heaven to the center of the universe, for this is perhaps impossible, but its passing takes place through the multiplication of itself and the infinite generation of light (*lumen*). This light (*lumen*), expanded and brought together from the first body toward the center of the universe, gathered together the mass existing below the first body; and since the first body could no longer be lessened on account of its being completely actualized and unchangeable, and since, too, there could not be a space that was empty, it was necessary that in the very gathering together of this mass the outermost parts should be drawn out and expanded. Thus the inner parts of the aforesaid mass came to be more dense and the outer parts more rarefied; and so great was the power of this light (*lumen*) gathering together—and in the very act of gathering, separating—that the outermost parts of the mass contained below the first body were drawn out and rarefied to the highest degree. Thus in the outermost parts of the mass in question, the second sphere came into being, completely actualized and susceptible of no further impression. The completeness of actualization and the perfection of the second sphere consist in this that light (*lumen*) is begotten from the first sphere and that light (*lux*) which is simple in the first sphere is doubled in the second.

Just as the light (*lumen*) begotten from the first body completed the actualization of the second sphere and left a denser mass below the second sphere, so the light (*lumen*) begotten from the second sphere completed the actualization of the third sphere, and through its gathering left below this third sphere a mass of even greater density. This process of simultaneously gathering together and separating continued in this way until the nine heavenly spheres were completely actualized and there was gathered together below the ninth and lowest sphere the dense mass which constitutes the matter of the four elements. But the lowest sphere, the sphere of the moon, which also gives forth light (*lumen*) from itself, by its light (*lumen*) gathered together the mass contained below itself and, by gathering it together, thinned out and expanded its outermost parts. The power of this light (*lumen*), however, was not so great that by drawing together it could expand the outermost parts of this mass to the highest degree. On this account every part of the mass was left imperfect and capable of being gathered together and expanded. The highest part of this mass was expanded, although not to the greatest possible extent. Nevertheless by its expansion it became fire, although remaining still the matter of the elements. This element giving forth light from itself and drawing together the mass contained below it expanded its outermost parts, but not to as great an extent as the fire was expanded, and in this way it produced air. Air, also, in bringing forth from itself, a spiritual body or a bodily spirit, and drawing together what is contained within itself, and by drawing together, expanding its outer parts, produced water and earth. But because water retained more of the power of drawing together than of the power of expanding, water as well as earth was left with the attribute of weight.

In this way, therefore, the thirteen spheres of this sensible world were brought into being. Nine of them, the heavenly spheres, are not subject to change, increase, generation or corruption because they are completely actualized. The other four spheres have the opposite mode of being, that is, they are subject to change, increase, generation and corruption, because they are not completely actualized. It is clear that every higher body, in virtue of the light (*lumen*) which proceeds from it, is the form (species) and perfection of the body that comes after it. And just as unity is potentially every number that comes after it, so the first body, through the multiplication of its light, is every body that comes after it.

Earth is all the higher bodies because all the higher lights come together in it. For this reason earth is called Pan by the poets, that is "the whole," and it is also given the name Cybele, which is almost like *cubile*, from cube (*cubus*) that is, a solid. The reason for this is that earth, that is to say, Cybele, the mother of all the gods, is the most compact of all bodies, because, although the higher lights are gathered together in it, nevertheless they do not have their source in the earth through its own operations, but the light (*lumen*) of any sphere whatever can be educed from it into act and operation. Thus every one of the gods will be begotten from it as from a kind of mother. The intermediate bodies have a twofold relationship. Towards lower bodies they have the same relation as the first heaven has to all other things, and they are related to the higher bodies as earth is related to all other things. And thus in a certain sense each thing contains all other things.

The form (*species*) and perfection of all bodies is light, but in the higher bodies it is more spiritual and simple, whereas in the lower bodies it is more corporeal and multiplied. Furthermore, all bodies are not of the same form (*species*) even though they all proceed from light, whether simple or multiplied, just as all numbers are not the same in form (*species*) despite the fact that they are all derived from unity by a greater or lesser multiplication.

This discussion may perhaps clarify the meaning of those who say that "all things are one by the perfection of one light" and also the meaning of those who say that "things which are many are many through the multiplication of light itself in different degrees."

But since lower bodies participate in the form of the higher bodies, the lower body because it participates in the same form as the higher body, receives its motion from the same incorporeal moving power by which the higher body is moved. For this reason the incorporeal power of intelligence or soul, which moves the first and highest sphere with a diurnal motion, moves all the lower heavenly spheres with this same diurnal motion. But in proportion as these spheres are lower they receive this motion in a more weakened state, because in proportion as a sphere is lower the purity and strength of the first corporeal light is lessened in it.

But although the elements participate in the form of the first heaven, nevertheless they are not moved by the mover of the first heaven with a diurnal motion. Although they participate in that first light, they are not subject to the first moving power since that light in them is impure, weak, and far removed from the purity which it has in the first body, and also because they possess the denseness of matter which is the principle of resistance and stubbornness. Nevertheless, there are some who think that the sphere of fire rotates with a diurnal motion, and they take the rotating motion of comets to be an indication of this. They say also that this motion extends even to the waters of the sea, in such a way that the tide of the seas proceeds from it. But all sound philosophers say that the earth is free from this motion.

In this same way, too, the spheres that come after the second sphere, which is usually called the eighth when we compute from the earth upward, all share in the motion of this second sphere because they participate in its form. Indeed this motion is proper to each of them in addition to the diurnal motion.

But because the heavenly spheres are completely actualized and are not receptive of rarefaction or condensation, light (*lux*) in them does not incline the parts of matter either away from the center so as to rarefy them, or toward the center to condense them. On this account the heavenly spheres are not receptive of up or down motion but only of circular motion by an intellectual moving power, which by directing its glance upon them in a corporeal way revolves the spheres themselves in a circular corporeal motion. But because the elements are incompletely actualized and subject to rarefaction and condensation, the light (*lumen*) which is in them inclines them away from the center so as to rarefy them, or toward the center so as to condense them. And on this account they are naturally capable of being moved in an upward or downward motion.

The highest body, which is the simplest of all bodies, contains four constituents, namely form, matter, composition and the composite. Now the form being the simplest holds the position of unity. But matter on account of its twofold potency, namely its susceptibility to impressions and its receptiveness of them, and also on account of its denseness which belongs fundamentally to matter but which is primarily and principally characteristic of a thing which is a duality, is rightly allotted the nature of a duality. But composition has a trinity in itself because there appears in it informed matter and materialized form and that which is distinctive of the composition, which is found in every composite as a third constituent distinct from matter and form. And that which is the composite proper, over and above these three constituents, is classed as a quaternary. There is, therefore, in the first body, in which all other bodies exist virtually, a quaternary and therefore the number of the remaining bodies is basically not more than ten. For the unity of the form, the duality of the matter, the trinity of the composition and the quaternity of the composite when they are added make a total of ten. On this account ten is the number of the bodies of the spheres of the world, because the sphere of the elements, although it is divided into four, is nevertheless one by its participation in earthly corruptible nature.

From these considerations it is clear that ten is the perfect number in the universe, because every perfect whole has something in it corresponding to form and unity, and something corresponding to matter and duality, something corresponding to composition and trinity, and something corresponding to the composite and quaternity. Nor is it possible to add a fifth to these four. For this reason every perfect whole is ten.

On this account it is manifest that only five proportions found in these four numbers, one, two, three, four, are suited to composition and to the harmony that gives stability to every composite. For this reason these five proportions are the only ones that produce harmony in musical melodies, in bodily movements, and in rhythmic measures.

This is the end of the treatise on light of the Bishop of Lincoln.

ROGER BACON
ca. 1214–ca. 1292

Born somewhere in England, Roger Bacon studied at the universities of Oxford and Paris. By 1237, he was teaching at Paris—one of the first to lecture on the newly rediscovered works of Aristotle. After ten years spent studying theology and teaching Aristotle, Bacon returned to England. In Oxford, he encountered the writings and perhaps even the person of Robert Grosseteste. Bacon joined the Franciscans, but he soon found himself in trouble with them. He naively accepted the work of the apocalyptic extremist Joachim of Floris, which made Bacon's own work suspect. Sometimes Bacon was too blunt in criticizing his superiors, claiming that the first cause of human ignorance was undue reverence for authority. The Franciscan General, St. Bonaventure, ordered him not to publish. In 1266, Pope Clement IV asked to see Bacon's work. Hoping to find papal support, Bacon wrote his *Opus Majus* and sent it to Rome. Unfortunately, Clement died before he could intervene on Bacon's behalf. Without the pope's patronage, Bacon's novel teachings—and his candid assessment of fellow teachers—led to his imprisonment. Continuing to write, he spent as many as fourteen of his last years in prison.

The works of Aristotle that Bacon taught, despite their empirical orientation, did not always lead to an emphasis on what we call "science." Aristotle advocated inductive reasoning from observed particulars to universals. But many thirteenth-century philosophers accepted not only Aristotle's observational method, but also his observational *conclusions* as well. With Aristotle's conclusions *given*, these philosophers saw little need for more empirical data and so considered further scientific inquiry pointless. And whereas Aristotle had been motivated to study natural phenomena to discover their purpose or *entelechy,* medieval theologians believed they already knew the entelechy of all of nature—the service of God's purposes. With God's purposes known, there seemed little reason for Aristotelian exploration.

However, some theologians granted that if human sin or reason's incompetence keeps us from knowing God's purposes, empirical testing can be useful in the quest for ends. Whereas one cannot know the *ultimate* purposes of God by reason alone, one can know *something* of God's purposes by examining God's creation. Ironically, Franciscan skepticism about human ability to know divine purposes was a factor in the rise of experimental science. Bacon, for example, argued that experiments were a way of overcoming the sinful errors of previous thinkers.

Like his later namesake, Sir Francis Bacon, Roger Bacon was more of an advocate for than a practitioner of empirical science. Roger Bacon did not actually perform many experiments, and his writings mix science with astrology and alchemy. But he did argue for experience as a major component in scientific knowledge, and he agreed with Grosseteste on the importance of mathematics for science. More important, he saw the practical applications of science and predicted the invention of automobiles, airplanes, and submarines.

The *Opus Majus* calls for educational reform and provides a blueprint. The selections given here, in the Robert Belle Burke translation, argue for the general importance of science, the necessity of mathematics in science, and science's need for experience as well as reason. Our selections end with Bacon's famous claim that the most important characteristic of science is that it "investigates by experiment."

*   *   *

For works on Bacon, see John Henry Bridges, *The Life & Work of Roger Bacon: An Introduction to the Opus Majus* (London: William & Norgate, 1914); William Romaine Newbold, *The Cipher of Roger Bacon* (Philadelphia: University of Pennsylvania Press, 1928); Evalyn Westacott, *Roger Bacon in Life and Legend* (New York: Philosophical Library, 1953); and the collection of essays, A.G. Little, ed., *Roger Bacon Essays* (Oxford: Clarendon Press, 1914).

For works on medieval science, see Alistair Cameron Crombie, *Augustine to Galileo: Medieval and Early Modern Science,* two volumes, 2nd edition (Garden City, NY: Doubleday, 1959); Charles Homer Haskins, *Studies in the History of Mediaeval Science* (New York: F. Ungar, 1960); Richard C. Dales, *The Scientific Achievement of the Middle Ages* (Philadelphia: University of Pennsylvania Press, 1973); and David C. Lindberg, *The Beginnings of Western Science: The European Scientific Tradition in Philosophical, Religious, and Institutional Context, 600 B.C. to A.D. 1450* (Chicago: University of Chicago Press, 1992). Of special interest is P.L. Jacob, *Science and Literature in the Middle Ages and the Renaissance* (New York: F. Ungar, 1964), which includes several hundred wood engravings.

THE OPUS MAJUS (in part)

PART IV OF THIS PLEA

FIRST DISTINCTION, IN THREE CHAPTERS

Chapter 1: In Which Is Shown the Power of Mathematics in the Sciences and in the Affairs and Occupations of this World

After making it clear that many famous roots of knowledge depend on the mastery of the languages through which there is an entrance into knowledge on the part of the Latins, I now wish to consider the foundations of this same knowledge as regards the great sciences, in which there is a special power in respect to the other sciences and the affairs of this world. There are four great sciences, without which the other sciences cannot be known nor a knowledge of things secured. If these are known any one can make glorious progress in the power of knowledge without difficulty and labor, not only in human sciences, but in that which is divine. The virtue of each of these sciences will be touched upon not only on account of knowledge itself, but in respect to the other matters aforesaid. Of these sciences the gate and key is mathematics, which the saints discovered at the beginning of the world, as I shall show, and which has always been used by all the saints and sages more than all other sciences. Neglect of this branch now for thirty or forty years has destroyed the whole system of study of the Latins. Since he who is ignorant of this cannot know the other sciences nor the affairs of this world, as I shall prove. And what is worse men ignorant of this do not perceive their own ignorance, and therefore do not seek a remedy. And on the contrary the knowledge of this science prepares the mind and elevates it to a certain knowledge of all things, so that if one learns the roots of knowledge placed about it and rightly applies them to the knowledge of the other sciences and matters, he will then be able to know all that follows without error and doubt, easily and effectually. For without these neither what precedes nor what follows can be known; whence they perfect what precedes and regulate it, even as the end perfects those things pertaining to it, and they arrange and open the way to what follows. This I now intend to intimate through authority and reason; and in the first place I intend to do so in the human sciences and in the matters of this world, and then in divine knowledge, and lastly according as they are related to the Church and the other three purposes.

* * *

Roger Bacon, *The Opus Majus of Roger Bacon,* Part IV, Chapters 1, 3; Part VI, Chapters 1–2, translated by Robert Belle Burke (Philadelphia: University of Pennsylvania Press, 1928).

Chapter 3: In Which It Is Proved by Reason that Every Science Requires Mathematics

What has been shown as regards mathematics as a whole through authority, can now be shown likewise by reason. And I make this statement in the first place, because other sciences use mathematical examples, but examples are given to make clear the subjects treated by the sciences; wherefore ignorance of the examples involves an ignorance of the subjects for the understanding of which the examples are adduced. For since change in natural objects is not found without some augmentation and diminution nor do these latter take place without change, Aristotle was not able to make clear without complications the difference between augmentation and change by any natural example, because augmentation and diminution go together always with change in some way; wherefore he gave the mathematical example of the rectangle which augmented by a gnomon* increases in magnitude and is not altered in shape. This example cannot be understood before the twenty-second proposition of the sixth book of the *Elements*. For in that proposition of the sixth book it is proved that a smaller rectangle is similar in every particular to a larger one and therefore a smaller one is not altered in shape, although it becomes larger by the addition of the gnomon.

Secondly, because comprehension of mathematical truths is innate, as it were, in us. For a small boy, as Tullius states in the first book of the *Tusculan Disputations*, when questioned by Socrates on geometrical truths, replied as though he had learned geometry. And this experiment has been tried in many cases, and does not hold in other sciences, as will appear more clearly from what follows. Wherefore since this knowledge is almost innate, and as it were precedes discovery and learning, or at least is less in need of them than other sciences, it will be first among sciences and will precede others disposing us toward them; since what is innate or almost so disposes toward what is acquired.

Thirdly, because this science of all the parts of philosophy was the earliest discovered. For this was first discovered at the beginning of the human race. Since it was discovered before the flood and then later by the sons of Adam, and by Noah and his sons, as is clear from the prologue to the *Construction of the Astrolabe* according to Ptolemy, and from Albumazar in the larger introduction to astronomy, and from the first book of the *Antiquitics*, and this is true as regards all its parts, geometry, arithmetic, music, astronomy. But this would not have been the case except for the fact that this science is earlier than the others and naturally precedes them. Hence it is clear that it should be studied first, that through it we may advance to all the later sciences.

Fourthly, because the natural road for us is from what is easy to that which is more difficult. But this science is the easiest. This is clearly proved by the fact that mathematics is not beyond the intellectual grasp of any one. For the people at large and those wholly illiterate know how to draw figures and compute and sing, all of which are mathematical operations. But we must begin first with what is common to the laity and to the educated; and it is not only hurtful to the clergy, but disgraceful and abominable that they are ignorant of what the laity knows well and profitably. Fifthly, we see that the clergy, even the most ignorant, are able to grasp mathematical truths, although they are unable to attain to the other sciences. Besides, a man by listening once or twice can learn more about this science with certainty and reality without error, than he can by listening ten

---

*[That which is added to three sides of a parallelogram to produce a larger parallelogram of the same shape.]

times about the other parts of philosophy, as is clear to one making the experiment. Sixthly, since the natural road for us is to begin with things which befit the state and nature of childhood, because children begin with facts that are better known by us and that must be acquired first. But of this nature is mathematics, since children are first taught to sing, and in the same way they can learn the method of making figures and of counting, and it would be far easier and more necessary for them to know about numbers before singing, because in the relations of numbers in music the whole theory of numbers is set forth by example, just as the authors on music teach, both in ecclesiastical music and in philosophy. But the theory of numbers depends on figures, since numbers relating to lines, surfaces, solids, squares, cubes, pentagons, hexagons, and other figures, are known from lines, figures, and angles. For it has been found that children learn mathematical truths better and more quickly, as is clear in singing, and we also know by experience that children learn and acquire mathematical truths better than the other parts of philosophy. For Aristotle says in the sixth book of the *Ethics* that youths are able to grasp mathematical truths quickly, not so matters pertaining to nature, metaphysics, and morals. Wherefore the mind must be trained first through the former rather than through these latter sciences. Seventhly, where the same things are not known to us and to nature, there the natural road for us is from the things better known to us to those better known to nature, or known more simply; and more easily do we grasp what is better known to ourselves, and with great difficulty we arrive at a knowledge of those things which are better known to nature. And the things known to nature are erroneously and imperfectly known by us, because our intellect bears the same relation to what is so clear to nature, as the eye of the bat to the light of the sun, as Aristotle maintains in the second book of the *Metaphysics;* such, for example, are especially God and the angels, and future life and heavenly things, and creatures nobler than others, because the nobler they are the less known are they to us. And these are called things known to nature and known simply. Therefore, on the contrary, where the same things are known both to us and to nature, we make much progress in regard to what is known to nature and in regard to all that is there included, and we are able to attain a perfect knowledge of them. But in mathematics only, as Averroës says in the first book of the *Physics* and in the seventh of the *Metaphysics* and in his commentary on the third book of the *Heavens and the World,* are the same things known to us and to nature or simply. Therefore as in mathematics we touch upon what is known fully to us, so also do we touch upon what is known to nature and known simply. Therefore we are able to reach directly an intimate knowledge of that science. Since, therefore, we have not this ability in other sciences, clearly mathematics is better known. Therefore the acquisition of this subject is the beginning of our knowledge.

Likewise, eighthly, because every doubt gives place to certainty and every error is cleared away by unshaken truth. But in mathematics we are able to arrive at the full truth without error, and at a certainty of all points involved without doubt; since in this subject demonstration by means of a proper and necessary cause can be given. Demonstration causes the truth to be known. And likewise in this subject it is possible to have for all things an example that may be perceived by the senses, and a test perceptible to the senses in drawing figures and in counting, so that all may be clear to the senses. For this reason there can be no doubt in this science. But in other sciences, the assistance of mathematics being excluded, there are so many doubts, so many opinions, so many errors on the part of man, that these sciences cannot be unfolded, as is clear since demonstration by means of a proper and necessary cause does not exist in them from their own nature because in natural phenomena, owing to the genesis and destruction of their proper causes as well as of the effects, there is no such thing as necessity. In metaphysics there can be no demonstration except through effect, since spiritual facts are discovered through corporeal effects and the creator through the creature, as is clear in that science. In morals there cannot be demonstrations from proper causes, as Aristotle teaches. And likewise neither in matters pertaining to logic nor in grammar, as is clear, can there be very convincing demonstrations because of the weak nature of the material concerning which those sciences treat. And therefore in mathematics alone are there demonstrations of the most convincing kind through a necessary cause. And therefore here alone can a man arrive at the truth from the nature of this science. Likewise in the other sciences there are doubts and opinions and contradictions on our part, so that we scarcely agree on the most trifling question or in a single sophism; for in these sciences there are from their nature no processes of drawing figures and of reckonings, by which all things must be proved true. And therefore in mathematics alone is there certainty without doubt.

Wherefore it is evident that if in other sciences we should arrive at certainty without doubt and truth without error, it behooves us to place the foundations of knowledge in mathematics, in so far as disposed through it we are able to reach certainty in other sciences and truth by the exclusion of error. This reasoning can be made clearer by comparison, and the principle is stated in the ninth book of Euclid. The same holds true here as in the relation of the knowledge of the conclusion to the knowledge of the premises, so that if there is error and doubt in these, the truth cannot be arrived at through these premises in regard to the conclusion, nor can there be certainty, because doubt is not verified by doubt, nor is truth proved by falsehood, although it is possible for us to reason from false premises, our reasoning in that case drawing in inference and not furnishing a proof; the same is true with respect to sciences as a whole; those in which there are strong and numerous doubts and opinions and errors, I say at least on our part, should have doubts of this kind and false statements cleared away by some science definitely known to us, and in which we have neither doubts nor errors. For since the conclusions and principles belonging to them are parts of the sciences as a whole, just as part is related to part, as conclusion to premises, so is science related to science, so that a science which is full of doubts and besprinkled with opinions and obscurities, cannot be rendered certain, nor made clear, nor verified except by some other science known and verified, certain and plain to us, as in the case of a conclusion reached through premises. But mathematics alone, as was shown above, remains fixed and verified for us with the utmost certainty and verification. Therefore by means of this science all other sciences must be known and verified.

Since we have now shown by the peculiar property of that science that mathematics is prior to other sciences, and is useful and necessary to them, we now proceed to show this by considerations taken from its subject matter. And in the first place we so conclude, because the natural road for us is from sense perception to the intellect, since if sense perception is lacking, the knowledge related to that sense perception is lacking also, according to the statement in the first book of the *Posterior Analytics,* since as sense perception proceeds so does the human intellect. But quantity is especially a matter of sense perception, because it pertains to the common sense and is perceived by the other senses, and nothing can be perceived without quantity, wherefore the intellect is especially able to make progress as respects quantity. In the second place, because the very act of intelligence in itself is not completed without continuous quantity, since Aristotle states in his book on *Memory and Recollection* that our whole intellect is associated with continuity and time. Hence we grasp quantities and bodies by a direct perception of the intellect, because their forms are present in the intellect. But the forms of incorporeal things are not so perceived by our intellect; or if such forms are produced in it, according to Avicenna's statement in the third book of the

Metaphysics, we, however, do not perceive this fact owing to the more vigorous occupation of our intellect in respect to bodies and quantities. And therefore by means of argumentation and attention to corporeal things and quantities we investigate the idea of incorporeal things, as Aristotle does in the eleventh book of the *Metaphysics*. Wherefore the intellect will make progress especially as regards quantity itself for this reason, that quantities and bodies as far as they are such belong peculiarly to the human intellect as respects the common condition of understanding. Each and every thing exists as an antecedent for some result, and this is true in higher degree of that which has just been stated.

Moreover, for full confirmation the last reason can be drawn from the experience of men of science; for all scientists in ancient times labored in mathematics, in order that they might know all things, just as we have seen in the case of men of our own times, and have heard in the case of others who by means of mathematics, of which they had an excellent knowledge, have learned all science. For very illustrious men have been found, like Bishop Robert of Lincoln and Friar Adam de Marisco, and many others, who by the power of mathematics have learned to explain the causes of all things, and expound adequately things human and divine. Moreover, the sure proof of this matter is found in the writings of those men, as, for example, on impressions such as the rainbow, comets, generation of heat, investigation of localities on the earth and other matters, of which both theology and philosophy make use. Wherefore it is clear that mathematics is absolutely necessary and useful to other sciences.

These reasons are general ones, but in particular this point can be shown by a survey of all the parts of philosophy disclosing how all things are known by the application of mathematics. This amounts to showing that other sciences are not to be known by means of dialectical and sophistical argument as commonly introduced, but by means of mathematical demonstrations entering into the truths and activities of other sciences and regulating them, without which they cannot be understood, nor made clear, nor taught, nor learned. If any one in particular should proceed by applying the power of mathematics to the separate sciences, he would see that nothing of supreme moment can be known in them without mathematics. But this simply amounts to establishing definite methods of dealing with all sciences, and by means of mathematics verifying all things necessary to the other sciences. But this matter does not come within the limits of the present survey.

*   *   *

PART VI OF THIS PLEA

It Is Also the Sixth Part of the Opus Majus, on Experimental Science

CHAPTER 1

Having laid down fundamental principles of the wisdom of the Latins so far as they are found in language, mathematics, and optics, I now wish to unfold the principles of experimental science, since without experience nothing can be sufficiently known. For there are two modes of acquiring knowledge, namely, by reasoning and experience. Reasoning draws a conclusion and makes us grant the conclusion, but does not make the conclusion certain, nor does it remove doubt so that the mind may rest on the intuition of truth, unless the mind discovers it by the path of experience; since many have the arguments relating to what can be known, but because they lack experience they neglect the arguments, and neither avoid what is harmful nor follow what is good. For if a man who has never seen fire should prove by adequate reasoning that fire burns and injures things and destroys them, his mind would not be satisfied thereby, nor would he avoid fire, until he placed his hand or some combustible substance in the fire, so that he might prove by experience that which reasoning taught. But when he has had actual experience of combustion his mind is made certain and rests in the full light of truth. Therefore reasoning does not suffice, but experience does.

This is also evident in mathematics, where proof is most convincing. But the mind of one who has the most convincing proof in regard to the equilateral triangle will never cleave to the conclusion without experience, nor will he heed it, but will disregard it until experience is offered him by the intersection of two circles, from either intersection of which two lines may be drawn to the extremities of the given line; but then the man accepts the conclusion without any question. Aristotle's statement, then, that proof is reasoning that causes us to know is to be understood with the proviso that the proof is accompanied by its appropriate experience, and is not to be understood of the bare proof. His statement also in the first book of the *Metaphysics* that those who understand the reason and the cause are wiser than those who have empiric knowledge of a fact, is spoken of such as know only the bare truth without the cause. But I am here speaking of the man who knows the reason and the cause through experience. These men are perfect in their wisdom, as Aristotle maintains in the sixth book of the *Ethics,* whose simple statements must be accepted as if they offered proof, as he states in the same place.

He therefore who wishes to rejoice without doubt in regard to the truths underlying phenomena must know how to devote himself to experiment. For authors write many statements, and people believe them through reasoning which they formulate without experience. Their reasoning is wholly false. For it is generally believed that the diamond cannot be broken except by goat's blood, and philosophers and theologians misuse this idea. But fracture by means of blood of this kind has never been verified, although the effort has been made, and without that blood it can be broken easily. For I have seen this with my own eyes, and this is necessary, because gems cannot be carved except by fragments of this stone. Similarly it is generally believed that the castors employed by physicians are the testicles of the male animal. But this is not true, because the beaver has these under its breast, and both the male and female produce testicles of this kind. Besides these castors the male beaver has its testicles in their natural place; and therefore what is subjoined is a dreadful lie, namely, that when the hunters pursue the beaver, he himself knowing what they are seeking cuts out with his teeth these glands. Moreover, it is generally believed that hot water freezes more quickly than cold water in vessels, and the argument in support of this is advanced that contrary is excited by contrary, just like enemies meeting each other. But it is certain that cold water freezes more quickly for any one who makes the experiment. People attribute this to Aristotle in the second book of the *Meteorologics;* but he certainly does not make this statement but he does make one like it, by which they have been deceived, namely, that if cold water and hot water are poured on a cold place, as upon ice, the hot water freezes more quickly, and this is true. But if hot water and cold are placed in two vessels, the cold will freeze more quickly. Therefore all things must be verified by experience.

But experience is of two kinds; one is gained through our external senses, and in this way we gain our experience of those things that are in the heavens by instruments made for this purpose, and of those things here below by means attested by our vision. Things that do not belong in our part of the world we know through other scientists who have had experience of them. As, for example, Aristotle on the authority of Alexander sent two thousand men through different parts of the world to gain experimental knowledge of all things that are on the surface of the earth, as Pliny bears witness in his *Natural History*. This experience is both human and philosophical, as far as man can act in accordance with the grace given him; but this experience does not suffice him, because it does not give full attestation in regard to things corporeal owing to its difficulty and does not touch at all on things spiritual. It is necessary, therefore, that the intellect of man should be otherwise aided, and for this reason the holy patriarchs and prophets, who first gave sciences to the world, received illumination within and were not dependent on sense alone. The same is true of many believers since the time of Christ. For the grace of faith illuminates greatly, as also do divine inspirations, not only in things spiritual, but in things corporeal and in the sciences of philosophy; as Ptolemy states in the *Centilogium*, namely, that there are two roads by which we arrive at the knowledge of facts, one through the experience of philosophy, the other through divine inspiration, which is far the better way, as he says.

Moreover, there are seven stages of this internal knowledge, the first of which is reached through illuminations relating purely to the sciences. The second consists in the virtues. For the evil man is ignorant, as Aristotle says in the second book of the *Ethics*. Moreover, Algazel says in his *Logic* that the soul disfigured by sins is like a rusty mirror, in which the species of objects cannot be seen clearly; but the soul adorned with virtues is like a well-polished mirror, in which the forms of objects are clearly seen. For this reason true philosophers have labored more in morals for the honor of virtue, concluding in their own case that they cannot perceive the causes of things unless they have souls free from sins. Such is the statement of Augustine in regard to Socrates in the eighth book of the *City of God*, Chapter III. Wherefore the Scripture says, "in a malevolent soul, etc." For it is not possible that the soul should rest in the light of truth while it is stained with sins, but like a parrot or magpie it will repeat the words of another which it has learned by long practice. The proof of this is that the beauty of truth known in its splendor attracts men to the love of it, but the proof of love is the display of a work of love. Therefore he who acts contrary to the truth must necessarily be ignorant of it, although he may know how to compose very elegant phrases, and quote the opinions of other people, like an animal that imitates the words of human beings, and like an ape that relies on the aid of men to perform its part, although it does not understand their reason. Virtue, therefore, clarifies the mind, so that a man comprehends more easily not only moral but scientific truths. I have proved this carefully in the case of many pure young men, who because of innocency of soul have attained greater proficiency than can be stated, when they have had sane advice in regard to their study. Of this number is the bearer of this present treatise, whose fundamental knowledge very few of the Latins have acquired. For since he is quite young, about twenty years of age, and very poor, nor has he been able to have teachers, nor has he spent one year in learning his great store of knowledge, nor is he a man of great genius nor of a very retentive memory, there can be no other cause except

Master with Students, engraving after a fifteenth-century miniature. Roger Bacon objected
to the Scholastic style of education depicted here, arguing that scientific experimentation
is necessary for a proper education. (*Corbis-Bettmann*)

the grace of God, which owing to the purity of his soul has granted to him those things
that it has as a rule refused to show to all other students. For as a spotless virgin he has
departed from me, nor have I found in him any kind of mortal sin, although I have examined him carefully, and he has, therefore, a soul so bright and clear that with very
little instruction he has learned more than can be estimated. And I have striven to aid in
bringing it about that these two young men should be useful vessels in God's Church,
to the end that they may reform by the grace of God the whole course of study of the
Latins.

The third stage consists in the seven gifts of the Holy Spirit, which Isaiah enu-
merates. The fourth consists in the beatitudes, which the Lord defines in the Gospels.
The fifth consists in the spiritual senses. The sixth consists in fruits, of which is the
peace of God which passes all understanding. The seventh consists in raptures and
their states according to the different ways in which people are caught up to see many
things of which it is not lawful for a man to speak. And he who has had diligent training in these experiences or in several of them is able to assure himself and others not
only in regard to things spiritual, but also in regard to all human sciences. Therefore

since all the divisions of speculative philosophy proceed by arguments, which are either based on a point from authority or on the other points of argumentation except this division which I am now examining, we find necessary the science that is called experimental. I wish to explain it, as it is useful not only to philosophy, but to the knowledge of God, and for the direction of the whole world; just as in the preceding divisions I showed the relationship of the languages and sciences to their end, which is the divine wisdom by which all things are disposed.

Chapter 2

Since this Experimental Science is wholly unknown to the rank and file of students, I am therefore unable to convince people of its utility unless at the same time I disclose its excellence and its proper signification. This science alone, therefore, knows how to test perfectly what can be done by nature, what by the effort of art, what by trickery, what the incantations, conjurations, invocations, deprecations, sacrifices, that belong to magic, mean and dream of, and what is in them, so that all falsity may be removed and the truth alone of art and nature may be retained. This science alone teaches us how to view the mad acts of magicians, that they may be not ratified but shunned, just as logic considers sophistical reasoning.

This science has three leading characteristics with respect to other sciences. The first is that it investigates by experiment the notable conclusions of all those sciences. For the other sciences know how to discover their principles by experiments, but their conclusions are reached by reasoning drawn from the principles discovered. But if they should have a particular and complete experience of their own conclusions, they must have it with the aid of this noble science. For it is true that mathematics has general experiments as regards its conclusions in its figures and calculations, which also are applied to all sciences and to this kind of experiment, because no science can be known without mathematics. But if we give our attention to particular and complete experiments and such as are attested wholly by the proper method, we must employ the principles of this science which is called experimental. I give as an example the rainbow and phenomena connected with it, of which nature are the circle around the sun and the stars, the streak (*virga*) also lying at the side of the sun or of a star, which is apparent to the eye in a straight line, and is called by Aristotle in the third book of the *Meteorologics* a perpendicular, but by Seneca a streak, and the circle is called a corona, phenomena which frequently have the colors of the rainbow. The natural philosopher discusses these phenomena, and the writer on Perspective has much to add pertaining to the mode of vision that is necessary in this case. But neither Aristotle nor Avicenna in their *Natural Histories* has given us a knowledge of phenomena of this kind, nor has Seneca, who composed a special book on them. But Experimental Science attests them.

BONAVENTURE
1221–1274

Born Giovanni Fidanza in 1221, St. Bonaventure came from Tuscany in what is now central Italy. As a boy, Bonaventure was healed of a serious illness, and his mother attributed the healing to St. Francis of Assisi. As a young man, Bonaventure went to study at the University of Paris and there joined the Franciscan Order. Following completion of his baccalaureate studies, Bonaventure composed his *Commentary on the "Sentences" of Peter Lombard* between 1250 and 1252.* In 1255, Bonaventure became a victim of the conflict between the "seculars" (priests who did not belong to religious orders) and the "regulars" (priests who did). The growing influence of the mendicant orders at the University of Paris led to a backlash by the seculars. The seculars excluded Bonaventure and St. Thomas Aquinas, his Dominican counterpart, from the faculty. It took the direct intervention of the pope in 1257 before the regulars were allowed to return to the university staff.

By then, however, Bonaventure was no longer teaching. Early in 1257, he had been appointed Minister General of the Franciscan Order. While he held this post, Bonaventure also found time to write a number of works, including a series of Lenten reflections on the Ten Commandments, *De Decem Praeceptis*. In 1273, Bonaventure was made Cardinal Bishop of Albano. He attended the Coun-

---

*In the twelfth century, Peter Lombard wrote the *Sentences*—a theological textbook that gathered the opinions of the great theologians and grouped them into four sections: on God, on creation, on the incarnation, and on redemption. While the work itself was not original, its carefulness and system inspired a number of important commentaries.

cil of Lyons during the following year. He died while in Lyons and was buried there in the presence of Pope Gregory X.

Bonaventure had grave doubts about the use of Aristotle's philosophy. He did accept a number of Aristotelian concepts, such as the necessity of experience to know the sensible world. He also used the Aristotelian categories of his time, such as substance, accident, form, and matter. But Bonaventure could not accept two of Aristotle's fundamental teachings. In the first place, Aristotle had rejected the Platonic notion of Forms. Bonaventure held that Augustine's reworking of this Platonic concept was correct and that the Divine Exemplars (Augustine's "Forms") were the proper basis for metaphysics. In the selection given here from *The Mind's Road to God,* translated by George Boas, Bonaventure uses these Platonic notions to explain the ascension of the soul to mystical union with God. Second, Bonaventure rejected the Aristotelian doctrine that the universe was eternal. Our selections on the eternity of the world, translated by Paul M. Byrne, present some of Bonaventure's arguments. It is important to note that in both cases Bonaventure was not content to appeal to theology alone—he sought to persuade by rational argument as well.

But beyond rejecting particular Aristotelian doctrines, Bonaventure believed it impossible that any pagan philosophy could adequately describe even the natural world. Indeed, the idea of a "natural world" itself is an abstraction, since the world is God's creation. Only when metaphysics acknowledges God's activity can truth be found. Even though the natural philosopher can prove God's existence and unity (and Bonaventure produced several such proofs), without a theological understanding of that unity, the philosopher will err.

*   *   *

The best general introduction to Bonaventure's life and teaching remains Étienne Gilson, *The Philosophy of St. Bonaventure,* translated by Dom Illtyd Trethowan and F.J. Sheed (New York: Sheed and Ward, 1938). Jacques Guy Bougerol, *Introduction to the Works of Bonaventure,* translated by Jose de Vinck (Paterson, NJ: St. Anthony Guild Press, 1964) also provides a general introduction, whereas Mary Bernetta Quinn, *To God Alone the Glory: A Life of St. Bonaventure* (Westminster, MD: Newman Press, 1962) gives a laudatory biography. For a comparison of Bonaventure and his more famous contemporary Thomas Aquinas, see Robert W. Shahan and Francis J. Kovach, eds., *Bonaventure & Aquinas: Enduring Philosophers* (Norman: University of Oklahoma Press, 1976).

There are a number of doctoral dissertations on Bonaventure, including Mary Rachael Dady, *The Theory of Knowledge of Saint Bonaventure* (Washington, DC: Catholic University of America Press, 1939), and Michael P. Malloy, *Civil Authority in Medieval Philosophy: Lombard, Aquinas, and Bonaventure* (Lanham, MD: University Press of America, 1985). The Franciscan Institute (of the appropriately named St. Bonaventure, New York) has produced monographs such as that of Emma Jane Marie Spargo, *The Category of the Aesthetic in the Philosophy of Saint Bonaventure* (1953). But most of these dissertations and monographs are too difficult for the beginning student (and often include long untranslated Latin passages).

THE MIND'S ROAD TO GOD (in part)

PROLOGUE

1. To begin with, the first principle from Whom all illumination descends as from the Father of Light, by Whom are given all the best and perfect gifts [James, 1, 17], the eternal Father do I call upon through His Son, our Lord Jesus Christ, that by the intercession of the most holy Virgin Mary, mother of God Himself and of our Lord, Jesus Christ, and of the blessed Francis, our father and leader, He may enlighten the eyes of our mind to guide our feet into the way of that peace "which surpasses all understanding" [Eph., 1, 17; Luke, 1, 79; Phil., 4, 7], which peace our Lord Jesus Christ has announced and given to us; which lesson our father Francis always taught, in all of whose preaching was the annunciation of peace both in the beginning and in the end, wishing for peace in every greeting, yearning for ecstatic peace in every moment of contemplation, as a citizen of that Jerusalem of which that man of peace said, with those that hated peace he was peaceable [Ps., 119, 7], "Pray ye for the things that are for the peace of Jerusalem" [Ps., 121, 6]. For he knew that the throne of Solomon was nowise save in peace, since it is written, "His place is in peace and His abode in Sion" [Ps., 75, 3].

2. Since, then, following the example of the most blessed father Francis, I breathlessly sought this peace, I, a sinner, who have succeeded to the place of that most blessed father after his death, the seventh Minister General of the brothers, though in all ways unworthy—it happened that by the divine will in the thirty-third year after the death of that blessed man I ascended to Mount Alverna as to a quiet place, with the desire of seeking spiritual peace; and staying there, while I meditated on the ascent of the mind to God, amongst other things there occurred that miracle which happened in the same place to the blessed Francis himself, the vision namely of the winged Seraph in the likeness of the Crucified. While looking upon this vision, I immediately saw that it signified the suspension of our father himself in contemplation and the way by which he came to it.

3. For by those six wings are rightly to be understood the six stages of illumination by which the soul, as if by steps or progressive movements, was disposed to pass into peace by ecstatic elevations of Christian wisdom. The way, however, is only through the most burning love of the Crucified, Who so transformed Paul, "caught up into the third heaven" [II Cor., 12, 2], into Christ, that he said, "With Christ I am nailed to the cross, yet I live, now not I, but Christ liveth in me" [Gal., 2, 19]; who therefore so absorbed the mind of Francis that his soul was manifest in his flesh and he bore the most holy stigmata of the Passion in his body for two years before his death. Therefore the symbol of the six-winged Seraph signifies the six stages of illumination, which begin with God's creatures and lead up to God, to Whom no one can enter properly save through the Crucified. For he who does not enter by the door but otherwise, he is

St. Bonaventure, *The Mind's Road to God*, translated by George Boas (New York: Macmillan/Library of the Liberal Arts, 1953), Prologue and Chapters 1–3.

a thief and a robber [John, 10, 1] But if anyone does enter by this door, he shall go in and go out and shall find pastures [John, 9]. Because of this John says in his Apocalypse [22, 14], "Blessed are they that wash their robes in the blood of the Lamb, that they may have a right to the Tree of Life and may enter in by the gates into the City"; as if he were to say that one cannot enter into the heavenly Jerusalem through contemplation unless one enter through the blood of the Lamb as through a gate. For one is not disposed to contemplation which leads to mental elevation unless one be with Daniel a man of desires [Dan., 9, 23]. But desires are kindled in us in two ways: by the cry of prayer, which makes one groan with the murmuring of one's heart, and by a flash of apprehension by which the mind turns most directly and intensely to the rays of light [Ps., 37, 9].

4. Therefore to the cry of prayer through Christ crucified, by Whose blood we are purged of the filth of vice, do I first invite the reader, lest perchance he should believe that it suffices to read without unction, speculate without devotion, investigate without wonder, examine without exultation, work without piety, know without love, understand without humility, be zealous without divine grace, see without wisdom divinely inspired. Therefore to those predisposed by divine grace, to the humble and the pious, to those filled with compunction and devotion, anointed with the oil of gladness [Ps., 44, 8], to the lovers of divine wisdom, inflamed with desire for it, to those wishing to give themselves over to praising God, to wondering over Him and to delighting in Him, do I propose the following reflections, hinting that little or nothing is the outer mirror unless the mirror of the mind be clear and polished.

Bestir yourself then, O man of God, you who previously resisted the pricks of conscience, before you raise your eyes to the rays of wisdom shining in that mirror, lest by chance you fall into the lower pit of shadows from the contemplation of those rays.

5. I have decided to divide my treatise into seven chapters, heading them with titles so that their contents may be the more easily understood. I ask therefore that one think rather of the intention of the writer than of his work, of the sense of the words rather than the rude speech, of truth rather than beauty, of the exercise of the affections rather than the erudition of the intellect. That such may come about, the progress of these thoughts must not be perused lightly, but should be meditated upon in greatest deliberation.

THE MENDICANT'S VISION IN THE WILDERNESS

CHAPTER 1

Of the Stages in the Ascent to God and of His Reflection in His Traces in the Universe

1. Blessed is the man whose help is from Thee. In his heart he hath disposed to ascend by steps, in the vale of tears, in the place which he hath set [Ps., 83, 6]. Since beatitude is nothing else than the fruition of the highest good, and the highest good is above us, none can be made blessed unless he ascend above himself, not by the ascent of his body but by that of his heart. But we cannot be raised above ourselves except by

a higher power raising us up. For howsoever the interior steps are disposed, nothing is accomplished unless it is accompanied by divine aid. Divine help, however, comes to those who seek it from their hearts humbly and devoutly; and this means to sigh for it in this vale of tears, aided only by fervent prayer. Thus prayer is the mother and source of ascent (*sursum-actionis*) in God. Therefore Dionysius, in his book, *Mystical Theology* [ch. 1, 1], wishing to instruct us in mental elevation, prefaces his work by prayer. Therefore let us pray and say to the Lord our God, "Conduct me, O Lord, in Thy way, and I will walk in Thy truth; let my heart rejoice that it may fear Thy name" [Ps., 85, 11].

2. By praying thus one is enlightened about the knowledge of the stages in the ascension to God. For since, relative to our life on earth, the world is itself a ladder for ascending to God, we find here certain traces [of His hand], certain images, some corporeal, some spiritual, some temporal, some aeviternal; consequently some outside us, some inside. That we may arrive at an understanding of the First Principle, which is most spiritual and eternal and above us, we ought to proceed through the traces which are corporeal and temporal and outside us; and this is to be led into the way of God. We ought next to enter into our minds, which are the eternal image of God, spiritual and internal; and this is to walk in the truth of God. We ought finally to pass over into that which is eternal, most spiritual, and above us, looking to the First Principle; and this is to rejoice in the knowledge of God and in the reverence of His majesty.

3. Now this is the three days' journey into the wilderness [Ex., 3, 18]; this is the triple illumination of one day, first as the evening, second as the morning, third as noon; this signifies the threefold existence of things, as in matter, in [creative] intelligence, and in eternal art, wherefore it is said, *Be it made, He made it,* and *It was so done* [Gen., 1]; and this also means the triple substance in Christ, Who is our ladder, namely, the corporeal, the spiritual, and the divine.

4. Following this threefold progress, our mind has three principal aspects. One refers to the external body, wherefore it is called animality or sensuality; the second looks inward and into itself, wherefore it is called spirit; the third looks above itself, wherefore it is called mind. From all of which considerations it ought to be so disposed for ascending as a whole into God that it may love Him with all its mind, with all its heart, and with all its soul [Mark, 12, 30]. And in this consists both the perfect observance of the Law and Christian wisdom.

5. Since, however, all of the aforesaid modes are twofold—as when we consider God as the alpha and omega, or in so far as we happen to see God in one of the aforesaid modes as *through* a mirror and *in* a mirror, or as one of those considerations can be mixed with the other conjoined to it or may be considered alone in its purity—hence it is necessary that these three principal stages become sixfold, so that as God made the world in six days and rested on the seventh, so the microcosm by six successive stages of illumination is led in the most orderly fashion to the repose of contemplation. As a symbol of this we have the six steps to the throne of Solomon [III Kings, 10, 19]; the Seraphim whom Isaiah saw have six wings; after six days the Lord called Moses out of the midst of the cloud [Ex., 24, 16]; and Christ after six days, as is said in Matthew [17, 1], brought His disciples up into a mountain and was transfigured before them.

6. Therefore, according to the six stages of ascension into God, there are six stages of the soul's powers by which we mount from the depths to the heights, from the external to the internal, from the temporal to the eternal—to wit, sense, imagination, reason, intellect, intelligence, and the apex of the mind, the illumination of conscience (*Synteresis*). These stages are implanted in us by nature, deformed by sin, re-

formed by grace, to be purged by justice, exercised by knowledge, perfected by wisdom.

7. Now at the Creation, man was made fit for the repose of contemplation, and therefore God placed him in a paradise of delight [Gen., 2, 16]. But turning himself away from the true light to mutable goods, he was bent over by his own sin, and the whole human race by original sin, which doubly infected human nature, ignorance infecting man's mind and concupiscence his flesh. Hence man, blinded and bent, sits in the shadows and does not see the light of heaven unless grace with justice succor him from concupiscence, and knowledge with wisdom against ignorance. All of which is done through Jesus Christ, Who of God is made unto us wisdom and justice and sanctification and redemption [I Cor., 1, 30]. He is the virtue and wisdom of God, the Word incarnate, the author of grace and truth—that is, He has infused the grace of charity, which, since it is from a pure heart and good conscience and unfeigned faith, rectifies the whole soul in the threefold way mentioned above. He has taught the knowledge of the truth according to the triple mode of theology—that is, the symbolic, the literal, and the mystical—so that by the symbolic we may make proper use of sensible things, by the literal we may properly use the intelligible, and by the mystical we may be carried aloft to supermental levels.

8. Therefore he who wishes to ascend to God must, avoiding sin, which deforms nature, exercise the above-mentioned natural powers for regenerating grace, and do this through prayer. He must strive toward purifying justice, and this in intercourse; toward the illumination of knowledge, and this in meditation; toward the perfection of wisdom, and this in contemplation. Now just as no one comes to wisdom save through grace, justice, and knowledge, so none comes to contemplation save through penetrating meditation, holy conversation, and devout prayer. Just as grace is the foundation of the will's rectitude and of the enlightenment of clear and penetrating reason, so, first, we must pray; secondly, we must live holily; thirdly, we must strive toward the reflection of truth and, by our striving, mount step by step until we come to the high mountain where we shall see the God of gods in Sion [Ps., 83, 8].

9. Since, then, we must mount Jacob's ladder before descending it, let us place the first rung of the ascension in the depths, putting the whole sensible world before us as a mirror, by which ladder we shall mount up to God, the Supreme Creator, that we may be true Hebrews crossing from Egypt to the land promised to our fathers; let us be Christians crossing with Christ from this world over to the Father [John, 13, 1]; let us also be lovers of wisdom, which calls to us and says, "Come over to me, all ye that desire me, and be filled with my fruits" [Ecclesiasticus, 24, 26]. For by the greatness of the beauty and of the creature, the Creator of them may be seen [Wisdom, 13, 5].

10. There shine forth, however, the Creator's supreme power and wisdom and benevolence in created things, as the carnal sense reports trebly to the inner sense. For the carnal sense serves him who either understands rationally or believes faithfully or contemplates intellectually. Contemplating, it considers the actual existence of things; believing, it considers the habitual course of things; reasoning, it considers the potential excellence of things.

11. In the first mode, the aspect of one contemplating, considering things in themselves, sees in them weight, number, and measure [Wisdom, 11, 21]—weight, which directs things to a certain location; number, by which they are distinguished from one another; and measure, by which they are limited. And so one sees in them mode, species, and order; and also substance, power, and operation. From these one can rise as from the traces to understanding the power, wisdom, and immense goodness of the Creator.

12. In the second mode, the aspect of a believer considering this world, one reaches its origin, course, and terminus. For by faith we believe that the ages are fashioned by the Word of Life [Hebr., 11, 3]; by faith we believe that the ages of the three laws—that is, the ages of the law of Nature, of Scripture, and of Grace—succeed each other and occur in most orderly fashion; by faith we believe that the world will be ended at the last judgment—taking heed of the power in the first, of the providence in the second, of the justice of the most high principle in the third.

13. In the third mode, the aspect of one inquiring rationally, one sees that some things merely are; others, however, are and live; others, finally, are, live, and discern. And the first are lesser things, the second midway, and the third the best. Again, one sees that some are only corporeal, others partly corporeal and partly spiritual, from which it follows that some are entirely spiritual and are better and more worthy than either of the others. One sees, nonetheless, that some are mutable and corruptible, as earthly things; others mutable and incorruptible, as celestial things, from which it follows that some are immutable and incorruptible, as the supercelestial things.

From these visible things, therefore, one mounts to considering the power and wisdom and goodness of God as being, living, and understanding; purely spiritual and incorruptible and immutable.

14. This consideration, however, is extended according to the sevenfold condition of creatures, which is a sevenfold testimony to the divine power, wisdom, and goodness, as one considers the origin, magnitude, multitude, beauty, plenitude, operation, and order of all things. For the *origin* of things, according to their creation, distinction, and beauty, in the work of the six days indicates the divine power producing all things from nothing, wisdom distinguishing all things clearly, and goodness adorning all things generously. *Magnitude* of things, either according to the measure of their length, width, and depth, or according to the excellence of power spreading itself in length, breadth, and depth, as appears in the diffusion of light, or again according to the efficacy of its inner, continuous, and diffused operation, as appears in the operation of fire—magnitude, I say, indicates manifestly the immensity of the power, wisdom, and goodness of the triune God, Who exists unlimited in all things through His power, presence, and essence. *Multitude* of things, according to the diversity of genus, species, and individuality, in substance, form, or figure, and efficacy beyond all human estimation, clearly indicates and shows the immensity of the aforesaid traits in God. *Beauty* of things, according to the variety of light, figure, and color in bodies simple and mixed and even composite, as in the celestial bodies, minerals, stones and metals, plants and animals, obviously proclaims the three mentioned traits. *Plenitude* of things—according to which matter is full of forms because of the seminal reasons; form is full of power because of its activity; power is full of effects because of its efficiency—declares the same manifestly. *Operation,* multiplex inasmuch as it is natural, artificial, and moral, by its very variety shows the immensity of that power, art, and goodness which indeed are in all things the cause of their being, the principle of their intelligibility, and the order of their living. *Order,* by reason of duration, situation, and influence, as prior and posterior, upper and lower, nobler and less noble, indicates clearly in the book of creation the primacy, sublimity, and dignity of the First Principle in relation to its infinite power. The order of the divine laws, precepts, and judgments in the Book of Scripture indicates the immensity of His wisdom. The order of the divine sacraments, rewards, and punishments in the body of the Church indicates the immensity of His goodness. Hence order leads us most obviously into the first and highest, most powerful, wisest, and best.

15. He, therefore, who is not illumined by such great splendor of created things is blind; he who is not awakened by such great clamor is deaf; he who does not praise God because of all these effects is dumb; he who does not note the First Principle from such great signs is foolish. Open your eyes therefore, prick up your spiritual ears, open your lips, and apply your heart, that you may see your God in all creatures, may hear Him, praise Him, love and adore Him, magnify and honor Him, lest the whole world rise against you. For on this account the whole world will fight against the unwise [Prov., 5, 21]; but to the wise will there be matter for pride, who with the Prophet can say, "Thou hast given me, O Lord, a delight in Thy doings: and in the works of Thy hands I shall rejoice [Ps., 91, 5]. . . . How great are Thy works, O Lord; Thou hast made all things in wisdom; the earth is filled with Thy riches" [Ps., 103, 24].

CHAPTER 2

Of the Reflection of God in His Traces in the Sensible World

1. But since with respect to the mirror of sensible things it happens that God is contemplated not only *through* them, as by His traces, but also *in* them, in so far as He is in them by essence, potency, and presence; and to consider this is higher than the preceding; therefore a consideration of this sort holds next place as a second step in contemplation, by which we should be led to the contemplation of God in all creatures which enter into our minds through the bodily senses.

2. Let it be noted then that this world, which is called the "macrocosm," enters our souls, which are called the "microcosm," through the doors of the five senses, according to the apprehension, delectation, and judgment of sensible things themselves. This is apparent as follows: In the world some things are generating, some generated, some governing the former and the latter. The generating are simple bodies, celestial bodies, and the four elements. For from the elements, by virtue of the light which reconciles the contrariety of elements in mixtures, there can be generated and produced whatsoever things are generated and produced through the operation of a natural power. But the generated are bodies composed of the elements, like minerals, vegetables, sensible things, and human bodies. The rulers of the former and the latter are spiritual substances, either conjoined entirely, as are the animal souls; or conjoined though separable, as are the rational spirits; or entirely separated, as are the celestial spirits, which philosophers call "intelligences," but we "angels." These, according to the philosophers, move the celestial bodies; and thus there is attributed to them the administration of the universe by taking over from the First Cause, that is God, their active influence, which they pour out in accordance with the work of governing, which looks to the natural harmony of things. According to the theologians, however, there is attributed to them the rule of the universe in accordance with the power of the supreme God with respect to the work of reparation, wherefore they are called "ministering spirits," sent to minister to them who shall receive the inheritance of salvation [Hebr., 1, 14].

3. Therefore, man, who is called a "microcosm," has five senses like five doors, through which enters into his soul the cognition of all that is in the sensible world. For through sight enter the transparent (*sublimia*), luminous, and other colored bodies; through touch the solid and terrestrial bodies; by the three intermediate senses the intermediates, as by taste the aqueous, by hearing the aerial, by odor the

vaporous—all of which have something of a humid nature, something aerial, something fiery or warm, as appears in the smoke which is freed from incense.

There enter then through these doors, not only simple bodies, but also composite, mixed from these. But since by sense we perceive not only these particular sensibles, which are light, sound, odor, savor, and the four primary qualities which touch apprehends, but also the common sensibles, which are number, magnitude, figure, rest, and motion, and since everything which is moved is moved by something, and some are self-moved and remain at rest, as the animals, it follows that when through these five senses we apprehend the motion of bodies, we are led to the cognition of spiritual movers, as through an effect we are led to a knowledge of its causes.

4. As far as the three kinds of things are concerned, this whole sensible world enters into the human soul through *apprehension*. The external sensibles, however, are what first enter the soul through the five doors of the senses. They enter, I say, not through their substance, but through their similitudes. These are first generated in the medium, and from the medium are generated in the organ and pass from the external organ into the internal, and from there into the apprehensive power. And thus the generation of the [sensible] species in the medium and from the medium into the organ and the reaction of the apprehensive power to it [the species] produce the apprehension of all those things which the soul apprehends from without.

5. Upon this apprehension, if it be of the appropriate thing, there follows *delight*. Sense, however, takes delight in an object perceived through an abstracted similitude either by reason of its beauty, as in sight; or by reason of its agreeableness, as in odor and hearing; or by reason of wholesomeness, as in taste and touch, speaking with appropriation. All delight, however, is by reason of proportion. But since a species is form, power, and operation, according to whether it is thought of as related to the principle from which it comes, to the medium through which it passes, or to the end for which it acts, therefore proportion may be considered in similitude, inasmuch as it is a species or form and thus is called *speciositas* [beauty], because beauty is nothing other than numerical equality or a certain relation of parts with agreeable color. Or else proportion may be considered as potency or power, and thus it is called "suavity," for active power does not exceed immoderately the powers of the recipient, since the senses are pained by extremes and delight in the mean. Or it may be considered, by thinking of species, as efficacy and impression, which is proportional when the agent by impression supplies what the recipient lacks; and this is to save and nourish it, which appears especially in taste and touch. And thus through delight the external pleasures enter into the soul by similitudes in a triple mode of delighting.

6. After the delight of apprehension comes *judgment*. By this we not only judge whether something is white or black, for this pertains to a special sense, not only whether it is healthful or harmful, for this pertains to the inner sense, but also why something is delightful. And in this act the question is raised about the reasons for our delight which sense derives from the object. This happens when we ask why something is beautiful, pleasant, and wholesome. And it is discovered that the answer is equality of proportion. Equality, however, is the same in the great and the small, and is not spread out through a thing's dimensions; nor does it change and pass away when there is alteration through change or motion. Therefore it abstracts from place, time, and motion, and thus is unchangeable, illimitable, without ends, and in all ways spiritual. Judgment is, therefore, an action which causes the sensible species, received sensibly through sense, to enter the intellective faculty by purification and abstraction. And thus the whole world can enter into the human soul through the doors of the senses by the three aforesaid operations.

7. These all, however, are traces in which we can see the reflection of our God. For since the apprehended species is a likeness produced in the medium and then impressed upon the organ itself, and by means of that impression leads to its principle and source—that is to say, to the object of knowledge—manifestly it follows that the eternal light generates out of itself a likeness or coequal radiance which is consubstantial and coeternal. And He Who is the image and likeness of the invisible God [Col., l, 15] and "the brightness of His glory and the figure of His substance" [Hebr., 1, 3], He Who is everywhere through His primal generation, as an object generates its likeness in the whole medium, is united by the grace of union to an individual of rational nature—as a species to a corporeal organ—so that by that union He may lead us back to the Father as to the primordial source and object. If then all knowable things can generate their likeness (*species*), obviously they proclaim that in them as in a mirror can be seen the eternal generation of the Word, the Image, and the Son, eternally emanating from God the Father.

8. In this way the species, delighting us as beautiful, pleasant, and wholesome, implies that in that first species is the primal beauty, pleasure, and wholesomeness in which is the highest proportionality and equality to the generator. In this is power, not through imagination, but entering our minds through the truth of apprehension. Here is impression, salubrious and satisfying, and expelling all lack in the apprehending mind. If, then, delight is the conjunction of the harmonious, and the likeness of God alone is the most highly beautiful, pleasant, and wholesome, and if it is united in truth and in inwardness and in plenitude which employs our entire capacity, obviously it can be seen that in God alone is the original and true delight, and that we are led back to seeking it from all other delights.

9. By a more excellent and immediate way are we led by judgment into seeing eternal truths more surely. For if judgment comes about through the reason's abstracting from place, time, and change, and therefore from dimension, succession, and transmutation, by the immutable, illimitable, and endless reason, and if there is nothing immutable, illimitable, and endless except the eternal, then all which is eternal is God or is in God. If, then, all things of which we have more certain judgments are judged by this mode of reasoning, it is clear that this is the reason of all things and the infallible rule and light of truth, in which all things shine forth infallibly, indestructibly, indubitably, irrefragably, unquestionably, unchangeably, boundlessly, endlessly, indivisibly, and intellectually. And therefore those laws by which we make certain judgments concerning all sensible things which come into our consideration—since they [the laws] are infallible and indubitable rules of the apprehending intellect—are indelibly stored up in the memory as if always present, are irrefragable and unquestionable rules of the judging intellect. And this is so because, as Augustine says [*Lib. Arb.*, II, ch. 4], no one judges these things except by these rules. It must thus be true that they are incommutable and incorruptible since they are necessary, and boundless since they are illimitable, endless since eternal. Therefore they must be indivisible since intellectual and incorporeal, not made but uncreated, eternally existing in eternal art, by which, through which, and in accordance with which all things possessing form are formed. Neither, therefore, can we judge with certainty except through that which was not only the form producing all things but also the preserver of all and the distinguisher of all, as the being who preserves the form in all things, the directing rule by which our mind judges all things which enter into it through the senses.

10. This observation is extended by a consideration of the seven different kinds of number by which, as if by seven steps, we ascend to God. Augustine shows this in his book *On the True Religion* and in the sixth book *On Music,* wherein he assigns the

differences of the numbers as they mount step by step from sensible things to the Maker of all things, so that God may be seen in all.

For he says that numbers are in bodies and especially in sounds and words, and he calls these *sonorous*. Some are abstracted from these and received into our senses, and these he calls *heard*. Some proceed from the soul into the body, as appears in gestures and bodily movements, and these he calls *uttered*. Some are in the pleasures of the senses which arise from attending to the species which have been received, and these he calls *sensual*. Some are retained in the memory, and these he calls *remembered*. Some are the bases of our judgments about all these, and these he calls *judicial,* which, as has been said above, necessarily transcend our minds because they are infallible and incontrovertible. By these there are imprinted on our minds the *artificial* numbers which Augustine does not include in this classification because they are connected with the judicial numbers from which flow the uttered numbers out of which are created the numerical forms of those things made by art. Hence, from the highest through the middle to the lowest, there is an ordered descent. Thence do we ascend step by step from the sonorous numbers by means of the uttered, the sensual, and the remembered.

Since, therefore, all things are beautiful and in some way delightful, and beauty and delight do not exist apart from proportion, and proportion is primarily in number, it needs must be that all things are rhythmical (*numerosa*). And for this reason number is the outstanding exemplar in the mind of the Maker, and in things it is the outstanding trace leading to wisdom. Since this is most evident to all and closest to God, it leads most directly to God as if by the seven differentiae. It causes Him to be known in all corporeal and sensible things while we apprehend the rhythmical, delight in rhythmical proportions, and through the laws of rhythmical proportions judge irrefragably.

11. From these two initial steps by which we are led to seeing God in His traces, as if we had two wings falling to our feet, we can determine that all creatures of this sensible world lead the mind of the one contemplating and attaining wisdom to the eternal God; for they are shadows, echoes, and pictures, the traces, simulacra, and reflections of that First Principle most powerful, wisest, and best; of that light and plenitude; of that art productive, exemplifying, and ordering, given to us for looking upon God. They are signs divinely bestowed which, I say, are exemplars or rather exemplifications set before our yet untrained minds, limited to sensible things, so that through the sensibles which they see they may be carried forward to the intelligibles which they do not see, as if by signs to the signified.

12. The creatures of this sensible world signify the invisible things of God [Rom., 1, 20], partly because God is of all creation the origin, exemplar, and end, and because every effect is the sign of its cause, the exemplification of the exemplar, and the way to the end to which it leads; partly from its proper representation; partly from prophetic prefiguration; partly from angelic operation; partly from further ordination. For every creature is by nature a sort of picture and likeness of that eternal wisdom, but especially that which in the book of Scripture is elevated by the spirit of prophecy to the prefiguration of spiritual things. But more does the eternal wisdom appear in those creatures in whose likeness God wished to appear in angelic ministry. And most specially does it appear in those which He wished to institute for the purpose of signifying which are not only signs according to their common name but also Sacraments.

13. From all this it follows that the invisible things of God are clearly seen, from the creation of the world, being understood by the things that are made; so that those who are unwilling to give heed to them and to know God in them all, to bless Him and to love Him, are inexcusable [Rom., 1, 20], while they are unwilling to be carried forth

from the shadows into the wonderful light of God [I Cor., 15, 57]. But thanks be to God through Jesus Christ our Lord, Who has transported us out of darkness into His wonderful light, when through these lights given from without we are disposed to reenter into the mirror of our mind, in which the divine lights shine [I Peter, 2, 9].

CHAPTER 3

Of the Reflection of God in His Image Stamped upon our Natural Powers

1. The two steps mentioned above, by leading us to God by means of His Traces, whereby He shines forth in all creatures, have led us to the point of entering into ourselves, that is, into our minds in which the divine image shines. Now in the third place, as we enter into ourselves, as if leaving the vestibule and coming into the sanctum, that is, the outer part of the tabernacle, we should strive to see God through a mirror. In this mirror the light of truth is shining before our minds as in a candelabrum, for in it gleams the resplendent image of the most blessed Trinity.

Enter then into yourselves and see, for your mind loves itself most fervently. Nor could it love itself unless it knew itself. Nor would it know itself unless it remembered itself, for we receive nothing through intelligence which is not present to our memory. And from this be advised, not with the eye of the flesh but with that of reason, that your soul has a threefold power. Consider then the operations and the functions of these three powers, and you will be able to see God in yourselves as in an image, which is to see through a glass darkly [I Cor., 13, 12].

2. The operation of memory is retention and representation, not only of things present, corporeal, and temporal, but also of past and future things, simple and eternal. For memory retains the past by recalling it, the present by receiving it, the future by foreseeing it. It retains the simple, as the principles of continuous and discrete quantities—the point, the instant, the unit—without which it is impossible to remember or to think about those things whose source is in these. Nonetheless it retains the eternal principles and the axioms of the sciences and retains them eternally. For it can never so forget them while it uses reason that it will not approve of them when heard and assent to them, not as though it were perceiving them for the first time, but as if it were recognizing them as innate and familiar, as appears when someone says to another, "One must either affirm or deny," or, "Every whole is greater than its part," or any other law which cannot be rationally contradicted.

From the first actual retention of all temporal things, namely, of the past, present, and future, it has the likeness of eternity whose indivisible present extends to all times. From the second it appears that it is not only formed from without by images [phantasms], but also by receiving simple forms from above and retaining them in itself—forms which cannot enter through the doors of the senses and the images of sensible things. From the third it follows that it has an undying light present to itself in which it remembers unchangeable truths. And thus, through the operations of the memory, it appears that the soul itself is the image of God and His likeness, so present to itself and having Him present that it receives Him in actuality and is susceptible of receiving Him in potency, and that it can also participate in Him.

3. The operation of the intellect is concerned with the meaning of terms, propositions, and inferences. The intellect, however, understands the meaning of terms when it comprehends what anything is through its definition. But a definition must be made by higher terms and these by still higher, until one comes to the highest and

most general, in ignorance of which the lower cannot be defined. Unless, therefore, it is known what is Being-in-itself, the definition of no special substance can be fully known. Nor can Being-in-itself be known unless it be known along with its conditions: the one, the true, the good. Since being, however, can be known as incomplete or complete, as imperfect or perfect, as potential or actual, as relative or absolute, as partial or total, as transient or permanent, as dependent or independent, as mixed with non-being or as pure, as contingent or necessary (*per se*), as posterior or prior, as mutable or immutable, as simple or composite; since privations and defects can be known only through affirmations in some positive sense, our intellect cannot reach the point of fully understanding any of the created beings unless it be favored by the understanding of the purest, most actual, most complete, and absolute Being, which is simply and eternally Being, and in which are the principles of all things in their purity. For how would the intellect know that a being is defective and incomplete if it had no knowledge of being free from all defect? And thus for all the aforesaid conditions.

The intellect is said to comprehend truly the meaning of propositions when it knows with certitude that they are true. And to know this is simply to know, since error is impossible in comprehension of this sort. For it knows that such truth cannot be otherwise than it is. It knows, therefore, that such truth is unchangeable. But since our mind itself is changeable, it cannot see that truth shining forth unchangeably except by some light shining without change in any way; and it is impossible that such a light be a mutable creature. Therefore it knows in that light which enlighteneth every man that cometh into this world [John, 1, 9], which is true light and the Word which in the beginning was with God [John, 1, 1].

Our intellect perceives truly the meaning of inference when it sees that a conclusion necessarily follows from its premises. This it sees not only in necessary terms but also in contingent. Thus if a man is running, a man is moving. It perceives, however, this necessary connection, not only in things which are, but also in things which are not. Thus if a man exists, it follows that if he is running, he is moved. And this is true even if the man is not existing. The necessity of this mode of inference comes not from the existence of the thing in matter, because that is contingent, nor from its existence in the soul, because then it would be a fiction if it were not in the world of things. Therefore it comes from the archetype in eternal art according to which things have an aptitude and a comportment toward one another by reason of the representation of that eternal art. As Augustine says in his *On True Religion* [Ch. 39, 72], "The light of all who reason truly is kindled at that truth and strives to return to it." From which it is obvious that our intellect is conjoined with that eternal truth so that it cannot receive anything with certainty except under its guidance. Therefore you can see the truth through yourself, the truth that teaches you, if concupiscence and phantasms do not impede you and place themselves like clouds between you and the rays of truth.

4. The operation of the power of choice is found in deliberation, judgment, and desire. Deliberation is found in inquiring what is better, this or that. But the better has no meaning except by its proximity to the best. But such proximity is measured by degrees of likeness. No one, therefore, can know whether this is better than that unless he knows that this is closer to the best. But no one knows that one of two things is more like another unless he knows the other. For I do not know that this man is like Peter unless I know or am acquainted with Peter. Therefore the idea of the good must be involved in every deliberation about the highest good.

Certain judgment of the objects of deliberation comes about through some law. But none can judge with certainty through law unless he be certain that that law is right and that he ought not to judge it. But the mind judges itself. Since, then, it cannot judge the law it employs in judging, that law is higher than our minds; and through this higher law one makes judgments according to the degree with which it is impressed upon it. But there is nothing higher than the human mind except Him Who made it. Therefore our deliberative faculty in judging reaches upward to divine laws if it solves its problems completely.

Now desire is of that which especially moves one. But that especially moves one which is especially loved. But happiness is loved above all. But happiness does not come about except through the best and ultimate end. Human desire, therefore, seeks nothing unless it be the highest good or something which leads to it or something which has some resemblance to it. So great is the force of the highest good that nothing can be loved except through desire for it by a creature which errs and is deceived when it takes truth's image and likeness for the truth.

See then how close the soul is to God and how memory in its operations leads to eternity, intelligence to truth, the power of choice to the highest goodness.

5. Following the order and origin and comportment of these powers, we are led to the most blessed Trinity itself. From memory arises intelligence as its offspring, for then do we know when a likeness which is in the memory leaps into the eye of the intellect, which is nothing other than a word. From memory and intelligence is breathed forth love, which is the tie between the two. These three—the generating mind, the word, and love—are in the soul as memory, intelligence, and will, which are consubstantial, co-equal, and coeval, mutually immanent. If then God is perfect spirit, He has memory, intelligence, and will; and He has both the begotten Word and spirated Love. These are necessarily distinguished, since one is produced from the other—distinguished, not essentially or accidentally, but personally. When therefore the mind considers itself, it rises through itself as through a mirror to the contemplation of the Blessed Trinity—Father, Word, and Love—three persons coeternal, coequal, and consubstantial; so that each one is in each of the others, though one is not the other, but all three are one God.

6. This consideration which the soul has of its threefold and unified principle through the trinity of its powers, by which it is the image of God, is supported by the light of knowledge which perfects it and informs it, and represents in three ways the most blessed Trinity. For all philosophy is either natural or rational or moral. The first deals with the cause of being, and therefore leads to the power of the Father. The second deals with the principle of understanding, and therefore leads to the wisdom of the Word. The third deals with the order of living, and therefore leads to the goodness of the Holy Spirit.

Again, the first is divided into metaphysics, mathematics, and physics. The first concerns the essences of things; the second, numbers and figures; the third, natures, powers, and extensive operations. Therefore the first leads to the First Principle, the Father; the second, to His image, the Son; the third, to the gift of the Holy Spirit.

The second is divided into grammar, which gives us the power of expression; logic, which gives us skill in argumentation; rhetoric, which makes us skillful in persuasion or stirring the emotions. And this similarly images the mystery of the most blessed Trinity.

The third is divided into individual, family, and political [problems]. And therefore the first images the First Principle, which has no birth; the second, the family relationship of the Son; the third, the liberality of the Holy Spirit.

7. All these sciences have certain and infallible rules, like rays of light descending from the eternal law into our minds. And thus our minds, illumined and suffused by such great radiance, unless they be blind, can be led through themselves alone to the contemplation of that eternal light. The irradiation and consideration of this light holds the wise suspended in wonder; and, on the other hand, it leads into confusion the foolish, who do not believe that they may understand. Hence this prophecy is fulfilled: "Thou enlightenest wonderfully from the everlasting hills. All the foolish of heart were troubled" [Ps., 75, 5–6].

ON THE ETERNITY OF THE WORLD
(selections)

COMMENTARY ON THE "SENTENCES" OF PETER LOMBARD

D. 1, P. 1, A. 1, Q. 2

The question is: Has the world been produced in time or from eternity. That it has not been produced in time is shown:

1. By two arguments based on motion, the first of which is demonstrative in the following way: *Before every motion and change, there is the motion of the first moveable thing (primum mobile);* but everything which begins to be begins by way of motion or change; therefore that motion (viz., of the first moveable thing) is before all that which begins to be. But that motion could not have preceded itself or its movable thing (mobile); therefore it could not possibly have a beginning. The first proposition is a basic one and its proof is as follows: It is a basic principle in philosophy that "in every kind the complete is prior to the incomplete of that kind"; but movement toward place is the more perfect among all the kinds of motion inasmuch as it is the motion of a complete being, and circular motion is both the swifter and the more perfect among all the kinds of local motion; but the motion of the heaven is of this kind, therefore most perfect, therefore the first. Therefore it is evident that, etc.

2. This is likewise shown by an absurdity consequent upon the alternative. *Everything which comes to be comes to be through motion or change;* consequently, if motion comes to be it comes to be through motion or change, and with regard to this latter motion the question is similarly raised. Therefore, either there is to be an infinite regress or a positing of some motion lacking a beginning; if the motion, then also the movable thing and, consequently, also the world.

From C. Vollert, L. Kendzierski, and P.M. Byrne, editors and translators, *St. Thomas Aquinas, Siger of Brabant, St. Bonaventure: On the Eternity of the World* (Milwaukee, WI: Marquette University Press, 1964). This selection was translated by Paul M. Byrne. Reprinted by permission of Marquette University Press.

3. Similarly, a demonstrative argument based on time is as follows: *Everything which begins to be either begins to be in an instant or in time.* If, therefore, the world begins to be, it does so either in an instant or in time. But before every time there is time, and time is before every instant. Consequently there is time before all those things which have begun to be. But it could not have been before the world and motion; therefore the world has not had a beginning. The first proposition is *per se* known. The second, namely that before every time there is time, is evident from the fact that if it is flowing, it was of necessity flowing beforehand. Similarly, it is evident that there is time before every instant since time is a circular measure suited to the motion and the movable thing; but every point in a circle is a beginning even as it is an end; therefore every instant of time is a beginning of the future even as it is a terminus of the past. Accordingly, before every "now" there has been a past. It is evident, therefore, etc.

4. Again, this is shown by the absurdity consequent upon the alternative. If time is produced, it is produced either in time or in an instant; therefore in time. But in every time there is a prior and a posterior, both a past and a future. Consequently, if time has been produced in time, there has been time before every time, and this is impossible. Therefore, etc.

These are Aristotle's arguments based on the character of the world itself.

5. Besides these, there are other arguments based on the character of the producing cause. In general, these can be reduced to two, the first of which is demonstrative and the second based on the absurdity consequent upon the alternative. The first is as follows: *Given all adequate and actual cause, the effect is given;* but God from eternity has been the adequate and actual cause of this world; therefore, etc. The major premise is *per se* known. The minor, namely that God is the adequate cause, is evident. Since He needs nothing extrinsic for the creating of the world, but only the power, wisdom and goodness which have been most perfect in God from eternity, evidently He has, from eternity, been the adequate cause. That He has also been the actual cause is evident as follows: God is pure act and is His own act of willing, as Aristotle says; and our philosophers (*Sancti*) say that He is His own acting. It follows, therefore, etc.

6. Also, by the absurdity of the alternative. Everything which begins to act or produce, when it was not producing beforehand, passes from rest into act. If, therefore, God begins to produce the world, He passes from rest into act; but all such things are subject to rest and change or mutability. Therefore God is subject to rest and mutability. This, however, contradicts His absolute goodness and absolute simplicity, and, consequently, is impossible. It is to blaspheme God; and to say that the world has had a beginning amounts to the same thing.

These are arguments which the commentators and more recent men (*moderniores*) have added over and beyond the arguments of Aristotle; or, at least, they are reducible to these.

But there are arguments to the contrary, based on *per se* known propositions of reason and philosophy:

1. The first of these is: *It is impossible to add to the infinite.* This is *per se* evident because everything which receives an addition becomes more; "but nothing is more than infinite." If the world lacks a beginning, however, it has had an infinite duration, and consequently there can be no addition to its duration. But this is certainly false because every day a revolution is added to a revolution; therefore, etc. If you were to say that it is infinite in past time and yet is actually finite with respect to the present, which now is, and, accordingly, that it is in this respect, in which it is finite, that the "more" is to be found, it is pointed out to you that, to the contrary, it is in the past that the "more"

is to be found. This is an infallible truth: If the world is eternal, then the revolutions of the sun in its orbit are infinite in number. Again, there have necessarily been twelve revolutions of the moon for every one of the sun. Therefore the moon has revolved more times than the sun, and the sun an infinite number of times. Accordingly, that which exceeds the infinite as infinite is discovered. But this is impossible; therefore, etc.

2. The second proposition is: *It is impossible for the infinite in number to be ordered.* For every order flows from a principle toward a mean. Therefore, if there is no first, there is no order; but if the duration of the world or the revolutions of the heaven are infinite, they do not have a first; therefore they do not have an order, and one is not before another. But since this is false, it follows that they have a first. If you say that it is necessary to posit a limit (*statum*) to all ordered series only in the case of things ordered in a causal relation, because among causes there is necessarily a limit, I ask why not in other cases. Moreover, you do not escape in this way. For there has never been a revolution of the heaven without there being a generation of animal from animal. But an animal is certainly related causally to the animal from which it is generated. If, therefore, according to Aristotle and reason it is necessary to posit a limit among those things ordered in a causal relation, then in the generation of animals it is necessary to posit a first animal. And the world has not existed without animals; therefore, etc.

3. The third proposition is: *It is impossible to traverse what is infinite.* But if the world had no beginning, there has been an infinite number of revolutions; therefore it was impossible for it to have traversed them; therefore impossible for it to have come down to the present. If you say that they (i.e., numerically infinite revolutions) have not been traversed because there has been no first one, or that they well could be traversed in an infinite time you do not escape in this way. For I shall ask you if any revolution has infinitely preceded today's revolution or none. If none, then all are finitely distant from this present one. Consequently, they are all together finite in number and so have a beginning. If some one is infinitely distant, then I ask whether the revolution immediately following it is infinitely distant. If not, then neither is the former (infinitely) distant since there is a finite distance between the two of them. But if it (i.e., the one immediately following) is infinitely distant, then I ask in a similar way about the third, the fourth, and so on to infinity. Therefore, one is no more distant than another from this present one, one is not before another, and so they are all simultaneous.

4. The fourth proposition is: *It is impossible for the infinite to be grasped by a finite power.* But if the world had no beginning, then the infinite is grasped by a finite power; therefore, etc. The proof of the major is *per se* evident. The minor is shown as follows. I suppose that God alone is with a power actually infinite and that all other things have limitation. Also I suppose that there has never been a motion of the heaven without there being a created spiritual substance who would either cause or, at least, know it. Further, I also suppose that a spiritual substance forgets nothing. If, therefore, there has been, at the same time as the heaven, any spiritual substance with finite power, there has been no revolution of the heaven which he would not know and which would have been forgotten. Therefore, he is actually knowing all of them and they have been infinite in number. Accordingly, a spiritual substance with finite power is grasping simultaneously an infinite number of things. If you assert that this is not unsuitable because all the revolutions, being of the same species and in every way alike, are known by a single likeness, there is the objection that not only would he have known the rotations, but also their effects as well, and these various and diverse effects are infinite in number. It is clear, therefore, etc.

5. The fifth proposition is: *It is impossible that there be simultaneously an infinite number of things.* But if the world is eternal and without a beginning, then there has been an infinite number of men, since it would not be without there being men—for all things are in a certain way for the sake of man and a man lasts only for a limited length of time. But there have been as many rational souls as there have been men, and so an infinite number of souls. But, since they are incorruptible forms, there are as many souls as there have been; therefore an infinite number of souls exist. If this leads you to say that there has been a transmigration of souls or that there is but the one soul for all men, the first is an error in philosophy, because, as Aristotle holds, "appropriate act is in its own matter." Therefore, the soul, having been the perfection of one, cannot be the perfection of another, even according to Aristotle. The second position is even more erroneous since much less is it true that there is but the one soul for all.

6. The last argument to this effect is: *It is impossible for that which has being after non-being to have eternal being,* because this implies a contradiction. But the world has being after non-being. Therefore it is impossible that it be eternal. That it has being after non-being is proven as follows: everything whose having of being is totally from another is produced by the latter out of nothing; but the world has its being totally from God; therefore the world is out of nothing. But not out of nothing as a matter (*materialiter*); therefore out of nothing as an origin (*originaliter*). It is evident that everything which is totally produced by something differing in essence has being out of nothing. For what is totally produced is produced in its matter and form. But matter does not have that out of which it would be produced because it is not out of God (*ex Deo*). Clearly, then, it is out of nothing. The minor, viz., that the world is totally produced by God, is evident from the discussion of another question.

CONCLUSION

Whether positing that all things have been produced out of nothing would imply saying that the world is eternal or has been produced eternally.

I answer: It has to be said that to maintain that the world is eternal or eternally produced by claiming that all things have been produced out of nothing is entirely against truth and reason, as the last of the above arguments proves; and it is so against reason that I do not believe that any philosopher, however slight his understanding, has maintained this. For such a position involves an evident contradiction. But, with the eternity of matter presupposed, to maintain an eternal world seems reasonable and understandable, and this by way of two analogies which can be drawn. For the procession of earthly things from God is after the fashion of an imprint (*vestigium*). Accordingly, if a foot and the dust in which its print were formed were eternal, nothing would prevent our understanding that the footprint is coeternal with the foot and, nevertheless, it still would be an imprint from the foot. If matter, or the potential principle, were in this fashion coeternal with the maker, what would keep that imprint from being eternal? Rather, on the contrary, it would seem quite fitting that it should be.

Again, another reasonable analogy offers itself. For, from God the creature proceeds as a shadow, the Son as brightness. But as soon as there is light, there is immediately brightness, and immediately shadow if there should be an opaque object in its way. If, therefore, matter, as opaque, is coeternal with the maker, just as it is reasonable to posit the Son, the brightness of the Father, to be coeternal, so it seems reasonable that creatures or the world, shadow in relation to the Highest Light, is eternal. Moreover, this view is more reasonable than its contrary, viz., that matter has been eternally incomplete, without form or the divine influence, as certain philosophers have maintained. In fact, it is more reasonable to such an extent that even that outstanding philosopher, Aristotle, has fallen into this error, according to the charges of our philosophers (*Sancti*), the exposition of the commentators, and the apparent meaning of his text.

On the other hand, modern scholars say that the Philosopher has never thought this nor did he intend to prove that the world had no beginning *in any way at all,* but rather that it did not begin *by way of a natural motion.*

Which of these interpretations is the truer one I do not know. This one thing I do know, that if he held that the world has not begun *according to nature,* he maintained what is true, and his arguments based on motion and time are conclusive. But if he thought that it has *in no way begun,* he has clearly erred, as has been shown above by many arguments. Moreover, in order to avoid self-contradiction, he had to maintain either that the world has not been made, or that it has not been made out of nothing. In order to avoid an actual infinity, however, he had to hold for either the corruption of the rational soul, or its unicity, or its transmigration; thus, in any case, he had to destroy its beatitude. So it is that this error has both a bad beginning and the worst of endings.

1. To the first objection, regarding motion, viz., that there is a first among all motions and changes because there is a most perfect one, it must be granted as true with respect to *natural* motions and changes and there is nothing against it. But with respect to the *supernatural* change, through which that *mobile* (i.e., the heaven) has proceeded into being, it is not true. For this latter change precedes every created thing, and so precedes the *primum mobile* and, of course, its motion.

2. To the objection, every motion passes into being through motion, it must be answered that motion does not pass into being *through itself* nor *in itself,* but *with another* and *in another.* And since God has, in the same instant, made the *mobile* and, as mover, acted upon the *mobile,* then He has cocreated the motion with the *mobile.* If, however, you were to seek further with regard to that creating, it must be said that there a limit is reached as in the very first of things. Further on, this will be made better known.

3. To the third objection, regarding the "now" of time, it must be said that just as there is a two-fold indicating of a point in a circle, either when the circle is being made or after it has been made, and just as when it is being made there is a placing and indicating of a first point but when it already is there is no locating of a first, so also with regard to time there is a twofold acceptance of the "now." In the very production of time, there has been a first "now" before which there has been no other and which was the beginning of time in which all things are said to have been produced. But with respect to time after it has been made, it is true that it is the terminus of the past and it is in the fashion of a circle. But things have not been produced in this way in a time already complete. Thus it is clear that the Philosopher's arguments do not at all establish this conclusion. With regard to the statement that before every time is time, this is true in terms of dividing time from within, but not in the sense of preceding as outside time.

4. To the objection concerning time, as to when has it begun, it must be said that it began in its own beginning (*principium*). But the source (*principium*) of time is the instant or "now"; and so it began in an instant. Also, the argument: Time has not been in an instant and so has not begun in an instant does not stand because things which are successive are not in their own beginning. This same thing can be said in another way

since there are two ways of speaking about time, either according to its essence or according to its being (*esse*). If one speaks of it according to its essence, then the "now" is the whole essence of time, and that has begun to be with the mobile thing, not in another "now" but in its own self since it has been established in the very beginning and thus it has not had another measure. If one speaks of it according to its being, then it has begun with the motion of change, viz., it has not begun by way of creation, but rather through the change of the changeable, and especially of the *primum mobile*.

5. To the objection based on the adequacy and actuality of the cause, it must be said that the adequate cause of any effect is of two kinds, either as operative through its *nature* or as operative through *will and reason*. If operative through *nature,* then, as soon as it is, it produces its effect. On the other hand, if operative through *will,* even though it be adequate, it is not necessarily operative as soon as it is, since a cause of this sort is operative by way of wisdom and discernment and so takes suitability into account. Therefore, inasmuch as eternity did not befit the nature of the creature itself, it was not fitting that God should grant this most excellent of states to any thing. Accordingly, the divine will, which operates by way of wisdom, has produced the world not from eternity but in time, since, as He has produced, so has He disposed and so has He willed. For He has willed from eternity to produce then when He has produced, just as I will now to hear Mass tomorrow. It is thus evident that the adequacy of the cause is not pertinent to this question.

Similarly with regard to actuality, it must be said that a cause can be in act in two ways, either in itself, as if I were to say: The sun shines, or in its effect (*in effectu*), as if I were to say: The sun illumines. In the first way God has always been in act, since He is pure act unadulterated by the merely possible. In the other way He is not always in act, for He has not always been producing.

6. To the sixth objection: If from being nonproducing He has become producing, He has changed from rest to act, it must be said that there is a type of agent in which action and production add something over and beyond the agent and producer. Such an agent is changed in some way when from nonacting it becomes acting, and in this case rest precedes operation and by operation completion is achieved. But there is another agent which is its own action, and nothing at all is added to such an agent when it produces nor does anything come to be in it which it was not beforehand. An agent of this sort neither receives completion in operating nor is it idle in nonoperating, nor, when from nonproducing it comes to be producing, is it changed from rest to act. But such is God, even according to the philosophers, who have asserted God to be the most simple of beings. It is evident, therefore, that their argument is a foolish one. For if He had produced things from eternity in order to avoid idleness, then He would not be, *without things,* the perfect good, nor consequently would He *with things,* since that which is most perfect is perfect by its own self. Moreover, if because of His immutability it were necessary that things be from eternity, then He could produce nothing new now. And what kind of God would He be who is now essentially incapable of anything? All these consequences imply nonsense rather than philosophy or an argumentation.

If you were to ask how this is to be understood, viz., that God acts by His own self and yet does not begin to act, the answer would have to be that, even though this cannot be fully understood because of the conjoined imagination, nevertheless it can be established by argumentation necessitating assent; and anyone who withdraws from sense experience in order to consider the intelligibles will, to some extent perceive it. For if anyone were to ask whether an angel could make a pottery cup or throw a stone in spite of no hands, the answer would be that he could because he is capable, by his own power alone and without an organ, of what the soul is capable of with the body and its members. If, therefore, an angel, because of its simplicity and perfection, exceeds man to such an extent that he can do, without an organ as a means, that for which man necessarily requires an organ, can even do through one [power] what man is capable of only through many, how much more can God, Who is at the very limit of the whole of simplicity and perfection, produce all things without any means by the command of His own will which is nothing other than Himself, and thereby remain immutable in producing! In this way a man can be led to an understanding of this truth. But that man will grasp it more perfectly who can consider these two aspects of his Maker, namely that He is most perfect and most simple. Because He is most perfect, all the perfections there are are to be attributed to Him; because most simple, these introduce no diversity into Him, and accordingly no change or mutability. So it is, "remaining at rest He causes all things to be moved."

*   *   *

CONFERENCES ON THE HEXAEMERON

IV, 13

The sixth division is into cause and caused; and here there are many errors. For some say that the world has been from eternity. Wise men agree that something could not come to be from nothing and in this way be from eternity, since it is necessarily the case that, just as when a thing passes into nothing it ceases to be, so also when it comes to be from nothing it begins to be. But some seem to have posited an unoriginated matter; from this it follows that God does not make anything. For He does not make matter, since it is unoriginated. Nor does He make form since either it comes to be from something or from nothing; not from matter since the being (*essentia*) of form cannot come from the being (*essentia*) of matter; and not from nothing since, as they suppose, God can make nothing from nothing. But let perish the notion that the power of God has matter as its supporting foundation.

*   *   *

V, 29

And it is in this way that the Philosopher proceeds to prove the world eternal on the basis that circular local motion, because it is perfect, precedes every motion and change. But I answer: It must be said that the perfect is before the diminished when speaking of the simply perfect, but not when speaking of the perfect in a genus, as is the case with local motion.

THOMAS AQUINAS
1225–1274

—◄◉►—

Saint Thomas Aquinas was indisputably the greatest of the medieval philosophers. He was born in his family's castle of Roccasecca near the town of Aquino, about halfway between Rome and Naples. The seventh son of the Count of Aquino, Landolfo, and his wife Teodora, at the age of 5 Thomas was sent to the Benedictine monastery of Monte Casino, where his uncle was the abbot. His parents hoped he would get a good education at the monastery and perhaps one day become abbot of Monte Casino. However, political struggles between the pope and the emperor made the monastery unsafe, and at age 14 Thomas moved to the Imperial University in Naples.

At this university, Thomas came under the influence of the Dominicans, a mendicant, or begging, order of friars. Even though the Dominicans were admired by many for their religious commitment, Thomas's family was appalled when in 1244 he announced his plans to join the order. They considered the Dominicans religious fanatics, virtually a cult, with none of the sophistication, prestige, or power of the long-established Benedictines. At his parents' instigation, Thomas's brothers kidnapped him and held him captive in the family castle. For a year they tried reasoning, shouting, intimidating—even tempting him with a prostitute—but Thomas would not be swayed. He eventually managed to escape and became a Dominican friar.

Thomas went to Paris, where he studied with Albertus Magnus (Albert the Great), an advocate of the newly rediscovered Aristotelian writings, and he even followed his teacher to Cologne to continue his study of Aristotle. As a student, Thomas was so stolid and methodical that many of his peers thought he was dull or downright stupid. Given his deliberate manner and his portly build, his classmates dubbed him "the Dumb Ox." But Albertus saw his potential and turned this cruel epithet into a prophecy, saying, "You call him a Dumb Ox; I tell you the Dumb Ox will bellow so loud his bellowing will fill the world." In 1252, Thomas returned to Paris for graduate studies, eventually receiving the magistrate (doctorate) in theology in 1256.

On concluding his studies, it seemed natural that Thomas would join the faculty of the University of Paris. However, scholars from the mendicant orders were held in suspicion by the regular faculty of the university. Along with the great Franciscan friar Bonaventure, Thomas was not allowed to teach in Paris until the pope himself intervened.

The rest of Thomas's life was spent teaching in France and Italy and writing extensively on philosophical and theological subjects. His complete works in Latin comprise twenty-five volumes. Thomas was also called upon to intervene in several disputes. In addition to defending his Dominican order, he was forced to articulate a middle position between those who rejected Aristotelian philosophy as anti-Christian and those who accepted Aristotle (or, rather, a version of Averroës' interpretation of Aristotle) too uncritically. Throughout his writings, Thomas negotiated a middle path of critical admiration for Aristotle.

Like other Christian thinkers, Thomas was concerned with the relation between reason and faith. Using basically Aristotelian categories, Thomas taught that natural reason could establish some of the truths of religion (such as the existence, unity, and goodness of God), but other truths were accessible only through faith. Contrary to some of the Latin Averroists, Thomas taught that there

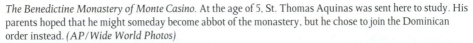

The Benedictine Monastery of Monte Casino. At the age of 5, St. Thomas Aquinas was sent here to study. His parents hoped that he might someday become abbot of the monastery, but he chose to join the Dominican order instead. *(AP/Wide World Photos)*

was no conflict between the teachings of philosophy and those of theology. To use a later analogy, Thomas believed that "the book of nature" (i.e., the created world) and the "Book of Scripture" were in perfect harmony.

In December 1273, Thomas suddenly stopped writing, apparently the result of a mystical experience. He reported to a friend that "all I have written seems like straw to me." A few months later, he was called to a church council in Lyon, France. On the way there his health forced him to stop at Fossanova (south of Rome) where he died on March 7, 1274, at the age of 49.

Three years after his death, several of Thomas's teachings were condemned by the Bishop of Paris. However, the condemnation did not stand long, and in 1323, Saint Thomas Aquinas was canonized. In 1879, Pope Leo XII commended the study of Aquinas's philosophy in an encyclical, *Aeterni Patris*. This papal proclamation did not launch a revival of Thomism, as is often said, but it did lend an enormous prestige to the study of Thomas and his work. The encyclical praises the saint in the highest terms: "As far as man is concerned, reason can now hardly rise higher than she rose, borne up in the flight of Thomas; and Faith can hardly gain more help from reason than those which Thomas gave her." Despite the encouragement of Leo XII and others, not all Catholic philosophers are by any means Thomists; many twentieth-century Catholic thinkers have shown more interest in existentialism and phenomenology. Today Thomas is studied and admired as much by Protestants and non-Christians as he is by Catholics.

*   *   *

Thomas's most famous work, the *Summa Theologica,* is one of the most comprehensive and systematic works of theology ever written. It has often been likened in its complexity and grandeur to a Gothic cathedral. This monumental classic is divided into four sections that, collectively, include 512 "Questions." Each Question raises a topic or area of investigation and is, in turn, made up of several "Articles" that explore specific concerns. These Articles range from abstract philosophical issues, such as "Whether one can intend two things at the same time," to such minutiae of theology as "Whether one angel can speak to another in such a way that others will not know what he is saying." Each Article is examined in the same manner, beginning with a question, offering an answer that Thomas considers inadequate, then supporting this answer with several "objections." At this point, a quotation or argument that contradicts the position taken thus far is introduced with the words "On the contrary (*sed contra*) . . ." The dramatic tension between two opposing positions is then resolved by the author's concise and straightforward *Respondeo,* or "I answer that . . . ," which introduces his own view. In presenting his answer, Thomas tries to avoid directly denying the preceding objections, seeing them instead as limited truths that his *Respondeo* supersedes. Finally, Thomas moves on to answer, one by one, each of the initial objections. (The reader should keep in mind that the *first* things Thomas says about a subject are the *opposite* of the position he will subsequently defend.)

The extensive selections from the *Summa Theologica* given here include readings from Thomas's "Treatise on God" (including his famous "Five Ways" or five arguments for God's existence); "Treatise on Creation" (including his argument that the world was created in time); "Treatise on Man" (including a discussion of the nature of the soul, his theory of knowledge, and his refutation of Averroës); "Treatise on Human Acts" (including his definition of happiness and his argument for free will); "Treatise on Habits" (with his presentation of the virtues); "Treatise on Law" (describing the kinds of law); and "Treatise on War" (describing his arguments for a just war). The translation is that of the Fathers of the English Dominican Province.

Two shorter works, *The Principles of Nature,* and *On Being and Essence,* both translated by Robert P. Goodwin, are given here complete. Both these treatises were written in Paris between 1252 and 1256 and show Thomas's original metaphysical thinking about questions of existence. They also demonstrate that even though Thomas used Aristotelian categories, he was an original thinker, going beyond the work of his ancient Greek predecessor.

*   *   *

The classic introductions to Thomas Aquinas are F.C. Copleston, *Aquinas* (Baltimore, MD: Penguin Books, 1955), and Étienne Gilson, *The Christian Philosophy of St. Thomas Aquinas* (New York: Random House, 1956). More recent helpful studies include Josef Pieper, *Guide to Thomas Aquinas* (New York: Pantheon, 1962); Ralph McInerny, *St. Thomas Aquinas* (Boston: Twayne, 1977); Anthony Kenny, *Aquinas* (New York: Hill and Wang, 1980); Brian Davies, *The Thought of Thomas Aquinas* (Oxford: Oxford University Press, 1992); Jean-Pierre Torrell, *Saint Thomas Aquinas, Volume I: The Person and His Work* (Washington, DC: Catholic University of America Press, 1996); and Thomas F. O'Meara, *Thomas Aquinas, Theologian* (Notre Dame, IN: Notre Dame University Press, 1997). James A. Weisheipl, *Friar Thomas D'Aquino: His Life, Thought, and Works* (Garden City, NY: Doubleday, 1974) offers a biography. G.K. Chesterton's impressionistic study entitled *St. Thomas Aquinas: The "Dumb Ox"* (1933; reprinted New York: Doubleday Image, 1956) is also a good place to become acquainted with Thomas. For a discussion of recent interpretation of Thomas Aquinas's work, see Fergus Karr, *Aquinas: Conflicting Versions of Thomism* (Oxford: Basil Blackwell, 2000). For collections of general essays, see Anthony Kenny, ed., *Aquinas: A Collection of Critical Essays* (Garden City, NY: Anchor Doubleday, 1969); Norman Kretzmann and Eleonore Stump, eds., *The Cambridge Companion to Aquinas* (Cambridge: Cambridge University Press, 1993); and Scott MacDonald and Eleonore Stump, *Aquinas's Moral Theory* (Ithaca, NY: Cornell University Press, 1999).

There are many studies on aspects of Thomas's thought. For example, a sampling of works on the "Five Ways" includes A.G.N. Flew, *God and Philosophy* (London: Hutchinson, 1966); Anthony Kenny, *The Five Ways: St. Thomas Aquinas' Proofs of God's Existence* (London: Routledge & Kegan Paul, 1969); Richard Swinburne, *The Existence of God* (Oxford: Clarendon Press, 1979); and J.L. Mackie, *The Miracle of Theism: Arguments for and against the Existence of God* (Oxford: Clarendon Press, 1982).

SUMMA THEOLOGICA (in part)

FIRST PART

TREATISE ON GOD

QUESTION 1: THE NATURE AND EXTENT OF SACRED DOCTRINE

To place our purpose within proper limits, it is necessary first to investigate the nature and extent of this sacred doctrine. Concerning this there are ten points of inquiry:—

(1) Whether it is necessary? (2) Whether it is a science? (3) Whether it is one or many? (4) Whether it is speculative or practical? (5) How it is compared with other sciences? (6) Whether it is a wisdom? (7) What is its subject-matter? (8) Whether it is a matter of argument? (9) Whether it rightly employs metaphors and similes? (10) Whether the Sacred Scripture of this doctrine may be expounded in different senses?

First Article

WHETHER, BESIDES PHILOSOPHY, ANY FURTHER DOCTRINE IS REQUIRED?

We Proceed Thus to the First Article:—

Objection 1. It seems that, besides philosophical science we have no need of any further knowledge. For man should not seek to know what is above reason: *Seek not the things that are too high for thee* (Ecclus. iii. 22). But whatever is not above reason is fully treated of in philosophical science. Therefore any other knowledge besides philosophical science is superfluous.

Obj. 2. Further, knowledge can be concerned only with being, for nothing can be known save what is true; and all that is, is true. But everything that is, is treated of in philosophical science—even God Himself, so that there is a part of philosophy called theology, or the divine science, as Aristotle has proved (*Metaph.* vi). Therefore, besides philosophical science, there is no need of any further knowledge.

On the contrary, It is written (2 Tim. iii. 16): *All Scripture inspired of God is profitable to teach, to reprove, to correct, to instruct in justice.* Now Scripture inspired of God is no part of philosophical science, which have been built up by human reason. Therefore it is useful that besides philosophical science there should be other knowledge—*i.e.,* inspired of God.

From St. Thomas Aquinas, *Summa Theologica,* Treatise on God (Part I, Q. 1 & 2; Q. 3, A.4; Q. 8, A.1; Q. 13, a. 2, 5); Treatise on Creation (Part I, Q. 46, a. 1, 2); Treatise on Man (Part I, Q. 75, a. 2; Q. 76, a. 1, 2, 4; Q. 84, a. 5, 6; Q. 85, a. 1, 2; Q. 86. a. 1); Treatise on Human Acts (Part I–II, Q. 2, a. 8; Q. 3, a. 4, 5, 8; Q. 5, a. 5; Q. 10, a. 2; Q. 13, a. 6); Treatise on Habits (Part I–II, Q. 61, a. 1, 2; Q. 62, a. 1, 2, 3); Treatise on Law (Part I–II, Q. 94, a. 2, 4, 5; Q. 95, a. 1, 2; Q. 96, a. 2); Treatise on War (Part II–II, q. 40, a. 1), translated by the Fathers of the English Dominican Province (New York: Benziger Brothers, 1947). Reprinted by permission.

I answer that, It was necessary for man's salvation that there should be a knowledge revealed by God, besides philosophical science built up by human reason. Firstly, indeed, because man is directed to God as to an end that surpasses the grasp of his reason: *The eye hath not seen, O God, besides Thee, what things Thou hast prepared for them that wait for Thee* (Isa. lxvi. 4). But the end must first be known by men who are to direct their thoughts and actions to the end. Hence it was necessary for the salvation of man that certain truths which exceed human reason should be made known to him by divine revelation. Even as regards those truths about God which human reason could have discovered, it was necessary that man should be taught by a divine revelation; because the truth about God such as reason could discover would only be known by a few, and that after a long time, and with the admixture of many errors. Whereas man's whole salvation, which is in God, depends upon the knowledge of this truth. Therefore, in order that the salvation of men might be brought about more fitly and more surely, it was necessary that they should be taught divine truths by divine revelation. It was therefore necessary that, besides philosophical science built up by reason there should be a sacred science learned through revelation.

Reply Obj. 1. Although those things which are beyond man's knowledge may not be sought for by man through his reason, nevertheless, once they are revealed by God they must be accepted by faith. Hence the sacred text continues, *For many things are shown to thee above the understanding of man* (Ecclus. iii. 25). And in this sacred science consists.

Reply Obj. 2. Sciences are differentiated according to the various means through which knowledge is obtained. For the astronomer and the physicist both may prove the same conclusion—that the earth, for instance, is round: the astronomer by means of mathematics (*i.e.,* abstracting from matter), but the physicist by means of matter itself. Hence there is no reason why those things which may be learned from philosophical science, so far as they can be known by natural reason, may not also be taught us by another science so far as they fall within revelation. Hence theology included in sacred doctrine differs in kind from that theology which is part of philosophy.

Second Article

WHETHER SACRED DOCTRINE IS A SCIENCE?

We Proceed Thus to the Second Article:—

Objection 1. It seems that sacred doctrine is not a science. For every science proceeds from self-evident principles. But sacred doctrine proceeds from articles of faith which are not self-evident, since their truth is not admitted by all: *For all men have not faith* (2 Thess. iii. 2). Therefore sacred doctrine is not a science.

Obj. 2. Further, no science deals with individual facts. But this sacred science treats of individual facts, such as the deeds of Abraham, Isaac, and Jacob, and such like. Therefore sacred doctrine is not a science.

On the contrary, Augustine says (*De Trin.* xiv. 1), *to this science alone belongs that whereby saving faith is begotten, nourished, protected, and strengthened.* But this can be said of no science except sacred doctrine. Therefore sacred doctrine is a science.

I answer that, Sacred doctrine is a science. We must bear in mind that there are two kinds of sciences. There are some which proceed from a principle known by the natural light of the intelligence, such as arithmetic and geometry and the like. There are some which proceed from principles known by the light of a higher science: thus the science of perspective proceeds from principles established by geometry, and music from principles established by arithmetic. So it is that sacred doctrine is a science, because it proceeds from principles established by the light of a higher science, namely, the science of God and the blessed. Hence, just as the musician accepts on authority the principles taught him by the mathematician, so sacred science is established on principles revealed by God.

Reply Obj. 1. The principles of any science are either in themselves self-evident, or reducible to the conclusions of a higher science; and such, as we have said, are the principles of sacred doctrine.

Reply Obj. 2. Individual facts are treated of in sacred doctrine, not because it is concerned with them principally: but they are introduced rather both as examples to be followed in our lives (as in moral sciences), and in order to establish the authority of those men through whom the divine revelation, on which this sacred scripture or doctrine is based, has come down to us.

Third Article

WHETHER DOCTRINE IS ONE SCIENCE?

We Proceed Thus to the Third Article:—

Objection 1. It seems that sacred doctrine is not one science; for according to the Philosopher (*Poster.* i) *that science is one which treats only of one class of subjects.* But the creator and the creature, both of whom are treated of in sacred doctrine, cannot be grouped together under one class of subjects. Therefore sacred doctrine is not one science.

Obj. 2. Further, in sacred doctrine we treat of angels, corporeal creatures, and human morality. But these belong to separate philosophical sciences. Therefore sacred doctrine cannot be one science.

On the contrary, Holy Scripture speaks of it as one science: *Wisdom gave him the knowledge [scientiam] of holy things* (Wisd. x. 10).

I answer that, Sacred doctrine is one science. The unity of a faculty or habit is to be gauged by its object, not indeed, in its material aspect, but as regards the precise formality under which it is an object. For example, man, ass, stone agree in the one precise formality of being colored; and color is the formal object of sight. Therefore, because Sacred Scripture considers things precisely under the formality of being divinely revealed, whatever has been divinely revealed possesses the one precise formality of the object of this science; and therefore is included under sacred doctrine as under one science.

Reply Obj. 1. Sacred doctrine does not treat of God and creatures equally, but of God primarily; and of creatures only so far as they are referable to God as their beginning or end. Hence the unity of this science is not impaired.

Reply Obj. 2. Nothing prevents inferior faculties or habits from being differentiated by something which falls under a higher faculty or habit as well; because the higher faculty or habit regards the object in its more universal formality, as the object of the *common sense* is whatever affects the senses, including, therefore, whatever is visible or audible. Hence the *common sense,* although one faculty, extends to all the objects of the five senses. Similarly, objects which are the subject-matter of different philosophical sciences can yet be treated of by this one single sacred science under one aspect precisely so far as they can be included in revelation. So that in this way sacred doctrine bears, as it were, the stamp of the divine science, which is one and simple, yet extends to everything.

Fourth Article

WHETHER SACRED DOCTRINE IS A PRACTICAL SCIENCE?

We Proceed Thus to the Fourth Article:—

Objection 1. It seems that sacred doctrine is a practical science; for a practical science is that which ends in action according to the Philosopher (*Metaph.* ii). But sacred doctrine is ordained to action: *Be ye doers of the word, and not hearers only* (Jas. i. 22). Therefore sacred doctrine is a practical science.

Obj. 2. Further, sacred doctrine is divided into the Old and the New Law. But law implies a moral science, which is a practical science. Therefore sacred doctrine is a practical science.

On the contrary, Every practical science is concerned with human operations; as moral science is concerned with human acts, and architecture with buildings. But sacred doctrine is chiefly concerned with God, whose handiwork is especially man. Therefore it is not a practical but a speculative science.

I answer that, Sacred doctrine, being one, extends to things which belong to different philosophical sciences, because it considers in each the same formal aspect, namely so far as they can be known through divine revelation. Hence, although among the philosophical sciences one is speculative and another practical, nevertheless sacred doctrine includes both; as God, by one and the same science, knows both Himself and His works. Still, it is speculative rather than practical, because it is more concerned with divine things than with human acts; though it does treat even of these latter, inasmuch as man is ordained by them to the perfect knowledge of God, in which consists eternal bliss. This is a sufficient answer to the Objections.

Fifth Article

WHETHER SACRED DOCTRINE IS NOBLER THAN OTHER SCIENCES?

We Proceed Thus to the Fifth Article:—

Objection 1. It seems that sacred doctrine is not nobler than other sciences; for the nobility of a science depends on the certitude it establishes. But other sciences, the principles of which cannot be doubted, seem to be more certain than sacred doctrine; for its principles—namely, articles of faith—can be doubted. Therefore other sciences seem to be nobler.

Obj. 2. Further, it is the sign of a lower science to depend upon a higher; as music depends upon arithmetic. But sacred doctrine does in a sense depend upon the philosophical sciences; for Jerome observes, in his Epistle to Magnus, *that the ancient doctors so enriched their books with the ideas and phrases of the philosophers, that thou knowest not what more to admire in them, their profane erudition or their scriptural learning.* Therefore sacred doctrine is inferior to other sciences.

On the contrary, Other sciences are called the handmaidens of this one: *Wisdom sent her maids to invite to the tower* (Prov. ix. 3).

I answer that, Since this science is partly speculative and partly practical, it transcends all others speculative and practical. Now one speculative science is said to be nobler than another, either by reason of its greater certitude, or by reason of the higher worth of its subject-matter. In both these respects this science surpasses other speculative sciences; in point of greater certitude, because other sciences derive their certitude from the natural light of human reason, which can err; whereas this derives its certitude from the light of the divine knowledge, which cannot be misled: in point of the higher worth of its subject-matter, because this science treats chiefly of those things which by their sublimity transcend human reason; while other sciences consider only those things which are within reason's grasp. Of the practical sciences, that one is nobler which is ordained to a further purpose, as political science is nobler than military science; for the good of the army is directed to the good of the State. But the purpose of this science, in so far as it is practical, is eternal bliss; to which as to an ultimate end the purposes of every practical science are directed. Hence it is clear that from every standpoint it is nobler than other sciences.

Reply Obj. 1. It may well happen that what is in itself the more certain may seem to us the less certain on account of the weakness of our intelligence, "which is dazzled by the clearest objects of nature; as the owl is dazzled by the light of the sun" (*Metaph.* ii. lect. i). Hence the fact that some happen to doubt about articles of faith is not due to the uncertain nature of the truths, but to the weakness of human intelligence; yet the slenderest knowledge that may be obtained of the highest things is more desirable than the most certain knowledge obtained of lesser things, as is said in *de Animalibus* xi.

Reply Obj. 2. This science can in a sense depend upon the philosophical sciences, not as though it stood in need of them, but only in order to make its teaching clearer. For it accepts its principles not from other sciences; but immediately from God, by revelation. Therefore it does not depend upon other sciences as upon the higher, but makes use of them as of the lesser, and as handmaidens: even so the master sciences make use of the sciences that supply their materials, as political of military science. That it thus uses them is not due to its own defect or insufficiency, but to the defect of our intelligence, which is more easily led by what is known through natural reason (from which proceed the other sciences), to that which is above reason, such as are the teachings of this science.

Sixth Article

WHETHER THIS DOCTRINE IS THE SAME AS WISDOM?

We Proceed Thus to the Sixth Article:—

Objection 1. It seems that this doctrine is not the same as wisdom. For no doctrine which borrows its principles is worthy of the name of wisdom; seeing that the wise man directs, and is not directed (*Metaph.* i). But this doctrine borrows its principles. Therefore this science is not wisdom.

Obj. 2. Further, it is a part of wisdom to prove the principles of other sciences. Hence it is called the chief of sciences, as is clear in *Ethic.* vi. But this doctrine does not prove the principles of other sciences. Therefore it is not the same as wisdom.

Obj. 3. Further, this doctrine is acquired by study, whereas wisdom is acquired by God's inspiration; so that it is numbered among the gifts of the Holy Spirit (Isa. xi. 2). Therefore this doctrine is not the same as wisdom.

On the contrary, It is written (Deut. iv. 6): *This is your wisdom and understanding in the sight of nations.*

I answer that, This doctrine is wisdom above all human wisdom; not merely in any one order, but absolutely. For since it is the part of a wise man to arrange and to judge, and since lesser matters should be judged in the light of some higher principle, he is said to be wise in any one order who considers the highest principle in that order: thus in the order of building he who plans the form of the house is called wise and architect, in opposition to the inferior laborers who trim the wood and make ready the stones: *As a wise architect I have laid the foundation* (1 Cor. iii. 10). Again, in the order of all human life, the prudent man is called wise, inasmuch as he directs his acts to a fitting end: *Wisdom is prudence to a man* (Prov. x. 23). Therefore he who considers absolutely the highest cause of the whole universe, namely God, is most of all called wise. Hence wisdom is said to be the knowledge of divine things, as Augustine says (*De Trin.* xii. 14). But sacred doctrine essentially treats of God viewed as the highest cause—not only so far as He can be known through creatures just as philosophers knew Him—*That which is known of God is manifest in them* (Rom. i. 19)—but also so far as He is known to Himself alone and revealed to others. Hence sacred doctrine is especially called wisdom.

Reply Obj. 1. Sacred doctrine derives its principles not from any human knowledge, but from the divine knowledge, through which, as through the highest wisdom, all our knowledge is set in order.

Reply Obj. 2. The principles of other sciences either are evident and cannot be proved, or are proved by natural reason through some other science. But the knowledge proper to this science comes through revelation, and not through natural reason. Therefore it has no concern to prove the principles of other sciences, but only to judge of them. Whatsoever is found in other sciences contrary to any truth of this science, must be condemned as false: *Destroying counsels and every height that exalteth itself against the knowledge of God* (2 Cor. x. 4, 5).

Reply Obj. 3. Since judgment appertains to wisdom, the twofold manner of judging produces a twofold wisdom. A man may judge in one way by inclination, as whoever has the habit of a virtue judges rightly of what concerns that virtue by his very inclination towards it. Hence it is the virtuous man, as we read, who is the measure and rule of human acts. In another way, by knowledge, just as a man learned in moral science might be able to judge rightly about virtuous acts, though he had not the virtue. The first manner of judging divine things belongs to that wisdom which is set down among the gifts of the Holy Ghost: *The spiritual man judgeth all things* (1 Cor. ii. 15). And Dionysius says (Div. Nom. ii.): *Hierotheus is taught not by mere learning, but by experience of divine things.* The second manner of judging belongs to this doctrine, which is acquired by study, though its principles are obtained by revelation.

Seventh Article

WHETHER GOD IS THE OBJECT OF THIS SCIENCE?

We Proceed Thus to the Seventh Article:—

Objection 1. It seems that God is not the object of this science. For in every science the nature of its object is presupposed. But this science cannot presuppose the essence of God, for Damascene says (*De Fid. Orth.* 1. iv): *It is impossible to define the essence of God.* Therefore God is not the object of this science.

Obj. 2. Further, whatever conclusions are reached in any science must be comprehended under the object of the science. But in Holy Writ we reach conclusions not only concerning God, but concerning many other things, such as creatures and human morality. Therefore God is not the object of this science.

On the contrary, The object of the science is that of which it principally treats. But in this science the treatment is mainly about God; for it is called theology, as treating of God. Therefore God is the object of this science.

I answer that, God is the object of this science. The relation between a science and its object is the same as that between a habit or faculty and its object. Now properly speaking the object of a faculty or habit is the thing under the aspect of which all things are referred to that faculty or habit, as man and stone are referred to the faculty of sight in that they are colored. Hence colored things are the proper objects of sight. But in sacred science all things are treated of under the aspect of God; either because they are God Himself; or because they refer to God as their beginning and end. Hence it follows that God is in very truth the object of this science. This is clear also from the principles of this science, namely, the articles of faith, for faith is about God. The object of the principles and of the whole science must be the same, since the whole science is contained virtually in its principles. Some, however, looking to what is treated of in this science, and not to the aspect under which it is treated, have asserted the object of this science to be something other than God—that is, either things and signs; or the works of salvation; or the whole Christ, as the head and members. Of all these things, in truth, we treat in this science, but so far as they have reference to God.

Reply Obj. 1. Although we cannot know in what consists the essence of God, nevertheless in this science we make use of His effects, either of nature or of grace, in place of a definition, in regard to whatever is treated of in this science concerning God; even as in some philosophical sciences we demonstrate something about a cause from its effect, by taking the effect in place of a definition of the cause.

Reply Obj. 2. Whatever other conclusions are reached in this sacred science are comprehended under God, not as parts or species or accidents, but as in some way related to Him.

Eighth Article

WHETHER SACRED DOCTRINE IS A MATTER OF ARGUMENT?

We Proceed Thus to the Eighth Article:—

Objection 1. It seems this doctrine is not a matter of argument. For Ambrose says (*De Fide*, 1): *Put arguments aside where faith is sought.* But in this doctrine faith especially is sought: *But these things are written that you may believe* (John xx. 31). Therefore sacred doctrine is not a matter of argument.

Obj. 2. Further, if it is a matter of argument, the argument is either from authority or from reason. If it is from authority, it seems unbefitting its dignity, for the proof from authority is the weakest form of proof. But if from reason, this is unbefitting its end, because, according to Gregory (*Homil.* 26), *faith has no merit in those things of which human reason brings its own experience.* Therefore sacred doctrine is not a matter of argument.

On the contrary, The Scripture says that a bishop should *embrace that faithful word which is according to doctrine, that he may be able to exhort in sound doctrine and to convince the gainsayers* (Tit. i. 9).

I answer that, As other sciences do not argue in proof of their principles, but argue from their principles to demonstrate other truths in these sciences: so this doctrine does not argue in proof of its principles, which are the articles of faith, but from them it goes on to prove something else; as the Apostle from the resurrection of Christ argues in proof of the general resurrection (1 Cor. xv). However, it is to be borne in mind, in regard to the philosophical sciences, that the inferior sciences neither prove their principles nor dispute with those who deny them, but leave this to a higher science; whereas the highest of them, viz., metaphysics, can dispute with one who denies its principles, if only the opponent will make some concession; but if he concede nothing, it can have no dispute with him, though it can answer his objections. Hence Sacred Scripture, since it has no science above itself, can dispute with one who denies its principles only if the opponent admits some at least of the truths obtained through divine revelation; thus we can argue with heretics from texts in Holy Writ, and against those who deny one article of faith we can argue from another. If our opponent believes nothing of divine revelation, there is no longer any means of proving the articles of faith by reasoning, but only of answering his objections—if he has any—against faith. Since faith rests upon infallible truth, and since the contrary of a truth can never be demonstrated, it is clear that the arguments brought against faith cannot be demonstrations, but are difficulties that can be answered.

Reply Obj. 1. Although arguments from human reason cannot avail to prove what must be received on faith, nevertheless this doctrine argues from articles of faith to other truths.

Reply Obj. 2. This doctrine is especially based upon arguments from authority, inasmuch as its principles are obtained by revelation: thus we ought to believe on the authority of those to whom the revelation has been made. Nor does this take away from the dignity of this doctrine, for although the argument from authority based on human reason is the weakest, yet the argument from authority based on divine revelation is the strongest. But sacred doctrine makes use even of human reason, not, indeed, to prove faith (for thereby the merit of faith would come to an end), but to make clear other things that are put forward in this doctrine. Since therefore grace does not destroy nature, but perfects it, natural reason should minister to faith as the natural bent of the will ministers to charity. Hence the Apostle says: *Bringing into captivity every understanding unto the obedience of Christ* (2 Cor. x. 5). Hence sacred doctrine makes use also of the authority of philosophers in those questions in which they were able to know the truth by natural reason, as Paul quotes a saying of Aratus: *As some also of your own poets said: For we are also His offspring* (Acts xvii. 28). Nevertheless, sacred doctrine makes use of these authorities as extrinsic and probable arguments; but properly uses the authority of the canonical Scriptures as an incontrovertible proof, and the authority of the doctors of the Church as one that may properly be used, yet merely as probable. For our faith rests upon the revelation made to the apostles and prophets, who wrote the canonical books, and not on the revelations (if any such there are) made to other doctors. Hence Augustine says (*Epist. ad Hieron.* xix. 1): *Only those books of Scripture which are called canonical have I learned to hold in such honor as to believe their authors have not erred in any way in writing them. But other authors I so read as not to deem anything in their works to be true, merely on account of their having so thought and written, whatever may have been their holiness and learning.*

Ninth Article

WHETHER HOLY SCRIPTURE SHOULD USE METAPHORS?

We Proceed Thus to the Ninth Article:—

Objection 1. It seems that Holy Scripture should not use metaphors. For that which is proper to the lowest science seems not to befit this science, which holds the highest place of all. But to proceed by the aid of various similitudes and figures is proper to poetry, the least of all the sciences. Therefore it is not fitting that this science should make use of such similitudes.

Obj. 2. Further, this doctrine seems to be intended to make truth clear. Hence a reward is held out to those who manifest it: *They that explain me shall have life everlasting* (Ecclus. xxiv. 31). But by such similitudes truth is obscured. Therefore to put forward divine truths by likening them to corporeal things does not befit this science.

Obj. 3. Further, the higher creatures are, the nearer they approach to the divine likeness. If therefore any creature be taken to represent God, this representation ought chiefly to be taken from the higher creatures, and not from the lower; yet this is often found in the Scriptures.

On the contrary, It is written (Osee xii. 10): *I have multiplied visions, and I have used similitudes by the ministry of the prophets.* But to put forward anything by means of similitudes is to use metaphors. Therefore this sacred science may use metaphors.

I answer that, It is befitting Holy Writ to put forward divine and spiritual truths by means of comparisons with material things. For God provides for everything according to the capacity of its nature. Now it is natural to man to attain to intellectual truths through sensible objects, because all our knowledge originates from sense. Hence in Holy Writ spiritual truths are fittingly taught under the likeness of material things. This is what Dionysius says (*Cæl. Hier.* i): *We cannot be enlightened by the divine rays except they be hidden within the covering of many sacred veils.* It is also befitting Holy Writ, which is proposed to all without distinction of persons—*To the wise and to the unwise I am a debtor* (Rom. i. 14)—that spiritual truths be expounded by means of figures taken from corporeal things, in order that thereby even the simple who are unable by themselves to grasp intellectual things may be able to understand it.

Reply Obj. 1. Poetry makes use of metaphors to produce a representation, for it is natural to man to be pleased with representations. But sacred doctrine makes use of metaphors as both necessary and useful.

Reply Obj. 2. The ray of divine revelation is not extinguished by the sensible imagery wherewith it is veiled, as Dionysius says (*Cæl. Hier.* i); and its truth so far remains that it does not allow the minds of those to whom the revelation has been made, to rest in the metaphors, but raises them to the knowledge of truths; and through those to whom the revelation has been made others also may receive instruction in these matters. Hence those things that are taught metaphorically in one part of Scripture, in other parts are taught more openly. The very hiding of truth in figures is useful for the exercise of thoughtful minds, and as a defence against the ridicule of the impious, according to the words *Give not that which is holy to dogs* (Matth. vii. 6).

Reply Obj. 3. As Dionysius says (*loc. cit.*), it is more fitting that divine truths should be expounded under the figure of less noble than of nobler bodies, and this for three reasons. Firstly, because thereby men's minds are the better preserved from error. For then it is clear that these things are not literal descriptions of divine truths, which might have been open to doubt had they been expressed under the figure of nobler bodies, especially for those who could think of nothing nobler than bodies. Secondly, because this is more befitting the knowledge of God that we have in this life. For what He is not is clearer to us than what He is. Therefore similitudes drawn from things farthest away from God form within us a truer estimate that God is above whatsoever we may say or think of Him. Thirdly, because thereby divine truths are the better hidden from the unworthy.

Tenth Article

WHETHER IN HOLY SCRIPTURE A WORD MAY HAVE SEVERAL SENSES?

We Proceed Thus to the Tenth Article:—

Objection 1. It seems that in Holy Writ a word cannot have several senses, historical or literal, allegorical, tropological or moral, and anagogical. For many different senses in one text produce confusion and deception and destroy all force of argument. Hence no argument, but only fallacies, can be deduced from a multiplicity of propositions. But Holy Writ ought to be able to state the truth without any fallacy. Therefore in it there cannot be several senses to a word.

Obj. 2. Further, Augustine says (*de util. cred.* iii) that *the Old Testament has a fourfold division as to history, etiology, analogy, and allegory.* Now these four seem altogether different from the four divisions mentioned in the first objection. Therefore it does not seem fitting to explain the same word of Holy Writ according to the four different senses mentioned above.

Obj. 3. Further, besides these senses, there is the parabolical, which is not one of these four.

On the contrary, Gregory says (Moral. xx. 1): *Holy Writ by the manner of its speech transcends every science, because in one and the same sentence, while it describes a fact, it reveals a mystery.*

I answer that, The author of Holy Writ is God, in whose power it is to signify His meaning, not by words only (as man also can do), but also by things themselves. So, whereas in every other science things are signified by words, this science has the property, that the things signified by the words have themselves also a signification. Therefore that first signification whereby words signify things belongs to the first sense, the historical or literal. That signification whereby things signified by words have themselves also a signification is called the spiritual sense, which is based on the literal, and presupposes it. Now this spiritual sense has a threefold division. For as the Apostle says (Heb. x. 1) the Old Law is a figure of the New Law, and Dionysius says (*Cæl. Hier.* i) *the New Law itself is a figure of future glory.* Again, in the New Law, whatever our Head has done is a type of what we ought to do. Therefore, so far as the things of the Old Law signify the things of the New Law, there is the allegorical sense; so far as the things done in Christ, or so far as the things which signify Christ, are types of what we ought to do, there is the moral sense. But so far as they signify what relates to eternal glory, there is the anagogical sense. Since the literal sense is that which the author intends, and since the author of Holy Writ is God. Who by one act comprehends all things by His intellect, it is not unfitting, as Augustine says (*Confess.* xii), if, even according to the literal sense, one word in Holy Writ should have several senses.

Reply Obj. 1. The multiplicity of these senses does not produce equivocation or any other kind of multiplicity, seeing that these senses are not multiplied because one word signifies several things; but because the things signified by the words can be themselves types of other things. Thus in Holy Writ no confusion results, for all the senses are founded on one—the literal—from which alone can any argument be drawn, and not from those intended in allegory, as Augustine says (*Epist.* xlviii). Nevertheless, nothing of Holy Scripture perishes on account of this, since nothing necessary to faith is contained under the spiritual sense which is not elsewhere put forward by the Scripture in its literal sense.

Reply Obj. 2. These three—history, etiology, analogy—are grouped under the literal sense. For it is called history, as Augustine expounds *(loc. cit.),* whenever anything is simply related; it is called etiology when its cause is assigned, as when Our Lord gave the reason why Moses allowed the putting away of wives—namely, on account of the hardness of men's hearts; it is called analogy whenever the truth of one text of Scripture is shown not to contradict the truth of another. Of these four, allegory alone stands for the three spiritual senses. Thus Hugh of S. Victor *(Sacram.* iv. 4 *Prolog.)* includes the anagogical under the allegorical sense, laying down three senses only—the historical, the allegorical, and the tropological.

Reply Obj. 3. The parabolical sense is contained in the literal, for by words things are signified properly and figuratively. Nor is the figure itself, but that which is figured, the literal sense. When Scripture speaks of God's arm, the literal sense is not that God has such a member, but only what is signified by this member, namely, operative power. Hence it is plain that nothing false can ever underlie the literal sense of Holy Writ.

QUESTION 2: THE EXISTENCE OF GOD

Because the chief aim of sacred doctrine is to teach the knowledge of God, not only as He is in Himself, but also as He is the beginning of things and their last end, and especially of rational creatures, as is clear from what has been already said, therefore, in our endeavor to expound this science, we shall treat: (1) Of God; (2) Of the rational creature's advance towards God; (3) Of Christ, Who as man, is our way to God.

In treating of God there will be a threefold division:—

For we shall consider (1) Whatever concerns the Divine Essence; (2) Whatever concerns the distinctions of Persons; (3) Whatever concerns the procession of creatures from Him.

Concerning the Divine Essence, we must consider:—

(1) Whether God exists? (2) The manner of His existence, or, rather, what is *not* the manner of His existence; (3) Whatever concerns His operations—namely, His knowledge, will, power.

Concerning the first, there are three points of inquiry:—

(1) Whether the proposition "God exists" is self-evident? (2) Whether it is demonstrable? (3) Whether God exists?

First Article

Whether the Existence of God Is Self-Evident?

We Proceed Thus to the First Article:—

Objection 1. It seems that the existence of God is self-evident. Now those things are said to be selfevident to us the knowledge of which is naturally implanted in us, as we can see in regard to first principles. But as Damascene says (*De Fid. Orth.* i. 1, 3), *the knowledge of God is naturally implanted in all.* Therefore the existence of God is self-evident.

Obj. 2. Further, those things are said to be self-evident which are known as soon as the terms are known, which the Philosopher (1 *Poster.* iii) says is true of the first principles of demonstration. Thus, when the nature of a whole and of a part is known, it is at once recognized that every whole is greater than its part. But as soon as the signification of the word "God" is understood, it is at once seen that God exists. For by this word is signified that thing than which nothing greater can be conceived. But that which exists actually and mentally is greater than that which exists only mentally. Therefore, since as soon as the word "God" is understood it exists mentally, it also follows that it exists actually. Therefore the proposition "God exists" is self-evident.

Obj. 3. Further, the existence of truth is self-evident. For whoever denies the existence of truth grants that truth does not exist: and if truth does not exist, then the proposition "Truth does not exist" is true: and if there is anything true, there must be truth. But God is truth itself: *I am the way, the truth, and the life* (John xiv. 6). Therefore "God exists" is self-evident.

On the contrary, No one can mentally admit the opposite of what is self-evident; as the Philosopher (*Metaph.* iv., lect. vi) states concerning the first principles of demonstration. But the opposite of the proposition "God is" can be mentally admitted: *The fool said in his heart, There is no God* (Ps. lii. 1). Therefore, that God exists is not self-evident.

I answer that, A thing can be self-evident in either of two ways; on the one hand, self-evident in itself, though not to us; on the other, self-evident in itself, and to us. A proposition is self-evident because the predicate is included in the essence of the subject, as "Man is an animal," for animal is contained in the essence of man. If, therefore the essence of the predicate and subject be known to all, the proposition will be self-evident to all; as is clear with regard to the first principles of demonstration, the terms of which are common things that no one is ignorant of, such as being and non-being, whole and part, and such like. If, however, there are some to whom the essence of the predicate and subject is unknown, the proposition will be self-evident in itself, but not to those who do not know the meaning of the predicate and subject of the proposition. Therefore, it happens, as Boethius says (*Hebdom., the title of which is: "Whether all that is, is good"),* "that there are some mental concepts self-evident only to the learned, as that incorporeal substances are not in space." Therefore I say that this proposition, "God exists," of itself is self-evident, for the predicate is the same as the subject; because God is His own existence as will be hereafter shown (Q. 3, A. 4). Now because we do not know the essence of God, the proposition is not self-evident to us; but needs to be demonstrated by things that are more known to us, though less known in their nature—namely, by effects.

Reply Obj. 1. To know that God exists in a general and confused way is implanted in us by nature, inasmuch as God is man's beatitude. For man naturally desires happiness, and what is naturally desired by man must be naturally known to him. This, however, is not to know absolutely that God exists; just as to know that someone is approaching is not the same as to know that Peter is approaching, even though it is Peter who is approaching; for many there are who imagine that man's perfect good which is happiness, consists in riches, and others in pleasures, and others in something else.

Reply Obj. 2. Perhaps not everyone who hears this word "God" understands it to signify something than which nothing greater can be thought, seeing that some have believed God to be a body. Yet, granted that everyone understands that by this word "God" is signified something than which nothing greater can be thought, nevertheless, it does not therefore follow that he understands that what the word signifies exists actually, but only that it exists mentally. Nor can it be argued that it actually exists, unless it be admitted that there actually exists something than which nothing greater can be thought; and this precisely is not admitted by those who hold that God does not exist.

Reply Obj. 3. The existence of truth in general is self-evident but the existence of a Primal Truth is not self-evident to us.

Second Article

WHETHER IT CAN BE DEMONSTRATED THAT GOD EXISTS?

We Proceed Thus to the Second Article:—

Objection 1. It seems that the existence of God cannot be demonstrated. For it is an article of faith that God exists. But what is of faith cannot be demonstrated, because a demonstration produces scientific knowledge; whereas faith is of the unseen (Heb. xi. 1). Therefore it cannot be demonstrated that God exists.

Obj. 2. Further, the essence is the middle term of demonstration. But we cannot know in what God's essence consists, but solely in what it does not consist; as Damascene says (*De Fid. Orth.* i. 4). Therefore we cannot demonstrate that God exists.

Obj. 3. Further, if the existence of God were demonstrated, this could only be from His effects. But His effects are not proportionate to Him, since He is infinite and His effects are finite; and between the finite and infinite there is no proportion. Therefore, since a cause cannot be demonstrated by an effect not proportionate to it, it seems that the existence of God cannot be demonstrated.

On the contrary, The Apostle says: *The invisible things of Him are clearly seen, being understood by the things that are made* (Rom. i. 20). But this would not be unless the existence of God could be demonstrated through the things that are made; for the first thing we must know of anything is, whether it exists.

I answer that, Demonstration can be made in two ways: One is through the cause, and is called *a priori,* and this is to argue from what is prior absolutely. The other is through the effect, and is called a demonstration *a posteriori;* this is to argue from what is prior relatively only to us. When an effect is better known to us than its cause, from the effect we proceed to the knowledge of the cause. And from every effect the existence of its proper cause can be demonstrated, so long as its effects are better known to us; because since every effect depends upon its cause, if the effect exists, the cause must pre exist. Hence the existence of God, in so far as it is not self-evident to us, can be demonstrated from those of His effects which are known to us.

Reply Obj. 1. The existence of God and other like truths about God, which can be known by natural reason, are not articles of faith, but are preambles to the articles; for faith presupposes natural knowledge, even as grace presupposes nature, and perfection supposes something that can be perfected. Nevertheless, there is nothing to prevent a man, who cannot grasp a proof, accepting, as a matter of faith, something which in itself is capable of being scientifically known and demonstrated.

Reply Obj. 2. When the existence of a cause is demonstrated from an effect, this effect takes the place of the definition of the cause in proof of the cause's existence. This is especially the case in regard to God, because, in order to prove the existence of anything, it is necessary to accept as a middle term the meaning of the word, and not its essence, for the question of its essence follows on the question of its existence. Now the names given to God are derived from His effects; consequently, in demonstrating the existence of God from His effects, we may take for the middle term the meaning of the word "God."

Reply Obj. 3. From effects not proportionate to the cause no perfect knowledge of that cause can be obtained. Yet from every effect the existence of the cause can be clearly demonstrated, and so we can demonstrate the existence of God from His effects; though from them we cannot perfectly know God as He is in His essence.

Third Article

WHETHER GOD EXISTS?

We Proceed Thus to the Third Article:—

Objection 1. It seems that God does not exist; because if one of two contraries be infinite, the other would be altogether destroyed. But the word "God" means that He is infinite goodness. If, therefore, God existed, there would be no evil discoverable; but there is evil in the world. Therefore God does not exist.

Obj. 2. Further, it is superfluous to suppose that what can be accounted for by a few principles has been produced by many. But it seems that everything we see in the world can be accounted for by other principles, supposing God did not exist. For all natural things can be reduced to one principle, which is nature; and all voluntary things can be reduced to one principle, which is human reason, or will. Therefore there is no need to suppose God's existence.

On the contrary, It is said in the person of God: *I am Who am* (Exod. iii. 14).

I answer that, The existence of God can be proved in five ways.

The first and more manifest way is the argument from motion. It is certain, and evident to our senses, that in the world some things are in motion. Now whatever is in motion is put in motion by another, for nothing can be in motion except it is in potentiality to that towards which it is in motion; whereas a thing moves inasmuch as it is in act. For motion is nothing else than the reduction of something from potentiality to actuality. But nothing can be reduced from potentiality to actuality, except by something in a state of actuality. Thus that which is actually hot, as fire, makes wood, which is potentially hot, to be actually hot, and thereby moves and changes it. Now it is not possible that the same thing should be at once in actuality and potentiality in the same respect, but only in different respects. For what is actually hot cannot simultaneously be potentially hot; but it is simultaneously potentially cold. It is therefore impossible that in the same respect and in the same way a thing should be both mover and moved, *i.e.,* that it should move itself. Therefore, whatever is in motion must be put in motion by another. If that by which it is put in motion be itself put in motion, then this also must needs be put in motion by another, and that by another again. But this cannot go on to infinity, because then there would be no first mover, and, consequently, no other mover; seeing that subsequent movers move only inasmuch as they are put in motion by the first mover; as the staff moves only because it is put in motion by the hand. Therefore it is necessary to arrive at a first mover, put in motion by no other; and this everyone understands to be God.

The second way is from the nature of the efficient cause. In the world of sense we find there is an order of efficient causes. There is no case known (neither is it, indeed, possible) in which a thing is found to be the efficient cause of itself; for so it would be prior to itself, which is impossible. Now in efficient causes it is not possible to go on to infinity, because in all efficient causes following in order, the first is the cause of the intermediate cause, and the intermediate is the cause of the ultimate cause, whether the intermediate cause be several, or one only. Now to take away the cause is to take away the effect. Therefore if there be no first cause among efficient causes, there will be no ultimate, nor any intermediate cause. But if in efficient causes it is possible to go on to infinity, there will be no first efficient cause, neither will there be an ultimate effect, nor any intermediate efficient causes; all of which is plainly false. Therefore it is necessary to admit a first efficient cause, to which everyone gives the name of God.

The third way is taken from possibility and necessity, and runs thus. We find in nature things that are possible to be and not to be, since they are found to be generated, and to corrupt, and consequently, they are possible to be and not to be. But it is impossible for these always to exist, for that which is possible not to be at some time is not. Therefore, if everything is possible not to be, then at one time there could have been nothing in existence. Now if this were true, even now there would be nothing in existence, because that which does not exist only begins to exist by something already existing. Therefore, if at one time nothing was in existence, it would have been impossible for anything to have begun to exist; and thus even now nothing would be in existence—which is absurd. Therefore, not all beings are merely possible, but there must exist something the existence of which is necessary. But every necessary thing either has its necessity caused by another, or not. Now it is impossible to go on to infinity in necessary things which have their necessity caused by another, as has been already proved in regard to efficient causes. Therefore we cannot but postulate the existence of some being having of itself its own necessity, and not receiving it from another, but rather causing in others their necessity. This all men speak of as God.

The fourth way is taken from the gradation to be found in things. Among beings there are some more and some less good, true, noble, and the like. But "more" and "less" are predicated of different things, according as they resemble in their different ways something which is the maximum, as a thing is said to be hotter according as it more nearly resembles that which is hottest; so that there is something which is truest, something best, something noblest, and, consequently, something which is uttermost being; for those things that are greatest in truth are greatest in being, as it is written in *Metaph.* ii. Now the maximum in any genus is the cause of all in that genus; as fire, which is the maximum of heat, is the cause of all hot things. Therefore there must also be something which is to all beings the cause of their being, goodness, and every other perfection; and this we call God.

The fifth way is taken from the governance of the world. We see that things which lack intelligence, such as natural bodies, act for an end, and this is evident from their acting always, or nearly always, in the same way, so as to obtain the best result. Hence it is plain that not fortuitously, but designedly, do they achieve their end. Now whatever lacks intelligence cannot move towards an end, unless it be directed by some being endowed with knowledge and intelligence; as the arrow is shot to its mark by the archer. Therefore some intelligent being exists by whom all natural things are directed to their end; and this being we call God.

Reply Obj. 1. As Augustine says (*Enchir.* xi): *Since God is the highest good, He would not allow any evil to exist in His works, unless His omnipotence and goodness were such as to bring good even out of evil.* This is part of the infinite goodness of God, that He should allow evil to exist, and out of it produce good.

Reply Obj. 2. Since nature works for a determinate end under the direction of a higher agent, whatever is done by nature must needs be traced back to God, as to its first cause. So also whatever is done voluntarily must also be traced back to some higher cause other than human reason or will, since these can change and fail; for all things that are changeable and capable of defect must be traced back to an immovable and self-necessary first principle, as was shown in the body of the *Article.*

QUESTION 3: OF THE SIMPLICITY OF GOD

*   *   *

Fourth Article

WHETHER ESSENCE AND EXISTENCE ARE THE SAME IN GOD?

We proceed thus to the Fourth Article:—

Objection 1. It seems that essence and existence are not the same in God. For if it be so, then the divine being has nothing added to it. Now being to which no addition is made is universal being which is predicated of all things. Therefore it follows that God is being in general which can be predicated of everything. But this is false: *For men gave the incommunicable name to stones and wood* (Wisd. xiv. 21). Therefore God's existence is not His essence.

Obj. 2. Further, we can know whether God exists as said above (Q. 2, A. 2) ; but we cannot know what He is. Therefore God's existence is not the same as His essence-that is, as His quiddity or nature.

On the contrary, Hilary says (Trin. vii): *In God existence is not an accidental quality, but subsisting truth.* Therefore what subsists in God is His existence.

I answer that, God is not only His own essence, as shown in the preceding article, but also His own existence. This may be shown in several ways. First, whatever a thing has besides its essence must be caused either by the constituent principles of that essence (like a property that necessarily accompanies the species—as the faculty of laughing is proper to a man—and is caused by the constituent principles of the species), or by some exterior agent,—as heat is caused in water by fire. Therefore, if the existence of a thing differs from its essence, this existence must be caused either by some exterior agent or by its essential principles. Now it is impossible for a thing's existence to be caused by its essential constituent principles, for nothing can be the sufficient cause of its own existence, if its existence is caused. Therefore that thing, whose existence differs from its essence, must have its existence caused by another. But this cannot be true of God; because we call God the first efficient cause. Therefore it is impossible that in God His existence should differ from His essence. Secondly, existence is that which makes every form or nature actual; for goodness and humanity are spoken of as actual, only because they are spoken of as existing. Therefore, existence must be compared to essence, if the latter is a distinct reality, as actuality to potentiality. Therefore, since in God there is no potentiality, as shown above (A. 1), it follows that in Him essence does not differ from existence. Therefore His essence is His existence. Thirdly, because, just as that which has fire, but is not itself fire, is on fire by participation; so that which has existence but is not existence, is a being by participation. But God is His own essence, as shown above (A. 3) ; if, therefore, He is not His own existence He will be not essential, but participated being. He will not therefore be the first being—which is absurd. Therefore God is His own existence, and not merely His own essence.

Reply Obj. 1. A thing that has nothing added to it can be of two kinds. Either its essence precludes any addition; thus, for example, it is of the essence of an irrational animal to be without reason. Or we may understand a thing to have nothing added to it, inasmuch as its essence does not require that anything should be added to it; thus the genus animal is without reason, because it is not of the essence of animal in general to have reason; but neither is it to lack reason. And so the divine being has nothing added to it in the first sense; whereas universal being has nothing added to it in the second sense.

Reply Obj. 2. To be can mean either of two things. It may mean the act of essence, or it may mean the composition of a proposition effected by the mind in joining a predicate to a subject. Taking to be in the first sense, we cannot understand God's existence nor His essence; but only in the second sense. We know that this proposition which we form about God when we say God is, is true; and this we know from His effects (Q. 2, A. 2).

*   *   *

QUESTION 8: THE EXISTENCE OF GOD IN THINGS

First Article

WHETHER GOD IS IN ALL THINGS?

We proceed thus to the First Article:—

Objection 1. It seems that God is not in all things. For what is above all things is not in all things. But God is above all, according to the Psalm (cxii. 4), The Lord is high above all nations, etc. Therefore God is not in all things.

Obj. 2. Further, what is in anything is thereby contained. Now God is not contained by things, but rather does He contain them. Therefore God is not in things; but things are rather in Him. Hence Augustine says (*Octog. Tri. Quæst.,* qu. 20), that *in Him things are, rather than He is in any place.*

Obj. 3. Further, the more powerful an agent is, the more extended is its action. But God is the most powerful of all agents. Therefore His action can extend to things which are far removed from Him; nor is it necessary that He should be in all things.

Obj. 4. Further, the demons are beings. But God is not in the demons; for there is no fellowship between light and darkness (2 Cor. vi. 14). Therefore God is not in all things.

On the contrary, A thing is wherever it operates. But God operates in all things, according to Isa. xxvi. 12, *Lord . . . Thou hast wrought all our works in* [Vulg., *for*] *us.* Therefore God is in all things.

I answer that, God is in all things; not, indeed, as part of their essence, nor as an accident; but as an agent is present to that upon which it works. For an agent must be joined to that wherein it acts immediately, and touch it by its power; hence it is proved in *Physic.* vii that the thing moved and the mover must be joined together. Now since God is very being by His own essence, created being must be His proper effect; as to ignite is the proper effect of fire. Now God causes this effect in things not only when they first begin to be, but as long as they are preserved in being; as light is caused in the air by the sun as long as the air remains illuminated. Therefore as long as a thing has being, God must be present to it, according to its mode of being. But being is in-nermost in each thing and most fundamentally inherent in all things since it is formal in respect of everything found in a thing, as was shown above (Q. 7, A. 1). Hence it must be that God is in all things, and innermostly.

Reply Obj. 1. God is above all things by the excellence of His nature; nevertheless, He is in all things as the cause of the being of all things; as was shown above in this article.

Reply Obj. 2. Although corporeal things are said to be in another as in that which contains them, nevertheless spiritual things contain those things in which they are; as the soul contains the body. Hence also God is in things as containing them: nevertheless by a certain similitude to corporeal things, it is said that all things are in God; inasmuch as they are contained by Him.

Reply Obj. 3. No action of an agent, however powerful it may be, acts at a distance, except through a medium. But it belongs to the great power of God that He acts immediately in all things. Hence nothing is distant from Him, as if it could be without God in itself. But things are said to be distant from God by the unlikeness to Him in nature or grace; as also He is above all by the excellence of His own nature.

Reply Obj. 4. In the demons there is their nature which is from God, and also the deformity of sin which is not from Him; therefore, it is not to be absolutely conceded that God is in the demons, except with the addition, *inasmuch as they are beings.* But in things not deformed in their nature, we must say absolutely that God is.

*   *   *

QUESTION 13: THE NAMES OF GOD

*   *   *

Second Article

Whether Any Name Can Be Applied to God Substantially?

We Proceed Thus to the Second Article:—

Objection 1. It seems that no name can be applied to God substantially. For Damascene says (*De Fid. Orth.* i. 9): *Everything said of God signifies not His sub-*

stance, but rather shows forth what He is not; or expresses some relation, or something following from His nature or operation.

Obj. 2. Further, Dionysius says (*Div. Nom.* i): *You will find a chorus of holy doctors addressed to the end of distinguishing clearly and praiseworthily the divine processions in the denomination of God.* Thus the names applied by the holy doctors in praising God are distinguished according to the divine processions themselves. But what expresses the procession of anything, does not signify its essence. Therefore the names applied to God are not said of Him substantially.

Obj. 3. Further, a thing is named by us according as we understand it. But God is not understood by us in this life in His substance. Therefore neither is any name we can use applied substantially to God.

On the contrary, Augustine says (*De Trin.* vi): *The being of God is the being strong, or the being wise, or whatever else we may say of that simplicity whereby His substance is signified.* Therefore all names of this kind signify the divine substance.

I answer that, Negative names applied to God or signifying His relation to creatures manifestly do not at all signify His substance, but rather express the distance of the creature from Him, or His relation to something else, or rather, the relation of creatures to Himself.

But as regards absolute and affirmative names of God, as *good, wise,* and the like, various and many opinions have been given. For some have said that all such names, although they are applied to God affirmatively, nevertheless have been brought into use more to express some remotion from God, rather than to express anything that exists positively in Him. Hence they assert that when we say that God lives, we mean that God is not like an inanimate thing; and the same in like manner applies to other names; and this was taught by Rabbi Moses. Others say that these names applied to God signify His relationship towards creatures: thus in the words, *God is good,* we mean, God is the cause of goodness in things; and the same rule applies to other names.

Both of these opinions, however, seem to be untrue for three reasons. First because in neither of them can a reason be assigned why some names more than others are applied to God. For He is assuredly the cause of bodies in the same way as He is the cause of good things; therefore if the words *God is good,* signified no more than, *God is the cause of good things,* it might in like manner be said that God is a body, inasmuch as He is the cause of bodies. So also to say that He is a body implies that He is not a mere potentiality, as is primary matter. Secondly, because it would follow that all names applied to God would be said of Him by way of being taken in a secondary sense, as healthy is secondarily said of medicine, forasmuch as it signifies only the cause of health in the animal which primarily is called healthy. Thirdly, because this is against the intention of those who speak of God. For in saying that God lives, they assuredly mean more than to say that He is the cause of our life, or that He differs from inanimate bodies.

Therefore we must hold a different doctrine—viz., that these names signify the divine substance, and are predicated substantially of God, although they fall short of a full representation of Him. Which is proved thus. For these names express God, so far as our intellects know Him. Now since our intellect knows God from creatures, it knows Him as far as creatures represent Him. Now it was shown above (Q. 4, A. 2) that God prepossesses in Himself all the perfections of creatures, being Himself simply and universally perfect. Hence every creature represents Him, and is like Him so far as it possesses some perfection: yet it represents Him not as something of the same species or genus, but as the excelling principle of whose form the effects fall short, although they derive some kind of likeness thereto, even as the forms of inferior bodies represent the power of the sun. This was explained above (Q. 4, A. 3), in treating of the divine perfection. Therefore the aforesaid names signify the divine substance, but in an imperfect manner, even as creatures represent it imperfectly. So when we say, *God is good,* the meaning is not, *God is the cause of goodness, or, God is not evil;* but the meaning is, *Whatever good we attribute to creatures, preexists in God,* and in a more excellent and higher way. Hence it does not follow that God is good, because He causes goodness; but rather, on the contrary, He causes goodness in things because He is good; according to what Augustine says (*De Doctr. Christ.* i. 32), *Because He is good, we are.*

Reply Obj. 1. Damascene says that these names do not signify what God is, forasmuch as by none of these names is perfectly expressed what He is; but each one signifies Him in an imperfect manner, even as creatures represent Him imperfectly.

Reply Obj. 2. In the significance of names, that from which the name is derived is different sometimes from what it is intended to signify, as for instance this name stone *(lapis)* is imposed from the fact that it hurts the foot *(lædit pedem),* but it is not imposed to signify that which hurts the foot, but rather to signify a certain kind of body; otherwise everything that hurts the foot would be a stone.* So we must say that these kinds of divine names are imposed from the divine processions; for as according to the diverse processions of their perfections, creatures are the representations of God, although in an imperfect manner; so likewise our intellect knows and names God according to each kind of procession; but nevertheless these names are not imposed to signify the procession themselves, as if when we say *God lives,* the sense were, *life proceeds from Him;* but to signify the principle itself of things, in so far as life pre-exists in Him, although it pre-exists in Him in a more eminent way than can be understood or signified.

Reply Obj. 3. We cannot know the essence of God in this life, as He really is in Himself; but we know Him accordingly as He is represented in the perfections of creatures; and thus the names imposed by us signify Him in that manner only.

*   *   *

Fifth Article

WHETHER WHAT IS SAID OF GOD AND OF CREATURES
IS UNIVOCALLY PREDICATED OF THEM?

We Proceed Thus to the Fifth Article:—

Objection 1. It seems that the things attributed to God and creatures are univocal. For every equivocal term is reduced to the univocal, as many are reduced to one: for if the name *dog* be said equivocally of the barking dog, and of the dogfish, it must be said of some univocally—viz., of all barking dogs; otherwise we proceed to infinitude. Now there are some univocal agents which agree with their effects in name and definition, as man generates man; and there are some agents which are equivocal, as the sun which causes heat, although the sun is hot only in an equivocal sense. Therefore it seems that the first agent to which all other agents are reduced, is an univocal agent: and thus what is said of God and creatures, is predicated univocally.

---

*This refers to the Latin etymology of the word *lapis,* which has no place in English.

Obj. 2. Further, there is no similitude among equivocal things. Therefore as creatures have a certain likeness to God, according to the word of Genesis (i. 26), *Let us make man to our image and likeness,* it seems that something can be said of God and creatures univocally.

Obj. 3. Further, measure is homogeneous with the thing measured. But God is the first measure of all beings. Therefore God is homogeneous with creatures; and thus a word may be applied univocally to God and to creatures.

On the contrary, Whatever is predicated of various things under the same name but not in the same sense, is predicated equivocally. But no name belongs to God in the same sense that it belongs to creatures; for instance, wisdom in creatures is a quality, but not in God. Now a different genus changes an essence. Since the genus is part of the definition; and the same applies to other things. Therefore whatever is said of God and of creatures is predicated equivocally.

Further, God is more distant from creatures than any creatures are from each other. But the distance of some creatures makes any univocal predication of them impossible, as in the case of those things which are not in the same genus. Therefore much less can anything be predicated univocally of God and creatures; and so only equivocal predication can be applied to them.

I answer that, Univocal predication is impossible between God and creatures. The reason of this is that every effect which is not an adequate result of the power of the efficient cause, receives the similitude of the agent not in its full degree, but in a measure that falls short, so that what is divided and multiplied in the effects resides in the agent simply, and in the same manner; as for example the sun by the exercise of its one power produces manifold and various forms in all inferior things. In the same way, as said in the preceding article, all perfections existing in creatures divided and multiplied, pre-exist in God unitedly. Thus, when any term expressing perfection is applied to a creature, it signifies that perfection distinct in idea from other perfections; as, for instance, by this term *wise* applied to a man, we signify some perfection distinct from a man's essence, and distinct from his power and existence, and from all similar things; whereas when we apply it to God, we do not mean to signify anything distinct from His essence, or power, or existence. Thus also this term *wise* applied to man in some degree circumscribes and comprehends the thing signified; whereas this is not the case when it is applied to God, but it leaves the thing signified as incomprehended, and as exceeding the signification of the name. Hence it is evident that this term *wise* is not applied in the same way to God and to man. The same rule applies to other terms. Hence no name is predicated univocally of God and of creatures.

Neither, on the other hand, are names applied to God and creatures in a purely equivocal sense, as some have said. Because if that were so, it follows that from creatures nothing could be known or demonstrated about God at all; for the reasoning would always be exposed to the fallacy of equivocation. Such a view is against the philosophers, who proved many things about God, and also against what the Apostle says: *The invisible things of God are clearly seen being understood by the things that are made* (Rom. 1. 20). Therefore it must be said that these names are said of God and creatures in an analogous sense, that is, according to proportion.

Now names are thus used in two ways: either according as many things are proportionate to one, thus for example *healthy* is predicated of medicine and urine in relation and in proportion to health of a body, of which the former is the sign and the latter the cause: or according as one thing is proportionate to another, thus *healthy* is said of medicine and animal, since medicine is the cause of health in the animal body. And in this way some things are said of God and creatures analogically, and not in a purely equivocal nor in a purely univocal sense. For we can name God only from creatures (A. 1). Thus, whatever is said of God and creatures, is said according to the relation of a creature to God as its principle and cause, wherein all perfections of things pre-exist excellently. Now this mode of community of idea is a mean between pure equivocation and simple univocation. For in analogies the idea is not, as it is in univocals, one and the same, yet it is not totally diverse as in equivocals; but a term which is thus used in a multiple sense signifies various proportions to some one thing; thus *healthy* applied to urine signifies the sign of animal health, and applied to medicine signifies the cause of the same health.

Reply Obj. 1. Although equivocal predications must be reduced to univocal, still in actions the non-univocal agent must precede the univocal agent. For the non-univocal agent is the universal cause of the whole species, as for instance the sun is the cause of the generation of all men; whereas the univocal agent is not the universal efficient cause of the whole species (otherwise it would be the cause of itself, since it is contained in the species), but is a particular cause of this individual which it places under the species by way of participation. Therefore the universal cause of the whole species is not an univocal agent: and the universal cause comes before the particular cause. But this universal agent, whilst it is not univocal, nevertheless is not altogether equivocal, otherwise it could not produce its own likeness, but rather it is to be called an analogical agent, as all univocal predications are reduced to one first non-univocal analogical predication, which is being.

Reply Obj. 2. The likeness of the creature to God is imperfect, for it does not represent one and the same generic thing (Q. 4, A. 3).

Reply Obj. 3. God is not the measure proportioned to things measured; hence it is not necessary that God and creatures should be in the same genus.

The arguments adduced in the contrary sense prove indeed that these names are not predicated univocally of God and creatures; yet they do not prove that they are predicated equivocally.

*   *   *

TREATISE ON CREATION

QUESTION 46: OF THE BEGINNING OF THE DURATION OF CREATURES

*   *   *

First Article

WHETHER THE UNIVERSE OF CREATURES ALWAYS EXISTED?

We Proceed Thus to the First Article:—

Objection 1. It would seem that the universe of creatures, called the world, had no beginning, but existed from eternity. For everything which begins to exist, is a possible being before it exists: otherwise it would be impossible for it to exist. If therefore the world began to exist, it was a possible being before it began to exist. But possible being is matter, which is in potentiality to existence, which results from a form, and to non-existence, which results from privation of form. If therefore the world began to exist, matter must have existed before the world. But matter cannot exist without form: while the matter of the world with its form is the world. Therefore the world existed before it began to exist: which is impossible.

Obj. 2. Further, nothing which has power to be always, sometimes is and sometimes is not; because so far as the power of a thing extends so long it exists. But every incorruptible thing has power to be always; for its power does not extend to any determinate time. Therefore no incorruptible thing sometimes is, and sometimes is not: but everything which has a beginning at some time is, and at some time is not; therefore no incorruptible thing begins to exist. But there are many incorruptible things in the world, as the celestial bodies and all intellectual substances. Therefore the world did not begin to exist.

Obj. 3. Further, what is unbegotten has no beginning. But the Philosopher (*Phys.* i, text. 82) proves that matter is unbegotten, and also (*De Cælo et Mundo* i, text. 20) that the heaven is unbegotten. Therefore the universe did not begin to exist.

Obj. 4. Further, a vacuum is where there is not a body, but there might be. But if the world began to exist, there was first no body where the body of the world now is; and yet it could be there, otherwise it would not be there now. Therefore before the world there was a vacuum; which is impossible.

Obj. 5. Further, nothing begins anew to be moved except through either the mover of the thing moved being otherwise than it was before. But what is otherwise now than it was before, is moved. Therefore before every new movement there was a previous movement. Therefore movement always was; and therefore also the thing moved always was, because movement is only in a movable thing.

Obj. 6. Further, every mover is either natural or voluntary. But neither begins to move except by some pre-existing movement. For nature always moves in the same manner: hence unless some change precede either in the nature of the mover, or in the movable thing, there cannot arise from the natural mover a movement which was not there before. And the will, without itself being changed, puts off doing what it proposes to do; but this can be only by some imagined change, at least on the part of time. Thus he who wills to make a house tomorrow, and not today, awaits something which will be tomorrow, but is not today; and at least awaits for today to pass, and for tomorrow to come; and this cannot be without change, because time is the measure of movement. Therefore it remains that before every new movement, there was a previous movement; and so the same conclusion follows as before.

Obj. 7. Further, whatever is always in its beginning, and always in its end, cannot cease and cannot begin; because what begins is not in its end, and what ceases is not in its beginning. But time always is in its beginning and end, because there is no time except now which is the end of the past and the beginning of the future. Therefore time cannot begin or end, and consequently neither can movement, the measure of which is time.

Obj. 8. Further, God is before the world either in the order of nature only, or also by duration. If in the order of nature only, therefore, since God is eternal, the world also is eternal. But if God is prior by duration; since what is prior and posterior in duration constitutes time, it follows that time existed before the world, which is impossible.

Obj. 9. Further, if there is a sufficient cause, there is an effect; for a cause to which there is no effect is an imperfect cause, requiring something else to make the effect follow. But God is the sufficient cause of the world; being the final cause, by reason of His goodness, the exemplar cause by reason of His wisdom, and the efficient cause, by reason of His power as appears from the above (Q. 44, AA. 2, 3, 4). Since therefore God is eternal, the world also is eternal.

Obj. 10. Further, eternal action postulates an eternal effect. But the action of God is His substance, which is eternal. Therefore the world is eternal.

On the contrary, It is said (Jo. xvii. 5), *Glorify Me, O Father, with Thyself with the glory which I had before the world was;* and (Prov. vii. 22), *The Lord possessed Me in the beginning of His ways, before He made anything from the beginning.*

I answer that, Nothing except God can be eternal. And this statement is far from impossible to uphold: for it has been shown above (Q. 19, A. 4) that the will of God is the cause of things. Therefore things are necessary, according as it is necessary for God to will them, since the necessity of the effect depends on the necessity of the cause (*Metaph.* v, text. 6). Now it was shown above (Q. 19, A. 3), that, absolutely speaking, it is not necessary that God should will anything except Himself. It is not therefore necessary for God to will that the world should always exist; but the world exists forasmuch as God wills it to exist, since the being of the world depends on the will of God, as on its cause. It is not therefore necessary for the world to be always; and hence it cannot be proved by demonstration.

Nor are Aristotle's reasons (*Phys.* viii) simply, but relatively, demonstrative— viz., in order to contradict the reasons of some of the ancients who asserted that the world began to exist in some quite impossible manner. This appears in three ways. Firstly, because, both in *Phys.* viii and in *De Cælo* i, text. 101, he premises some opinions, as those of Anaxagoras, Empedocles and Plato, and brings forward reasons to refute them. Secondly, because wherever he speaks of this subject, he quotes the testimony of the ancients, which is not the way of a demonstrator, but of one persuading of what probable. Thirdly, because he expressly says (*Topic.* i. 9), that there are dialectical problems, about which we have nothing to say from reason, as, *whether the world is eternal.*

Reply Obj. 1. Before the world existed it was possible for the world to be, not, indeed, according to a passive power which is matter, but according to the active power of God; and also, according as a thing is called absolutely possible, not in relation to any power, but from the sole habitude of the terms which are not repugnant to each other; in which sense possible is opposed to impossible, as appears from the Philosopher (*Metaph.* v, text. 17).

Reply Obj. 2. Whatever has power always to be, from the fact of having that power, cannot sometimes be and sometimes not be; but before it received that power, it did not exist.

Hence this reason, which is given by Aristotle (*De Cælo* i, text. 120), does not prove simply that incorruptible things never began to exist; but that they did not begin by the natural mode whereby things generated and corruptible begin.

Reply Obj. 3. Aristotle (*Phys.* i, text. 82) proves that matter is unbegotten from the fact that it has not a subject from which to derive its existence; and (*De Cælo et Mundo* i, text. 20) he proves that heaven is ungenerated, forasmuch as it has no contrary from which to be generated. Hence it appears that no conclusion follows either way, except that matter and heaven did not begin by generation, as some said, especially about heaven. But we say that matter and heaven were produced into being by creation, as appears above (Q. 44, A. 1 ad 2).

Reply Obj. 4. The notion of a vacuum is not only *in which is nothing,* but also implies a space capable of holding a body and in which there is not a body, as appears from Aristotle (*Phys.* iv., text. 60). Whereas we hold that there was no place or space before the world was.

Reply Obj. 5. The first mover was always in the same state: but the first movable thing was not always so, because it began to be whereas hitherto it was not. This, however, was not through change, but by creation, which is not change, as said above (Q. 45, A. 2 ad 2). Hence it is evident that this reason, which Aristotle gives (*Phys.* viii), is valid against those who admitted the existence of eternal movable things, but not eternal movement, as appears from the opinions of Anaxagoras and Empedocles. But we hold that from the moment that movable things began to exist movement also existed.

Reply Obj. 6. The first agent is a voluntary agent. And although He had the eternal will to produce some effect, yet He did not produce an eternal effect. Nor is it necessary for some change to be presupposed, not even on account of imaginary time. For we must take into consideration the difference between a particular agent, that presupposes something and produces something else, and the universal agent, who produces the whole. The particular agent produces the form, and presupposes the matter; and hence it is necessary that it introduce the form in due proportion into a suitable matter. Hence it is correct to say that it introduces the form into such matter, and not into another, on account of the different kinds of matter. But it is not correct to say so of God Who produces form and matter together: whereas it is correct to say of Him that He produces matter fitting to the form and to the end. Now, a particular agent presupposes time just as it presupposes matter. Hence it is correctly described as acting in time *after* and not in time *before,* according to an imaginary succession of time after time. But the universal agent who produces the thing and time also, is not correctly described as acting now, and not before, according to an imaginary succession of time succeeding time, as if time were presupposed to His action; but He must be considered as giving time to His effect as much as and when He willed, and according to what was fitting to demonstrate His power. For the world leads more evidently to the knowledge of the divine creating power, if it was not always, than if it had always been; since everything which was not always manifestly has a cause; whereas this is not so manifest of what always was.

Reply Obj. 7. As is stated (*Phys.* iv., text. 99), *before* and *after* belong to time, according as they are in movement. Hence beginning and end in time must be taken in the same way as in movement. Now, granted the eternity of movement, it is necessary that any given moment in movement be a beginning and an end of movement; which need not be if movement has a beginning. The same applies to the *now* of time. Thus it appears that the idea of the instant now, as being always the beginning and end of time, presupposes the eternity of time and movement. Hence Aristotle brings forward this reason (*Phys.* viii., text. 10) against those who asserted the eternity of time, but denied the eternity of movement.

Reply Obj. 8. God is prior to the world by priority of duration. But the word *prior* signifies priority not of time, but of eternity.—Or we may say that it signifies the eternity of imaginary time, and not of time really existing; thus, when we say that above heaven there is nothing, the word *above* signifies only an imaginary place, according as it is possible to imagine other dimensions beyond those of the heavenly body.

Reply Obj. 9. As the effect follows from the cause that acts by nature, according to the mode of its form, so likewise it follows from the voluntary agent, according to the form preconceived and determined by the agent, as appears from what was said above (Q. 19, A. 4; Q. 41, A. 2). Therefore, although God was from eternity the sufficient cause of the world, we should not say that the world was produced by Him, except as preordained by His will—that is, that it should have being after not being, in order more manifestly to declare its author.

Reply Obj. 10. Given the action, the effect follows according to the requirement of the form, which is the principle of action. But in agents acting by will, what is conceived and preordained is to be taken as the form, which is the principle of action. Therefore from the eternal action of God an eternal effect did not follow; but such an effect as God willed, an effect, to wit, which has being after not being.

Second Article

WHETHER IT IS AN ARTICLE OF FAITH THAT THE WORLD BEGAN?

We Proceed Thus to the Second Article:—

Objection 1. It would seem that it is not an article of faith but a demonstrable conclusion that the world began. For everything that is made has a beginning of its duration. But it can be proved demonstratively that God is the effective cause of the world; indeed this is asserted by the more approved philosophers. Therefore it can be demonstratively proved that the world began.

Obj. 2. Further, if it is necessary to say that the world was made by God, it must therefore have been made from nothing, or from something. But it was not made from something; otherwise the matter of the world would have preceded the world; against which are the arguments of Aristotle (*De Cælo* i), who held that heaven was ungenerated. Therefore it must be said that the world was made from nothing; and thus it has being after not being. Therefore it must have begun.

Obj. 3. Further, everything which works by intellect, works from some principle, as appears in all kinds of craftsmen. But God acts by intellect: therefore His work has a principle. The world, therefore, which is His effect did not always exist.

Obj. 4. Further, it appears manifestly that certain arts have developed, and certain countries have begun to be inhabited at some fixed time. But this would not be the case if the world had been always. Therefore it is manifest that the world did not always exist.

Obj. 5. Further, it is certain that nothing can be equal to God. But if the world had always been, it would be equal to God in duration. Therefore it is certain that the world did not always exist.

Obj. 6. Further, if the world always was, the consequence is that infinite days preceded this present day. But it is impossible to pass through an infinite medium. Therefore we should never have arrived at this present day; which is manifestly false.

Obj. 7. Further, if the world was eternal, generation also was eternal. Therefore one man was begotten of another in an infinite series. But the father is the efficient cause of the son (*Phys.* ii., text. 29). Therefore in efficient causes there could be an infinite series, which is disproved (*Metaph.* ii., text. 5).

Obj. 8. Further, if the world and generation always were, there have been an infinite number of men. But man's soul is immortal: therefore an infinite number of human souls would actually now exist, which is impossible. Therefore it can be known with certainty that the world began, and not only is it known by faith.

On the contrary, The articles of faith cannot be proved demonstratively, because faith is of things *that appear not* (Heb. xi. 1). But that God is the Creator of the world: hence that the world began, is an article of faith; for we say, *I believe in one God,* etc. And again, Gregory says *(Hom.* i. *in Ezech.),* that Moses prophesied of the past, saying, *In the beginning God created heaven and earth: in which words the newness of the world is stated. Therefore the newness of the world is known only by revelation; and therefore it cannot be proved demonstratively.*

I answer that, By faith alone do we hold, and by no demonstration can it be proved, that the world did not always exist, as was said above of the mystery of the Trinity (Q. 32, A. 1). The reason of this is that the newness of the world cannot be demonstrated on the part of the world itself. For the principle of demonstration is the essence of a thing. Now everything according to its species is abstracted from *here* and *now;* whence it is said that universals are everywhere and always. Hence it cannot be demonstrated that man, or heaven, or a stone were not always. Likewise neither can it be demonstrated on the part of the efficient cause, which acts by will. For the will of God cannot be investigated by reason, except as regards those things which God must will of necessity; and what He wills about creatures is not among these, as was said above (Q. 19, A. 3). But the divine will can be manifested by revelation, on which faith rests. Hence that the world began to exist is an object of faith, but not of demonstration or science. And it is useful to consider this, lest anyone, presuming to demonstrate what is of faith, should bring forward reasons that are not cogent, so as to give occasion to unbelievers to laugh, thinking that on such grounds we believe things that are of faith.

Reply Obj. 1. As Augustine says (*De Civ. Dei* xi. 4), the opinion of philosophers who asserted the eternity of the world was twofold. For some said that the substance of the world was not from God, which is an intolerable error; and therefore it is refuted by proofs that are cogent. Some, however, said that the world was eternal, although made by God. For they hold that the world has a beginning, not of time, but of creation, so that in a certain hardly intelligible way it was always made. *And they try to explain their meaning thus* (*De Civ. Dei* x. 31): *for as, if the foot were always in the dust from eternity, there would always be a footprint which without doubt was caused by him who trod on it, so also the world always was, because its Maker always existed.* To understand this we must consider that the efficient cause, which acts by motion, of necessity precedes its effect in time; because the effect is only in the end of the action, and every agent must be the principle of action. But if the action is instantaneous and not successive, it is not necessary for the maker to be prior to the thing made in duration, as appears in the case of illumination. Hence they say that it does not follow necessarily if God is the active cause of the world, that He should be prior to the world in duration; because creation, by which He produced the world, is not a successive change, as was said above (Q. 45, A. 2).

Reply Obj. 2. Those who would say that the world was eternal, would say that the world was made by God from nothing, not that it was made after nothing, according to what we understand by the word creation, but that it was not made from anything; and so also some of them do not reject the word creation, as appears from Avicenna (*Metaph.* ix, text. 4).

Reply Obj. 3. This is the argument of Anaxagoras (as quoted in *Phys.* viii., text. 15). But it does not lead to a necessary conclusion, except as to that intellect which deliberates in order to find out what should be done, which is like movement. Such is the human intellect, but not the divine intellect (Q. 14, AA. 7, 12).

Reply Obj. 4. Those who hold the eternity of the world hold that some region was changed an infinite number of times, from being uninhabitable to being inhabitable and vice versa, and likewise they hold that the arts, by reason of various corruptions and accidents, were subject to an infinite variety of advance and decay. Hence

Aristotle says (*Meteor.* i), that it is absurd from such particular changes to hold the opinion of the newness of the whole world.

Reply Obj. 5. Even supposing that the world always was, it would not be equal to God in eternity, as Boethius says (*De Consol.* v. 6); because the divine Being is all being simultaneously without succession; but with the world it is otherwise.

Reply Obj. 6. Passage is always understood as being from term to term. Whatever bygone day we choose, from it to the present day there is a finite number of days which can be passed through. The objection is founded on the idea that, given two extremes, there is an infinite number of mean terms.

Reply Obj. 7. In efficient causes it is impossible to proceed to infinity *per se*—thus, there cannot be an infinite number of causes that are *per se* required for a certain effect; for instance, that a stone be moved by a stick, the stick by the hand, and so on to infinity. But it is not impossible to proceed to infinity *accidentally* as regards efficient causes; for instance, if all the causes thus infinitely multiplied should have the order of only one cause, their multiplication being accidental, as an artificer acts by means of many hammers accidentally, because one after the other may be broken. It is accidental, therefore, that one particular hammer acts after the action of another; and likewise it is accidental to this particular man as generator to be generated by another man; for he generates as a man, and not as the son of another man. For all men generating hold one grade in efficient causes—viz., the grade of a particular generator. Hence it is not impossible for a man to be generated by man to infinity; but such a thing would be impossible if the generation of this man depended upon this man, and on an elementary body, and on the sun, and so on to infinity.

Reply Obj. 8. Those who hold the eternity of the world evade this reason in many ways. For some do not think it impossible for there to be an actual infinity of souls, as appears from the *Metaphysics* of Algazel, who says that such a thing is an accidental infinity. But this was disproved above (Q. 7, A. 4). Some say that the soul is corrupted with the body. And some say that of all souls only one will remain. But others, as Augustine says, asserted on this account a circuit of souls—viz., that souls separated from their bodies return again thither after a course of time; a fuller consideration of which matters will be given later (Q. 75, A. 6; Q. 76, A. 2; Q. 118, A. 6). But be it noted that this argument considers only a particular case. Hence one might say that the world was eternal, or at least some creature, as an angel, but not man. But we are considering the question in general, as to whether any creature can exist from eternity.

* * *

Treatise on Man

QUESTION 75: OF MAN WHO IS COMPOSED OF A SPIRITUAL AND A CORPOREAL SUBSTANCE: AND IN THE FIRST PLACE CONCERNING WHAT BELONGS TO THE ESSENCE OF THE SOUL

* * *

Three Orders of Society, from *L'image du monde*, Franco-Flemish, late-thirteenth century. This detail from an illustrated manuscript page shows the hierarchy of medieval society with monk, knight, and peasant. (*British Museum*)

Second Article

WHETHER THE HUMAN SOUL IS SOMETHING SUBSISTENT?

We Proceed Thus to the Second Article:—

Objection 1. It would seem that the human soul is not something subsistent. For that which subsists is said to be *this particular thing*. Now *this particular thing* is said not of the soul, but of that which is composed of soul and body. Therefore the soul is not something subsistent.

Obj. 2. Further, everything subsistent operates. But the soul does not operate; for, as the Philosopher says (*De Anima* i. 4), *to say that the soul feels or understands is like saying that the soul weaves or builds.* Therefore the soul is not subsistent.

Obj. 3. Further, if the soul were subsistent, it would have some operation apart from the body. But it has no operation apart from the body, not even that of understanding: for the act of understanding does not take place without a phantasm, which cannot exist apart from the body. Therefore the human soul is not something subsistent.

On the contrary, Augustine says (*de Trin.* x. 7): *Whoever understands that the nature of the soul is that of a substance and not that of a body, will see that those who maintain the corporeal nature of the soul, are led astray through associating with the soul those things without which they are unable to think of any nature—i.e., imaginary pictures of the corporal things.* Therefore the nature of the human intellect is not only incorporeal, but it is also a substance, that is, something subsistent.

I answer that, It must necessarily be allowed that the principle of intellectual operation which we call the soul, is a principle both incorporeal and subsistent. For it is clear that by means of the intellect man can have knowledge of all corporeal things. Now whatever knows certain things cannot have any of them in its own nature; because that which is in it naturally would impede the knowledge of anything else. Thus we observe that a sick man's tongue being vitiated by a feverish and bitter humor, is insensible to anything sweet and everything seems bitter to it. Therefore if the intellectual principle contained the nature of a body it would be unable to know all bodies. Now every body has its own determinate nature. Therefore it is impossible for the intellectual principle to be a body. It is likewise impossible for it to understand by means of a bodily organ; since the determinate nature of that organ would impede knowledge of all bodies; as when a certain determinate color is not only in the pupil of the eye, but also in a glass vase, the liquid in the vase seems to be of that same color.

Therefore the intellectual principle which we call the mind or the intellect has the operation *per se* apart from the body. Now only that which subsists can have an operation *per se.* For nothing can operate but what is actual: wherefore a thing operates according as it is; for which reason we do not say that heat imparts heat, but that what is hot gives heat. We must conclude, therefore, that the human soul, which is called the intellect or the mind, is something incorporeal and subsistent.

Reply Obj. 1. *This particular thing* can be taken in two senses. Firstly, for anything subsistent; secondly, for that which subsists, and is complete in a specific nature. The former sense excludes the inherence of an accident or of a material form; the latter excludes also the imperfection of the part, so that a hand can be called *this particular thing* in the first sense, but not in the second. Therefore as the human soul is a part of human nature, it can indeed be called *this particular thing,* in the first sense, as being something subsistent; but not in the second, for in this sense, what is composed of body and soul is said to be *this particular thing.*

Reply Obj. 2. Aristotle wrote those words as expressing not his own opinion, but the opinion of those who said that to understand is to be moved, as is clear from the context. Or we may reply that to operate *per se* belongs to what exists *per se.* But for a thing to exist *per se,* it suffices sometimes that it be not inherent, as an accident or a material form; even though it be part of something. Nevertheless, that is rightly said to subsist *per se,* which is neither inherent in the above sense nor part of anything else. In this sense, the eye or the hand cannot be said to subsist *per se;* nor can it for that reason be said to operate *per se.* Hence the operation of the parts is through each part attributed to the whole. For we say that the man sees with the eye, and feels with the hand and, and not in the same sense as when we say that what is hot gives heat by its heat; for heat, strictly speaking, does not give heat. We may therefore say that the soul understands, as the eye sees; but it is more correct to say that man understands through the soul.

Reply Obj. 3. The body is necessary for intellect, not as its origin of action, but on the part of the object; for the phantasm is to the intellect what color is to the sight. Neither does such a dependence on the body prove the intellect to be non-subsistent; otherwise it would follow that an animal is not subsistent, since it requires external objects of the senses in order to perform its act of perception.

*   *   *

QUESTION 76: OF THE UNION OF BODY AND SOUL

*   *   *

First Article

WHETHER THE INTELLECTUAL PRINCIPLE IS UNITED TO THE BODY AS ITS FORM?

We Proceed Thus to the First Article:—

Objection 1. It seems that the intellectual principle is not united to the body as its form. For the Philosopher says (*De Anima* iii. 4) that "the intellect is separate," and that it is not the act of any body. Therefore it is not united to the body as its form.

Obj. 2. Further, every form is determined according to the nature of the matter of which it is the form; otherwise no proportion would be required between matter and form. Therefore if the intellect were united to the body as its form since every body has a determinate nature it would follow that the intellect has a determinate nature; and thus, it would not be capable of knowing all things, as is clear from what has been said (Q. 75, A. 2), which is contrary to the notion of intellect. Therefore the intellect is not united to the body as its form.

Obj. 3. Further, whatever receptive power is an act of a body receives a form materially and individually; for what is received must be received according to the mode of the receiver. But the form of the thing understood is not received into the intellect materially and individually, but rather immaterially and universally; otherwise the intellect would not be capable of the knowledge of immaterial and universal objects, but only of individuals, like the senses. Therefore the intellect is not united to the body as its form.

Obj. 4. Further, power and action have the same subject; for the same subject is what can, and does, act. But the intellectual action is not the action of a body, as appears from above (Q. 75, A. 2). Therefore neither is the intellectual power a power of the body. But virtue or power cannot be more abstract or more simple than the essence from which the virtue or power is derived. Therefore neither is the substance of the intellect the form of a body.

Obj. 5. Further, whatever has *per se* being is not united to the body as its form, because a form is that by which a thing is, so that the very being of a form does not belong to the form by itself. But the intellectual principle has *per se* being and is subsistent, as was said above (Q. 75, A. 2). Therefore it is not united to the body as its form.

Obj. 6. Further, whatever exists in a thing by reason of its nature exists in it always. But to be united to matter belongs to the form by reason of its nature. For form is the act of matter not by any accidental quality, but by its own essence; otherwise matter and form would not make a thing substantially one, but only accidentally one. Therefore a form cannot be without its own proper matter. But the intellectual principle, since it is incorruptible, as was shown above (Q. 75, A. 6), remains separate from the body after the dissolution of the body. Therefore the intellectual principle is not united to the body as its form.

On the contrary, According to the Philosopher (*Metaph.* vii. 2), difference is derived from the form. But the difference which constitutes man is *rational* which is applied to man on account of his intellectual principle. Therefore the intellectual principle is the form of man.

I answer that, We must assert that the intellect which is the principle of intellectual operation is the form of the human body. For that whereby primarily anything acts is a form of the thing to which the act is to be attributed; for instance, that whereby a body is primarily healed is health and that whereby the soul knows primarily is knowledge; hence health is a form of the body, and knowledge is a form of the soul. The reason is because nothing acts except so far as it is in act; hence a thing acts by that whereby it is in act. Now it is clear that the first thing by which the body lives is the soul. And as life appears through various operations in different degrees of living things, that whereby we primarily perform each of all these vital actions is the soul. For the soul is the primary principle of our nourishment, sensation, and local movement; and likewise of our understanding. Therefore this principle by which we primarily understand, whether it be called the intellect or the intellectual soul, is the form of the body. This is the demonstration used by Aristotle (*De Anima* ii. 2).

But if anyone say that the intellectual soul is not the form of the body he must first explain how it is that this action of understanding is the action of this particular man; for each one is conscious that it is himself who understands. Now an action may be attributed to anyone in three ways, as is clear from the Philosopher. "For a thing is said to move or act either by virtue of its whole self, for instance, as a physician heals; or by virtue of a part, as a man sees by his eye; or through an accidental quality, as when we say that something that is white build, because it is accidental to the builder to be white" (*Phys.* v. 1) So when we say that Socrates or Plato understands, it is clear that this is not attributed to him accidentally, since it is ascribed to him as man, which is predicated of him essentially. We must therefore say either that Socrates understands by virtue of his whole self, as Plato maintained, holding that man is an intellectual soul, or that the intellect is a part of Socrates. The first cannot stand, as was shown above (Q. 75, A. 4), for this reason, that it is one and the same man who is conscious both that he understands, and that he senses. But one cannot sense without a body; therefore the body must be some part of man. It remains therefore that the intellect by which Socrates understands is a part of Socrates, so that in some way it is united to the body of Socrates.

The Commentator [Averroës] held that this union is through the intelligible species, as having a double subject: in the possible intellect, and in the phantasms which are in the corporeal organs (*De Anima* iii, Comm. 5). Thus through the intelligible species the possible intellect is linked to the body of this or that particular man. But this link or union does not sufficiently explain the fact that the act of the intellect is the act of Socrates. This can be clearly seen from comparison with the sensitive power, from which Aristotle proceeds to consider things relating to the intellect. For the relation of phantasms to the intellect is like the relation of colours to the sense of sight, as he says in the book on the *Soul* (iii. 7). Therefore, as the species of colours are in the sight, so are the species of phantasms in the possible-intellect. Now it is clear that because the colours, the likenesses of which are in the sight, are on a wall, the action of seeing is not attributed to the wall, for we do not say that the wall sees, but rather that it is seen. Therefore, from the fact that the species of phantasms are in the possible intellect it does not follow that Socrates, in whom are the phantasms, understands, but that he or his phantasms are understood.

Some, however, tried to maintain that the intellect is united to the body as its mover, and hence that the intellect and body form one thing so that the act of the intellect could be attributed to the whole. This is groundless however, for many reasons. First, because the intellect does not move the body except through desire, the movement of which presupposes the operation of the intellect. The reason therefore why Socrates understands is not because he is moved by his intellect, but rather, contrariwise, he is moved by his intellect because he understands. Secondly, because, since Socrates is an individual in a nature of one essence composed of matter and form, if the intellect be not the form, it follows that it must be outside the essence, and then the intellect is to the whole Socrates as a mover to the thing moved. The act of intellect however remains in the agent, and does not pass into something else, as does the action of heating. Therefore the act of understanding cannot be attributed to Socrates for the reason that he is moved by his intellect. Thirdly, because the action of a mover is never attributed to the thing moved, except as to an instrument; as the action of a carpenter to a saw. Therefore if understanding is attributed to Socrates, as the action of what moves him, it follows that it is attributed to him as to an instrument. This is contrary to the teaching of the Philosopher, who holds that understanding is not possible through a corporeal instrument (*De Anima* iii. 4). Fourthly, because, although the action of a part be attributed to the whole, as the action of the eye is attributed to a man, yet it is never attributed to another part, except perhaps accidentally; for we do not say that the hand sees because the eye sees. Therefore if the intellect and Socrates are united in the above manner, the action of the intellect cannot be attributed to Socrates. If, however, Socrates be a whole composed of a union of the intellect with whatever else belongs to Socrates, while nevertheless the intellect is united to those other things only as a mover, it follows that Socrates is not one absolutely, and consequently neither a being absolutely, for a thing is a being according as it is one.

There remains, therefore, no other explanation than that given by Aristotle (*De Anima* ii. 2)—namely, that this particular man understands because the intellectual principle is his form. Thus from the very operation of the intellect it is made clear that the intellectual principle is united to the body as its form.

The same can be clearly shown from the nature of the human species. For the nature of each thing is shown by its operation. Now the proper operation of man as man is to understand, because he thereby surpasses all other animals. From this, too, Aristotle concludes (*Ethic.* x. 7) that the ultimate happiness of man must consist in this operation as properly belonging to him. Man must therefore derive his species from that which is the principle of this operation. But the species of anything is derived from its form. It follows therefore that the intellectual principle is the proper form of man.

But we must observe that the nobler a form is, the more it rises above corporeal matter, the less it is merged in matter, and the more it excels matter by its power and its operation; hence we find that the form of a mixed body has another operation not caused by its elemental qualities. And the higher we advance in the nobility of forms, the more we find that the power of the form excels the elementary matter; as the vegetative soul excels the form of the metal, and the sensitive soul excels the vegetative soul. Now the human soul is the highest and noblest of forms. Therefore it excels corporeal matter in its power by the fact that it has an operation and a power in which corporeal matter has no share whatever. This power is called the intellect.

It is well to remark that if anyone holds that the soul is composed of matter and form, it would follow that in no way could the soul be the form of the body. For since the form is an act, and matter is only a being in potency, that which is composed of matter and form cannot be the form of another by virtue of itself as a whole. But if it is a form by virtue of some part of itself, then that part which is the form we call the soul, and that of which it is the form we call the first thing animated, as was said above (Q. 75, A. 5).

Reply Obj. 1. As the Philosopher Says (*Phys.* ii. 2), the ultimate natural form to which the consideration of the natural philosopher is directed, namely, the human soul, is indeed separate; yet it exists in matter. He proves this from the fact that "man and the sun generate man from matter." It is separate indeed according to its intellectual power, because the intellectual power does not belong to a corporeal organ, as the power of seeing is the act of the eye; for understanding is an act which cannot be performed by a corporeal organ, like the act of seeing. But it exists in matter so far as the soul itself, to which this power belongs, is the form of the body, and the term of human generation. And so the Philosopher says (*De Anima* ii. 2) that "the intellect is separate" because it is not the power of a corporeal organ.

From this it is clear how to answer the *Second and Third objections.* For, in order that man may be able to understand all things by means of his intellect, and that his intellect may understand all things immaterial and universal, it is sufficient that the intellectual power be not the act of the body.

Reply Obj. 4. The human soul, by reason of its perfection, is not a form merged in matter, or entirely embraced by matter. Therefore there is nothing to prevent one of its powers not being the act of the body, although the soul is essentially the form of the body.

Reply Obj. 5. The soul communicates that being in which it subsists to the corporeal matter, out of which, combined with the intellectual soul, there results unity of being so that the being of the whole composite is also the being of the soul. This is not the case with other nonsubsistent forms. For this reason the human soul retains its own being after the dissolution of the body, though this is not so with other forms.

Reply Obj. 6. To be united to the body pertains to the soul by reason of itself, as it pertains to a light body by reason of itself to be raised up. And as a light body remains light when removed from its proper place, retaining meanwhile an aptitude and an inclination for its proper place, so the human soul retains its proper being when separated from the body, having an aptitude and a natural inclination to be united to the body.

Second Article

WHETHER THE INTELLECTUAL PRINCIPLE IS MULTIPLIED ACCORDING
TO THE NUMBER OF BODIES?

We Proceed Thus to the Second Article:—

Objection 1. It would seem that the intellectual principle is not multiplied according to the number of bodies, but that there is one intellect in all men. For an immaterial substance is not multiplied in number within one species. But the human soul is an immaterial substance; since it is not composed of matter and form, as was shown above (Q. 75, A. 5). Therefore there are not many human souls in one species. But all men are of one species. Therefore there is but one intellect in all men.

Obj. 2. Further, when the cause is removed, the effect is also removed. Therefore, if human souls were multiplied according to the number of bodies, it follows that the bodies being removed, the number of souls would not remain; but from all the souls there would be but a single remainder. This is heretical; for it would do away with the distinction of rewards and punishments.

Obj. 3. Further, if my intellect is distinct from your intellect, my intellect is an individual, and so is yours; for individuals are things which differ in number but agree in one species. Now whatever is received into anything must be received according to the condition of the receiver. Therefore the species of things would be received individually into my intellect, and also into yours: which is contrary to the nature of the intellect which knows universals.

Obj. 4. Further, the thing understood is in the intellect which understands. If, therefore, my intellect is distinct from yours, what is understood by me must be distinct from what is understood by you; and consequently it will be reckoned as something individual, and be only potentially something understood; so that the common intention will have to be abstracted from both; since from things diverse something intelligible common to them may be abstracted. But this is contrary to the nature of the intellect; for then the intellect would seem not to be distinct from the imagination. It seems, therefore, to follow that there is one intellect in all men.

Obj. 5. Further, when the disciple receives knowledge from the master, it cannot be said that the master's knowledge begets knowledge in the disciple, because then also knowledge would be an active form, such as heat is, which is clearly false. It seems, therefore, that the same individual knowledge which is in the master is communicated to the disciple; which cannot be, unless there is one intellect in both. Seemingly, therefore, the intellect of the disciple and master is but one; and, consequently, the same applies to all men.

Obj. 6. Further, Augustine (*De Quant. Animae* xxxii) says: *If I were to say that there are many human souls, I should laugh at myself.* But the soul seems to be one chiefly on account of the intellect. Therefore there is one intellect of all men.

On the contrary, The Philosopher says (*Phys.* ii. 3) that the relation of universal causes to universals is like the relation of particular causes to individuals. But it is impossible that a soul, one in species, should belong to animals of different species. Therefore it is impossible that one individual intellectual soul should belong to several individuals.

I answer that, It is absolutely impossible for one intellect to belong to all men. This is clear if, as Plato maintained, man is the intellect itself. For it would follow that Socrates and Plato are one man; and that they are not distinct from each other, except by something outside the essence of each. The distinction between Socrates and Plato would be no other than that of one man with a tunic and another with a cloak; which is quite absurd.

It is likewise clear that this is impossible if, according to the opinion of Aristotle (*De Anima* ii. 2), it is supposed that the intellect is a part or a power of the soul which is the form of man. For it is impossible for many distinct individuals to have one form, as it is impossible for them to have one existence, for the form is the principle of existence.

Again, this is clearly impossible, whatever one may hold as to the manner of the union of the intellect to this or that man. For it is manifest that, supposing there is one principal agent, and two instruments, we can say that there is one agent absolutely, but several actions; as when one man touches several things with his two hands, there will be one who touches, but two contacts. If, on the contrary, we suppose one instrument and several principal agents, we might say that there are several agents, but one act; for example, if there be many drawing a ship by means of a rope; there will be many drawing, but one pull. If, however, there is one principal agent, and one instrument, we say that there is one agent and one action, as when the smith strikes with one hammer, there is one striker and one stroke. Now it is clear that no matter how the intellect is united or coupled to this or that man, the intellect has the precedence of all the other things which appertain to man; for the sensitive powers obey the intellect, and are at its service. Therefore, if we suppose two men to have several intellects and one sense,—for instance, if two men had one eye,—there would be several seers, but one sight. But if there is one intellect, no matter how diverse may be all those things of which the intellect makes use as instruments, in no way is it possible to say that Socrates and Plato are otherwise than one understanding man. And if to this we add that to understand, which is the act of the intellect, is not affected by any organ other than the intellect itself; it will further follow that there is but one agent and one action: that is to say that all men are but one "understander," and have but one act of understanding, in regard, that is, of one intelligible object.

However, it would be possible to distinguish my intellectual action from yours by the distinction of the phantasms—that is to say, were there one phantasm of a stone in me, and another in you—if the phantasm itself, as it is one thing in me and another in you, were a form of the possible intellect; since the same agent according to divers forms produces divers actions; as, according to divers forms of things with regard to the same eye, there are divers visions. But the phantasm itself is not a form of the possible intellect; it is the intelligible species abstracted from the phantasm that is a form. Now in one intellect, from different phantasms of the same species, only one intelligible species is abstracted; as appears in one man, in whom there may be different phantasms of a stone; yet from all of them only one intelligible species of a stone is abstracted; by which the intellect of that one man, by one operation, understands the nature of a stone, notwithstanding the diversity of phantasms. Therefore, if there were one intellect for all men, the diversity of phantasms which are in this one and that one would not cause a diversity of intellectual operation in this man and that man. It follows, therefore, that it is altogether impossible and unreasonable to maintain that there exists one intellect for all men.

Reply Obj. 1. Although the intellectual soul, like an angel, has no matter from which it is produced, yet it is the form of a certain matter; in which it is unlike an angel. Therefore, according to the division of matter, there are many souls of one species; while it is quite impossible for many angels to be of one species.

Reply Obj. 2. Everything has unity in the same way that it has being; consequently we must judge of the multiplicity of a thing as we judge of its being. Now it is clear that the intellectual soul, by virtue of its very being, is united to the body as its form; yet, after the dissolution of the body, the intellectual soul retains its own being. In like manner the multiplicity of souls is in proportion to the multiplicity of bodies; yet, after the dissolution of the bodies, the souls retain their multiplied being.

Reply Obj. 3. Individuality of the intelligent being, or of the species whereby it understands, does not exclude the understanding of universals; otherwise, since separate intellects are subsistent substances, and consequently individual, they could not understand universals. But the materiality of the knower, and of the species whereby it knows, impedes the knowledge of the universal. For as every action is according to the mode of the form by which the agent acts, as heating is according to the mode of the heat; so knowledge is according to the mode of the species by which the knower knows. Now it is clear that common nature becomes distinct and multiplied by reason of the individuating principles which come from the matter. Therefore if the form, which is the means of knowledge, is material—that is, not abstracted from material conditions—its likeness to the nature of a species or genus will be according to the distinction and multiplication of that nature by means of individuating principles; so that knowledge of the nature of a thing in general will be impossible. But if the species be abstracted from the conditions of individual matter, there will be a likeness of the nature without those things which make it distinct and multiplied; thus there will be knowledge of the universal. Nor does it matter, as to this particular point, whether there be one intellect or many; because, even if there were but one, it would necessarily be an individual intellect, and the species whereby it understands, an individual species.

Reply Obj. 4. Whether the intellect be one or many, what is understood is one; for what is understood is in the intellect, not according to its own nature, but according to its likeness; *for the stone is not in the soul, but its likeness is,* as is said, *De Anima* iii. 8. Yet it is the stone which is understood, not the likeness of the stone; except by a reflection of the intellect on itself: otherwise, the objects of sciences would not be things, but only intelligible species. Now it happens that different things, according to different forms, are likened to the same thing. And since knowledge is begotten according to the assimilation of the knower to the thing known, it follows that the same thing may happen to be known by several knowers; as is apparent in regard to the senses; for several see the same color, according to different likenesses. In the same way several intellects understand one object understood. But there is this difference, according to the opinion of Aristotle, between the sense and the intelligence—that a thing is perceived by the sense according to the disposition which it has outside the soul—that is, in its individuality; whereas the nature of the thing understood is indeed outside the soul but the mode according to which it exists outside the soul is not the mode according to which it is understood. For the common nature is understood as apart from the individuating principles; whereas such is not its mode of existence outside the soul. But, according to the opinion of Plato, the thing understood exists outside the soul in the same conditions as those under which it is understood; for he supposed that the natures of things exist separate from matter.

Reply Obj. 5. One knowledge exists in the disciple and another in the master. How it is caused will be shown later on (Q. 117, A. 1).

Reply Obj. 6. Augustine denies a plurality of souls, that would involve a plurality of species.

*   *   *

Fourth Article

WHETHER IN MAN THERE IS ANOTHER FORM BESIDES THE INTELLECTUAL SOUL?

We Proceed Thus to the Fourth Article:—

Objection 1. It would seem that in man there is another form besides the intellectual soul. For the Philosopher says (*De Anima* ii. 1), that *the soul is the act of a physical body which has life potentially.* Therefore the soul is to the body as a form of matter. But the body has a substantial form by which it is a body. Therefore some other substantial form in the body precedes the soul.

Obj. 2. Further, man moves himself as every animal does. Now everything that moves itself is divided into two parts, of which one moves, and the other is moved, as the Philosopher proves (*Phys.* viii. 5). But the part which moves is the soul. Therefore the other part must be such that it can be moved. But primary matter cannot be moved (*ibid.* v. 1), since it is a being only potentially; indeed everything that is moved is a body. Therefore in man and in every animal there must be another substantial form, by which the body is constituted.

Obj. 3. Further, the order of forms depends on their relation to primary matter; for *before* and *after* apply by comparison to some beginning. Therefore if there were not in man some other substantial form besides the rational soul, and if this were to inhere immediately to primary matter; it would follow that it ranks among the most imperfect forms which inhere to matter immediately.

Obj. 4. Further, the human body is a mixed body. Now mingling does not result from matter alone; for then we should have mere corruption. Therefore the forms of the elements must remain in a mixed body; and these are substantial forms. Therefore in the human body there are other substantial forms besides the intellectual soul.

On the contrary, Of one thing there is but one substantial being. But the substantial form gives substantial being. Therefore of one thing there is but one substantial form. But the soul is the substantial form of man. Therefore it is impossible for there to be in man another substantial form besides the intellectual soul.

I answer that, If we suppose that the intellectual is not united to the body as its form, but only as its motor, as the Platonists maintain, it would necessarily follow that in man there is another substantial form, by which the body is established in its being as movable by the soul. If, however, the intellectual soul be united to the body as its substantial form, as we have said above (A. 1), it is impossible for another substantial form besides the intellectual soul to be found in man.

In order to make this evident, we must consider that the substantial form differs from the accidental form in this, that the accidental form does not make a thing to be *simply,* but to be *such,* as heat does not make a thing to be simply, but only to be hot. Therefore by the coming of the accidental form a thing is not said to be made or generated simply, but to be made such, or to be in some particular condition—and in like manner, when an accidental form is removed, a thing is said to be corrupted, not simply, but relatively. Now the substantial form gives being simply; therefore by its coming a thing is said to be generated simply; and by its removal to be corrupted simply. For this reason, the old natural philosophers, who held that primary matter was some actual being—for instance, fire or air, or something of that sort—maintained that nothing is generated simply, or corrupted simply; and stated that *every becoming is nothing but an alteration,* as we read, *Phys.* i. 4. Therefore, if besides the intellectual soul there pre-existed in matter another substantial form by which the subject of the soul were made an actual being, it would follow that the soul does not give being simply; and consequently that it is not the substantial form: and so at the advent of the soul there would not be simple generation; nor at its removal simple corruption, all of which is clearly false.

Whence we must conclude, that there is no other substantial form in man besides the intellectual soul; and that the soul, as it virtually contains the sensitive and nutritive souls, so does it virtually contain all inferior forms, and itself alone does whatever the imperfect forms do in other things. The same is to be said of the sensitive soul in brute animals, and of the nutritive soul in plants, and universally of all more perfect forms with regard to the imperfect.

Reply Obj. 1. Aristotle does not say that the soul is the act of a body only, but *the act of a physical organic body which has life potentially;* and that this potentiality *does not reject the soul.* Whence it is clear that when the soul is called the act, the soul itself is included; as when we say that heat is the act of what is hot, and light of what is lucid; not as though lucid and light were two separate things, but because a thing is made lucid by the light. In like manner, the soul is said to be the *act of a body,* etc., because by the soul it is a body, and is organic, and has life potentially. Yet the first act is said to be in potentiality to the second act, which is operation; for such a potentiality *does not reject*—that is, does not exclude—the soul.

Reply Obj. 2. The soul does not move the body by its essence, as the form of the body, but by the motive power, the act of which presupposes the body to be already actualized by the soul: so that the soul by its motive power is the part which moves; and the animate body is the part moved.

Reply Obj. 3. We observe in matter various degrees of perfection, as existence, living, sensing, and understanding. Now what is added is always more perfect. Therefore that form which gives matter only the first degree of perfection is the most imperfect; while that form which gives the first, second, and third degree, and so on, is the most perfect: and yet it inheres to matter immediately.

Reply Obj. 4. Avicenna held that the substantial forms of the elements remain entire in the mixed body; and that the mixture is made by the contrary qualities of the elements being reduced to an average. But this is impossible, because the various forms of the elements must necessarily be in various parts of matter—for the distinction of which we must suppose dimensions, without which matter cannot be divisible. Now matter subject to dimension is not to be found except in a body. But various bodies cannot be in the same place. Whence it follows that elements in the mixed body would be distinct as to situation. And then there would not be a real mixture which is in respect of the whole; but only a mixture apparent to sense, by the juxtaposition of particles.

Averroës maintained that the forms of elements, by reason of their imperfection, are a medium between accidental and substantial forms, and so can be *more* or *less;* and therefore in the mixture they are modified and reduced to an average, so that one form emerges from them. But this is even still more impossible. For the substantial being of each thing consists in something indivisible, and every addition and subtraction varies the species, as in numbers, as stated in *Metaph.* viii. (Did. vii. 3); and consequently it is impossible for any substantial form to receive *more* or *less.* Nor is it less impossible for anything to be a medium between substance and accident.

Therefore we must say, in accordance with the Philosopher (*De Gener.* i. 10), that the forms of the elements remain in the mixed body, not actually but virtually. For the proper qualities of the elements remain, though modified, and in them is the power of the elementary forms. This quality of the mixture is the proper disposition for the substantial form of the mixed body; for instance, the form of a stone, or of any sort of soul.

* * *

QUESTION 84: HOW THE SOUL WHILE UNITED TO THE BODY UNDERSTANDS CORPOREAL THINGS BENEATH IT

* * *

Fifth Article

WHETHER THE INTELLECTUAL SOUL KNOWS MATERIAL THINGS IN THE ETERNAL TYPES?

We Proceed Thus to the Fifth Article:—

Objection 1. It would seem that the intellectual soul does not know material things in the eternal types. For that in which anything is known must itself be known more and previously. But the intellectual soul of man, in the present state of life, does not know the eternal types: for it does not know God in Whom the eternal types exist, but is *united to God as to the unknown,* as Dionysius says (*Myst. Theolog.* i). Therefore the soul does not know all in the eternal types.

Obj. 2. Further, it is written (Rom. i. 20) that *the invisible things of God are clearly seen . . . by the things that are made.* But among the invisible things of God are the eternal types. Therefore the eternal types are known through creatures and not the converse.

Obj. 3. Further, the eternal types are nothing else but ideas, for Augustine says (QQ. 83, qu. 46) that *ideas are permanent types existing in the Divine mind.* If therefore we say that the intellectual soul knows all things in the eternal types, we come back to the opinion of Plato who said that all knowledge is derived from them.

On the contrary, Augustine says (*Confess.* xii. 25): *If we both see that what you say is true, and if we both see that what I say is true, where do we see this, I pray? Neither do I see it in you, nor do you see it in me: but we both see it in the unchangeable truth which is above our minds.* Now the unchangeable truth is contained in the eternal types. Therefore the intellectual soul knows all true things in the eternal types.

I answer that, As Augustine says (*De Doctr. Christ.* ii. 11): *If those who are called philosophers said by chance anything that was true and consistent with our faith, we must claim it from them as from unjust possessors. For some of the doctrines of the heathens are spurious imitations or superstitious inventions, which we must be careful to avoid when we renounce the society of the heathens.* Consequently whenever Augustine, who was imbued with the doctrines of the Platonists, found in their teaching anything consistent with faith, he adopted it: and those things which he found contrary to faith he amended. Now Plato held, as we have said above (A. 4), that the forms of things subsist of themselves apart from matter; and these he called ideas, by participation of which he said that our intellect knows all things: so that just as corporeal matter by participating, the idea of a stone becomes a stone, so our intellect, by participating the same idea, has knowledge of a stone. But since it seems contrary to faith that forms of things should subsist of themselves, outside the things themselves and apart from matter, as the Platonists held, asserting that *per se* life or *per se* wisdom are creative substances, as Dionysius relates (*Div. Nom.* xi); therefore Augustine (QQ. 83, *loc. cit.*), for the ideas defended by Plato, substituted the types of all creatures existing in the Divine mind, according to which types all things are made in themselves, and are known to the human soul. When, therefore, the question is asked: Does the human soul know all things in the eternal types? we must reply that one thing is said to be known in another in two ways. First, as in an object itself known; as one may see in a mirror the images of things reflected therein. In this way the soul, in the present state of life, cannot see all things in the eternal types; but the blessed who see God, and all things in Him, thus know all things in the eternal types. Secondly, one thing is said to be known in another as in a principle of knowledge: thus we might say that we see in the sun what we see by the sun. And thus we must needs say that the human soul knows all things in the eternal types, since by participation of these types we know all things. For the intellectual light itself which is in us, is nothing else than a participated likeness of the uncreated light in which are contained the eternal types. Whence it is written (Ps. iv. 6, 7), *Many say: Who showeth us good things?* which question the Psalmist answers, *The light of Thy countenance, O Lord, is signed upon us,* as though he were to say: By the seal of the Divine light in us, all things are made known to us.

But since besides the intellectual light which is in us, intelligible species, which are derived from things, are required in order for us to have knowledge of material things; therefore this same knowledge is not due merely to a participation of the eternal types, as the Platonists held, maintaining that the mere participation of ideas sufficed for knowledge. Wherefore Augustine says (*De Trin.* iv. 16): *Although the philosophers prove by convincing arguments that all things occur in time according to the eternal types, were they able to see in the eternal types, or to find out from them how many kinds of animals there are and the origin of each? Did they not seek for this information from the story of times and places?*

But that Augustine did not understand all things to be known in their *eternal types* or in *the unchangeable truth,* as though the eternal types themselves were seen, is clear from what he says (QQ. 83, *loc. cit.*)—viz., that *not each and every rational soul can be said to be worthy of that vision,* namely, of the eternal types, but only those that are holy and pure, such as the souls of the blessed.

From what has been said the objections are easily solved.

Sixth Article

WHETHER INTELLECTUAL KNOWLEDGE IS DERIVED FROM SENSIBLE THINGS?

We Proceed Thus to the Sixth Article:—

Objection 1. It would seem that intellectual knowledge is not derived from sensible things. For Augustine says (QQ. 83, qu. 9) that *we cannot expect to learn the fullness of truth from the senses of the body.* This he proves in two ways. First, because *whatever the bodily senses reach, is continually being changed; and what is never the same cannot be perceived.* Secondly, because, *whatever we perceive by the body, even when not present to the senses, may be present to the imagination, as when we are asleep or angry: yet we cannot discern by the senses, whether what we perceive be the sensible object or the deceptive image thereof. Now nothing can be perceived which cannot be distinguished from its counterfeit.* And so he concludes that we cannot expect to learn the truth from the senses. But intellectual knowledge apprehends the truth. Therefore intellectual knowledge cannot be conveyed by the senses.

Obj. 2. Further, Augustine says (*Gen. ad lit.* xii. 16): *We must not think that the body can make any impression on the spirit, as though the spirit were to supply the place of matter in regard to the body's action; for that which acts is in every way more excellent than that which it acts on.* Whence he concludes that *the body does not cause its image in the spirit, but the spirit causes it in itself.* Therefore intellectual knowledge is not derived from sensible things.

Obj. 3. Further, an effect does not surpass the power of its cause. But intellectual knowledge extends beyond sensible things: for we understand some things which cannot be perceived by the senses. Therefore intellectual knowledge is not derived from sensible things.

On the contrary, The Philosopher says (*Metaph.* i. 1; *Poster.* ii. 15) that the principle of knowledge is in the senses.

I answer that, On this point the philosophers held three opinions. For Democritus held that *all knowledge is caused by images issuing from the bodies we think of and entering into our souls,* as Augustine says in his letter to Dioscorus (cxviii. 4). And Aristotle says *(De Somn. et Vigil.)* that Democritus held that knowledge is caused by a *discharge of images.* And the reason for this opinion was that both Democritus and the other early philosophers did not distinguish between intellect and sense, as Aristotle relates (*De Anima* iii. 3). Consequently, since the sense is affected by the sensible, they thought that all our knowledge is affected by this mere impression brought about by sensible things. Which impression Democritus held to be caused by a discharge of images.

Plato, on the other hand, held that the intellect is distinct from the senses: and that it is an immaterial power not making use of a corporeal organ for its action. And since the incorporeal cannot be affected by the corporeal, he held that intellectual knowledge is not brought about by sensible things affecting the intellect, but by separate intelligible forms being participated by the intellect, as we have said above (AA. 4, 5). Moreover he held that sense is a power operating of itself. Consequently neither is sense, since it is a spiritual power, affected by the sensible: but the sensible organs are affected by the sensible, the result being that the soul is in a way roused to form within itself the species of the sensible. Augustine seems to touch on this opinion (*Gen. ad lit.* xii. 24) where he says that the *body feels not, but the soul through the body, which it makes use of as a kind of messenger, for reproducing within itself what is announced from without.* Thus according to Plato, neither does intellectual knowledge proceed from sensible knowledge, nor sensible knowledge exclusively from sensible things; but these rouse the sensible soul to the sentient act, while the senses rouse the intellect to the act of understanding.

Aristotle chose a middle course. For with Plato he agreed that intellect and sense are different. But he held that the sense has not its proper operation without the co-operation of the body; so that to feel is not an act of the soul alone, but of the *composite*. And he held the same in regard to all the operations of the sensitive part. Since, therefore, it is not unreasonable that the sensible objects which are outside the soul should produce some effect in the *composite*, Aristotle agreed with Democritus in this, that the operations of the sensitive part are caused by the impression of the sensible on the sense: not by a discharge, as Democritus said, but by some kind of operation. For Democritus maintained that every operation is by way of a discharge of atoms, as we gather from *De Gener.* i. 8. But Aristotle held that the intellect has an operation which is independent of the body's co-operation. Now nothing corporeal can make an impression on the incorporeal. And therefore in order to cause the intellectual operation, according to Aristotle, the impression caused by the sensible does not suffice, but something more noble is required, *for the agent is more noble than the patient,* as he says (*ibid.* 5). Not, indeed, in the sense that the intellectual operation is effected in us by the mere impression of some superior beings, as Plato held; but that the higher and more noble agent which he calls the active intellect, of which we have spoken above (Q. 79, AA. 3, 4), causes the phantasms received from the senses to be actually intelligible, by a process of abstraction.

According to this opinion, then, on the part of the phantasms, intellectual knowledge is caused by the senses. But since the phantasms cannot of themselves affect the passive intellect, and require to be made actually intelligible by the active intellect, it cannot be said that sensible knowledge is the total and perfect cause of intellectual knowledge, but rather that it is in a way the material cause.

Reply Obj. 1. Those words of Augustine mean that we must not expect the entire truth from the senses. For the light of the active intellect is needed, through which we achieve the unchangeable truth of changeable things, and discern things themselves from their likeness.

Reply Obj. 2. In this passage Augustine speaks not of intellectual but of imaginary knowledge. And since, according to the opinion of Plato, the imagination has an operation which belongs to the soul only, Augustine, in order to show that corporeal images are impressed on the imagination, not by bodies but by the soul, uses the same argument as Aristotle does in proving that the active intellect must be separate, namely, because *the agent is more noble than the patient.* And without doubt, according to the above opinion, in the imagination there must needs be not only a passive but also an active power. But if we hold, according to the opinion of Aristotle, that the action of the imagination is an action of the *composite,* there is no difficulty; because the sensible body is more noble than the organ of the animal, in so far as it is compared to it as a being in act to a being in potentiality; even as the object actually colored is compared to the pupil which is potentially colored. It may, however, be said, although the first impression of the imagination is through the agency of the sensible, since *fancy is movement produced in accordance with sensation* (*De Anima* iii. 3), that nevertheless there is in man an operation which by synthesis and analysis forms images of various things, even of things not perceived by the senses. And Augustine's words may be taken in this sense.

Reply Obj. 3. Sensitive knowledge is not the entire cause of intellectual knowledge. And therefore it is not strange that intellectual knowledge should extend further than sensitive knowledge.

*   *   *

QUESTION 85: OF THE MODE AND ORDER OF UNDERSTANDING

*   *   *

First Article

WHETHER OUR INTELLECT UNDERSTANDS CORPOREAL AND MATERIAL THINGS BY ABSTRACTION FROM PHANTASMS?

We Proceed Thus to the First Article:—

Objection 1. It would seem that our intellect does not understand corporeal and material things by abstraction from the phantasms. For the intellect is false if it understands an object otherwise than as it really is. Now the forms of material things do not exist as abstracted from the particular things represented by the phantasms. Therefore, if we understand material things by abstraction of the species from the phantasm, there will be error in the intellect.

Obj. 2. Further, material things are those natural things which include matter in their definition. But nothing can be understood apart from that which enters into its definition. Therefore material things cannot be understood apart from matter. Now matter is the principle of individualization. Therefore material things cannot be understood by abstraction of the universal from the particular, which is the process whereby the intelligible species is abstracted from the phantasm.

Obj. 3. Further, the Philosopher says (*De Anima* iii. 7) that the phantasm is to the intellectual soul what color is to the sight. But seeing is not caused by abstraction of species from color, but by color impressing itself on the sight. Therefore neither does the act of understanding take place by abstraction of something from the phantasm, but by the phantasm impressing itself on the intellect.

Obj. 4. Further, the Philosopher says (*De Anima* iii. 5) there are two things in the intellectual soul—the passive intellect and the active intellect. But it does not belong to the passive intellect to abstract the intelligible species from the phantasm, but to receive them when abstracted. Neither does it seem to be the function of the active intellect which is related to the phantasm, as light is to color; since light does not abstract anything from color, but rather streams on to it Therefore in no way do we understand by abstraction from phantasms.

Obj. 5. Further, the Philosopher (*De Anima* iii. 7) says that *the intellect understands the species in the phantasm;* and not, therefore, by abstraction.

On the contrary, The Philosopher says (*De Anima* iii. 4) that *things are intelligible in proportion as they are separable from matter.* Therefore material things must needs be understood according as they are abstracted from matter and from material images, namely, phantasms.

I answer that, As stated above (Q. 84, A. 7), the object of knowledge is proportionate to the power of knowledge. Now there are three grades of the cognitive powers. For one cognitive power, namely, the sense, is the act of a corporeal organ. And therefore the object of every sensitive power is a form as existing in corporeal matter. And since such matter is the principle of individuality, therefore every power of the sensitive part can only have knowledge of the individual. There is another grade of cognitive power which is neither the act of a corporeal organ, nor in any way connected with corporeal matter; such is the angelic intellect, the object of whose cognitive power is therefore a form existing apart from matter: for though angels know material things, yet they do not know them save in something immaterial, namely, either in themselves or in God. But the human intellect holds a middle place: for it is not the act of an organ; yet it is a power of the soul which is the form of the body, as is clear from what we have said above (Q. 76, A. 1). And therefore it is proper to it to know a form existing individually in corporeal matter, but not as existing in this individual matter. But to know what is in individual matter, not as existing in such matter, is to abstract the form from individual matter which is represented by the phantasms. Therefore we must needs say that our intellect understands material things by abstracting from the phantasms; and through material things thus considered we acquire some knowledge of immaterial things, just as, on the contrary, angels know material things through the immaterial.

But Plato, considering only the immateriality of the human intellect, and not its being in a way united to the body, held that the objects of the intellect are separate ideas; and that we understand not by abstraction, but by participating things abstract, as stated above (Q. 84, A. 1).

Reply Obj. 1. Abstraction may occur in two ways: First, by way of composition and division; thus we may understand that one thing does not exist in some other, or that it is separate therefrom. Secondly, by way of simple and absolute consideration; thus we understand one thing without considering the other. Thus for the intellect to abstract one from another things which are not really abstract from one another, does, in the first mode of abstraction, imply falsehood. But, in the second mode of abstraction, for the intellect to abstract things which are not really abstract from one another, does not involve falsehood, as clearly appears in the case of the senses. For if we understood or said that color is not in a colored body, or that it is separate from it, there would be error in this opinion or assertion. But if we consider color and its properties, without reference to the apple which is colored; or if we express in word what we thus understand, there is no error in such an opinion or assertion, because an apple is not essential to color, and therefore color can be understood independently of the apple. Likewise, the things which belong to the species of a material thing, such as a stone, or a man, or a horse, can be thought of apart from the individualizing principles which do not belong to the notion of the species. This is what we mean by abstracting the universal from the particular, or the intelligible species from phantasm; that is, by considering the nature of the species apart from its individual qualities represented by the phantasms. If, therefore, the intellect is said to be false when it understands a thing otherwise than as it is, that is so, if the word *otherwise* refers to the thing understood; for the intellect is false when it understands a thing otherwise than as it is; and so the intellect would be false if it abstracted the species of a stone from its matter in such a way as to regard the species as not existing in matter, as Plato held. But it is not so, if the word *otherwise* be taken as referring to the one who understands. For it is quite true that the mode of understanding, in one who understands, is not the same as the mode of a thing in existing: since the thing understood is immaterially in the one who understands, according to the mode of the intellect, and not materially, according to the mode of a material thing.

Reply Obj. 2. Some have thought that the species of a natural thing is a form only, and that matter is not part of the species. If that were so, matter would not enter into the definition of natural things. Therefore it must be said otherwise, that matter is twofold, common, and *signate* or individual; common, such as flesh and bone; and individual, as this flesh and these bones. The intellect therefore abstracts the species of a natural thing from the individual sensible matter, but not from the common sensible matter; for example, it abstracts the species of man from *this flesh and these bones,* which do not belong to the species as such, but to the individual (*Metaph.* vii, Did. vi. 10), and need not be considered in the species: whereas the species of man cannot be abstracted by the intellect from *flesh and bones.*

Mathematical species, however, can be abstracted by the intellect from sensible matter, not only from individual, but also from common matter; not from common intelligible matter, but only from individual matter. For sensible matter is corporeal matter as subject to sensible qualities, such as being cold or hot, hard or soft, and the like: while intelligible matter is substance as subject to quantity. Now it is manifest that quantity is in substance before other sensible qualities are. Hence quantities, such as number, dimension, and figures, which are the terminations of quantity, can be considered apart from sensible qualities; and this is to abstract them from sensible matter; but they cannot be considered without understanding the substance which is subject to the quantity; for that would be to abstract them from common intelligible matter. Yet they can be considered apart from this or that substance; for that is to abstract them from individual intelligible matter. But some things can be abstracted even from common intelligible matter, such as *being, unity, power, act,* and the like; all these can exist without matter, as is plain regarding immaterial things. Because Plato failed to consider the twofold kind of abstraction, as above explained (*ad* 1), he held that all those things which we have stated to be abstracted by the intellect are abstract in reality.

Reply Obj. 3. Colors, as being in individual corporeal matter, have the same mode of existence as the power of sight: and therefore they can impress their own image on the eye. But phantasms, since they are images of individuals, and exist in corporeal organs, have not the same mode of existence as the human intellect, and therefore have not the power of themselves to make an impression on the passive intellect. This is done by the power of the active intellect which by turning towards the phantasm produces in the passive intellect a certain likeness which represents, as to its specific conditions only, the thing reflected in the phantasm. It is thus that the intelligible species is said to be abstracted from the phantasm; not that the identical form which previously was in the phantasm is subsequently in the passive intellect, as a body transferred from one place to another.

Reply Obj. 4. Not only does the active intellect throw light on the phantasm: it does more; by its own power it abstracts the intelligible species from the phantasm. It throws light on the phantasm, because, just as the sensitive part acquires a greater power by its conjunction with the intellectual part, so by the power of the active intellect the phantasms are made more fit for the abstraction therefrom of intelligible intentions. Furthermore, the active intellect abstracts the intelligible species from the phantasm, forasmuch as by the power of the active intellect we are able to disregard the conditions of individuality, and to take into our consideration the specific nature, the image of which informs the passive intellect.

Reply Obj. 5. Our intellect both abstracts the intelligible species from the phantasms, inasmuch as it considers the natures of things in universal, and, nevertheless, understands these natures in the phantasms, since it cannot understand even the things of which it abstracts the species, without turning to the phantasm, as we have said above (Q. 84, A. 7).

Second Article

WHETHER THE INTELLIGIBLE SPECIES ABSTRACTED FROM THE PHANTASM IS RELATED TO OUR INTELLECT AS THAT WHICH IS UNDERSTOOD?

We Proceed Thus to the Second Article:—

Objection 1. It would seem that the intelligible species abstracted from the phantasm is related to our intellect as that which is understood. For the understood in act is in the one who understands: since the understood in act is the intellect itself in act. But nothing of what is understood is in the intellect actually understanding, save the abstracted intelligible species. Therefore this species is what is actually understood.

Obj. 2. Further, what is actually understood must be in something; else it would be nothing. But it is not in something outside the soul: for, since what is outside the soul is material, nothing therein can be actually understood. Therefore what is actually understood is in the intellect. Consequently it can be nothing else than the aforesaid intelligible species.

Obj. 3. Further, the Philosopher says (1 *Peri Herm.* i) that *words are signs of the passions in the soul.* But words signify the things understood, for we express by word what we understand. Therefore these passions of the soul, viz., the intelligible species, are what is actually understood.

On the contrary, The intelligible species is to the intellect what the sensible image is to the sense. But the sensible image is not what is perceived, but rather that by which sense perceives. Therefore the intelligible species is not what is actually understood, but that by which the intellect understands.

I answer that, Some have asserted that our intellectual faculties know only the impression made on them; as, for example, that sense is cognizant only of the impression made on its own organ. According to this theory, the intellect understands only its own impression namely, the intelligible species which it has received, so that this species is what is understood.

This is, however, manifestly false for two reasons. First, because the things we understand are the objects of science; therefore if what we understand is merely the intelligible species in the soul, it would follow that every science would not be concerned with objects outside the soul, but only with the intelligible species within the soul; thus, according to the teaching of the Platonists all science is about ideas, which they held to be actually understood. Secondly, it is untrue, because it would lead to the opinion of the ancients who maintained that *whatever seems, is true,* and that consequently contradictories are true simultaneously. For if the faculty knows its own impression only, it can judge of that only. Now a thing seems, according to the impression made on the cognitive faculty. Consequently the cognitive faculty will always judge of its own impression as such; and so every judgment will be true: for instance, if taste perceived only its own impression, when anyone with a healthy taste perceives that honey is sweet, he would judge truly; and if anyone with a corrupt taste perceives that honey is bitter, this would be equally true; for each would judge according to the impression on his taste. Thus every opinion would be equally true; in fact, every sort of apprehension.

Therefore it must be said that the intelligible species is related to the intellect as that by which it understands: which is proved thus. There is a twofold action (*Metaph.* ix, Did. viii. 8), one which remains in the agent; for instance, to see and to understand; and another which passes into an external object; for instance, to heat and to cut; and each of these actions proceeds in virtue of some form. And as the form from which proceeds an act tending to something external is the likeness of the object of the action, as heat in the heater is a likeness of the thing heated; so the form from which proceeds an action remaining in the agent is the likeness of the object. Hence that by which the sight sees is the likeness of the visible thing; and the likeness of the thing understood, that is, the intelligible species, is the form by which the intellect understands. But since the intellect reflects upon itself, by such reflection it understands both its own act of intelligence, and the species by which it understands. Thus the intelligible species is that which is understood secondarily; but that which is primarily understood is the object, of which the species is the likeness. This also appears from the opinion of the ancient philosophers, who said that *like is known by like.* For they said that the soul knows the earth outside itself, by the earth within itself; and so of the rest. If, therefore, we take the species of the earth instead of the earth, according to Aristotle (*De Anima* iii. 8), who says *that a stone is not in the soul, but only the likeness of the stone;* it follows that the soul knows external things by means of its intelligible species.

Reply Obj. 1. The thing understood is in the intellect by its own likeness; and it is in this sense that we say that the thing actually understood is the intellect in act, because the likeness of the thing understood is the form of the intellect, as the likeness of a sensible thing is the form of the sense in act. Hence it does not follow that the intelligible species abstracted is what is actually understood; but rather that it is the likeness thereof.

Reply Obj. 2. In these words *the thing actually understood* there is a double implication:—the thing which is understood, and the fact that it is understood. In like manner the words *abstract universal* imply two things, the nature of a thing and its abstraction or universality. Therefore the nature itself to which it occurs to be understood, abstracted or considered as universal is only in individuals; but that it is understood, abstracted or considered as universal is in the intellect. We see something similar to this in the senses. For the sight sees the color of the apple apart from its smell. If therefore it be asked where is the color which is seen apart from the smell, it is quite clear that the color which is seen is only in the apple: but that it be perceived apart from the smell, this is owing to the sight, forasmuch as the faculty of sight receives the likeness of color and not of smell. In like manner humanity understood is only in this or that man; but that humanity be apprehended without conditions of individuality, that is, that it be abstracted and consequently considered as universal, occurs to humanity inasmuch as it is brought under the consideration of the intellect, in which there is a likeness of the specific nature, but not of the principles of individuality.

Reply Obj. 3. There are two operations in the sensitive part. One, in regard of impression only, and thus the operation of the senses takes place by the senses being impressed by the sensible. The other is formation, inasmuch as the imagination forms for itself an image of an absent thing, or even of something never seen. Both of these operations are found in the intellect. For in the first place there is the passion of the passive intellect as informed by the intelligible species; and then the passive intellect thus informed forms a definition, or a division, or a composition, expressed by a word. Wherefore the concept conveyed by a word is its definition; and a proposition conveys the intellect's division or composition. Words do not therefore signify the intelligible species themselves; but that which the intellect forms for itself for the purpose of judging of external things.

*   *   *

QUESTION 86: WHAT OUR INTELLECT KNOWS IN MATERIAL THINGS

*   *   *

First Article

WHETHER OUR INTELLECT KNOWS SINGULARS?

We Proceed Thus to the First Article:—

Objection 1. It would seem that our intellect knows singulars. For whoever knows composition, knows the terms of composition. But our intellect knows this composition; *Socrates is a man:* for it belongs to the intellect to form a proposition. Therefore our intellect knows this singular, Socrates.

Obj. 2. Further, the practical intellect directs to action. But action has relation to singular things. Therefore the intellect knows the singular.

Obj. 3. Further, our intellect understands itself. But in itself it is a singular, otherwise it would have no action of its own; for actions belong to singulars. Therefore our intellect knows singulars.

Obj. 4. Further, a superior power can do whatever is done by an inferior power. But sense knows the singular. Much more, therefore, can the intellect know it.

On the contrary, The Philosopher says (*Phys.* i. 5), that *the universal is known by reason; and the singular is known by sense.*

I answer that, Our intellect cannot know the singular in material things directly and primarily. The reason of this is that the principle of singularity in material things is individual matter, whereas our intellect, as we have said above (Q. 85, A. 1), understands by abstracting the intelligible species from such matter. Now what is abstracted from individual matter is the universal. Hence our intellect knows directly the universal only. But indirectly, and as it were by a kind of reflection, know the singular, because, as we have said above (Q. 85, A. 7), even after abstracting the intelligible species, the intellect, in order to understand, needs to turn to the phantasms in which it understands the species, as is said *De Anima* iii. 7. Therefore it understands the universal directly through the intelligible species, and indirectly the singular represented by the phantasm. And thus it forms the proposition, *Socrates is a man.* Wherefore the reply to the first objection is clear.

Reply Obj. 2. The choice of a particular thing to be done is as the conclusion of a syllogism formed by the practical intellect, as is said *Ethic.* vii. 3. But a singular proposition cannot be directly concluded from a universal proposition, except through the medium of a singular proposition. Therefore the universal principle of the practical intellect does not save through the medium of the particular apprehension of a sensitive part, as is said *De Anima* iii. 11.

Reply Obj. 3. Intelligibility is incompatible with the singular not as such, but as material, for nothing can be understood otherwise than immaterially. Therefore if there be an immaterial singular such as the intellect, there is no reason why it should not be intelligible.

Reply Obj. 4. The higher power can do what the lower power can, but in a more eminent way. Wherefore what the sense knows materially and concretely, which is to know the singular directly, the intellect knows immaterially and in the abstract, which is to know the universal.

* * *

FIRST PART OF THE SECOND PART (I–II)

TREATISE ON HUMAN ACTS

* * *

QUESTION 2: OF THOSE THINGS IN WHICH MAN'S HAPPINESS CONSISTS

* * *

Eighth Article

WHETHER ANY CREATED GOOD CONSTITUTES MAN'S HAPPINESS?

We Proceed Thus to the Eighth Article:—

Objection 1. It would seem that some created good constitutes man's happiness. For Dionysius says (*Div. Nom.* vii) that Divine wisdom *unites the ends of first things to the beginnings of second things,* from which we may gather that the summit of a lower nature touches the base of the higher nature. But man's highest good is happiness. Since then the angel is above man in the order of nature, as stated in the First Part (Q. 111, A. 1), it seems that man's happiness consists in man somehow reaching the angel.

Obj. 2. Further, the last end of each thing is that which, in relation to it, is perfect: hence the part is for the whole, as for its end. But the universe of creatures which is called the macrocosm, is compared to man who is called the microcosm (*Phys.* viii. 2), as perfect to imperfect. Therefore man's happiness consists in the whole universe of creatures.

Obj. 3. Further, man is made happy by that which lulls his natural desire. But man's natural desire does not reach out to a good surpassing his capacity. Since then man's capacity does not include that good which surpasses the limits of all creation, it seems that man can be made happy by some created good. Consequently some created good constitutes man's happiness.

On the contrary, Augustine says (*De Civ. Dei* xix. 26): *As the soul is the life of the body, so God is man's life of happiness: of Whom it is written: "Happy is that people whose God is the Lord"* (Ps. cxliii. 15).

I answer that, It is impossible for any created good to constitute man's happiness. For happiness is the perfect good, which lulls the appetite altogether; else it would not be the last end, if something yet remained to be desired. Now the object of the will, *i.e.,* of man's appetite, is the universal good; just as the object of the intellect is the universal true. Hence it is evident that naught can lull man's will, save the universal good. This is to be found, not in any creature, but in God alone; because every creature has goodness by participation. Wherefore God alone can satisfy the will of man, according to the words of Ps. cii. 5: *Who satisfieth thy desire with good things.* Therefore God alone constitutes man's happiness.

Reply Obj. 1. The summit of man does indeed touch the base of the angelic nature, by a kind of likeness; but man does not rest there as in his last end, but reaches out to the universal fount itself of good, which is the common object of happiness of all the blessed, as being the infinite and perfect good.

Reply Obj. 2. If a whole be not the last end, but ordained to a further end, then the last end of a part thereof is not the whole itself, but something else. Now the universe of creatures, to which man is compared as part to whole, is not the last end, but is ordained to God, as to its last end. Therefore the last end of man is not the good of the universe, but God himself.

Reply Obj. 3. Created good is not less than that good of which man is capable, as of something intrinsic and inherent to him: but it is less than the good of which he is capable, as of an object, and which is infinite. And the participated good which is in an angel, and in the whole universe, is a finite and restricted good.

*   *   *

QUESTION 3: WHAT IS HAPPINESS?

*   *   *

Fourth Article

WHETHER, IF HAPPINESS IS IN THE INTELLECTIVE PART, IT IS AN OPERATION OF THE INTELLECT OR OF THE WILL?

We Proceed Thus to the Fourth Article:—

Objection 1. It would seem that happiness consists in an act of the will. For Augustine says (*De Civ. Dei* xix. 10, 11), that man's happiness consists in peace; wherefore it is written (Ps. cxlvii. 3): *Who hath placed peace in thy end.* But peace pertains to the will. Therefore man's happiness is in the will.

Obj. 2. Further, happiness is the supreme good. But good is the object of the will. Therefore happiness consists in an operation of the will.

Obj. 3. Further, the last end corresponds to the first mover: thus the last end of the whole army is victory, which is the end of the general, who moves all the men. But the first mover in regard to operations is the will: because it moves the other powers, as we shall state further on (Q. 9, AA. 1, 3). Therefore happiness regards the will.

Obj. 4. Further, if happiness be an operation, it must needs be man's most excellent operation. But the love of God, which is an act of the will, is a more excellent operation than knowledge, which is an operation of the intellect, as the Apostle declares (1 Cor. xiii). Therefore it seems that happiness consists in an act of the will.

Obj. 5. Further, Augustine says (*De Trin.* xiii. 5) that *happy is he who has whatever he desires, and desires nothing amiss.* And a little further on (6) he adds: *He is almost happy who desires well, whatever he desires: for good things make a man happy, and such a man already possesses some good—i.e., a good will.* Therefore happiness consists in an act of the will.

On the contrary, Our Lord said (Jo. xvii. 3): *This is eternal life: that they may know Thee, the only true God.* Now eternal life is the last end, as stated above (A. 2 *ad* 1). Therefore man's happiness consists in the knowledge of God, which is an act of the intellect.

I answer that, As stated above (Q. 2, A. 6) two things are needed for happiness: one, which is the essence of happiness: the other, that is, as it were, its proper accident, *i.e.,* the delight connected with it. I say, then, that as to the very essence of happiness, it is impossible for it to consist in an act of the will. For it is evident from what has been said (AA. 1, 2; Q. 2, A. 7) that happiness is the attainment of the last end. But the attainment of the end does not consist in the very act of the will. For the will is directed to the end, both absent, when it desires it; and present, when it is delighted by resting therein. Now it is evident that the desire itself of the end is not the attainment of the end, but is a movement towards the end: while delight comes to the will from the end being present; and not conversely, is a thing made present, by the fact that the will delights in it. Therefore, that the end be present to him who desires it, must be due to something else than an act of the will.

This is evidently the case in regard to sensible ends. For if the acquisition of money were through an act of the will, the covetous man would have it from the very moment that he wished for it. But at that moment it is far from him; and he attains it, by grasping it in his hand, or in some like manner; and then he delights in the money got. And so it is with an intelligible end. For at first we desire to attain an intelligible end; we attain it, through its being made present to us by an act of the intellect; and then the delighted will rests in the end when attained.

So, therefore, the essence of happiness consists in an act of the intellect: but the delight that results from happiness pertains to the will. In this sense Augustine says (*Conf.* x. 23) that happiness is *joy in truth,* because, to wit, joy itself is the consummation of happiness.

Reply Obj. 1. Peace pertains to man's last end, not as though it were the very essence of happiness; but because it is antecedent and consequent thereto: antecedent, in so far as all those things are removed which disturb and hinder man in attaining the last end: consequent, inasmuch as, when man has attained his last end, he remains at peace, his desire being at rest.

Reply Obj. 2. The will's first object is not its act: just as neither is the first object of the sight, vision, but a visible thing. Wherefore, from the very fact that happiness belongs to the will, as the will's first object, it follows that it does not belong to it as its act.

Reply Obj. 3. The intellect apprehends the end before the will does: yet motion towards the end begins in the will. And therefore to the will belongs that which last of all follows the attainment of the end, viz., delight or enjoyment.

Reply Obj. 4. Love ranks above knowledge in moving, but knowledge precedes love in attaining: *for naught is loved save what is known,* as Augustine says (*De Trin.*

x. 1). Consequently we first attain an intelligible end by an act of the intellect; just as we first attain a sensible end by an act of sense.

Reply Obj. 5. He who has whatever he desires, is happy, because he has what he desires: and this indeed is by something other than the act of his will. But to desire nothing amiss is needed for happiness, as a necessary disposition thereto. And a good will is reckoned among the good things which make a man happy, forasmuch as it is an inclination of the will: just as a movement is reduced to the genus of its terminus, for instance, *alteration* to the genus *quality.*

Fifth Article

WHETHER HAPPINESS IS AN OPERATION OF THE SPECULATIVE, OR OF THE PRACTICAL INTELLECT?

We Proceed Thus to the Fifth Article:—

Objection 1. It would seem that happiness is an operation of the practical intellect. For the end of every creature consists in becoming like God. But man is like God, by his practical intellect, which is the cause of things understood, rather than by his speculative intellect, which derives its knowledge from things. Therefore man's happiness consists in an operation of the practical intellect rather than of the speculative.

Obj. 2. Further, happiness is man's perfect good. But the practical intellect is ordained to the good rather than the speculative intellect, which is ordained to the true. Hence we are said to be good, in reference to the perfection of the practical intellect, but not in reference to the perfection of the speculative intellect, according to which we are said to be knowing or understanding. Therefore man's happiness consists in an act of the practical intellect rather than of the speculative.

Obj. 3. Further, happiness is a good of man himself. But the speculative intellect is more concerned with things outside man; whereas the practical intellect is concerned with things belonging to man himself, viz., his operations and passions. Therefore man's happiness consists in an operation of the practical intellect rather than of the speculative.

On the contrary, Augustine says (*De Trin.* i. 8) that *contemplation is promised us, as being the goal of all our actions, and the everlasting perfection of our joys.*

I answer that, Happiness consists in an operation of the speculative rather than of the practical intellect. This is evident for three reasons. First because if man's happiness is an operation, it must needs be man's highest operation. Now man's highest operation is that of his highest power in respect of its highest object: and his highest power is the intellect, whose highest object is the Divine Good, which is the object, not of the practical, but of the speculative intellect. Consequently happiness consists principally in such an operation, viz., in the contemplation of Divine things. And since that *seems to be each man's self, which is best in him,* according to *Ethic.* ix. 8, and x. 7, therefore such an operation is most proper to man and most delightful to him.

Secondly, it is evident from the fact that contemplation is sought principally for its own sake. But the act of the practical intellect is not sought for its own sake but for the sake of action: and these very actions are ordained to some end. Consequently it is evident that the last end cannot consist in the active life which pertains to the practical intellect.

Thirdly, it is again evident, from the fact that in the contemplative life man has something in common with things above him, viz., with God and the angels, to whom he is made like by happiness. But in things pertaining to the active life, other animals also have something in common with man, although imperfectly.

Therefore the last and perfect happiness, which we await in the life to come, consists entirely in contemplation. But imperfect happiness, such as can be had here, consists first and principally in contemplation, but secondarily, in an operation of the practical intellect directing human actions and passions, as stated in *Ethic.* x. 7, 8.

Reply Obj. 1. The asserted likeness of the practical intellect to God is one of proportion; that is to say, by reason of its standing in relation to what it knows, as God does to what He knows. But the likeness of the speculative intellect to God is one of union and *information;* which is a much greater likeness.—And yet it may be answered that, in regard to the principal thing known, which is His Essence, God has not practical but merely speculative knowledge.

Reply Obj. 2. The practical intellect is ordained to good which is outside of it: but the speculative intellect has good within it, viz., the contemplation of truth. And if this good be perfect, the whole man is perfected and made good thereby: such a good the practical intellect has not; but it directs man thereto.

Reply Obj. 3. This argument would hold, if man himself were his own last end; for then the consideration and direction of his actions and passions would be his happiness. But since man's last end is something outside of him, to wit, God, to Whom we reach out by an operation of the speculative intellect; therefore man's happiness consists in an operation of the speculative intellect rather than of the practical intellect.

*   *   *

Eighth Article

WHETHER MAN'S HAPPINESS CONSISTS IN THE VISION OF THE DIVINE ESSENCE?

We Proceed Thus to the Eighth Article:—

Objection 1. It would seem that man's happiness does not consist in the vision of the Divine Essence. For Dionysius says (*Myst. Theol.* i) that by that which is highest in his intellect, man is united to God as to something altogether unknown. But that which is seen in its essence is not altogether unknown. Therefore the final perfection of the intellect, namely, happiness, does not consist in God being seen in His Essence.

Obj. 2. Further, the higher perfection belongs to the higher nature. But to see His own Essence is the perfection proper to the Divine intellect. Therefore the final perfection of the human intellect does not reach to this, but consists in something less.

On the contrary, It is written (1 Jo. iii. 2): *When He shall appear, we shall be like to Him; and we shall see Him as He is.*

I answer that, Final and perfect happiness can consist in nothing else than the vision of the Divine Essence. To make this clear, two points must be observed. First, that man is not perfectly happy, so long as something remains for him to desire and seek: secondly, that the perfection of any power is determined by the nature of its object. Now the object of the intellect is *what a thing is, i.e.,* the essence of a thing, according to *De Anima* iii. 6. Wherefore the intellect attains perfection, in so far as it knows the essence of a thing. If therefore an intellect know the essence of some effect, whereby it is not possible to know the essence of the cause, *i.e.* to know of the cause *what it is;* that intellect cannot be said to reach that cause simply, although it may be able to gather from the effect the knowledge that the cause is. Consequently, when man knows an effect, and knows that it has a cause, there naturally remains in man the desire to know about that cause, *what it is.* And this desire is one of wonder, and causes inquiry, as is stated in the beginning of the *Metaphysics* (i. 2). For instance, if a man, knowing the eclipse of the sun, consider that it must be due to some cause, and know not what that cause is, he wonders about it, and from wondering proceeds to inquire. Nor does this inquiry cease until he arrive at a knowledge of the essence of the cause.

If therefore the human intellect, knowing the essence of some created effect, knows no more of God than *that He is;* the perfection of that intellect does not yet reach simply the First Cause, but there remains in it the natural desire to seek the cause. Wherefore it is not yet perfectly happy. Consequently, for perfect happiness the intellect needs to reach the very Essence of the First Cause. And thus it will have its perfection through union with God as with that object, in which alone man's happiness consists, as stated above (AA. 1, 7; Q. 2, A. 8).

Reply Obj. 1. Dionysius speaks of the knowledge of wayfarers journeying towards happiness.

Reply Obj. 2. As stated above (Q. 1, A. 8), the end has a twofold acceptation. First, as to the thing itself which is desired: and in this way, the same thing is the end of the higher and of the lower nature, and indeed of all things, as stated above *(ibid.).* Secondly, as to the attainment of this thing; and thus the end of the higher nature is different from that of the lower, according to their respective habitudes to that thing. So then the happiness of God, Who, in understanding his Essence, comprehends It, is higher than that of a man or angel who sees It indeed, but comprehends It not.

*   *   *

QUESTION 5: OF THE ATTAINMENT OF HAPPINESS

*   *   *

Fifth Article

WHETHER MAN CAN ATTAIN HAPPINESS BY HIS NATURAL POWERS?

We Proceed Thus to the Fifth Article:—

Objection 1. It would seem that man can attain Happiness by his natural powers. For nature does not fail in necessary things. But nothing is so necessary to man as that by which he attains the last end. Therefore this is not lacking to human nature. Therefore man can attain Happiness by his natural powers.

Obj. 2. Further, since man is more noble than irrational creatures, it seems that he must be better equipped than they. But irrational creatures can attain their end by their natural powers. Much more therefore can man attain Happiness by his natural powers.

Obj. 3. Further, Happiness is a *perfect operation,* according to the Philosopher (*Ethic.* vii. 13). Now the beginning of a thing belongs to the same principle as the perfecting thereof. Since, therefore, the imperfect operation, which is as the beginning in human operations, is subject to man's natural power, whereby he is master of his own actions; it seems that he can attain to perfect operation, *i.e.,* Happiness, by his natural powers.

On the contrary, Man is naturally the principle of his action, by his intellect and will. But final Happiness prepared for the saints, surpasses the intellect and will of man; for the Apostle says (1 Cor. ii. 9): *Eye hath not seen, nor ear heard, neither hath it entered into the heart of man, what things God hath prepared for them that love Him.* Therefore man cannot attain Happiness by his natural powers.

I answer that, Imperfect happiness that can be had in this life, can be acquired by man by his natural powers, in the same way as virtue, in whose operation it consists: on this point we shall speak further on (Q. 63). But man's perfect Happiness, as stated above (Q. 3, A. 8), consists in the vision of the Divine Essence. Now the vision of God's Essence surpasses the nature not only of man, but also of every creature, as was shown in the First Part (Q. 12, A. 4). For the natural knowledge of every creature is in keeping with the mode of his substance: thus it is said of the intelligence (*De Causis;* Prop. viii.) that *it knows things that are above it, and things that are below it, according to the mode of its substance.* But every knowledge that is according to the mode of created substance, falls short of the vision of the Divine Essence, which infinitely surpasses all created substance. Consequently neither man, nor any creature, can attain final Happiness by his natural powers.

Reply Obj. 1. Just as nature does not fail man in necessaries, although it has not provided him with weapons and clothing, as it provided other animals, because it gave him reason and hands, with which he is able to get these things for himself; so neither did it fail man in things necessary, although it gave him not the wherewithal to attain Happiness: since this it could not do. But it did give him freewill, with which he can turn to God, that He may make him happy. *For what we do by means of our friends, is done, in a sense, by ourselves* (*Ethic.* iii. 3).

Reply Obj. 2. The nature that can attain perfect good, although it needs help from without in order to attain it, is of more noble condition than a nature which cannot attain perfect good, but attains some imperfect good, although it need no help from without in order to attain it, as the Philosopher says (*De Cælo* ii. 12). Thus he is better disposed to health who can attain perfect health, albeit by means of medicine, than he who can attain but imperfect health, without the help of medicine. And therefore the rational creature, which can attain the perfect good of happiness, but needs the Divine assistance for the purpose, is more perfect than the irrational creature, which is not capable of attaining this good, but attains some imperfect good by its natural powers.

Reply Obj. 3. When imperfect and perfect are of the same species, they can be caused by the same power. But this does not follow of necessity, if they be of different species: for not everything, that can cause the disposition of matter, can produce the final perfection. Now the imperfect operation, which is subject to man's natural power, is not of the same species as that perfect operation which is man's happiness: since operation takes its species from its object. Consequently the argument does not prove.

*   *   *

QUESTION 10: OF THE MANNER IN WHICH THE WILL IS MOVED

*   *   *

Second Article

WHETHER THE WILL IS MOVED, OF NECESSITY, BY ITS OBJECT?

We Proceed Thus to the Second Article:—

Objection 1. It seems that the will is moved, of necessity, by its object. For the object of the will is compared to the will as mover to movable, as stated in *De Anima* iii. 10. But a mover, if it be sufficient, moves the movable of necessity. Therefore the will can be moved of necessity by its object.

Obj. 2. Further, just as the will is an immaterial power, so is the intellect: and both powers are ordained to a universal object, as stated above (A. 1 *ad* 3). But the intellect is moved, of necessity, by its object: therefore the will also, by its object.

Obj. 3. Further, whatever one wills, is either the end, or something ordained to an end. But, seemingly, one wills an end necessarily: because it is like the principle in speculative matters, to which principle one assents of necessity. Now the end is the reason for willing the means; and so it seems that we will the means also necessarily. Therefore the will is moved of necessity by its object.

On the contrary, The rational powers, according to the Philosopher (*Metaph.* ix. 2) are directed to opposites. But the will is a rational power, since it is in the reason, as stated in *De Anima* iii. 9. Therefore the will is directed to opposites. Therefore it is not moved, of necessity, to either of the opposites.

I answer that, The will is moved in two ways: first, as to the exercise of its act; secondly, as to the specification of its act, derived from the object. As to the first way, no object moves the will necessarily, for no matter what the object be, it is in man's power not to think of it, and consequently not to will it actually. But as to the second manner of motion, the will is moved by one object necessarily, by another not. For in the movement of a power by its object, we must consider under what aspect the object moves the power. For the visible moves the sight, under the aspect of color actually visible. Wherefore if color be offered to the sight, it moves the sight necessarily: unless one turns one's eyes away; which belongs to the exercise of the act. But if the sight were confronted with something not in all respects colored actually, but only so in some respects, and in other respects not, the sight would not of necessity see such an object: for it might look at that part of the object which is not actually colored, and thus it would not see it. Now just as the actually colored is the object of sight, so is good the object of the will. Wherefore if the will be offered an object which is good universally and from every point of view, the will tends to it of necessity, if it wills anything at all; since it cannot will the opposite. If, on the other hand, the will is offered an object that is not good from every point of view, it will not tend to it of necessity. And since lack of any good whatever, is a non-good, consequently, that good alone which is perfect and lacking in nothing, is such a good that the will cannot not-will it: and this is Happiness. Whereas any other particular goods, in so far as they are lacking in some good, can be regarded as non-goods: and from this point of view, they can be set aside or approved by the will, which can tend to one and the same thing from various points of view.

Reply Obj. 1. The sufficient mover of a power is none but that object that in every respect presents the aspect of the mover of that power. If, on the other hand, it is lacking in any respect, it will not move of necessity, as stated above.

Reply Obj. 2. The intellect is moved, of necessity, by an object, which is such as to be always and necessarily true: but not by that which may be either true or false— viz., by that which is contingent: as we have said of the good.

Reply Obj. 3. The last end moves the will necessarily, because it is the perfect good. In like manner whatever is ordained to that end, and without which the end cannot be attained, such as *to be* and *to live,* and the like. But other things without which the end can be gained, are not necessarily willed by one who wills the end: just as he who assents to the principle, does not necessarily assent to the conclusions, without which the principles can still be true.

*   *   *

QUESTION 13: OF CHOICE, WHICH IS AN ACT OF THE WILL WITH REGARD TO THE MEANS

*   *   *

Sixth Article

WHETHER MAN CHOOSES OF NECESSITY OR FREELY?

We Proceed Thus to the Sixth Article:—

Objection 1. It would seem that man chooses of necessity. For the end stands in relation to the object of choice, as the principle of that which follows from the principles, as declared in *Ethic.* vii. 8. But conclusions follow of necessity from their principles. Therefore man is moved of necessity from (willing) the end to the choice (of the means).

Obj. 2. Further, as stated above (A. 1 *ad* 2), choice follows the reason's judgment of what is to be done. But reason judges of necessity about some things: on account of the necessity of the premises. Therefore it seems that choice also follows of necessity.

Obj. 3. Further, if two things are absolutely equal, man is not moved to one more than to the other; thus if a hungry man, as Plato says (cf. *De Cælo* ii. 13), be confronted on either side with two portions of food equally appetizing and at an equal distance, he is not moved towards one more than to the other; and he finds the reason of this in the immobility of the earth in the middle of the world. Now, if that which is equally (eligible) with something else cannot be chosen, much less can that be chosen which appears as less (eligible). Therefore if two or more things are available, of which one appears to be more (eligible), it is impossible to choose any of the others. Therefore that which appears to hold the first place is chosen of necessity. But every act of choosing is in regard to something that seems in some way better. Therefore every choice is made necessarily.

On the contrary, Choice is an act of a rational power; which according to the Philosopher (*Metaph.* ix. 2) stands in relation to opposites.

I answer that, Man does not choose of necessity. And this is because that which is possible not to be, is not of necessity. Now the reason why it is possible not to choose, or to choose, may be gathered from a twofold power in man. For man can will and not will, act and not act; again, he can will this or that, and do this or that. The reason of this is seated in the very power of the reason. For the will can tend to whatever the reason can apprehend as good. Now the reason can apprehend as good, not only this, viz., *to will or to act,* but also this, viz., *not to will* or *not to act.* Again, in all particular goods, the reason can consider an aspect of some good, and the lack of some good, which has the aspect of evil: and in this respect, it can apprehend any single one of such goods as to be chosen or to be avoided. The perfect good alone, which is Happiness, cannot be apprehended by the reason as an evil, or as lacking in any way. Consequently man wills Happiness of necessity, nor can he will not to be happy, or to be unhappy. Now since choice is not of the end, but of the means, as stated above (A. 3); it is not of the perfect good, which is Happiness, but of other particular goods. Therefore man chooses not of necessity, but freely.

Reply Obj. 1. The conclusion does not always of necessity follow from the principles, but only when the principles cannot be true if the conclusion is not true. In like manner, the end does not always necessitate in man the choosing of the means, because the means are not always such that the end cannot be gained without them; or, if they be such, they are not always considered in that light.

Reply Obj. 2. The reason's decision or judgment of what is to be done is about things that are contingent and possible to us. In such matters the conclusions do not follow of necessity from principles that are absolutely necessary but from such as are so conditionally; as, for instance, *If he runs, he is in motion.*

Reply Obj. 3. If two things be proposed as equal under one aspect, nothing hinders us from considering in one of them some particular point of superiority, so that the will has a bent towards that one rather than towards the other.

* * *

TREATISE ON HABITS

QUESTION 61: OF THE CARDINAL VIRTUES

* * *

First Article

WHETHER THE MORAL VIRTUES SHOULD BE CALLED CARDINAL OR PRINCIPAL VIRTUES?

We Proceed Thus to the First Article:—

Objection 1. It would seem that moral virtues should not be called cardinal or principal virtues. For *the opposite members of a division are by nature simultaneous* (Categor. x), so that one is not principal rather than another. Now all the virtues are opposite members of the division of the genus *virtue.* Therefore none of them should be called principal.

Obj. 2. Further, the end is principal as compared to the means. But the theological virtues are about the end; while the moral virtues are about the means. Therefore the theological virtues, rather than the moral virtues, should be called principal or cardinal.

Obj. 3. Further, that which is essentially so is principal in comparison with that which is so by participation. But the intellectual virtues belong to that which is essentially rational: whereas the moral virtues belong to that which is rational by participation, as stated above (Q. 58, A. 3). Therefore the intellectual virtues are principal, rather than the moral virtues.

On the contrary, Ambrose in explaining the words, *Blessed are the poor in spirit* (Luke vi. 20) says: *We know that there are four cardinal virtues, viz., temperance, justice, prudence, and fortitude.* But these are moral virtues. Therefore the moral virtues are cardinal virtues.

I answer that, When we speak of virtue simply, we are understood to speak of human virtue. Now human virtue, as stated above (Q. 56, A. 3), is one that answers to the perfect idea of virtue, which requires rectitude of the appetite: for such like virtue not only confers the faculty of doing well, but also causes the good deed done. On the other hand, the name virtue is applied to one that answers imperfectly to the idea of virtue, and does not require rectitude of the appetite: because it merely confers the faculty of doing well without causing the good deed to be done. Now it is evident that the perfect is principal as compared to the imperfect: and so those virtues which imply rectitude of the appetite are called principal virtues. Such are the moral virtues, and prudence alone, of the intellectual virtues, for it is also something of a moral virtue, as was clearly shown above (Q. 57, A. 4). Consequently, those virtues which are called principal or cardinal are fittingly placed among the moral virtues.

Reply Obj. 1. When a univocal genus is divided into its species, the members of the division are on a par in the point of the generic idea; although considered in their nature as things, one species may surpass another in rank and perfection, as man in respect of other animals. But when we divide an analogous term, which is applied to several things, but to one before it is applied to another, nothing hinders one from ranking before another even in the point of the generic idea; as the notion of being is applied to substance principally in relation to accident. Such is the division of virtue into the various kinds of virtue: since the good defined by reason is not found in the same way in all things.

Reply Obj. 2. The theological virtues are above man, as stated above (Q. 58, A. 3 *ad* 3). Hence they should properly be called not human, but *super-human* or godlike virtues.

Reply Obj. 3. Although the intellectual virtues, except in prudence, rank before the moral virtues, in the point of their subject, they do not rank before them as virtues; for a virtue, as such, regards good, which is the object of the appetite.

Second Article

WHETHER THERE ARE FOUR CARDINAL VIRTUES?

We Proceed Thus to the Second Article:—

Objection 1. It would seem that there are not four cardinal virtues. For prudence is the directing principle of the other moral virtues, as is clear from what has been said above (Q. 58, A. 4). But that which directs other things ranks before them. Therefore prudence alone is a principal virtue.

Obj. 2. Further, the principal virtues are, in a way, moral virtues. Now we are directed to moral works both by the practical reason, and by a right appetite, as stated in *Ethic.* vi. 2. Therefore there are only two cardinal virtues.

Obj. 3. Further, even among the other virtues one ranks higher than another. But in order that a virtue be principal, it needs not to rank above all the others, but above some. Therefore it seems that there are many more principal virtues.

On the contrary, Gregory says (*Moral.* ii): *The entire structure of good works is built on four virtues.*

I answer that, Things may be numbered either in respect of their formal principles, or according to the subjects in which they are: and either way we find that there are four cardinal virtues.

For the formal principle of the virtue of which we speak now is good as defined by reason; which good can be considered in two ways. First, as existing in the very act of reason: and thus we have one principal virtue, called *Prudence.*—Secondly, according as the reason puts its order into something else; either into operations, and then we have *Justice;* or into passions, and then we need two virtues. For the need of putting the order of reason into the passions is due to their thwarting reason: and this occurs in two ways. First, by the passions inciting to something against reason; and then the passions need a curb, which we call *Temperance.* Secondly, by the passions withdrawing us from following the dictate of reason, e.g., through fear of danger or toil: and then man needs to be strengthened for that which reason dictates, lest he turn back; and to this end there is *Fortitude.*

In like manner, we find the same number if we consider the subjects of virtue. For there are four subjects of the virtue we speak of now: viz., the power which is rational in its essence, and this is perfected by *Prudence;* and that which is rational by participation, and is threefold, the will, subject of *Justice,* the concupiscible faculty, subject of *Temperance,* and the irascible faculty, subject of *Fortitude.*

Reply Obj. 1. Prudence is the principal of all virtues simply. The others are principal, each in its own genus.

Reply Obj. 2. That part of the soul which is rational by participation is threefold, as stated above.

Reply Obj. 3. All the other virtues among which one ranks before another, are reducible to the above four, both as to the subject and as to the formal principle.

*   *   *

QUESTION 62: OF THE THEOLOGICAL VIRTUES

*   *   *

First Article

WHETHER THERE ARE ANY THEOLOGICAL VIRTUES?

We Proceed Thus to the First Article:—

Objection 1. It would seem that there are not any theological virtues. For according to *Phys.* vii., text. 17, virtue is the disposition of a perfect thing to that which is best: and by perfect, I mean that which is disposed according to nature. But that which is Divine is above man's nature. Therefore the theological virtues are not virtues of a man.

Obj. 2. Further, theological virtues are quasi-Divine virtues. But the Divine virtues are exemplars, as stated above (Q. 61, A. 5), which are not in us but in God. Therefore the theological virtues are not virtues of man.

Obj. 3. Further, the theological virtues are so called because they direct us to God, Who is the first beginning and last end of all things. But by the very nature of his reason and will, man is directed to his first beginning and last end. Therefore there is no need for any habits of theological virtue, to direct the reason and will to God.

On the contrary, The precepts of the Law are about acts of virtue. Now the Divine Law contains precepts about the acts of faith, hope, and charity: for it is written (*Ecclus.* ii. 8, *seqq.*): *Ye that fear the Lord believe Him,* and again, *hope in Him,* and again, *love Him.* Therefore faith, hope, and charity are virtues directing us to God. Therefore they are theological virtues.

I answer that, Man is perfected by virtue, for those actions whereby he is directed to happiness, as was explained above (Q. 5, A. 7). Now man's happiness is twofold, as was also stated above (*ibid.,* A. 5). One is proportionate to human nature, a happiness, to wit, which man can obtain by means of his natural principles. The other is a happiness surpassing man's nature, and which man can obtain by the power of God alone, by a kind of participation of the Godhead, about which it is written (2 Pet. i. 4) that by Christ we are made *partakers of the Divine nature.* And because such happiness surpasses the capacity of human nature, man's natural principles which enable him to act well according to his capacity, do not suffice to direct man to this same happiness. Hence it is necessary for man to receive from God some additional principles, whereby he may be directed to supernatural happiness, even as he is directed to his connatural end, by means of his natural principles, albeit not without the Divine assistance. Such like principles are called *theological virtues:* first, because their object is God, inasmuch as they direct us aright to God: secondly, because they are infused in us by God alone: thirdly, because these virtues are not made known to us, save by Divine revelation, contained in Holy Writ.

Reply Obj. 1. A certain nature may be ascribed to a certain thing in two ways. First, essentially: and thus these theological virtues surpass the nature of man. Secondly, by participation, as kindled wood partakes of the nature of fire: and thus, after a fashion, man becomes a partaker of the Divine Nature, as stated above: so that these virtues are proportionate to man in respect of the Nature of which he is made a partaker.

Reply Obj. 2. These virtues are called Divine, not as though God were virtuous by reason of them, but because of them God makes us virtuous, and directs us to Himself. Hence they are not exemplar but exemplate virtues.

Reply Obj. 3. The reason and will are naturally directed to God, inasmuch as He is the beginning and end of nature, but in proportion to nature. But the reason and will, according to their nature, are not sufficiently directed to Him in so far as He is the object of supernatural happiness.

Second Article

WHETHER THE THEOLOGICAL VIRTUES ARE DISTINCT FROM THE INTELLECTUAL AND MORAL VIRTUES?

We Proceed Thus to the Second Article:—

Objection 1. It would seem that the theological virtues are not distinct from the moral and intellectual virtues. For the theological virtues, if they be in a human soul, must needs perfect it, either as to the intellective, or as to the appetitive part. Now the virtues which perfect the intellective part are called intellectual; and the virtues which perfect the appetitive part, are called moral. Therefore, the theological virtues are not distinct from the moral and intellectual virtues.

Obj. 2. Further, the theological virtues are those which direct us to God. Now, among the intellectual virtues there is one which directs us to God: this is wisdom, which is about Divine things, since it considers the highest cause. Therefore the theological virtues are not distinct from the intellectual virtues.

Obj. 3. Further, Augustine (*De Moribus Eccl.* xv) shows how the four cardinal virtues are the order of love. Now love is charity, which is a theological virtue. Therefore the moral virtues are not distinct from the theological.

On the contrary, That which is above man's nature is distinct from that which is according to his nature. But the theological virtues are above man's nature; while the intellectual and moral virtues are in proportion to his nature, as clearly shown above (Q. 58, A. 3). Therefore they are distinct from one another.

I answer that, As stated above (Q. 54, A. 2 *ad* 1), habits are specifically distinct from one another in respect of the formal difference of their objects. Now the object of the theological virtues is God Himself, Who is the last end of all, as surpassing the knowledge of our reason. On the other hand, the object of the intellectual and moral virtues is something comprehensible to human reason. Wherefore the theological virtues are specifically distinct from the moral and intellectual virtues.

Reply Obj. 1. The intellectual and moral virtues perfect man's intellect and appetite according to the capacity of human nature; the theological virtues, supernaturally.

Reply Obj. 2. The wisdom which the Philosopher (*Ethic.* vi. 3, 7) reckons as an intellectual virtue, considers Divine things so far as they are open to the research of human reason. Theological virtue, on the other hand, is about those same things so far as they surpass human reason.

Reply Obj. 3. Though charity is love, yet love is not always charity. When, then, it is stated that every virtue is the order of love, this can be understood either of love in the general sense, or of the love of charity. If it be understood of love, commonly so called, then each virtue is stated to be the order of love, in so far as each cardinal virtue requires ordinate emotions; and love is the root and cause of every emotion, as stated above (Q. 27, A. 4; Q. 28, A. 6 *ad* 2; Q. 41, A. 2 *ad* 1).—If, however, it be understood of the love of charity, it does not mean that every other virtue is charity essentially: but that all other virtues depend on charity in some way, as we shall show further on (Q. 65, AA. 2, 4; II–II, Q. 23, A. 7).

Third Article

WHETHER FAITH, HOPE, AND CHARITY ARE FITTINGLY RECKONED AS THEOLOGICAL VIRTUES?

We Proceed Thus to the Third Article:—

Objection 1. It would seem that faith, hope, and charity are not fittingly reckoned as three theological virtues. For the theological virtues are in relation to Divine happiness, what the natural inclination is in relation to the connatural end. Now among the virtues directed to the connatural end there is but one natural virtue, viz., the understanding of principles. Therefore there should be but one theological virtue.

Obj. 2. Further, the theological virtues are more perfect than the intellectual and moral virtues. Now faith is not reckoned among the intellectual virtues, but is something less than a virtue, since it is imperfect knowledge. Likewise hope is not reckoned among the moral virtues, but is something less than a virtue, since it is a passion. Much less therefore should they be reckoned as theological virtues.

Obj. 3. Further, the theological virtues direct man's soul to God. Now man's soul cannot be directed to God, save through the intellective part, wherein are the intellect and will. Therefore there should be only two theological virtues, one perfecting the intellect, the other, the will.

On the contrary, The Apostle says (1 Cor. xiii. 13): *Now there remain faith, hope, charity, these three.*

I answer that, As stated above (A. 1), the theological virtues direct man to supernatural happiness in the same way as by the natural inclination man is directed to his connatural end. Now the latter happens in respect of two things. First, in respect of the reason or intellect, in so far as it contains the first universal principles which are known to us by the natural light of the intellect, and which are reason's starting-point, both in speculative and in practical matters. Secondly, through the rectitude of the will which tends naturally to good as defined by reason.

But these two fall short of the order of supernatural happiness, according to 1 Cor. ii. 9: *The eye hath not seen, nor ear heard, neither hath it entered into the heart of man, what things God hath prepared for them that love Him.* Consequently in respect of both the above things man needed to receive in addition something supernatural to direct him to a supernatural end. First, as regards the intellect, man receives certain supernatural principles, which are held by means of a Divine light: these are the articles of faith, about which is faith.—Secondly, the will is directed to this end, both as to the movement of intention, which tends to that end as something attainable,—and this pertains to hope,—and as to a certain spiritual union, whereby the will is so to speak, transformed into that end,—and this belongs to charity. For the appetite of a thing is moved and tends towards its connatural end naturally; and this movement is due to a certain conformity of the thing with its end.

Reply Obj. 1. The intellect requires intelligible species whereby to understand: consequently there is need of a natural habit in addition to the power. But the very nature of the will suffices for it to be directed naturally to the end, both as to the intention of the end and as to its conformity with the end. But the nature of the power is insufficient in either of these respects, for the will to be directed to things that are above its nature. Consequently there was need for an additional supernatural habit in both respects.

Reply Obj. 2. Faith and hope imply a certain imperfection: since faith is of things unseen, and hope, of things not possessed. Hence faith and hope, in things that are subject to human power, fall short of the notion of virtue. But faith and hope in things which are above the capacity of human nature surpass all virtue that is in proportion to man, according to 1 Cor. i. 25: *The weakness of God is stronger than men.*

Reply Obj. 3. Two things pertain to the appetite, viz., movement to the end, and conformity with the end by means of love. Hence there must needs be two theological virtues in the human appetite, namely, hope and charity.

*   *   *

Treatise on Law

QUESTION 94: OF THE NATURAL LAW

*   *   *

Second Article

Whether the Natural Law Contains Several Precepts, or One Only?

We Proceed Thus to the Second Article:—

Objection 1. It would seem that the natural law contains, not several precepts, but one only. For law is a kind of precept, as stated above (Q. 92, A. 2). If therefore there were many precepts of the natural law, it would follow that there are also many natural laws.

Obj. 2. Further, the natural law is consequent to human nature. But human nature, as a whole, is one; though, as to its parts, it is manifold. Therefore, either there is but one precept of the law of nature, on account of the unity of nature as a whole; or there are many, by reason of the number of parts of human nature. The result would be that even things relating to the inclination of the concupiscible faculty belong to the natural law.

Obj. 3. Further, law is something pertaining to reason, as stated above (Q. 90, A. 1). Now reason is but one in man. Therefore there is only one precept of the natural law.

On the contrary, The precepts of the natural law in man stand in relation to practical matters, as the first principles to matters of demonstration. But there are several first indemonstrable principles. Therefore there are also several precepts of the natural law.

I answer that, As stated above (Q. 91, A. 3), the precepts of the natural law are to the practical reason, what the first principles of demonstrations are to the speculative reason; because both are self-evident principles. Now a thing is said to be self-evident in two ways: first, in itself; secondly, in relation to us. Any proposition is said to be selfevident in itself, its predicate is contained in the notion of the subject: although, to one who knows not the definition of the subject, it happens that such a proposition is not self-evident. For instance, this proposition, *Man is a rational being,* is, in its very nature, self-evident, since who says *man,* says *a rational being:* and yet to one who knows not what a man is, this proposition is not self-evident. Hence it is that, as Boethius says *(De Hebdom.),* certain axioms or propositions are universally self-evident to all; and such are those propositions whose terms are known to all, as, *Every whole is greater than its part,* and, *Things equal to one and the same are equal to one another.* But some propositions are self-evident only to the wise, who understand the meaning of the terms of such propositions: thus to one who understands that an angel is not a body, it is self-evident that an angel is not circumscriptively in a place: but this is not evident to the unlearned, for they cannot grasp it.

Now a certain order is to be found in those things that are apprehended universally. For that which, before aught else, falls under apprehension, is *being,* the notion of which is included in all things whatsoever a man apprehends. Wherefore the first indemonstrable principle is that *the same thing cannot be affirmed and denied at the same time,* which is based on the notion of being and not-being: and on this principle all others are based, as is stated in *Metaph.* iv, text. 9. Now as being is the first thing that falls under the apprehension simply, so *good* is the first thing that falls under the apprehension of the practical reason, which is directed to action: since every agent acts for an end under the aspect of good. Consequently the first principle in the practical reason is one founded on the notion of good, viz., that *good is that which all things seek after.* Hence this is the first precept of law, that *good is to be done and pursued, and evil is to be avoided.* All other precepts of the natural law are based upon this: so that whatever the practical reason naturally apprehends as man's good (or evil) belongs to the precepts of the natural law as something to be done or avoided.

Since, however, good has the nature of an end, and evil, the nature of a contrary, hence it is that all those things to which man has a natural inclination, are naturally apprehended by reason as being good, and consequently as objects of pursuit, and their contraries as evil, and objects of avoidance. Wherefore according to the order of natural inclinations, is the order of the precepts of the natural law. Because in man there is first of all an inclination to good in accordance with the nature which he has in common with all substances: inasmuch as every substance seeks the preservation of its own being, according to its nature: and by reason of this inclination, whatever is a means of preserving human life, and of warding off its obstacles, belongs to the natural law. Secondly, there is in man an inclination to things that pertain to him more specially, according to that nature which he has in common with other animals: and in virtue of this inclination, those things are said to belong to the natural law, *which nature has taught to all animals,* such as sexual intercourse, education of offspring and so forth. Thirdly, there is in man an inclination to good, according to the nature of his reason, which nature is proper to him: thus man has a natural inclination to know the truth about God, and to live in society: and in this respect, whatever pertains to this inclination belongs to the natural law; for instance, to shun ignorance, to avoid offending those among whom one has to live, and other such things regarding the above inclination.

Reply Obj. 1. All these precepts of the law of nature have the character of one natural law, inasmuch as they flow from one first precept.

Reply Obj. 2. All the inclinations of any parts whatsoever of human nature, *e.g.,* of the concupiscible and irascible parts, in so far as they are ruled by reason, belong to the natural law, and are reduced to one first precept, as stated above: so that the precepts of the natural law are many in themselves, but are based on one common foundation.

Reply Obj. 3. Although reason is one in itself, yet it directs all things regarding man; so that whatever can be ruled by reason, is contained under the law of reason.

*   *   *

Fourth Article

WHETHER THE NATURAL LAW IS THE SAME IN ALL MEN?

We Proceed Thus to the Fourth Article:—

Objection 1. It would seem that the natural law is not the same in all. For it is stated in the Decretals (*Dist.* i) that *the natural law is that which is contained in the*

Law and the Gospel. But this is not common to all men; because, as it is written (Rom. x. 16), *all do not obey the gospel.* Therefore the natural law is not the same in all men.

Obj. 2. Further, *Things which are accordingly to the law are said to be just,* as stated in *Ethic.* v. But it is stated in the same book that nothing is so universally just as not to be subject to change in regard to some men. Therefore even the natural law is not the same in all men.

Obj. 3. Further, as stated above (AA. 2, 3), to the natural law belongs everything to which a man is inclined according to his nature. Now different men are naturally inclined to different things; some to the desire of pleasures, others to the desire of honors, and other men to other things. Therefore there is not one natural law for all.

On the contrary, Isidore says (*Etym.* v. 4): *The natural law is common to all nations.*

I answer that, As stated above (AA. 2, 3), to the natural law belongs those things to which a man is inclined naturally: and among these it is proper to man to be inclined to act according to reason. Now the process of reason is from the common to the proper, as stated in *Phys.* i. The speculative reason, however, is differently situated in this matter, from the practical reason. For, since the speculative reason is busied chiefly with necessary things, which cannot be otherwise than they are, its proper conclusions, like the universal principles, contain the truth without fail. The practical reason, on the other hand, is busied with contingent matters, about which human actions are concerned: and consequently, although there is necessity in the general principles, the more we descend to matters of detail, the more frequently we encounter defects. Accordingly then in speculative matters truth is the same in all men, both as to principles and as to conclusions: although the truth is not known to all as regards the conclusions, but only as regards the principles which are called *common notions.* But in matters of action, truth or practical rectitude is not the same for all, as to matters of detail, but only as to the general principles: and where there is the same rectitude in matters of detail, it is not equally known to all.

It is therefore evident that, as regards the general principles whether of speculative or of practical reason, truth or rectitude is the same for all, and is equally known by all. As to the proper conclusions of the speculative reason, the truth is the same for all, but is not equally known to all: thus it is true for all that the three angles of a triangle are together equal to two right angles, although it is not known to all. But as to the proper conclusions of the practical reason, neither is the truth or rectitude the same for all, nor, where it is the same, is it equally known by all. Thus it is right and true for all to act according to reason: and from this principle it follows as a proper conclusion, that goods entrusted to another should be restored to their owner. Now this is true for the majority of cases: but it may happen in a particular case that it would be injurious, and therefore unreasonable, to restore goods held in trust; for instance if they are claimed for the purpose of fighting against one's country. And this principle will be found to fail the more, according as we descend further into detail, e.g., if one were to say that goods held in trust should be restored with such and such a guarantee, or in such and such a way; because the greater the number of conditions added, the greater the number of ways in which the principle may fail, so that it be not right to restore or not to restore.

Consequently we must say that the natural law, as to general principles, is the same for all, both as to rectitude and as to knowledge. But as to certain matters of detail, which are conclusions, as it were, of those general principles, it is the same for all in the majority of cases, both as to rectitude and as to knowledge; and yet in some few cases it may fail, both as to rectitude, by reason of certain obstacles (just as natures subject to generation and corruption fail in some few cases on account of some obstacle), and as to knowledge, since in some the reason is perverted by passion, or evil habit, or an evil disposition of nature; thus formerly, theft, although it is expressly contrary to the natural law, was not considered wrong among the Germans, as Julius Caesar relates (*De Bello Gall.* vi).

Reply Obj. 1. The meaning of the sentence quoted is not that whatever is contained in the Law and the Gospel belongs to the natural law, since they contain many things that are above nature; but that whatever belongs to the natural law is fully contained in them. Wherefore Gratian, after saying that *the natural law is what is contained in the Law and the Gospel,* adds at once, by way of example, *by which everyone is commanded to do to others as he would be done by.*

Reply Obj. 2. The saying of the Philosopher is to be understood of things that are naturally just, not as general principles, but as conclusions drawn from them, having rectitude in the majority of cases, but failing in a few.

Reply Obj. 3. As, in man, reason rules and commands the other powers, so all the natural inclinations belonging to the other powers must needs be directed according to reason. Wherefore it is universally right for all men, that all their inclinations should be directed according to reason.

Fifth Article

WHETHER THE NATURAL LAW CAN BE CHANGED?

We Proceed Thus to the Fifth Article:—

Objection 1. It would seem that the natural law can be changed. Because on Ecclus. xvii. 9, *He gave them instructions, and the law of life,* the gloss says: *He wished the law of the letter to be written, in order to correct the law of nature.* But that which is corrected is changed. Therefore the natural law can be changed.

Obj. 2. Further, the slaying of the innocent, adultery, and theft are against the natural law. But we find these things changed by God: as when God commanded Abraham to slay his innocent son (Gen. xxii. 2); and when he ordered the Jews to borrow and purloin the vessels of the Egyptians (Exod. xii. 35); and when He commanded Osee to take to himself *a wife of fornications* (Osee i. 2). Therefore the natural law can be changed.

Obj. 3. Further, Isidore says (*Etym.* v. 4) that *the possession of all things in common, and universal freedom, are matters of natural law.* But these things are seen to be changed by human laws. Therefore it seems that the natural law is subject to change.

On the contrary, It is said in the Decretals (*Dist.* v): *The natural law dates from the creation of the rational creature. It does not vary according to time, but remains unchangeable.*

I answer that, A change in the natural law may be understood in two ways. First, by way of addition. In this sense nothing hinders the natural law from being changed: since many things for the benefit of human life have been added over and above the natural law, both by the Divine law and by human laws.

Secondly, a change in the natural law may be understood by way of subtraction, so that what previously was according to the natural law, ceases to be so. In this sense, the natural law is altogether unchangeable in its first principles: but in its secondary principles, which, as we have said (A. 4), are certain detailed proximate conclusions drawn from the first principles, the natural law is not changed so that what it prescribes be not right in most cases. But it may be changed in some particular cases of rare occurrence, through some special causes hindering the observance of such precepts, as stated above (A. 4).

Reply Obj. 1. The written law is said to be given for the correction of the natural law, either because it supplies what was wanting to the natural law; or because the natural law was perverted in the hearts of some men, as to certain matters, so that they esteemed those things good which are naturally evil; which perversion stood in need of correction.

Reply Obj. 2. All men alike, both guilty and innocent, die the death of nature: which death of nature is inflicted by the power of God on account of original sin, according to 1 Kings ii. 6: *The Lord killeth and maketh alive.* Consequently, by the command of God, death can be inflicted on any man, guilty or innocent, without any injustice whatever.—In like manner adultery is intercourse with another's wife; who is allotted to him by the law emanating from God. Consequently intercourse with any woman, by the command of God, is neither adultery nor fornication.—The same applies to theft, which is the taking of another's property. For whatever is taken by the command of God, to Whom all things belong, is not taken against the will of its owner, whereas it is in this that theft consists.—Nor is it only in human things, that whatever is commanded by God is right; but also in natural things, whatever is done by God, is, in some way, natural, as stated in the First Part (Q. 105, A. 6 *ad* 1).

Reply Obj. 3. A thing is said to belong to the natural law in two ways. First, because nature inclines thereto: *e.g.,* that one should not do harm to another. Secondly, because nature did not bring in the contrary: thus we might say that for man to be naked is of the natural law, because nature did not give him clothes, but art invented them. In this sense, *the possession of all things in common and universal freedom* are said to be of the natural law, because, to wit, the distinction of possessions and slavery were not brought in by nature, but devised by human reason for the benefit of human life. Accordingly the law of nature was not changed in this respect, except by addition.

*   *   *

QUESTION 95: OF HUMAN LAW

*   *   *

First Article

WHETHER IT WAS USEFUL FOR LAWS TO BE FRAMED BY MEN?

We Proceed Thus to the First Article:—

Objection 1. It would seem that it was not useful for laws to be framed by men. Because the purpose of every law is that man be made good thereby, as stated above (Q. 92, A. 1). But men are more to be induced to be good willingly by means of admonitions, than against their will, by means of laws. Therefore there was no need to frame laws.

Obj. 2. Further, as the Philosopher says (*Ethic.* v. 4), *men have recourse to a judge as to animate justice.* But animate justice is better than inanimate justice, which is contained in laws. Therefore it would have been better for the execution of justice to be entrusted to the decision of judges, than to frame laws in addition.

Obj. 3. Further, every law is framed for the direction of human actions, as is evident from what has been stated above (Q. 90, AA. 1, 2). But since human actions are about singulars, which are infinite in number, matters pertaining to the direction of human actions cannot be taken into sufficient consideration except by a wise man, who looks into each one of them. Therefore it would have been better for human acts to be directed by the judgment of wise men, than by the framing of laws. Therefore there was no need of human laws.

On the contrary, Isidore says (*Etym.* v. 20): *Laws were made that in fear thereof human audacity might be held in check, that innocence might be safeguarded in the midst of wickedness, and that the dread of punishment might prevent the wicked from doing harm.* But these things are most necessary to mankind. Therefore it was necessary that human laws should be made.

I answer that, As stated above (Q. 63, A. 1; Q. 94, A. 3), man has a natural aptitude for virtue; but the perfection of virtue must be acquired by man by means of some kind of training. Thus we observe that man is helped by industry in his necessities, for instance, in food and clothing. Certain beginnings of these he has from nature, viz., his reason and his hands; but he has not the full complement, as other animals have, to whom nature has given sufficiency of clothing and food. Now it is difficult to see how man could suffice for himself in the matter of this training: since the perfection of virtue consists chiefly in withdrawing man from undue pleasures, to which above all man is inclined, and especially the young, who are more capable of being trained. Consequently a man needs to receive this training from another, whereby to arrive at the perfection of virtue. And as to those young people who are inclined to acts of virtue, by their good natural disposition, or by custom, or rather by the gift of God, paternal training suffices, which is by admonitions. But since some are found to be depraved, and prone to vice, and not easily amenable to words, it was necessary for such to be restrained from evil by force and fear, in order that, at least, they might desist from evil-doing, and leave others in peace, and that they themselves, by being habituated in this way, might be brought to do willingly what hitherto they did from fear, and thus become virtuous. Now this kind of training, which compels through fear of punishment, is the discipline of laws. Therefore, in order that man might have peace and virtue, it was necessary for laws to be framed: for, as the Philosopher says (Polit. i. 2), *as man is the most noble of animals if he be perfect in virtue, so is he the lowest of all, if he be severed from law and righteousness;* because man can use his reason to devise means of satisfying his lusts and evil passions, which other animals are unable to do.

Reply Obj. 1. Men who are well disposed are led willingly to virtue by being admonished better than by coercion: but men who are evilly disposed are not led to virtue unless they are compelled.

Reply Obj. 2. As the Philosopher says (*Rhet.* i. 1), *it is better that all things be regulated by law, than left to be decided by judges: and this for three reasons. First, because it is easier to find a few wise men competent to frame right laws, than to find the many who would be necessary to judge aright of each single case.—Secondly, because those who make laws consider long beforehand* what laws to make; whereas judgment on each single case has to be pronounced as soon as it arises: and it is easier for man to see what is right, by taking many instances into consideration, than by considering one solitary fact.—Thirdly, because lawgivers judge in the abstract and of future events; whereas those who sit in judgment judge of things present, towards which they are affected by love, hatred, or some kind of cupidity; wherefore their judgment is perverted.

Since then the animated justice of the judge is not found in every man, and since it can be deflected, therefore it was necessary, whenever possible, for the law to determine how to judge, and for very few matters to be left to the decision of men.

Reply Obj. 3. Certain individual facts which cannot be covered by the law *have necessarily to be committed to judges,* as the Philosopher says in the same passage: for instance, *concerning something that has happened or not happened,* and the like.

Second Article

WHETHER EVERY HUMAN LAW IS DERIVED FROM THE NATURAL LAW?

We Proceed Thus to the Second Article:—

Objection 1. It would seem that not every human law is derived from the natural law. For the Philosopher says (*Ethic.* v. 7) that *the legal just is that which originally was a matter of indifference.* But those things which arise from the natural law are not matters of indifference. Therefore the enactments of human laws are not all derived from the natural law.

Obj. 2. Further, positive law is contrasted with natural law, as stated by Isidore (*Etym.* v. 4) and the Philosopher (*Ethic.* v, *loc. cit.*). But those things which flow as conclusion from the general principles of the natural law belong to the natural law, as stated above (Q. 94, A. 4). Therefore that which is established by human law does not belong to the natural law.

Obj. 3. Further, the law of nature is the same for all; since the Philosopher says (*Ethic.* v. 7) that *the natural just is that which is equally valid everywhere.* If therefore human laws were derived from the natural law, it would follow that they too are the same for all: which is clearly false.

Obj. 4. Further, it is possible to give a reason for things which are derived from the natural law. But *it is not possible to give the reason for all the legal enactments of the lawgivers,* as the jurist says. Therefore not all human laws are derived from the natural law.

On the contrary, Tully says (*Rhetor.* ii): *Things which emanated from nature and were approved by custom, were sanctioned by fear and reverence for the laws.*

I answer that, As Augustine says (*De Lib. Arb.* i. 5), *that which is not just seems to be no law at all: wherefore the force of a law depends on the extent of its justice. Now in human affairs a thing is said to be just, from being right, according to the rule of reason. But the first rule of reason is the law of nature, as is clear from what has been stated* above (Q. 91, A. 2 *ad* 2). Consequently every human law has just so much of the nature of law, as it is derived from the law of nature. But if in any point it deflects from the law of nature, it is no longer a law but a perversion of law.

But it must be noted that something may be derived from the natural law in two ways: first, as a conclusion from premises, secondly, by way of determination of certain generalities. The first way is like to that by which, in sciences, demonstrated conclusions are drawn from the principles: while the second mode is likened to that whereby, in the arts, general forms are particularized as to details: thus the craftsman needs to determine the general form of a house to some particular shape. Some things are therefore derived from the general principles of the natural law, by way of conclusions; *e.g.,* that *one must not kill* may be derived as a conclusion from the principle that one should do harm to no man: while some are derived therefrom by way of determination; *e.g.,* the law of nature has it that the evil-doer should be punished; but that he be punished in this or that way, is a determination of the law of nature.

Accordingly both modes of derivation are found in the human law. But those things which are derived in the first way, are contained in human law not as emanating therefrom exclusively, but have some force from the natural law also. But those things which are derived in the second way, have no other force than that of human law.

Reply Obj. 1. The Philosopher is speaking of those enactments which are by way of determination or specification of the precepts of the natural law.

Reply Obj. 2. This argument avails for those things that are derived from the natural law, by way of conclusions.

Reply Obj. 3. The general principles of the natural law cannot be applied to all men in the same way on account of the great variety of human affairs: and hence arises the diversity of positive laws among various people.

Reply Obj. 4. These words of the Jurist are to be understood as referring to decisions of rulers in determining particular points of the natural law: on which determinations the judgment of expert and prudent men is based as on its principles; in so far, to wit, as they see at once what is the best thing to decide.

Hence the Philosopher says (*Ethic.* vi. 11) that in such matters, *we ought to pay as much attention to the undemonstrated sayings and opinions of persons who surpass us in experience, age and prudence, as to their demonstrations.*

*   *   *

QUESTION 96: OF THE POWER OF HUMAN LAW

*   *   *

Second Article

WHETHER IT BELONGS TO THE HUMAN LAW TO REPRESS ALL VICES?

We Proceed Thus to the Second Article:—

Objection 1. It would seem that it belongs to human law to repress all vices. For Isidore says (*Etym.* v. 20) that *laws were made in order that, in fear thereof, man's audacity might be held in check.* But it would not be held in check sufficiently, unless all evils were repressed by law. Therefore human law should repress all evils.

Obj. 2. Further, the intention of the lawgiver is to make the citizens virtuous. But a man cannot be virtuous unless he forbear from all kinds of vice. Therefore it belongs to human law to repress all vices.

Obj. 3. Further, human law is derived from the natural law, as stated above (Q. 95, A. 2). But all vices are contrary to the law of nature. Therefore human law should repress all vices.

On the contrary, We read in *De Lib. Arb.* i. 5: *It seems to me that the law which is written for the governing of the people rightly permits these things, and that Divine providence punishes them.* But Divine providence punishes nothing but vices. Therefore human law rightly allows some vices, by not repressing them.

I answer that, As stated above (Q. 90, AA. I, 2), law is framed as a rule or measure of human acts. Now a measure should be homogeneous with that which it measures, as stated in *Metaph.* x, text. 3, 4, since different things are measured by different measures. Wherefore laws imposed on men should also be in keeping with their condition, for, as Isidore says (*Etym.* v. 21), law should be *possible both according to nature, and according to the customs of the country.* Now possibility or faculty of action is due to an interior habit or disposition: since the same thing is not possible to one who has not a virtuous habit, as is possible to one who has. Thus the same is not possible to a child as to a full-grown man: for which reason the law for children is not the same as for adults, since many things are permitted to children, which in an adult are punished by law or at any rate are open to blame. In like manner many things are permissible to men not perfect in virtue, which would be intolerable in a virtuous man.

Now human law is framed for a number of human beings, the majority of whom are not perfect in virtue. Wherefore human laws do not forbid all vices, from which the virtuous abstain, but only the more grievous vices, from which it is possible for the majority to abstain; and chiefly those that are to the hurt of others, without the prohibition of which human society could not be maintained: thus human law prohibits murder, theft and such like.

Reply Obj. 1. Audacity seems to refer to the assailing of others. Consequently it belongs to those sins chiefly whereby one's neighbor is injured: and these sins are forbidden by human law, as stated.

Reply Obj. 2. The purpose of human law is to lead men to virtue, not suddenly, but gradually. Wherefore it does not lay upon the multitude of imperfect men the burdens of those who are already virtuous, viz., that they should abstain from all evil. Otherwise these imperfect ones, being unable to bear such precepts, would break out into yet greater evils: thus it is written (Prov. xxx. 33): *He that violently bloweth his nose, bringeth out blood;* and (Matth. ix. 17) that if *new wine,* i.e., precepts of a perfect life, *is put into old bottles,* i.e., into imperfect men, *the bottles break, and the wine runneth out,* i.e., the precepts are despised, and those men, from contempt, break out into evils worse still.

Reply Obj. 3. The natural law is a participation in us of the eternal law: while human law falls short of the eternal law. Now Augustine says (*De Lib. Arb.* i. 5): *The law which is framed for the government of states, allows and leaves unpunished many things that are punished by Divine providence. Nor, if this law does not attempt to do everything, is this a reason why it should be blamed for what it does.* Wherefore, too, human law does not prohibit everything that is forbidden by the natural law.

*   *   *

SECOND PART OF THE SECOND PART (II–II)

TREATISE ON WAR

* * *

QUESTION 40: OF WAR

* * *

First Article

WHETHER IT IS ALWAYS SINFUL TO WAGE WAR?

We Proceed Thus to the First Article:—

Objection 1. It would seem that it is always sinful to wage war. Because punishment is not inflicted except for sin. Now those who wage war are threatened by Our Lord with punishment, according to Matth. xxvi. 52: *All that take the sword shall perish with the sword.* Therefore all wars are unlawful.

These statues from niches in the west facade of Reims Cathedral show a monk giving communion to a faithful knight. In the *Summa Theologica*, St. Thomas Aquinas argues that war is justified for a Christian if (1) the war is declared by a sovereign, (2) there is a just cause for the war, and (3) the warriors have a proper intention for fighting. Thomas's just war theory continues to be influential today. (*Art Resource*)

Obj. 2. Further, whatever is contrary to a Divine precept is a sin. But war is contrary to a Divine precept, for it is written (Matth. v. 39): *But I say to you not to resist evil;* and (Rom. xii. 19): *Not revenging yourselves, my dearly beloved, but give place unto wrath.* Therefore war is always sinful.

Obj. 3. Further, nothing, except sin, is contrary to an act of virtue. But war is contrary to peace. Therefore war is always a sin.

Obj. 4. Further, the exercise of a lawful thing is itself lawful, as is evident in scientific exercises. But warlike exercises which take place in tournaments are forbidden by the Church, since those who are slain in these trials are deprived of ecclesiastical burial. Therefore it seems that war is a sin in itself.

On the contrary, Augustine says in a sermon on the son of the centurion [*Ep. ad Marcel.,* cxxxviii.]: *If the Christian Religion forbade war altogether, those who sought salutary advice in the Gospel would rather have been counselled to cast aside their arms, and to give up soldiering altogether. On the contrary, they were told: "Do violence to no man; . . . and be content with your pay."* [Luke iii. 14] *If he commanded them to be content with their pay, he did not forbid soldiering.*

I answer that, In order for a war to be just, three things are necessary. First, the authority of the sovereign by whose command the war is to be waged. For it is not the business of a private individual to declare war, because he can seek for redress of his rights from the tribunal of his superior. Moreover it is not the business of a private individual to summon together the people, which has to be done in wartime. And as the care of the common weal is committed to those who are in authority, it is their business to watch over the common weal of the city, kingdom or province subject to them. And just as it is lawful for them to have recourse to the sword in defending that common weal against internal disturbances, when they punish evil-doers, according to the words of the Apostle (Rom. xiii. 4): *He beareth not the sword in vain: for he is God's minister, an avenger to execute wrath upon him that doth evil;* so too, it is their business to have recourse to the sword of war in defending the common weal against external enemies. Hence it is said to those who are in authority (Ps. lxxxi. 4): *Rescue the poor: and deliver the needy out of the hand of the sinner;* and for this reason Augustine says (*Contra Faust.* xxii. 75): *The natural order conducive to peace among mortals demands that the power to declare and counsel war should be in the hands of those who hold the supreme authority.*

Secondly, a just cause is required, namely that those who are attacked, should be attacked because they deserve it on account of some fault. Wherefore Augustine says (QQ. in Hept., qu. x, super Jos.): *A just war is wont to be described as one that avenges wrongs, when a nation or state has to be punished, for refusing to make amends for the wrongs inflicted by its subjects, or to restore what it has seized unjustly.*

Thirdly, it is necessary that the belligerents should have a rightful intention, so that they intend the advancement of good, or the avoidance of evil. Hence Augustine says *De Verb. Dom: True religion looks upon as peaceful those wars that are waged not for motives of aggrandizement or cruelty, but with the object of securing peace, of punishing evil-doers, and of uplifting the good.* For it may happen that the war is declared by the legitimate authority, and for a just cause, and yet be rendered unlawful through a wicked intention. Hence Augustine says (*Contra Faust.* xxii. 74): *The passion for inflicting harm, the cruel thirst for vengeance, an unpacific and relentless spirit, the fever of revolt, the lust of power, and such like things, all these are rightly condemned in war.*

Reply Obj. 1. As Augustine says (*Contra Faust.* xxii. 70): *To take the sword is to arm oneself in order to take the life of anyone, without the command or permission of superior or lawful authority.* On the other hand, to have recourse to the sword (as a private person) by the authority of the sovereign or judge, or (as a public person) through zeal for justice, and by the authority, so to speak, of God, is not to *take the sword,* but to use it as commissioned by another, wherefore it does not deserve punishment. And yet even those who make sinful use of the sword are not always slain with the sword, yet they always perish with their own sword, because, unless they repent, they are punished eternally for their sinful use of the sword.

Reply Obj. 2. Such like precepts, as Augustine observes (*De Serm. Dom. in Monte* i. 19), should always be borne in readiness of mind, so that we be ready to obey them, and, if necessary, to refrain from resistance or self-defense. Nevertheless it is necessary sometimes for a man to act otherwise for the common good, or for the good of those with whom he is fighting. Hence Augustine says (*Ep. ad Marcellin.* cxxxviii): *Those whom we have to punish with a kindly severity, it is necessary to handle in many ways against their will. For when we are stripping a man of the lawlessness of sin, it is good for him to be vanquished, since nothing is more hopeless than the happiness of sinners, whence arises a guilty impunity, and an evil will, like an internal enemy.*

Reply Obj. 3. Those who wage war justly aim at peace, and so they are not opposed to peace, except to the evil peace, which Our Lord *came not to send upon earth* (Matth. x. 34). Hence Augustine says (*Ep. ad Bonif.* clxxxix): *We do not seek peace in order to be at war, but we go to war that we may have peace. Be peaceful, therefore, in warring, so that you may vanquish those whom you war against, and bring them to the prosperity of peace.*

Reply Obj. 4. Manly exercises in warlike feats of arms are not all forbidden, but those which are inordinate and perilous, and end in slaying or plundering. In olden times warlike exercises presented no such danger, and hence they were called *exercises of arms* or bloodless wars, as Jerome states in an epistle.

THE PRINCIPLES OF NATURE

Chapter 1. Being in Potency and Being in Act

(1) There are certain things which can exist but do not, and others which do exist. Those which can be are said to exist *in potency*, whereas those which are, are said to exist in act. Now there are two ways of existing in act: to exist *essentially* or *substantially* (as when a man exists), and to exist *accidentally* (as when a man exists as white). The former is to exist without qualification, whereas the latter is to exist in a qualified way.

St. Thomas Aquinas, *Selected Writings of St. Thomas Aquinas*, translated by Robert P. Goodwin (New York: Macmillan/Library of the Liberal Arts, 1965).

(2) Something is in potency to both the ways of existing in act. Sperm and menstrual blood, for example, are in potency to being man, whereas a man is in potency to being white. Both that which is in potency to exist substantially, and that which is in potency to exist accidently, can, like the sperm and the man, respectively, be called matter. They differ, however, in this: the matter that is in potency to exist substantially is called *matter from which*, whereas the matter that is in potency to exist accidentally is called *matter in which*. Likewise, properly speaking, what is in potency to exist substantially is called *prime matter*, whereas what is in potency to exist accidentally is called a *subject*. Accordingly, accidents are said to be in a subject, but substantial form is not spoken of in this way. Wherefore matter differs from subject, inasmuch as a subject does not have an act of existing from that which accrues to it, but is complete with an act of existing in itself; for example, a man does not have an act of existing from whiteness. But matter has an act of existing from what accrues to it, because of itself it exists incompletely. Hence, simply put, form makes matter exist, whereas an accident does not make a subject exist. The subject, however, makes an accident exist. Occasionally, however, one term is substituted for the other—that is, matter for subject, and vice versa.

(3) Moreover, just as everything in potency can be called matter, so anything from which something exists, either substantially or accidentally, can be called a form as man, since he is potentially white, becomes actually white through whiteness, and the sperm, since it is potentially man, becomes actually man through the soul. Because form makes something exist actually, it is said to be an act. What makes something exist substantially is called *substantial form*, and what makes something exist accidentally is called *accidental form*.

(4) As generation is a movement to form, there are two kinds of generation corresponding to the two kinds of form: *generation simply* corresponds to substantial form, and *qualified generation* corresponds to accidental form. For when a substantial form is introduced, something is said to have come into being without qualification, as we have said. For example, a man comes into being, or a man is generated. When, however, an accidental form is introduced, something is said not to have come into being, but to have become this. For example, when a man becomes white, we do not say that the man comes into being or is generated without qualification, but rather that the man becomes, or is made, white.

(5) There are two kinds of corruption opposed to these two kinds of generation: *corruption simply and qualified corruption*. Generation simply and corruption simply occur only in the genus *substance*, whereas qualified generation and qualified corruption occur in all other genera. Furthermore, as generation is a kind of passage from not-existing to existing, and, conversely, corruption a passage from existing to not-existing, generation does not arise from any nonentity but from a nonentity which is a being in potency. For example, a statue comes from bronze, which is a statue in potency, not in act.

(6) Therefore, three things are required for generation: namely, a being in potency, which is matter; a state of not-existing in act, which is privation; and that through which something comes to be actually, which is form. Thus when a statue is made from bronze, the bronze, which is in potency to the form *statue*, is the matter. The lack of configuration or arrangement is the privation.

(7) The shape from which it gets the name *statue* is the form. This is, however, not a substantial form because the bronze, before the advent of that form, had an act of existing, and its act of existing does not depend upon that shape. It is an accidental form, as are all artificial forms; for art works only on what is already constituted as existing by nature.

CHAPTER 2. MATTER, FORM, AND PRIVATION

(8) Therefore, there are three principles of nature: matter, form, and privation. One of these, form, is that toward which generation moves, whereas the other two lie on the side of that from which generation proceeds. Hence, matter and privation refer to the same subject, but according to different aspects. For the very same thing is both bronze and deprived-of-a-certain-shape before the advent of the form. But it is said to be bronze for one reason, and deprived-of-a-shape for another. Wherefore privation is said to be, not an essential principle, but an accidental one, since it coincides with matter. Thus we say that a physician builds accidentally, for he does not build by virtue of being a physician but because he is a builder; this characteristic resides in the same subject along with his medical skill.

(9) Now accidents are of two kinds: *necessary,* which are not separated from a certain kind of thing, like risibility from man, and *non-necessary,* which are so separated, as is whiteness from man. Accordingly, although privation is an accidental principle, it does not follow that it is unnecessary for generation. For matter is never lacking privation: inasmuch as it is under one form, it is deprived of another, and vice versa. For example, in fire there is the privation of air; in air there is the privation of fire.*

(10) Although generation is from not-existing, one should realize that we maintain, not that negation is a principle, but rather that privation is, for negation does not determine a subject for itself. Lack of sight can be attributed even to nonentities, for example, "Chimeras do not see." Likewise, we can attribute it to beings that are not meant to see, such as a stone. But privation is attributed only to a determinate subject in which the missing perfection is meant to be. For example, blindness is attributed only to those things that were born to see.

(11) Moreover, it is in accordance with the fact that generation does not arise from non-being simply, but from non-being which is in some subject—and not just any subject, but a determined one—that privation is said to be a principle. For not everything which is not-burning will burn, but only those things that are apt to burn. Privation differs, however, from the other principles, which are principles both in being and in becoming. For something to become a statue, bronze and finally the figure of a statue are necessary. Moreover, when the statue does actually exist, both of these exist. Privation, however, is a principle in becoming but not in being, because while the statue is coming into being the statue cannot exist. For if it did already exist, the statue could not come into being, since what comes to be exists only successively, as do time and change. But when the statue exists, no privation of *statue* is present in it. Just as affirmation and negation cannot exist simultaneously, so neither can privation and the form of which it is the privation. Accordingly, privation is an accidental principle, as has previously been explained; the other two are essential principles.

---

*Aquinas is using here a very ancient theory of "chemical elements." He elaborates upon his notion of element below, paragraphs 21 and 22. The theory has a long history, dating back at least to the pre-Socratic philosopher Empedocles (ca. 484–424 B.C.), who had claimed that the things of experience are composed in various ways of four opposed and irreducible elements: fire, water, earth, and air. Many subsequent Greek thinkers, including Aristotle, maintained this division, and Aquinas continues in this tradition. Modern chemistry continues this tradition in a modified way, at least in the sense that it, too, sees all physical realities to be made up of, and reducible to, approximately one hundred elements, which are chemically irreducible to one another.

(12) From what has been said it is evident that matter differs by definition from form and privation. For matter is that in which both form and privation are understood, as one shape and the lack of another shape are understood in bronze. Indeed, sometimes matter is given a name which includes a privation and sometimes not. So bronze, when it is the matter of a statue, does not connote a privation, because in saying "bronze" we do not include in our comprehension the lack of an arrangement or shape. But flour, since it is matter with respect to bread, includes the privation of the form of bread, because in saying "flour," one signifies that lack of disposition or ordination which is opposed to the form of bread. And so, because in generation the matter or subject remains but the privation and the composite of matter and privation do not, therefore matter that does not include privation is permanent, whereas matter that does is transient.

(13) We should realize, however, that some matter includes a form, like the bronze which is the matter of a statue. Bronze itself is a composite of matter and form. Accordingly, since it possesses matter, bronze cannot be called prime matter. Only that matter which is understood without any form or privation, but which is subject to form and privation, is called prime matter, inasmuch as there is no other matter prior to it. It is also called "hyle."*

(14) Since all cognition and every definition are through form, it follows that prime matter can be known or defined, not of itself, but through the composite. Accordingly, we know prime matter as that which is related to all forms and privations, as bronze is related to the form of a statue and to the privation of some shape. It is called *primary* without qualification. Something can be called "prime matter" with respect to a certain genus, as water is prime matter to the genus of liquids. But this is not primary without qualification, because it is a composite of matter and form; hence there is a matter prior to it.

(15) We should note that prime matter, and even form, are neither generated nor corrupted, inasmuch as every generation is from something to something. That from which generation arises is matter; that to which it proceeds is form. If, therefore, matter and form were generated, there would have to be a matter of matter and a form of form *ad infinitum*. Hence, properly speaking, only composites are generated.

(16) We should note also that prime matter is said to be numerically one in all things. Something can be said to be numerically one in two ways. First, it can be numerically one if it has one numerically determinate form, like Socrates. Prime matter is not said to be numerically one in this way, since in itself it does not have any form. Something can be numerically one in another way, that is, if it lacks the dispositions through which numerical differences occur. Prime matter is said to be numerically one in this way, since it is understood without dispositions by which numerical differences occur.

(17) Finally we note that although prime matter does not in itself have any form or privation, as in the nature of bronze there is neither shape nor the lack of shape, nevertheless prime matter never exists without form and privation. Sometimes it is under one form, sometimes it is under another. But matter cannot exist of itself, since of itself it possesses no form. It does not exist in act, since existing in act occurs only through a form, but exists only in potency. Hence whatever exists in act cannot be called prime matter.

---

*The term "hyle" is a transliteration of a Greek word meaning "matter" or "material."

CHAPTER 3. CAUSES, PRINCIPLES, AND ELEMENTS

(18) From what has been said, it is evident that there are three principles of nature: matter, form, and privation. These alone, however, are not sufficient for generation. For what is in potency cannot reduce itself to act. Bronze, which is in potency to being a statue, does not make itself be a statue, but needs an agent which draws out the form of statue from potency to act. For form cannot draw itself out from potency to act. Here I am speaking of the form of the thing generated, which we have already said is the term of generation. This form exists only when a change is completed, but the agent itself exists only during the becoming—that is, while the thing is coming to be. There is required, therefore, besides form and matter, another principle which acts. This is called the *efficient* or *moving cause,* or agent, or that from which the motion begins.

(19) Because, as Aristotle states in Book Two of the *Metaphysics,* everything that acts, acts only when intending something, a fourth principle is required—that is, what is intended by the agent. This is called the *end.* And although every agent, be it natural or voluntary, intends an end, we should realize nevertheless that it does not follow that every agent knows or deliberates about the end. Knowing the end is necessary for those whose actions are not determined, but for whom opposed goals are possible, as is the case for voluntary agents. These, therefore, must know the end, through which knowledge they determine their actions. However, the actions of natural agents are determined; hence, there is no necessity for their choosing the means to their end. Avicenna offers the example of the cithara* player, who need not deliberate as to which notes form a chord by striking each individually, since they are predetermined. If the player did deliberate, there would be a delay between the notes, producing an arpeggio. Furthermore, deliberation is especially apparent in the voluntary agent, as opposed to the natural agent. So an even stronger argument can be made if one sees that if a voluntary agent (whose deliberation is especially evident) does not always deliberate, then, certainly, neither does the natural agent. Therefore, it is possible for a natural agent to intend an end without deliberating about it. To intend in this way is nothing more than to have a natural inclination toward something.

(20) From what has been said it is evident that there are four causes, namely, material, efficient, formal, and final. Moreover, although "principle" and "cause" are said quasi-interchangeably, as is maintained in Book Five of the *Metaphysics,* nevertheless, Aristotle in his *Physics* contends that there are four causes and three principles. Furthermore, he holds that causes are both extrinsic and intrinsic. Matter and form are said to be intrinsic to a thing inasmuch as they are constitutive parts of a thing, whereas the efficient and the final causes are called extrinsic, since they are external to the thing. But he accepts only intrinsic causes as principles. Privation is not included among the causes, for, as has been said, it is an accidental principle. When we speak of four causes, therefore, we mean essential causes. Accidental causes, however, are reduced to essential ones, since everything that is accidental is reduced to that which is essential.

(21) But although Aristotle contends in Book One of the *Physics* that principles are intrinsic causes, nevertheless, as he states in Book Eleven of the *Metaphysics,* principle is properly said to be an extrinsic cause, whereas those causes which are parts of

---

*An ancient musical instrument resembling a lyre, and a precursor of the zither.

a thing—that is, the intrinsic causes—are called *elements*. However, both can be said to be causes, although sometimes one is taken for the other. For every cause can be said to be a principle, and every principle a cause. But cause appears to connote something more than what is commonly said to be a principle, inasmuch as anything that is prior, whether or not something else follows from it, can be said to be a principle. An artisan is called the principle of a knife, for example, because a knife comes into being as a result of his activity. But when something is changed from black to white, black is said to be the principle of that motion, just as, universally, anything from which change commences is called a principle. Black, however, is not that from which the being of white follows. Something prior is said to be a cause only when the existence of what is posterior follows from it. Hence, a cause is said to be that from whose existing another follows. Accordingly, what is prior by way of being that from which motion starts cannot be called an essential cause, even if it is called a principle. This is the reason for including privation among principles, but not among causes. A privation is that from which generation begins. It can, however, be called an accidental cause, inasmuch as it coincides with matter, as was explained above.

(22) *Element* is predicated properly only of those causes which enter into the composition of a thing, and which are properly material; every material cause, moreover, is not properly said to be an element but only that one which is involved in a thing's primary composition. Thus we do not speak of limbs as elements of man, because his limbs are composed of other things. We do claim, however, that earth and water are elements; for these are not composed of other bodies, rather it is from these that the first composition of natural bodies results. Hence Aristotle, in Book Five of his *Metaphysics*, says that an element is "an immanent, specifically irreducible entity of which a thing is primarily composed." The explanation of the phrase, "of which a thing is primarily composed" is clear from what we have already said. The word "immanent" is used to differentiate an element from that other kind of matter which is totally destroyed by generation, like the bread which is the matter of blood. Blood is generated only if bread is destroyed. Bread does not remain in blood, and therefore it cannot be said to be an element of blood. But elements must remain in some way, since they are not entirely destroyed, as is stated in the book *On Generation*. The phrase "specifically irreducible" differentiates the elements from those materials having parts diverse in form—that is, in species—like a hand, whose parts are flesh and bone, which are specifically different. But an element is not divided into specifically diverse parts; any part of the element water, for example, is water. Nor is it necessary for an element to be undivided quantitatively in order to be an element. It suffices that it not be divided specifically. If it is not divided in any way, it is also called an element, as letters are said to be elements of words. From all that we have said it is clear, therefore, that a principle is in some way more than a cause, and a cause more than an element. This is, indeed, what the Commentator [Averroës] contends in his comment on the fifth book of the *Metaphysics*.

CHAPTER 4. THE RELATIONSHIPS BETWEEN CAUSES

(23) Having seen that there are four kinds of cause, it is also necessary to see that it is not impossible for the same thing to have several causes, like a statue, which has both bronze and an artisan as causes. The artisan is the efficient cause, and the bronze the material one. Nor is it impossible for the same thing to be the cause of contraries,

as the pilot is the cause of both the safety and the sinking of his ship. He is the cause of the latter by his absence, and of the former by his presence.

(24) It should be understood also that it is possible for the same thing to be a cause and to be caused, with respect to the same thing but in different ways. For example, taking a walk is the efficient cause of health, while health is the final cause of taking a walk, inasmuch as taking a walk is sometimes done for the sake of health. Likewise, the body is the matter of the soul, and the soul is the form of the body. The efficient cause is said to be a cause with respect to the end, since the end does not exist in act unless the agent acts; but the end is said to be the cause of the efficient cause, since the latter does not operate except through the intention of an end. Hence, an efficient cause is the cause of that which is the end, as in the example of taking a walk for one's health. It does not, however, make the end be an end, and therefore it is not the cause of the causality of the end—that is, it does not make the end be a final cause. A physician, for example, produces actual health, but he does not establish health as an end. Moreover, the end does not cause that which is the efficient cause, rather, it is a cause of the efficient cause's being an efficient cause. For health—and I mean the health resulting from the physician's ministrations—does not make a physician be a physician; it causes him to be an efficient cause. Hence, the end is the cause of the causality of the efficient cause, for it makes the efficient cause be an efficient cause. Similarly, it makes the matter be matter, and form be form, since matter receives a form only for some end, and a form perfects matter only for an end. Wherefore the end is said to be the cause of causes, inasmuch as it is the cause of the causality of all the causes. Matter is also said to be the cause of a form, inasmuch as a form does not exist except in matter. Similarly, form is the cause of matter, inasmuch as matter does not actually exist except through form. Matter and form are mutually related, as the second book of the *Physics* states. They are related to the composite, as parts are to the whole and as the simple is to the complex.

(25) Every cause, insofar as it is a cause, is naturally prior to what is caused. We should realize, however, that priority can have two forms, as Aristotle says in Book Sixteen of *On Animals*. Accordingly, a thing can be called prior and posterior, and a cause can be called caused, with respect to the same thing. For one thing can be called prior to another in generation and time, or in substance and completeness. Therefore, since the operation of nature proceeds from the imperfect to the perfect and from the incomplete to the complete, the imperfect is prior to the perfect in generation and time, but the perfect is prior to the imperfect in substance. For example, a man can be said to be prior to a boy in substance and completeness, whereas a boy is prior to a man in generation and time. But, although in things generable the imperfect is prior to the perfect, and potency prior to act—considering, in one and the same thing, that what is prior is imperfect rather than perfect, and in potency rather than in act—nevertheless, speaking without qualification, what is in act and perfect must be prior. This follows because what reduces a potency to act is in act, and what perfects the imperfect is itself perfect. Matter, indeed, is prior to form in generation and time, inasmuch as that to which something is added is prior to that which is added. But form is prior to matter in substance and in fully constituted being, because matter has complete existence only through form. Similarly, the efficient cause is prior to the end in generation and time, since the motion to the end comes about by the efficient cause; but the end is prior to the efficient cause as such in substance and completeness, since the action of the efficient cause is completed only through the end. Therefore, the material and the efficient causes are prior by way of generation, whereas form and end are prior by way of perfection.

(26) It should be noted that necessity is of two kinds: *absolute* and *conditional*. Necessity is indeed absolute when it proceeds from causes which are prior by way of generation, that is, from the material and efficient causes. For example, the necessity of death stems from matter—that is, from the disposition of composing contraries; therefore it is said to be absolute because there is no impediment to it. This is also called the necessity of matter. However, conditional necessity proceeds from causes posterior in generation, that is, from form and end. Accordingly, we say that conception must take place if a man is to be generated. This necessity is said to be conditional, because it is not necessary without qualification for some particular woman to conceive. However, conception is necessary under this condition, namely, if a man is to be generated. This is called the necessity of the end.

(27) We should also realize that three of the causes—form, end, and efficient cause—can coincide. The generation of fire offers a clear example of this. Fire generates fire; therefore fire is an efficient cause, insofar as it generates. Fire is a form, insofar as it makes that which formerly was in potency be in act. Finally, fire is an end, insofar as it is intended by the agent and insofar as the operation of the agent is terminated in it. There are, however, two kinds of ends, namely, the end of the generation process and the end of the thing generated. Both of these ends are evident in producing a knife. The form *knife* is the end of the generating process; but cutting, which is the knife's operation, is the end of the thing generated—that is, the knife.

(28) Sometimes the end of the generating process coincides with the two other above-mentioned causes: form and efficient cause. This occurs when generation proceeds from one thing to another thing that is similar in species to the first, as when a man generates a man, or an olive tree an olive tree. It is not possible, however, for the end of the thing generated to coincide with the form and the efficient cause; yet we should realize that the end and the form are numerically identical, inasmuch as the form of the thing generated and the end of the generation are numerically the same. The end of the generating process and the efficient cause coincide in species, but not in number. For it is impossible for the maker and the thing made to be the same in number; but they can be the same in species. For example, when a man generates a man, the man generating and the man generated are diverse in number, but the same in species.

(29) Matter does not coincide with any of the other causes, since, by reason of the fact that it is being in potency, matter is by nature imperfect. The other causes, however, since they are in act, have the nature of something perfect. The perfect and the imperfect do not coincide.

CHAPTER 5. OTHER DIVISIONS OF THE CAUSES

(30) Wherefore, having seen that there are four causes, namely, efficient, material, formal, and final, we should also realize that each of these causes can be divided in many ways. There exist what are called *prior* and *posterior* causes. For example, both the physician's art and the physician himself are causes of health, but the art is a prior cause and the physician a posterior one. The same division is true of the formal cause and the other causes. Note also that we should always reduce a question to the first cause. If we were to ask, "Why is the man healthy?" we would answer, "Because the physician healed him." Continuing, we would ask, "But by what means did the physician heal?"—"Through the art of healing that he possesses."

(31) Moreover, we must understand that *proximate cause* means the same as *posterior cause*, and *remote cause* the same as *prior cause*. Accordingly, these two divisions of causes—prior and posterior, and remote and proximate—signify the same thing. Furthermore, we should observe that the more universal cause is always called the remote cause, while the more particular cause is called the proximate cause. For example, the proximate form of man is his definition, that is, *rational mortal animal;* but animal is more remote, and substance even further removed. For all superior things are forms of inferior ones. Similarly, the proximate matter of a statue is bronze, while the remote matter is metal, and the more remote is body.

(32) There is likewise another division of causes: into *essential* and *accidental* causes. A cause is called essential when it causes something by reason of its being what it is, as, for example, the builder is the cause of a house, and the wood is the matter of a bench. A cause is called accidental when it happens to coincide with an essential cause. This may be illustrated by a grammarian who builds something. The grammarian is said to be an accidental cause of a building, not insofar as he is a grammarian, but insofar as being a grammarian is accidental to building. The same is true of the other causes.

(33) In addition, certain causes are *simple,* and others *composite*. A cause is called simple when it alone is said to be the cause, be it essential (as when we say that the builder is the cause of the house) or accidental (as when we say that the physician is the cause of the house). However, we would be speaking of a composite cause when both are called the cause, as when we say that the builder-physician is the cause of the house. A simple cause can also be defined, according to Avicenna, as that which causes without being united with another, like bronze which causes the statue without the addition of any other matter. Further illustrations might be the physician who produces health, or the fire that warms. A cause is called composite when many things must unite into being a cause, as not one man, but many, are the cause of the motion of a ship, and not one stone, but many are the matter of the house.

(34) In addition, certain causes are *actual,* and others *potential*. A cause is actual when it is actually causing the thing, like a builder when he builds, or the bronze from which a statue is being made. A potential cause is one which, although not actually causing the thing, nevertheless can cause something, like a builder when he is not building. It should be understood in speaking of actual causes that what causes and what is caused must exist simultaneously, such that if the one exists, the other does also. For if there is an actual builder, he must be building, and if actual building is going on, the builder must be a builder in act. This is not necessary, however, in those causes which are causes only in potency.

(35) Moreover, we should realize that a universal cause is related to a universal effect, while a singular cause is related to a singular effect. For example, the builder is the cause of the house, while *this* builder is the cause of *this* house.

CHAPTER 6. UNITY AND DIVERSITY WITHIN CAUSES

(36) It should be understood that in speaking of the intrinsic principles matter and form, there are a similarity and a difference of principles, according to the similarity and the difference of things resulting from the principles. Certain things are the same numerically, like Socrates (when Socrates is being pointed at) and this man. Others are diverse numerically but the same specifically, like Socrates and Plato, who, although they are the same in human species, nevertheless differ numerically. Further,

certain things are different specifically, but the same generically, like a man and an ass, which are the same in the genus *animal*. Still others are diverse generically but the same only according to an analogy, like substance and quantity, which do not agree in any genus but are similar only analogously; for they are alike only in being. Being is not a genus, however, since it is predicated, not univocally, but analogously.

(37) To grasp this one should understand that something can be predicated of many things in three ways: *univocally, equivocally*, and *analogously*. A univocal predication occurs when something is predicated according to the same name and the same nature, that is, definition, as animal is predicated both of man and of ass. Each is called an animal and each is an animated substance capable of sensation, which is the definition of an animal. Equivocal predication occurs when something is predicated of several things according to the same name but diverse natures, like *dog,* said of a barking animal and of a stellar constellation. These agree in name only, not in definition or signification, for what is signified by a name is the definition, as is stated in the fourth book of the *Metaphysics*. An analogous predication occurs when something is predicated of several things which have diverse natures, but which are related to some one thing, as *healthy* is predicated of an animal body, of urine, and of medicine, although it does not wholly signify the same thing in all. For *healthy* is predicated of urine as of a sign of health; of a body, as of its subject; of medicine, as of its cause. Nevertheless, each of these is related to the one end, health.

(38) Sometimes things which are similar analogously—that is, through a proportion, a comparison, or an agreement—are such by being related to one end. The example above is an instance of this. At other times things are analogous by being related to one agent. For example, *physician* is predicated of one who heals through his training; of one who heals without training, like a midwife; and even of the instruments used. But it is predicated of all of them in relation to one agency, which in this case is the healing art. At still other times many things are similar analogously by attribution to one subject, as *being,* is said of substance, quantity, quality, and the other predicaments. Quantity and the others are called being, but not for the same reason that substance is. All the others are called being inasmuch as they are related to substance, which indeed is their subject. Therefore, *being* is said first of substance and only secondarily of the others. Consequently, being is not the genus of substance and quantity, because no genus is predicated of some of its species first, and of others secondarily. Being is predicated analogously; and this is what we meant when we claimed that substance and quantity differ generically but are analogously the same.

(39) Therefore, of those things which are numerically the same, both the matter and the form are numerically the same, as [both matter and form] of Tullius and of Cicero. Of those which are specifically the same but numerically diverse, the matter and the form are not numerically the same, but are specifically the same, as [those] of Socrates and of Plato. Similarly, of those things which are generically the same, their principles are generically the same, like the soul and the body of an ass and of a horse, which differ specifically but are the same generically. Likewise, of those things which are similar only in an analogous way, their principles are only analogously or proportionately similar. For matter and form and privation, or even potency and act, are principles of substance and of the other genera. Nevertheless, the matter of a substance and that of quantity, and likewise the form and the privation, differ generically, but agree only according to a proportion, which consists in this: just as the matter of a substance is related to the substance in the nature of matter, so too is the matter of quantity related to quantity. Accordingly, just as substance is the cause of all the other things, so the principles of substance are the principles of all the others.

ON BEING AND ESSENCE

Preface

A small error in the beginning of something is a great one at the end, as the Philosopher claims in the first book of his *On the Heavens*. Moreover, being and essence are what the intellect first conceives, as Avicenna maintains in the first book of his *Metaphysics*. Hence we ought to state what the terms "essence" and "being" signify, how they are found in diverse things, and, finally, how they are related to logical intentions, namely, genus, species, and difference. We proceed in this way in order to avoid the errors which follow from being ignorant of *being* and *essence,* and to reveal their difficulty.

Chapter 1

Since a knowledge of simple things must be acquired from those that are complex, and since a knowledge of prior things must be acquired from those that are posterior—so that beginning with easier matters a discipline might more suitably proceed—we must, therefore, begin with the meaning of *being* and then take up the meaning of *essence*.

As the Philosopher states in the fifth book of the *Metaphysics,* it must be understood that *being through itself* is used in two ways. In one way it is divided into the ten genera. In another way it signifies the truth of propositions. The difference between these two is that, according to the latter way, *being* can be attributed to anything concerning which an affirmative proposition can be formed, even if it posits nothing in reality. In this way even privations and negations are called beings; for we say that an affirmation *is* opposed to a negation, and that blindness *is* in the eye. But in the former way, *being* can be said only of something which exists in reality. Accordingly, in the first way, blindness and things of this kind are not beings. Therefore, the term "essence" is not derived from *being* said in the second way, for, in this way, some things are said to be beings which do not have an essence, as is evident in privations. *Essence,* however, is derived from being said in the first way. Hence the Commentator, in the same place, says that *being* used in the first way signifies the essence of a thing. As we have noted, because *being* used in this way is divided into ten genera, *essence* must signify something common to all natures, through which natures diverse beings are placed in diverse genera and species. Thus, for example, humanity is the essence of man, and so with others.

Moreover, that through which something is constituted in its proper genus or species is what is signified by the definition that declares what a thing is. Hence, philosophers have substituted the name "quiddity" for that of "essence." It is what the Philosopher frequently calls "the *what* a thing was to be," that is, that through which something is a certain kind of being. It is called *form,* moreover, inasmuch as "form"

St. Thomas Aquinas, *Selected Writings of St. Thomas Aquinas,* translated by Robert P. Goodwin (New York: Macmillan/Library of the Liberal Arts, 1965).

signifies the certitude of anything, as Avicenna says in the third book of his *Metaphysics*. It is also called by the name "nature," when the latter is understood according to the first of those four senses which Boethius establishes in the book *De Duabus Naturis* is, when *nature* is said of anything that can be grasped intellectually in some way. For a thing is intelligible only through its definition and essence. Accordingly, the Philosopher, in the fifth book of the *Metaphysics,* states that every substance is a nature. Yet the term *nature,* taken in this sense, seems to signify the essence of a thing inasmuch as it possesses an ordering to its proper operations, since no thing is devoid of its proper operation. The term "quiddity," however, is used to signify the definition. But "essence" is used inasmuch as it designates that through which and in which a being has the act of existing.

But because being is asserted absolutely and primarily of substances, and secondarily and in a relative sense of accidents, it follows also that essence is truly and properly in substances, but is in accidents only in a certain way and in a qualified sense. Some substances indeed are simple, and some are composite. Essence is present in both, but it exists more truly and in a nobler way in simple substances, inasmuch as they have their acts of existing in a nobler way. For simple substances are the cause of composite ones—at least the first substance, God, is. However, because the essences of simple substances are more hidden from us, we must therefore begin with essences of composite ones, so that our study might proceed more suitably from easier things.

CHAPTER 2

In composite substances both the matter and the form are known, as soul and body are known in man. Moreover, neither one of them alone can be called essence. For it is clear that the matter alone of a thing is not its essence, because through its essence a thing both is knowable, and is established in a species and a genus. But matter is neither a principle of knowledge nor that by which something is determined in a genus or species. On the contrary, a thing is so determined by that by which it is in act. Nor can it be said that form alone is the essence of a composite substance, although some try to assert this.

From what we have said, it is evident that essence is that which is signified by the definition of a thing. Moreover, the definition of natural substances contains not only form, but also matter; otherwise there would be no difference between definitions in physics and in mathematics. Nor can it be said that matter is put in the definition of a natural substance as something added to its essence, or as a being outside of its essence, because this kind of definition is proper to accidents, which do not have a perfect essence. Hence the definition of an accident must include its subject, which is outside its genus.

Clearly, then, essence includes matter and form. One cannot, however, say that essence signifies a relationship between matter and form, or something superadded to them, since this would necessarily be an accident or something extraneous to the thing; nor would the thing be known through it. None of these features is suitable for an essence. By form, which is the act of matter, matter is made a being in act and an individual substance. Hence what is superadded does not make matter be in act without qualification, but rather makes matter be actually such, just as accidents do. For example, whiteness makes something be actually white. Accordingly, when such a form is acquired, one says that something is generated in a qualified way, not absolutely.

Consequently, in the case of composite substances, the term "essence" signifies the composite of matter and form. This, too, agrees with Boethius' commentary on the *Categories,* where he says that ⟨*ousia*⟩ signifies a composite. ⟨*Ousia*⟩ among the Greeks is the same as *essence* for us, as Boethius himself says in the book *De Duabus Naturis.* Avicenna also says that the quiddity of composite substances is itself a composition of form and matter. The Commentator also says in his comment on the seventh book of the *Metaphysics,* "The nature which species have in things that can be generated is a certain mean, that is, a composite of matter and form." Reason, too, agrees with this, because the existing of a composite substance is not simply the act of the form alone, nor of the matter alone, but of the composite itself. Moreover, essence is that according to which a thing is said to be. Hence it is necessary that an essence, by which a thing is denominated a being, be neither the form alone nor the matter alone, but both, although the form in its own way is the cause of this act of existing. We find the same thing in other things constituted by a plurality of principles, for a thing gets its name, not from one or another of these principles alone, but from what embraces both of them. This is evident in the case of flavors. Sweetness is caused by the action of heat spreading moisture. Although heat, in this way, is the cause of sweetness, nevertheless a body is not called sweet because of heat, but because of flavor, which embraces both heat and moisture.

But, since the principle of individuation is matter, it might seem to follow that essence, which embraces in itself both matter and form simultaneously, is particular only and not universal. From this it would follow that universals would not have a definition, if essence is that which is signified by a definition. Accordingly, it should be known that matter in just any way is not held to be the principle of individuation. Only designated matter is. By *designated matter* I mean matter considered under determinate dimensions. This matter, however, is not included in the definition of a man insofar as he is a man, but would be included in the definition of Socrates, if Socrates had a definition. Undesignated matter, however, is included in the definition of man. We do not include in man's definition this bone or this flesh, but bone and flesh absolutely, which are the undesignated matter of man. Thus, it is evident that the essence of Socrates and the essence of man differ only in that one is designated and the other is not. Hence the Commentator says in his commentary on the seventh book of the *Metaphysics,* "Socrates is nothing other than animality and rationality, which are his quiddity." So also the essence of a genus and of a species differ according as one is designated and the other not, although a different mode of designation is used in regard to this and to the preceding case, because the designation of an individual with respect to his species is through matter determined by dimensions, whereas the designation of a species with respect to its genus is through a constitutive difference taken from the form of the thing.

However, this determination or designation, which is in the species with respect to the genus, is not through something in the essence of the species that is in no way in the essence of the genus. Rather, whatever is in the species is in the genus in an undetermined fashion. For if *animal* were not the whole that is man, but only a part, *animal* would not be predicated of man, since no integral part is predicated of its whole.

How this occurs can be seen if we consider how *body,* understood as part of an animal, differs from *body* understood as a genus. For it is impossible for body to be a genus in the same way as it is an integral part. Therefore this term "body" is understood in many ways. Body is said to be in the genus substance inasmuch as it has a nature such that three dimensions can be designated in it. Indeed, these three designated dimensions themselves are body according as it is in the genus of quantity.

Moreover, it happens in things that what has one perfection may also possess a further perfection. This is evident in man, since he has both a sensitive nature and, beyond that, an intellectual nature. Similarly, to this perfection of having a form such that three dimensions can be designated in it, can be added another perfection, such as life or the like. It is possible, therefore, for this term "body" to signify a certain thing having such a form as there follows precisely and exclusively the capacity of having designated in it three dimensions. Hence from this form no further perfection would follow. If something else were added, it would be outside the meaning of *body* so understood. In this way body is an integral and material part of an animal, because in this way soul will be extrinsic to what is signified by the term "body" and will be an addition to body itself, so that an animal will be constituted from these two, body and soul, as from parts.

The term "body" can also mean a certain something having a form such that three dimensions can be designated in it, whatever that form be, and whether or not a more ultimate perfection can arise from it. Body in this sense is the genus *animal* because nothing is understood in *animal* which is not contained implicitly in body. For the soul is not another form distinct from that through which three dimensions can be designated in that thing. Therefore, when it was said that body is such that it has a form according to which three dimensions can be designated in it, body was understood, no matter what form it possesses, whether it be animality, or rockness, or any other. Thus the form *animal* is contained implicitly in the form *body,* according as body is its genus. Such also is the relationship of animal to man. If "animal" names only a certain thing which has the perfection of sensing or being moved by a principle existing within it known in precision from any other perfection, then the addition of any further perfection would be related to animal as a part, and not as implicitly contained in the notion of animal. In this way *animal* would not be a genus. It is a genus insofar as it signifies anything from whose form can arise sensation and motion, whatever that form be, whether a sensitive soul only, or a sensitive and rational one. Therefore, a *genus* signifies indeterminately that whole which is in the species, for it does not signify matter alone. *Difference* likewise signifies a whole and does not signify the form alone. A definition, too, signifies the whole, as does even the species. They do this, however, in various ways. A genus signifies the whole as a certain determination, designating what is material in the thing, exclusive of the determination proper to the form. Hence genus is derived from matter, although it is not matter. This is evident from the fact that something is said to be a body from its perfection according to which three dimensions can be designated in it. This perfection is related materially to further perfection. On the other hand, a difference signifies the whole as a certain determination taken determinately from the form, without determinate matter being included in its primary notion. This is evident from the usage of "animate," or that which has a soul, for what this is, whether body or something else, is not determined. Accordingly, Avicenna says that genus is not understood in the difference as part of its essence, but only as a being outside its essence, just as a subject is contained in the understanding of properties. Therefore, too, the genus, properly speaking, is not predicated of the difference, as the Philosopher says in the third book of the *Metaphysics* and in the fourth book of the *Topics*, except perhaps in the way a subject is predicated of a property. But the definition or species includes both, namely, determinate matter, designated by the term "genus," and determinate form, designated by the term "difference."

On the basis of what we have just said, it is clear why genus, species, and difference are related proportionately to matter, form, and the composite in nature, although the former are not the same as the latter. The genus is not matter, but is taken from matter and signifies the whole; and the difference is not the form, but is taken from form as signifying the whole. Accordingly we say that a man is a rational animal, but not that he is composed of animal and rational, as we say that a man is composed of body and soul. For man is said to be composed of body and soul after the manner of a third thing that is constituted of two things, and identical with neither of them. For a man is neither a soul nor a body. However, if man is said to be composed in some way of animal and rational, it is not as a third thing from two other things, but as a third notion from two other notions. For the notion *animal* lacks the determination of a special form which expresses the nature of the thing, inasmuch as animal is matter with respect to the ultimate perfection. However, the notion of this difference, rational, consists in the determination of the special form. The notion of species or definition is constituted from these two notions. Therefore, just as the things which compose are not predicated of the thing composed of them, so neither are constitutive notions predicated of the notion constituted from them. For we do not say that a definition is "genus" or difference.

Although "genus" signifies the whole essence of the species, nevertheless it is not necessary that the diverse species in the same genus have the same essence. This is so because the unity of genus proceeds from its very indetermination or indifference. This is not to say, however, that what is signified by "genus" is numerically one nature in diverse species, to which nature some other thing which is the difference is added, determining it as the form determines matter which is numerically one. It is a question, rather, of "genus" signifying a certain form—not, however, this one or that one determinately. The difference expresses this determinately, and it is none other than the one signified indeterminately by the genus. And this is why the Commentator says in the twelfth book of the *Metaphysics* that prime matter is said to be one through the removal of all forms, whereas genus is said to be one through the community of the form signified. It is therefore evident that through the addition of the difference, which thereby removes that indetermination which was the cause of the unity of the genus, essentially diverse species remain.

Now because the nature of the species is, as we have stated, indeterminate with respect to the individual, as is the nature of a genus with respect to the species, it therefore follows that just as a genus, insofar as it is predicated of a species, implies (although indistinctly) in its signification everything determinate in the species, so also the species, as predicated of an individual, must signify (although indistinctly) all that is essentially in the individual. In this way the essence of Socrates is signified by the name "man." Accordingly, *man* is predicated of Socrates. But if the nature of a species is signified in precision from designated matter, which is the principle of individuation, then it will be related to the individual after the manner of a part. In this way the essence of Socrates is signified by the term "humanity." For humanity signifies that whereby man is a man. But designated matter is not that whereby man is a man. Therefore, in no way is designated matter included among those things by which a man is a man. Hence, since humanity includes in its conception only those things by which a man is man, it is clear that designated matter is excluded or precluded from its signification. In addition, since a part is not predicated of the whole, so humanity is predicated of neither man nor Socrates. Accordingly, Avicenna says that the quiddity of a composite is not the composite of which it is the quiddity, even if the quiddity itself is a composite. Hence, although humanity is composite, it is nevertheless not identified with man. Indeed, it must be received in something, which is designated matter.

As has been said, the designation of a species with respect to the genus is through the form, and the designation of an individual with respect to the species is through the matter. Because of this the term signifying that whence the nature of the genus is taken, in precision from the determinate form perfecting the species, must signify the material part of the whole itself, as body is the material part of man. However, the term signifying that whence the nature of the species is taken in precision from designated matter, signifies the formal part.

Therefore, humanity is signified as a certain form, and is said to be the form of the whole—not, however, as something superadded to the essential parts, namely form and matter, as the form house is superadded to its integral parts, but rather as a form which is a whole, that is, a form embracing matter. It is, nevertheless, signified in precision from those things according to which matter is apt to be designated. In this way it is clear that the terms "man" and "humanity" signify the essence *man,* but in diverse ways, as has been said. For the term "man" signifies the essence *man* as a whole, inasmuch as it does not prescind from the designation of matter but contains it implicitly and in an indistinct way, just as genus was said to contain the difference. Accordingly, the term "man" is predicated of individuals. The term "humanity," however, signifies the essence man as a part, since it contains in its signification only what is in man insofar as he is man, and prescinds from all designation of matter. Hence humanity cannot be predicated of individual men. On account of this, the term "essence" is sometimes predicated of a thing, as when it is said that Socrates is an essence, and sometimes it is denied of a thing, as when it is said that the essence of Socrates is not Socrates.

CHAPTER 3

Having seen, therefore, what is signified in composite substances by the term "essence," we should see how this term is related to the notions of genus, species, and difference. Inasmuch as what belongs to the character *genus, species,* or *difference* is predicated of this designated singular, it is impossible for the character *universal,* namely of a genus or species, to belong to an essence according as it is signified after the manner of a part, as by the term "humanity" or "animality." This is why Avicenna says that rationality is not a difference* but the principle of a difference; and by the same token, humanity is not a species, nor is animality a genus. Similarly, it is not possible to say that the character *genus* and *species* is proper to the essence, where essence is a certain thing existing outside of the singulars, as the Platonists proposed; for then the genus and the species would not be predicated of this individual. One cannot say that Socrates is something separated from himself, nor can one say that what is separated aids in the cognition of this singular. Therefore, we are left with saying that the character *genus* or *species* belongs to an essence according as it is signified as the whole, as by the terms "man" or "animal," insofar as it implicitly and indistinctly contains all that is in the individual.

Nature or essence, understood in this sense, can be considered in two ways. One way is according to its own proper character. This is an absolute consideration of nature. In this way nothing is true of it except what is proper to it as such. Hence the attribution to it of anything belonging to others would be false. As an example, *rational* and *animal,* and whatever else is included in man's definition, are proper to man as

---

*The problem to which St. Thomas addresses himself in this chapter is the status in being of species, genus, difference, etc.: What reality does, for example, human nature, as such, have? This is the so-called problem of universals.

man. Neither white nor black, however, nor anything else of this sort which is not in the notion of humanity, belongs to man as man. Accordingly, if the question arises whether the nature so considered can be said to be one or many, neither should be conceded, because each is extrinsic to the notion of humanity, and either can happen to it. For if plurality were included within its notion, the nature *man* could never be one, although it is one insofar as it is in Socrates. Similarly, if unity were included in its notion, then Socrates and Plato would be one and the same, and the nature could not be multiplied in many.

Nature can be considered, however, in another way: according to the act of existing which it has in this or that individual. When so considered, something is predicated of the nature accidentally, in virtue of that in which it exists; it is said, for example, that man is white because Socrates is white. The condition of being white, however, is not proper to man as man.

Now, this nature has two acts of existing: one in singular things, another in the soul. And according to each, accidents follow upon the aforesaid nature. In addition, the nature, in singulars, has many acts of existing according to the diversity of singulars. Yet according to the first consideration, that is, an absolute one, no act of existing is due the nature. For it is false to say that the essence of man, as man, has the act of existing in this singular inasmuch as, if it were proper to man as man to exist in this singular, man would never exist outside it. Similarly, if it pertained to a man as man not to exist in this singular, then man would never exist in this singular. But it is true to say that it is not proper to man as man to exist in this or that singular, or in a soul. It is, therefore, evident that the nature of man considered absolutely abstracts from every act of existing, but in such a way, however, that no act of existing is excluded by way of precision. Now it is this nature so considered which is predicated of all individuals.

Nevertheless, it cannot be said that the character *universal* belongs to nature so understood, because community and unity belong to the character *universal,* whereas neither of these belong to human nature considered absolutely. For if community were included in the notion of man, community would be found whenever humanity was found. But this is false, because in Socrates no community is found. On the contrary, whatever is in him is individuated. Similarly, it cannot be said that the character *genus* or *species* accrues to human nature according as it exists in individuals, because human nature in individuals does not possess such a unity as to be something that is one belonging to all, which the character *universal* demands. It remains, therefore, that the character species accrues to human nature as it exists in the intellect. For human nature itself exists in the intellect in abstraction from all individuating conditions. Thus it has a uniform relation to all individuals outside the soul, inasmuch as it is equally the similitude of all and leads to the cognition of all inasmuch as they are men. And since the nature has such a relationship to all individuals, the intellect forms the notion of species and attributes it to the nature. Hence the Commentator says in the first book of the *De Anima* that it is the intellect which makes universality in things. Avicenna makes the same claim in his *Metaphysics*. Hence, although this nature existing in the intellect has the character *universal* inasmuch as it is compared to things which are outside of the mind, since it is the similitude of all of them, nevertheless, according as it exists in this or that intellect, it is a certain particular species understood by the intellect.

For this reason, the defect in the Commentator's reasoning in the third book of the *De Anima* is evident. He chose to conclude to the unity of an intellect for all men from the universality of the known form. This view is defective because the form is not universal according as it exists in the intellect, but inasmuch as it refers to things as their similitude. So also if there were one corporeal statue representing many men, that image or species of the statue would still be properly singular, since it would exist in this matter. It would, however, have the character *community,* inasmuch as it would be the common representation of many.

Since it belongs to human nature absolutely considered to be predicated of Socrates, and since the character *species* does not belong to it absolutely considered, but is among the accidents which follow upon it according as it exists in the intellect, therefore the term "species" is not predicated of Socrates, as in the sentence, "Socrates is a species." This would necessarily happen if the character *species* were proper to man according as it exists in Socrates, or according to its absolute consideration, that is, as man. For whatever belongs to man as man is predicated of Socrates. To be predicated, however, belongs essentially to genus, since it is posited in the definition of genus. For predication is something which is accomplished by the action of the intellect composing and dividing, and has for its foundation in the real thing itself the unity of those things one of which is said of the other. Hence, the character *predicability* can be included in the nature of this kind of intention, that is, genus, which is similarly accomplished by an act of the intellect. Nonetheless, that to which the intellect attributes the intention *predicability,* composing it with another, is not the intention itself, *genus.* It is rather that to which the intellect attributes the intention *genus,* as the *what* that is signified by this term "animal."

It is evident, therefore, how an essence or nature is related to the character *species,* for the character *species* does not belong to essence or nature considered absolutely, nor is the character *species* one of the accidents which follow upon it according as it exists outside the soul, like whiteness or blackness. The character *species* is included among the accidents which follow upon it according as it exists in the intellect. The characters *genus* and *difference* also belong to nature so considered.

CHAPTER 4

It now remains for us to see the way in which essence is found in separated substances, namely, the soul, the intelligences, and the First Cause.

Although all hold that the first cause is simple, nevertheless certain men try to introduce a composition of form and matter into intelligences and the soul. Avicebron,* the author of the *Fons Vitae,* appears to be the originator of this position. This is contrary to the common views of the philosophers, for they call them substances separated from matter, and prove that they exist without any matter. The strongest argument for this position is from the power of understanding present in these substances. For we see that forms are actually intelligible only insofar as they are separated from matter and material conditions. Nor can they be made actually intelligible except through the power of an intelligent substance according as they are received in this substance, and are effected through it. It is, therefore, necessary that every substance capable of intellectual understanding be completely free of matter such that it have no matter as part of itself, nor be like a form impressed on matter, as material forms are.

Nor can anyone maintain that not all matter impedes intelligibility, but that only corporeal matter does. If this impeding were of the nature of corporeal matter only,

---

*Avicebron or Ibn Gabirol, Solomon ben Judah (ca. 1021–1058), a Spanish Jewish poet and Neoplatonic philosopher.

then matter would have to impede intelligibility because of its corporeal form, since matter is not called corporeal except insofar as it exists under a corporeal form. But this is impossible because, like other forms, even a corporeal form is actually intelligible when abstracted from matter. Hence, in no way whatsoever can there be a composition of form and matter in the soul or in an intelligence such that their essence would be understood in the same way as essence in corporeal substances. There is in them, however, a composition of form and act of existing. Wherefore, in the comment on the ninth proposition in the book *De Causis*,* it is said that an intelligence is something having form and an act of existing. Form is understood there as the simple quiddity or nature itself.

How this can be so is plain enough. Whatever things are related to each other in such a way that one causes the other to be, that thing which has the nature *cause* can have the act of existing without the other thing, but not vice versa. Such is the relation between matter and form, because form gives existence to matter. It is, therefore, impossible for matter to exist without some form, but it is not impossible for some form to exist without matter. For the form, as form, is not dependent upon matter. However, if some forms are found which can exist only in matter, this happens to them because of their distance from the first principle, which is first and pure act. Accordingly, those forms which are nearest to the first principle are forms subsisting of themselves without matter. As has just been said, form, according to every genus of form, may not need matter; and the intelligences are forms of this kind. Hence, it is not necessary that the essences or quiddities of these substances be other than the form itself. In this, therefore, the essences of composite substances and of simple substances differ, since the essence of a composite substance is not the form alone but includes both form and matter, whereas the essence of a simple substance is the form alone.

This accounts for two other differences. One is that the essence of composite substances can be signified as a whole or as a part. This occurs because of the designation of matter as has just been said. Therefore, not in just any way is the essence of a composite thing predicated of the composite thing itself. For it is not possible to say that a man is his quiddity. But the essence of a simple thing, which is its form, cannot be signified except as the whole, since there is nothing in the essence besides the form, as it were to receive the form. Therefore, in whatever way it is taken, the essence of simple substances is predicated of the simple substances. Accordingly, Avicenna says that "the quiddity of simple substances is the simple substance itself," inasmuch as there is nothing else receiving it.

The second difference is that the essences of composite things, inasmuch as they are received in designated matter, are multiplied according to the division of matter. It happens, therefore, that some are the same in species but different in number. But since the essence of simple substances is not received in matter, no such multiplication is possible. Therefore, among these substances there cannot be many individuals of the same species. Rather, there are as many species as there are individuals, as Avicenna expressly states.

Although substances of this kind are simply forms without matter, nonetheless they are not in every way simple, as pure acts are. They do have an admixture of potency, which is evident in the following way. Whatever is extraneous to the concept of

---

Liber de Causis, an anonymous compilation of extracts from the *Elements of Theology* by Proclus (410–485), a synthesizer of Neoplatonic doctrines, especially those of Plotinus (ca. 205–270).

an essence or quiddity is adventitious, and forms a composition with the essence, since no essence can be understood without those things which are its parts. On the other hand, every essence or quiddity can be understood without its act of existing being understood. I can understand what a man or phoenix* is, and yet not know whether or not it exists in the nature of things. Therefore, it is evident that the act of existing is other than essence or quiddity. This is true, unless, perhaps, there is something whose quiddity is its very act of existing. This thing would have to be unique and primary, since it would be impossible for anything to be multiplied except by the addition of some difference, as the nature *genus* is multiplied into species; or by a form being received in diverse matters, as the nature *species* is multiplied in different individuals; or by one being absolute, and the other being received in something. For example, if there were a certain "separated" heat it would be distinct, in virtue of its very separation from the heat which is not separated. If, however, something is posited which is simply its own act of existing such that it would be subsistent existence itself, this existence cannot receive the addition of a difference, because then it would not be simply an act of existing, but an act of existing plus this certain form. Even less would it receive the addition of matter, because then it would not be subsistent existence, but material existence. Hence, there remains only one such thing that is its own act of existing. Accordingly, in anything other than it, the act of existing must necessarily be other than its quiddity or nature or form. Hence, among the intelligences, their acts of existing must be other than their forms. Therefore, it is said that intelligences are forms and acts of existing.

Whatever belongs to something is either caused by the principles of its nature, like risibility in man, or accrues to it from some extrinsic principle, like the light in the air, which is caused by the sun. It is impossible that the act of existing itself be caused by the form or quiddity—and by "caused" I mean as by an efficient cause—for then something would be the cause of itself and produce itself in existence, which is impossible. It is therefore necessary that everything whose act of existing is other than its nature have its act of existing from another. And because everything which exists through another is reduced to that which exists through itself, as to a first cause, there must be something which causes all things to exist, inasmuch as it is subsistent existence alone. Otherwise we would proceed to infinity in causes, since everything which is not a subsistent act of existing has a cause for its act of existing, as we have just said. It is evident, therefore, that an intelligence is a form and an act of existing, and that it has its act of existing from the First Being which is existence only; and this is the First Cause, God.

Everything that receives something from another is in potency with respect to what is received, and what is received in it is its act. Therefore, that quiddity or form which an intelligence is must be in potency with respect to the act of existing, which it receives from God. And that act of existing is received as an act. Thus potency and act are found in intelligences, but not (except equivocally) matter and form. Hence, even *to suffer, to receive, to be subject to,* and all other things of this kind which seem proper to things in virtue of their matter, belong equivocally to intellectual and corporeal substances, as the Commentator states in his commentary on the third book of the *De Anima.* Likewise, because the quiddity of an intelligence is as has been said, the intelligence itself, its quiddity or essence, therefore, is itself that which is; and its act of existing, received from God, is that by which it subsists in the nature of things.

---

*A bird described in Egyptian mythology; a symbol of immortality.

The Gothic Cathedral

a. *The Cathedral of Notre Dame de Chartres,* Chartres, France, begun in the 1140s. The word "Gothic" was originally a perjorative term coined by Renaissance thinkers who considered this style to be a barbaric break from classical tradition. The two towers shown here, for example, are not symmetrical. Even though the overall design of the cathedral may not be symmetrical, each of its elements was designed to reflect the harmony and beauty of God's creation. (*Lauros-Giraudon/Art Resource*)

b. *Interior, Chartres Cathedral.* By using pointed arches, it was possible to make soaring open spaces in the nave (main sanctuary) of the Gothic cathedral. The weight was shifted downward instead of outward. (*Bildarchiv Foto Marburg/Art Resource*)

Because of this, certain men contend that a substance of this kind is composed of that by which it is and that which it is, or as Boethius says, of what is and the act of existing.

Inasmuch as potency and act are found in intelligences, there will be no difficulty in discovering multitude among the intelligences. This would be impossible if there were no potency in them. Hence, the Commentator says in his commentary on the third book of the *De Anima* that if the nature of the possible intellect were unknown to us we could not find multitude in the separated substances. The distinction between them, therefore, is in accordance with the degree of potency and act, such that a superior intelligence which is nearer to the first being would have more act and less potency; and so on with the others. This terminates in the human soul, which holds the lowest grade among intellectual substances. Hence, its possible intellect is related to intelligible forms as prime matter, which holds the lowest grade among sensible beings, is related to sensible forms, as the Commentator says in his commentary on the third book of the *De Anima*. Accordingly, the Philosopher compares it to a writing tablet on which nothing is written, because it has a greater degree of potency than the other intelligible substances. The human soul, then, is so near to material things that the material thing is drawn to participate in its act of existing; thus from body and soul there results one act of existing in one composite, although that act of existing, insofar as it is the soul's, does not depend upon the body. Then, after that form which is the soul, there are other forms having more potency and having a greater propinquity to matter, to the extent that their acts of existing are not without matter. Among these, too, order and grade are found, all the way down to the primary forms of the elements, which are closest to matter. Hence, they have no operations except in accordance with the demands of their active and passive qualities, and of other qualities by which matter is disposed to form.

CHAPTER 5

From what has been seen previously, it is evident how essence is found in diverse things: for we found among substances a threefold mode of possessing an essence.

There is something, God, Whose essence is its very act of existing. Accordingly, some philosophers argue that God does not have a quiddity or essence because His essence is nothing other than His act of existing. From this it follows that He is not in any genus, since everything that is in a genus necessarily has a quiddity distinct from its act of existing. This, in turn, follows from the fact that the quiddity or nature of a genus or species is not distinguished according to the character *nature* in those things

---

c. Flying Buttresses at Reims Cathedral, ca. 1230–1235, by Villard De Honnecourt. To leave the interior unencumbered, the remaining outward stresses were often buttressed from outside the building. In some cathedrals exterior buttresses could not be built directly along the outside walls because of side aisles. Instead they were built outside the side aisles and connected to the pillars of the nave by stone ribs. These supporting ribs appear to "fly" over the side aisles. (*Villard de Honnecourt/Giraudon, Art Resource*)
d. The Rose Window, Notre Dame Cathedral, Paris, thirteenth century. By using pointed arches and flying buttresses, the walls of a cathedral did not have to bear the weight of the roof. Instead they could be used as screens for stained glass ornamentation such as this. (*Giraudon/Art Resource*)

of which there is a genus or species, but according to the act of existing which is diverse in diverse things. If we say that God is only an act of existing, we do not necessarily fall into the error of those who have stated that God is that universal existence by which each thing formally exists. The act of existing which God is is such that no addition can be made to it. Hence, by its very purity, His act of existing is distinct from every other act of existing. A comparable situation would be this: if there were a certain separated color, it would, by its very separation, be distinct from the color not separated. Wherefore, it is stated in the commentary on the ninth proposition of the book *De Causis* that the individuation of the first cause, which is only an act of existing, is through its pure goodness. However, just as the notion of existing-in-general does not include any addition, neither does it include any precision of addition; for if this were so, nothing in which something were added over and above the act of existing could be understood to exist. Similarly, even though He is only an act of existing, this does not necessitate that He be deficient in other perfections and excellences. Indeed, God possesses the perfections which are in all genera, because of which He is said to be perfect without qualification, as the Philosopher and the Commentator state in the fifth book of the *Metaphysics*. He has these perfections, however, in a more excellent way than other things, because in Him they are one, while in other things they are diverse. This is so because all these perfections belong to Him according to His simple act of existing, just as, if someone were able to perform the operations of all the qualities in virtue of one quality, He would, in that one quality, have all qualities; so God possesses all perfections in His very act of existing.

Essence is found in a second way in created intellectual substances in which their essence is other than their acts of existing, although their essence is without matter. Hence, their acts of existing are not absolute, but received, and, therefore, limited and restricted to the capacity of the receiving nature. Nonetheless, their nature or quiddity is absolute and not received in any matter. Therefore, the book *De Causis* maintains that intelligences are infinite from below and finite from above. For they are limited as to their acts of existing, which are received from something higher. They are not limited from below, since their forms are not limited to the capacity of some matter receiving them. Hence, there is not found among such substances a multitude of individuals in one species, as has been said, except in the case of the human soul because of the body to which it is united. And although its individuation depends on the body as the occasion for its beginning, since it does not acquire an individuated act of existing except in the body whose act it is, nevertheless individuation would not necessarily cease if the body were removed. For since the human soul possesses absolutely the act of existing, which is individuated in being received, and from which union the soul is made the form of this body, that act of existing always remains individuated. Accordingly, Avicenna says that the individuation and the multitude of souls depend on the body as to its source, but not on the body as to its end. Moreover, inasmuch as quiddity in these substances is not identical with the act of existing, they can therefore be assigned a category; and because of this, genus, species, and differences are found in them, although the differences proper to them are hidden to us. Even in sensible things essential differences themselves are unknown. They are, therefore, signified through accidental differences which arise from essential ones, just as a cause is signified by its effect; for example, *biped* is proposed as the difference of man. However, the proper accidents of immaterial substances are unknown to us; hence, their differences cannot be signified by us either through themselves or through accidental differences.

One must realize, however, that genus and difference cannot be taken in the same way in these substances and in sensible substances. In sensible substances, genus is taken from what is material in the thing, whereas difference is taken from what is formal in it. Hence Avicenna says in the beginning of his book *De Anima* that form in things composed of matter and form "is the simple difference of what is constituted from it." This is so not because the form itself is the difference, but rather because it is the principle of the difference, as he states in his *Metaphysics*. Such a difference is called the simple difference, inasmuch as it is taken from that which is a part of the quiddity of the thing—that is, from the form. Moreover, since immaterial substances are simple quiddities, a difference in them cannot be taken from that which is a part of the quiddity, but from the whole quiddity. Therefore, in the beginning of the *De Anima*, Avicenna states that only species whose essence is composed of matter and form have a simple difference. Likewise among them the genus is taken from the whole essence, but in a different way. For one separated substance agrees with the others in immateriality; they differ from each other in grade of perfection according to their withdrawal from potency or approach to pure act. And therefore, a genus among them is taken from what follows upon them inasmuch as they are immaterial, like intellectuality or something of that sort. Their difference, unknown to us, is taken from that which follows in them the grade of perfection.

These differences need not be accidental, because they are according to a greater and a lesser perfection, which do not diversify a species. For a grade of perfection in the reception of the same form does not diversify a species, like being more white or less white in participating in a whiteness of the same nature. A diverse grade of perfection in the participated forms or natures themselves does diversify a species, just as nature advances through grades from plants to animals by way of certain things which are midway between animals and plants, according to the Philosopher in his eighth book of the *De Animalibus*.

The division of intellectual substances, moreover, need not always be through two genuine differences, because this cannot happen in all things, as the Philosopher says in the eleventh book of the *De Animalibus*.

The third way in which an essence is found is in substances composed of matter and form, wherein also the act of existing is received and limited inasmuch as they have it from another, and their nature or quiddity is received in designated matter. Therefore, they are limited from above and from below. Moreover, multiplication of individuals in one species is possible among them because of the division through designated matter. And how essence in these is related to logical intentions has been explained above.

CHAPTER 6

Having declared how essence is found in all substances, it now remains for us to see how essence is in accidents. As has been said, because essence is what is signified through a definition, accidents must have an essence in the same way that they have a definition. However, they have an incomplete definition, for they cannot be defined except by positing the subject in their definition. This is so because they do not, of themselves, have the act of existing independently of the subject, but, just as a substantial act of existing follows upon a composition of matter and form, so an accidental act of existing follows upon addition of an accident to a subject. Therefore, neither the substantial form itself, nor matter, has a complete essence because in the definition of substantial form one must include that of which it is the form. Thus its definition is through the addition of something extrinsic to its class, as is the definition of an accidental form. In the definition of the soul, therefore, the natural philosopher, who considers the soul only insofar as it is the form of the physical body, includes body.

There is, however, this difference between substantial and accidental forms: just as a substantial form does not have through itself an absolute act of existing without that to which it is added, so neither does that to which it is added, namely, matter. Therefore, from their union arises that act of existing in which the thing subsists through itself, and from them is produced something that is one through itself. Hence a certain essence results from their union. Thus, although form, when considered in itself, does not have the complete nature *essence,* nevertheless, it is part of a complete essence. On the other hand, that to which an accident is added is a being complete in itself, subsisting in its own act of existing, which act naturally precedes the added accident. Therefore, an added accident, from its union with that to which it is added, does not cause the act of existing in which the thing subsists and through which the thing is a being through itself; but it does cause a certain second existence, without which the subsisting thing can be understood to exist, as "first" can be understood without "second." Hence, from the union of accident and subject there is not produced something that is one through itself, but something that is accidentally one. And so from their union no distinctive essence results, as results from the union of form and matter. Because of this, an accident neither has the character of a complete essence, nor is part of a complete essence; rather, just as it is a being in a qualified sense, so it has an essence in a qualified sense.

Now what is said maximally and most truly in any genus is the cause of those which are posterior in that genus; for example, fire, which is at the extreme of heat, is the cause of heat in hot things, as is stated in the second book of the *Metaphysics.* Accordingly, substance, which is first in the genus *being,* having essence in the truest and fullest sense, must be the cause of accidents, which participate secondarily and in a qualified way in the character of being.

This happens in diverse ways, however. Inasmuch as the parts of a substance are matter and form, certain accidents follow principally upon the form; others, upon the matter. Moreover, there is some form whose act of existing does not depend upon matter, as the intellective soul. Matter, however, has the act of existing only through form. Hence, among the accidents which follow upon form, there is something that does not have any communication with matter, namely, understanding, which does not occur through a corporeal organ, as the Philosopher proves in the third book of the *De Anima.* Indeed, others among those accidents following upon the form do have a communication with matter, as hearing and the like. No accident, however, follows upon the matter without a communication of the form.

There is, moreover, a certain diversity among those accidents which follow upon matter. Certain of them follow upon matter according to an order which they have to a special form; for example, in animals, male and female, whose diversity is reduced to matter, as is stated in the tenth book of the *Metaphysics.* Accordingly, if the animal form is removed, the aforesaid accidents do not remain, except in an equivocal sense. There are others which follow upon matter according to an order which they have to a general form. Hence, if the special form is removed, they nevertheless remain in it, like the blackness of an African's skin, which depends upon a mixture of the elements and not upon the soul. It, therefore, remains in it after death. And because each thing is individuated by matter but is located in a genus or species by its form, accidents which follow upon matter, therefore, are accidents of the individual, according to which individuals of the same species differ from each other. Accidents which follow the form, however, are proper attributes of the genus or species; hence, they are found in all participants in the nature of the genus or species. For example, risibility follows the form in man, since laughter arises from a certain knowledge in a man's soul.

One should understand likewise that accidents are caused sometimes by the essential principles according to a perfect act, like the heat in fire, which is always actually hot. Sometimes they are caused according to an aptitude only, with completion occurring by the action of an exterior agent; for example, lucency in the air, which is completed by a bright external body. Among these, the aptitude is an inseparable accident, whereas the complement, which comes from some principle which is outside the essence of the thing, or which does not enter into the constitution of the thing, will be separable, as being moved and the like.

It should be known, therefore, that in accidents, genus, species, and difference are understood differently from the way they are understood in substances. For in substances, something that is one through itself is brought about from substantial form and matter, with one certain nature resulting from their union, which properly is placed in the predicament *substance*. Therefore, in substances, concrete names which signify the composite are properly said to be in the genus, as a species or genus; for example, *man* or *animal*. However, neither the form nor the matter is in the predicament in this way except by reduction, as a principle is said to be in a genus. But something that is one through itself does not come about from the union of accident and subject. Hence, from their union there does not result any nature to which the intention *genus* or *species* can be attributed. Accordingly, accidental names said concretely, like *white* and *musical,* are not placed in a category, as species or genus are, except by reduction. They are placed in a category only according as they are signified abstractly, like *whiteness* or *music*.

In addition, because accidents are not composed of matter and form, genus in them cannot be taken from matter, nor difference from form, as in composite substances. Their first genus must be taken from the very mode of existing, according as *being* is said diversely, with certain priorities and posteriorities, of the ten genera of predicaments. Accordingly, quantity is called being inasmuch as it is the measure of a substance; quality, insofar as it is a disposition of a substance; and so on for the others, as the Philosopher says in the fourth book of the *Metaphysics*. On the other hand, differences in accidents are taken from the diversity of the principles by which they are caused. So, because proper attributes are caused by the proper principles of the subject, the subject, therefore, is included in their definition in place of a difference. This is true if they are defined in any absolute way, according as they are properly in a genus; for example, it is said that snubness is curvature of the nose. But the converse is true, if their definition is taken according as they are said concretely. Then a subject is placed in their definition as a genus, since then they would be defined after the manner of composite substances wherein the character genus is taken from matter. Accordingly, we say that a snub nose is a curved nose. The same is true if one accident is the principle of another accident, as action, passion, and quantity are the principles of relation. Therefore, in the fifth book of his *Metaphysics,* the Philosopher divides relation according to this. But because the proper principles of accidents are not always evident, we sometimes take the differences of accidents from their effects; for example, *contractive* and *expansive* are called differences of color, and are caused by the abundance or scarcity of light which produce diverse species of color.*

It is evident, therefore, how essence is found in substances and in accidents, in composite substances and in simple substances, and how universal intentions of logic are found in all these. An exception was made, however, of the first principle, which is the ultimate in simplicity, and to which, because of its simplicity, the character *genus, species,* and consequently *definition,* does not belong. This brings us to the end and consummation of this discourse.

---

*Color for St. Thomas, following Aristotle, was a species of the genus sense quality, and had two contraries, white and black, between which all other colors were situated.

LATE MEDIEVAL PHILOSOPHY

◄─◄○►─►

Whereas Thomas Aquinas lived during a period of relative calm and well-being, the century and a half following his death was one of tumult and upheaval. As a part of the often vicious conflict between church and state, Philip IV of France captured Pope Boniface VIII in 1303 and soon thereafter moved the papal court to Avignon, France—the so-called Babylonian Captivity of the Church. Beginning in 1347, the bubonic plague, or Black Death, struck Western Europe. Responses to the plague ranged from fanatical anti-intellectual apocalypticism to self-indulgent hedonism. Some even blamed the plague on intellectuals such as Thomas, saying they provoked divine wrath by explaining God's ways rationally; others simply counseled, "Let us eat, drink, and be merry, for tomorrow we die." Many turned to superstition or to scapegoating Jews. At the same time, England and France were involved in the Hundred Years' War (1337–1453), which brought enormous casualties. Between the plague and the war, in the years from 1300 to 1450, the population of Western Europe was reduced by half—perhaps by as much as two-thirds. In 1378, the Great Schism divided the Catholic church as the Italians reinstituted the papacy in Rome, while a second pope reigned in Avignon. For over thirty years, rival popes condemned and excommunicated one another. In 1409, an attempt to end the schism with a compromise pope led only to a third pope and thus a third claimant to St. Peter's universal chair. Finally, in 1417 the church united around one pope ruling in Rome. But by now the power and prestige of the papacy had been severely diminished, and a hundred years later, in the Protestant Reformation, the Western church split decisively.

The philosophy of this period reflects a growing skepticism about natural theology, that is, about the ability of reason to know truths concerning God. John Duns Scotus began this process as he tended to reduce the competence of theology to supernatural revelation alone, dismissing the natural theology of Thomas. William of Ockham took this tendency further, claiming philosophy and theology to be separate realms with separate rules. The transitional thinker Nicholas Cusanas claimed that knowledge was at best mere conjecture and that contradictories are compatible in reality: God, especially, incorporates all contradictions, all opposites, within Himself. In addition, mystics such as Meister Eckhart and Catherine of Siena argued for a nonrational way of knowing God.

*   *   *

For general surveys of medieval philosophy, which include the later period, see Maurice De Wulf, *History of Mediaeval Philosophy* (New York: Dover, 1952); Étienne Gilson, *History of Christian Philosophy in the Middle Ages* (New York: Random House, 1955); Armand A. Maurer, *Medieval Philosophy* (New York: Random House, 1962); and John Marenbon, ed., *Medieval Philosophy* (London: Routledge, 1998). The following volumes of Frederick Copleston's *A History of Philosophy* deal with this period: *Volume II, Medieval Philosophy, Part II, Albert the Great to Duns Scotus* (1950; reprinted Garden City, NY: Image Doubleday, 1962); *Volume III, Late Medieval and Renaissance Philosophy, Part I, Ockham to the Speculative Mystics* and *Part II, The Revival of Platonism to Suárez* (both 1953; reprinted Garden City, NY: Image Doubleday, 1963); and the later single volume, *A History of Medieval Philosophy* (New York: Harper & Row, 1972). Ray C. Petry, ed., *Late Medieval Mysticism* (Philadelphia: Westminster Press, 1957); Gordon Leff, *The Dissolution of the Medieval Outlook: An Essay on Intellectual and Spiritual Change in the Fourteenth Century* (New York: New York University Press, 1976), and John Marenbon, *Later Medieval Philosophy (1150–1350): An Introduction* (London: Routledge & Kegan Paul, 1987) give surveys of the late-medieval period, whereas Norman Kretzmann et al., eds., *The Cambridge History of Later Medieval Philosophy: From the Rediscovery of Aristotle to the Disintegration of Scholasticism 1100–1600* (Cambridge: Cambridge University Press, 1982), offers thematic essays.

JOHN DUNS SCOTUS
ca. 1265–1308

Not much is known about the early life of John Duns Scotus except that he was born in Scotland. He later became a Franciscan friar and taught at Cambridge, Oxford, and Paris. In 1303, he was banished from Paris because he sided with Pope Boniface VIII against King Philip IV. Within a year, he was back in Paris, and in 1305 he became regent master of theology. Two years later, he was transferred to Cologne, where he died in 1308.

Scotus managed to write a number of books during his short life—twelve Latin volumes in a seventeenth-century edition—though some work, previously thought his, is now believed to be that of his followers. Scotus's abstract metaphysical speculations and technical terminology are extremely difficult to understand. It is not surprising, then, that later thinkers called him the "Subtle Doctor." The followers of John Duns Scotus were so intent on following his subtlety that Renaissance thinkers mocked them as "Dunsmen"—from which we get our word "dunce." Despite this epithet, there are those, such as the poet Gerard Manley Hopkins, and the philosophers Charles Sanders Peirce and Martin Heidegger, who have found Scotus's thought penetrating and profound.

Scotus disagreed with Thomas Aquinas on a number of issues including the doctrine of analogy, the nature of individuation, and the limits of natural theology. But the most important difference between these two thinkers concerned the relative importance of intellect and will. A later philosopher, Christopher Devlin, explains that for Thomas the mind is like

a limpid and motionless pool in which both the nature of the surrounding objects and the movements of the heavens can be clearly discerned. Everything is reflected in a two-dimensional surface, and yet there is no mistaking the differences of depth and distance, there is no confusion between earth and heaven.

But, Devlin says, when Scotus considers Thomas's understanding of the mind,

> He complains that if [the rational mind] is regarded as a closed circle sufficient unto itself, it does not adequately represent the human soul. The human soul is not co-extensive with reason or understanding . . . it is a mistake to regard the other powers of the soul simply as functions or adjuncts to understanding. There is a power of the soul which is below understanding, but which has better evidence of the soul's origin, and there is a power of the soul which is above understanding and which is more in touch with the soul's destiny. The secret entrance to the pool is the point where the unconscious begins to influence the conscious mind. The secret exit is the point where the soul finds that its intellectual powers extended to their fullest have still failed to satisfy it, and that it must bring a higher faculty into play. In this way he returns to, and hopes to reinstate St. Augustine's hierarchy of memory, understanding and will. He sees these powers as the one soul operating on different levels of consciousness.*

Our first selection, from *A Treatise on God as First Principle,* presents Scotus's argument for God's existence as the "one nature which is simply first." Here Scotus argues from possibility to a necessary being. Our second selection is from *Reportata Parisiensia,* the lectures notes of Scotus's Parisian students. This brief passage argues that "being," not God, is the subject of metaphysics, emphasizing the distinction between philosophy and theology. The final selection, from the "Prologue" to the *Ordinatio,* presents a discussion of the relationship between reason and faith. Following an exposition of reasoning to the contrary, Scotus argues for the necessity of revealed knowledge. In so doing, Scotus distances himself from the natural theology of Thomas and further separates reason and revelation. All three of these excerpts are translated by Allan B. Wolter.

*   *   *

For years, Charles R.S. Harris's *Duns Scotus,* two volumes (1927; reprinted New York: Humanities Press, 1959) was the standard work, but this study includes material now known to be unauthentic. For more recent work on Duns Scotus, see Efrem Bettoni, *Duns Scotus: The Basic Principles of His Philosophy,* translated by Bernardine Bonansea (Washington, DC: Catholic University of America Press, 1961); Allan B. Wolter, *The Philosophical Theology of John Duns Scotus* (Ithaca, NY: Cornell University Press, 1990); and, especially, Richard Cross, *Duns Scotus* (Oxford: Oxford University Press, 1999). For a collection of essays, see John K. Ryan and Bernardine M. Bonansea, eds., *John Duns Scotus* (Washington, DC: Catholic University of America Press, 1965). The Philosophy Series by the Franciscan Institute Publications includes several specialized studies on Duns Scotus, though they may prove difficult for the beginning student.

---

*Anne Fremantle, *The Age of Belief: The Medieval Philosophers* (New York: New American Library, 1954), pp. 181–82.

A TREATISE ON GOD AS FIRST PRINCIPLE (in part)

CHAPTER 3

3.1 The triple primacy of the First Principle.

3.2 O Lord, our God, you have proclaimed yourself to be the first and last. Teach your servant to show by reason what he holds with faith most certain, that you are the most eminent, the first efficient cause and the last end.

3.3 We would like to select three of the six essential orders referred to earlier, the two of extrinsic causality and the one of eminence and, if you grant us to do so, to demonstrate that in these three orders there is some one nature which is simply first. I say one "nature" advisedly, since in this third chapter these three ways of being first will be shown to characterize not a unique singular or what is but one in number, but a unique essence or nature. Numerical unity, however, will be discussed later.

3.4 (First conclusion) *Some nature among beings can produce an effect.*

3.5 This is shown to be so because something can be produced and therefore something can be productive. The implication is evident from the nature of correlatives. Proof of the antecedent: (1) Some nature is contingent. It is possible for it to exist after being nonexistent, not of itself, however, or by reason of nothing, for in both these cases a being would exist by reason of what is not a being. Therefore it is producible by another. (2) Some nature too is changeable or mobile, since it can lack some perfection it is able to have. The result of the change then can begin to be and thus be produced.

3.6 In this conclusion, as in some of those which follow, I could argue in terms of the actual thus. Some nature is producing since some nature is produced, because some nature begins to exist, for some nature is contingent and the result of motion. But I prefer to propose conclusions and premises about the possible. For once those about the actual are granted, those about the possible are also conceded, but the reverse is not the case. Also those about the actual are contingent, though evident enough, whereas those about the possible are necessary. The former concern the being as existing whereas the latter can pertain properly to a being considered even in terms of its essentials. The existence of this essence, of which efficiency is now established, will be proved later.

3.7 (Second conclusion) *Something able to produce an effect is simply first, that is to say, it neither can be produced by an efficient cause nor does it exercise its efficient causality in virtue of anything other than itself.*

3.8 It is proved from the first conclusion that something can produce an effect. Call this producer A. If A is first in the way explained, we have immediately what we seek to prove. If it is not such, then it is a posterior agent either because it can be produced by something else or because it is able to produce its effect only in virtue of some agent other than itself. To deny the negation is to assert the affirmation. Let us assume that this being is not first and call it B. Then we can argue of B as we did of A.

Duns Scotus, *A Treatise on God as First Principle,* translated by Allan B. Wolter (Chicago: Franciscan Herald Press, 1969). Reprinted by permission.

Either we go on *ad infinitum* so that each thing in reference to what precedes it in the series will be second; or we shall reach something that has nothing prior to it. However, an infinity in the ascending order is impossible; hence a primacy is necessary because whatever has nothing prior is not posterior to anything posterior to itself, for the second conclusion of chapter two does away with a circle in causes.

3.9 An objection is raised here on the grounds that those who philosophize admit that an infinity is possible in an ascending order, as they themselves were wont to assume infinite generators of which none is first but each is second to some other, and still they assume no circle in causes. In ruling out this objection I declare that the philosophers did not postulate the possibility of an infinity in causes essentially ordered, but only in causes accidentally ordered, as is evident from Avicenna's *Metaphysics*, B. VI, chapter five, where he speaks of an infinity of individuals in a species.

3.10 But to show what I have in mind, I will explain what essentially ordered and accidentally ordered causes are. Here recall that it is one thing to speak of incidental causes (*causae per accidens*) as contrasted with those which are intended to cause a given effect (*causae per se*). It is quite another to speak of causes which are ordered to one another essentially or of themselves (*per se*) and those which are ordered only accidentally (*per accidens*). For in the first instance, we have merely a one-to-one comparison, [namely] of the cause to that which is caused. A *per se* cause is one which causes a given effect by reason of its proper nature and not in virtue of something incidental to it. In the second instance, two causes are compared with each other insofar as they are causes of the same thing.

3.11 *Per se* or essentially ordered causes differ from accidentally ordered causes in three respects. The first difference is that in essentially ordered causes, the second depends upon the first precisely in the act of causing. In accidentally ordered causes this is not the case, although the second may depend upon the first for its existence or in some other way. The second difference is that in essentially ordered causes the causality is of another nature and order, inasmuch as the higher cause is the more perfect, which is not the case with accidentally ordered causes. This second difference is a consequence of the first, since no cause in the exercise of its causality is essentially dependent upon a cause of the same nature as itself, for to produce anything one cause of a given kind suffices. A third difference follows, viz. that all essentially ordered causes are simultaneously required to cause the effect, for otherwise some causality essential to the effect would be wanting. In accidentally ordered causes this simultaneity is not required.

3.12 What we intend to show from this is that an infinity of essentially ordered causes is impossible, and that an infinity of accidentally ordered causes is also impossible unless we admit a *terminus* in an essentially ordered series. Therefore there is no way in which an infinity in essentially ordered causes is possible. And even if we deny the existence of an essential order, an infinity of causes is still impossible. Consequently in any case there is something able to produce an effect which is simply first. Here three propositions are assumed. For the sake of brevity, call the first A, the second B and the third C.

3.13 The proof of these: first, A is proved. (1) If the totality of essentially ordered causes were caused, it would have to be by a cause which does not belong to the group, otherwise it would be its own cause. The whole series of dependents then is dependent and upon something which is not one of the group. (2) [If this were not so], an infinity of essentially ordered causes would be acting at the same time (a consequence of the third difference mentioned above). Now no philosopher assumes this.

(3) Thirdly, to be prior, according to Bk. V of the *Metaphysics,* a thing must be nearer the beginning. Consequently, where there is no beginning, nothing can be essentially prior to anything else. (4) Fourthly, by reason of the second difference, the higher cause is more perfect in its causality, therefore what is infinitely higher is infinitely more perfect, and hence of infinite perfection in its causing. Therefore it does not cause in virtue of another, because everything of this kind is imperfect in its causality, since it depends upon another to produce its effect. (5) Fifthly, inasmuch as to be able to produce something does not imply any imperfection—a point evident from conclusion eight of chapter two—it follows that this ability can exist in some nature without imperfection. But if every cause depends upon some prior cause, then efficiency would never be found without imperfection. Consequently, an independent power to produce something can exist in some nature and this is simply first. Therefore, such an efficient power is possible and this suffices for now, since we shall prove later from that that it exists in reality. And so A becomes evident from these five arguments.

3.14 Proof of B: If we assume an infinity of accidentally ordered causes, it is clear that these are not concurrent, but one succeeds another so that the second, though it is in some way from the preceding, does not depend upon it for the exercise of its causality. For it is equally effective whether the preceding cause exists or not. A son in turn may beget a child just as well whether his father be dead or alive. But an infinite succession of such causes is impossible unless it exists in virtue of some nature of infinite duration from which the whole succession and every part thereof depends. For no change of form is perpetuated save in virtue of something permanent which is not a part of that succession, since everything of this succession which is in flux is of the same nature. Something essentially prior to the series, then, exists, for everything that is part of the succession depends upon it, and this dependence is of a different order from that by which it depends upon the immediately preceding cause where the latter is a part of the succession. Therefore B is evident.

3.15 Proof of C: From the first conclusion, some nature is able to produce an effect. But if an essential order of agents be denied, then this nature capable of causing does not cause in virtue of some other cause, and even if we assume that in one individual it is caused, nevertheless in some other it will not be caused, and this is what we propose to prove to be true of the first nature. For if we assume that in every individual this nature is caused, then a contradiction follows if we deny the existence of an essential order, since no nature that is caused can be assumed to exist in each individual in such a way that it is included in an accidental order of causes without being at the same time essentially ordered to some other nature. This follows from B.

3.16 (Third conclusion) *If what is able to cause effectively is simply first, then it is itself incapable of being caused, since it cannot be produced and is independently able to produce its effects.*

3.17 This is clear from the second conclusion, for if such a being could cause only in virtue of something else or if it could be produced, then either a process *ad infinitum* or a circle in causes would result, or else the series would terminate in some being which cannot be produced and yet independently is able to produce an effect. This latter being I call "first," and from what you grant, it is clear that anything other than this is not first. Furthermore, it follows that if the first cannot be produced, then it has no causes whatsoever, for it cannot be the result of a final cause (from conclusion two of chapter two)—nor of a material cause (from the sixth conclusion of the same)—nor of a formal cause (from the seventh conclusion there). Neither can it be caused by matter and form together (from the eighth conclusion there).

3.18 (Fourth conclusion) *A being able to exercise efficient causality which is simply first actually exists, and some nature actually existing is capable of exercising such causality.*

3.19 Proof of this: Anything to whose nature it is repugnant to receive existence from something else, exists of itself if it is able to exist at all. To receive existence from something else is repugnant to the very notion of a being which is first in the order of efficiency, as is clear from the third conclusion. And it can exist, as is clear from the second conclusion. Indeed, the fifth argument there which seems to be less conclusive than the others established this much. The other proofs there can be considered in the existential mode—in which case they concern contingent, though manifest facts—or they can be understood of the nature, the quiddity and possibility, in which case the conclusions proceed from necessary premises. From all this it follows that an efficient cause which is first in the unqualified sense of the term can exist of itself, for what does not actually exist of itself is incapable of existing of itself. Otherwise a nonexistent being would cause something to exist; but this is impossible, even apart from the fact that in such a case the thing would be its own cause and hence could not be entirely uncaused. Another way to establish this fourth conclusion would be to argue from the impropriety of a universe that would lack the highest possible degree of being.

3.20 As a corollary of this fourth conclusion, note that not only is such a cause prior to all others, but that it would be contradictory to say that another is prior to it. And insofar as such a cause is first, it exists. This is proved in the same way as was the fourth conclusion. The very notion of such a being implies its inability to be caused. Therefore, if it can exist, owing to the fact that to be is not contradictory to it, then it follows that it can exist of itself and consequently that it does exist of itself.

3.21 (Fifth conclusion) *A being unable to be caused is of itself necessarily existent.*

3.22 Proof: By excluding every cause of existence other than itself, whether it be intrinsic or extrinsic, we make it impossible for it not to be. Proof: Nothing can be nonexistent unless something either positively or privatively incompatible with it can exist, for one of two contradictories is always true. But nothing can be either positively or privatively incompatible with a being which cannot be caused, because it would be either of itself or from another. Not the first way, for then it would exist of itself—from the fourth conclusion,—so that there would be two incompatible things, and for that reason neither would exist, since you admit that the uncausable is nonexistent because of this incompatible element and vice versa. Neither can the incompatible be from another, because nothing caused has a more intense or potent existence from a cause than an uncausable thing has of itself, since the former is dependent in existing whereas the uncausable is not. Furthermore the possibility of the causable being does not entail its actual existence as is the case with the uncausable. Nothing incompatible with what is already a being can come from a cause unless it receive from that cause a being more intense or powerful than is the being of that which is incompatible with it.

3.23 (Sixth conclusion) *It is the characteristic of but one nature to have necessary being of itself.*

3.24 This is proved thus: If two natures of themselves could be necessary being, then this necessity of existing would be a common feature. And this they would share by reason of some essential or generic kind of entity in addition to which they would differ by reason of their ultimate actual formalities. Now two inconsistencies follow from this. To begin with, each will be a necessary being first of all through that common nature which is the less actual, rather than through that distinctive nature which is the more actual. For were it necessary being also by reason of its distinctive nature, then it will be necessary being twice over, because that distinguishing nature does not formally include the common nature, even as a [specific] difference does not include the genus. It seems impossible however, that the less actual be the primary reason why something is necessary, and that it is neither primarily nor *per se* necessary by reason of what is more actual. The second impossibility is that neither of the two would necessarily exist by virtue of that common nature which is presumed to be the primary reason why each is necessary. For that nature is insufficient to account for the existence of either nature, since every nature is what it is by reason of its ultimate formal constituent. But it is precisely what—to the exclusion of all else—accounts for a thing's actual existence, that is the reason for its being necessary. If you say that the common nature suffices for existence apart from the distinguishing natures, then it follows that the common nature of itself exists actually and without any distinguishing features, and therefore cannot be distinguished, since the necessary being already existing is not in potency to being [different kinds of things] in an unqualified sense [in the way] that the generic being in a species is simply that *kind* of thing.

3.25 Besides, two natures included under a common class are unequal. Proof of this is to be found among the different kinds of things into which a genus is divided. But if the two such natures are unequal, one will be of a more perfect being than the other. Nothing however is more perfect than a being having necessary existence of itself.

3.26 Moreover, if there were two natures having necessary being of themselves, neither would depend upon the other for existence and consequently no essential order would exist between them. One of them, therefore, would not belong to this universe, for there is nothing in the universe which is not related by an essential order to the other beings, for the unity of the universe stems from the order of its parts. Here it is objected that inasmuch as each is related to the parts of the universe through the order of eminence, this suffices for unity. To the contrary: One is not so ordered to the other, for a more perfect existence characterizes the more eminent nature. Nothing however is more perfect than a being having necessary existence of itself. What is more, one of two is not ordered to the parts of the universe, because if the universe is one, then it is characterized by a single order and this obtains where there is but one first. Proof: If you assume there are two first natures, since there is a dual term of reference, the nature next to the first has no unique order or dependence and the same is true of each subsequent nature. And thus through the whole universe there will be two orders, and hence two universes. Or else where will be an order only to one necessary being, but not to the other. If one proceeds reasonably, then, it seems he ought not to postulate anything for no apparent need, or whose entity is not clearly revealed by reason of some order to other things,—for, according to *Physics,* Bk. I, more than one thing should not be postulated where one suffices. Now we show there is a necessary being in the universe from the uncausable, and this in turn from what is first in causing, and the latter from what is caused. But from these effects there is no apparent necessity for assuming several first causing natures; furthermore, this is impossible, as will be shown later in the fifteenth conclusion of this third chapter. Therefore it is not necessary to assume that there are several things which are uncaused and necessarily exist. With reason, then, they are not postulated.

3.27 Concerning the final cause I propose four conclusions similar to the first four in this chapter about a being able to produce an effect. They are also proved in a similar way. The first of these is this: (Seventh conclusion) *Among beings some nature is able to function as final cause.*

3.28 Proof: Since something is producible (from the proof of the first conclusion of this chapter), something is able to be ordered to an end. The implication is clear. . . . That an essential order is involved is even more evident here than in the case of the efficient cause. . . .

3.29 (Eighth conclusion) *Something able to be an end is simply ultimate, that is to say, it can neither be ordained to something else nor exercise its finality in virtue of something else.*

3.30 This is proved by five arguments similar to those advanced for the second conclusion of this third chapter.

3.31 (Ninth conclusion) *Such an ultimate end cannot be caused in any way.*

3.32 This is proved from the fact that it cannot be ordained for another end; otherwise it would not be ultimate. It follows further that it cannot be caused by an efficient cause (from conclusion four of chapter two and also from what was said above in the proof for the third conclusion of the present chapter).

3.33 (Tenth conclusion) *The being which can be an ultimate end actually exists, and that this primacy pertains to some actually existing nature.*

3.34 The proof for this is like that used for the fourth conclusion of chapter three. Corollary: It is first to such an extent that it is impossible that anything should be prior to it. This is proved in the same fashion as the corollary to the fourth conclusion above.

REPORTATA PARISIENSIA (in part)

[BEING AS THE SUBJECT AND GOD AS THE GOAL OF METAPHYSICS]

We must first see whether metaphysics, the first and highest of the naturally acquired habits perfecting man's intellect in the present life, has God as its first object.

On this point there is a controversy between Avicenna and Averroës. Avicenna claims that God is not the subject of metaphysics, because no science proves [the existence of] its own subject. The metaphysician, however, proves that God exists. Averroës reproves Avicenna in his final comment on the *Physics,* Book 1, because he wishes, by using the same major premise against Avicenna, to prove that God and the pure spirits are the subject of metaphysics, and that God's existence is not proved in metaphysics, since it is only by means of motion, which pertains to the science of natural philosophy, that any kind of pure spirit can be proved to exist.

John Duns Scotus, *Reportata Parisiensia,* prol. qiii, art. i (VIVES, vol. xxii, 46a–47b) in *Duns Scotus Philosophical Writings,* translated by Allan Wolter (New York: Macmillan/Library of Liberal Arts, 1962), pp. 10–13.

It seems to me, however, that of the two, Avicenna has spoken better. Wherefore I argue against Averroës as follows. The proposition they both hold, viz. "No science proves the existence of its subject" is true, because of the priority the subject holds in regard to the science. For if the subject were posterior to the science, then its existence would have to be established in some lower science, where it would be conceived under some inferior aspect which is inadequate for its role as the object [of the higher science]. Now a subject enjoys a greater priority over the lower than over the higher science. If the highest science, therefore, cannot prove that its subject exists, it is even less possible for a lower science to do so.

Or to put the argument in another way, if the philosopher of nature can prove that God exists, then God's existence is a conclusion of natural philosophy. Now if metaphysics cannot prove the existence of God in this way, then God's existence is presupposed as a principle in metaphysics. Consequently, a conclusion of natural philosophy is a principle of metaphysics, and therefore the philosophy of nature is prior to metaphysics.

Again, if a certain property can exist only in virtue of such and such a cause, from every such property that appears in the effect, we can infer the existence of the cause. Now it is not just such properties of the effect as are treated in the philosophy of nature that are possible only on condition that God exists, for the same is true of the properties treated of in metaphysics. Not only does motion presuppose a mover, but a being that is posterior presupposes one that is prior. Consequently, from the priority that exists among beings the existence of the First Being can be inferred, and this can be done in a more perfect way than the existence of a Prime Mover can be established in natural philosophy. We can infer, then, in metaphysics from act and potency, finiteness and infinity, multitude and unity, and many other such metaphysical properties, that God or the First Being exists.

So far as this article is concerned, then, I say that God is not the subject of metaphysics, because, as has been proved above in the first question, there is but one science that has God as its first subject, and this is not metaphysics. And this is proved in the following manner. Of every subject, also of a subordinate science, it is known through the senses that it is of such a nature that to exist is not repugnant to it, as is evident of the subject of optics, for the existence of a visible line is grasped immediately from the senses. Just as principles are grasped immediately once the terms are apprehended through the medium of the senses, so likewise if a subject is not to be posterior to, or less known than, its principle, it must needs be grasped through the senses. But no proper notion that we can form of God is apprehended immediately by man's intellect in this life. Therefore, we can have no naturally acquired science about God under some notion proper to Himself. Proof of the minor: The first [proper] concept we have of God is that He is the First Being. But this notion is not grasped through the senses, but we must first ascertain that the union of these two terms is compatible. Before we can know this compatibility, however, it is necessary that we demonstrate that some being is first. Therefore, etc.

Hence, I concede with Avicenna that God is not the subject of metaphysics. The Philosopher's statement, (*Metaphysics*, Book I) that metaphysics is concerned with the highest causes, presents no difficulty. For he speaks here as he did in the *Prior Analytics*, Book I, where he says: "First it is necessary to determine with what *[Prior Analytics]* is concerned and what it has to do. It is concerned with demonstration and has to do with the demonstrative branch of learning, that is with the general science of demonstrating or syllogising." Hence, "concerned with" denotes properly the circumstance of the final cause just as much as it does that of the material cause. Wherefore, metaphysics is concerned with the highest causes as its end. In knowing them, metaphysical science attains its goal.

PROLOGUE TO THE ORDINATIO

PART 1. THE NECESSITY OF REVEALED KNOWLEDGE. DOES MAN IN HIS PRESENT STATE NEED TO BE SUPERNATURALLY INSPIRED WITH SOME KNOWLEDGE?

1. The question is raised whether man in his present state needs to be supernaturally inspired with some special knowledge he could not attain by the natural light of the intellect.

[The Pro and Con]

That he needs none, I argue as follows:*
[Arg. 1] Every faculty which has something common as its primary object, is as competent by nature in regard to everything contained under this object as it is with regard to what is of itself the natural object. This is proved by the case of the primary object of vision and the other things contained under it. And thus we may proceed inductively with the other faculties and their primary objects. Reason also proves the same, for the primary object is that which is equal to the faculty in question. But if this notion, namely, of the primary object, were verified of something that is beyond the natural competency of the faculty, the object would not be equal to, but would exceed the faculty. The major then is evident. The natural primary object of our intellect is being qua being. Therefore, our intellect is able to know naturally any being whatsoever and consequently also any intelligible nonentity, for "affirmation explains denial." Therefore, etc. Proof of the minor: Avicenna in the first book of the *Metaphysics* says: "'Being' and 'thing' are impressed first upon the soul. Neither can they be revealed through other notions." But if the primary object of the intellect were anything other than these, then "being" and "thing" could be made known through this other notion. But this is impossible.

2. [Arg. 2] Furthermore, the sense needs no supernatural knowledge in its present state; therefore, neither does the intellect. The antecedent is evident. Proof of the consequence: "Nature leaves out nothing necessary" (*On the Soul,* III). Now, if this is true of things that are imperfect, all the more does it hold for things that are perfect.

---

*For the refutation of these arguments see ¶90–94.

Translation by Allan B. Wolter. Reprinted from *Franciscan Studies,* Vol. XI, No. 3–4, 1951, by permission.

Consequently, if the inferior faculties lack nothing necessary for their function and the attainment of their end, all the more is this true of the higher faculty. Therefore, etc.

3. [Arg. 3] Furthermore, if some such knowledge were necessary, it would be so only because the faculty with its purely natural endowments is disproportionate to an object knowable only under such conditions. Therefore, an additional factor is required that the faculty may be made equal to the object. Now this other factor is either natural or supernatural. If natural, then the two combined are still disproportionate to the primary object. If this factor is supernatural, then the faculty is disproportionate to it; and so on *ad infinitum*. But since we cannot proceed to infinity according to *Metaphysics* II, it is necessary to stop with the first [*viz.* something natural], and admit that the intellective faculty is proportionate to everything that can be known and in any way in which it can be known. Therefore, etc.

4. *To the Contrary:*

"All doctrine divinely inspired is useful for arguing . . . etc." (*Tim. 3*).

Furthermore, it is said of wisdom: "No one can know its way, but He who knows all things knows it" (*Bar. 3*). Therefore, no other can have wisdom save from Him who knows all things. So much for the necessity of revelation. As to the fact thereof, he adds: "He [God] gave it to Jacob, His child, and to Israel, His beloved."—referring to the Old Testament—and the following: "After these things, He was seen on earth and talked with men."—referring to the New Testament.

[I. Controversy between the Philosophers and Theologians]

5. In this question we are faced with the controversy between the philosophers and theologians. The philosophers insist on the perfection of nature and deny supernatural perfection. The theologians, on the other hand, recognize the deficiency of nature and the need of grace and supernatural perfection.

[A. Opinion of the Philosophers]

The philosophers, then, would say that no supernatural knowledge is necessary for man in his present state, but that all the knowledge he needs could be acquired by the action of natural causes. In support of this, they cite from various places both the authority and the reasoning of the Philosopher.

6. [First argument]* The first is that passage in the third book *On the Soul,* where he [Aristotle] says that "the agent intellect is that by which [the intellect] makes all things; the possible intellect is that by which it becomes all things." From this I argue as follows. Once a natural agent and patient are put together and not impeded, action necessarily follows, for an action depends essentially only upon these factors as prior causes. But in regard to every intelligible object, the agent intellect is active and the possible intellect receptive. They are naturally in the soul and are not impeded. This is evident. By their natural power, then, an act of knowledge regarding any intelligible object whatsoever is possible.

7. [Second argument]** This is confirmed by reason. Every natural passive faculty has some corresponding natural agent. Otherwise the passive faculty would seem to have no purpose in nature, since nothing in the realm of nature could reduce it to act. But the possible intellect is a passive faculty with regard to any intelligible object whatsoever. Some natural active power, consequently, corresponds to it. The thesis

*This argument is answered in ¶72.
**This argument is answered in ¶73–78.

therefore follows. The minor is evident, since the possible intellect naturally seeks to know whatever can be known. Also it is naturally perfected by such knowledge. By nature then it is capable of receiving any knowledge whatsoever.

8. [Third argument]* Furthermore, speculative science is divided into mathematics, physics and metaphysics according to the *Metaphysics,* VI. And from the proof for this, which is given there, no other speculative science seems possible, since in these sciences the whole of being is considered, both in itself and in all its divisions. Now just as a speculative science other than these three would not be possible, neither is any practical science possible other than those acquired sciences that have to do with functional and productive activity. Consequently, practical acquired sciences suffice to perfect the practical intellect and speculative acquired sciences, the speculative intellect.

9. [Fourth argument]** Furthermore, anyone capable by nature of knowing a principle can know naturally the conclusions included in that principle. This I prove from the fact that the knowledge of the conclusions depends solely upon an understanding of the principle and the deduction of the conclusion from the principle, as is evident from the definition of "to know" in the *Posterior Analytics,* I. Now, the deduction is manifest of itself, as is clear from the definition of the perfect syllogism in the *Prior Analytics.* "Such a syllogism needs nothing either for being, or for appearing, evidently necessary." Consequently if the principles be known, everything needed for a knowledge of the conclusion is there. And so the major is clear.

10. Now we know naturally the first principles in which all conclusions are virtually contained. Hence, we can also know naturally all the conclusions that can be known.

Proof of the first part of the minor. Since the terms of the first principles are most common, it follows that they can be known naturally, for according to the first book of the *Physics,* we know first what is most common. But according to *Posterior Analytics,* I: "we know and understand principles in so far as we know their terms." We can know first principles then naturally.

11. Proof of the second part of the minor. Since the terms of the first principles are most common, when they are distributed, they are distributed in regard to all the concepts that fall under them. Now in first principles, such terms are taken universally and therefore they extend to all particular concepts. Consequently, they include the terms of all particular conclusions.

[B. Refutation of the Opinion of the Philosophers]

12. Three arguments can be raised against this opinion.*** ([Marginal note by Scotus:] By natural reason nothing supernatural can be shown to exist in the wayfarer, nor can it be proved that anything supernatural is necessarily required for his perfection. Neither can one who has something supernatural know it is in him. Here then it is impossible to use natural reason against Aristotle. If one argues from beliefs, it is no argument against a philosopher since the latter does not concede a premise taken on faith. Hence, these reasons which are here urged against him have as one premise something believed or proved from something believed. Therefore, they are nothing more than theological persuasions from beliefs to a belief.)

---

*This argument is answered in ¶79–82.
**This argument is answered in ¶83–89.
***Scotus actually adduces five arguments, but only accepts the first three as valid.

13. [First principal argument] The first way is this. Every agent who acts knowingly needs a distinct knowledge of his destiny or end. I prove this, because every agent acting for the sake of an end, acts from a desire of the end. Now everything that is an agent in virtue of itself acts for the sake of an end. Therefore, every such agent seeks its end in a way proper to itself. Just as an agent that acts by its nature must desire the end for which it must act, so also the agent that acts knowingly. For the latter is also an agent in virtue of itself, according to the second book of the *Physics*. The major then is clear.

But man can have no definite knowledge of his end from what is natural; therefore, he needs some supernatural knowledge thereof.

14. The minor is evident, first, because the Philosopher, following natural reason, maintained that perfect happiness consists in the acquired knowledge of the pure Spirits, as he apparently wishes to say in the *Ethics,* book I and book X. Or if he does not categorically assert that this is our highest possible perfection, at least natural reason can argue to no other, so that on this basis alone, we will either err or be in doubt about our specific end. Hence, it is with some doubt in mind that he says in the first book of the *Ethics,* "If there be any gift of the gods, it is reasonable that it be happiness."

15. Secondly, the same minor is proved by reason. For we know the proper end only of such substances whose manifest actions show us that such an end is in accord with such a nature. Now of all the actions that we experience or know to exist in our nature at present, there are none that reveal that the vision of the pure Spirits is in accord with our nature. Naturally then we are unable to know definitely that this end is befitting our nature.

16. So much at least is sure, we cannot know definitely by natural reason certain conditions that make the end more desirable and cause us to seek it more fervently. For even granting that reason could prove that the face-to-face vision and enjoyment of God are the end of man, it still could not be inferred that these will be his forever or that they pertain to him as a whole, namely in body and soul, as will be pointed out in book IV, distinction 43. And yet the fact that such a good will never cease is something that renders the end more attractive than if it were something transient. Also, it is more desirable to possess this good with a complete [human] nature than with the soul apart from the body, as is clear from Augustine, *On Genesis,* XIII. It is necessary to know these and similar conditions associated with our end, if we are to seek it efficaciously. Still natural reason is insufficient in this regard. Therefore, supernaturally given knowledge is required.

17. [Second principal reason] The second argument runs in this fashion. Everyone who knowingly acts for the sake of an end, needs to know how and in what way such an end may be attained. In addition, he must know all that is necessary for this end. Thirdly, he must know that this is all that is required. The first is clear, because if one knows not how or in what way the end is to be attained, he is also ignorant of the way in which he must dispose himself in order to attain it. The second is proved, for if one does not know all that is necessary for the end, he could fail to reach it because he did not know that a certain action was necessary for its attainment. So also with the third. If these means were not known to be sufficient, the doubt that there might be some unknown yet necessary factor, would keep one from efficaciously doing what was necessary.

18. But by natural reason one in this life is unable to know these three points. Proof that the first cannot be known. Beatitude is granted as the reward of merits which

God accepts as worthy of such a reward. In consequence, beatitude does not follow with natural necessity from any kind of acts we may be able to perform, but is something that is freely given by God, who accepts as meritorious certain acts directed toward Him. Now, this is not something that can be known naturally, as is clear from the fact that the philosophers erred in this matter when they claimed everything God does immediately He does with necessity. The two other points, at least, are clear enough. For the fact that the divine will accepts just such and such things as worthy of eternal life, as well as the fact that just these things suffice, is not something that natural reason can know. This acceptance of what is only contingently related to it depends solely upon the divine will. Therefore, etc.

19. [Objections to the first two principal reasons] Objections are raised against these two reasons. To the first: Every created nature depends essentially upon anything that in virtue of itself causes such a nature. By reason of this dependence, it is possible to know and to demonstrate by a simple demonstration of fact any such cause of a given effect, once the latter is known. Now, since the nature of man can be known naturally by man—for it is not disproportionate to his cognitive power—it follows that once this nature is known, its destiny also could be known naturally.

20. This reason is confirmed. For if the destiny of a less perfect nature can be known from a knowledge of that nature, this is no less possible in our case, since what is destined for an end depends upon that end no less in the present case than it does in the others.

21. For this same reason, too, the proposition assumed in the proof of the minor, namely "the end of a substance is known only through the actions of that substance," would also seem to be false, since, by a demonstration of simple fact, the end of a nature could be known from a knowledge of that nature in itself.

22. And if it be maintained that reason infers only that man could know naturally his natural goal but not that which is supernatural, against this is Augustine's statement: "To be able to have faith, just as to be able to possess charity, pertains to the nature of men, although to have faith, just as to have charity, is due to the grace that is given to the faithful" (*On the Predestination of the Saints*). Now, if the nature of man can be known naturally by man, then this ability in so far as it pertains to this nature, can also be known naturally. Consequently, it is also possible to know that such a nature can be ordained to an end for which charity and faith dispose it.

23. Likewise, man naturally seeks this goal which you call supernatural. Therefore, he is naturally ordained to it. This destiny, then, could be inferred from such an ordination just as it could be inferred from a knowledge of the nature ordained to such an end.

24. Also, according to Avicenna, it can be known naturally that *being* is the primary object of the intellect. And it is naturally knowable that this notion of being is verified most perfectly of God. The end of any power, however, is the very best of those things which come under its primary object, for only in such is there perfect rest and delight, according to the tenth book of the *Ethics*. Therefore, it can be known naturally that man according to his intellect is ordained to God as an end.

25. This reason is confirmed. For whoever can know any power naturally, is also able naturally to know what its primary object is. In addition he can know wherein the notion of this object is verified, as well as the fact that the most perfect of such things is the goal or end of this power. Now the mind knows itself, according to Augustine (*On the Trinity*). Therefore, it knows what its primary object is, and it knows that God does not fall outside its scope, for otherwise God would not be intelligible to this mind in any way. Consequently, the mind knows that God is the very best of those things in

which the notion of its primary object is to be found, and thus it knows that God is the goal of this faculty.

26. Against the second reason the following argument is adduced. If one extreme is known through the other, the media are also known. But those things necessary for reaching the goal are media between the nature and the end to be attained. Now, since the end could be known from a knowledge of the nature, as has been proved above [¶19], it seems that the media necessary to this end can also be known in a similar way.

27. This reason is confirmed. For just as is the case with other things, so here also there seems to be a necessary connection of things with this end. But in other cases such a connection with the end serves to make other things known, for instance, such and such things are inferred to be necessary for health from the notion of health. Therefore, etc.

28. [Reply to the Objections] To the first of these [cf. ¶19–21], I say that even though the argument is based on the notion of an end which is a final cause and not that of an end to be attained through some action—a distinction of ends that will be treated later—nevertheless, to this objection as well as to what follows according to Augustine [cf. ¶22], and to the third objection regarding the power and its primary object [cf. ¶24], a single reply can be given. All these assume that our nature or our intellective power can be known naturally by us. Now this is false, if understood of that proper and special aspect by reason of which our nature is ordered to such an end, and in virtue of which it is capable of [receiving] the highest grace and has God as its most perfect object. For neither our soul nor our nature are known by us in our present state except under some general notion that can be abstracted from what the senses can perceive, as will be made clear later in distinction 3. And to be ordained to this end, or to be able to possess grace or to have God as its most perfect object is not something that pertains to our nature under such a general notion.

29. Now to the form [cf. ¶19]. It is stated that from the being which is ordained to this end, the end itself can be demonstrated by a demonstration of simple fact. Now I say this is true only if the being ordained to the end is known precisely according to that proper aspect in virtue of which it has such a destiny. And so the minor is false. And when they try to prove it on the grounds that there is no disproportion, I say that although the mind is identified with itself, nevertheless it is not proportionate to itself as object, except according to general notions which can be abstracted from what can be pictured in the imagination.

30. As to the confirmation [cf. ¶20], I say that even with other substances, their proper ends (namely, those which they have in virtue of their proper natures) remain unknown unless there be some manifest actions from which an ordination to such an end might be inferred.

31. And from this, the answer to what is added against the proof of the minor is clear [cf. ¶21]. The proposition: "The proper end of a substance is known to us only through its manifest actions," is not false. For this proposition does not mean that the end could not be known in some other way. Indeed, it is true that if the substance were known in its proper nature, from such knowledge one could ascertain what causes this substance in virtue of itself. But no substance is known to us at present in this way and therefore, in this life, we are unable to infer the proper end of any substance except through the evident actions of this substance, which substance is known only confusedly and in general. In our case, however, the end can be proved from a knowledge of neither the nature nor its acts. Although the proof of the minor touches but one way, namely our ignorance of its acts, it presupposes the other, namely, our ignorance of the nature in itself.

32. To the second argument based on Augustine [cf. ¶22] I say that this ability to possess charity, in so far as it disposes one to love God in himself under His proper nature, is something that pertains to man according to a special aspect and not as common to himself and to what is perceptible by the senses. In consequence, this ability is not something about man that can be known naturally in this life, even as man himself is not known under that peculiar aspect in virtue of which he possesses this ability. And in this way I reply to the objection in so far as it can be used to support the principal claim [of the philosophers], namely that the minor of the first argument [of the theologians] [cf. ¶14–15] is false. But in so far as it is leveled against the reply regarding the natural and supernatural end [cf. ¶22], I answer: I concede that God is the natural end of man, but an end that must be attained supernaturally and not naturally. And this is what the following reason concerning natural desire proves, which proof I concede.

33. As to the other argument [cf. ¶24], what it assumed must be denied, namely that it can be known naturally that being is the primary object of the intellect and this in so far as no restriction is made regarding a being that can be perceived by the sense and one that cannot. It must also be denied that Avicenna says this is something that can be known naturally, for he has mixed his religion—that of Mohammed—with philosophical matters, and some things he states as philosophical and proved by reason; others as in accord with his religion. Wherefore, he expressly assumes in the ninth book of the *Metaphysics,* chapter 7, that the disembodied soul knows immaterial substances in themselves, and therefore these have to be placed under the primary object of the intellect. But it was not so according to Aristotle. For him, the primary object of our intellect is, or seems to be, the quiddity of what can be perceived by the senses. And by this he means either what is in itself perceptible by the senses or what falls under this designation. The latter is the quiddity which can be abstracted from what is perceptible to the senses.

34. However, I reply to what is cited from Augustine in confirmation of the argument [cf. ¶25]. His statement, I say, should be understood of the first act which of itself is fully sufficient for the second act, but its activity is hindered at present. On account of this hindrance, the second act in the present life is not elicited from the first. But more of this later.

35. Some may object to this answer on the grounds that man in the state of original justice could have known his nature, and therefore the destiny of this nature, as the argument for the first objection claims [cf. ¶19]. Therefore, this knowledge is not supernatural.

36. Also, the reply to the last reason might be questioned [cf. ¶33]. For if we are ignorant of what the primary object of the intellect is because the intellect is not known under each proper aspect according to which it regards such an object, it follows that we cannot know that any given thing is intelligible, because the power is not known under every proper aspect according to which it could consider any given thing as an intelligible object.

37. I reply: To the first [cf. ¶35]. It is necessary to point out what kind of knowledge man had in his original state, a topic which may be put off until later. But at least so far as man in his present state is concerned, it is called supernatural knowledge, because it exceeds man's natural power—natural, I understand, according to his fallen state.

38. As to the second [cf. ¶36], I concede that at present our knowledge of the soul or of some of its faculties is not so distinct that such knowledge could be used to ascertain that some intelligible object corresponds to it. But from the act which we experience, we conclude that the power and the nature to which this act belongs regards

as its object that which we perceive to be attained through the act in question. Hence, we do not infer the object of the faculty from a knowledge of the faculty in itself, but from the knowledge of the act we experience. But of a supernatural object we have neither kind of knowledge, and in consequence neither method of knowing the proper end of this nature is to be had.

39. The answer to the objection against the second reason is clear [cf. ¶26]. For the argument assumes something that has already been denied [cf. ¶28–29]. To the confirmation of this argument [cf. ¶27] I say that when the end follows naturally those things that lead to the end, and demands them naturally as prerequisites, then, such things could be inferred from the end. But in this case, these things do not follow naturally, but only in virtue of a [voluntary] acceptance on the part of the divine will, which reckons these merits as worthy of such an end.

40. [Third principal reason] A third main argument is raised against the opinion of the philosophers. The knowledge of pure Spirits is the most noble, because it has to do with the noblest class (*Metaphysics,* IV). Hence, the knowledge of their proper attributes is noblest and most necessary. For their proper attributes are more perfectly knowable than those attributes they have in common with objects perceptible to the senses. But these proper attributes cannot be known merely from what is purely natural. For, in the first place, if these properties were found to be treated in any science possible to us at present, it would be in metaphysics. But it is not possible for us naturally to have a science of the proper attributes of these pure Spirits, as is evident. And this is what the Philosopher maintains when he says in the first book of the *Metaphysics* that it is necessary for the wise man to know all things in some way, and not in particular. And he adds: "For he who knows universals, knows in a sense all things." Here he calls the metaphysician the "wise man," just as he calls philosophy "wisdom."

41. I prove the same thing in a second way. These properties are not known by a science or knowledge that gives the reason for the facts unless their proper subjects are known, for only the subjects give the reason for such proper attributes. Now the proper subjects of these attributes cannot be known naturally by us. Therefore, etc.

Neither can we know these properties from their effects by a demonstration of the simple fact. Proof: the effect leaves the intellect in doubt with regard to these properties or even leads it into error. This is clear with regard to the properties of the First Spiritual Substance itself, for it is a property of this [divine] Substance that it can be shared with three [Divine Persons]. But the effects [*viz.* creatures] do not reveal this property, because they are not from this Substance in so far as it is a Trinity. And if one were to argue from the effects to the cause, one would rather conclude the very opposite and so be in error. For in no effect is one nature associated with more than one *supposit.* It is also a property of this nature, in its external relations, to cause [its effects] contingently. And the effects lead one to infer the opposite view and to fall into error, as is evident from the opinion of philosophers who held that the First Cause causes necessarily whatever it produces. As to the properties of the other pure Spirits [*viz.* the angels or Intelligences], clearly the same holds. For effects rather lead one to conclude that they are necessary and everlasting beings, according to the philosophers, instead of contingent beings, which have come into existence after being non-existent. Again, these philosophers also seem to conclude on the basis of movement that the number of these pure Spirits corresponds with the number of movements of the heavenly bodies. Again, [they held that] these pure Spirits were naturally beatified and incapable of sin—all of which is absurd.

42. [Objection to the third principal reason] Against this reason I argue that whatever necessary knowledge regarding these pure Spirits we may have at present by

faith or what is commonly revealed could also be had by a knowledge that is natural. And I prove it in this way. We can comprehend naturally any necessary truths whose terms we can know naturally. Now we know naturally the terms of all necessary revealed truths. Therefore, etc.

43. Proof of the major. These necessary truths are either mediately or immediately [evident]. If immediately, then, they are known once the terms are known, according to the first book of the *Posterior Analytics*. If they are mediate truths, then we can conceive the middle term between them, since we can know the extremes. By joining this middle term with the two extremes, we have either mediate or immediate premises. If immediate, we argue as before. If mediate, the process of conceiving the middle term between the extremes and joining it with the latter continues until we come to truths that are immediately evident. In the last analysis, then, we shall arrive at necessary and immediate propositions, which are known from their terms and from which all other necessary truths follow. Hence, these mediate truths could be known naturally by us through those which are immediate.

44. Proof of the minor. If one who has faith contradicts one who has no faith, the two do not contradict each other in word only but according to the conceptual meaning, as is evident when the philosopher and theologian contradict each other regarding the proposition: "God is triune." Here, one denies and the other affirms not only the same name but also the same concept. Consequently, every simple concept that the theologian has, the philosopher also has.

45. [Reply to the objection] To this, I reply. There are certain truths about the pure Spirits that are immediate. Now I take one such primary and immediate truth, let us call it "a." In it are included many mediate truths, for instance, all those which affirm in particular what is common to the predicate of those things which are common to the subject, let us call them "b" and "c." These mediate truths are evident only through some immediate truth. Therefore, the former cannot be known unless the immediate truth is understood. If therefore some intellect could grasp the terms of "b" and combine them with one another in a proposition, but could not understand the terms of "a" nor, in consequence, the proposition "a" itself, then so far as this intellect is concerned, "b" would be a neutral proposition. It is known neither through itself, nor through the immediate proposition [*viz.* "a"], since in our assumption the latter remains unknown. And so it is with us. For we have certain concepts common to material and immaterial substances, and these we can put together into propositions. But these latter are not evident except through those immediate truths which concern the proper and special character of these quiddities. Now we do not conceive these quiddities under this aspect and therefore, neither do we know those general truths which involve the universal concepts.

46. For example: if someone were able to conceive a triangle not according to its proper notion as a triangle but only under the notion of "figure" abstracted from a quadrangle, it would be impossible for him to grasp that property by which a triangle is the first [of plane geometrical figures], because this property could be conceived only if it were abstracted from a triangle itself. He could, however, abstract the notion of "first" from other things that are first, e.g. of numbers. Although his intellect could form the proposition: "Some figure is first," because it could grasp the terms involved, still such a proposition would be neutral to him, because it is a mediate proposition included in this immediate proposition: "A triangle is first in this way." But he would be unable to know this immediate proposition because he cannot grasp its terms. Therefore, he is not able to understand the mediate proposition, which can be known from the immediate proposition alone.

47. Applying this to the argument [cf. ¶42], I deny the major. To the proof, I say that these necessary truths are mediately evident propositions. And when you say, "Therefore, we can conceive a medium between these extremes," I deny the consequence, because the medium between the extremes is at times essentially ordered, for example, when it is the essence of the extreme or is a prior attribute with regard to one that is posterior. Now a middle term through which one extreme can universally be inferred from the other is of this kind. I concede, therefore, that whoever can grasp the extremes can grasp such a middle term between them, because its concept is included in, or is the same as, that of the other extreme. But if the middle term is particular, and is contained under the other extremes and is not essentially related to these extremes, then it is not necessary that one who can conceive universal extremes, could conceive a means which is particular in regard to these extremes. So it is here. For the quiddity under its proper and particular aspect has some immediate attribute inhering in it, and is a middle term that is less universal than the common concept of which this attribute, conceived in general, is predicated. Therefore, it is not a medium for universally inferring the attribute of the common concept, but only in a particular case. This is evident in the above example [cf. ¶46], because it is not necessary that one who can conceive a figure in general and the general notion of being first, can conceive a triangle in particular, for a triangle is a medium contained under figure—a medium, I say, for concluding that a particular figure is first.

48. ([Note] This third argument [cf. ¶40] holds above all of the first immaterial substance [*viz.* God], for it is especially necessary to know God as a beatific object. Now the reply to the objection brought against it supposes that we conceive God naturally in the present life only in a concept that is common to Him and to what can be perceived by the senses, which is explained later in the first question of the third distinction. But even if this assumption were denied, it would still be necessary to maintain that any concept of God we could derive from creatures is imperfect, whereas that which could be had in virtue of His essence in itself would be perfect. Hence, what was said regarding the universal and particular notions [cf. ¶47], would also be valid for the perfect and imperfect notions in this other view.)

49. [Fourth principal reason] A fourth argument is this. Whatever is ordered to some end toward which it is not disposed, must be gradually disposed for this end. Man is ordered to a supernatural end toward which he is of himself indisposed. Therefore he needs to be gradually disposed to possess this end. This takes place by reason of some imperfect supernatural knowledge, which is maintained to be necessary. Therefore, etc.

50. But if it be objected that a perfect agent can remove any imperfection immediately and can act immediately, I reply that even if it could do so by its absolute power, still it is more perfect to make the creature active in attaining its perfection than to deprive it of any such activity. But man could have some activity in the attainment of his final perfection. Hence, it is more perfect that such be given him. But this could not be done without imparting some imperfect knowledge which precedes that perfect knowledge which he is ultimately destined to possess.

51. [Fifth principal argument] A fifth argument is this. Any agent that makes use of an instrument in acting, cannot in virtue of this instrument perform any action which exceeds [in perfection] the nature of the instrument. The light of the agent intellect, however, is an instrument which the soul at present uses to understand things naturally. In consequence, the soul, using this light, is not capable of any action that would exceed this light. Therefore, the soul is incapable of any knowledge that it does not attain in this way. But this light of itself is limited to knowledge by way of the senses. Now

the knowledge of many other things, however, is necessary for us at present. Therefore, etc.

52. This reason seems to militate against the position of the one who advanced it.* For according to this line of reasoning, the Uncreated Light would be unable to make use of the agent intellect as an instrument in producing a knowledge of pure truth. For such truth, according to him, cannot be ours through the senses without some special illumination. And so it follows that in knowing pure truth the light of the agent intellect plays no part at all, which seems hardly possible inasmuch as this illumination [by the agent intellect] is the most perfect of all intellectual activity. Consequently, the most perfect intellectual power in the soul should in some way concur with this action.

53. [Evaluation of the fourth and fifth reasons] These last two reasons [cf. ¶49–51] do not seem to be very efficacious. For the first would hold, if it were proved that man was destined for supernatural beatitude (the proof of which pertains to the questions of beatitude), and if, in addition, it were shown that natural knowledge does not dispose one sufficiently in our present state for the attainment of supernatural knowledge. The second reason begs two points, namely, that a knowledge of certain things unknowable by way of the senses, is necessary, and that the light of the agent intellect is limited to things that can be known by way of the senses.

54. The first three reasons appear to be more probable.

[C. Objection to the Opinion of the Theologians]

That no such knowledge, however, is necessary for salvation, I prove: Let us assume that someone is not baptized. When he grows up, he has no one to teach him. The affections [of his will], such as he is capable of, are good and in accord with what his natural reason tells him is right. What reason reveals to him as evil, he avoids.

Although God could visit such a one, teaching him the common law by man or angel even as He visited Cornelius, still let us assume that such an individual is taught by no one. Nevertheless, he will be saved. And even if he should be instructed later, before such instruction he is just and consequently, worthy of eternal life. For, by willing what is good, even before he is instructed, he merits grace which renders him just. And still he has no theology, not even in regard to the primary truths of faith. His is purely natural knowledge. Consequently, nothing that pertains to theology is, absolutely speaking, necessary for salvation.

55. [Reply] It could be said that such an individual, by willing what is good in general, merits *de congruo*** to be justified from original sin, and God does not deprive such a one of this gift of His liberality. Hence, He gives him the first grace without using the sacrament [i.e., baptism], because God is not constrained to make use of the sacraments. But grace is not [ordinarily] given without the habit of faith. Hence, such an individual actually possesses the habit of theology, even though this habit could not be reduced to act. Neither could such an individual be baptized unless first instructed. And even though it would not be a contradiction [for God] to give grace without faith, for these are distinct habits and reside in different faculties, nevertheless, just as in baptism these two are infused simultaneously, so, for the same reason, they could be given together in this case. For God is no less gracious toward one whom He justifies

---

*[Namely, Scotus's chief adversary, Henry of Ghent.]

**[A reward which is fitting even though there is no strict obligation in justice.]

without the sacraments, because of merit *de congruo,* than He is toward one whom He justifies through the reception of the sacrament without any merit on this individual's part. And thus it is possible for God by his absolute power to save anyone, and to enable him to merit glory without infused faith—if God were to give grace without faith—for once such an individual possessed grace, he could use it properly to will what he knew by natural reason and acquired faith (or by natural reason alone without acquired faith, if no one were to teach him). Nevertheless, according to God's usual way of acting, He does not give grace without first giving the habit of faith, for grace is not assumed to be infused unless faith is also infused. But this is not because of any necessity, as if grace without faith would not be sufficient, but because of the divine liberality which reforms the whole [soul, *viz.* intellect and will]. Then, too, many would be less perfectly inclined to assent to certain truths without infused faith.

56. Now, I say, there is a similar relation in the case of the habit of theology, which, when perfect, includes both an infused and an acquired faith of the articles [of the Creed] and of other things revealed by God in Scripture, so that there is not just infused faith, or just acquired faith, but both together. Hence, if we are speaking of the more fundamental or prior habit which theology includes, *viz.* infused faith, it is true, according to the usual way in which God acts, that theology is necessary for all, as a general rule. But it is not true that theology is necessary for all, if we understand by theology the second habit which it includes, *viz.* acquired faith. But if we speak of the necessity based on God's usual way of acting. Perhaps it is necessary for an adult who could have and is able to understand a teacher, that he have an acquired faith with regard to certain general truths.

[II. Solution to the Question]

57. To the question, then, I reply first by distinguishing in what sense something may be called supernatural. For a capacity to receive may be compared to the act which it receives or to the agent from which it receives [this act]. Viewed in the first way, this potentiality is either natural or violent or neither natural nor violent. It is called natural, if it is naturally inclined toward the form it receives. It is violent, if what it suffers is against its natural inclination. It is neither the one nor the other, if it is inclined neither to the form which it receives nor to its opposite. Now from this viewpoint, there is no supernaturality. But when the recipient is compared to the agent from which it receives the form, then there is naturalness if the recipient is referred to an agent which is naturally ordained to impress such a form in such a recipient. Supernaturalness is had, however, when the recipient is referred to an agent which does not impress this form upon this recipient naturally.

58. Before this distinction is applied to the case at hand, several arguments are brought to bear against it, first on the grounds that the distinction of "natural" and "violent" is based upon the recipient's relation to the agent and not merely to the form, and secondly on the count that the distinction of "natural" and "supernatural" is based upon the recipient's relation to the patient and not to the agent exclusively. I will not cite the arguments for these points here.

59. Nevertheless, the solution seems reasonable, because a cause which causes anything in virtue of itself is that cause whose presence is followed by the effect even when all other factors are excluded or varied. Now even though a form contrary to the inclination is induced only by means of some agent which does violence to the recipient, and even though a supernatural agent acts supernaturally only by inducing some

form, still the precise character of "violent" arises by virtue of the relation of the recipient to the form, whereas that of "supernatural" arises precisely in virtue of the relation of the recipient to the agent. This is proved from the fact that as long as the recipient and form remain what they are (*viz.* that the form can be received, but only contrary to the inclination of the recipient), then no matter how the agent is varied, violence is still done to the recipient. Similarly, when the agent and recipient are so related to each other that the recipient is altered only by an agent that does not act naturally (I say "only" to exclude any preparation by a natural agent), whatever be the form such an agent induces, it will be supernatural with regard to the recipient.

A second proof that such is the case is based not only on the induction [of the form] but on its permanency. A form which does violence to the recipient may remain in it without any external action, but not for a long time. Another remains naturally and for some time. [Hence, the external agent need not be taken into consideration.] Again, one form that endures is natural; another supernatural, but only by reason of the agent, so that if the latter were not taken into consideration, the form could not be called supernatural. But it might be called natural, because it perfects naturally, if the relation of the form to the recipient alone is considered.

60. Applying this to the question at issue, I say that if the possible intellect be compared to the knowledge that is actualized in it, no knowledge is supernatural to it, because the possible intellect is perfected by any knowledge whatsoever and is naturally inclined toward any kind of knowledge. But according to the second way of speaking, that knowledge is supernatural which is generated by some agent which by its very nature is not ordained to move the possible intellect in a natural manner.

61. In our present state, however, the possible intellect, according to the Philosopher, is ordained to be moved to knowledge by the agent intellect and the phantasm. Therefore, that knowledge alone is natural to it which is impressed by these agencies.

In virtue of these, however, all conceptual knowledge which one has in this life according to the common law, can be obtained, as is evident from the objections raised against the third principal reason [cf. ¶84]. Consequently, even though God by way of revelation could cause some special knowledge, as for instance, when one is rapt in ecstasy, still such supernatural knowledge is not necessary according to the common law.

62. It is different, however, with the truth of propositions, because as has been shown by the three reasons adduced against the first opinion [cf. ¶13ff.], even when the agent intellect and sense image are fully active, many propositions we need to know remain unknown or neutral. The knowledge of such propositions must be given to us in a supernatural manner, because no one could naturally discover them and teach them to others, for on natural grounds alone, if they are neutral to one, they are to all. The question of whether it would be possible, once such knowledge was originally imparted, for another to assent to these propositions on purely natural grounds will be discussed in book III, distinction 23. The original transmission of such knowledge, however, is called revelation. It is supernatural, therefore, since it is due to an agent that does not naturally move our intellect in its present state.

63. Another way in which an action or knowledge could be called supernatural would be because it is from an agent which takes the place of a supernatural object. For that object which is able to cause such propositions as "God is triune" and the like, is the divine essence known in its proper nature. Knowable in this way, it is a supernatural object. Whatever agent, then, causes some knowledge of truths which such an object would be able to make evident when known in its own nature, such an agent [I say] takes the place of this object. And if this agent would cause as perfect a knowledge of those truths as the object would cause if known in itself, then such an agent

would substitute perfectly for the object. But no matter how imperfect the knowledge caused by such an agent would be, it is still virtually contained in that perfect knowledge which the object would cause if known in itself.

64. And so it is in this case. For one who reveals that "God is triune" causes in the mind some knowledge of this truth, obscure though it be, a knowledge which concerns an object unknown in its proper nature. If this object were known properly, it would be able to produce a clear and perfect knowledge of this truth. In so far as this knowledge is obscure and is included eminently in the clear knowledge, as the imperfect is included eminently in the perfect, to that extent, then, the agent which reveals or causes the obscure truth, takes the place of the object that could cause a clear knowledge of the same. This is true especially when the agent could cause a knowledge of a certain truth only by taking the place of a certain object, and when it would be unable to make known a truth about this object by taking the place of some less perfect object that could naturally move our intellect. For no such inferior object virtually includes any knowledge of these truths, be it clear or obscure knowledge. Hence, it is necessary that the agent somehow take the place of a supernatural object, even when causing this obscure knowledge.

65. The difference between these two ways in which revealed knowledge is called supernatural is apparent if we consider each separately. Thus, if a supernatural agent would cause a knowledge of some natural object, for example, if it infused the knowledge of geometry in someone, this would be supernatural in the first way but not in the second. What is supernatural in the second way, however, is supernatural in both ways, for the second way implies the first, but not vice versa. However, where there is only the first type of supernatural [e.g. infused geometry], it is not impossible that what is supernatural could have been produced naturally [under other conditions]. Where something is supernatural in the second way, however, it is necessary that it be produced supernaturally, since it could not possibly be produced naturally.

[III. Concerning the Three Principal Reasons Against the Philosophers]

66. The three reasons upon which this solution is based are confirmed by arguments from authority. The first [cf. ¶13–16] is confirmed by the statement of Augustine in the *City of God*, XVIII, Chapter 41: "The philosophers, not knowing to what end these things were to be referred, were able to see some truth among the false things they asserted."

67. The second argument [cf. ¶17–18] is confirmed by Augustine in the *City of God*, XI, Chapter 2: "What good is it to know where one must go if one does not know how to get there?" In this the philosophers erred, for even though they handed on some truths regarding virtues, still their teaching was tainted with error, as he points out in the text quoted above. This is clear from their books. For Aristotle criticizes the polities devised by many another (*Politics* II), and yet his own polity is not without reproach, since he teaches that the gods are to be honored. "It is fitting," he says (*Politics* VII. ch. 7), "that honor be shown to the gods," and in the same book, Chapter 5: "There ought to be a law . . . that no deformed child shall be nursed."

68. The third argument [cf. ¶40–41] is confirmed by Augustine in the *City of God*, XI, Chapter 3: "We need the testimony of others concerning objects that lie beyond the reach of our own senses, since we cannot know them by our own testimony." And this confirms our main solution throughout [cf. ¶57–65], for those propositions which the argument declares to be neutral so far as we are concerned [cf. ¶40–41], cannot be believed by anyone on the basis of his own testimony, but he must have the testimony of someone who is above the whole of mankind.

69. It is doubtful just how this first revelation or imparting of such knowledge actually did or could have taken place. Was it by some interior or by some exterior communication, together with such signs as would suffice to cause assent? For the problem at hand, it is enough to point out that such knowledge could be supernaturally revealed in either way. But in neither way could it be imparted without error by man right from the beginning.

70. The objection is raised that these three reasons [cf. ¶13–41] refute themselves, for whatever they reveal as necessary to know is something that is true, since we can really know only what is true. Consequently, whatever these arguments reveal to be necessary for us to know—for example, that the end of man is the enjoyment of God in himself (first argument); that the manner of reaching Him is by way of merits which God accepts as worthy of such a reward (second argument); that God is triune and causes things contingently, etc. (third argument)—all these are shown to be true. Consequently, these reasons either are based solely on faith or a conclusion is drawn from them which is the very opposite of what they actually prove.

71. I reply that natural reason merely shows us that it is necessary for us to know definitely one part of this contradiction: "The enjoyment [of God] is [our] end; this enjoyment is not our end." In other words, our intellect must not remain in doubt or ignorance on this problem of whether such enjoyment is our end, for such would keep us from seeking the end. But natural reason does not reveal just which part we must know. In this way, then, the aforementioned reasons in so far as they are natural, reveal that one part of the contradiction must be true. Either it is this or it is that. But a definite answer is possible only from what we believe.

[IV. Reply to the Arguments of the Philosophers]

72. As to the arguments for the opinion of Aristotle, I say to the first [cf. ¶6] that knowledge depends upon the soul knowing and the object known, for according to Augustine (*On the Trinity,* IX, last chapter): "Knowledge is born of the knower and the known." Hence, even though the soul may possess sufficient active and passive faculties so far as its own activity in knowing is concerned, still it does not have in itself active powers that would suffice to take the place of the object's action for it is like a blank writing-tablet, as the third book, *On the Soul* tells us. Hence to say that the agent intellect is that by which [the mind] makes all things [known], is true only in so far as this "making" something known is an action of the soul and not in so far as it involves an action on the part of the object.

73. To the confirmation by reason [cf. ¶7], I say to the major that "nature" at times is taken in the sense of an intrinsic principle of movement and rest—as is described in the second book of the *Physics*—at other times, for a naturally active principle, in so far as nature is distinguished from art and deliberate intention on the basis of the different ways these proceed from their principle. In this latter sense, "nature" may or may not be intrinsic, just so long as it is natural [i.e., not deliberate or the result of art]. According to the first meaning of "nature," the major is not true, because not everything that is naturally passive has a corresponding intrinsic active principle or nature, for many things lack an intrinsic active power to produce some act they are able to receive naturally. If nature be taken in the second sense, the major is also false in certain instances, namely when a nature because of its excellence is naturally ordained to receive a perfection so eminent that it could be caused by an agent that is natural in the second sense. And so it is in our case.

74. To the proof given for the major, I say that the passive potency is not in vain for even though it could not be reduced to act by a natural agent as the principal cause,

still a natural agent can dispose it for such an act. And there is some agent in nature, i.e., in the universe as a whole, that can completely reduce it to act, namely the First or Supernatural Agent.

75. Someone may object that to be incapable of attaining its perfection through what is natural devaluates [our] nature, for according to the second book *On the Heavens and Earth:* "The more noble nature, the less it should lack." I reply: if our happiness consisted in the highest speculation that is naturally attainable, the Philosopher would not say our nature lacked anything necessary. But I admit that we can naturally possess such perfection at present. But I go further when I say that there is another higher form of speculation that can be received naturally. Consequently, nature in this regard is honored even more than if one were to claim that the highest possible perfection it could receive is that which is naturally attainable. Nor is it surprising that some nature has the ability to receive a perfection greater than that which lies within the reach of its own active causality.

76. The above citation from the second book *On the Heavens and Earth* is not to the point, because the Philosopher is speaking here of organs corresponding to the power of movement, if this be present in the stars. Now I concede universally that nature gives an organ to everything to which it gives an organic power (I am speaking of things that are not deformed). In our case, however, it is a question of giving a non-organic power, and still not giving naturally all the other requisites for the act. From the Philosopher's statement here, then, it can be said that if a nature can be ordained for a certain act or object, this nature has a natural faculty for the act and also a corresponding organ, if the faculty is organic. But the same cannot be said of the other requisites for the act.

77. The major [cf. ¶7] could be answered in another way, namely that it is true if one speaks of a natural passive potency with respect to an active power, but it is false if passive potency is taken with respect to the act received. The difference between these two is clear from the first part of the solution to this question [cf. ¶57].

78. The minor [cf. ¶7] is true in the second way [*viz.* if the possible intellect is taken in respect to the act received], but not in the first. There is a third and easy way of answering the minor, namely: to deny it. For even though absolutely speaking the possible intellect is naturally receptive of this intellection, this is not so in its present state. The reason for this, however, will be explained later in distinction 3.

79. To the third reason [cf. ¶8] see Thomas' reply in the *Summa* I, Question 1 where he says: "Sciences are diversified according to the diverse nature of their knowable objects. For both the astronomer and the physicist demonstrate the same conclusion, for example, that the earth is round. The astronomer does so by means of mathematics (i.e., abstracting from matter), but the physicist does so by means of the matter considered. Hence, there is no reason why the same things treated by the philosophical sciences inasmuch as they can be known by the light of natural reason, may not also be treated by another science inasmuch as they are known by the light of divine revelation."

To the contrary: If the knowledge of those things which can be known in theology is, or can be, treated in other sciences, even though it be in another light, it follows that theological knowledge of such things is unnecessary. The consequence is evident from his own example, for anyone who knows that the earth is round by means of physics has no absolute need of a mathematical knowledge [of the same].

80. This reply [of Thomas], to the third argument, however, is explained in this way. Habit is both a form and a habit. In so far as it is a habit, it is distinguished by

reason of the object. In so far as it is a form, however, it can be distinguished by reason of the active principle. Now principles are the efficient causes of a habit of knowledge. Consequently, even though the same object of knowledge (for example, that the earth is round), is not distinguished by reason of the object, there is still a distinction by reason of the different principles which the mathematician and physicist use to prove this. And so there will be a distinction of habits in so far as they are forms, but not in so far as they are habits.

81. To the contrary: Form is a common [or generic term] with reference to habit. Now it is impossible that anything be distinct by reason of some superior classification and yet not be distinct by reason of some subordinate classification. Therefore, it is impossible that anything be distinct by reason of form (and hence distinct in form) and still not be distinct by reason of habit. This is like saying that certain things differ as animals but not as men. Furthermore, he assumes that principles distinguish habits according to some other type of causality than as efficient principles, which is false. For if the distinguishing causes have any relation to habits, it is none other than as efficient causes. Furthermore, the [basic] reason always holds, for no matter how cognitive habits may be distinguished, so long as other habits are possible, there would still be no need of any one habit [e.g., theology], in the sense that without it knowledge would be impossible.

82. Therefore, I reply to the argument that even though these speculative sciences [*viz.* physics, mathematics and metaphysics] treat of all speculative things, they still do not exhaust all that can be known about these objects, for they fail to treat of what is proper to them, as has been made clear in the third argument against the first opinion. See above [cf. ¶40ff.].

83. The fourth argument [cf. ¶9] is answered in this way. First principles cannot be applied to any conclusions other than those which deal with what can be perceived by the senses, both because their terms are abstracted from sensible objects and so partake of their nature, and because the agent intellect, through which this application [of principles] takes place, is limited to objects that can be perceived by the senses.

84. To the contrary: The intellect is certain that these first principles are true not only of what can be perceived by the senses, but also of what cannot be so perceived. For the intellect has no doubt that contradictories cannot be simultaneously true of spiritual things any more than of material things. And there is no value in the statement that the term of the first principle is the "being" which is divided into the ten categories and does not apply to theological objects. For we have not the slightest doubt that contradictories are not simultaneously verified about God (e.g. God is happy; God is not happy, etc.) any more than of something white.

85. Another solution is offered, namely, that the conclusions follow from the major premises only when the latter are combined with a minor premise. But the minors to which they must be joined are not naturally evident.

To the contrary: The minors subsumed under the first principles predicate of the things subsumed, the subject terms of the first principles. But the terms of the first principles are known to be predicated about everything, for these terms are most common, therefore, etc.

86. Therefore, I reply that the second part of the minor [cf. ¶10] is false, *viz.* that all the conclusions that can be known are virtually included in the first principles. To the proof, I say that just as the subject terms are common, so also are those of the predicate. Therefore, when the subject terms, since they are distributed, stand for [supposit for] all things, they stand for them only in regard to the predicate terms, which are

most common. In virtue of such principles, then, only the most common predicates are known of those things which fall under such principles.

87. This is evident from reason, because the middle term cannot give the reason why any attribute inheres in its respective subject, unless the attribute in question is included virtually in the notion of the middle term. But the notion of the subject of a most common principle includes the reason for the inherence of only the most universal attributes and not those which are particular. Therefore, it is only under this most general aspect that such a subject can be the means or the reason why anything is known. But in addition to the most general attributes, there are many other attributes that can be known. Because these are not included in the attributes of the first principles, however, the latter will yield no knowledge of them. Consequently there are many things that can be known which are not included in the first principles.

This is clear from an example. Although the proposition: "Every whole is greater than its part," includes "A quarternion is greater than a binary" and other similar propositions with the same predicate, it does not include these: "A quarternion is twice as much as a binary" or "A ternary is one and a half times a binary," for these propositions would require some special middle terms which include them.

88. The third proof is from logic [cf. ¶86–87]. Although it is licit to descend from a universal affirmative subject, it is not licit to do so from the predicate. Now there are many predicates contained under the predicates of the first principles that can be known of those things which fall under the subjects of these principles. Therefore, these predicates are not known of these subjects through the first principles.

89. Against this it is objected: "Anything can be either affirmed or denied, but nothing can be both affirmed and denied." It follows: "Therefore, this is white or not white," so that it is permissible in this case to descend both from the predicate and from the subject.

I reply that this principle, "Anything can be affirmed or denied, etc. . . ." is equivalent to this: "Concerning anything one part of any contradiction is true and the other is false," where there is a double distribution [*viz.* "concerning anything" and "of any contradiction"], and it is lawful to descend from both distributed terms: "Therefore, of this thing, [one part] of this contradiction [is true, the other false; of that thing, one part of this contradiction is true, etc.; of that thing, one part of that contradiction is true, etc.] etc. But it is not lawful to descend [distributively] from a predicate with confused supposition," because it does not follow "Concerning everything, one part of every contradiction [is true and the other false], therefore, this part [is true and the other false]." And so it is with other principles. The predicate of a universal affirmative proposition always has only confused supposition, whether there is a double or only one distribution of the subject.

And in the example proposed it is clear that this still holds true. For it can be known of man that he is risible. From this principle "Of anything, etc. . . ." we can never infer anything more than: "Therefore, man is either risible or not risible." Hence, the other part of this disjunctive predicate will never be known of the subject through this principle. On the contrary another special principle is required such as the definition of the subject or the attribute, which is in truth a means and reason for knowing definitely that man is risible.

[Solution of the Initial Arguments]

90. To the arguments at the beginning.—To the first [cf. ¶1]: I distinguish natural objects. For a natural object can mean one which the faculty can attain naturally, i.e.,

by the action of causes that are naturally active, or it may mean an object toward which the faculty is naturally inclined, whether such an object can be naturally attained or not. The major, then, could be denied if natural is taken in the first sense, for the first object is equal to the faculty, and therefore this object is abstracted from everything concerning which the faculty is able to function. Still it does not follow necessarily that just because the intellect could know such a common object naturally, it could know everything contained under it, because the knowledge of some of the things contained is much more perfect than the confused knowledge of the common object itself. And so, even granting the minor in either sense of natural knowledge, the intended conclusion about what can be naturally attained does not follow, for the major is not true of the object that can be naturally attained.

91. Against this answer, I contend that it destroys itself. For according to him [Henry of Ghent], the primary object is one that is equal to the power. Now this is true: a power regards as its object [a] only those things of which the notion of its first object is verified and [b] anything of which this notion is verified. Therefore, it is impossible that something should be the primary natural object without everything of which it is verified being of itself a natural object. For grant the opposite and then the object is not naturally adequate but exceeds [the faculty] and something inferior is adequate and therefore the first object.

The reason given for [Henry's] answer, however, is a fallacy of figure of speech. For although, in so far as "being" is something that can be grasped by the intellect in a single act (as "man" can be grasped in one intellectual act), "being" can be known naturally (for this one concept of being in so far as it is a concept of one object is something natural), still it cannot be maintained that "being" is the primary object naturally attainable. For "being" is the first object in so far as it is included in all objects known of themselves, and as such it would be naturally attainable only if each of these objects were naturally attainable. Therefore, he [Henry] interchanges "this something," [without qualification], with "of a certain kind" when he argues: "Being is naturally knowable; therefore, being in so far as it is the first (i.e. adequate) object of the intellect, is naturally attainable." For the antecedent is true in so far as "being" is one single intelligible [object], e.g. a white thing, but the consequent makes a conclusion about being in so far as it is included in every intelligible object, and not "being" as conceived without this qualification.

92. To the argument, therefore, there is another, a real, answer, namely, the minor is false in regard to the object naturally attainable, but it is true in the other sense (namely the object to which the power is naturally ordered or inclined). In this way the quotation from Avicenna must be understood. (It will be pointed out later in distinction 3 what must be held to be the first object naturally attainable.) This answer is confirmed by Anselm in Chapter 4, *On Free Will:* "We have no power, I believe, which alone suffices for an act." By "power" he means what we commonly call a faculty, as is evident from his example about sight. Therefore, it is not unfitting that a power should be naturally ordered to an object which it cannot attain naturally by natural causes, any more than it is for a power or faculty to be ordained by its very nature [for an act] and nevertheless be unable to produce this act by itself alone.

93. As to the second argument [cf. ¶2], I deny its consequence. What is to be said of its proof, is clear from the reply given the second argument for the opinion of the Philosopher [cf. ¶73–74], because superior natures are ordained passively to receive something greater than they can actively produce. Consequently, their perfection cannot be achieved except by some supernatural agent. But this is not so with the perfec-

tion of less perfect things whose ultimate perfection could fall under the action of inferior agents.

94. As to the third [cf. ¶3], I say some of the propositions we must firmly hold to be true, are disproportionate to the possible intellect, that is to say, the intellect is not equal to being moved [to know them] by what can be known from sense images and the natural light of the agent intellect.

When you argue: "Therefore, the intellect becomes proportionate by means of something else," I concede that there is something else—both something that moves it (for, moved supernaturally by the one revealing, the intellect assents to this truth), and something else in the sense of a form (for there is the assent produced in the intellect, which is a kind of inclination in the intellect toward this object which brings the intellect into proportion with the latter).

But when you press further, "Is this 'something else' natural or supernatural?" I reply that it is supernatural, and this is so whether you understand this "something else" in the sense of agent or form.

When you infer: "Therefore, the intellect is disproportionate to it and must be made proportionate through something else," I declare that the intellect by its very nature is in obediential potency toward the agent, and thus is sufficiently proportionate to it to the extent that it can be moved by this agent. Also of itself, the intellect is capable of the act of assent caused by such an agent and this capability is natural. Hence, it is not necessary that it be proportioned by something in order that it be able to receive this assent.

Therefore, we stop not with the first [*viz.* something natural] but with the second [*viz.* something supernatural]. For this revealed truth of itself is insufficient to incline the intellect to assent to it, and hence neither the agent nor the patient is proportionate to this truth. But a supernatural agent suffices to incline the intellect toward this truth by causing in it the act of assent which makes the intellect proportionate to this truth. Hence, an additional something is not required to make the intellect proportionate to such an agent or to the form it impresses, in the same way that something is required in addition to the intellect that it be made proportionate to such an object in the twofold manner mentioned above.

WILLIAM OF OCKHAM
ca. 1285–1349

William was born in Ockham, Surrey, near London, between 1280 and 1290. He joined the Franciscan order as a young man. In 1309 or 1310, he went to Oxford, where his studies included the work of Duns Scotus. Despite his success as a student and, later, as a student lecturer, Ockham was denied a license to teach. The chancellor of the university accused him of heresy, even going to the papal court in Avignon, France, in 1323 to press charges. The following year Ockham was summoned to Avignon by Pope John XXII. The affair dragged on for four years. Meanwhile, Ockham kept writing and came into conflict with the pope again when he joined the general of his Franciscan order in advocating apostolic poverty.

In 1328, Ockham was forced to flee Avignon when the pope was prepared to condemn the Franciscan position on poverty. He eventually found refuge in Munich under the protection of Emperor Ludwig of Bavaria, who was angry with the pope for not recognizing his crown. Ockham reportedly told the emperor, "Defend me with your sword, and I will defend you with my pen."

Over the next twenty years, Ockham did indeed defend the emperor, arguing that imperial power flows from God through the people, not through the pope—a position that anticipated later political theories. Following Ludwig's death in 1347, Ockham sought reconciliation with the pope (now Clement VI), and a document of submission was drawn up. We do not know whether Ockham ever signed the document, for he died in 1349, apparently from the plague.

Ockham's philosophy reflects his times: He is much less optimistic than was Thomas Aquinas about the ability of human reason to understand the things of God. Ockham criticized the proofs for God's existence, arguing that theological truth can be known only by revelation, not reason. In so arguing, he separated philosophy from theology and reason from faith more completely than had any of his predecessors.

Ockham is probably best known for his "Law of Parsimony," or "Ockham's Razor." This principle has often been formulated as *entia non sunt multiplicanda praeter necessitatem,* "entities are not to be multiplied beyond necessity," though none of Ockham's known works contains that exact phrase.* Essentially this principle holds that we should always seek the simplest explanation, a principle still used by philosophers and scientists. Ockham was not the first to enunciate this principle: It can be found earlier in the writings of Thomas Aquinas,** Duns Scotus, and even, in embryonic form, in Aristotle.*** But the skill with which Ockham wielded this "razor" ensured its association with his name.

Ockham was especially effective in using his razor on the question of universals. Contrary to the moderate realism dominant in his day, Ockham saw no need to posit universals as real entities beyond individual things. This critique is clear in the selections on universals given here. Following some defining of terms, Ockham argues against the realist position and, with great care, against the position of the "Subtle Doctor," Duns Scotus. Ockham asserts that "in a particular substance there is nothing substantial except the particular form, the particular matter, or the composite of the two"—that is, there is no real universal apart from the particular thing.

In addition, representative passages on being, on knowledge, on God, and on politics are included. The final reading on politics—with its strong, though guarded, antipapal polemic—represents a marked departure from the political theory of John of Salisbury.

* * *

Marilyn McCord Adams's *William Ockham,* two volumes (Notre Dame, IN: University of Notre Dame Press, 1987) is the definitive introduction to Ockham, whereas Meyrick Heath Carré, *Realists and Nominalists* (London: Oxford University Press, 1946), and Sharon M. Kaye and Robert M. Martin, *On Ockham* (Belmont, CA: Wadsworth, 2001) provide helpful overviews. Specialized studies include E.A. Moody, *The Logic of William of Ockham* (1935; reprinted New York: Russell and Russell, 1965); Damascene Webering, *The Theory of Demonstration According to William Ockham* (St. Bonaventure, NY: Franciscan Institute, 1953); Herman Shapiro, *Motion, Time and Place According to William Ockham* (St. Bonaventure, NY: Franciscan Institute, 1957); Arthur Stephen McGrade, *The Political Thought of William of Ockham: Personal and Institutional Principles* (London: Cambridge University Press, 1974); and Rega Wood, *Ockham on the Virtues* (West Lafayette, IN: Purdue University Press, 1997). For collections of essays, see Philotheus Bohner, ed., *Collected Articles on Ockham* (St. Bonaventure, NY: Franciscan Institute, 1958) and Paul V. Spade, ed., *The Cambridge Companion to Ockham* (Cambridge: Cambridge University Press, 1999).

---

*Ockham's extant writings do include the phrases *pluralitas non est ponenda sine necessitate,* "plurality is not to be posited without necessity," and *frustra fit per plura quod potest fieri per pauciora,* "what can be explained by the assumption of fewer things is vainly explained by the assumption of more things." Perhaps applying his principle to its own formulation, we should say, "Why use many if few will do?"

**See his *Summa Theologica,* Part I, Q. 2, a. 3, obj. 2—page 348 in this volume.

***See *Postcrior Analytics* I.25, 86a33–35 and *Physics* I.4, 188a17–18; VIII.6, 259a8–12.

Plague Victim, from *Das Buch der Cirurgia,* 1497, by Hieronymus Brunschwig. Beginning in 1347 the Bubonic Plague, or "Black Death," struck western Europe. Transmitted by flea bite, the disease was characterized by enormous swelling or "buboes" in the groin or armpits. The patient in this woodcut has a large buboe on his armpit—a sure sign that he will be dead within two or three days. Apparently William of Ockham met such a fate in 1349. (*Library of Congress*)

ON UNIVERSALS

Summa Logicae, Part I

Chapter 14: On the Universal

It is not enough for the logician to have a merely general knowledge of terms; he needs a deep understanding of the concept of a term. Therefore, after discussing some general divisions among terms we should examine in detail the various headings under these divisions.

First, we should deal with terms of second intention and afterwards with terms of first intention. I have said that "universal," "genus," and "species" are examples of terms of second intention. We must discuss those terms of second intention which are called the five universals, but first we should consider the common term "universal." It is predicated of every universal and is opposed to the notion of a particular.

First, it should be noted that the term "particular" has two senses. In the first sense a particular is that which is one and not many. Those who hold that a universal is a certain quality residing in the mind which is predicable of many (not suppositing for itself, of course, but for the many of which it is predicated) must grant that, in this sense of the word, every universal is a particular. Just as a word, even if convention makes it common, is a particular, the intention of the soul signifying many is numerically one thing a particular; for although it signifies many things it is nonetheless one thing and not many.

In another sense of the word we use "particular" to mean that which is one and not many and which cannot function as a sign of many. Taking "particular" in this sense no universal is a particular, since every universal is capable of signifying many and of being predicated of many. Thus, if we take the term "universal" to mean that which is not one in number, as many do, then, I want to say that nothing is a universal. One could, of course, abuse the expression and say that a population constitutes a single universal because it is not one but many. But that would be puerile.

Therefore, it ought to be said that every universal is one particular thing and that it is not a universal except in its signification, in its signifying many things. This is what Avicenna means to say in his commentary on the fifth book of the *Metaphysics*. He says, "One form in the intellect is related to many things, and in this respect it is a universal; for it is an intention of the intellect which has an invariant relationship to anything you choose." He then continues, "Although this form is a universal in its relationship to individuals, it is a particular in its relationship to the particular soul in which it resides; for it is just one form among many in the intellect." He means to say that a universal is an intention of a particular soul. Insofar as it can be predicated of many things not for itself but for these many, it is said to be a universal; but insofar as it is a particular form actually existing in the intellect, it is said to be a particular. Thus "particular" is predicated of a universal in the first sense but not in the second. In the same way we say that the sun is a universal cause and, nevertheless, that it is really and truly a particular or individual cause. For the sun is said to be a universal cause because it is the cause of many things (i.e., every object that is generable and corruptible), but it is said to be a particular cause because it is one cause and not many. In the same way the intention of the soul is said to be a universal because it is a sign predicable of many things, but it is said to be a particular because it is one thing and not many.

But it should be noted that there are two kinds of universals. Some things are universal by nature; that is, by nature they are signs predicable of many in the same way that the smoke is by nature a sign of fire; weeping, a sign of grief; and laughter, a sign of internal joy. The intention of the soul, of course, is a universal by nature. Thus, no substance outside the soul, nor any accident outside the soul is a universal of this sort. It is of this kind of universal that I shall speak in the following chapters.

Other things are universals by convention. Thus, a spoken word, which is numerically one quality, is a universal; it is a sign conventionally appointed for the signification of many things. Thus, since the word is said to be common, it can be called a universal. But notice it is not by nature, but only by convention, that this label applies.

CHAPTER 15: THAT THE UNIVERSAL IS NOT A THING OUTSIDE THE MIND

But it is not enough just to state one's position; one must defend it by philosophical arguments. Therefore, I shall set forth some arguments for my view, and then corroborate it by an appeal to the authorities.

That no universal is a substance existing outside the mind can be proved in a number of ways:

No universal is a particular substance, numerically one; for if this were the case, then it would follow that Socrates is a universal; for there is no good reason why one substance should be a universal rather than another. Therefore no particular substance is a universal; every substance is numerically one and a particular. For every substance is either one thing and not many or it is many things. Now, if a substance is one thing and not many, then it is numerically one; for that is what we mean by "numerically one." But if, on the other hand, some substance is several things, it is either several particular things or several universal things. If the first alternative is chosen, then it follows that some substance would be several particular substances; and consequently that some substance would be several men. But although the universal would be distinguished from a single particular, it would not be distinguished from several particulars. If, however, some substance were to be several universal entities, I take one of those universal entities and ask, "Is it many things or is it one and not many?" If the second is the case then it follows that the thing is particular. If the first is the case then I ask, "Is it several particular things or several universal things?" Thus, either an infinite regress will follow or it will be granted that no substance is a universal in a way that would be incompatible with its also being a particular. From this it follows that no substance is a universal.

Again, if some universal were to be one substance existing in particular substances, yet distinct from them, it would follow that it could exist without them; for everything that is naturally prior to something else can, by God's power, exist without that thing; but the consequence is absurd.

Again, if the view in question were true, no individual would be able to be created. Something of the individual would pre-exist it, for the whole individual would not take its existence from nothing if the universal which is in it were already in something else. For the same reason it would follow that God could not annihilate an individual substance without destroying the other individuals of the same kind. If He were to annihilate some individual, he would destroy the whole which is essentially that individual and, consequently, He would destroy the universal which is in that thing and in others of the same essence. Consequently, other things of the same essence would not remain, for they could not continue to exist without the universal which constitutes a part of them.

Again, such a universal could not be construed as something completely extrinsic to the essence of an individual; therefore, it would belong to the essence of the individual; and, consequently, an individual would be composed of universals, so that the individual would not be any more a particular than a universal.

Again, it follows that something of the essence of Christ would be miserable and damned, since that common nature really existing in Christ would be damned in the damned individual; for surely that essence is also in Judas. But this is absurd.

Many other arguments could be brought forth, but in the interests of brevity, I shall dispense with them. Instead, I shall corroborate my account by an appeal to authorities.

First, in the seventh book of the *Metaphysics,* Aristotle is treating the question of whether a universal is a substance. He shows that no universal is a substance. Thus, he says, "It is impossible that substance be something that can be predicated universally."

Again, in the tenth book of the *Metaphysics,* he says, "Thus, if, as we argued in the discussions on substance and being, no universal can be a substance, it is not possible that a universal be a substance in the sense of a one over and against the many."

From these remarks it is clear that, in Aristotle's view, although universals can supposit for substances, no universal is a substance.

Again, the Commentator in his forty-fourth comment on the seventh book of the *Metaphysics* says, "In the individual, the only substance is the particular form and matter out of which the individual is composed."

Again, in the forty-fifth comment, he says, "Let us say, therefore, that it is impossible that one of those things we call universals be the substance of anything, although they do express the substances of things."

And, again, in the forty-seventh comment, "It is impossible that they (universals) be parts of substances existing of and by themselves."

Again, in the second comment on the eighth book of the *Metaphysics,* he says, "No universal is either a substance or a genus."

Again, in the sixth comment on the tenth book, he says, "Since universals are not substances, it is clear that the common notion of being is not a substance existing outside the mind."

Using these and many other authorities, the general point emerges: no universal is a substance regardless of the viewpoint from which we consider the matter. Thus, the viewpoint from which we consider the matter is irrelevant to the question of whether something is a substance. Nevertheless, the meaning of a term is relevant to the question of whether the expression "substance" can be predicated of the term. Thus, if the term "dog" in the proposition "The dog is an animal" is used to stand for the barking animal, the proposition is true; but if it is used for the celestial body which goes by that name, the proposition is false. But it is impossible that one and the same thing should be a substance from one viewpoint and not a substance from another.

Therefore, it ought to be granted that no universal is a substance regardless of how it is considered. On the contrary, every universal is an intention of the mind which, on the most probable account, is identical with the act of understanding. Thus, it is said that the act of understanding by which I grasp men is a natural sign of men in the same way that weeping is a natural sign of grief. It is a natural sign such that it can stand for men in mental propositions in the same way that a spoken word can stand for things in spoken propositions.

That the universal is an intention of the soul is clearly expressed by Avicenna in the fifth book of the *Metaphysics,* in which he comments, "I say, therefore, that there are three senses of 'universal.' For we say that something is a universal if (like 'man') it is actually predicated of many things; and we also call an intention a universal if it could be predicated of many." Then follows the remark, "An intention is also called a universal if there is nothing inconceivable in its being predicated of many."

From these remarks it is clear that the universal is an intention of the soul capable of being predicated of many. The claim can be corroborated by argument. For every one agrees that a universal is something predicable of many, but only an intention of the soul or a conventional sign is predicated. No substance is ever predicated of anything. Therefore, only an intention of the soul or a conventional sign is a universal; but I am not here using the term "universal" for conventional signs, but only for signs that are universals by nature. That substance is not capable of functioning as predicate is clear; for if it were, it would follow that a proposition would be composed of particular substances; and, consequently, the subject would be in Rome and the predicate in England which is absurd.

Furthermore, propositions occur only in the mind, in speech, or in writing; therefore, their parts can exist only in the mind, in speech, and in writing. Particular substances, however, cannot themselves exist in the mind, in speech, or in writing. Thus, no proposition can be composed of particular substances. Propositions are, however, composed of universals; therefore, universals cannot conceivably be substances.

CHAPTER 16: AGAINST SCOTUS' ACCOUNT OF THE UNIVERSAL

It may be clear to many that a universal is not a substance outside the mind which exists in, but is distinct from, particulars. Nevertheless, some want to claim that the universal is, in some way, outside the soul and in particulars; and while they do not want to say that a universal is really distinct from particulars, they say that it is formally distinct from particulars. Thus, they say that in Socrates there is human nature which is contracted to Socrates by an individual difference which is not really, but only formally, distinct from that nature. Thus, while there are not two things, one is not formally the other.

I do not find this view tenable:

First, in creatures there can never be any distinction outside the mind unless there are distinct things; if, therefore, there is any distinction between the nature and the difference, it is necessary that they really be distinct things. I prove my premise by the following syllogism: the nature is not formally distinct from itself; this individual difference is formally distinct from this nature; therefore, this individual difference is not this nature.

Again, the same entity is not both common and proper, but in their view the individual difference is proper and the universal is common; therefore, no universal is identical with an individual difference.

Again, opposites cannot be attributed to one and the same created thing, but *common* and *proper* are opposites; therefore, the same thing is not both common and proper. Nevertheless, that conclusion would follow if an individual difference and a common nature were the same thing.

Again, if a common nature were the same thing as an individual difference, there would be as many common natures as there are individual differences; and, consequently, none of those natures would be common, but each would be peculiar to the difference with which it is identical.

Again, whenever one thing is distinct from another it is distinguished from that thing either of and by itself or by something intrinsic to itself. Now, the humanity of Socrates is something different from the humanity of Plato; therefore, they are distinguished of and by themselves and not by differences that are added to them.

Again, according to Aristotle things differing in species also differ in number, but the nature of a man and the nature of a donkey differ in species of and by themselves; therefore, they are numerically distinguished of and by themselves; therefore, each of them is numerically one of and by itself.

Again, that which cannot belong to many cannot be predicated of many; but such a nature, if it really is the same thing as the individual difference, cannot belong to many since it cannot belong to any other particular. Thus, it cannot be predicable of many; but, then, it cannot be a universal.

Again, take an individual difference and the nature which it contracts. Either the difference between these two things is greater or less than the difference between two particulars. It is not greater because they do not differ really; particulars, however, do differ really. But neither is it less because then they would admit of one and the same definition, since two particulars, can admit of the same definition. Consequently, if one of them is, by itself, one in number, the other will also be.

Again, either the nature is the individual difference or it is not. If it is the difference I argue as follows: this individual difference is proper and not common; this individual difference is this nature; therefore this nature is proper and not common, but that is what I set out to prove. Likewise, I argue as follows: the individual difference is not formally distinct from the individual difference; the individual difference is the nature; therefore, the nature is not formally distinct from the individual difference. But if it be said that the individual difference is not the nature, my point has been proved; for it follows that if the individual difference is not the nature, the individual difference is not really the nature; for from the opposite of the consequent follows the opposite of the antecedent. Thus, if it is true that the individual difference really is the nature, then the individual difference is the nature. The inference is valid, for from a determinable taken with its determination (where the determination does not detract from or diminish the determinable) one can infer the determinable taken by itself; but "really" does not express a determination that detracts or diminishes. Therefore, it follows that if the individual difference is really the nature, the individual difference is the nature.

Therefore, one should grant that in created things there is no such thing as a formal distinction. All things which are distinct in creatures are really distinct and, therefore, different things. In regard to creatures modes of argument like the following ought never be denied: this is A; this is B; therefore, B is A; and this is not A; this is B; therefore, B is not A. Likewise, one ought never deny that, as regards creatures, there are distinct things where contradictory notions hold. The only exception would be the case where contradictory notions hold true because of some syncategorematic element or similar determination, but in the same present case this is not so.

Therefore, we ought to say with the philosophers that in a particular substance there is nothing substantial except the particular form, the particular matter, or the composite of the two. And, therefore, no one ought to think that in Socrates there is a humanity or a human nature which is distinct from Socrates and to which there is added an individual difference which contracts that nature. The only thing in Socrates which can be construed as substantial is this particular matter, this particular form, or the composite of the two. And, therefore, every essence and quiddity and whatever belongs to substance, if it is really outside the soul, is just matter, form, or the composite of these or, following the doctrine of the Peripatetics, a separated and immaterial substance.

*   *   *

SUMMA LOGICAE, PART II

CHAPTER 2: WHAT IS REQUIRED FOR THE TRUTH OF A SINGULAR NON-MODAL PROPOSITION

. . . We will first discuss singular non-modal present-tense propositions whose subjects and predicates are both in the nominative case and which are not equivalent to hypothetical propositions.

On this point it should be noted that for the truth of such a singular proposition which is not equivalent to several propositions it is not required that the subject and predicate be really identical, or that the predicate be in reality in the subject or that it really inhere in the subject, or that the predicate be united to the subject itself outside the mind. Thus, for the truth of "This is an angel" it is not required that the common term "angel" be really identical with what is posited as the subject, or that it be really in that subject, or anything of this sort. Rather, it is sufficient and necessary that the subject and predicate supposit for the same thing. And, therefore, if in "This is an angel" the subject and predicate supposit for the same thing, the proposition will be true. Thus, it is not asserted that this thing has angelhood or that angelhood is in it—or anything of this sort. Rather, it is asserted that this thing is truly an angel—not, indeed, that it is the predicate, but that it is that for which the predicate supposits.

Similarly, by means of propositions like "Socrates is a man" and "Socrates is an animal" it is not asserted that Socrates has humanity or animality. Nor is it asserted that humanity or animality is in Socrates, or that man or animal is in Socrates, or that animal is part of the quidditative concept of Socrates. Rather, it is asserted that Socrates is truly a man and is truly an animal. Nor, indeed, is it asserted that Socrates is the predicate "man" or the predicate "animal." Rather, it is asserted that he is a thing for which the predicate "man" or the predicate "animal" stands or supposits. For both of these predicates stand for Socrates.

From this it is clear that, literally speaking, all propositions such as these are false: "Man is of the quiddity of Socrates," "Man is of the essence of Socrates," "Humanity is in Socrates," "Socrates has humanity," "Socrates is a man in virtue of hu-

From *Ockham's Theory of Terms: Part II of the Summa Logicae* by William of Ockham, translated by Michael J. Loux. Copyright © 1974 by University of Notre Dame Press. Reprinted by permission.

manity"—and many other such propositions which are considered true, it seems, by everyone. Their falsity is obvious. For I take one of them, namely, "Humanity is in Socrates," and I ask: what does "humanity" stand for? Either for a thing or for an intention, i.e. by means of this proposition it is asserted either that a real extramental thing is in Socrates or that an intention of the soul is in Socrates. If it supposits for a thing, then I ask: for which thing? Either for Socrates, or for a part of Socrates, or for a thing which is neither Socrates nor a part of Socrates. If for Socrates, then the proposition is false, since nothing which is Socrates is in Socrates—for Socrates is not in Socrates, even though Socrates is Socrates. And in the same way humanity is not in Socrates but is Socrates, if "humanity" supposits for a thing which is Socrates. On the other hand, if "humanity" stands for a thing which is a part of Socrates, then the proposition is false, because anything which is a part of Socrates is either matter or form or a composite of matter and form—and just one human form and not another—or it is an integral part of Socrates. But humanity is no such part, as is clear inductively. For humanity is not an intellective soul. For if it were, then real humanity would have remained in Christ in the tomb, and humanity would have been really united to the Word in the tomb, and, consequently, he would really have been a man—which is false. Similarly, humanity is not matter. Nor is humanity the body of Socrates or his foot or his head, and so on for the other parts of Socrates. For no part of Socrates is humanity—rather, it is only a part of humanity. As a result, "humanity" cannot supposit for a part of Socrates. If it supposits for a thing which is neither Socrates nor a part of Socrates, then, since such a thing could only be an accident or some other thing which is not in Socrates, "humanity" would supposit for an accident of Socrates or for some other thing which is neither Socrates nor a part of Socrates—and it is clear that that is false. If, moreover, "humanity" supposits for an intention of the soul, then the proposition is clearly false. For an intention of the soul is not in Socrates. And so it is clear that "Humanity is in Socrates" is false no matter how it is understood.

One can argue in the same way with respect to all the other propositions noted above. For if man or humanity is of the essence of Socrates, I then ask: what does "man" or "humanity" supposit for? Either for Socrates, in which case it would be asserted that Socrates is of the essence of Socrates—which is not true. Or if it supposits for a thing other than Socrates, then it supposits either for a part of Socrates—but this cannot be, since no part of Socrates is a man or humanity—or for something else which is neither Socrates nor a part of Socrates—but it is clear that no such thing is a man or humanity unless it is Plato or John or some other man. And it is manifest that no man other than Socrates is of the essence of Socrates. On the other hand, if it supposits for an intention of the soul or for a spoken word, it is clear that in that case it is not of the essence of Socrates. And so it is obvious that all such propositions are literally false.

Now someone might claim that humanity is in Socrates and is of the essence of Socrates, and that, nevertheless, it is neither Socrates, nor matter, nor form, nor an integral part—rather, it is a common nature which enters into a composition with the individual difference of Socrates. Hence, it is a part of Socrates but neither matter nor form.

I argue against this view at length in several places, namely, in my commentaries on the first book of the *Sentences,* on the book of Porphyry, and on the *Categories.* At present I will offer some arguments against it.

The first is this. If humanity were something different from singular things and of the essence of singulars, then the same thing, while remaining unchanged, would be in many singular things. And so the same thing, while remaining naturally un-changed, would be in many distinct places without a miracle. But it is obvious that this is false.

Similarly, in that case the same thing, while remaining unchanged, would be damned in Judas and saved in Christ. And so there would be something miserable and damned in Christ—which is absurd.

Likewise, in that case God would not be able to annihilate an individual unless he annihilated or destroyed every individual of the same genus. For when something is annihilated, nothing of it remains and, as a result, such a common nature does not re-main. Consequently, no individual in which it is remains, and so each individual would be annihilated or destroyed.

Further, I take that humanity which you posit in Socrates and in every other man, and the donkeyhood which you posit in every donkey. And let that humanity be called A, so that A stands just for that humanity; and let that donkeyhood be called B, so that B stands just for that donkeyhood. Then I ask: are A and B just two things, or more than two things, or not more than one thing? It cannot be said that they are not more than one thing. For in that case necessarily either they are one thing, or neither A nor B is a thing, or A is not a thing, or B is not a thing. It is clear, even according to those who hold this position, that the first answer cannot be given. Nor can the second answer be given, since these same people deny it when they claim that humanity is a real thing and, likewise, donkeyhood. Nor can the third answer be given, since there is no more reason for claiming that B is not a thing than for claiming that A is not a thing, and conversely. Therefore, it is absolutely necessary to say that A and B are more than one thing. Further, it cannot be claimed that they are more than two things. For if they are more than two things and if they are not more than two universal things, then they are more singular things. And, as a result, they are not distinguished absolutely from singular things. Therefore, the only remaining alternative is that they are two things and no more. Consequently, each of them is one in number, since each will be one thing in such a way that it is not many things. And this is what it is to be one in number, namely, to be one thing and not many. For that ought to be the de-scription of being one in number. For if this were to be denied, I might just as easily claim that Socrates is not numerically one thing even if he is one thing and not many things.

Hence, it is the opinion of the Philosopher as well as the truth that the predicate "is one in species" or "is one or the same in genus" is never predicated except of an in-dividual or individuals, each of which is one in number. Thus, "Socrates and Plato are one in species" and "Socrates and this donkey are one in genus" are true. And nothing other than individuals is one in species or in genus. And so it is the case that that hu-manity which is posited in every man is one thing and not more than one thing and, consequently, that it is one in number. From this it follows that numerically one thing would be in every man.

Moreover, I think that in other places I have sufficiently responded to arguments which seem to contravene the view I have set forth.

Nor does it help to claim that the humanity of Socrates is only formally dis-tinct—and not really distinct—from Socrates. For such a distinction should not be posited in creatures, although it can in some sense be posited in the divinity. This is so because among creatures it is impossible to find any numerically one thing which is re-ally more than one thing and is each of those things, as is the case with God. For in God the divine essence is three persons and it is each of those persons, and yet one person is not another. For to say that the essence and a person are formally distinguished, in the true sense, is nothing other than to say that the essence is three persons and a person is not three persons. Similarly, I understand the proposition, "The essence and the Paternity are formally distinguished" to mean nothing other than the proposition "The essence is the Filiation and the Paternity is not the Filiation and yet the essence is the Paternity." Likewise, to say that the Paternity and the Active Procession are formally distinguished is nothing other than to say that the Paternity is not the Filiation and that the Active Procession is the Filiation and yet that the Paternity is the Active Procession.

And so, generally, when two things are truly said to be formally distinguished, this is nothing other than to say that something is truly affirmed of the one and truly denied of the other, and yet that one of those two things is truly affirmed of the other—without any variation or equivocation or verification for different things, as happens in particular and indefinite propositions. But this can never occur except when one simple thing is more than one thing, as a single divine essence is three persons and as a single Active Procession is the Paternity and the Filiation. And since it cannot happen among creatures that one thing is more than one thing and is each of them, a formal distinction ought not be posited in creatures. And so it is clear that it should not be claimed that the humanity of Socrates is formally—but not really—distinguished from Socrates. The same holds for propositions like "Animality is distinguished from a man," and so on for the others. In the commentary on the first book of the Sentences, distinction two I proved, moreover, that such a formal distinction must not be posited in creatures.

ON BEING

Summa Logicae, Part I

Chapter 38: On Being

Having dealt with terms of second intention and second imposition we shall turn our attention to those terms of first intention that are called the categories. But first we shall consider some expressions that are common to all things, both signs and things that are not signs. "Being" and "one" are terms of this sort.

It should first be noted that the term "being" has two senses. In one sense the term is used to correspond to one concept that is common to all things and is predicable *in quid* of everything in the way in which a transcendental is capable of being predicated *in quid*.

From *Ockham's Theory of Terms: Part I of the Summa Logicae* by William of Ockham, translated by Michael J. Loux. Copyright © 1974 by University of Notre Dame Press. Reprinted by permission.

One can prove that there is one common concept predicable of everything in the following way: if there is no one such common concept, then there are different concepts for different things.

Let us suppose that there are two such concepts, *A* and *B*. Following out this supposition, I can show that some concept more general than *A* and *B* is predicable of an object, *C*. Just as we can form the verbal propositions "*C* is *B*," "*C* is *A*," and "*C* is something," we can form three corresponding mental propositions. Two of these are dubious and one is certain; for someone can doubt which of the first two is true, while knowing that the third is true. If this is granted, I argue as follows: two of the propositions are dubious and one is certain. The three propositions all have the same subject; therefore, they have different predicates. Were it not so, one and the same proposition would be both certain and dubious; for in the present case the first two are dubious. But if they have different predicates, the predicate in "*C* is something" is not the predicate in either "*C* is *B*" or "*C* is *A*." It is, we can conclude, a different predicate. But it is clear that the relevant predicate is neither less general nor convertible with either *A* or *B*. It must therefore be more general. But this is what we set out to prove—that some concept of the mind, different from those that are logically subordinated to it, is common to everything. That must be granted. Just as one word is capable of being truly predicated of everything, there is some one concept of the mind that can be truly predicated of every object or of every pronoun referring to an object.

But while there is one concept common to everything, the term "being" is equivocal because it is not predicated of the items logically subordinated to it according to just one concept; several different concepts correspond to the term as I have indicated in my commentary on Porphyry.

Further, it should be noted that, as the Philosopher says in the fifth book of the *Metaphysics,* "Being is said both essentially and accidentally." In drawing this distinction the Philosopher should not be understood to mean that some things are beings *per se* and others, beings *per accidens*. What he is doing on the contrary is pointing to the different ways in which one thing can be predicated of another through the mediation of "to be." This is clear from the examples he uses. As he notes, we say that the musical is *per accidens* just, that the musical is *per accidens* a man, and that the musical is *per accidens* a builder. It should be clear from these examples that he is only distinguishing the different ways of predicating one thing of another, viz., *per accidens* and *per se*. It is clear that there are not two kinds of being, the *per se* and the *per accidens*. Everything is either a substance or an accident, but both substances and accidents are beings *per se*. This point holds even though we have *per se* and *per accidens* predication.

Similarly, being is divided into being in potency and being in act. This should not be understood to mean that there are two kinds of beings, those which do not exist in nature but could and those which actually exist in nature. By dividing being into potency and act in the fifth book of the *Metaphysics,* Aristotle means to show that the term "being" is predicated of some things by means of *de inesse* propositions and not by means of propositions equivalent to propositions of possibility. Thus "Socrates is a being" and "Whiteness is a being." Of other things, Aristotle wants to say, "being" is predicated only by means of a proposition of possibility or by a proposition equivalent to such. Thus "The Anti-Christ can be" and "The Anti-Christ is a being in potency." He wants to say that being like knowledge and sleep, can be predicated both potentially and actually. But note: things do not sleep or have knowledge except actually.

We will talk about the other divisions in being elsewhere. In the interests of brevity these remarks will suffice for the present.

ON KNOWLEDGE

QUODLIBETAL QUESTIONS

FIRST QUODLIBET

Question 13: *Whether that which is known by the understanding first according to a primacy of generation is the individual.*

For the negative: And it seems in the first place that it is not. For the universal is the first and proper object of the understanding. Therefore, in point of primacy of generation it is known first.

For the opposite: the object of sense and the object of understanding are absolutely the same. But the individual is the first object of sense by such a primacy. Therefore etc.

The meaning of the question must be stated first here. In the second place the question is to be answered.

FIRST ARTICLE

With respect to the first part it must be known that individual is taken here not as every thing which is one in number, for taken thus, each and every thing is individual. But it is taken to mean that thing which is one in number and is not a sign, whether natural or voluntary (or at good pleasure), common to many things, for the written word, the concept, and the spoken word, which are significative of many things, are not individuals, but only the thing which is not a common sign is individual.

In the second place [with respect to this first part] it must be known that this question is not understood to be about any knowledge whatsoever of the individual, for any universal knowledge taken thus is knowledge of the individual. For nothing is understood by such universal knowledge except an individual and individuals. However, such knowledge is common; but the question is understood to be about knowledge which is properly speaking simple and individual.

SECOND ARTICLE

Thesis 1

With respect to the second part, having supposed that the question is understood to be about knowledge properly individual, then I say first that, taking individual in the said manner to mean knowledge which is properly individual and simple, the individual is known first.

This is proved by the following reason, that the thing outside the soul which is not a sign is understood by such knowledge first. But every thing outside the soul is individual: therefore etc.

William of Ockham, *The Seven Quodlibeta.* From Richard McKeon, ed., *Selections from Medieval Philosophers* (NY: Charles Scribner's, 1929).

Moreover, the object precedes its own act and is first in the primacy of generation. But nothing precedes such an act except the individual: therefore etc.

Thesis 2

In the second place [with respect to the second part] I say that knowledge which is simple and peculiarly individual and first by such a primacy is intuitive knowledge. That this knowledge, however, is first, is evident because of the fact that abstractive individual knowledge presupposes intuitive knowledge in respect to the same object, and not conversely. Moreover, that it is properly and peculiarly individual is evident from the fact that it is caused immediately by the individual thing, or it is its nature to be caused by it, nor is it its nature to be caused by any other individual thing, even of the same species.

Thesis 3

In the third place, I say that the abstractive knowledge which is first by the primacy of generation and simple (1) is not knowledge peculiarly individual, but (2) on the contrary is sometimes, nay always, common knowledge.

(1) The first is evident because one does not have properly simple knowledge of any individual at the moment when specific knowledge of the individual can not be bad; but now and then there is such knowledge [i.e. abstractive knowledge which is not properly individual], as is clear in the case of something coming from a distance which causes a sensation by virtue of which I am able only to judge that that which is seen is a being. It is manifest that in that case the abstractive knowledge which I have first according to the primacy of generation is knowledge of being and of nothing lower. And consequently it is not a concept having to do with the species nor is it a proper concept of the individual.

(2) The second is clear because no abstractive simple knowledge is more the likeness of one thing than another in respect of like things, nor is it caused by a thing, nor is it its nature to be caused by it: therefore, no such knowledge is properly an individual knowledge; but all such knowledge is universal.

Problem 1

But perhaps there are some doubts at this point. First because it seems that intuitive knowledge is not proper knowledge, because whatever is given by intuitive knowledge is assimilated equally to one individual and to another which is like it, and it represents one individual equally with the rest. Therefore, it does not seem to be knowledge of one thing more than another.

Problem 2

The second doubt is that if first abstractive knowledge is occasionally a knowledge or concept of being, such as was given in the case of something coming from a distance, then in the same way first intuitive knowledge in the same situation will be knowledge of all being, because it is impossible that there be many simple proper concepts of the same thing. But I can have one perception of one thing coining from distant places, by which I only judge it to be being, another by which I judge it to be animal, a third by which I judge it to be man, a fourth by which I judge it to be Socrates. But these perceptions are not of different kinds [ratio]: therefore, all of them can not be proper notions of the same individual thing.

Problem 3

The third doubt is that it seems that first abstractive knowledge is most of all proper, since the object is approximated in the manner in which it should be, because we are able by the first abstractive knowledge to recall the same thing previously seen, which could not be done if abstractive proper knowledge were not had concerning the same thing previously seen.

Problem 4

The fourth doubt is that it seems from what has been said already, as if the concept of the genus could be abstracted from one individual, for example the concept of animal, as is evident in the case of one coming from distant places, since I have a perception such that I can judge by it that that is an animal.

Reply to Problem 1

I say, therefore, to the first of these doubts that intuitive knowledge is proper individual knowledge, not because of the greater assimilation to one thing than to another, but because it is caused naturally by the one and not by the other, nor can it be caused by the other. If you say that it can be caused by God alone, that is true, but it is the nature of such a perception to be caused by one created object and not by another. And if it is caused, it is always caused by one object and not by another. Whence it is no more called intuitive proper singular knowledge because of likeness, than it is called first abstractive knowledge, but only because of causality; nor can any other cause be assigned.

Reply to Problem 2

To the second doubt I say that sometimes those perceptions are of the same species and differ only as more and less perfect in the same species, as, if a concept were perceived from parts of the same reason or kind [ratio], in which there were no more accidents sensible to sight, then by the approximation of that visible, as for example white, perception is intensified and is made clearer. And in this way one and another individual can be caused, for such a perceived thing is being or body or color or whiteness. But you say that those things differ in species which can not, cause an effect of the same species; but clear and obscure vision are of this sort, therefore etc.: I say that whenever causes which are augmented and intensified can not cause an effect of the same species, they differ in species then and not otherwise. Now, however, this perception, when it is augmented and intensified, can accomplish every effect that clear sight can; and consequently they are of the same reason or of the same species. Yet clear perception and obscure perception are sometimes of different species, as for example when different objects are seen, as, if something were seen colored in different colors, according to a lesser and a greater approximation. But these perceptions are not of the same object but of different objects.

Reply to Problem 3

To the third doubt I say that by seeing something I have some proper abstractive knowledge; but this is not simple but composed from simples. And this composite notion is the beginning of recollection, for by it I recall Socrates, because I saw him formed thus or figured thus, colored thus, of such a length, breadth, and in such a place; and by that composition I recall that I have seen Socrates. But if you circumscribe all simple concepts except one, I no more recall Socrates because of it, than I recall another man extremely like him. Whence I can recall that I have bad sight of a man; but I do not know whether it is Plato or Socrates; and therefore a simple abstractive notion is not proper absolutely; but a composite notion can well be proper.

Reply to Problem 4

To the fourth doubt I say that the concept of genus is never abstracted from one individual. To the other argument [of this doubt] concerning something coming from distant places, I say that I judge it to be animal because I have previously the concept of animal, which concept is the genus; and therefore by the concept I am led to recollective knowledge. Whence if I did not previously have the concept of the genus of animal, I would judge only that this thing seen is something.

And if you ask what abstractive conception is first formed by the medium of intuitive knowledge, I say sometimes only the concept of that which is or being, sometimes the concept of genus, sometimes the concept of the most special species according to whether the object is less or more removed. The concept of that which is or being, however, is always impressed, because when the object is approximated in the required manner, the specific concept and the concept of being are caused at the same time by the individual thing without.

REPLY TO THE PRINCIPAL ARGUMENT

To the principal argument I say that the universal is the first object by the primacy of adequation, not by the primacy of generation.

ON GOD

Quodlibetal Questions

First Quodlibet

Question 1: *Can it be proved by natural reason that there is just one God?*

For the affirmative: Of one world there is just one ruler, according to *Metaphysics* 12 [10.1076a4]. But according to the Philosopher in *On the Heavens* 1 [8-9.276a18-279b3], it can be proved by natural reason that there is just one world. Therefore, it can

William of Ockham, *Quodlibetal Questions,* translated by Alfred J. Freddoso and Francis E. Kelley (New Haven, CT: Yale University Press, 1991). Reprinted by permission.

be proved by natural reason that there is just one ruler. But that ruler is God. Therefore, etc.

For the opposite: An article of the faith cannot be proved evidently.* But it is an article of the faith that there is just one God. Therefore, etc. In this question I will first explain what is to be understood by the name "God"; second, I will reply to the question.

FIRST ARTICLE

As for the first article, I claim that the name "God" can have various descriptions. One description is that God is something nobler and better than anything other than itself; a second description is that God is that than which nothing is better or more perfect.

SECOND ARTICLE

Thesis 1

As for the second article, I claim that if "God" is taken in accord with the first description, then it cannot be proved demonstratively that there is just one God. The reason for this is that if "God" is taken in this way, then it cannot be known evidently that God exists; therefore, if "God" is taken in this way, it cannot be known evidently that there is just one God. The consequence is obvious. The antecedent is proved from the fact that the proposition "God exists" is not known per se, since there are many who are in doubt about it; nor can it be proved from things that are known per se, since in every argument for that conclusion something will be accepted that is either doubtful or [merely] believed;** nor, it is clear, is the proposition in question known through experience. Therefore, etc.

Thesis 2

Second, I claim that if one could prove evidently that God exists, taking "God" in the first way, then the uniqueness of God could be proved evidently. The reason for this is that if there were two Gods, A and B, under this description, then A would be more perfect than anything other than himself; and so he would be more perfect than B, and B would be more imperfect than A. Similarly, B would be more perfect than A, since by hypothesis B is God. Consequently, B would be more perfect and more imperfect than A, and A more perfect and more imperfect than B—which is an obvious

---

*[For Ockham, the term "evident" (*evidens*) designates the highest grade of epistemic appraisal, so that an evident proposition is one that is as certain as any proposition can be. Accordingly, to prove a proposition evidently is to deduce it by evident rules of inference from propositions that are themselves evident. An article (or mystery) of the faith is by definition a proposition that cannot be rendered evident to us in this life.]

**[Here and in what follows, Ockham distinguishes between one's having evident knowledge (*scientia*) with respect to a proposition and one's merely believing it or having faith with respect to it. Belief, so taken, involves accepting on trust something that is not evident. On this construal, then, belief and evident knowledge are contraries.]

contradiction. Therefore, if one could prove evidently that God exists, taking "God" in this way, then the uniqueness of God could be proved evidently.

Thesis 3

Third, I claim that the uniqueness of God cannot be proved evidently if "God" is taken in the second way. And yet the negative proposition "The uniqueness of God (when 'God' is taken in this way) cannot be proved evidently" cannot itself be proved demonstratively, since the only way one can demonstrate that the uniqueness of God cannot be proved evidently is by refuting the arguments to the contrary. In the same way, it cannot be proved demonstratively that the stars are even in number, nor can the Trinity of persons [in God] be demonstrated; and yet the following negative propositions cannot be proved evidently: "It cannot be demonstrated that the stars are even in number," "The Trinity of persons cannot be demonstrated."

Thesis 4

Nonetheless, it should be noted that it can be demonstrated that God exists if "God" is taken in the second way mentioned above. For there would be an infinite regress if among the things that exist there were not something such that nothing else is prior to it or more perfect than it. But from this it does not follow that it can be demonstrated that there is just *one* such being. Instead, this is held only by faith.

*   *   *

ON POSSIBILITY AND GOD

My question is this: Is the inability to perform the impossible a characteristic of God that is prior [by nature] to the impossible's inability to be made by God?

[Arguments for and Against the Thesis]

It seems that God's inability to perform the impossible is the prior characteristic for the following reason. That God can make what is possible is prior to the possible's capacity to be made by God. In the same vein then God's inability to make the impossible should be prior to the impossible's inability to be made by God. The antecedent is evident from the fact that everything that pertains to God is prior to anything that pertains to a creature, and consequently also to anything that the creature gets from God. Therefore, since the ability to make the possible is a divine characteristic, this should pertain to God in some prior fashion than that the impossibility of being made by God should be a characteristic of a thing other than God.

To the contrary: Nothing that suggests any lack of perfection can be a primary attribute of God.

William Ockham, *Ordinatio (Sent. 1).* dist. 43. From *Medieval Philosophy: From St. Augustine to Nicholas of Cusa,* translated by A.B. Wolter and edited by John F. Wippel and Allan B. Wolter. Copyright 1969 by the Free Press.

[The View of Henry of Ghent]

One answer to the problem is this. Any attribute of God which signifies something that is not perfection purely and simply is not as such a primary attribute of God. But since something of this sort is attributed to a creature by virtue of its relationship to God, it is also attributed to God. Of such sort are those [divine] names which express God's relations to creatures and which are therefore predicated of God because creatures bear this relationship to him. For example, God is said to be a "Lord" because since time began he has had a "servant." And therefore "power over creatures" is an action-predicate ascribed to God because the creature in itself is a potential recipient of such action from its creator.

The additional point is made, however, that both the possible action on God's part and the recipient possibility of the creature can be viewed either subjectively or objectively. If God's power is viewed in terms of its subject, then it is prior to the potentiality of the creature, no matter how you look at the latter. The reason is that power so considered is a perfection purely and simply. Considered from the standpoint of its object, however, God's power is not such a perfection and therefore one can ascribe it to God only because the creature possesses a recipient capacity as regards God. Therefore it is said that absolutely speaking, this passive capacity is something a creature has only because God has the power to act. Consider these four relationships to what is possible, namely the two ways of viewing God's power to act (i.e. one which views this power as God's attribute, the other which sees it as a feature of the creature) and the two ways of viewing the recipient capacity of a creature (viz. as an attribute of the creature itself and as something which it has received from God). Now the following order obtains. God's power to act considered in itself is that from which the creature derives its recipient capacity considered in itself. A concomitant of this capacity is its relationship to God in virtue of which God in turn is said to have power with reference to the creature.

Against this view we can use his [Henry's] own counter-argument. For he claims elsewhere that we don't say, "It is impossible for God to do something because it is impossible for the thing in question to be done." Rather we assert the reverse, viz., "It is impossible for God to do this, therefore it is impossible for this to be done." Similarly one argues affirmatively that "Because it is possible for God to do this, therefore it is possible for this to be done" and not the reverse, viz., "It is possible for this to be done, therefore God can do it." This argument clearly gives God's power as regards creatures priority over the creature's recipient capacity as regards God and by implication it also gives God's inability to do the impossible priority over the impossible's inability to be done by God. And from this it is clear he would have to say that not everything which relates to creatures is ascribed to God because the creature is related to him, but rather the converse. Such relative attributes are ascribed to creatures because other relative attributes are ascribed to God.

Also, there is no more reason for ascribing to God some relationship to a creature on the grounds that the creature bears a relationship to him than there is for attributing something to a created cause on the grounds that its effect bears a relationship to such a cause. The minor is evident because according to him, when a created cause has a real relation, it follows that the cause is first altered in some real fashion before the effect is produced. It doesn't do to object that the parallel between God and the created cause breaks down since God bears only a logical and not a real relation [to the creature], whereas a cause is really related [to its effect]. For the impossibility of one real relation arising from another is no greater than for one logical relationship to arise from another. Hence the impossibility of a created cause acquiring a relationship because of a relationship in the effect is no greater than in the case of God, for God receives less in the way of both real and logical entities from a creature than does a created cause from its effect.

Similarly, if from one real aspect there does not arise a second corresponding real aspect, by the same token one logical relationship does not arise from another corresponding logical relation. But the relationship of a creature to God is a logical relationship, for there is certainly not something real involved, since what does not exist is not referred really. Therefore from this relationship a logical relationship of God to creatures does not arise.

Furthermore, against [Henry's] other point that God's power to act is prior to the creature's recipient capacity and that the former is a pure perfection, one can argue thus. No matter how you view it, one simply can't have an ability to do something apart from all reference to the something in question. Therefore this power to act is a power to act in regard to something. But this something is not God because God doesn't cause God, neither does God act upon God. Therefore this something is a creature. Hence God's ability to act no matter how you look at it involves a reference to the creature. Consequently, even as a primary attribute of God this power to act has reference to a creature. According to him [Henry], then, it would not be a perfection purely and simply.

A confirmatory argument: He says that just as the recipient capacity has two aspects, so also there are two aspects to the power to act, one of which refers this ability to God. Now I ask: just how is this relationship [i.e. power to act] referred to God? Either he is its foundation or he is the term [i.e. object over which the power is exercised]. If God is the foundation, then the relationship has another term and this can only be the creature; therefore this relationship has its term in a creature and consequently cannot be a primary attribute of God nor can it be a perfection purely and simply. If God is the term of the relationship, then since a thing is said to be able to act with reference to some recipient which is passive or submissive with respect to the action, it would follow that God would be passive, which is impossible. And so it is quite clear that this view contains inconsistencies.

[The View of Duns Scotus]

Another view is that the primary reason something is impossible is not to be found in God [but in the thing itself] which is simply impossible because it is inconsistent that what it is should happen. The explanation is this. Included in the simply impossible are incompatible elements which are such in virtue of their intelligible content or essential meanings. But viewed in terms of their originative source, these incompatibles flow from the same fountainhead as do these essential meanings. And hence the following logical order obtains. (1) In the first logical moment* the divine intellect

---

*Literally, an *instans naturae.* Though Scotus does not admit any temporal sequence or priority among those attributes God has from all eternity, he does believe one can distinguish a certain order of nature (i.e. a certain logical priority) among these attributes or properties in virtue of what they are. Knowledge of a creature's possibility does not logically entail a decision to create, but God's decision to create (made from all eternity) does entail knowledge of its possibility. If B entails A, but not vice versa, A is said to be prior by nature to B even when there is no temporal precedence. As one may number various moments of time to create a framework for discussing a temporal order of events, so Scotus distinguished various *instantia naturae* or "logical moments" to show the logical sequence of such nonmutual entailments.

produces a thing in that kind of existence it has as an intelligible object.* (2) In the second logical moment, the latter has possibility [i.e. can be actually realized] precisely by reason of what it is. Now just as God by his intellect produces the possible in its mode of being as a possible, so does he give this mode of being to each of the incompatible elements that make up an impossible. And these possibles produced [by the divine intellect] are mutually incompatible in virtue of what they are, so that they cannot exist together in one thing and from two such no third thing can be formed. Now this incompatibility which they possess precisely in virtue of what they are, they owe—in terms of its origins—to the divine intellect which produced them as possible modes of being. From the incompatibility of its elements the incompatibility of the figment as a whole follows. And from this it follows that it is impossible for any agent whatsoever to make it. And here the whole sequence ends. It does not end up with denying some kind of possibility to God.

Now some of [Scotus'] statements can be contested. First of all it does not seem proper to speak of the divine intellect "producing" the creature in a kind of intelligible existence. If all that a thing acquires through an action is a way of specifying or naming it in terms of an extrinsic frame of reference, whereas it gets nothing in the way of being or existence as such, then the thing in question is not "produced" through such an act. But a creature receives nothing as such from the fact it is known by God; it is just that one may denominate it with reference to something extrinsic to itself. It is the same as with the object of a created intellect which is not "produced" by being known, but has merely acquired a new name in terms of an extrinsic frame of reference. Consequently, the creature is not produced in intelligible being or existence.

Furthermore, were a creature produced in such a way, it would be precisely because it is known or because it was nothing before being produced, or because it was not intelligible before this. It is not because of the first, for then the divine essence would be produced in intelligible existence when it is known and then anyone knowing God would produce God in intelligible being. It is not because of the second reason, since a creature is still nothing even after it is known. Neither is it on account of the third, since it is not the case that the divine essence was intelligible prior to its self-knowledge.

Furthermore, according to him, nothing is produced in this kind of intelligible existence unless something is also produced in real existence. But when the creature is produced by the divine intellect, it is produced only in existence as an intelligible, and hence something else has to be produced in real existence. But nothing can be, as is clear inductively.

Furthermore, take what he says about a thing being produced in intelligible existence in the first logical moment and having existence as a possible in the second logical moment. To the contrary: I'll concede [for the purpose of argument] the first logical moment in which the intellect precedes the intelligible being of the creature. But I ask: At this moment is the creature possible or not possible? If it is possible, then it is

---

*Literally, "produces it in *esse intelligibili*." Like Meinong, Scotus distinguished between thinking or knowing and the "intelligible content" of the knowledge or thought. He speaks of the latter as having a "diminutive kind of existence." Since the intelligible content of any creature is limited, Scotus argued it would be derogatory to the infinite perfection of God's mind to make it in any way dependent upon the finite intelligibility of the creature. Like an artist who first gives his "creation" existence in his mind, God does not know the possible because it has some logically prior intelligibility, but he invests it with intelligibility by knowing it.

possible before it is produced in intelligible being. If it is not possible, then it is repugnant that the creature exist.

Furthermore, he says the sequence ends with the impossibility of any agent making it and not with some corresponding relationship in God. To the contrary: For every relationship of the possible creature to God there is a corresponding relationship in God to the creature as a possible mode of being. In the same way, to the negation of such a relationship there will be a corresponding negative relationship in God to the impossible; hence the sequence does not end with the latter. If one objects that in God there is no relationship correlative to the relationship of the possible creature to God, one can counter that either this relationship of the creature as a possible is real or it is logical. It is not real because it has no real foundation. Hence it is a logical relation which arises in virtue of the intellectual act of considering the creature with reference to God according to him [Scotus]. But the mind can just as well consider God with reference to the creature as the reverse; therefore, etc.

[Ockham's Own Opinion]

Therefore I answer the question in a different way. As a general rule to every related thing, if it be properly designated, there corresponds some correlative, and where the correlative terms are related as cause and effect, or as "ability to act" and "the capacity to be acted upon," the correlatives are by nature simultaneous. Because they are such and each entails the other, one is no more the cause of the other than vice versa.

Since father and son are simultaneous by nature in the way the Philosopher speaks of simultaneity of nature in the chapter on "relation" in the *Categoriae* [Chapter 7 (7b-15)] it follows that the son is not more a son than the father is a father, nor is the reverse true. Neither is it more the case that the son is because the father is, than it is that the father is because the son is. Neither is it more the case that *the son has a father because the father has a son* than it is that *the father has a son because the son has a father*. And when the mutual entailment holds precisely because of the nature of the correlatives, it is universally true that one proposition is no more the cause of the other than vice versa.

And when one asks whether the inability of doing the impossible is something God has prior to the impossible's inability to be made by God, I say that the inability to do the impossible is not something that God has prior to the impossible's inability to be done by God. Neither is the impossible's inability to be made by God prior to God's inability to do the impossible.

And in the same fashion I say of the affirmative form: the ability to do the possible or to create a creature is not something God has prior to the creature's ability to be made by God but they are simultaneous by nature in the same way that "to be able to make" and "to be able to be made" are simultaneous by nature, according to the Philosopher; that is to say, "Something can make" does not come before "Something can be made," neither is the reverse true.

Suppose one says that whatever a creature has, it has from God, therefore "to be possible" is something which belongs to it that is from God. "To be able to make something" is not something God gets from anything else, but has of himself, and whatever pertains to a thing of itself, pertains to it before anything it has by reason of something other than itself. Hence "to be able to make something" is something which pertains to God before "the ability to be made" pertains to the creature, and they are therefore not simultaneous. To this one should counter that whatever a creature has that is real, viz. as some inherent quality, it has from God as from its originative source. But not everything which pertains to it by way of predication does it have from God in this way, except in the same way one can speak of God having from God such predicates [as may be affirmed of him]. Because such predications when they are actually and really made, then they are from God.* And hence "to be possible" is something a creature has of itself, but it is not a real something inhering in the creature [like a real accident]. But the creature is truly possible of itself in the same way that man of himself is not an ass. Therefore arguments like the above do not hold except for those things which pertain to it in reality, in the way that a whole has its parts and its accidents. It is not a proper mode of speech to say that possible existence pertains to a creature, but to speak properly one ought to say that the creature is possible, not because anything pertains to it, but because it can exist in the real world.

[Reply to the Argument at the Beginning]

To the initial argument, I say that God is not able to make before a creature is able to be made. Indeed a creature's ability to be made has the same priority with God's being able to make it.

ON POLITICS (selections)

Eight Questions on the Power of the Pope

Question 2: The Origin of the Supreme Civil Power

CHAPTER 1

In the second place, the question is raised whether the supreme lay power derives the character strictly proper to it immediately from God. On this question there are two contrary opinions. According to one, the supreme lay power does not derive the power strictly proper to it immediately from God, because it derives it from God through the

---

*According to Aristotle, when a person makes an affirmation or mental judgment, a real or physical concomitant change takes place in the soul or mind. It acquires a new accidental entity which falls in the category of "quality." This new reality, Ockham points out, may be said to come from God as the first cause of all things created.

From *A Scholastic Miscellany: Anselm to Ockham,* edited and translated by Eugene R. Fairweather (Volume X: The Library of Christian Classics). First published in 1940 by SCM Press Ltd., London and The Westminster Press, Philadelphia. Used by permission of Westminster/John Knox Press.

mediation of papal power. For the pope possesses the fullness of power in temporal and spiritual matters alike, and therefore no one possesses any power save from him. The things alleged above [in Question I, Chapter 2] can be put forward in support of this opinion, and other reasons can also be offered. For it seems to some that, even though the pope did not have the fullness of power of this sort in temporal matters, it should still be said that the imperium* comes from him. From this it can be concluded that the supreme lay power—namely, the imperial power—derives the power proper to it from the pope, and not immediately from God, since it derives the power proper to it from him from whom it receives the imperium.

It remains to be proved, then, that the imperium comes from the pope, and this can be demonstrated in many ways. For the imperium comes from him to whom the keys of heavenly and earthly imperium were given; but the keys of heavenly and earthly imperium were given to Peter, and consequently to his successors, and therefore imperium comes from the pope. To state the point more fully, imperium comes from him who, by the ordinance of God (in whose power imperium most perfectly lies), is the first head and supreme judge of all mortals. Now by God's ordinance the pope, and not the emperor, is the first head and the judge of all mortals; the imperium, therefore, comes from the pope. Again, the imperium is derived from him who can depose the emperor; but the pope can depose the emperor, and therefore the imperium comes from the pope. Again, the imperium comes from him who can transfer the imperium from one nation to another; but the pope can do this and therefore the imperium is derived from the pope. Again, the imperium comes from him by whom the emperor, once elected, is examined, anointed, consecrated, and crowned. Now the emperor is examined, anointed, consecrated, and crowned by the pope; therefore, the imperium comes from the pope. Again, the imperium comes from him to whom the emperor takes an oath like a vassal; but the emperor executes an oath of fidelity and subjection to the pope, like a vassal of the latter and therefore the imperium comes from the pope. Again, the imperium comes from him who holds both swords, that is, the material and the spiritual. Now the pope possesses both swords, and therefore the imperium is derived from the pope. This seems to be Innocent IV's meaning when in a certain decretal he asserts that "the two swords of both administrations are held concealed in the bosom of the faithful Church"; for this reason, if anyone is not within that Church, he possesses neither. "Thus," he goes on, "both rights are believed to belong to Peter, since the Lord did not say to him, with reference to the material sword, 'Cast away,' but rather, 'Put up again thy sword into thy scabbard,' meaning, 'Do not employ it by thyself.'" Here he significantly expresses the name of the second, because this power of the material sword is implicit with the Church, but is made explicit by the emperor who receives it.

Again, the imperium is derived from him to whom the emperor stands in the relation of a son to his father, of a disciple to his master, of lead to gold, of the moon to the sun. Now the emperor stands in these relations to the pope; the imperium, therefore, comes from the pope. Again, the imperium is derived from him to whom the emperor is obliged to bow his head; but the emperor is bound to bow his head to the pope and therefore the imperium comes from the pope. Again, the imperium comes from him by whom, on his own authority and not by the ordinance of the emperor or of some other man, it ought to be ruled during a vacancy; but the pope does this when the imperium is vacant, and therefore the imperium is derived from the pope.

---

*["Empire," "imperial authority," "dominion," etc.]

[Chapters 2 and 3 have to do with different forms of the papal theory; Chapters 4 to 6 with different arguments for the imperial position.]

*   *   *

CHAPTER 7

Now that the above opinions have been considered, a reply should be made in accordance with them to the arguments alleged on the other side, and first to the points put forward above (in Chapter 1) against the view last stated. In answer to these, it is said that the imperium does not come from the pope, since after Christ's advent the imperium was derived from the same person as before; but before Christ's advent the imperium was not derived from the pope (as was alleged above), and therefore it has never afterward come from the pope.

But in reply to the first argument to the contrary, to the effect that, according to Pope Nicholas, Christ gave or committed to blessed Peter the rights of heavenly and earthly imperium together, it is said that Pope Nicholas' words are really to be expounded against the interpretation which at first glance appears to be proper, lest they seem to savor of heresy. The same holds for certain other things said by the same pope in the same chapter—for instance, when he says, "He alone established and founded and erected that Church," namely, the Roman, "on the rock of the faith just springing up," and when he says, "The Roman Church instituted all primates, whether the supreme dignity of any patriarch or the primacies of metropolitan sees, or the chairs of episcopates, or, for that matter, the dignity of churches of any order." Unless these words are somewhat discreetly interpreted, they seem to be contrary to the divine Scriptures and the writings of the holy Fathers, because Christ did not found the Roman Church upon the rock of the faith just springing up, since the Roman Church was not founded at the beginning of the faith, nor did it found all the other churches. For many churches were founded before the Roman Church, and many were raised up to ecclesiastical dignities even before the foundation of the Roman Church, for before the Roman Church existed blessed Matthias was elected to the dignity of apostleship (Acts 1:15–26). Seven deacons also were chosen by the apostles before the Roman Church began (Acts 6:1–6); also, before the Roman Church existed they "had peace throughout all Judea, and Galilee, and Samaria" (Acts 9:31). Before the Roman Church existed blessed Paul and Barnabas were raised to the apostolic dignity by God's command (Acts 13:1–3); before the Roman Church had the power of appointing prelates, Paul and Barnabas appointed presbyters throughout the several churches (Acts 14:22). Before the Roman Church had any authority, the apostles and elders held a general council (Acts 15:6ff.); also, before the Roman Church had the power of instituting prelates, blessed Paul said to the elders whom he had called from Ephesus (as we are told in Acts 20:17, 28): "Take heed to yourselves, and to the whole flock, wherein the Holy Ghost hath placed you bishops, to rule the church of God." Before the Roman Church held the primacy, the churches of Antioch were so multiplied that the disciples of Christ were first called Christians there (Acts 11:26); for this reason also blessed Peter had his see there before Rome, and thus he instituted churches and ecclesiastical dignities in the Antiochene church before he did so in the Roman. It is necessary, then, to attach a sound interpretation to the words of Pope Nicholas given above, lest they openly contradict the divine Scriptures. And, likewise, his other statements that follow, concerning the rights of heavenly and earthly imperium alike committed to blessed Peter, must be soundly expounded, lest they seem to savor of manifest heresy. For if they are construed as they sound at first hearing, two errors follow from them.

According to the first error, heavenly imperium comes from the pope, because Pope Nicholas says that Christ committed the rights of heavenly as well as earthly imperium to Peter. But it is certain that heavenly imperium does not come from the pope, particularly in the way in which some say, on account of that authoritative statement of Pope Nicholas, that earthly imperium is derived from the pope—namely, so that he who possesses the earthly imperium holds it as a fief from the pope—since it would be heretical to say that anyone held the heavenly imperium from the pope as a fief. Nor does the heavenly imperium come from the pope as its lord, as they claim that the earthly imperium comes from the pope as its lord, since the pope is merely in some sense the key bearer of the heavenly imperium, and in no sense its lord.

The second error which follows from Nicholas' words, understood as certain people understand them, is to the effect that all kingdoms are derived from the pope. It is recognized that this principle works to the disadvantage of all kings who do not pay homage to the pope for their kingdoms. For the king of France seems to err dangerously in faith when he makes no acknowledgment of a superior in temporal affairs.

These say, then, that the aforesaid words of Nicholas are to be interpreted in another way than their sound suggests. Thus they say that, just as according to Gregory, in the homily for the Common of virgins, the "kingdom of heaven" must sometimes be understood to refer to the Church Militant, so also the "heavenly imperium" can be understood to refer to the spiritually good in the Church Militant. Therefore, the spiritually evil in the Church can also be designated by the term, "earthly imperium," and the aforesaid words of Nicholas should be interpreted as meaning that Christ committed to blessed Peter some power over the good and over the evil in the Church. Or else, some say that by the "heavenly imperium" Pope Nicholas understands the "spirituals," whose "conversation is in heaven," and by the "earthly imperium" the "seculars," wrapped up in earthly business, and that he means that the pope has power over both.

Or else it is said that Christ committed to Peter the rights of heavenly imperium, in so far as in spiritual things he has power over wayfarers predestined to the heavenly imperium, and that he also committed to him the rights of earthly imperium, in so far as he made him superior in spiritual things to the earthly emperor, whom on occasion he can even coerce. Yet just as no one holds the heavenly imperium from the pope in fief, so also no one holds the earthly imperium in fief from him.

MEISTER ECKHART
ca. 1260–ca. 1328

The medieval mystic Johannes Eckhart was born at Hochheim in Thuringia, central Germany. As a young man, he entered the Dominican monastery at nearby Erfurt, where he began his studies for the priesthood. Over the next several years, he studied in Cologne and Paris. He received the degree of Master in Sacred Theology (hence the title "Meister") and taught at the University of Paris. From 1294, Eckhart held a number of administrative positions within the Dominican Order, eventually becoming Provincial of Saxony and Vicar of Bohemia. These administrative positions required numerous meetings, extensive travel, and voluminous correspondence. Despite his workload, Eckhart found time to write a book of advice, *Counsels on Discernment;* several speculative volumes, such as the *Book of Divine Comfort;* and a major theological work, *Opus Tripartitum*, most of which has been lost.

Eckhart was also a popular preacher, delivering a number of sermons as he traveled through Germany. Many of these sermons were preached in German rather than Latin. According to some scholars, by presenting his ideas in the vernacular, Eckhart did for German what Dante did for Italian: He gave the vernacular stature and prestige. In his most famous German sermon, reprinted here in the Raymond Bernard Blakney translation, Eckhart describes union with God in the core of the human soul. According to Eckhart, this core of the soul is the source of the soul's "agents": the intellect, the memory, and the will. Because they are only agents of the soul and not the soul itself, neither the intellect nor the will can adequately present God to us. Neither ideas *about* God nor willingness to accept God can bring union with God. Instead, we must withdraw from all agents and prepare a place of silence for God to enter. Once God has entered the core of the soul, human beings are divinized.

Whereas talk of "communion" with God is orthodox in Christian theology, teaching "union" with God has sometimes been considered to be immodest. Traditional Christian theology wants to maintain a respectful distinction between Creator and creation. Talk of union with God violates this tact. A later work (falsely) attributed to Eckhart indicates what the church feared: "Sir, rejoice with me, I have become God!" Eckhart's sermons eventually led to trouble with church authorities. Eckhart himself admitted that some of the ideas in his vernacular sermons were ill-expressed and that in translating theological ideas from Latin to German he may have made errors. But the Archbishop of Cologne believed the problem was deeper than mistranslation: Eckhart was a heretic. Eckhart's last years were spent fighting heresy charges. As Eckhart succinctly put it, "I am able to be in error, but I cannot be a heretic, for the first [i.e., error] belongs to the intellect, the second [i.e., heresy] to the will." Though he protested innocence until his death (around 1328), in 1329 Pope John XXII declared eleven of Eckhart's teachings suspect and seventeen heretical. Despite this papal condemnation, Eckhart's thought and writings continued to be influential in the later Middle Ages and are still consulted today.

*   *   *

For general works on mysticism, see the suggested readings in the introduction to Hildegard of Bingen (page 201). For a study of mystics in the late Middle Ages, see Ray C. Petry, *Late Medieval Mysticism* (Philadelphia: Westminster Press, 1957).

There are several anthologies of Eckhart's writings with commentary, including Meister Eckhart, *Meister Eckhart: An Introduction to the Study of His Works with an Anthology of His Sermons*, edited and translated by James M. Clark (London: Thomas Nelson and Sons, 1957), and Meister Eckhart, *Meister Eckhart: Mystic and Philosopher*, translated with commentary by Reiner Schürmann (Bloomington: Indiana University Press, 1978). For readings that explore Eckhart's work in the context of German mysticism, see James Midgley Clark, *The Great German Mystics, Eckhart, Tauler and Suso* (1949; reprinted New York: Russell and Russell, 1970); Jeanne Ancelet-Hustache, *Master Eckhart and the Rhineland Mystics*, translated by Hilda Graef (New York: Harper Torchbooks, 1957); and Oliver Davies, ed., *The Rhineland Mystics: Writings of Meister Eckhart, Johannes Tauler, and Jan van Ruusbroec and Selections from the Theologia Germanica and the Book of Spiritual Poverty* (New York: Crossroad, 1990). Specialized studies of various aspects of Eckhart's thought include C.F. Kelley, *Meister Eckhart on Divine Knowledge* (New Haven, CT: Yale University Press, 1977) and Frank J. Tobin, *Meister Eckhart: Thought and Language* (Philadelphia: University of Pennsylvania Press, 1986).

SERMON #1

This is Meister Eckhart from whom God hid nothing.

*For while all things were wrapped in peaceful silence and night was
in the midst of its swift course . . .*

—Wisdom of Solomon 18:14

Because the same One, who is begotten and born of God the Father, without ceasing in
eternity, is born today, within time, in human nature, we make a holiday to celebrate it.
St. Augustine says that this birth is always happening. And yet, if it does not occur in
me, how could it help me? Everything depends on that.

We intend to discuss, therefore, how it does occur in us, or how it is made perfect in a good soul, for it is in a good soul that God the Father is speaking his eternal
word. What I shall say applies to that perfect person who has turned to the way of God
and continues in it, and not to the natural undisciplined person who is far from this
birth and ignorant of it. This, then, is the saying of the wise man: "While all things
were wrapped in peaceful silence . . . a secret word leaped down from heaven, out of
the royal throne, to me." This sermon is to be on that word.

Three points are, then, noteworthy. The first is: where does God the Father speak
his word in the soul, or where does this birth take place—or what part of the soul is
susceptible to this act? It must be in the purest, noblest, and subtlest element the soul
can provide. Truly, if God could give the soul anything rarer out of his omnipotence,
and if the soul could have received into its nature anything nobler from him, he must
have awaited its coming to be born. Therefore the soul in which this birth is to happen
must have purity and nobility of life, and be unitary and self-contained; it must not be
dissipated in the multiplicity of things, through the five senses. What is more, it must
continue to be self-contained and unitary and of the utmost purity, for that is its station
and it disdains anything less.

The second part of this sermon will discuss what one should do about this act of
God, this inward utterance, this birth: whether it is necessary to co-operate in some
way to merit and obtain the birth. Should one construct an idea in his mind and think-
ingprocess and discipline himself by meditating upon it, to the effect that God is wise,
almighty, and eternal? Or should one withdraw from all thought and free his mind of
words, acts, and ideas, doing nothing but being always receptive to God and allowing
him to act? How shall one best serve the eternal birth?

The third part [of this sermon will discuss] the profitableness of this birth and
how great it is.

In the first place, please note that I shall support what I have to say by citations
from nature, which you may check for yourselves. Even though I believe more in the

Scriptures than I do in myself, I shall follow [this policy] because you will get more out of arguments based on evidence.

Let us take first the test: "Out of the silence, a secret word was spoken to me." Ah, Sir!—what is this silence and where is that word to be spoken? We shall say, as I have heretofore, [it is spoken] in the purest element of the soul, in the soul's most exalted place, in the core, yes, in the essence of the soul. The central silence is there, where no creature may enter, nor any idea, and there the soul neither thinks nor acts, nor entertains any idea, either of itself or of anything else.

Whatever the soul does, it does through agents. It understands by means of intelligence. If it remembers, it does so by means of memory. If it is to love, the will must be used and thus it acts always through agents and not within its own essence. Its results are achieved through an intermediary. The power of sight can be effectuated only through the eyes, for otherwise the soul has no means of vision. It is the same with the other senses. They are effectuated through intermediaries.

In Being, however, there is no action and, therefore, there is none in the soul's essence. The soul's agents, by which it acts, are derived from the core of the soul. In that core is the central silence, the pure peace, and abode of the heavenly birth, the place for this event: this utterance of God's word. By nature the core of the soul is sensitive to nothing but the divine Being, unmediated. Here God enters the soul with all he has and not in part. He enters the soul through its core and nothing may touch that core except God himself. No creature enters it, for creatures must stay outside in the soul's agents, from whence the soul receives ideas, behind which it has withdrawn as if to take shelter.

When the agents of the soul contact creatures, they take and make ideas and likenesses of them and bear them back again into the self. It is by means of these ideas that the soul knows about eternal creatures. Creatures cannot approach the soul except in this way and the soul cannot get at creatures, except, on its own initiative, it first conceives ideas of them. Thus the soul gets at things by means of ideas and the idea is an entity created by the soul's agents. Be it a stone, or a rose, or a person, or whatever it is that is to be known, first an idea is taken and then absorbed, and in this way the soul connects with the phenomenal world.

But an idea, so received, necessarily comes in from outside, through the senses. Thus the soul knows about everything but itself. There is an authority who says that the soul can neither conceive nor admit any idea of itself. Thus it knows about everything else but has no self-knowledge, for ideas always enter through the senses and therefore the soul cannot get an idea of itself. Of nothing does the soul know so little as it knows of itself, for lack of means. And that indicates that within itself the soul is free, innocent of all instrumentalities and ideas, and that is why God can unite with it, he, too, being pure and without idea, or likeness.

Whatever skill a master teacher may have, concede that skill to God, multiplied beyond measure. The wiser and more skillful a teacher is, the more simply, and with less artifice, he achieves his ends. Man requires many tools to do his visible work and, before he can finish it as he has conceived it, much preparation is required. It is the function and craft of the moon and sun to give light and they do it swiftly. When they emit their rays, all the ends of the world are filled with light in a moment. Higher than these are the angels who work with fewer instruments and also with fewer ideas. The highest seraph has only one. He comprehends as unity all that his inferiors see as manifold. But God needs no idea at all, nor has he any. He acts in the soul without instrument, idea, or likeness. He acts in the core of the soul, which no idea ever penetrated—but he alone—his own essence. No creature can do this.

How does God beget his Son in the soul? As a creature might, with ideas and likenesses? Not at all! He begets him in the soul just as he does in eternity—and not otherwise. Well, then, how? Let us see.

God has perfect insight into himself and knows himself up and down, through and through, not by ideas, but of himself. God begets his Son through the true unity of the divine nature. See! This is the way: he begets his Son in the core of the soul and is made One with it. There is no other way. If an idea were interposed, there could be no true unity. Man's whole blessedness lies in that unity.

Now you might say: "Naturally! But there is nothing to the soul but ideas." No! Not at all! If that was so, the soul could never be blessed, for even God cannot make a creature in which a perfect blessing is found. Otherwise, God himself would not be the highest blessing, or the best of ends, as it is his nature and will to be—the beginning and the end of everything. A blessing is not a creature nor is it perfection, for perfection [that is, in all virtues] is the consequence of the perfecting of life, and for that you must get into the essence, the core of the soul, so that God's undifferentiated essence may reach you there, without the interposition of any idea. No idea represents or signifies itself. It always points to something else, of which it is the symbol. And since man has no ideas, except those abstracted from external things through the senses, he cannot be blessed by an idea.

The second point [of this sermon] is this: What should a man do to secure and deserve the occurrence and perfection of this birth in his soul? Should he co-operate by imagining and thinking about God, or should he keep quiet, be silent and at peace, so that God may speak and act through him? Should he do nothing but wait until God does act? I repeat, as I have said before, that this exposition and this activity are for those good and perfect persons only, who have so absorbed the essence of virtue that virtue emanates from them without their trying to make it do so, and in whom the useful life and noble teachings of our Lord Jesus Christ are alive. Such persons know that the best life and the loftiest is to be silent and to let God speak and act through one.

When all the agents [of the soul] are withdrawn from action and ideation, then this word is spoken. Thus he said: "Out of the silence, a secret word was spoken to me." The more you can withdraw the agents of your soul and forget things and the ideas you have received hitherto, the nearer you are to [hearing the word] and the more sensitive to it you will be. If you could only become unconscious of everything all at once and ignore your own life, as St. Paul did when he could say: "Whether in the body, or out of it, I cannot tell. God knoweth!" His spirit had so far withdrawn all its agents that the body was forgotten. Neither memory nor intellect functioned, nor the senses, nor any [of the soul's] agents which are supposed to direct or grace the body. The warmth and energy of the body were suspended and yet it did not fail during the three days in which he neither ate nor drank. It was also this way with Moses, when he fasted forty days on the mountain and was none the worse for it. He was as strong on the last day as on the first. This is the way a man should diminish his senses and introvert his faculties until he achieves forgetfulness of things and self. So one authority said to his soul: "Draw back from the unrest of external actions," and also: "Fly from the storm of visible works and inward thoughts and hide yourself, for they only make turmoil."

Therefore, if God is to speak his word to the soul, it must be still and at peace, and then he will speak his word and give himself to the soul and not a mere idea, apart from himself. Dionysius says: "God has no idea of himself and no likeness, for he is intrinsic good, truth, and being." God does all that he does within himself and of himself in an instant. Do not imagine that when God made heaven and earth and all the creatures, that he made one today and another tomorrow. To be sure, Moses describes it thus, but he knew much better! He put it this way on account of the people who could neither understand nor conceive it otherwise. God did nothing more about it than just this: he willed and they were! God acts without instrumentality and without ideas. And the freer you are from ideas the more sensitive you are to his inward action. You are nearer to it in proportion as you are introverted and unself-conscious.

It was to this point that Dionysius instructed his disciple Timothy, saying: "My dear son Timothy, you should soar above self with untroubled mind, above all your faculties, characteristics, and states, up into the still, secret darkness, so that you may come to know the unknown God above all gods. Forsake everything. God despises ideas."

But now, perhaps you say: "What can God do in the core and essence [of the soul] without ideas?" I couldn't possibly know, for the agents of the soul deal only in ideas, taking things and naming them, each according to its own idea. A bird is not known [as such] on the human idea [pattern], and thus, since all ideas come from the outside, [what God is doing in the core of my soul] is hidden from me and that is a great benefit. Since the soul itself does not know, it wonders and, wondering, it seeks, for the soul knows very well that something is afoot, even though it does not know how or what. When a person learns the cause of anything, he soon grows tired of it and looks for something else to work out, and is constantly uneasy until he knows all about that, and thus he lacks steadfastness. Only this unknown knowledge keeps the soul steadfast and yet ever on the search.

The wise man said: "In the middle of the night, while all things were wrapped in silence, a secret word was spoken to me." It came stealthily, like a thief. What does he mean by a word that is secret or hidden? It is the nature of a word to reveal what is hidden. "It opened and shone before me as if it were revealing something and made me conscious of God, and thus it was called 'a word.' Furthermore it was not clear to me what it was, because it came with stealth like a whisper trying to explain itself through the stillness." See! As long as it is concealed, man will always be after it. It appears and disappears, which means that we shall plead and sigh for it.

St. Paul says that we are to hunt it and track it down and never give up till we get it. Once he was caught up into the third heaven of the knowledge of God and saw everything. When he came back he had forgotten nothing but it had so regressed into the core of his soul that he could not call it up to mind. It was covered up. Thus he felt constrained to pursue it within [his soul] and not without. It is always within and never outside—but always inward. When he was convinced of that, he said: "I am persuaded that neither death . . . nor any affliction can separate me from what I find within me."

One heathen authority once said something fine about this to another: "I am aware of something in myself whose shine is my reason. I see clearly that something is there, but what it is I cannot understand. But it seems to me that, if I could grasp it, I should know all truth." To which the other authority replied: "By all means keep after it! For if you do grasp it, you will possess the totality of all goods and life eternal!" St. Augustine also has something to say about this: "I am aware of something in myself, like a light dancing before my soul, and if it could be brought out with perfect steadiness, it would surely be life eternal. It hides, and then again, it shows. It comes like a thief, as if it would steal everything from the soul. But since it shows itself and draws attention, it must want to allure the soul and make the soul follow it, to rob the soul of self." One of the prophets also has something to say about this: "Lord, take from them their spirit and give them instead thy spirit!" This is what that loving soul meant when she said: "When Love said that word, my soul melted and flowed away. Where he comes in, I must go out!" That is also what Christ meant, when he said: "Whosoever shall forsake anything for my sake, shall receive again a hundredfold and whosoever will have me, must deny himself of everything and whosoever will serve me must follow me and not seek his own."

Now perhaps you are saying: "My dear sir! You are trying to reverse the natural course of the soul. It is the soul's nature to take things in through the senses and convert them into ideas. Do you want to reverse that sequence?"

No! But how do you know what precious things God has stored up in nature which have not yet been described—things still hidden? Those who write about the aristocracy of the soul can get no further than their natural intelligence will take them. They cannot get into the core and therefore much must remain hidden from them and unknown. The prophet said: "I will sit and be silent and listen to what God shall say in me." That this word comes "at night and in the darkness" is expressive of its hiddenness. St. John says: "The light shone in the darkness. It came unto its own. And to as many as received it, to them power was given to become the Sons of God."

See now the profit and fruit of this secret word and this darkness. Not only the Son of the heavenly Father is born in the darkness which is his own, but you, too, are born there, a son of the same heavenly Father, and to you also he gives power. Now see how great the profit is! For all the truth the authorities ever learned by their own intelligence and understanding, or ever shall learn up to the last of days, they never got the least part of the knowledge that is in the core [of the soul]. Let it be called ignorance or want of knowledge, still it has more in it than all wisdom and all knowledge without it, for this outward ignorance lures and draws you away from things you know about and even from yourself. That is what Christ meant when he said: "Whosoever forsaketh not himself and mother and father and all that is external is not worthy of me." It was as if he would say: "Whosoever will not depart from the externality of creatures cannot be born or received in this divine birth." By robbing yourself of self and all externalities you are admitted to the truth.

And I really believe it, and am sure that the person who is right in this matter will never be separated from God by any mode [of action] or anything else. I say that there is no way he can fall into deadly sin. He would rather suffer the most shameful death than commit the least of mortal sins, as did the saints. I say that he could not commit even a venial sin nor consent to one in himself or other people, if it could be prevented. He is so strongly attracted and drawn and accustomed to this way of life that he would not turn to another. All his mind and power are directed to this one end.

May God, newly born in human form, eternally help us, that we frail people, being born in him, may be divine. Amen.

Catherine of Siena
ca. 1347–1380

Saint Catherine was born in the central Italian city of Siena, the twenty-fourth of twenty-five children. Despite her family's expectations, Catherine was uninterested in marriage. Instead, she spent much of her youth in the nearby Dominican church, eventually receiving the Dominican habit at age 18. For the next three years, she was a recluse in her parents' home, leaving her room only for mass. Although she had no formal schooling, during this time she somehow learned to read. At 21, she reentered the world and began a lifelong practice of caring for the poor and ill. On several occasions, she ministered to those who had the plague, putting her life at great danger. In 1370, she had an ecstatic union with God, which she described as her "mystical death." But rather than leading to further isolation, this experience led her to deeper involvement in church reform and in church-state politics.

For the rest of her short life, Catherine acted as emissary for the pope in disputes with various city-states in Italy. While traveling on diplomatic missions, she also heard confessions, and as a woman she was given the rare privilege by Pope Gregory XI that those who confessed to her were to be absolved of their sins. She also found time to write a number of letters, which convey her basic ideas. During a break from church diplomacy in 1377, Catherine had another intense mystical experience, which led to her writing the *Dialogues*. The last years of her life were spent in a disappointing attempt to organize a new crusade to the Holy Land. In 1461, Catherine was canonized, and in 1970 she and the Spanish mystic St. Teresa of Avila (1515–1582) were the first women given the title "Doctor of the Church."

Among the many letters she wrote, the one reprinted here, translated by Suzanne Noffke, shows Catherine's emphasis on love. Catherine explains that God loves us only because God chooses to love us—there is no necessity in divine charity. Our highest calling is to love God and show our love by loving others. In propounding this doctrine of love, Catherine hints at the necessity of free will as a prerequisite for such love.

Our selection from Catherine's *Dialogues,* also translated by Suzanne Noffke, makes explicit this connection between free will and God's love. After an introduction and discussion of the nature of suffering, Catherine asserts that although God "created us without our help, he will not save us without our help" (*Dialogues,* 23). This notion of free will is clearly quite different from that of Augustine and Thomas Aquinas. Our selection concludes with Catherine's eloquent description of the soul's union with God.

Some have argued that the mystics are not really philosophers and should not be included in a study of philosophic classics. It is true that the mystics often used different forms of discourse to make their points—this is why I have included a vision from Hildegard, a sermon from Eckhart, and a letter from Catherine. It is also true that they often held unusual perspectives on the issues. But mystics such as Catherine address many of the classic philosophical questions of epistemology, metaphysics, and ethics and so can provide correctives to more rationalist colleagues.

*   *   *

For brief overviews of Catherine of Siena's thought, see the introduction to Catherine of Siena, *The Dialogue,* translated and introduced by Suzanne Noffke (New York: Paulist Press, 1980) and Cornelia Wolfskeel, "Catherine of Siena," in Mary Ellen Waithe, ed., *A History of Women Philosophers, Volume II: Medieval, Renaissance and Enlightenment Women Philosophers, 500–1600* (Dordrecht, The Netherlands: Kluwer Academic Publishers, 1989). There are a number of biographies of Catherine of Siena, beginning with Raymond of Capua, 1330–1399, who wrote *The Life of St. Catherine of Siena,* translated by George Lamb (New York: P.J. Kennedy, 1960). Studies in this century include Edmund G. Gardner, *Saint Catherine of Siena: A Study in the Religion, Literature, and History of the Fourteenth Century in Italy* (London: J.M. Dent, 1907); Augusta Theodosia Drane, *The History of St. Catherine of Siena and Her Companions,* 4th edition (London: Longmans, Green, 1915); Johannes Jørgensen, *Saint Catherine of Siena,* translated by Ingeborg Lund (London: Longmans, Green, 1939); Arrigo Levasti, *My Servant, Catherine,* translated by Dorothy M. White (Westminster, MD: Newman Press, 1954); Igino Giordani, *Catherine of Siena: Fire and Blood,* translated by Thomas J. Tobin (Milwaukee, WI: Bruce, 1959); and Joseph Marie Perrin, *Catherine of Siena,* translated by Paul Barrett (Westminster: Newman Press, 1965).

LETTER #58

TO MONNA MELINA, WIFE OF BARTOLOMEO BARBANI OF LUCCA

In the name of Jesus Christ crucified and of gentle Mary, mother of God's Son.

My daughter in Christ Jesus,

I Caterina, servant and slave of the servants of Jesus Christ, am writing to encourage you in his precious blood. I long to see you so transformed and fused into the fire of divine charity that nobody and nothing will ever separate you from it. You know, my dear beloved daughter, that to join two things together there must be nothing between them or there cannot be a perfect fusion. Now realize that this is how God wants our soul to be, without any selfish love of ourselves or of others in between, just as God loves us without anything in between. Freely and generously he loved us, gratuitously and not because he had to: he loved us without being loved. For us it is impossible to love the way God does. We are always obligated in duty to love since we are constantly being given a share in God's goodness and blessings. So we have to love with this second sort of love. But let this love be so clean and free that we love no one, nothing, spiritually or temporally, apart from God.

And if you say to me, "How can I have this sort of love?" I tell you, daughter, that we cannot have it or draw it from any source but the fountain of First Truth. At this fountain you will discover your soul's dignity and beauty. You will see the Word, the slain Lamb who gave himself as your ransom and as your food. And he was moved only by the fire of his charity and not by any service he could have received from us, from whom he had received nothing but offense. I am saying, then, that when we gaze into this fountain thirsty and hungry for virtue, we begin at once to drink. We do not see or love ourselves or anything else selfishly, because we see everything in the fountain of God's goodness. In him we love what we love, and we love nothing without him.

Now how could the soul who has seen such immeasurable goodness on God's part do anything but love? This, it seems, is what gentle First Truth invited us to when he cried out with heartfelt earnestness in the temple: "Let anyone who is thirsty come to me and drink, for I am the fountain of living water!" You see, daughter, it is the thirsty who are invited. He does not say, "anyone who is not thirsty," but "anyone who is thirsty." So God insists that we bring with us the vessel of our free will, with a thirst and willingness to love. Let's go, then, to the fountain of God's sweet goodness. There we shall discover the knowledge of ourselves and of God. And when we dip our vessel in, we shall draw out the water of divine grace, powerful enough to give us everlasting life.

But remember: we wouldn't be able to make any progress if we were burdened with a heavy load. This is why I don't want you to clothe yourself with love for me or anyone else, but to be clothed only in love for God. I'm telling you this because I know from your letter the pain you suffered at my departure. I want you to learn from gentle First Truth. Neither attachment to his mother nor to any of his disciples kept him from running like one in love to the shameful death of the cross, leaving Mary and his disciples behind. Yet he loved them immensely. And later on they left one another for the greater honor of God and other people's salvation, because their concern was not for themselves. They gave up their own consolations for God's praise and glory, as people who eat and savor souls. You must believe that when they were so distressed they would gladly have stayed with Mary, whom they loved so much. Yet they all left. For they did not love themselves or their neighbors or God selfishly. No, they loved God because he was supremely good and worthy of love, and themselves and their neighbors and everything else they loved in God.

Now this is how I want you and the others to love. Look at me only in terms of giving honor to God and your best efforts to your neighbors. For though we may feel a certain sadness when someone we love leaves us, still we accept it graciously if our love is true, rooted only in God's honor and concerned more for the salvation of souls than for ourselves. Now then, don't let me see any more sadness, because this would be an interference that would hinder your being conformed and united with Christ. It is because I think God asks us to give ourselves freely, as he did, that I said I want you and my other dear daughters to be transformed in and united with God by love, getting rid of any medium, anything that gets in between—except divine charity, which is a sweet and glorious medium that doesn't separate but unites.

Really, it seems just like the master mason. He gathers many stones and fits them together, and the result is called both "stones" and "a wall." He does this by using mortar as his medium. Without the medium the stones would fall apart more scattered and broken than ever. So now imagine how our soul has to gather all people and be united with them in love and desire for their salvation, so that they may be sharers in the blood of the Lamb. So here this wall stands—many people, yet they are one. This, it seems, is what Saint Paul was inviting us to when he said that many run the race, but only one wins, and the winner is the one who has used this medium, divine charity. But you could say to me what the disciples said to Christ when he said, "A little while and you shall not see me, and again a little while and you shall see me." They said, "What is he going to do, that he says, 'A little while and you shall not see me, and again a little while and you shall see me'?" So you could say, "First you tell us that God doesn't want anything between us and him, and now you tell us to put something in between!" My answer is that you must use the medium that doesn't put anything between us and God, the fire of divine charity, which becomes one with [God] as wood put into the fire. Would you say the wood remains wood? No, it becomes one with the fire. But if you were to use as medium your selfish love for yourself, you would be using a medium that would separate you from God, even though it is nothing (because sins have their root in nothing but selfish love and pleasure and enjoyment apart from God). For just as all virtue proceeds from charity, which gives it life, so all vice proceeds from selfish love, which deals death and eats away every virtue in the soul. This is why I said that God doesn't want anything between himself and us, and that any love not set in the true medium [of divine charity] does not last.

Run, my beloved daughters! Let's sleep no longer! I've felt sorry about your pain, and this is why I am giving you this remedy of loving God without anything between you and him. But if you still want poor wretched me as intermediary, I want to show you where to find me without being separated from this true love. Go with the dear loving Magdalen to the most sweet venerable cross. There you will find the Lamb and me, and there you can graze and feed and fulfill your desires. This is the way I want you to seek me and every created thing; let this cross be your standard and comfort. And don't imagine, because I am physically far away from you, that my affection and my concern for your salvation are far away. No, I am even closer than when I am there physically. Don't you know that the holy disciples had a greater awareness and knowledge of the Master after he had left them than before? They had been so taken up with his humanity that they hadn't looked beyond it. But after his departure they began to know and understand his goodness. This is why First Truth said, "I have to go; otherwise the Paraclete will not come to you." So I say I had to leave you so you would begin to seek God in truth and not through any intermediary. I tell you, you will be better off than before, if you enter into yourselves to ponder the words and teaching you have been given. In this way you will receive the fullness of grace by the very grace of God. I'll write no more, because I have no more time for writing.

I'm sending this letter primarily to you, Melina, and then to Caterina, Monna Chiara, Monna Bartolomea, Monna Lagina, and Monna Colomba. Warm greetings from all of us!

Keep living in God's holy and tender love.

THE DIALOGUE (in part)

PROLOGUE

In the Name of Christ Crucified and of Gentle Mary.

1. A soul rises up, restless with tremendous desire for God's honor and the salvation of souls. She has for some time exercised herself in virtue and has become accustomed to dwelling in the cell of self-knowledge in order to know better God's goodness toward her, since upon knowledge follows love. And loving, she seeks to pursue truth and clothe herself in it.

But there is no way she can so savor and be enlightened by this truth as in continual humble prayer, grounded in the knowledge of herself and of God. For by such prayer the soul is united with God, following in the footsteps of Christ crucified, and through desire and affection and the union of love he makes of her another himself. So Christ seems to have meant when he said, "If you will love me and keep my word, I will show myself to you, and you will be one thing with me and I with you." And we find similar words in other places from which we can see it is the truth that by love's affection the soul becomes another himself.

To make this clearer still, I remember having heard from a certain servant of God that, when she was at prayer, lifted high in spirit, God would not hide from her mind's eye his love for his servants. No, he would reveal it, saying among other things, "Open

Catherine of Sienna, *The Dialogue*, 1–3, 4, 7, 23, and 79. Reprinted from *Catherine of Siena* by Suzanne Noffker, O.P. © 1980 by The Missionary Society of St. Paul the Apostle in the State of New York. Used by permission of Paulist Press.

your mind's eye and look within me, and you will see the dignity and beauty of my reasoning creature. But beyond the beauty I have given the soul by creating her in my image and likeness, look at those who are clothed in the wedding garment of charity, adorned with many true virtues: They are united with me through love. So I say, if you should ask me who they are, I would answer," said the gentle loving Word, "that they are another me; for they have lost and drowned their own will and have clothed themselves and united themselves and conformed themselves with mine."

It is true, then, that the soul is united to God through love's affection.

Now this soul's will was to know and follow truth more courageously. So she addressed four petitions to the most high and eternal Father, holding up her desire for herself first of all—for she knew that she could be of no service to her neighbors in teaching or example or prayer without first doing herself the service of attaining and possessing virtue.

Her first petition, therefore, was for herself. The second was for the reform of holy Church. The third was for the whole world in general, and in particular for the peace of Christians who are rebelling against holy Church with great disrespect and persecution. In her fourth petition she asked divine providence to supply in general and in particular for a certain case which had arisen.

2. This desire of hers was great and continuous. But it grew even more when First Truth showed her the world's need and how storm tossed and offensive to God it is. And she had on her mind, besides, a letter she had received from her spiritual father, a letter in which he expressed pain and unbearable sadness over the offense against God, the damnation of souls, and persecutions against holy Church. All of this stirred up the flame of her holy desire with grief for the offense but with gladness in the hope by which she waited for God to provide against such great evils.

She found herself eager for the next day's Mass—it would be Mary's day—because in communion the soul seems more sweetly bound to God and better knows his truth. For then the soul is in God and God in the soul, just as the fish is in the sea and the sea in the fish. So when it was morning and time for Mass she took her place with eager desire. From her deep knowledge of herself, a holy justice gave birth to hatred and displeasure against herself, ashamed as she was of her imperfection, which seemed to her to be the cause of all the evils in the world. In this knowledge and hatred and justice she washed away the stains of guilt, which it seemed to her were, and which indeed were, in her own soul, saying, "O eternal Father, I accuse myself before you, asking that you punish my sins in this life. And since I by my sins am the cause of the sufferings my neighbors must endure, I beg you in mercy to punish me for them."

THE WAY OF PERFECTION

3. *Then eternal Truth seized her desire and drew it more strongly to himself. Just as in the Old Testament when sacrifice was offered to God a fire came and drew to himself the sacrifice that was acceptable to him, so gentle Truth did to that soul. He sent the fiery mercy of the Holy Spirit and seized the sacrifice of desire she had made of herself to him, saying:*

Do you not know, my daughter, that all the sufferings the soul bears or can bear in this life are not enough to punish one smallest sin? For an offense against me, infinite Good, demands infinite satisfaction. So I want you to know that not all sufferings given in this life are given for punishment, but rather for correction, to chastise the child who offends. However, it is true that a soul's desire, that is, true contrition and sorrow for sin, can make satisfaction. True contrition satisfies for sin and its penalty not by virtue of any finite suffering you may bear, but by virtue of your infinite desire. For God, who is infinite, would have infinite love and infinite sorrow.

The infinite sorrow God wills is twofold: for the offense you yourself have committed against your Creator, and for the offense you see on your neighbors' part. Because those who have such sorrow have infinite desire and are one with me in loving affection (which is why they grieve when they sin or see others sinning), every suffering they bear from any source at all, in spirit or in body, is of infinite worth, and so satisfies for the offense that deserved an infinite penalty. True, these are finite deeds in finite time. But because their virtue is practiced and their suffering borne with infinite desire and contrition and sorrow for sin, it has value.

So the glorious apostle Paul taught: "If I had an angelic tongue, knew the future, gave what is mine to the poor, and gave my body to be burned, but did not have charity, it would be worth nothing to me" (1 Cor. 13:1–3). Finite works are not enough either to punish or to atone unless they are seasoned with loving charity.

4. I have shown you, dearest daughter, that in this life guilt is not atoned for by any suffering simply as suffering, but rather by suffering borne with desire, love, and contrition of heart. The value is not in the suffering but in the soul's desire. Likewise, neither desire nor any other virtue has value or life except through my only-begotten Son, Christ crucified, since the soul has drawn love from him and in virtue follows his footsteps. In this way and in no other is suffering of value. It satisfies for sin, then, with gentle unitive love born from the sweet knowledge of my goodness and from the bitterness and contrition the heart finds in the knowledge of itself and its own sins. Such knowledge gives birth to hatred and contempt for sin and for the soul's selfish sensuality, whence she considers herself worthy of punishment and unworthy of reward. So you see, said gentle Truth, those who have heartfelt contrition, love for true patience, and that true humility which considers oneself worthy of punishment and unworthy of reward suffer with patience and so make atonement.

You ask me for suffering to atone for the offenses my creatures commit against me. And you ask for the will to know and love me, supreme Truth. Here is the way, if you would come to perfect knowledge and enjoyment of me, eternal Life: Never leave the knowledge of yourself. Then, put down as you are in the valley of humility you will know me in yourself, and from this knowledge you will draw all that you need.

No virtue can have life in it except from charity, and charity is nursed and mothered by humility. You will find humility in the knowledge of yourself when you see that even your own existence comes not from yourself but from me, for I loved you before you came into being. And in my unspeakable love for you I willed to create you anew in grace. So I washed you and made you a new creation in the blood that my only-begotten Son poured out with such burning love.

This blood gives you knowledge of the truth when knowledge of yourself leads you to shed the cloud of selfish love. There is no other way to know the truth. In so knowing me the soul catches fire with unspeakable love, which in turn brings continual pain. Indeed, because she has known my truth as well as her own sin and her neighbors' ingratitude and blindness, the soul suffers intolerably. Still, this is not a pain that troubles or shrivels up the soul. On the contrary, it makes her grow fat. For she suffers because she loves me, nor would she suffer if she did not love me.

Thus, as soon as you and my other servants come in this way to know my truth you will, for the glory and praise of my name, have to endure great trials, insults, and reproaches in word and in deed, even to the point of death. Behave, then, you and my other servants, with true patience, with sorrow for sin and love of virtue, for the glory and praise of my name. If you do, I shall be appeased for your sins and those of my other servants. The sufferings you endure will, through the power of charity, suffice to win both atonement and reward for you and for others. For you they will win the fruit of life: The stains of your foolishness will be blotted out, and I will no longer remember that you had ever offended me. As for others, because of your loving charity I will pardon them in proportion to their receptiveness.

More particularly, I will pardon both sin and punishment in those who humbly and reverently accept the teaching of my servants. How? They will come in this way to truly know and regret their sins, and so, because of my servants' prayer and desire they will receive (humbly, as I have said) the fruit of grace. And the more willing they are to exercise this grace with virtue, the more they will receive, but if they are less willing, they will receive less. So in general I am saying that through your desires they will receive both forgiveness and its gifts, unless their stubbornness is such that they despair. (Then I would reject them for scorning the blood by which they have so tenderly been bought.)

What fruit do they receive? Pressed by my servants' prayers, I look on them and give them light. I rouse the dog of conscience within them. I make them sensitive to the perfume of virtue and give them delight in the fellowship of my servants. Sometimes I allow the world to show them its true colors, letting them feel all sorts of emotions, so that they may know how inconstant it is and be more eager to seek their homeland in eternal life. The eye cannot see, nor the tongue tell, nor can the heart imagine how many paths and methods I have, solely for love and to lead them back to grace so that my truth may be realized in them!

I am constrained to this by the same immeasurable love with which I created them, as well as by prayers and desires and sufferings of my servants. I do not spurn their tears and sweat and humble prayers; no, I accept them, since it is I who make them love and fill them with grief over the damnation of souls.

But ordinarily I grant these others pardon of their sin only, not of its penalty. For they on their part are not disposed to receive my love and that of my servants with perfect love. Nor do they receive my servants' grief with bitterness or perfect contrition for the sin they have committed, but receive it with imperfect love and contrition. For this reason, such as these receive no pardon of the penalty but only of the sin itself. For not only the giver but also the receiver must be rightly disposed. And if these others are imperfect, they receive only imperfectly the perfect desires of those who offer them with pain to me on their behalf.

Why, then, did I tell you that they receive both pardon and its gifts? Such is the truth. Their sin is atoned for in the way I have told you, through the light of conscience and other means of which we have spoken. In other words, in this beginning of awareness they vomit out the filth of their sins, and so they receive the gift of grace. So it is with those who live in ordinary charity. If they accept what comes their way as correction without resisting the Holy Spirit's mercy, they receive the life of grace from him, leaving their sin behind.

But if, like fools, they are ungrateful and heedless of me and of my servants' labors, then what was given in mercy will at once turn to their judgment and ruin—not through any defect in mercy or in those who begged mercy for the ingrates, but only through their own wretchedness and hardness. They have, with the hand of free choice, encrusted their heart in a diamond rock that can never be shattered except by blood.

Still, I tell you, in spite of their hardness, let them while they still have time and free-dom to choose seek the blood of my Son and with that same hand let them pour it over the hardness of their heart: It will shatter the diamond and they will know the fruit of that blood which was paid out for them. But if they dawdle, time will run out and there will be no remedy at all, because they will have no return to show for the endowment they had from me. For I gave them memory to hold on to my blessings, and under-standing to see and know the truth, and will to love me, eternal Truth, once under-standing has known me.

This is the endowment I gave to all of you, and I your Father expect a return from it. But if you sell it in barter to the devil, the devil goes off with it and carries away everything you had acquired in this life. Then he fills your memory with delight-ful recollections of indecency, pride, avarice, selfish love for yourself, and hatred and contempt for your neighbors. (For the devil is a persecutor of my servants.) Your mind is darkened in these wretched things by your disordered will, and so in stench you reap eternal punishment, infinite punishment, for you would not atone for your guilt with contrition and contempt for sin.

So you see, suffering atones for sin not by reason of the finite pain but by reason of perfect contrition of the heart. And in those who have this perfect contrition it atones not only for the sin itself but for the penalty due that sin. But for most, as I have said, their suffering satisfies only for sin itself; for though they are freed from deadly sin and receive grace, if their contrition and love are not strong enough to satisfy for the penalty, they go to the pains of purgatory once they have passed beyond the second and final means.

Atonement is made, then, through the desire of the soul who is united to me, infi-nite Good, in proportion as love is perfect both in the one who prays with desire and in the one who receives. And my goodness will measure out to you with the very same measure that you give to me and that the other receives. So feed the flame of your de-sire and let not a moment pass without crying out for these others in my presence with humble voice and constant prayer. Thus I tell you and the spiritual father I have given you on earth: Behave courageously, and die to all your selfish sensuality!

*   *   *

7. I have told you how every sin is done by means of your neighbors, because it deprives them of your loving charity, and it is charity that gives life to all virtue. So that selfish love which deprives your neighbors of your charity and affection is the principle and foundation of all evil.

Every scandal, hatred, cruelty, and everything unbecoming springs from this root of selfish love. It has poisoned the whole world and sickened the mystic body of holy Church and the universal body of Christianity. For all virtues are built on charity for your neighbors. So I have told you, and such is the truth: Charity gives life to all the virtues, nor can any virtue exist without charity. In other words, virtue is attained only through love of me.

After the soul has come to know herself she finds humility and hatred for her selfish sensual passion, recognizing the perverse law that is bound up in her members and is always fighting against the spirit. So she rises up with hatred and contempt for that sensuality and crushes it firmly under the foot of reason. And through all the bless-ings she has received from me she discovers within her very self the breadth of my goodness. She humbly attributes to me her discovery of this self knowledge, because she knows that my grace has drawn her from darkness and carried her into the light of true knowledge. Having come to know my goodness, the soul loves it both with and without intermediary. I mean she loves it without the intermediary of herself or her own advantage. But she does have as intermediary that virtue which is conceived through love of me, for she sees that she cannot be pleasing or acceptable to me except by conceiving hatred of sin and love of virtue.

Virtue, once conceived, must come to birth. Therefore, as soon as the soul has conceived through loving affection, she gives birth for her neighbors' sake. And just as she loves me in truth, so also she serves her neighbors in truth. Nor could she do otherwise, for love of me and love of neighbor are one and the same thing: Since love of neighbor has its source in me, the more the soul loves me, the more she loves her neighbors.

Such is the means I have given you to practice and prove your virtue. The service you cannot render me you must do for your neighbors. Thus it will be evident that you have me within your soul by grace, when with tender loving desire you are looking out for my honor and the salvation of your neighbors by bearing fruit for them in many holy prayers.

I showed you earlier how suffering alone, without desire, cannot atone for sin. Just so, the soul in love with my truth never ceases doing service for all the world, universally and in particular, in proportion to her own burning desire and to the disposition of those who receive. Her loving charity benefits herself first of all, as I have told you, when she conceives that virtue from which she draws the life of grace. Blessed with this unitive love she reaches out in loving charity to the whole world's need for salvation. But beyond a general love for all people she sets her eye on the specific needs of her neighbors and comes to the aid of those nearest her according to the graces I have given her for ministry: Some she teaches by word, giving sincere and impartial counsel; others she teaches by her example—as everyone ought to—edifying her neighbors by her good, holy, honorable life.

These are the virtues, with innumerable others, that are brought to birth in love of neighbor. But why have I established such differences? Why do I give this person one virtue and that person another, rather than giving them all to one person? It is true that all the virtues are bound together, and it is impossible to have one without having them all. But I give them in different ways so that one virtue might be, as it were, the source of all the others. So to one person I give charity as the primary virtue, to another justice, to another humility, to another a lively faith or prudence or temperance or patience, and to still another courage.

These and many other virtues I give differently to different souls, and the soul is most at ease with that virtue which has been made primary for her. But through her love of that virtue she attracts all the other virtues to herself, since they are all bound together in loving charity.

The same is true of many of my gifts and graces, virtue and other spiritual gifts, and those things necessary for the body and human life. I have distributed them all in such a way that no one has all of them. Thus have I given you reason—necessity, in fact—to practice mutual charity. For I could well have supplied each of you with all your needs, both spiritual and material. But I wanted to make you dependent on one another so that each of you would be my minister, dispensing the graces and gifts you have received from me. So whether you will it or not, you cannot escape the exercise of charity! Yet, unless you do it for love of me, it is worth nothing to you in the realm of grace.

So you see, I have made you my ministers, setting you in different positions and in different ranks to exercise the virtue of charity. For there are many rooms in my house. All I want is love. In loving me you will realize love for your neighbors, and if you love your neighbors you have kept the law. If you are bound by this love you will do everything you can to be of service wherever you are.

*   *   *

23. *Here the eternal Truth was showing that, although he had created us without our help, he will not save us without our help. He wants us to set our wills with full freedom to spending our time in true virtue. So he continued:*

You must all keep to this bridge, seeking the glory and praise of my name through the salvation of souls, bearing up under pain and weariness, following in the footsteps of this gentle loving Word. There is no other way you can come to me.

You are the workers I have hired for the vineyard of holy Church. When I gave you the light of holy baptism I sent you by my grace to work in the universal body of Christianity. You received your baptism within the mystic body of holy Church by the hands of my ministers, and these ministers I have sent to work with you. You are to work in the universal body. They, however, have been placed within the mystic body to shepherd your souls by administering the blood to you through the sacraments you receive from them, and by rooting out from you the thorns of deadly sin and planting grace within you. They are my workers in the vineyard of your souls, ambassadors for the vineyard of holy Church.

Each of you has your own vineyard, your soul, in which your free will is the appointed worker during this life. Once the time of your life has passed, your will can work neither for good nor for evil; but while you live it can till the vineyard of your soul where I have placed it. This tiller of your soul has been given such power that neither the devil nor any other creature can steal it without the will's consent, for in holy baptism the will was armed with a knife that is love of virtue and hatred of sin. This love and hatred are to be found in the blood. For my only-begotten Son gave his blood for you in death out of love for you and hatred for sin, and through that blood you receive life in holy baptism.

So you have this knife for your free will to use, while you have time, to uproot the thorns of deadly sin and to plant the virtues. This is the only way you can receive the fruit of the blood from these workers I have placed in holy Church. For they are there, as I have told you, to uproot deadly sin from the vineyard of your soul and to give you grace by administering the blood to you through the sacraments established in holy Church.

So if you would receive the fruit of this blood, you must first rouse yourself to heartfelt contrition, contempt for sin, and love for virtue. Otherwise you will not have done your part to be fit to be joined as branches to the vine that is my only-begotten Son, who said, "I am the true vine and you are the branches. And my Father is the gardener."

Indeed I am the gardener, for all that exists comes from me. With power and strength beyond imagining I govern the whole world: Not a thing is made or kept in order without me. I am the gardener, then, who planted the vine of my only-begotten Son in the earth of your humanity so that you, the branches, could be joined to the vine and bear fruit.

Therefore, if you do not produce the fruit of good and holy deeds you will be cut off from this vine and you will dry up. For those who are cut off from this vine lose the life of grace and are thrown into the eternal fire, just as a branch that fails to bear fruit is cut off the vine and thrown into the fire, since it is good for nothing else. So those who are cut off because of their offenses, if they die still guilty of deadly sin, will be thrown into the fire that lasts forever, for they are good for nothing else.

Such people have not tilled their vineyards. They have, in fact, destroyed them—yes, and other people's as well. Not only did they fail to set out any good plants of virtue, but they even dug out the seed of grace that they had received with the light of holy baptism, when they had drunk of the blood of my Son—that wine poured out for you by this true vine. They dug out this seed and fed it to beasts, that is, to their countless sins. And they trampled it underfoot with their disordered will, and so offended me and brought harm to their neighbors as well as to themselves.

But that is not how my servants act, and you should be like them, joined and engrafted to this vine. Then you will produce much fruit, because you will share the vital sap of the vine. And being in the Word, my Son, you will be in me, for I am one with him and he with me. If you are in him you will follow his teaching, and if you follow his teaching you will share in the very being of this Word—that is, you will share in the eternal Godhead made one with humanity, whence you will draw that divine love which inebriates the soul. All this I mean when I say that you will share in the very substance of the vine.

* * *

79. I said that these souls are given the feeling [of my presence] never to lose it. But I do leave in another fashion. The soul that is chained within the body is incapable of constantly experiencing union with me, and because of her incapacity I withdraw—not my grace nor its feeling, but the union. For once souls have risen up in eager longing, they run in virtue along the bridge of the teaching of Christ crucified and arrive at the gate with their spirits lifted up to me. When they have crossed over and are inebriated with the blood and aflame with the fire of love, they taste in me the eternal Godhead, and I am to them a peaceful sea with which the soul becomes so united that her spirit knows no movement but in me. Though she is mortal she tastes the reward of the immortals, and weighed down still with the body she receives the lightness of the spirit. Often, therefore, the body is lifted up from the ground because of the perfect union of the soul with me, as if the heavy body had become light.

It is not because its heaviness has been taken away, but because the union of the soul with me is more perfect than the union between the soul and the body. And for this reason the strength of the spirit united with me lifts the body's weight off the ground, and the body is, as it were, immobile, so completely bedraggled by the soul's emotion that (as you recall having heard about several persons) it would have been impossible to go on living had not my goodness encircled it with strength.

So I want you to know that it is a greater marvel to see the soul not leaving the body in this union than to see a host of dead bodies resurrected. This is why I withdraw that union for a while and make the soul return to the vessel that is her body, so that the body's feeling, which had been completely lost because of the soul's emotion, returns. For the soul does not really leave the body (this happens only in death), but her powers and emotions are united with me in love. Therefore the memory finds itself filled with nothing but me. The understanding is lifted up as it gazes into my Truth. The will, which always follows the understanding, loves and unites itself with what the eye of understanding sees.

When these powers are gathered and united all together and immersed and set afire in me, the body loses its feeling. For the eye sees without seeing; the ear hears without hearing; the tongue speaks without speaking (except that sometimes, because of the heart's fullness, I will let the tongue speak for the unburdening of the heart and for the glory and praise of my name, so that it speaks without speaking); the hand touches without touching; the feet walk without walking. All the members are bound and busied with the bond and feeling of love. By this bond they are subjected to reason and joined with the soul's emotion so that, as if against their own nature, they all cry out to me the eternal Father with one voice, asking to be separated from the soul, and the soul from the body. And so the soul cries out in my presence with the glorious Paul, "O unfortunate me! Who will free me from my body? For I have a perverse law that is fighting against my spirit!" (Rom. 7:24, 23).

Paul was speaking not only of the fight that sensual feeling puts up against the spirit, for he had, as it were, been given a guarantee by my word when he was told, "Paul, my grace is enough for you" (2 Cor. 12:9). Why then did he say it? Because Paul felt himself bound up in the vessel of his body, and this blocked him off for a time from seeing me. In other words, until the hour of his death his eye was bound so that he could not see me, the eternal Trinity, with the vision of the blessed immortals who forever offer glory and praise to my name. Instead he found himself among mortals who are constantly offending me, deprived of seeing me as I really am.

He and my other servants do see me and enjoy me, though not as I really am but in loving charity and in other ways as my goodness pleases to reveal myself to you. Still, every vision the soul receives while in the mortal body is a darkness when compared with the vision the soul has when separated from the body. So it seemed to Paul that his sense of sight was fighting against his spiritual vision. In other words, his human feeling of his body's bulk was a block to the eye of his understanding and was keeping him from seeing me face to face. His will, it seemed to him, was bound so that he could not love as much as he longed to love, for all love in this life is imperfect until it reaches its perfection.

Not that Paul's love (or that of my other true servants) was imperfect in relation to grace and the perfection of love, for he was perfect. But he was at the same time imperfect in that his love lacked its fulfillment, and so he suffered. For if his desire had been filled with what he loved he would not have been suffering. But because love, while in the mortal body, does not perfectly possess what it loves, it suffers.

Once, however, the soul is separated from the body, her longing is fulfilled and so she loves without suffering. She is sated, but her satiety is far removed from boredom. Though sated she is hungry, but her hunger is far removed from pain. For once the soul is separated from the body, her vessel is filled up in me in truth, so steadied and strengthened that she can desire nothing but that she has it. Because she desires to see me, she sees me face to face. Because she desires to see my name glorified and praised in my holy ones, she sees it, both in the angelic nature and in the human.

NICHOLAS CUSANAS
1401–1464

Nicholas Cusanas (or "Nicholas of Cusa") was born in Cusa (or Kues) on the Moselle River in Germany. As a boy, he studied with the Brothers of the Common Life in Deventer, Holland, a group that put special emphasis on piety and humility. From there he went on to study philosophy at Heidelberg (1416), canon (or church) law at Padua (1417–1423), and theology at Cologne (1425). He received a doctorate in canon law at Padua and was ordained a priest in 1426. Soon after his ordination, Nicholas became involved in a number of legal matters related to church reform. He first supported the "conciliar" movement, which advocated the primacy of church councils over the pope. But disillusionment with the Council of Basel's inability to reform the church led him to side with the pope. He was sent by the Holy See on various missions, including the (temporarily) successful negotiations on reunification with the Eastern Church in Byzantium. For his efforts he was rewarded by being made a cardinal in 1448 and being given the bishopric of Brixen in 1450, positions he held until his death in 1464.

In his attempt to synthesize reason and faith, Nicholas returned to the Neoplatonic tradition of the early Middle Ages and the mysticism of Meister Eckhart. In particular, he was taken by the Neoplatonic mystical belief that there is a faculty of intuition or intelligence that is above reason. The Aristotelian understanding of reason, which his predecessors had used, begins with the *law of noncontradiction*. This law states that contradictories cannot be true of the same thing at the same time. But Nicholas claimed that this law is not true; there is a "coincidence of opposites" in all particular entities, but especially in God. Using language that would later be echoed by the German philosopher Hegel, Nicholas claimed that reason cannot grasp the divine Absolute. We need to recognize the "ignorance" of reason and "see incomprehensively" by means of the higher faculty of intuition.

Nicholas develops this idea in his most famous work, *On Learned Ignorance*. There he argues that God's essence is paradoxical and cannot be known. In the opening chapters of this work, given here in the Jasper Hopkins translation, Nicholas asserts that God is both Absolute Maximum and Absolute Minimum and draws out the implications of this position. He goes on to say that although God is beyond our reason, since we cannot comprehend the Absolute Maximum, we can have an ignorance about God that is "learned" and "sacred." Our selection ends with the last chapter from Book I, in which Nicholas emphasizes the *via negativa*, the "way of negation," which gives us incomprehensible truth about God by telling us what God is not.

*   *   *

Henry Bett, *Nicholas of Cusa* (London: Methuen, 1932), provides the classic study of Nicholas, whereas Jasper Hopkins, *A Concise Introduction to the Philosophy of Nicholas of Cusa*, 2nd edition (Minneapolis: University of Minnesota Press, 1980) and Pauline Moffitt Watts, *Nicolaus Cusanus, A Fifteenth-Century Vision of Man* (Leiden, The Netherlands: E.J. Brill, 1982) give more recent introductions. For specialized studies, see Paul E. Sigmund, *Nicholas of Cusa and Medieval Political Thought* (Cambridge, MA: Harvard University Press, 1963); James E. Biechler, *The Religious Language of Nicholas of Cusa* (Missoula, MT: Scholars Press, 1975); and Ronald Levao, *Renaissance Minds and Their Fictions: Cusanus, Sidney, Shakespeare* (Berkeley: University of California Press, 1985). For a recent collection of essays, see Gerald Christianson and Thomas M. Izbicki, eds., *Nicholas of Cusa, in Search of God and Wisdom* (Leiden, The Netherlands: E.J. Brill, 1991).

ON LEARNED IGNORANCE (in part)

Chapter 1: How It Is That Knowing Is Not-Knowing.

We see that by the gift of God there is present in all things a natural desire to exist in the best manner in which the condition of each thing's nature permits this. And [we see that all things] act toward this end and have instruments adapted thereto. They have an innate sense of judgment which serves the purpose of knowing. [They have this] in order that their desire not be in vain but be able to attain rest in that [respective] object which is desired by the propensity of each thing's own nature. But if perchance affairs

Reprinted, by permission, from Jasper Hopkins, *Nicholas of Cusa on Learned Ignorance: A Translation and an Appraisal of De Docta Ignorantia,* Chapters 1–4, 26 (Minneapolis, MN: Banning Press, 2nd edition, 2nd printing, 1990).

La Primavera ("*The Allegory of Spring*"), ca. 1482. Botticelli (1445–1510) shows the eternal spring of Venus' garden of Hesperides. Like Nicholas Cusanas, Botticelli was heavily influenced by Neoplatonism and his paintings are usually interpreted in Neoplatonic terms. (For example, there are nine figures in this work just as there are nine Enneads of Plotinus.) (*Alinari/Art Resource*)

turn out otherwise, this [outcome] must happen by accident—as when sickness misleads taste or an opinion misleads reason. Wherefore, we say that a sound, free intellect knows to be true that which is apprehended by its affectionate embrace. (The intellect insatiably desires to attain unto the true through scrutinizing all things by means of its innate faculty of inference.) Now, that from which no sound mind can withhold assent is, we have no doubt, most true. However, all those who make an investigation judge the uncertain proportionally, by means of a comparison with what is taken to be certain. Therefore, every inquiry is comparative and uses the means of comparative relation. Now, when, the things investigated are able to be compared by means of a close proportional tracing back to what is taken to be [certain], our judgment apprehends easily; but when we need many intermediate steps, difficulty arises and hard work is required. These points are recognized in mathematics, where the earlier propositions are quite easily traced back to the first and most evident principles but where later propositions [are traced back] with more difficulty because [they are traced back] only through the mediation of the earlier ones.

Therefore, every inquiry proceeds by means of a comparative relation, whether an easy or a difficult one. Hence, the infinite, qua infinite, is unknown; for it escapes all comparative relation. But since comparative relation indicates an agreement in some one respect and, at the same time, indicates an otherness, it cannot be understood independently of number. Accordingly, number encompasses all things related comparatively. Therefore, number, which is a necessary condition of comparative relation, is present not only in quantity but also in all things which in any manner whatsoever can agree or differ either substantially or accidentally. Perhaps for this reason Pythagoras deemed all things to be constituted and understood through the power of numbers.

Both the precise combinations in corporeal things and the congruent relating of known to unknown surpass human reason—to such an extent that Socrates seemed to himself to know nothing except that he did not know. And the very wise Solomon maintained that all things are difficult and unexplainable in words. And a certain other man of divine spirit says that wisdom and the seat of understanding are hidden from the eyes of all the living. Even the very profound Aristotle, in his First Philosophy, asserts that in things most obvious by nature such difficulty occurs for us as for a night owl which is trying to look at the sun. Therefore, if the foregoing points are true, then since the desire in us is not in vain, assuredly we desire to know that we do not know. If we can fully attain unto this [knowledge of our ignorance], we will attain unto learned ignorance. For a man even one very well versed in learning—will attain unto nothing more perfect than to be found to be most learned in the ignorance which is distinctively his. The more he knows that he is unknowing, the more learned he will be. Unto this end I have undertaken the task of writing a few things about learned ignorance.

Chapter 2: Preliminary Clarification of What Will Follow.

Since I am going to discuss the maximum learning of ignorance, I must deal with the nature of Maximality. Now, I give the name "Maximum" to that than which there cannot be anything greater. But fulness befits what is one. Thus, oneness—which is also being—coincides with Maximality. But if such oneness is altogether free from all relation and contraction, obviously nothing is opposed to it, since it is Absolute Maximality. Thus, the Maximum is the Absolute One which is all things. And all things are in the Maximum (for it is the Maximum); and since nothing is opposed to it, the Minimum likewise coincides with it, and hence the Maximum is also in all things. And because it is absolute, it is, actually, every possible being; it contracts nothing from things, all of which [derive] from it. In the first book I shall strive to investigate—incomprehensibly above human reason—this Maximum, which the faith of all nations indubitably believes to be God. [I shall investigate] with the guidance of Him "who alone dwells in inaccessible light."

Secondly, just as Absolute Maximality is Absolute Being, through which all things are that which they are, so from Absolute Being there exists a universal oneness of being which is spoken of as "a maximum deriving from the Absolute [Maximum]"—existing from it contractedly and as a universe. This maximum's oneness is contracted in plurality, and it cannot exist without plurality. Indeed, in its universal oneness this maximum encompasses all things, so that all the things which derive from the Absolute [Maximum] are in this maximum and this maximum is in all [these] things. Nevertheless, it does not exist independently of the plurality in which it is present, for it does not exist without contraction, from which it cannot be freed. In the second book I will add a few points about this maximum, viz., the universe.

Thirdly, a maximum of a third sort will thereafter be exhibited. For since the universe exists-in-plurality only contractedly, we shall seek among the many things the one maximum in which the universe actually exists most greatly and most perfectly as in its goal. Now, such [a maximum] is united with the Absolute [Maximum], which is the universal end; [it is united] because it is a most perfect goal, which surpasses our every capability. Hence, I shall add some points about this maximum, which is both contracted and absolute and which we name *Jesus,* blessed forever. [I shall add these points] according as Jesus Himself will provide inspiration.

However, someone who desires to grasp the meaning must elevate his intellect above the import of the words rather than insisting upon the proper significations of words which cannot be properly adapted to such great intellectual mysteries. Moreover, it is necessary to use guiding illustrations in a transcendent way and to leave behind perceptible things, so that the reader may readily ascend unto simple intellectuality. I have endeavored, for the purpose of investigating this pathway, to explain [matters] to those of ordinary intelligence as clearly as I could. Avoiding all roughness of style, I show at the outset that learned ignorance has its basis in the fact that the precise truth is inapprehensible.

CHAPTER 3: THE PRECISE TRUTH IS INCOMPREHENSIBLE.

It is self-evident that there is no comparative relation of the infinite to the finite. Therefore, it is most clear that where we find comparative degrees of greatness, we do not arrive at the unqualifiedly Maximum; for things which are comparatively greater and lesser are finite; but, necessarily, such a Maximum is infinite. Therefore, if anything is posited which is not the unqualifiedly Maximum, it is evident that something greater can be posited. And since we find degrees of equality (so that one thing is more equal to a second thing than to a third, in accordance with generic, specific, spatial, causal, and temporal agreement and difference among similar things), obviously we cannot find two or more things which are so similar and equal that they could not be progressively more similar *ad infinitum*. Hence, the measure and the measured—however equal they are—will always remain different.

Therefore, it is not the case that by means of likenesses a finite intellect can precisely attain the truth about things. For truth is not something more or something less but is something indivisible. Whatever is not truth cannot measure truth precisely. (By comparison, a noncircle [cannot measure] a circle, whose being is something indivisible.) Hence, the intellect, which is not truth, never comprehends truth so precisely that truth cannot be comprehended infinitely more precisely. For the intellect is to truth as [an inscribed] polygon is to [the inscribing] circle. The more angles the inscribed polygon has the more similar it is to the circle. However, even if the number of its angles is increased ad infinitum, the polygon never becomes equal [to the circle] unless it is resolved into an identity with the circle. Hence, regarding truth, it is evident that we do not know anything other than the following: viz., that we know truth not to be precisely comprehensible as it is. For truth may be likened unto the most absolute necessity (which cannot be either something more or something less than it is), and our intellect may be likened unto possibility. Therefore, the quiddity of things, which is the truth of beings, is unattainable in its purity; though it is sought by all philosophers, it is found by no one as it is. And the more deeply we are instructed in this ignorance, the closer we approach to truth.

CHAPTER 4: THE ABSOLUTE MAXIMUM, WITH WHICH THE MINIMUM COINCIDES, IS UNDERSTOOD INCOMPREHENSIBLY.

Since the unqualifiedly and absolutely Maximum (than which there cannot be a greater) is greater than we can comprehend (because it is Infinite Truth), we attain unto it in no other way than incomprehensibly. For since it is not of the nature of those things which can be comparatively greater and lesser, it is beyond all that we can conceive. For whatsoever things are apprehended by the senses, by reason, or by intellect differ both within themselves and in relation to one another—[differ] in such way that there is no precise equality among them. Therefore, Maximum Equality, which is neither other than nor different from anything, surpasses all understanding. Hence, since the absolutely Maximum is all that which can be, it is altogether actual. And just as there cannot be a greater, so for the same reason there cannot be a lesser, since it is all that which can be. But the Minimum is that than which there cannot be a lesser. And since the Maximum is also such, it is evident that the Minimum coincides with the Maximum. The foregoing [point] will become clearer to you if you contract maximum and minimum to quantity. For maximum quantity is maximally large; and minimum quantity is maximally small. Therefore, if you free *maximum* and *minimum* from *quantity*—by mentally removing *large* and *small*—you will see clearly that maximum and minimum coincide. For *maximum* is a superlative just as *minimum* is a superlative. Therefore, it is not the case that absolute quantity is maximum quantity rather than minimum quantity; for in it the minimum is the maximum coincidingly.

Therefore, opposing features belong only to those things which can be comparatively greater and lesser; they befit these things in different ways; [but they do] not at all [befit] the absolutely Maximum, since it is beyond all opposition. Therefore, because the absolutely Maximum is absolutely and actually all things which can be (and is so free of all opposition that the Minimum coincides with it), it is beyond both all affirmation and all negation. And it is not, as well as is, all that which is conceived to be; and it is, as well as is not, all that which is conceived not to be. But it is a given thing in such way that it is all things; and it is all things in such way that it is no thing; and it is maximally a given thing in such way that it is it minimally. For example, to say "God, who is Absolute Maximality, is light" is [to say] no other than "God is maximally light in such way that He is minimally light." For Absolute Maximality could not be actually all possible things unless it were infinite and were the boundary of all things and were unable to be bounded by any of these things—as, by the graciousness of God, I will explain in subsequent sections. However, the [absolutely Maximum] transcends all our understanding. For our intellect cannot, by means of reasoning, combine contradictories in their Beginning, since we proceed by means of what nature makes evident to us. Our reason falls far short of this infinite power and is unable to connect contradictories, which are infinitely distant. Therefore, we see incomprehensibly, beyond all rational inference, that Absolute Maximality (to which nothing is opposed and with which the Minimum coincides) is infinite. But "maximum" and "minimum," as used in this [first] book, are transcendent terms of absolute signification, so that in their absolute simplicity they encompass—beyond all contraction to quantity of mass or quantity of power—all things.

*   *   *

CHAPTER 26: NEGATIVE THEOLOGY.

The worshipping of God, who is to be worshipped in spirit and in truth, must be based upon affirmations about Him. Accordingly, every religion, in its worshipping, must mount upward by means of affirmative theology. [Through affirmative theology] it worships God as one and three, as most wise and most gracious, as Inaccessible Light, as Life, Truth, and so on. And it always directs its worship by faith, which it attains more truly through learned ignorance. It believes that He whom it worships as one is All-in-one, and that He whom it worships as Inaccessible Light is not light as is corporeal light, to which darkness is opposed, but is infinite and most simple Light, in which darkness is Infinite Light; and [it believes] that Infinite Light always shines within the darkness of our ignorance but [that] the darkness cannot comprehend it. And so, the theology of negation is so necessary for the theology of affirmation that without it God would not be worshipped as the Infinite God but, rather, as a creature. And such worship is idolatry; it ascribes to the image that which befits only the reality itself. Hence, it will be useful to set down a few more things about negative theology.

Sacred ignorance has taught us that God is ineffable. He is so because He is infinitely greater than all nameable things. And by virtue of the fact that [this] is most true, we speak of God more truly through removal and negation—as [teaches] the greatest Dionysius, who did not believe that God is either Truth or Understanding or Light or anything which can be spoken of. (Rabbi Solomon and all the wise follow Dionysius.) Hence, in accordance with this negative theology, according to which [God] is only infinite, He is neither Father nor Son nor Holy Spirit. Now, the Infinite qua Infinite is neither Begetting, Begotten, nor Proceeding. Therefore, when Hilary of Poitiers distinguished the persons, he most astutely used the expressions "Infinity in the Eternal," "Beauty in the Image," and "Value in the Gift." He means that although in eternity we can see only infinity, nevertheless since the infinity which is eternity is negative infinity, it cannot be understood as Begetter but [can] rightly [be understood as] eternity, since "eternity" is affirmative of oneness, or maximum presence. Hence, [Infinity-in-the-Eternal is] the Beginning without Beginning. "Beauty in the Image" indicates the Beginning from the Beginning. "Value in the Gift" indicates the Procession from these two.

All these things are very well known through the preceding [discussion]. For although eternity is infinity, so that eternity is not a greater cause of the Father than is infinity: nevertheless, in a manner of considering, eternity is attributed to the Father and not to the Son or to the Holy Spirit; but infinity is not [attributed] to one person more than to another. For according to the consideration of oneness infinity is the Father; according to the consideration of equality of oneness it is the Son; according to the consideration of the union [of the two it is] the Holy Spirit. And according to the simple consideration of itself infinity is neither the Father nor the Son nor the Holy Spirit. Yet, infinity (as also eternity) is each of the three persons, and, conversely, each person is infinity (and eternity)—not, however, according to [the simple] consideration [of itself], as I said. For according to the consideration of infinity God is neither one nor many. Now, according to the theology of negation, there is not found in God anything other than infinity. Therefore, according to this theology [God] is not knowable either in this world or in the world to come (for in this respect every created thing is darkness, which cannot comprehend Infinite Light), but is known only to Himself.

From these [observations] it is clear (1) that in theological matters negations are true and affirmations are inadequate, and (2) that, nonetheless, the negations which remove the more imperfect things from the most Perfect are truer than the others. For example, it is truer that God is not stone than that He is not life or intelligence; and [it is truer that He] is not drunkenness than that He is not virtue. The contrary [holds] for affirmations; for the affirmation which states that God is intelligence and life is truer than [the affirmation that He is] earth or stone or body. All these [points] are very clear from the foregoing. Therefrom we conclude that the precise truth shines incomprehensibly within the darkness of our ignorance. This is the learned ignorance we have been seeking and through which alone, as I explained, [we] can approach the maximum, triune God of infinite goodness—[approach Him] according to the degree of our instruction in ignorance, so that with all our might we may ever praise Him, who is forever blessed above all things, for manifesting to us His incomprehensible self.

EPILOGUE: GIOVANNI PICO DELLA MIRANDOLA
1463–1494

◄O►

In the late-1300s, some Italian thinkers began to talk about a rebirth or "renaissance." They wrote disparagingly of the "Middle" or "Dark Ages," depicting it as a period of barbarian ignorance from which they had just emerged. They saw themselves as awakening to their classical past and continuing the civilizing work of the ancient Greeks and Romans.

Although there are few scholars today who would not modify this self-characterization, there does seem to have been something different about the late-medieval/early-modern period. Whereas the medievals had access to some classical texts, the Renaissance thinkers had a wide, and often contradictory, variety of ancient Greek and Roman works. Whereas the philosophers of the Middle Ages tended to use ancient materials to reinforce their Christian beliefs, the early-modern thinkers found new uses for these ancient texts. But most important, whereas the Middle Ages tended to be vertically oriented, focusing on God and God's Kingdom, the early-modern period became more and more horizontally oriented, examining the created world and celebrating its most important inhabitants, human beings.

The person who most typifies this use of ancient texts to express the importance and "dignity of man" is Count Giovanni Pico della Mirandola. Pico was born in Mirandola, near Ferrara, northern Italy. The son of a minor Italian prince, his education included a variety of subjects and a diversity of institutions. In 1477, he went to the University of Bologna to study canon (church) law. After two years, he moved to study philosophy at the universities of Ferrara and Padua. Finally in 1482, he concluded his studies by examining Hebrew and Arabic thought while in Florence and Paris.

Pico believed it was possible to reconcile the seeming contradictions among the various systems of thought he had studied. Drawing out what he considered the best in each thinker and system he encountered, he developed a philosophy known as "syncretism." Syncretism holds that all schools of philosophy have some truth and so should be examined and defended; but no system of thought has all the truth, and so one must also expose the errors in each scheme.

Applying his philosophy of syncretism, in 1486 Pico drew up a list of nine hundred true theses (or propositions), using various Greek, Arabic, Hebrew, and Roman thinkers who summarized his views. He invited scholars from all over Europe to come to Rome, where he would defend his positions against all challengers. However, the disputation never occurred. Pope Innocent VIII suspended the debate and appointed a commission to investigate the nine hundred theses. Seven of the propositions were subsequently declared unorthodox and six more held to be dangerous. Pico publicly protested the decision by publishing a defense of his positions. This succeeded only in infuriating the pope. The pope condemned all nine hundred propositions, reportedly commenting, "That young man wants someone to burn him." Pico fled to France but was arrested there by papal envoys. Through the intervention of friends in Italy, Pico was released by the French king. He spent the rest of his short life in Florence under the protection of the powerful Medici family.

The *Oration on the Dignity of Man* was intended as an introductory speech for the proposed debate in Rome. In the selection reprinted here, translated by Charles Glenn Wallis, Pico exhibits his syncretistic willingness to draw from many different sources. Quoting from a wide variety of writings, he argues that God has given all creatures besides humans a unique, fixed nature. They have a certain kind of being that they cannot change. But we as human beings do not have a given being—we alone have the freedom to choose what we will become. Even though we can choose to become animals or "couch potatoes" or angelic philosophers, it is the ability to *choose* that gives us dignity.

*   *   *

Pico's life was chronicled by his nephew in the difficult-to-find Giovanni Francesco Pico, *Giovanni Pico della Mirandola: His Life by His Nephew Giovanni Francesco Pico,* translated by Sir Thomas More, edited by J.M. Rigg (London: D. Nutt, 1890). For a general overview of Pico, see William G. Craven, *Giovanni Pico della Mirandola, Symbol of His Age: Modern Interpretations of a Renaissance Philosopher* (Geneve: Droz, 1981).

For collections of primary source readings in Renaissance philosophy, see Ernst Cassirer, Paul O. Kristeller, and John H. Randall, Jr., eds., *The Renaissance Philosophy of Man* (Chicago: University of Chicago Press, 1948), and Arturo B. Fallico and Herman Shapiro, eds., *Renaissance Philosophy,* two volumes (New York: Random House, 1967–1969). For general studies of Renaissance thought, see Ernst Cassirer, *The Individual and Cosmos in Renaissance Philosophy,* translated by Mario Domandi (New York: Harper & Row, 1963); Paul O. Kristeller, *Renaissance Thought and Its Sources* (New York: Columbia University Press, 1979); Charles B. Schmitt, Quentin Skinner, and Eckhard Kessler, eds., *The Cambridge History of Renaissance Philosophy* (Cambridge: Cambridge University Press, 1988); and Brian P. Copenhaver and Charles B. Schmitt, *Renaissance Philosophy,* Vol. 3 of *History of Western Philosophy* (Oxford: Oxford University Press, 1992).

ORATION ON THE DIGNITY OF MAN
(in part)

Now the highest Father, God the master-builder, had, by the laws of his secret wisdom, fabricated this house, this world which we see, a very superb temple of divinity. He had adorned the super-celestial region with minds. He had animated the celestial globes with eternal souls; he had filled with a diverse throng of animals the cast-off and residual parts of the lower world. But, with the work finished, the Artisan desired that there be someone to reckon up the reason of such a big work, to love its beauty, and to wonder at its greatness. Accordingly, now that all things had been completed, as Moses and Timaeus testify, He lastly considered creating man. But there was nothing in the archetypes from which He could mold a new sprout, nor anything in His store-houses which He could bestow as a heritage upon a new son, nor was there an empty judiciary seat where this contemplator of the universe could sit. Everything was filled up; all things had been laid out in the highest, the lowest, and the middle orders. But it did not belong to the paternal power to have failed in the final parturition, as though exhausted by childbearing; it did not belong to wisdom, in a case of necessity, to have been tossed back and forth through want of a plan; it did not belong to the loving-kindness which was going to praise divine liberality in others to be forced to condemn itself. Finally, the best of workmen decided that that to which nothing of its very own could be given should be, in composite fashion, whatsoever had belonged individually to each and every thing. Therefore He took up man, a work of indeterminate form; and, placing him at the midpoint of the world, He spoke to him as follows:

"We have given to thee, Adam, no fixed seat, no form of thy very own, no gift peculiarly thine, that thou mayest feel as thine own, have as thine own, possess as thine own the seat, the form, the gifts which thou thyself shalt desire. A limited nature in other creatures is confined within the laws written down by Us. In conformity with thy free judgment, in whose hands I have placed thee, thou art confined by no bounds; and thou wilt fix limits of nature for thyself. I have placed thee at the center of the world, that from there thou mayest more conveniently look around and see whatsoever is in the world. Neither heavenly nor earthly, neither mortal nor immortal have We made thee. Thou, like a judge appointed for being honorable, art the molder and maker of thyself; thou mayest sculpt thyself into whatever shape thou dost prefer. Thou canst grow downward into the lower natures which are brutes. Thou canst again grow upward from thy soul's reason into the higher natures which are divine."

O great liberality of God the Father! O great and wonderful happiness of man! It is given him to have that which he chooses and to be that which he wills. As soon as brutes are born, they bring with them, "from their dam's bag," as Lucilius, says, what they are going to possess. Highest spirits have been, either from the beginning or soon after, that which they are going to be throughout everlasting eternity. At man's birth the Father placed in him every sort of seed and sprouts of every kind of life. The seeds that each man cultivates will grow and bear their fruit in him. If he cultivates vegetable seeds, he will become a plant. If the seeds of sensation, he will grow into brute. If

Pico della Mirandola, *On the Dignity of Man,* translated by Charles Glenn Wallis (Englewood Cliffs, NJ: Prentice Hall, 1985).

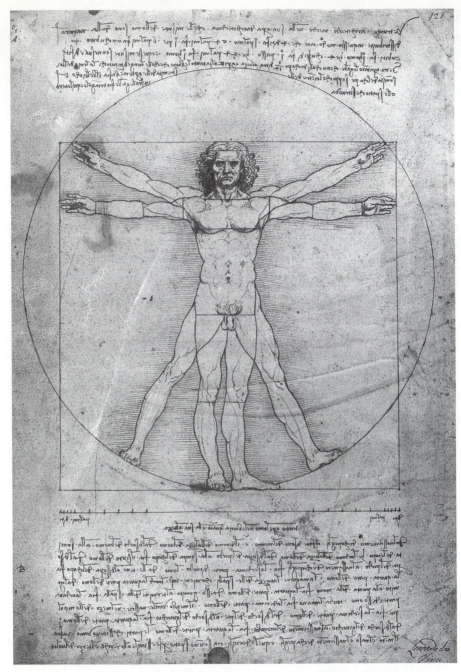

Study of Human Proportions, by Leonardo da Vinci (1452–1519). Like Pico, Leonardo enjoyed the patronage of Lorenzo de Medici; and also like Pico, Leonardo celebrated the "dignity of man" and exuberantly exhibited his own ability. (© *1991 Archivi Alinari/Art Resource*)

rational, he will come out a heavenly animal. If intellectual, he will be an angel, and a son of God. And if he is not contented with the lot of any creature but takes himself up into the center of his own unity, then, made one spirit with God and settled in the solitary darkness of the Father, who is above all things, he will stand ahead of all things. Who does not wonder at this chameleon which we are? Or who at all feels more wonder at anything else whatsoever? It was not unfittingly that Asclepius the Athenian said that man was symbolized by Prometheus in the secret rites, by reason of our nature sloughing its skin and transforming itself; hence metamorphoses were popular among the Jews and the Pythagoreans. For the more secret Hebrew theology at one time reshapes holy Enoch into an angel of divinity, whom they call *malach hashechina,* and at other times reshapes other men into other divinities. According to the Pythagoreans, wicked men are deformed into brutes and, if you believe Empedocles, into plants too. And copying them, Mohammed often had it on his lips that he who draws back from divine law becomes a brute. And his saying so was reasonable: for it is not the rind which makes the plant, but a dull and non-sentient nature; not the hide which makes a beast of burden, but a brutal and sensual soul; not the spherical body which makes the heavens, but right reason; and not a separateness from the body but a spiritual intelligence which makes an angel. For example, if you see a man given over to his belly and crawling upon the ground, it is a bush not a man that you see. If you see anyone blinded by the illusions of his empty and Calypso-like imagination, seized by the desire of scratching, and delivered over to the senses, it is a brute not a man that you see. If you come upon a philosopher winnowing out all things by right reason, he is a heavenly not an earthly animal. If you come upon a pure contemplator, ignorant of the body, banished to the innermost places of the mind, he is not an earthly, not a heavenly animal; he more superbly is a divinity clothed with human flesh.

Who is there that does not wonder at man? And it is not unreasonable that in the Mosaic and Christian holy writ man is sometimes denoted by the name "all flesh" and at other times by that of "every creature"; and man fashions, fabricates, transforms himself into the shape of all flesh, into the character of every creature. Accordingly, where Evantes the Persian tells of the Chaldaean theology, he writes that man is not any inborn image of himself, but many images coming in from the outside: hence that saying of the Chaldaeans: *enosh hu shinuy vekamah tevaoth baal chayim,* that is, man is an animal of diverse, multiform, and destructible nature.

But why all this? In order for us to understand that, after having been born in this state so that we may be what we will to be, then, since we are held in honor, we ought to take particular care that no one may say against us that we do not know that we are made similar to brutes and mindless beasts of burden. But rather, as Asaph the prophet says: "Ye are all gods, and sons of the most high," unless by abusing the very indulgent liberality of the Father, we make the free choice, which he gave to us, harmful to ourselves instead of helpful toward salvation. Let a certain holy ambition invade the mind, so that we may not be content with mean things but may aspire to the highest things and strive with all our forces to attain them: for if we will to, we can. Let us spurn earthly things; let us struggle toward the heavenly. Let us put in last place whatever is of the world; and let us fly beyond the chambers of the world to the chamber nearest the most lofty divinity. There, as the sacred mysteries reveal, the seraphim, cherubim, and thrones occupy the first places. Ignorant of how to yield to them and unable to endure the second places, let us compete with the angels in dignity and glory. When we have willed it, we shall be not at all below them.